Future Forms and Design for Sustainable Cities

Future Forms and Design for Sustainable Cities

Mike Jenks and Nicola Dempsey

Routledge
Taylor & Francis Group

LONDON AND NEW YORK

Architectural
Press

Architectural Press is an imprint of Routledge

2 Park Square, Milton Park, Abingdon, Oxon OX14 4RN
711 Third Avenue, New York, NY 10017, USA

Routledge is an imprint of the Taylor & Francis Group, an informa business

First edition 2005

British Library Cataloguing in Publication Data
A catalogue record for this book is available from the British Library

Library of Congress Cataloging-in-Publication Data
A catalog record for this book is available from the Library of Congress

ISBN–13: 978-0-7506-6309-0
ISBN–10: 0-7506-6309-X

For information on all Architectural Press publications
visit our website at www.routledge.com

Contents

Contributors   xi

Acknowledgements   xiii

Introduction   **1**

    Mike Jenks and Nicola Dempsey

Section One – The Big Picture: Cities and Regions   **11**

1.   Back to the City: A Route to Urban Sustainability   13
    Bob Giddings, Bill Hopwood, Mary Mellor and Geoff O'Brien

2.   The Intelligent City: Ubiquitous Network or Humane Environment?   31
    Guy Briggs

3.   Towards the Spatial Sustainability of City-regions: A Comparative
    Study of Tokyo and Randstad   55
    Akiko Okabe

4.   The Multi-modal Urban Region: A Concept to Combine
    Environmental and Economic Goals   73
    Luca Bertolini

5.   Creating a Sustainable City Region   95
    Raymond Green

6.   Forecasting the Sustainability of Alternative Plans: The Cambridge
    Futures Experience   113
    Marcial Echenique

Section Two – Designing for Sustainable Urban Form at High and Lower Densities 135

7. The City and the Megastructure 137
   Justyna Karakiewicz

8. High-density, High-rise and Multiple and Intensive Land Use in Hong Kong: A Future City Form for the New Millennium 153
   Stephen Lau, Jun Wang, R. Giridharan and S. Ganesan

9. From Central Business District to New Downtown: Designing Future Sustainable Urban Forms in Singapore 167
   Perry Pei-Ju Yang

10. Towards a Sustainable City: Rebuilding Lower Manhattan 185
    Beverly Willis

11. Upper City Transformations: A New Strategy for High-density Development 207
    Ineke Hulshof

12. Sustainable Cells of Urbanism: Regenerative Theory and Practice 221
    Tom J. Bartuska and Bashir A. Kazimee

13. Sustainable Urbanity in a Powerful but Fragile Landscape 245
    Ferdinand S. Johns

14. Envisioning the Future: Sustainable Models for Rural Communities 263
    Helena Webster and Peter Williams

Section Three – Aspects of Design for Sustainable Urban Forms 285

15. The Language and Meaning of Density 287
    Mike Jenks and Nicola Dempsey

16. Urban Densities, Quality of Life and Local Facility Accessibility in Principal Japanese Cities 311
    Kiyonobu Kaido

17. Emerging Work Patterns and Their Implication on the Strategy and Planning of Work Environments 339
    Nicola Gillen

18. Solar Cities: The Oxford Solar Initiative 355
    Susan Roaf, Manuel Fuentes and Rajat Gupta

19. Quantification of Urban Solar Access 371
    John Mardaljevic

20. A Comparative Sustainability Assessment and Indication of Future
     Housing Trends in Hong Kong   393
     Alex Amato, Richard Frewer and Steven Humphrey

Conclusion: Future Forms for City Living?   **413**

     Nicola Dempsey and Mike Jenks

Index   439

Contributors

Alex Amato
Assistant Professor
Department of Architecture
The University of Hong Kong
Hong Kong SAR
People's Republic of China

Tom J. Bartuska
Professor of Architecture
School of Architecture
Washington State University
Washington DC, USA

Luca Bertolini
Lecturer
Amsterdam Study Centre for the
Metropolitan Environment
University of Amsterdam
Amsterdam,
The Netherlands

Guy Briggs
Associate Director
EDAW
London, UK

Nicola Dempsey
PhD Researcher
Oxford Institute for Sustainable
Development
School of the Built Environment
Oxford Brookes University
Oxford, UK

Marcial Echenique
Professor of Land Use and Transport
Studies
The Martin Centre for Architectural
and Urban Studies
University of Cambridge
Cambridge, UK

Richard Frewer
Chair Professor
Department of Architecture
The University of Hong Kong
Hong Kong SAR
People's Republic of China

Manuel Fuentes
Research Associate
Oxford Institute for Sustainable
Development
School of the Built Environment
Oxford Brookes University
Oxford, UK

S. Ganesan
Professor
Department of Architecture
The University of Hong Kong
Hong Kong SAR
People's Republic of China

Bob Giddings
Principal Lecturer
School of the Built Environment
Northumbria University
Newcastle-on-Tyne, UK

Nicola Gillen
Workplace Consultant and Architect
DEGW
London, UK

R. Giridharan
PhD Researcher
Department of Architecture
The University of Hong Kong
Hong Kong SAR
People's Republic of China

Raymond Joseph Green
Vice-President
Town and Country Planning Association
London, UK

Rajat Gupta
Postdoctoral Research Fellow
Oxford Institute for Sustainable
Development
School of the Built Environment
Oxford Brookes University
Oxford, UK

Bill Hopwood
Researcher
Sustainable Cities Research Institute
Northumbria University
Newcastle-on-Tyne, UK

Ineke Hulshof
Architect
Stichting Bovenstad
Uppercity Foundation
Hulshof Architecten
Rotterdam, The Netherlands

Steven Humphrey
Assistant Director
Davis Langdon and Seah Management
Ltd. (Hong Kong Office)
Hong Kong SAR
People's Republic of China

Mike Jenks
Professor Emeritus and Co-Director of the
Oxford Institute for Sustainable
Development
Oxford Brookes University
Oxford, UK

Ferdinand S. Johns
Professor of Architecture
School of Architecture
Montana State University
Montana, USA

Kiyonobu Kaido
Professor
Faculty of Urban Science
Meijo University
Japan

Justyna Karakiewicz
Associate Professor
Department of Architecture
The University of Hong Kong
Hong Kong SAR
People's Republic of China

Bashir A. Kazimee
Professor of Architecture
School of Architecture
Washington State University
Washington DC, USA

Stephen Siu Yu Lau
Associate Professor, Hon. Director
Center for Architecture and Urban Design
for China and Hong Kong
Department of Architecture
The University of Hong Kong
Hong Kong SAR
People's Republic of China

John Mardaljevic
Senior Research Fellow
Institute of Energy and Sustainable
Development De Montfort University
Leicester, UK

Mary Mellor
Professor and Lecturer
Sustainable Cities Research Institute
Northumbria University
Newcastle-on-Tyne, UK

Geoff O'Brien
Senior Lecturer in Environmental
Management and Planning
School of Applied and Molecular
Sciences
Northumbria University
Newcastle-on-Tyne, UK

Akiko Okabe
Architect
Assistant Professor
Chiba University
Chiba, Japan

Perry Pei-Ju Yang
Assistant Professor
Department of Architecture
School of Design and Environment
National University of Singapore
Singapore

Susan Roaf
Professor
Oxford Institute for Sustainable
Development
School of the Built Environment
Oxford Brookes University
Oxford, UK

Jun Wang
MPhil Researcher
Department of Architecture
The University of Hong Kong
Hong Kong SAR
People's Republic of China

Helena Webster
Reader in Architecture
Department of Architecture
School of the Built Environment
Oxford Brookes University
Oxford, UK

Peter Williams
Architectural Assistant
PRP Architects
Surrey, UK

Beverly Willis
Architect
President, Beverly Willis Architecture
Foundation
President, Architecture Research
Institute, Inc.
New York, NY, USA

Captions for photos on reverse of section inter-leafs

Figure Section 1: Urban networks, the Randstadt, Netherlands (Source: Ministry of Housing, Spatial Planning and the Environment (2001) *Summary: Making Space: Sharing Space*, Fifth National policy Document on Spatial Planning 2000–2020, The Hague, Netherlands, p32.)

Figure Section 2: Innovative housing design, Java Island, Amsterdam (Source: Mike Jenks)

Figure Section 3: High density cycle park! (Source: Mike Jenks)

Figure Conclusion: Mass Rapid transit – the Skytrain, Bangkok (Source: Mike Jenks)

Acknowledgements

Our thanks go to all those involved in the writing and production of this book. We owe a debt of gratitude to all the contributors for their chapters and for their forbearance in the long time it has taken to be finally published. Our thanks go to Dan Saunders who produced the cover image and to Shibu Raman for producing the drawings for Chapter 5. We thank the Dutch Ministry of Housing, Physical Planning and Environment for supporting the preparation of this book, in particular Japp van Staalduine. Our appreciation goes to IUPEA colleagues and our colleagues at the Oxford Institute for Sustainable Development. And finally, we would like to give our warmest thanks to Margaret Jenks and Dan Saunders for all their support and patience over the weekends lost to editorial tasks.

Mike Jenks and Nicola Dempsey

Introduction

The future for our cities is dependent on the actions of today. In particular, achieving cities that are sustainable is an imperative in our rapidly urbanizing world. In 1950 30% of the world's population lived in urban areas. By 2003 that proportion had risen to 48%, and it is very likely that the watershed of over half will be reached when this book is published. The predictions are that by 2030, 61% of the population will be urban (United Nations, 2004). Envisioning such a future is no easy matter. One of the conclusions reached by Williams *et al.* as to how a sustainable urban form can be achieved was the need for the development of 'new ways of conceiving the future built environment' (2000, p. 354).

The aim of this book is to present the reader with examples of the latest research into different urban forms and the ways in which they can be designed to be more sustainable. The pursuit of sustainability has been placed on the agenda of governments and non-governmental organizations after the 1972 UN Conference on the Human Environment, and more recently by the World Commission on Environment and Development (1987) and the 1992 Earth Summit in Rio. It has been stated by these, and other, bodies that cities must be economically viable, socially equitable and contribute to environmental protection of all species: adhering to the concept of the *Three Pillars of Sustainable Development* (United Nations, 2002). In many countries, policy has been adopted with long-term urban sustainability as its focus, and there are many examples of this translated into practice (Edwards, 1999; Beatley, 2000; European Commission, 2001; Sorensen *et al.*, 2004).

This book presents some of the diverse aspects that are inextricably bound up with, and strongly influence, the scope of sustainable urban planning and design. A great deal has been written about the influences that can be said to affect the urban form, such as the technological, social, economic, institutional, geographical and physical (e.g. Norgaard, 1994; Jenks *et al.*, 1996; Jenks and Burgess, 2000; Williams *et al.*, 2000; Wheeler, 2003). These aspects are inter-related and interdependent as they all facilitate and influence sustainable urban planning and design in varying degrees. The chapters that follow add to the debate, examining ideas drawn from research and practice at different scales of the built environment from the urban region to the neighbourhood level in a number of different countries. The different scales at which sustainable ideas are discussed are reflected in the three major sections of the book.[1]

Section One

The chapters in Section One of this book discuss different (spatial) urban concepts, with particular reference to the city region. The chapters draw on research to assess how emerging conceptual ideas work when put into practice through a range of policy and planning strategies, with the ultimate objective of achieving urban sustainability.

The first chapter by Giddings *et al.* outlines the important role that the city's character and content have to play in establishing that city as a viable, sustainable, urban form. While cities have always experienced varying degrees of indiscriminate and unregulated change, it is suggested that a concerted effort should be made to incorporate the city's distinctiveness and evolving nature into a strategy of urban sustainability. They suggest that establishing the social, economic and environmental dimensions of sustainability can contribute to the recovery of a city's urban spirit and the re-emergence of a clear delineation between the currently blurred boundaries of the rural and the urban. One of the ways in which this is possible is by considering the city as part of a wider urban region: a concept that is discussed in several chapters in this section.

The second chapter by Briggs also considers the intangible nature of the city in his discussion of the concept of the intelligent city; that is, how the form of cities, the culture and habits of its citizens may be affected by advances in communication technology. He draws together the discussions of city intelligence and urban sustainability, illustrating how one cannot exist without the other. According to Briggs, the intelligent city has 'social equity as its focus', putting 'people back at the centre of the urban agenda', mirroring the *Brundtland* definition of sustainability. He suggests that adaptability is key to the intelligent, sustainable city and highlights the need for indicators to measure and monitor change, in an effort to help ensure the city's long-term sustainability.

Okabe notes in the following chapter that the reality of current living spheres has already extended beyond the city limits. Recognizing that the sustainable city limits itself spatially, Okabe looks at the monocentric and polycentric configurations of two established urban regions, Tokyo in Japan and the Randstad in the Netherlands. Like Giddings *et al.* she discusses the importance of the spatial form of the city, in terms of the distinction between the urban and the rural, which, it is argued, allows for a more inclusive analysis of the phenomena of counter-urbanization and re-urbanization. Okabe suggests that the polycentric urban system is a more sustainable form than the monocentric.

Bertolini also discusses the Randstad region, examining the transport planning policy and design in relation to a key dimension of sustainability – the integration of environmental and economic goals. He concentrates on how to design for good accessibility and efficient transportation with minimal environmental damage. The future policy plan alternatives for the Randstad region that have been proposed by the Dutch Government are evaluated to illustrate the scope for policy development within a conceptual framework. Bertolini suggests that a scenario which radically improves the performance of public transport, improves mobility and increases access to employment whilst reducing carbon dioxide emissions, best fulfils the goal of minimizing environmental damage and maximizing accessibility.

Green considers the city region in the context of the UK. He discusses the unsustainable nature of city regions in their current state with specific reference to dispersal and urban sprawl, a need for meaningful urban regeneration and the growing environmental footprint of cities. By widening the planning canvas from city to region, a more sustainable urban environment might be achieved. Focussing on two UK cities,

Sheffield and Bristol, Green presents a five-stage guide to improving transport and accessibility in the city region. He concludes that achieving a successful, sustainable city region can only be achieved with a shift of focus in policy from the compact city to the wider regional scale.

The final chapter in this section addresses the measurement of prediction of sustainability in alternative plans. Echenique demonstrates how is it possible to measure the three necessary pillars of sustainability – environmental, social and economic – with reference to the *Cambridge Futures Project*. Seven alternative plans for the city and surroundings area are modelled, discussed and assessed predictively in relation to sustainability indicators. The discussion illustrates how the model is a powerful tool for decision-making and a means of engendering meaningful public debate and consultation.

The depth of discussion given to the urban region highlights the changing spatial form of the urban environment and illustrates that there is a range of strategies through which urban sustainability can be achieved.

Section Two

The issue of density is central to the design of the sustainable urban form. Where sustainable objectives include the efficient use of land, good accessibility to employment, and key services and facilities through public transport use, walking and cycling, high density would seem to be a fundamental prerequisite (Jenks *et al.*, 1996). However, the design of the sustainable urban form cannot be restricted to high-density development alone. Lower densities are a reality in many places and it is suggested that they will continue to be (Breheny, 1997). Sustainable design must then be adaptable to the specific requirements of a particular urban form, be it high or low density.

The first five chapters in this section discuss, and give examples of, design in high (or 'higher') density urban areas. Karakiewicz discusses Hong Kong and characterizes the high-density developments as megastructures. The megastructure is defined as any development that can exist as a self-contained community with all the necessary functions of the city available. Karakiewicz discusses how Hong Kong's megastructures are not the result of urban theory, but rather have developed out of necessary provision for a growing population. In this way, they can adapt to the needs of residents and of the wider city to which they must remain connected to be a significant sustainable urban form.

Lau *et al.* examine high-rise and *multiple intensive land use (MILU)* in Hong Kong. MILU maximizes land resources in a compact urban form through the mixing of land uses, intensification and connection to an efficient public transport system and pedestrian infrastructure. Vertical intensification, illustrated by towers over 200 m high, and the 'sky city', exemplified by the multi-layering of vehicular and pedestrian movement, are two design concepts making use of the third and fourth dimensions (space above and below ground, and time, respectively). Lau *et al.* conclude that they are socially acceptable sustainable urban forms in Hong Kong which, as proponents of high-density lifestyle, correspond to cultural needs.

The concept of the 24-hour city is discussed in the next chapter by Yang. In Singapore, the central business district (CBD) shuts down after working hours, rendering it unsustainable. Yang explores design ideas for future downtown urban forms in response to the challenges of competitive urban revitalization. Three sustainable proposals are presented which comprise mixed uses, new homes, urban parks and university campuses, achieved through an 'urban design studio' workshop process. Yang underlines the need for rethinking urbanism in relation to the wider social and economic context as well as integrating the needs of the user into the design solution.

The business district of Lower Manhattan, New York is the subject of the chapter by Willis. The damage caused by the disaster of September 11 extended well beyond the destruction of the World Trade Centre. This chapter considers the surrounding area and provides guiding principles for its rebuilding, prompted by the work of the coalition, Civic Alliance to Rebuild Downtown New York. It is suggested that this rebuilding requires consideration as to how Lower Manhattan should function physically, economically and socially in a 21st century context, and how it could be rebuilt in a sustainable manner. Willis argues that sustainable design must take into account the need for a supportive infrastructure for New Yorkers, their daily activities and the underlying character of the area, as well as the economic dimension in terms of the expansion of knowledge-based industries and tourism.

Hulshof concentrates on a sustainable design concept which makes use of existing urban roofspace to intensify development without creating a need for further space, helping to reduce urban sprawl and preserve open space. This research was inspired by the installation of a functional sculpture in Rotterdam, the *Bamboo Summit City*. Hulshof outlines design proposals for high-density Dutch cities which have a considerable amount of unused roof space. These proposals show how existing urban roof-top areas can be transformed to incorporate workable 'uppercities'.

The final three chapters consider how sustainable development can be achieved within a low-density context. Bartuska and Kazimee discuss how principles of sustainable planning and design have been applied to the small town of Pullman in the USA. The study models the ecological (or biological) variables including air, water, food, energy and human ecology as primary indicators of sustainable community development. Strategies were established at different spatial scales, corresponding to the differing needs of the region, the city, the district and neighbourhood, down to the design of the dwelling unit. The authors suggest that as this regenerative proposal is based upon an holistic model of sustainability, the principles demonstrated in Pullman can be applied to other larger urban areas.

The following chapter concentrates on sustainable development in the low-density town of Bozeman in the USA. Johns presents strategies and design prototypes, which, he suggests, illustrate how a low-density town within fragile environmental surroundings can be made more sustainable. Bozeman is located in the Gallatin valley where, because of the fragility of the natural environment, the majority of future development will be limited to existing settlement areas. Johns admits that the proposals put forward are quite modest, and correspond to American individualism and the consumer-driven market-based system. Some of the proposals discussed by Johns include a pedestrian-oriented neighbourhood centre, commercial area infill and the development of low-density residential clusters.

The final chapter in this section, by Webster and Williams, reports on a design project undertaken by staff and students of Cambridge University and the Massachusetts Institute of Technology, called the *Cambridge Futures Project*. Through a design case study process, issues raised by the creation of sustainable rural communities in the Cambridge region were closely scrutinized. The aim of the project was to examine whether innovative change in public policy and spatial design could create sustainable environments. The authors examine some of those changes including the establishment of a charitable trust as opposed to developer-led action. The result provides a clear vision for a future sustainable settlement according to Webster and Williams, who highlight how the design of the physical infrastructure can make an important contribution to long-term environmental sustainability as well as providing a sense of place for residents.

Section Three

The previous sections offer some holistic arguments for achieving sustainable development, and illustrate how different urban forms have particular requirements that must be taken into account for sustainability to occur. There are, however, other aspects which can have an impact on the design of the sustainable urban form. This section considers some of these aspects which include changing work patterns, renewable energy use and assessment of the sustainability of high-rise buildings.

Despite being a ubiquitous term often used in definitions of the 'compact city', the term 'density' is surprisingly little understood. The chapter by Jenks and Dempsey attempts to demystify the meaning of density by tracing some of the ideas behind housing density standards in the UK. The authors highlight the difficulties in measuring density, due to the fact that there being no common methodology or definition. When analysed over time, the key government documentation provides density standards, especially for 'high' densities, that have remarkable similarities, and yet the recommended urban forms associated with the standards vary enormously. An explanation for this variety is suggested: density is a relative concept that is culturally determined, depending on the dominant contemporaneous ideas of the time.

The next chapter by Kaido continues the discussion of density, with regard to research conducted into high-density living and the relationship it has with accessibility. One of the claimed advantages of compact, high-density development is that facilities are more accessible, thus reducing the need to travel. This chapter draws on research from Japan which compares densely inhabited districts in 49 cities. The results show that there is an inherent danger associated with relying on simple theories when applied to the complexities of real urban environments. It is not enough to make the assumption that high density will, by default, lead to high levels of accessibility. Kaido argues that there are other variables that need to be taken into account, such as planning policies and car ownership, as they can also have a significant impact on the success of the compact, sustainable urban form.

The chapter by Gillen also examines accessibility in cities, in relation to the workplace. Work patterns are changing and, with them, demands on good work environment. Gillen argues that the main requirement that workers have is for increased communication connections to one another. This chapter explores the impact of communications on the workplace and how new technology can be extrapolated to guide the design of the city. Gillen suggests that virtual and physical space have distinct yet complementary roles to play in the city; and as such, aspects including accessibility, public space and privacy encompass a further dimension for sustainable urban design.

Roaf *et al.* consider the application of strategies and technologies for the use of renewable energies in a community-wide framework in the UK. The scope for the building industry to reduce current levels of carbon dioxide emissions is considerable and the authors suggest that significant emission reductions are achievable with relative ease. The reported research involves two pilot studies in Oxford: equipping a small area of houses with photovoltaics with a single connection to the grid, and plans for a solar suburb. The research also involves the testing of public opinion towards the implementation of the two initiatives: part of the collaborative approach adopted by the *Oxford Solar Initiative*.

The next chapter by Mardaljevic also considers solar energy, in terms of solar access and social sustainability. The quality of life in dense urban areas can be affected by the amount of daylight and sunlight that one has access to, particularly in public spaces. Mardaljevic suggests that solar access can influence people's perceptions of the city: gloomy and unattractive as opposed to well lit and bright. Traditional methods of estimating solar access in urban areas are critically examined, and a new schema is proposed to quantify urban solar access with examples demonstrating the application. Solar access prediction represents an important advance for sustainable design in a climate where policies are calling for higher densities and public open space is at a premium.

The final chapter in this section discusses the sustainability of buildings. In the context of urban sustainability, having the ability to assess the sustainability of buildings is imperative. This chapter uses the extreme case of high-density, high-rise housing in Hong Kong as a case study. Three housing blocks are compared: one private, one social and one at the conceptual design stage (the Integer Concept tower). Embodied and operational energy, construction waste and costs, as well as recycling are modelled to give an analysis of the sustainability of the building's full life cycle. Although in its early stages, Amato *et al.* suggest that this model has the potential to help the construction industry and designers make sustainable decisions when building in urban areas.

The chapters in this section present different aspects that have a direct or indirect impact on the sustainability of the urban form. Ensuring that similar aspects (such as changing travel patterns or changes in policy) are adequately accounted for in urban design now and in the future is fundamental to the achievement of urban sustainability.

Conclusion: future forms for city living

The conclusion briefly draws together the research and practice discussed in the book. Together with reference to additional schemes and proposals, it adds to the research in the chapters with examples of large-scale designs proposed and/or implemented over the past decade or so. This offers some indication to planners and designers of sustainable urban forms that might be achievable in the future.

Note

1. The chapters in this book have been adapted from a selection of papers drawn from a major international symposium held in September 2002 in Oxford, UK. This was the fifth symposium of the International Urban Planning and Environment Association, entitled *Achieving Sustainable Urban Environments: Future Forms for City Living*. These chapters were selected from the 'futures' theme, one of the six themes in the symposium.

References

Beatley, T. (2000) *Green Urbanism: Learning from European Cities*, Island Press, Washington D.C.

Breheny, M. (1997) Urban Compaction: Feasible and Acceptable? *Cities* **14(4)**: 209–217.

Edwards, B. (1999) *Sustainable Architecture: European Directives and Building Design*, 2nd edition, Architectural Press, Oxford.

European Commission (2001) *Environment 2010: Our Future, Our Choice: the Sixth EU Environmental Action Programme 2001–2010*, Office for Official Publications of the European Communities, Luxembourg.

Jenks, M. and Burgess, R. (2000) *Compact Cities: Sustainable Urban Forms for Developing Countries*, Spon Press, London.

Jenks, M., Burton, E. and Williams, K. (1996) *The Compact City: A Sustainable Urban Form?*, E & FN Spon, London.

Norgaard, RB. (1994) *Development Betrayed: The End of Progress and a Coevolutionary Revisioning of the Future*, Routledge, London.

Sorensen, A., Marcotullio, PJ. and Grant, J., eds. (2004) *Towards Sustainable Cities: East Asian, North American and European Perspectives on Managing Urban Regions*, Ashgate, Aldershot.

United Nations (2002) *Report of the World Summit on Sustainable Development: Johannesburg, South Africa, 26 August–4 September*, United Nations, New York.

United Nations (2004) *World Urbanization Prospects: The 2003 Revision*, UN Department of Economic and Social Affairs, New York.

Wheeler, SM. (2003) The evolution of Urban Form in Portland and Toronto: Implications for Sustainability Planning. *Local Environment*, **8(3)**: 317–336.

Williams, K., Burton, E. and Jenks, M. (2000) Achieving Sustainable Urban Form: Conclusions. In: *Achieving Sustainable Urban Form* (eds. Williams, K., Burton, E. and Jenks, M.), E & FN Spon, London.

World Commission on Environment and Development (WCED) (1987) *Our Common Future*, Oxford University Press, Oxford.

Section One

The Big Picture: Cities and Regions

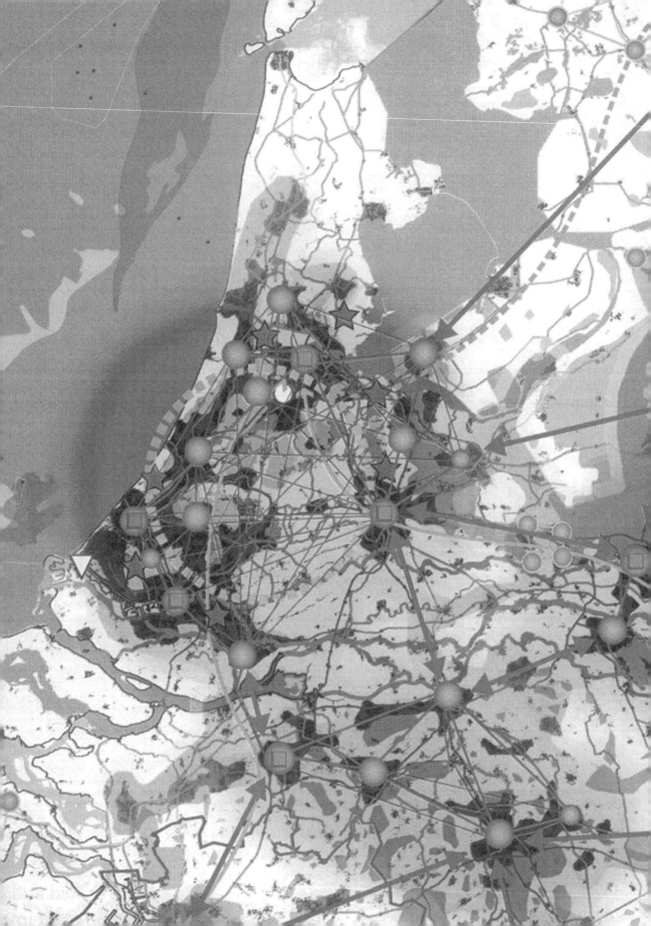

1

Bob Giddings, Bill Hopwood, Mary Mellor and Geoff O'Brien

Back to the City: A Route to Urban Sustainability

Introduction

The character of the city has been changing for as long as people have been urban dwellers. Its diverse functions have included marketplace, theatrical stage, place of execution and the city has been the setting for revolutions, uprisings, coronations, massacres, celebrations . . . the list is long. Whether or not one has an over-romantic notion of the city, unquestionably the city has long been the backdrop for much human activity. In the past few decades, the environmental and social consequences of the concentrated patterns of human activity in the urban environment have been highlighted and debated, with the suggestion that present living arrangements in Western cities are unsustainable. This chapter offers some insight into the ways that the city and its form have changed over the years. It also outlines how the power over, and responsibility for, the changes in the city has shifted as the functions of the city also shift. The city should not be dismissed in the search for another more sustainable, alternative form. On the contrary, the characteristics of the city should be recognized, capitalized and built upon. Cities convey something special about civilization itself that should not be spread too thinly and reduced to banal, lifeless, endless sprawl. This chapter suggests that it is important to recognize and support the character, content and distinctiveness of cities before modern economic and political trends destroy their essence through commodification and standardization.

The changing character of the city

Cities and society have developed and flourished in an almost symbiotic manner. The latin word for city is *civitas*, from which the words *civilization* and *citizenship* are derived. Take, for example, British cities prior to the Industrial Revolution. Despite being home to the minority of the population, these cities often physically dominated their surroundings and exerted immense influence over all spheres of human endeavour. From their beginnings, cities were places of manufacture and commerce, often developing in locations suited to a particular economic activity such as on trade routes or near useful resources such as coal. There was a tension in the division of wealth and power between the country landowners, and the city-based merchants and rulers, but over time the latter prevailed, as cities grew physically larger and, thanks to additions to the workforce, also economically more powerful. The British Census of 1851 showed that, for the first time, more people were living in urban areas than rural, at 54% of the population (Best, 1979).

Today, globally about 2.6 billion people live in cities of up to 5 million inhabitants with an additional 400 million living in some 40 large urban areas, often called mega-cities, of over 5 million inhabitants (Angotti, 1993; Sassen, 2000). Two-thirds of the population of Europe lives in cities and urban areas that occupy about 1% of the land area (Stanners and Bordeau, 1995). With their concentrated population, diversity of skills and growing demands, cities stimulated economic growth. Often this was led by the consumption patterns of a privileged stratum, made up of the few new rich, who often lived in close proximity to the many in abject poverty (Best, 1979). Some would argue that this wide gulf between the rich and the poor has never disappeared.

The social role of the city

As well as being the seats of power, wealth and knowledge, cities have also been catalysts for social change and revolution. They have been the source of most of the enduring changes that underpin human freedoms including the development of politics (from the Greek word *polis* meaning city), the centre of revolutions that have helped to shape the modern world and the struggles for human rights. Arguably cities are the birthplace of democracy which, we would argue, is a vital feature of sustainability.

The essence of cities is that they have always contained a myriad of diverse and intense connections and activities; where people live, work, shop and play, meeting the needs of economic production and social reproduction (Smith, 2002). They bring together people from many different backgrounds and cultures. This can be purely in terms of physical proximity but also in the creation of space for fusing ideas, styles and activities. They are centres for many cultural forms. Without romanticizing their history, which has its grim share of oppression, hunger, crime and pollution, cities have been the driving force for innovation, social improvement, cultural activity and diversity (Figure 1.1).

Urban space has always been a place for the community rather than the individual, and public buildings, such as those for government, education, culture and commerce, play an important role in providing a focus for citizens and communities. They provide emotional attraction for both citizens and visitors, embodying political and cultural activities, giving significance and providing landmarks in time and space. They link the past, present and future, become reassuringly familiar to local people and stimulating for visitors. Lozano (1990) argues that the city is a realm with a high level of culture linked with the most civilized expression of social behaviour. Mumford (1970) described the city as the most advanced work of art of human civilization.

The changing form of the city

Historically, cities have had complex spatial layouts reflecting the multiplicity of human exchanges. They have been alive with the richness of patterns and symbols that fulfil many psychological and spiritual needs. For example, the sense of enclosure and spatial definition provided by medieval walls satisfied more than just a need for defensive protection; they also provided psychological stimulation and physical comfort (Lozano, 1990). The need to pattern human surroundings is as valid today as it was in medieval times, and this is particularly recognized by Alexander and Lynch (Lynch, 1960; Alexander *et al.*, 1977; Alexander, 1987). Their ideas about legibility are based on a vivid and integrated physical setting that can provide the raw

Figure 1.1
The city as a myriad of diverse
and intense activities – the
driving force for cultural activity:
Venice, 2002.
(*Source*: Bob Giddings.)

material for a symbolic and collective community memory. The layouts, landmarks and public spaces all contribute to each city's distinctive sense of identity (Figures 1.2 and 1.3).

From cities to urban sprawl

The last two centuries have seen a transformation in cities from being relatively contained, to widespread urban sprawl. This has been a worldwide phenomenon. The strengthening of international capital has led to the concentration of economic power in a number of global centres of finance and highly

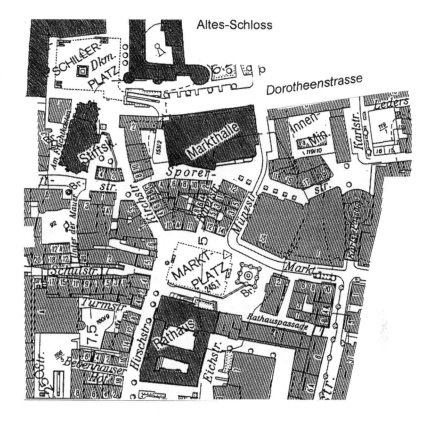

specialized services, such as London, Frankfurt and New York (Sassen, 2001; Smith, 2002). The decisions taken in these global cities, as seats of government, international markets and the locations of many corporate headquarters, are often of greater significance than decisions taken by governments at a regional or even national level. At the same time some older industrial cities such as Detroit and Manchester have seen their influence dwindle as manufacturing becomes less important (Sassen, 2001; Smith, 2002). As production has moved location or closed down, there has been a trend of population migration away from the cities to the suburbs, smaller towns and semi-rural areas (Turok, 1999).

The combined actions of economic power and planning have undermined the importance of distinct spaces and landmarks that originally contributed to the establishment of the character and spaces of cities. Many urban patterns and traditional connections have been weakened or lost, slashed by mega redesigns that ignored centuries of evolution. Cities have been scarred by major road networks, which occupy large areas of land, fragment and blight neighbourhoods destroying local

Figure 1.3
The square as a place for
chance meetings, a focal point
in the city, a recognizable
landmark and a junction of
various routes: Verona, 1999.
(*Source*: Bob Giddings.)

social interchange and disconnecting travellers from their surroundings (Appleyard, 1981). Sprawl, car traffic, zoning and major redevelopments have destroyed the fabric of streets, buildings and spaces, often replacing diversity with large single-use structures which can have a hostile or imposing presence. In the process of modernization, urban communities have lost the richness of patterns and symbols that made each city distinct. Lozano's concept of cities (1990), as the setting of culture and civilized behaviour, is becoming increasingly fragile.

Suburban sprawl has meant that the edge of cities is often blurred with miles of semi-suburban semi-rural hinterland of shopping malls, office parks and housing developments that constitutes neither city nor countryside. In many cases huge conurbations have obliterated any notion of the city (Bookchin, 1995). People often live miles from where they work, shop or go for leisure activities. The traditional connection of the exchange of goods between cities and their neighbouring countryside is also lost with resources being shipped from all parts of the world to service the undifferentiated urbanized communities.

Commodifying cities

Today's modern landmarks reflect the values of commercialism, where offices and retail units have replaced the library and the town hall, often in physical stature as well as importance to the city (nowadays expressed in terms of financial returns). These bland new buildings neither connect with the city's public, social or physical fabric nor reflect its identity or individuality. Bookchin (1995) has argued that when there is a physical loss of 'city-ness' in favour of huge, bland conurbations there is a parallel loss of citizenship. Active citizenship is discouraged and replaced by the role of consumer or, at best, passive voter. Power is concentrated in the hands of large companies, and government largely acts in their favour.

Recent trends in global economics and telecommunications have led to the assertion that place no longer matters. With no apparent need for a physical focal point for activities, it would seem that cities could suffer dramatically. The possibilities of teleworking and Internet-based consuming would appear to make it possible to return to a more rural lifestyle. However, this runs counter to the international trend of increased urban living. Urban areas continue to grow and there is strong evidence that at least some cities are still as important as ever because they provide rich social connections, high densities of people and skills, as well as being centres of power, decisions and infrastructure. Gillen, for example, discusses the significance of city as a necessary *physical hub* for people whose work patterns are becoming increasingly more oriented around technology-based networks.[1]

The last few years have seen a growing emphasis on the importance of cities with policies, for example in the UK, to encourage city living through calls for improvements to the quality of urban design and support for public space (Urban Task Force, 1999; DETR, 2000a, 2000b). However, many of these proposals do not tackle the deep-rooted trends that undermine the socio-economic quality or environmental sustainability of urban life. Much of the emphasis is on external appearance with less consideration for the content and use of buildings and spaces. The pace and scope of development has often been driven by property developers, with no interests within the city, so that the urban scale and appearance is defined more by the needs of capital (Smith, 2002). As governments have abandoned Keynesian or social-democratic policy in favour of neo-liberalism, the priority of policy has moved from meeting social needs to attracting and meeting the needs of capital (ibid). Privatization and budget cuts have limited the role for public planning and construction leaving the private sector as the main initiator and producer thereby determining the character and priorities of developments. The role of city authorities is mainly in support of the private sector, striving to attract investors, to support property development and increasingly to encourage the private provision of services.

Instead of concentrating on the needs of the existing populations of cities the emphasis has been on place marketing and gentrification (Borja and Castells, 1997). Almost universally, the policy aim of cities is to attract international capital to invest, higher-paid executives and professionals to settle and tourists to visit. The main benefit for some city authorities has been an increase in property tax income (Hackworth and Smith, 2001). Almost all cities now have major marketing strategies. For many, this includes the widespread transformation of former docks from places of work into exclusive islands of leisure with expensive flats, bars and restaurants. Cities are now being sold as a commodity to be consumed, rather than a place where production, living and consumption take place (Philo and Kearns, 1993). The notion of cities as a complex cultural expression and as a set of buildings and spaces in which a range of activities occur is being superseded as cities theme themselves.

Ironically the drive for image in city redevelopment often ignores or undermines what is distinct about each city, including its social character, urban landscape and economic focus. The global reach of retail chains and trends of international style also diminish the rooted distinctiveness of place. The result is urban theme parks rather than real living and working places. These trends undermine diversity, increase social divisions, diminish culture and close off spaces for genuinely local businesses.

Bianchini (1991) and Worpole (1992) criticize the declining quality of life and public space in British cities due to the omnipresence of retail superstores, the domination of cars and the privatization of services. They identified art and culture as the primary factors in improving the quality of city life. However, far from their proposals for local art set in, and used for, the community, culture and the arts are instead being used to create images in the marketing of cities. Instead of being rooted in the vernacular, art and culture are offered primarily as commercialized leisure and an incentive for tourists to visit. In the process, urban history has been transformed into heritage. An *image* of historic cityscapes and workplaces may be recreated but the real function and roots of community and industry have been lost (Figure 1.4). Behind the glossy image is a remaindered population living in poverty and largely ignored (Holcom, 1993).

This disjointed glossy imaging is illustrated in urban regeneration and large-scale redevelopment which is often based on retail and commercialized leisure and culture – hotels, multiplex cinemas, entertainment complexes, sports stadiums, art galleries and conference centres. It is claimed that such developments will strengthen the local economy and make it more attractive to visitors. The architecture of such

Figure 1.4
The commodification of heritage, with open-topped bus and recreated history pre-packaged for tourists: Oxford, 2004. (*Source*: Mike Jenks.)

buildings is often grandiose and disrupts the existing urban fabric (Figure 1.5). These buildings seldom connect to the actual needs and character of an area nor strengthen its legibility. Economically they usually do not develop the local economy. They may draw in visitors; however, they often only pass through local neighbourhoods that have been blighted or socially changed (Gratz and Mintz, 1998). What is being done to establish the viability of the wider community?

The economic trends of neo-liberalism have increased social polarization and inequality (Hamnett, 1996; Borja and Castells, 1997; Sassen, 2001). While elites need people willing to work for low wages, they do not want them living nearby. Gentrification intensifies polarization and feeds antagonism. The existing population of working class, and sometimes minority ethnic

Figure 1.5
Grandiose architecture and glossy image but not connected to needs of the area and ignores the poor: Petronas Towers, Kuala Lumpur, 1996.
(*Source*: Bob Giddings.)

communities, are either alienated as a remainder community surrounded by affluence or pushed out to somewhere else. New central or prestige area housing does not cater for families or for lower-paid workers. In some cases, tenants of social housing live in estates starved of repairs and investment next door to expensive new flats. Often the new housing is not part of the wider community but is exclusive, in gated developments, which cut existing connections and restrict access to residents (Figure 1.6). City-centre housing should be neither a dormitory for the rich and childless nor an isolated enclave for the privileged. Successful cities should provide a diversity of

Figure 1.6
Gated housing developments are on the increase not only in the UK, but also worldwide: Newcastle and Shanghai. (*Sources*: Bob Giddings and Pacific Productions.)

housing, all with good quality surroundings, including homes for families, affordable properties to rent and buy.

Sustaining cities in the face of change

The future form of cities and the strategies that they should adopt in a global economy and information age is still being debated (Graham and Marvin, 1996; Borja and Castells, 1997). A highly attractive alternative for cities to the current unregulated, indiscriminate change taking place is urban sustainability (Wackernagel and Rees, 1996), based on the principles of allowing present generations to meet their needs without compromising the ability of future generations to meet theirs (WCED, 1987). Within the present economic framework there is no incentive for cities to take responsibility for the externalized damage of their activities. Redevelopments that only address a superficial image do not provide any socio-economic or environmental solutions. In contrast to the strategy of city-image enhancement, sustainable development offers a very different approach.

A foundation to urban sustainability is the overriding objective to achieve a high quality of life for the whole community within a socio-economic framework that minimizes the impact of the city on the local and global environment. For it to be successfully realized, the city must tackle the dimensions of sustainability: social, ecological, as well as economic. Sustainable cities ensure well-being and a good quality of life for citizens, are environmentally friendly, and socially integrated and just.

There is no shortage of ideas for how environmental sustainability can be achieved:

- **use of renewable energy and a dramatic increase in energy efficiency**
- **recycling and reuse of materials**
- **food production within cities**
- **an end to edge-of-town retail, leisure and business development to protect the countryside and retaining jobs in cities**

Urban density is cited as a potential proponent of sustainability, offering opportunities for increased energy savings and reducing the need for travel. What is missing is the political question of how such a strategy could be implemented (assuming that sustainability as a strategy will be imposed on the city). In this context there has been much less consideration of the social, economic, political and cultural policies that underlie the process by which urban sustainability could be attained.

s towards sustainability is an
)eing and quality of life for all.
egarded as being inextricably
dents, rather than simply as
.ssession of commodities. The
society and the environment
tion that one cannot exist
rity and culture depend on
?000; Giddings *et al.*, 2002).
:entrates on the production
ms of monetary value. This
market economy of family
id prioritizes profit rather
1 the production of goods
Figure 1.7).

also important that the
) not connect with their
y will have ecological
there is much greater
rials from within city
d global markets and a
ation exports, then the
surroundings will be
and distinct character
lections, with a built

form rooted in sociability and inclusion, this will aid the countryside to re-establish its own identity.

If considered as city regions, cities can benefit their rural hinterland through mutually beneficial exchanges. While getting food, energy and water from their surroundings, they in turn provide other vital components of sustainability including health services, festivals, education and manufactured goods. Often the best way to strengthen the centre of cities is to support the existing local people, business, activities and culture. They enhance the quality of the environment without gentrification, encourage walking, support public places and buildings, and design for people (Figure 1.8). While this may not appeal to the property developer, it is a necessary organic step to re-connect the city to its wider region in a durable and sustainable way, while supporting the distinctiveness of places, rich in diversity and activity (Jacobs, 1994; Gratz and Mintz, 1998).

As Healey (1998) has pointed out, place does matter, contrary to the claims of some neo-liberals and advocates of globalization. Sense of place and community is the soul of the cities and the principles of a renaissance of cities celebrate that experience. Cities need their unique sense of being a distinct place, yet many cities have had this undermined by urbanization and urban sprawl. The distinction between city and countryside needs to be redefined without returning to the simplicities of medieval walls. While the countryside should be accessible to city residents, the countryside should primarily be a place of work and life which are connected to the landscape. If rural dwellers are oriented to a city lifestyle based on car commuting, the land becomes merely an object of consumption and the attractive nature of the land is compromised with traffic, pollution and increased road infrastructure.

The need for meaningful citizen participation

Crucial to the development of a sustainable city is the commitment and will of the population. There is a growing trend in government to conclude that the market is an accurate reflection of individual choices and an appropriate way of influence decisions. There is an emphasis on people as consumers rather than as citizens. For Bookchin (1995), the erosion of citizenship would mean the end of cities. He has argued for a change in politics to reclaim citizenship, public involvement in decision-making and deep-rooted democracy. Gentrification and

Figure 1.8
Vastra Hamnen Bo01 –
sustainable urban design
creating identity, using
renewable energy, recycling
waste and water, encouraging
sustainable transport use, and
involving local people with a
broadband community
network: Malmo, 2003.
(*Source*: Nicholas Low.)

privatization run counter to strengthening local democracy in the way they produce exclusion and polarization. The notion of cities with areas reserved for the affluent professional classes where other, generally poorer classes, are effectively excluded, or where cities are themed for the benefit of the consumer, is one that portrays a false image and prohibits effective, meaningful civic engagement.

Sustainable cities need active involvement of the people; they need active citizens (Selman and Parker, 1997; Taylor, 2000). Local Agenda 21 recognized that some 70% of the actions required to achieve sustainability needed to be done locally (UNCED, 1992). As Camagni *et al.* (1998) point out, policy-making and decision-taking need to be focused at the local level. Active citizen involvement implies a fundamental change to politics and political structures. Local government needs to be more than modernized; it needs to be transformed into a vibrant dynamic and challenging forum of debate, based on public involvement. Instead of responding to falling turn-out only by seeking to make voting easier, people need to be reconnected to the democratic process by having more reason to vote. Local government needs enhancing with a return of the powers that have been stripped away by budget cuts, centralization of power, and privatization of facilities and services. City governments need the ability to make decisions, including economic issues and taxation that are connected to the local population. This might include allowing a greater local tax and the ability to make choices on spending. Examples already exist such as the participatory budget process in Porto Alegre in Brazil (Wainwright, 2003). Reforming the funding process for local government will begin to re-connect the elector with the elected. This reform needs to go beyond the rhetoric of partnership which does not fundamentally empower citizens and communities; there needs to be real power in the hands of residents.

Conclusion: Do cities have a future?

Urbanization is certainly the future but a question mark hangs over what kind of future the city can look forward to. Despite technological advances and an explosion in wealth, human societies are becoming increasingly divided, socially and economically. Much of the strain of these social divisions is focused on the cities. Urbanized humanity is also placing increasing burdens on the planetary ecological support systems and without marked changes in patterns of consumption many ecosystems will not survive.

This chapter has argued that cities can provide a rich and varied quality of life for all of its citizens, but that this depends upon changes being made to the ways in which cities are funded and governed. The primary focus of the city needs to be its people, operating at a human scale, rich in symbolism and with spaces and places for social interaction and the daily business of life. Technological advances may assist in solving some of the challenges for cities, but they are not a panacea. What is needed is a new debate on the future of cities that will challenge many of the present political and economic norms.

The city has a long history and has been the major source of human culture, innovation and democratic rights. The key is to build on its essential characteristics and make them relevant for today. The possibility of a continuation of present trends of unsustainable economic growth, increased social fragmentation and environmental degradation is neither an acceptable nor sustainable option. Without change, human societies will find themselves having to survive in a polluted world where social relations are severely damaged and economies have collapsed. For many communities this is already the case. The adaptability of the city is unquestioned. It is the adaptability of its citizens, decision-makers and urban policy within that city that will be put to the test in the pursuit of sustainability. Society needs to challenge the view that the market economy is the main form of socio-economic organization that can successfully provide for a society (Hutchinson *et al.*, 2002). Cities should be places where the interaction and participation of citizens enable them to meet their own needs and aspirations, and those of the wider community, as well as allowing future generations to meet theirs. If citizens can collectively recover the character of cities as a source of democratic reinvigoration and creative energy, solutions to the challenges of sustainability may well emerge.

Note

1. See Section Three of this book, Gillen, N. *Emerging Work Patterns and their Implication on the Strategy and Planning of Work Environments*.

References

Alexander, C. (1987) *A New Theory of Urban Design*, Oxford University Press, New York.

Alexander, C., Ishikawa, S., Silverstein, M., Jacobson, M., Fiksdahl-King, I. and Angel, S. (1977) *A Pattern Language*, Oxford University Press, New York.

Angotti, T. (1993) *Metropolis 2000: Planning, Poverty and Politics*, Routledge, London.

Appleyard, D. (1981) *Livable Streets*, California University Press, Berkeley.

Best, G. (1979) *Mid-Victorian Britain 1851–75*, Fontana Press, London.

Bianchini, F. (1991) *City Centres, City Cultures: The Role of the Arts in the Revitalisation of Towns and Cities*, CLES, Manchester.

Bookchin, M. (1995) *From Urbanization to Cities: Toward a New Politics of Citizenship*, Cassell, London.

Borja, J. and Castells, M. (1997) *Local and Global: Management of Cities in the Information Age*, Earthscan, London.

Camagni, R., Capello, R. and Nijkamp, P. (1998) Towards Sustainable City Policy: An Economy-Environment Technology Nexus. *Ecological Economics*, **24**: 103–118.

Davidson, J. (2000) Sustainable Development: Business As Usual or a New Way of Living. *Environmental Ethics*, **22**: 25–42.

Department of the Environment, Transport and the Regions (DETR) (2000a) *Our Towns and Cities: The Future: Delivering the Urban Renaissance*, Stationery Office, Norwich.

Department of the Environment, Transport and the Regions (DETR) (2000b) *By Design: Urban Design in the Planning System, Towards Better Practice*, Thomas Telford, London.

Giddings, B., Hopwood, B. and O'Brien, G. (2002) Environment, Economy and Society: Fitting Them Together into Sustainable Development. *Sustainable Development*, **10**: 187–196.

Graham, S. and Marvin, S. (1996) *Telecommunications and the City: Electronic Spaces, Urban Places*, Routledge, London.

Gratz, R. and Mintz, N. (1998) *Cities Back for the Edge: New Life for Downtown*, John Wiley, New York.

Hackworth, J. and Smith, N. (2001) The changing state of gentrification. *Tijdschrift voor Economische en Sociale Geografie*, **92(4)**: 464–477.

Hamnett, C. (1996) Social Polarisation, Economic Restructuring and Welfare State Regimes. *Urban Studies*, **33(8)**: 1407–1430.

Healey, P. (1998) Collaborative Planning in a Stakeholder Society. *Town Planning Review* **69(1)**: 1–21.

Holcom, B. (1993) Revising place: de- and re-constructing the image of the industrial city. In: *Selling Places: The City as Cultural Capital, Past and Present* (eds. Kearns, G. and Philo, C.), Pergamon Press, Oxford.

Hutchinson, F., Mellor, M. and Olsen, W. (2002) *The Politics of Money: Towards Sustainability and Economic Democracy*, Pluto, London.

Jacobs, J. (1994) *The Death and Life of Great American Cities*, Penguin, London.

Lozano, E. (1990) *Community Design and the Culture of Cities*, Cambridge University Press, Cambridge.

Lynch, K. (1960) *The Image of the City*, MIT Press, Cambridge, Massachusetts.

Mumford, L. (1970) *Culture of Cities*, Harvest Book, New York.

Philo, C. and Kearns, G. (1993) Culture, History Capital: A Critical Introduction to the Selling of Places. In: *Selling Places: The City as Cultural Capital, Past and Present* (eds. Kearns, G. and Philo, C.), Pergamon Press, Oxford.

Sassen, S. (2000) *Cities in a World Economy*, Pine Forge Press, Thousand Oaks.

Sassen, S. (2001) *The Global City*, Princeton University Press, London.

Selman, P. and Parker, J. (1997) Citizenship, Civicness and Social Capital in Local Agenda 21. *Local Environment*, **2(2)**: 171–184.

Smith, N. (2002) New Globalism, New Urbanism: Gentrification as Global Urban Strategy. *Antipode*, **34(3)**: 427–450.

Stanners, D. and Bordeau, P., eds. (1995) *Europe's Environment – The Dobris Assessment*, European Environment Agency, Copenhagen.

Taylor, M. (2000) Communities in the Lead: Organisational Capacity and Social Capital. *Urban Studies*, **37(5)**: 1019–1035.

Turok, I. (1999) *The Jobs Gap in Britain's Cities: Employment Loss and Labour Market Consequences*, Policy Press, Bristol.

United Nations Conference on Environment and Development (UNCED) (1992) *Agenda 21; Programme of Action for Sustainable Development: The Final Text of Agreements Negotiated by Governments at the United Nations Conference on Environment and Development (UNCED), 3–14 June 1992, Rio de Janeiro, Brazil,* UN Publications, New York.

Urban Task Force (1999) *Towards an Urban Renaissance*, E & FN Spon, London.

Wackernagel, M. and Rees, WE. (1996) *Our Ecological Footprint: Reducing Human Impact on Earth*, New Society Publishers, Gabriola Island, Canada.

Wainwright, H. (2003) *Reclaim the City: Experiments in Popular Democracy*, Verso, London.

World Commission on Environment and Development (WCED) (1987) *Our Common Future*, Oxford University Press, Oxford.

Worpole, K. (1992) *Towns for People*, Open University Press, Buckingham.

The Intelligent City: Ubiquitous Network or Humane Environment

Introduction

The 'new' (or knowledge) economy is redefining the city for the 21st century. This has significant implications for the way we live, work and move around our cities. In the pursuit of sustainable urban form, the notion of 'the intelligent city' is invaluable because it shares the theoretical foundations of sustainability. In this discussion, city intelligence refers to the capacity of the city to adequately serve the requirements of its inhabitants, matching its potential to their aspirations, which is not unlike the sustainable principle of fulfilling the needs of the present generation. The 'intelligent city' is not a new concept: in its broadest sense, city intelligence is something that is intrinsic to the *traditional* city form, which is derived from its physical context, the culture and habits of its citizens, and available technology. 'Intelligence' is not, nor should it be, simply a measure of the effectiveness of a communications network.

If the requirements of the intelligent city are changing, then we will need to reconsider how we (re)create our cities. This has implications both for urban policy and for the processes we undertake to develop urban accommodation. A shift in emphasis from quantitative to qualitative is needed; as well as a broader focus in the local planning system, changing from a site-specific adversarial approach to one that is more contextual, and consensus based. This approach should enable the development of a new model for the sustainable intelligent city, incorporating an understanding of the management of overlapping functions, and the potential for intensification of space and time. The aim would be to create a framework to allow for local action that is integrated into city-wide, regional and indeed global visions.

In this chapter a series of strategic questions will be posed and answered in order to define what is meant by 'city intelligence'. An attempt will be made to reposition the concept of the intelligent city, decoupling it from issues of digital infrastructure and information communications technology, and instead to re-align it with a broader approach that embodies longer-term issues and sustainable values. To do this, the notion of the intelligent city will be examined from a number of perspectives, which are organized into three parts. Firstly, the derivation and definitions of city intelligence will be established. Secondly, the link between intelligence and sustainability will be discussed as will the extent to which both concepts overlap. The implications for urban intelligence of the new economic context defined by the knowledge economy will also be examined here. Finally, the implications for policy and the development process are outlined, including a review of some indicators for measuring city intelligence.

Intelligent city definitions and derivation of its concept

The concept of 'city intelligence' can be and has been interpreted in many different ways: from referring simply to the level of digital infrastructure provision to the idea of the city as a functioning being in and of itself, capable of autonomous reaction to stimuli. This relationship with the provision of digital infrastructure arises largely through the derivation of the concept from studies concerning intelligent buildings. The first applications of the term 'intelligent building' in the 1980s were extremely technocentric, and it was only towards the end of this decade that the concept began to be expanded beyond technological terminology.

A series of 'intelligent building' studies carried out during the 1990s by design consultancy DEGW and others, examined the effectiveness of buildings to provide environments suited to the changing nature of work, and the changing real estate priorities of international corporations (DEGW, 1992, 1999; Harrison *et al.*, 1998). The capacity of buildings to cope with the increasing requirements for integrated digital information and communications technology played a part in this; however, over the course of the studies the emphasis slowly changed. Building intelligence was redefined:

> . . . in a way that focussed on how buildings and technology can support an organization [and that] ... the building technologies should serve the needs of the occupants rather than controlling or limiting them.
>
> Harrison *et al.*, 1998, p. 134

More importantly, a pivotal aspect that these studies introduced to the concept of building intelligence was the issue of responsiveness to change:

> In the IBE [Intelligent Buildings in Europe] method the building shell is rated in terms of one overall characteristic – its adaptability to meet changing needs over time. This is seen as fundamental to the concept of building intelligence . . .
>
> Harrison *et al.*, 1998, p. 134

This final intelligent building study decoupled the definition from the requirements of IT, stating that 'an intelligent building does not have to involve high levels of technology' (Harrison *et al.*, 1998, p. 146). Instead the study related building intelligence to location, including issues of ease of access and the level of local amenity provision. This evaluation enabled the definition of four intelligent building types, shown in Figure 2.1.

The study also began to examine how the concept of intelligence might be extended out beyond the building to describe a wider area. Intrinsic to this concept was the idea of the organization as a network, as business organizations dispersed themselves and their functions around buildings, so they would need an 'intelligent area' in which to function (Figure 2.2). This was interpreted as suggesting that intelligence operates across a range of scales, from a single building to a multiple city region (Figure 2.3).

The definitions from these studies have two basic flaws when applied to the wider area:

- They retain a technocratic (or digital) focus
- They focus on the requirements of business organizations

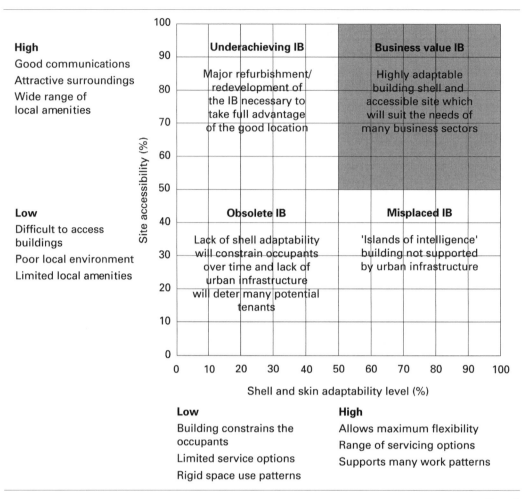

High

Good communications

Attractive surroundings

Wide range of
local amenities

Low

Difficult to access
buildings

Poor local environment

Limited local amenities

Site accessibility (%)

Underachieving IB

Major refurbishment/
redevelopment of
the IB necessary to
take full advantage
of the good location

Business value IB

Highly adaptable
building shell and
accessible site which
will suit the needs of
many business sectors

Obsolete IB

Lack of shell adaptability
will constrain occupants
over time and lack of
urban infrastructure
will deter many potential
tenants

Misplaced IB

'Islands of intelligence'
building not supported
by urban infrastructure

Shell and skin adaptability level (%)

Low

Building constrains the
occupants

Limited service options

Rigid space use patterns

High

Allows maximum flexibility

Range of servicing options

Supports many work patterns

Figure 2.1
Intelligent buildings (IB) in
South-East Asia.
(*Source:* Harrison *et al.*, 1998;
DEGW, 1999[1])

In recognition of these flaws, the models were developed
further to incorporate a wider understanding of the requirements
of urban inhabitants, and the processes they undertake. The
final model developed in the DEGW studies defined a set of
intelligent city attributes, related to the primary goals of living,
moving and working (Figure 2.4). Each of these goals is
broken down into a series of sub-tasks, from which the
attributes are derived. The model recognized the significant
role that infrastructure has, and suggested that it should be
extended to include telecommunications systems. The study
also recognized that effective management is equally crucial
to maintaining this infrastructure and to long-term urban
success.

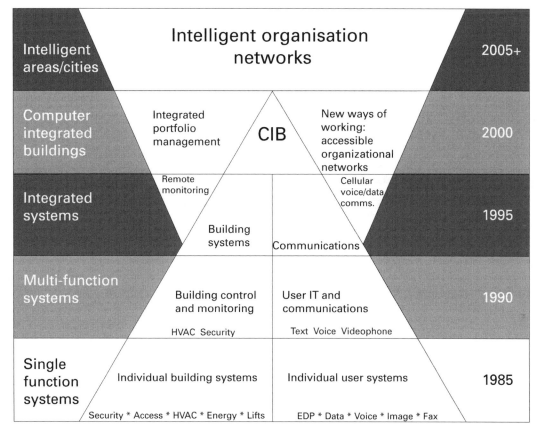

	Intelligent organisation networks		2005+

Figure 2.2
The CIB is intrinsically about systems. The intelligent building has emerged as different building systems have become integrated. The next step is to integrate systems across buildings to create intelligent organizational networks based in intelligent areas.
(*Source*: DEGW, 1999.)
Note: HVAC refers to heating, ventilation and air conditioning systems; EDP refers to electronic data processing.

Redefining the intelligent city

Although a useful starting point, the output from this study remains rather mechanistic, simply providing attributes rather than deriving a useful and workable definition of the intelligent city. To refine the concepts contained in this model, we need to examine further:

- the city's fundamental role
- the relationship between its fabric and processes
- the key attributes that enable the city to successfully realize its role

Cities exist because of two major human requirements (or drivers): to facilitate transaction and to enable freedom. The origin of the city as a physical construct lies in trade or the economics of exchange, and the exchange of ideas and goods remains one of the fundamental driving forces behind city

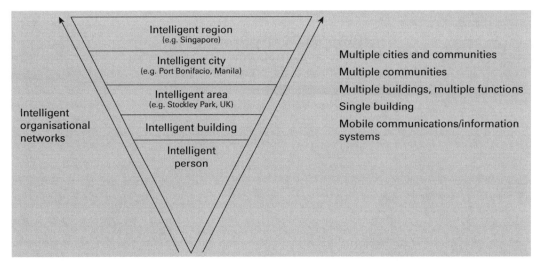

Figure 2.3
If intelligent (business) areas
are possible, then the concept
can surely be extended to larger,
or more heterogeneous,
communities, cities or even
regions? (*Source*: DEGW, 1992,
1999.)

Goals	Tasks	Intelligent city attributes		
Living	Shelter Leisure Learning Caring	Urban infrastructure and masterplan	Information network	Urban management strategy
		Houses		
		Hotels		
		Hospitals		
		Learning environments		
		Work environments		
		Retail facilities		
Moving	People Goods Information	Entertainment facilities		
		Airports		
		Railway stations		
		Bus stations		
		Freight distribution centres		
		Road/rail networks		
Working		Transportation vehicles		
		Green spaces		
		Outdoor facilities		

Figure 2.4
The DEGW Intelligent City Model,
demonstrating particular
attributes of intelligent cities, in
the broad functional categories
of living, moving and working.
(*Source*: Harrison *et al.*, 1998;
DEGW, 1992, 1999.)

growth. No city is static – if a city is not growing, it is by default stagnating (Jacobs, 1969). How effectively a city facilitates this economic function is therefore a key measure of city intelligence. But exchange is not confined to the economic

Figure 2.5
The traditional market is more than simply a place of exchange of goods; it is also a meeting place, where both social and economic interchange takes place. (*Source*: Guy Briggs.)

sphere. Cities exist equally to facilitate social interchange. Both of these attributes can be described as transactions, which further illustrate the first of the primary drivers for the existence of cities as: *Creating the conditions for social and economic transaction* (Figure 2.5).

The second primary driver relates to freedom. Historically in the west (and currently in the developing world) large-scale urbanization has been driven by a desire to escape from the constraints of agrarian subsistence survival. Movement to the cities promised rural dwellers a level of freedom that a rural lifestyle was incapable of supporting. Historically, cities were places where indentured serfs might flee the bonds of feudal

landlords, or where those driven off the land would attempt to make a new life. Cities have also long been associated with insurrection and rebellion, still in evidence today with, for example, annual international demonstrations against global capitalism (Ackroyd, 2000).

The city offers its citizens the freedom to associate with whomever they wish, the freedom to congregate in large numbers, to express political ideas and affiliations, and to express ideas (Figure 2.6) that may not be common to the majority. In Soho (London) annually, on a particular Saturday in August, a gathering of sado–masochists march through the streets, demonstrating, with cracking whips, outlandish leather and latex costumes, handcuffs and chains, their right to practise their personal delights, carefully escorted by politely attendant policemen. If these were attempted in a small town it would cause a riot. The city enables this and many other freedoms, which encapsulates the second primary driver for the existence of cities: *to enable freedom of association and expression.*

If the city's fundamental roles are to facilitate transaction and to enable freedom, city intelligence will be a measure of how well it does this. This leads to a definition of the intelligent city that goes beyond the concept of wired (or wireless) networked space. It stops short of defining the city as a sentient being, but it does gain something from the implication contained in the word 'intelligence'. The idea of the city as an organism, although it conjures up images drawn from science fiction fantasy, allows the elaboration of a definition of city intelligence

Figure 2.7
The built fabric of the city is only half the equation, without the social, cultural and political processes, the city's fabric is but an empty shell. (*Source*: Guy Briggs.)

far more complex than that referred to by measurements of digital infrastructure (Kane, 1999; Shutz, 1999).

Digital infrastructure is but one aspect of the city's physical fabric (Figure 2.7), which also includes its transport infrastructure, its utilities and its building stock. This is the city as container, a passive vessel. But such a view is one-dimensional. A broader concept of the city, derived from the sense of the city as organism, would consider it to be a network of systems, a complex structure of interwoven organizational forms. The city is both container and contained the sum of its fabric and the human processes that shape and are shaped by this fabric. The city is the intersection of its people, their processes and the physical place.

To draw an analogy with the digital world, the city's physical fabric is its 'hardware'. The 'software' that brings it alive and allows it to function is the collection of human organizational systems (Figure 2.8) that construct the city its social networks; cultural infrastructure; economic base and infrastructure; and institutional infrastructure, including political and planning mechanisms.

At its broadest level, city intelligence is the capability of this network of organizational systems to function effectively, and successfully, over a period of time. It is reliant on compatibility between the city's functional objectives (its 'business plan'), and the provision of hard and soft infrastructure to service these objectives. References to 'city intelligence' should measure how effectively the city (fabric, networks and systems)

39

Figure 2.8
The city's container is complemented by the organizational systems that take place within it, one of which is the political system, illustrated here by a demonstration in Trafalgar Square, London. (*Source*: Guy Briggs.)

facilitates the functioning of human socio-cultural and economic systems, and allows their evolution. In short, the successful (or intelligent) city matches aspirations (demand) and resources (supply).

In a world of constant change, the basis for a city's long-term success, and therefore maintaining its intelligent status, lies in the adaptability of its fabric, processes and systems. It is this aspect that makes city intelligence and urban sustainability mutually dependent concepts.

Urban intelligence, sustainability and the new context: intelligent cities and sustainability?

This understanding of what constitutes city intelligence leads to a consideration of the city from a holistic viewpoint as the sum of a number of systems: namely economic, social and environmental. These systems are fundamentally integrated, and the health of the city overall relies on achieving a dynamic balance between these potentially competing interests. The city is not static; it is a dynamic system in which the key to its long-term health and success, or its intelligence, will be its capacity to adapt to change. Like any ecological system, the key to this capacity is diversity.

Anyone with even a modest understanding of the principles of sustainability will recognize that the factors described above are as fundamental to sustainability definitions and theory as they are to city intelligence. The Darwinian concept of adaptability is the primary link between these two concepts. City intelligence will measure the capability of a city through the adaptability of its systems (its fabric and processes) to fulfil its fundamental role, ensuring that its citizens are capable of carrying out their transactions and living in freedom. Sustainability will measure the extent to which the city is capable of doing so without negatively affecting the wider environment, or the future capacity of the city to continue to fulfil its role in the same way. Although different in emphasis, these two concepts need to be considered together. Urban sustainability must be rooted in the concept of urban intelligence. If a city is not to some extent intelligent, then its sustainability is irrelevant, but if a city is not sustainable, then it will not remain intelligent for long.

Yet the requirements for city intelligence evolve as one might expect from a Darwinian concept. What made a city intelligent (and for that matter sustainable) in the past will not necessarily do so today or in the future. The traditional city form is derived from the surrounding physical context, available technology and the culture and habits of its inhabitants. In the long term, the sustainability of the traditional city was dependent on satisfying the needs and desires of its citizens, while remaining within (or expanding) the carrying capacity of the local hinterland. The cities that thrived and prospered into the modern age (incidents of politics and war aside) were those that best facilitated expansion through trade and expression, and that were able to adapt continually to changing economic or socio-cultural circumstances; that is, those that were most 'intelligent'. Intrinsic to this definition of intelligence was urban competition; in other words, competition for resources, people and trade.

The urban context has changed. Three factors are profoundly altering the potential for any city to remain successful in the long term:

- **The shift to the knowledge economy and its consequences, especially in terms of the increasing requirements for autonomy and interaction of knowledge workers**

- **The increasing globalization of trade, labour, culture and politics, as well as the new opportunities created by digital communications and information sharing systems**

- **The increasingly important systemic inter-relationships between different cities and places**

The changing context has resulted in both the expansion and change in structure of cities' hinterlands. Cities are globally connected in an increasingly complex web of links, through

Figure 2.9
A 900-person capacity dining
hall in Chinatown, New York,
replicating those in Hong Kong,
and a symbol of the
globalization of culture and
opportunity in the
contemporary world.
(*Source*: Guy Briggs.)

their production systems, finance, resource usage and in the environmental problems that they cause and suffer. Urban hinterlands now overlap, and in many cases one city will be part of another's hinterland, and vice versa (Figure 2.9). Under these circumstances, where cities around the world, which form part of a greater dynamic system, collaboration, not competition, is the key to success, and specialization is only sustainable within a broader regional framework (Harrison *et al.*, 2004).

The new context: the knowledge economy

The key factor in the new urban context outlined above is the fundamental economic shift that began to emerge in the late 1980s. This new context, sometimes called the 'New Economy', but more appropriately referred to as the 'Knowledge Economy' is becoming the defining paradigm of the way we live and work in the 21st century (Harrison *et al.*, 2004). The most obvious manifestation of this is the Internet, and its influence on business and economic production has been extraordinary (Shapiro *et al.*, 2000). However, the changes brought about by this new economic paradigm run far deeper than the emergence of a single digital tool. The knowledge economy is not just about the digitization of economic processes, but embraces three contemporary economic revolutions:

- **A revolution in the use of technology in business, based on information and telecommunications technologies**

- The formation of an integrated world economy through globalization
- The emergence of entirely new forms of economic production and management, to the extent that the output of the information economy is now a significant part of the global economy, and a major contributor to real US economic growth (Shapiro *et al.*, 2000)

At the same time, two simultaneous spatial phenomena have taken place, and these will have major implications for 21st century urbanism. Firstly, economic activities are becoming spatially dispersed, and this trend will continue as people have the opportunity to work anywhere, at anytime (Harrison *et al.*, 2004). And secondly, knowledge workers require an increasing level of interaction with one another to achieve their project goals. This interaction does not necessarily require face-to-face communication. However, the natural social gregariousness of humans, coupled with the value created by informal, unplanned and unpredictable interaction, is likely to increase the need of people to come together in physical space (Harrison *et al.*, 2004). This is particularly evident at top management level, where new forms of territorial centralization of control are emerging.

At its broadest level, the knowledge economy is about creative people coming together to add value to work, through the exchange of information to generate new ideas. Keynesian economics supposed that consumption would be the driving force of the economy, yet current theory suggests that ideas that is new ways of thought leading to technological advances and inventions will be the economic driving force of the future. It will become necessary therefore to reverse the attitude that considers the environment and society as serving the economy, rather than the other way around. Economic growth will become dependent on doing more with less, or doing without (Hansen, 1999).

The two spatial trends identified above will therefore have major implications for cities. The increasing dispersal of economic functions, the ability to work anywhere and at anytime, provides a renewed emphasis on the quality of place as a primary factor in locational choice. At the same time the territorial centralization that is emerging for continued social interaction implies a new strategic role for particular cities that are able to position themselves at the centre of this new paradigm. What these two implications have in common, is an emerging focus on people as the primary variable.

The intelligent city will aim to position itself as a key site of the knowledge economy. Whether the aim is to capture the increasing dispersal of economic operations and talent, or to emerge as one of the centres of power and control, is irrelevant to this discussion, and more likely to depend on factors of history and scale. Either option will require the city to meet the business requirements of the new economic paradigm. In summary these are:

- employing the right people
- increasing interaction and communication
- promoting accessibility, openness and convenience
- achieving flexibility of operation: functional, financial and physical
- maintaining and promoting value through image differentiation (Harrison *et al.*, 2004)

If a city is to effectively provide for these business requirements, it will need to address them in terms of both its hard and soft systems that is, its fabric and processes. It is self-evident that a city will need to provide appropriate infrastructural conditions, including digital networks, but what is less well understood is the need for cities to address more generic needs such as requirements for diversity, intensification and the city's quality of place.

As history has demonstrated, few cities can grow or even survive in the long term through specialization. Cities will need to attract and provide for a diversity of organizations and cultures, through maintaining diversity in its neighbourhoods, buildings and spaces, including a range of public to private space. Providing for diversity increases the agility of the workplace, building, development or city; in other words, its ability to be flexible in the face of change is critical.

At the same time, competing (and co-operating) knowledge industry organizations will seek to concentrate functions and people in a particular locale. Intensification of the city through increasing its density, especially at central locations, through the promotion of effective transport networks and by ensuring that transport accessibility and densification are related which maximizes the potential of high-value locations, increases the potential for activity and interaction, and optimizes infrastructure provision. This facilitates the clustering of related economic functions, and allows more effective access to goods and services. This is not a new idea; research by Newman and Kenworthy (1989), amongst others, has demonstrated the link between transport and urban form, in particular car dependence and urban sprawl. This has been picked up in key policy documents in the UK, such as the influential report by the Urban Task Force (1999), and the Sustainable Communities Plan (ODPM, 2003). However, it seems to be an idea that has been overlooked as cities spread out to merge with the suburbs, which in turn can blend into peri-urban business parks. It is also intrinsically linked to the next factor, identity.

City identity, or sense of place, will become increasingly important for two reasons. Highly educated workers are becoming increasingly discerning of their own value and therefore more confident in demanding better terms; this increasing mobility of the workforce allows a greater focus on quality of life issues. These factors create a greater demand for access to, and therefore provision of, cultural and leisure amenities. Attracting the increasingly mobile workforce requires that cities achieve differentiation not by specialization, but by enhancing their quality of place.

Achieving the intelligent city: a focus on social sustainability

Conventional approaches to sustainability pit environmental protection against economic development. But a holistic approach to the question will find that the greatest hurdles to achieving sustainability lie neither in the environmental or economic spheres, but in the social. Global environmental problems have their origin in local action, and changes to the global environment have significant local impacts. Cities are open social systems integrated into the broader systems of the global economy and global environment. They are increasingly indistinct from their hinterlands and are globally connected to one another in a progressively more complex web of links: in production systems, finance, resource usage, and through the environmental problems caused, and suffered, by them.

Achieving social sustainability is a prerequisite both for environmental and economic (Figure 2.10) sustainability, which will by necessity take place in the urban realm (Wu, 1998). Despite being closely associated with crime and vandalism, deprivation, unemployment, deteriorating infrastructure, inner-city decay, socio-economic problems and neighbourhood collapse (i.e. the most serious symptoms of unsustainable development), the city nevertheless provides the greatest opportunities for their remedy.

Figure 2.10
The urban environment may be the scene of great socio-economic inequity, especially in the developing world with its large populations of urban poor, but the city is also the place of greatest opportunity, and therefore the environment in which we are most likely to achieve global social equity.
(*Source:* Guy Briggs.)

The concept of urban intelligence puts people back at the centre of the urban agenda. By definition, urban intelligence has social sustainability as its focus. The environmental agenda that generally drives sustainability processes is very often divorced from its *Brundtland* origins, where it was expressed in terms of the need for development to ensure greater social sustainability (locally and globally), while acknowledging the limitations imposed by the environmental context (to paraphrase the definition of sustainability set out in the report of the 1987 Brundtland Commission[2]).

If cities are to strive for sustainability, urban governance and policy should be directed at achieving urban intelligence. This will require a major shift, especially in the UK, so that these two aspects, process (governance) and tool (policy), become more strategic and more integrated, with the aim of being facilitatory rather than directive. The primary arena in which this shift will take place is in planning policy, which sets the framework within which other strategic policies are realized.

The intelligent city and planning policy

In the UK especially, apart from broad strategic aims set out in unitary development plans, planning policy is essentially reactive and confrontational.[3] The planning system will need to shift from defining possible products and acceptable standards, to becoming the process enabler, by working to articulate ambitions for development and acting to manage the process. Re-orienting policy towards process, rather than product, is the means to achieving effective policy in tune with the requirements of urban intelligence. The current focus of the planning system is largely based on the physical (or environmental) system, the process container, at the expense of the requirements of urban processes. The focus of the planning system should be to set strategic goals, and then to work with both developer and user organizations to ensure that the city enables transaction and freedom for residents and organizations.

Policy as a system must integrate with other systems that make up the city, and become flexible enough to accommodate, and even drive, development and change. Adaptability is the vital attribute of the intelligent city, and the adaptability of buildings and infrastructure is as much a function of the planning regime as it is of available construction technologies and financial mechanisms.

Measuring change

The Planning and Compulsory Purchase Bill, currently progressing through parliament, will make the achievement of sustainable development a clear and definite duty of the planning system, and its changes are to be welcomed. However, it does not go far enough in shaking up the planning system as a policy framework. The primary evidence for this is its emphasis on speeding up the process by which planning applications are made. This will certainly be welcomed by business people and developers, but fails to recognize that for the majority of citizens, who are unlikely ever to go through the planning application process, their experience of the planning system is only indirect, and through the resulting created environment.

The challenge for planners will be to recognize that the best results are obtained through an iterative process. By working closely with users, developers and professionals, planners will be able to shift from policy definition to implementation in a seamless briefing process. Policy should be seen as a brief, rather than as proscription (setting out ambitions, defining targets and articulating quality levels), instead of defining how things should or should not be done. The aim of policy as a brief is to create frameworks for development that are flexible and comprehensive, and based on consensus at every decision-making stage. These frameworks can exist across a range of scales, from city-wide strategic visions to site-specific development briefs.

Orientating policy delivery around the development process, rather than its products, requires that we redefine the indicators used to measure the current status of our cities (supply), and to determine success in meeting future ambitions (demand), in terms of the requirements of urban intelligence. There are many indicator sets in existence, and new ones are constantly emerging. Achieving a completely comprehensive and wide-ranging set of indicators is neither necessary nor desirable. Such indicator sets can become a hindrance to change, operating as a checklist rather than as a stimulant to intelligent action (Harrison *et al.*, 2004). It is more important that indicators become more focused, and targeted to measuring the *right* things. Using a limited set of the right indicators should enable policy makers and implementers to think laterally, provoking unexpected results and responses.

To indicate the relative advantages and disadvantages of urban indicators, three examples are discussed here. The first of these was established by urban development consultancy *Londonomics*, undertaking a review of town centre performance and regeneration in 2000. According to this review, urban success results from the interaction of four linked elements, which they term '*Intelligent City Indicators*'. These are as follows:

- *Economy*: concerned with turnover, investment and employment, and measured over time against turnover per unit of floor space, number of planning applications, business starts and closures, retail expenditure and demographics
- *Accessibility*: concerned with transport, and measured through infrastructural capacity versus extent of congestion
- *Property*: concerned with space, and measuring return, take-up (a function of demand) and change of use, against vacancy rates, comparative yield, intensity of land use, building quality and open space
- *Environment*: concerned with safety and security, ambience and conviviality, and local partnership and commitment assessed in terms of availability (the number of hours the environment is active), sense of place, cleanliness, amenities and key attractions

It should be noted that the economy is placed first amongst this set, with the implication that the health of the system is reliant on the buoyancy of the economy. Although relatively straightforward, the major shortcoming of this indicator set is its largely quantitative aspect of the supply and demand equation.

A consortium lead by *The London School of Economics* completed a study in September 2002 by the name of PASTILLE

(*Promoting Action for Sustainability Through Indicators at the Local Level in Europe*). The indicators put together during this study are quite different in their emphasis to those developed by *Londonomics*. They do not directly refer to urban intelligence, but the aim was to produce a tool that would assist local authorities with city planning and resource management. This emphasis on effective resource management, through changing demand circumstances, implies that the indicators should assist cities to 'be intelligent'.

PASTILLE has produced 10 key indicators, heading 10 indicator sets, which are:

- satisfaction with local community services
- local contribution to global climatic change
- local mobility and passenger transportation
- availability of local public open areas and local services
- quality of local outdoor air
- children's journeys to and from school
- sustainable management of local authority and businesses
- noise pollution
- sustainable land use
- availability of products promoting sustainability

The value of indicators of this type is in measuring the effectiveness of delivery of local authority services on the ground. They do not address strategic issues, such as the aspirations of the city's residents and businesses, the suitability of the city's transport system or the system of city governance. But for the purposes of the intelligent city, the set is unduly long, concentrating on issues of detail, and is of less use in determining a city's intelligence than is the indicators compiled by *Londonomics*.

The key question is: What will the indicators tell us? Indicators potentially provide a great deal of information, enabling current performance of particular aspects to be benchmarked against past performance and desired targets. But they do not provide us with any indication of the availability of choices for reaching alternative futures. As well as being primarily concerned with quantitative measures, the main problem with this type of indicator set, for the purposes of determining city intelligence, is that they are largely concerned with supply issues and do not address demand, thereby ignoring the major indicator of the overall quality of place.

A focus on quality

The final indicator example does just this, and is from the *Brookings Institution* in Washington, D.C. A report written for the *Brookings Center* on *Urban and Metropolitan Policy* (Florida and Gates, 2001), examined what attracted knowledge industry businesses to particular urban centres in the US. The most important factor to emerge was *people*, or more specifically, a high level of talent in the particular location (referred to by the companies concerned as 'high human capital'). The key factors in locational choice for industry have traditionally been access to raw materials, markets and labour, with labour ranked always third. What the report demonstrated was that in the knowledge economy, labour has become the significant variable in locational choice. Industries are now following labour, rather than the other way around. What is now of particular interest to cities, is: What will make them attractive to the knowledge economy labour pool?

Florida and Gates developed a theory which states that a city's diversity, or level of tolerance towards a wide range of people, is the key to its success in attracting talented people. To measure this they established a series of diversity indices, with three top-level indicators: the *gay index* which measures the representation of *gay male couples*; the *bohemian index* which records numbers of artists, musicians, writers, actors, directors and designers; and the *foreign born index* which measures the representation of immigrants. A fourth index consolidates the three to provide a *composite diversity index*.

The indices were based on the 1990 census numbers for the US's 50 largest cities (by population), and compared to the *Milken Institute's Tech Pole*, which measures the concentration of high technology and growth, based on 1998 figures. The measure of high-tech growth is taken as a leading indication of future city success. The comparison demonstrated that the leading indicator for an area's potential to attract high-tech growth is the presence of a large gay population, although all three indicators showed a high correlation with future high-tech growth. The composite indicator showed the most consistent correlation. The authors found that *diversity of human capital is a key component of the ability to attract and retain high-tech industry* (Florida and Gates, 2001, p. 6).

It is the conclusion that the authors were able to draw from their results that is the most important aspect of these indicators. They

Figure 2.11
Successful (and intelligent) cities will embrace diversity, both culturally and ethnically. (*Source*: Guy Briggs.)

did not suppose that high-tech jobs were chasing gay males or bohemian musicians, but rather that people in high-tech jobs are drawn to places that are inclusive, open minded and culturally creative. A cosmopolitan and diverse local population indicates these urban attributes. The significant message here is that what attracts people to live in cities is becoming the most important factor in determining economic success. The huge advantage of this particular set of indicators is that they focus on people and demand, they are essentially qualitative, and they link quality of place with urban success (Figure 2.11).

Conclusion

This chapter sets out to examine the concept of the intelligent city, seeking to broaden the common understanding of the intelligent city as a digitally networked environment. Changing this notion requires the posing of critical questions about the fundamental role of the city, and to examine its structure as both fabric and process. Through these the city is defined as a holistic system, in which adaptability is the key to its long-term success.

The questions that have been posed indicate that the intelligent city is not a new concept, but that as a measure of success, the intelligent city has been around for a lengthy period of time, although not defined as such. Although the vital ingredient of an intelligent city remains its ability to match aspirations and resources, the factors that gave a traditional city its intelligence are not necessarily those that are of relevance today. The context of urban success has changed. Globalization and the arrival of the knowledge economy have ushered in a series of revolutions in the relationship of cities to one another, and of people to cities.

Although the knowledge economy is still in its infancy, its fundamental differentiator is the shift in emphasis – from the manufacture of goods to the creation of ideas – as the primary economic product. This, with its associated revolution in communications technology, will overturn the traditional requirement for labour to follow industry. But people still need to come together for face-to-face collaboration, and will do this where it is most convenient, and most pleasant. We are already seeing a renewed emphasis on the quality of place in particular cities, and it is these cities that are likely to emerge as key sites of the knowledge economy.

These factors have profound implications for policy, and for policy makers. Policy must shift in emphasis from the specification of satisfactory products, to the definition of ambitions and management of the process, while protecting diverse interests. Nowhere is this more necessary than in planning policy and urban development process. Policy makers will need to become more proactive, and policy more iterative, rather than relying on the current reactive process. To assist this process, we will need to change the way we try to understand cities. Achieving effective process facilitation requires the development of a new set of intelligent city indicators, both to define the current status of a particular city (issues of supply) and to assess its ambitions (demand).

Effective intelligent city indicators will be simple to apply, will link supply and demand, and will be qualitative in essence. They will also examine the intelligent city in terms of its long-term sustainability, and may be used to predict future development needs. In this way we will develop a new model of the 'sustainable city' – incorporating an understanding of the management of overlapping functions, and the potential for intensification of space and time to enable local action that is integrated into city-wide, regional and even global visions.

Investigations into the sustainability of the built environment, and programmes for action to address the problems such investigations identify, too often get caught up in the detail. Solutions often concentrate on the environmental attributes of an individual building without sufficient understanding of broader strategic frameworks, of systemic attributes, or of the drivers and consequences of individual actions. This contradicts the fundamental meaning of sustainability, and can only be addressed by rooting the issues within a broader framework of theory and action. By linking urban sustainability to city intelligence, we will begin to develop a framework that can attribute real, relative value, better enabling the achievement of the aims of the sustainability agenda.

Conventional arguments state that cities are the antithesis of sustainable development, as massive consumers and producers of waste (Girardet, 1992). However, contrasting arguments would consider cities as both the natural human environment for the 21st century, and the arena in which sustainability can best be achieved. If the route to sustainable development is through social sustainability, the city is where this will happen. If sustainability relies on an economy of means, then it is in cities, which allow for effectiveness of process through the concentration of resources, overlap and built-in redundancy, that we will achieve a sustainable future.

Notes

1. The *Intelligent Buildings in South-East Asia* study scored the intelligence of buildings on a matrix, categorizing them into four intelligent building types, according to the quality of the building itself as well as its location within the city. Buildings falling into the bottom left quadrant are redundant and poorly located, while those in the bottom right are good buildings in the wrong place. In the top left are poor buildings in good locations. A truly 'intelligent' building will be one that is both well located and of good quality, and these will fit into the top right quadrant (Harrison *et al.*, 1998; DEGW, 1999).

2. The World Commission on Environment and Development was created as a result of General Assembly Resolution 38/161 adopted at the 38th Session of the United Nations in autumn 1983.

3. Although this may seem a controversial statement, primary evidence for this is the large number of planning enquiries that are held each year, from which, it seems, only lawyers benefit. These are most often adversarial engagements in which the planning authority will argue against a particular development, while its proponents will argue in favour.

References

Ackroyd, P. (2000) *London, The Biography*, Chatto and Windus, London.

DEGW (London) and Teknibank (Milan) in association with The European Intelligent Building Group (1992) *The Intelligent Building in Europe*, The British Council for Offices, Reading.

DEGW, Ove Arup and Partners, and Northcroft, in association with The Council on Tall Buildings and Urban Habitat (Grupo Brasil and Edison Musa Arquitetos Addociados) (1999) *Intelligent Buildings in Latin America*, unpublished Multi Client Study.

Florida, R. and Gates, G. (2001) *Technology and Tolerance: The Importance of Diversity to High Technology Growth*, The Brookings Institution, Washington.

Girardet, H. (1992) *The Gaia Atlas of Cities, New Directions of Sustainable Urban Living*, Gaia Books, London.

Hansen, S. (1999) Economic Initiatives and Sustainable Development: An Assessment of Possibilities and Limitations. In: *Towards Sustainable Development: on the Goals of Development and the Conditions of Sustainability* (eds. Lafferty, W.M. and Langhelle, O.), Macmillan, Basingstoke.

Harrison, A., Loe, E. and Read, J. (1998) *Intelligent Buildings in South East Asia*, E & FN Spon, London.

Harrison, A., Wheeler, P. and Whitehead, C. (2004) *Distributed Workplace: Sustainable Work Environments*, Routledge, London.

Jacobs, J. (1969) *The Economy of Cities*, Random House, New York.

Kane, M. (1999) Sustainability Concepts: From Theory to Practice. In: *Sustainability in Question: The Search for a Conceptual Framework* (eds. Kohn, J., Gowdy, J., Hinterberger, F. and Van der Straaten, J.), E Elgar, Cheltenham.

Newman, P. and Kenworthy, J. (1989) *Cities and Automobile Dependence: an international sourcebook*, Gower, Aldershot.

Office of the Deputy Prime Minister (ODPM) (2003) *Sustainable Communities: building for the future*, Office of the Deputy Prime Minister, London.

Shapiro, R., Price, L. and Mayer, J. (2000) *Digital Economy 2000*, US Department of Commerce, Washington.

Shutz, J. (1999) Organising Diversity. In: *Sustainability in Question: The Search for a Conceptual Framework* (eds. Kohn, J., Gowdy, J., Hinterberger, F. and Van der Straaten, J.), E Elgar, Cheltenham.

Urban Task Force (1999) *Towards an Urban Renaissance*, E & FN Spon, London.

Wu, C. (1998) *The Concept of Urban Social Sustainability: Co-ordinating Everyday Life and Institutional Structures in London*, unpublished PhD thesis, London School of Economics.

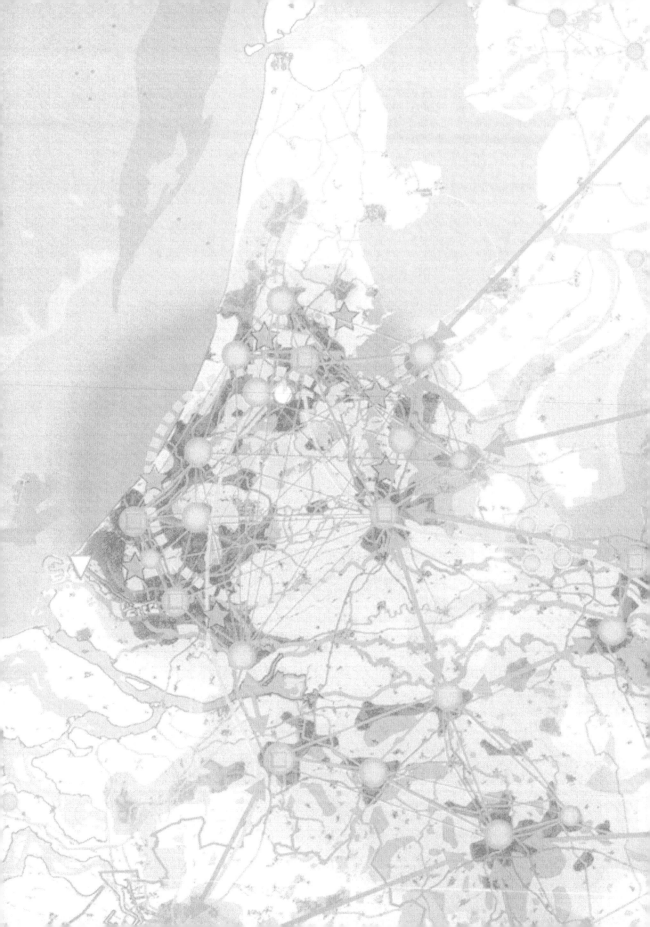

3

Akiko Okabe

Towards the Spatial Sustainability of City-regions: A Comparative Study of Tokyo and Randstad

Introduction: the city-region

One of the main debates in urban planning today is centred on whether the high-density compact city is more sustainable than a diffused low-density settlement. While it can be argued that urban development does not necessarily predicate the physical expansion of urbanized areas, it can also be argued that there are pragmatic limitations to restricting development to urban areas, to the exclusion of rural areas. Land-use management methods have historically been confined to traditional planning practices, which have controlled important factors such as the residential density adopted and the degree of mixed-use activity in a given area. This chapter attempts to overcome these limitations by introducing the concept of the city-region as a spatial scale for urban development.

Within the city-region scale, both monocentric development with a single-metropolitan core, and polycentric development consisting of closely located, administratively independent cities, can be appropriate models. In the spatial economy, the virtues of a polycentric accumulation of economic, activities in the wider urban-region may outweigh those of monocentric accumulation *en masse*.

This chapter sets out to illustrate why the polycentric city-region should be more attractive and sustainable compared with the monocentric when considering the city-region as both a living and working sphere. Two case studies, Tokyo and Randstad, are referred to. Tokyo in Japan is the largest example of monocentric urban development in the world, which has its origin as a single-core city, has greatly expanded and can now be considered on a regional scale. Randstad in the Netherlands is based on a polycentric urban system composed of several cities and has become a highly urbanized, well-connected region. This chapter redefines both Tokyo and Randstad as city-regions and discusses the idea that the growing interest in sustainability should lead both city-regions towards a similar spatial form despite their distinct differences.

This chapter is composed of five sections. Firstly, the reason why Tokyo and Randstad have been selected is discussed, taking into account the global developments. Secondly, the importance of discussing the city-region as a sustainable *spatial* form, rather than a sustainable *urban* form is examined. Thirdly, the spatial configuration of the two city-regions is analysed through maps of the same scale in which the spatial distribution of built-up and green areas is visualized. Fourthly, the ways in which Tokyo and Randstad are transforming their spatial structures in order to achieve environmental sustainability as well as economic and socio-cultural sustainability is explored. And finally, by way of a conclusion, three necessary conditions of sustainable city-regions are proposed.

Why Tokyo and Randstad?

Tokyo has often been compared with other large cities such as New York, London or Paris. Sassen (1991), for example, designated New York, London and Tokyo as the three global cities, defined by the considerable economic influence that they have on other cities and countries on a worldwide scale. However, Tokyo is physically too large for a direct comparison of its spatial form with that of other global cities in developed countries. Recognizing the key role of cities in an increasingly globalized world, Scott (2000) introduced the concept of 'global city-regions' with the aim of incorporating 'the notion of the wider metropolitan-region as an emerging political–economic unit with increasing autonomy of action on the national and world stages'. It is the objective of this chapter to redefine Tokyo as a global city-region.

The potential of global cities is basically judged by their population and their economic activities. It could be argued that the debate on global cities seems to be instinctively based on the premise that cities are formed by a single-central metropolitan core and its immediate surroundings. Sassen's three global cities all have a mononuclear structure in common. However, when the focus is put on the wider region, the synergic power caused by a number of overlapping conurbations can be taken into account (Scott, 2000). For example, the agglomeration of the Pearl River Delta in China is composed of different conurbations, each of them originally having a distinct degree of autonomy, after which they rapidly transformed into one whole independent economic unit. This is not a classic case of megalopolis as identified by Gottman in the 1960s, rather it represents a new spatial form of a wider metropolitan-region on a global scale (Castells, 1996). The region of Randstad is also a good example of polycentric development, encompassing well-established, economically comparable cities, which now form an important economic region in the Netherlands.

The competition between cities to increase economic activity with consequent expansion in urban populations, in many cases, has led to the formation of large urban agglomerations. However, when a city-region with a large territorial surface becomes more globally competitive than the traditional city form, two issues come to light. Firstly, the spatial distribution of populations and economic activities within the region must be explored and planned, and secondly, a balance must be struck between economic efficiency and an improved quality of life.

In this chapter, Tokyo has been selected as an example of a monocentric city-region and Randstad as an example of a polycentric city-region.

Spatial considerations of the 'city-region'

The debate on sustainable urban form has been limited to the scope of urban areas alone, to the exclusion of rural areas. However, the reality of locating urban residential areas has already extended well beyond the city limits. Whilst people who live in rural areas may access urban services on a daily basis, it can also be beneficial for urban dwellers to take advantage of nearby rural areas. This has been analysed by the French urbanist

Ascher, who theorized that urban functions should be diffused over the entire region but with the physical distinction of urban and rural areas, introducing the theory of 'Metapolis' (Ascher, 1995). Jacobs, whose work has centred on the city as the measurable form, developed her theory of the city-region as an economic functional unit in her work, *Cities and the Wealth of Nations* (1984).

Especially in densely populated territories, such as those in which Tokyo and Randstad are located, the distinction between the urban and the rural is losing its meaning. Rural areas do not necessarily depend economically on agriculture. Due to a highly developed transport infrastructure and the information society, urban functions are increasingly spread out over a wider urban- and/or rural-region. Regions or city-regions are arising both as a framework for sustainable planning and for policy-making (Orlfield, 1997; Simmonds and Hack, 2000; Salet *et al.*, 2003). The urbanization process has been described as a series of consecutive stages. Suburbanization, which has historically occurred in many cities after the initial phase of urbanization, has been perceived as a physical invasion of the rural by the urban. Urban sprawl 'occurs not on a *tabula rasa* landscape but rather on a peopled and working rural landscape' (Savage and Lapping, 2003). Such counter-urbanization has taken place for different reasons which may range from poor living conditions, to nationally planned suburban developments, to the pursuit of a perceived higher quality of life away from the city. With counter-urbanization (suburbanization, de-urbanization or whatever term is used to describe the movement of people away from the city), urban functions spread homogeneously, arguably weakening both urban and rural characteristics. It then becomes more difficult to distinguish between an urban and a rural area, at least if judged by the economic activities, and the services and facilities provided.

If reurbanization follows counter-urbanization, it has been argued that a cyclical process of urbanization is complete, leading towards sustainable development (Hall and Hay, 1980). However, the transition from counter-urbanization to reurbanization does not seem to be a simple enough process for clear parameters to be identified in the urbanization process. In his research on regional systems in North Italy, Dematteis detected that 'between 1980 and 1990, this urban de-concentration (de-urbanization) process continues, but in a more selective way which can be described as 'concentrated

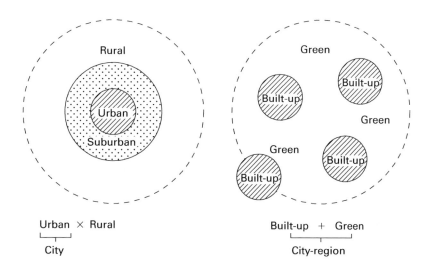

Figure 3.1
The urbanization process and the city-region.

de-concentration' (1998). If a city-region is considered as a framework, this phenomenon can be analysed more effectively. Furthermore, a framework can facilitate the identification of those qualitative characteristics of the urban and rural, and the symbiosis between built-up and green areas. This is becoming more and more pressing as the distinction between urban and rural continues to blur (see Figure 3.1).

Randstad and Tokyo: spatial configuration

The significance of the city-region varies at different scales. At the local level, it is possible to find examples of several municipalities cooperating in order to reach a critical mass of 200,000–300,000 inhabitants, which is enough to support sophisticated urban functions. In France, *Communautés d'Agglomération*, or municipal coalitions, are established to reach a mass of 15,000 inhabitants. In Japan, many municipality unifications are negotiated in order to reach a mass of 150,000–300,000 inhabitants, which, it is suggested, will maximize administrative efficiency. At the other end of the scale, city-regions on a mega-regional level are emerging, such as the 'blue banana' which covers the area from London to France and Italy, and aspires to be a mega-region with 80 million inhabitants (Brunet, 1989) (Figure 3.2). Another example is the *Japanese Pacific Belt* which stretches from Tokyo through Nagoya and Osaka to Fukuoka for a distance of about 800 km. In Europe, 'at the broadest geographical scale, there is continued growth of

Figure 3.2
The 'blue banana.'

polycentric mega-urban regions. . . . But, at a finer geographical scale within these regions, there is a noticeable geographical deconcentration from the most heavily urbanised areas which form their cores' (Hall, 2001). The globalized world is now experiencing a complex dynamism caused by different layers of city-regions which have distinct scales of development (both within the region itself and compared to other city-regions) which are spatially integrated.

Randstad

The comparison of Tokyo with Randstad focuses on city-regions at a wider regional level which extends to a spatial area with a diameter of 100 km. Kloosterman and Lambregts (2001) define polycentric urban-regions as having the following three conditions: a number of historically and spatially distinct cities which are closely located, none of which is a clear hegemony, and which have maintained their own administrative independence. Randstad is located at the heart of Europe and is a classic example of a city-region based on a polycentric urban

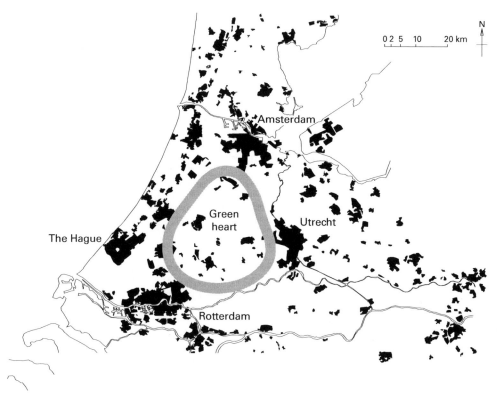

Figure 3.3
The Randstad and its green heart.

system on a greater regional level. It covers an area of 7–8000 km^2 which is accessible within 1 hour by high-speed transport infrastructure. The polycentric urban system is composed of four main cities: Amsterdam (the state capital), The Hague (the seat of the Dutch government), Rotterdam (an international port) and Utrecht (the convention and service centre in the middle of the country). These four principal cities have different urban functions. The population of each city is no more than 1 million inhabitants but the population of the city-region as a whole reaches 6 million. Randstad is well known for its protected green area in the middle, dubbed the green heart (Figure 3.3). The cities are located on its edge ('Rand' in Dutch).

Randstad is economically strong enough to compete with monocentric cities such as London or Paris, the largest in Europe. The primary competitive edge that Randstad holds is due to its privileged location within Europe. But the green heart of the area can be highlighted as a uniquely competitive factor. The existence of the green heart and the polycentric urban system with medium-sized cities ensures that urban life is always close to a rural area, which is impossible to achieve in large, monocentric metropolis. After the Second World War through to the 1980s, Dutch authorities had controlled urban development from encroaching on the green area, in an effort to maintain the traditional Dutch landscape (VROM, 2000). The green heart would not have survived if these strict controls had not existed. Meanwhile, 'the Randstad maintains major links with other economic centres in the world through its harbors (Rotterdam) and airports (Amsterdam Schiphol).... The Randstad has seven universities. Furthermore, the four cities, Amsterdam, Rotterdam, The Hague and Utrecht, excel in social and cultural amenities, museums, theatres and conference centres' (Tummers and Schrijnen, 2000). People living in polycentric Randstad have similar levels of accessibility to urban functions as people living in a large monocentric metropolis with the same overall agglomeration mass. Furthermore, a polycentric region would be arguably more flexible in adapting to the changing work, consumption and family patterns that have emerged over recent years. For instance, households consisting of two working adults have become more commonplace and there is no reason why both should be commuting to the same central urban area. In a polycentric region, accessibility to employment can easily be facilitated by the strategic residential location for couples working in different cities (Evans and Taylor, 2001).

Tokyo

The Tokyo wider metropolitan region, which extends over four prefectures (Tokyo, Saitama, Kanagawa and Chiba), comprises an area with a diameter of 100 km and has a population of approximately 30 million. Tokyo is a city that originally had a monocentric structure (see Figure 3.4). Just before the Second World War, the Yamanote line, a circular railway route 35 km in circumference, was completed which contributed to the post-war creation of subcentres, such as Shinjuku, Shibuya and Ikebukuro, responding to the rapid growth of the city towards the west. Today, the historic core district of Tokyo incorporates these subcentres, which together, make up the large monocentric core of the greater metropolitan-region. The adjacent local cities have been absorbed into the greater Tokyo region. Historically, these local cities, Saitama, Chiba, Hachijoji-Tama and Kawasaki-Yokohama, developed independently of Tokyo. During the rapid economic growth of Japan in the 1960s and 1970s, these local cities were transformed into 'dormitory-towns' of Tokyo.

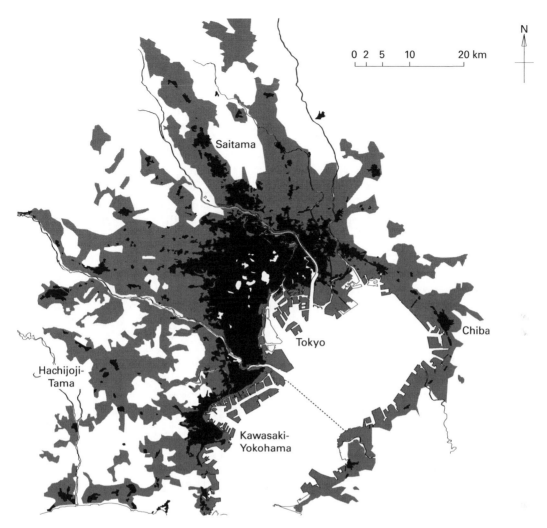

Figure 3.4
Tokyo greater and wider
metropolitan regions.

The majority of employed people living in these local cities commuted daily to the centre of Tokyo, coming home only to sleep at night. The over-concentration of urban functions in the single-business core led to urban problems, such as soaring office rents, housing shortages, overcrowded public transportation and traffic congestion.

In the second half of the 1980s, Japan experienced a spectacular economic boom, well known as 'bubble economy', characterized by huge increases in land values which forced the development strategy of Tokyo metropolitan-region to change. During this time, the 'dormitory-towns' of Tokyo were given a strategic role as new functional cores of economic activity in the expectation of further development of the wider

63

Tokyo region. To ameliorate the over-concentration of urban functions, it was proposed to promote the business core cities (Yokohama, Saitama, Hachijoji and Chiba) at the edge of Tokyo, by transferring business functions from the central core to the edge cities, and make it possible to live and work there. Both the central and metropolitan governments have taken steps to decentralize the urban functions of Tokyo in the *Tokyo Metropolitan Planning* and the *Tokyo City Planning Policies*.

The policy to reinforce the polycentric structure of Tokyo's wider region has worked effectively to a certain extent. In the centre of Tokyo, employment has decreased and office buildings reduced in number. However, when the Japanese economy moved in recession after the bubble period, the decentralization policy was questioned and the demand to reinforce the economic activity in the centre grew. Those who support the concentrated accumulation in the single-central core of Tokyo insist that the external economy favourable to business activities results from financial and administrative functions being highly concentrated, and thus Tokyo could be more competitive in the global market. At the same time, they say that the deficiency caused by the over-concentration could be minimized by introducing measures, such as a congestion charge (Hatta and Yashiro, 1995).

Having experienced rapid urbanization since the Second World War, it has been questioned whether being a monocentric concentration or a polycentric diffusion would be the more appropriate urban form for Tokyo. That is, should Tokyo pursue the benefits produced by the concentration of economic facilities in the business centre core, or should it distribute urban functions to the existing business core cities scattered in suburban Tokyo and therefore avoid the deficiencies caused by over-concentrated accumulation?

As a means of comparing Randstad with Tokyo, a map of Randstad was superimposed upon that of Tokyo (Figure 3.5). This shows that the monocentric core of Tokyo spatially fits within the green heart of Randstad. If we imagine Tokyo with its densely built-up centre substituted by green, open space, the four local cities (Saitama, Chiba, Hachijoji-Tama and Kawasaki-Yokohama) absorbed into the Tokyo metropolitan wider region lie along the edge of this green heart where the four major cities of Randstad are also spatially situated. This simulation clearly reveals the hidden polycentric structure of Tokyo.

Figure 3.5
Tokyo with Randstad's green
heart superimposed.

Towards sustainability

Tokyo is facing an ageing society and depopulation.
Depopulation has led to economic decline by weakening its
competitiveness in the global market. However, a decrease in
population can be dealt with as an opportunity to improve the
quality of life in the densely populated and continuous, built-
up area. Depopulation means more physical space per person
and also makes it possible to provide more green spaces. To
ensure an urban life with access to green spaces, the
'Renovation program for the Tokyo and Hanshin Area'[1]
suggests the insertion of 'environmental infrastructures'. These
infrastructures consist of green networks in homogeneously
spread built-up areas (Figure 3.6). This programme is based on
the assumption that the population in 2050 will have decreased
to the same level as in 1975 and the elderly will have increased
to account for 30% of the population.

There is a problem in that urbanization seems to be an
irreversible process. Many medium-sized cities in Japan have

Green network

Figure 3.6
Renovation programme
for the Tokyo area.
(*Source*: Land Use Agency,
2000.)

already experienced a decrease in population, nevertheless, the urban sprawl process is still continuing. Once it has materialized, the built-up area appears to spread like an oil spill, whose surface is very difficult to reduce. It would be more realistic to insert new green areas into existing built-up areas. The renovation programme proposes the strategic connection of small green areas and the creation of a green network extended over the whole territory of the wider Tokyo region (Ishikawa, 2001). Also, the networked environmental infrastructure will divide the continuous, built-up area into smaller units of mixed uses. The present trends of depopulation and an ageing society could mean future citizens of Tokyo will experience an attractive lifestyle in compact living areas close to water and green areas. This reveals the potential merits of a polycentric system for its higher quality of life and as a sustainable urban form.

Statistics show that the demands on transport for connection between the medium-sized cities (which form the outer ring) are increasing more rapidly than the transport demand between the metropolitan core and suburban sub-cores (Tokyo Metropolitan Government, 1998). A network-based transportation system is now required, in place of the modern transport infrastructure with a radial pattern, to support the increasingly dispersed traffic within the region. These observations reveal that the polycentric system would be more suitable for the future society in the Tokyo wider region.

The regeneration programme led by the Japanese Central Government has given priority to a different policy direction by the establishment of an *Urban Renaissance Headquarters* within the Prime Minister's Cabinet in May 2001. The initial task was the introduction of the *Urban Renaissance Special Measure Law* that came into force in June 2002. The committee that prepared for its introduction presented an action-oriented report entitled 'Towards regeneration of the Tokyo area' in November 2000. This report admits the importance of polycentricity in the Tokyo wider region and refers broadly to an environmental infrastructure. However, the *Urban Renaissance Headquarters* gives absolute priority towards the use of urban regeneration to reactivate the Japanese economy on a very short-term basis. The fruit of this urban regeneration policy is more than 30 skyscrapers in the central district of Tokyo, with the expectation that increased construction demand will improve the economic situation (Igarashi and Ogawa, 2003). As a result, urban policy is reinforcing the concentration of urban functions and social segregation in the monocentric core.

The Tokyo wider region seeks a delicate balance that allows the coexistence of a monocentric and a polycentric system. However, lacking efficient planning regulations, market-motivated development promotes the monocentric system. Hall and Pfeiffer (2000) suggest that 'In market or mixed economies, planning regulations tend to work best when they are consistent with market behaviour. . . . Land-use regulations that ignore such market-behavioural tendencies are not likely to succeed'. However, they also admit that 'planning sometimes has to work against trends too, when they become self-destructive and blind to the needs of the wider society' (Hall and Pfeiffer, 2000). This reality of Tokyo demonstrates that it is quite difficult to recreate a contrast between built-up and green areas, and to shift towards polycentricity without imposing more planning controls, even if both public and private sectors agree that it is indispensable to achieve well-balanced sustainability.

Randstad, with its advantageous geographical situation, is receiving strong pressure for further urban development, particularly after the establishment of the single market in Europe. The Dutch National Government has adopted a new strategy 'seeing the Randstad not only as the main economic area of the Netherlands, but also as a key area in north-west Europe, thanks to its position at the mouth of the Rhine and the Maas in the increased reality of the open market of the EU' (Kreukels, 2003). One might say that Randstad is currently at something of a crossroads, having to maintain a balance between continued economic performance and environmental considerations. The physical urban–rural balance that has ensured the polycentric urban system has arguably reached its saturation point. The typical Dutch landscape, which has always had a clear distinction between urban and rural areas, is rapidly disappearing. Discussions began in the 1990s as to whether Randstad should be developed as a single-large metropolis in the future. The green heart has also experienced a qualitative transformation. While it has lost a lot of its agricultural economic base, the demand for recreation and sport is increasing. There is a significant demand for housing in rural and village areas because of its attractive living environment and high-quality landscape (VROM, 2001).

The *Fifth Memorandum of Spatial Planning* has designated this polycentric city-region 'Delta-Metropolis' (VROM, 2001) rather than Randstad.[2] 'Delta-Metropolis' is an expression of the objective to promote better integration between parts of the Randstad area, enabling it to operate more as one coherent unit' (VROM, 2001). It declares that 'spatial integration is achieved by strengthening the networks of relationships' and emphasizes the importance of the green network as well as the infrastructure network. However, the image of Randstad as a well-balanced polycentric urban system with green space in the middle and green buffer zones between component cities seems to be fading as its physical aspect is approaching that of a wider metropolitan-region developed from a monocentric urban system.

The other difficult task of dealing with market-motivated development, without losing the traditional landscape of compact built-up areas on a green carpet, is being intelligently explored. Planning applications and programmes for new developments are permitted more easily as long as the overall green area is not reduced; compensation for lost green spaces is required through the greening of brownfield sites. This means a radical shift from strict and static land-use planning to more flexible and dynamic management of the city-region.

Conclusion

The two strategies of Randstad and Tokyo outlined in this paper converge in the same image of sustainable city-regions which, to be effective, must have the following three characteristics in common:

- **A polycentric system keeping one coherent regional unit**
- **A clear contrast between built-up and green areas**
- **Flexible and dynamic management**

The convergent images of future Tokyo and Randstad show that a sustainable spatial form requires a regional unity with a polycentric structure. It is obvious that city-regions based on a network of small- to medium-sized cities, such as the case of Randstad, should adopt a polycentric urban system. This chapter has revealed that the global city of Tokyo is also attempting to shift from a monocentric towards a polycentric urban system, indicating its adaptability as an urban planning model.

If economic efficiency is the primary goal, it is almost impossible to judge which is more appropriate for the city-region: polycentricism or monocentrism. However, if we consider that quality of life forms a basic element of regional competitiveness, polycentrism can provide a high quality of life within a compact sphere, through good access to green spaces. Clear contrast between built-up and green areas ensures a lifestyle that can enjoy the benefits of both the compact city and green open spaces. Connections are required as well as separations. The component urban cores should be well connected to one another by public transport and information infrastructures that should be as efficient as those in large, monocentric cities. An efficient public transport system will help to achieve well-connected city-regions with component urban cores that are physically separated from one another.

For Tokyo and Randstad, it will be the flexibility of polycentricity as a model that ensures its success. Modern land-use planning in Randstad is no longer able to maintain the contrast of the urban and the rural. The polycentric model should be adopted to achieve the virtues of both a high-density compact city and a low-density settlement with large tracts of green space. In terms of the economic progress of the city-region, flexible management is necessary to react to market forces, as well as to strike a balance with environmental concerns.

Acknowledgement

Collaboration in preparing graphics for Figures 3.2–3.5: Akira Masuda.

Notes

1. A non-legally-binding report edited by a committee of experts organized by the ex-Land Use Agency (recently absorbed by the Ministry of Land and Transport).

2. Delta-Metropolis is a term attributed to town planner I.E. Frieling, which refers to the area which lies in the delta of the Rhine and Maas rivers.

References

Ascher, F. (1995) *Metapolis ou l'avenir des villes*, Ed. Odile Jacob, Paris.

Brunet, R. (1989) *Les Villes Européennes, La Documentation Francaise*, Reclus DATAR, Paris.

Castells, M. (1996) *The Rise of the Network Society*, Blackwell, Oxford.

Dematteis, G. (1998) Suburnanizacion y Periurbanizacion, Ciudades Anglosajonas y Ciudades Latinas. In: *La Ciudad Dispersa* (ed. Monclus F.J.), CCCB/Centre de Cultura Contemporània de Barcelona, Barcelona.

Evans, D. and Taylor, P.J. (2001) *The East Midlands Polycentric Urban Region: A Pilot Study*. Retrieved from the World Wide Web at http://www.lboro.ac.uk./gawc/gawc.html

Hall, P. (2001) *Urban Development and Research Needs in Europe: CERUM Report* 8.

Hall, P. and Hay, D. (1980) *Growth Centres in the European Urban System*, Heinemann, London.

Hall, P. and Pfeiffer, U. (2000) *Urban Future 21: A Global Agenda for Twenty-First Century Cities*, E & FN Spon, London.

Hatta, T. and Yashiro, N., eds. (1995) *Economy of the Tokyo Problem*, Tokyo University Press, Tokyo.

Igarashi, T. and Ogawa, A. (2003) *Questioning Urban Renaissance*, Iwanami, Tokyo.

Ishikawa, M. (2001) *Cities and Green-Land*, Iwanami, Tokyo.

Jacobs, J. (1984) *Cities and the Wealth of Nations*, Random House, New York.

Japanese Land Use Agency (2000) *Renovation Program for Wider Tokyo region and Wider Kyoto–Osaka–Kobe Region*, Japanese National Printing Bureau, Tokyo.

Kloosterman, R.C. and Lambregts, B. (2001) Clustering of Economic Activities in Polycentric Urban Regions: The Case of Randstad. *Urban Studies*, **38(4)**: 717–732.

Kreukels, A. (2003) Rotterdam and the South Wing of the Randstad. In: *Metropolitan Governance and Spatial Planning* (eds. Salet, W., Thornley, A. and Kreukels, A.), Spon Press, London, 189–201.

Orlfield, M. (1997) *American Metropolitics, The New Suburban Reality*, Brookings Institution Press, Washington.

Salet, W., Thornley, A. and Kreukels, A., eds. (2003) *Metropolitan Governance and Spatial Planning*, Spon Press, London.

Sassen, S. (1991) *The Global City: New York, London, Tokyo*, Princeton University Press, Princeton.

Savage, L. and Lapping, M. (2003) Sprawl and Its Discontents, the Rural Dimension. In: *Suburban Sprawl, Culture Theory and Politics* (eds. Lindstorm, M.J. and Bartling, H.), Rowman and Littlefield, Lanham.

Scott, A.J. (2000) Globalization and the Rise of City-Regions. *European Planning Studies*, **9(7)**: 813–826.

Simmonds, R. and Hack, G., eds. (2000) *Global City Regions, Their Emerging Forms*, Spon Press, London.

Tokyo Metropolitan Government (1998) *Planning of Tokyo*, Policy and Information Bureau, Tokyo Metropolitan Government, Tokyo.

Tummers, L.J.M. and Schrijnen, P.M. (2000) The Randstad. In: *Global City Regions, Their Emerging Forms* (eds. Simmonds, R. and Hack, G.), Spon Press, London, 66–79.

Urban Re-generation Committee of Japanese Government (2000) *Towards Regeneration of Tokyo Metropolitan Area* (unpublished). Retrieved from the World Wide Web at http://www.mlit.go.jp/crd/city/torikumi/suisin/tkteigen/tkteigenn.htm

VROM: Ministry of Housing, Spatial Planning and the Environment, The Netherlands (2000) *Compact Cities and Open Landscapes*, Ministry of Housing, Spatial Planning and the Environment, The Hague.

VROM: Ministry of Housing, Spatial Planning and the Environment, The Netherlands (2001) *Fifth Memorandum/Vijfde Nota over de Ruimtelijke Ordering*, Ministry of Housing, Spatial Planning and the Environment, The Hague.

4

Luca Bertolini

The Multi-modal Urban Region: A Concept to Combine Environmental and Economic Goals

Introduction

Environmental sustainability is seldom, if ever, the main goal of urban development. Other goals, such as improving local economic performance or social equity are often just as high, if not higher, on the political agenda. This means that in order to give environmental sustainability in urban development a chance, it needs to be combined with other objectives. A crucial question in this respect is how to combine economic and environmental objectives. This chapter addresses this issue by first considering the available evidence on the relationship between urban form and economic performance on one hand, and urban form and environmental sustainability on the other. In both cases the focus is on transport and land use features of cities. In the second part of the chapter a conceptual framework is introduced to help develop transport and land use policies that build upon this evidence. The main idea is that of the 'multi-modal urban region', or of an urban region where land use and transport policies are directed at matching the competitive advantages of each transport mode (the supply of mobility) to the spatial characteristics of different urban activities (the demand for mobility). Trends and plans in the Netherlands are used to illustrate and support this argument. Central to the discussion are not so much methods for the *evaluation* of policy alternatives, but rather than methods of *generating* policy alternatives, that is, ways of facilitating the policy *design process*. This is an often neglected, but arguably important, perspective. Research, design and policy challenges following from the proposed approach are introduced and briefly discussed as part of the conclusion.

Urban form and economic performance

Theoretical background

Academics, policy makers and spatial economists in particular, have long been interested in the relationship between urban form and economic performance. A number of theoretically well-founded findings can be elicited from this literature. All else being equal, a well-functioning city enhances its economic performance by reducing production costs such as those for gathering inputs and distributing outputs, for example, by shortening the journey times between company locations and worker's homes or between different functionally connected companies. The spatial enlargement of urban markets also translates into lower costs: it gives companies access to a larger pool of labour, whilst at the same time helping job seekers to find adequate work. A well-functioning city thus creates a more efficient-labour market, one in which it is easier to match jobs with skills. Similar benefits can also be obtained in other spatial markets, such as those for housing and services. In a more general sense, a well-functioning city generates favourable opportunities for exploiting economies of scales, such as those obtained from having the widest possible access to specialist personnel, intermediaries, customers and suppliers. Finally, a well-functioning city encourages the incubation and spread of knowledge and innovation (for overviews of these arguments see *inter alia*: McCann, 1995; Rietveld and Bruisma, 1998; Gordon and McCann, 2000; Cervero, 2001; Geurs and Ritsema van Eck, 2001).

A problem with most of these theoretically well-founded statements is that they are supported by relatively little empirical research. Furthermore, in most studies, the various aspects that make up the urban system (e.g. land use and transport) are examined separately rather than simultaneously. In addition, the relationships between economic performance and characteristics of the urban system (other than its size), are addressed only to a limited extent. One interesting exception is research conducted by Prud'homme and Lee (1999). This is discussed in the next section.

Urban form and economic performance

An empirical analysis

Since the groundbreaking contribution made by Alonso (1971), there has been a whole stream of research into the relationship between a city's size and its economic performance. The results are intriguing. Alonso's theory implies the existence of an optimum city size, but actual experiences are contradictory. Cities in different socio-economic contexts seem to be governed by different cost–benefit curves: a city like Tokyo, the largest in the world, may not yet have reached the limit of its expansion; but there are other, often far smaller ones elsewhere, in particular many capital cities in developing countries, which already seem to have grown to an unmanageable size. Prud'homme and Lee (1999) contended that other factors, not just size need to be taken into consideration in order to explain these differences. It is not the size of a city in itself that is significant, they argue, but rather the *actual extent of the spatial markets* involved in its economic functioning. It is not the number of jobs or workers cited in the municipal statistics that is important, but the number of actually *accessible* ones. In this respect, two further factors play a leading role in addition to the size of the city:

1. *The speed of its transport system*: the faster it is, the greater the spatial reach of those seeking jobs or workers
2. *The geographical spread or 'sprawl' of activities*: in this case, the greater the spread, the fewer jobs or workers within a given spatial reach

The combination of size, speed and spread determines what Prud'homme and Lee call the 'effective labour market,' the number of jobs or workers reachable within a certain time (t) in minutes. Particularly in large cities, this 'effective' labour market is often considerably smaller than the total labour market. In most cities, not all the jobs and workers are within what most people would consider to be an acceptable journey time. In the Paris conurbation, for example, the total size of the labour market is 5.1 million jobs, but its effective size according to Prud'homme and Lee's calculations is only 2.7 million for $t = 60$ minutes and just 1.2 million for $t = 45$ minutes. It is this

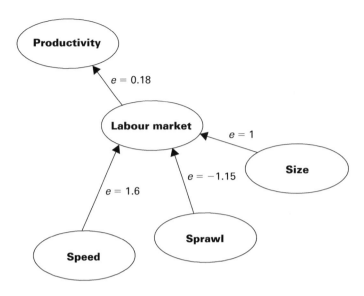

Figure 4.1
The efficiency of cities.
(*Source*: adapted from
Prud'homme and Lee, 1999.)

effective labour market size rather than its total size that has a direct relationship with a region's labour and other productivity dimensions. Prud'homme and Lee tested this hypothesis on a sample of 22 French cities. Figure 4.1 shows their conceptual framework and the elasticities (e) they found.

Such results have provoked a wealth of reactions. It has, for instance, been commented (see, for example, Geurs and Ritsema van Eck, 2001) that Prud'homme and Lee's sample was too small to make generalizations for other geographical contexts, and that extrapolation into the future of the relationships found could not be taken for granted. Even Prud'homme and Lee themselves urge caution. Nevertheless, the essence of their analysis appears to be quite robust, particularly regarding the direction of the relationships. Recent research by Cervero (2001) in the USA has confirmed Prud'homme and Lee's findings in general terms, albeit with rather lower elasticity figures.

However, a further comment needs to be made about these studies. Both Prud'homme and Lee (1999) and Cervero (2001) examine speed and spread as independent variables. But to what extent is this actually the case? Historical developments and research into human behaviour seem to point in another direction. Mobility appears to be constrained by travel time, rather than travel distance (see *inter alia* Zahavi, 1974; Hupkes, 1982; Downes and Emmerson, 1985; Schafer and Victor, 1997; WBCSD, 2001). The implication is that, when higher speeds give access to more attractive locations at a constant travel time and all else is equal, people and businesses will tend to move there, rather than to travel less. An increase in the average speed will be thus generally accompanied by an increase in the geographical spread. Conversely, spatial concentration often correlates with a decline in speed, caused by such factors as increased congestion. In other words, there seems to exist a certain trade-off between the two variables. The next section discusses this crucial relationship in more detail.

Key characteristics of the urban system

The dataset constructed by Kenworthy and Laube (1999) provides a useful framework for further discussion of the relationship between the speed and spread of urban spatial systems. Kenworthy and Laube collated, standardized and compared the characteristics of 46 cities in various parts of the world (see Table 4.1).

Table 4.1 shows a clear distinction between three types of cities in the industrialized world. In American cities, commuting speeds are on average higher, the distances travelled greater, and the land use densities lower. Wealthy Asian cities represent the other extreme: average travel speed is relatively low, distances are smaller and land uses are far more concentrated. These differences are matched by two distinctive modal split patterns: a car-dominated America and a public transport dominated Wealthy Asia. European cities are somewhere in between, with a relatively balanced modal split in travel between home and work.

What is important for this discussion is that these data show, as expected, a strong inverse relationship between, speed, on the one hand, and distances, on the other, and densities. As far as economic performance is concerned, no clear, direct relationship appears to exist between either speed or distance/density and gross regional product (GRP). Furthermore, while the American and European samples vary considerably in city size, there appears to be no significant link between size and other variables such as economic ones. However, other relationships seem much clearer. For example, Table 4.1 shows that how higher average speeds are consistently matched by a higher percentage of GRP being spent on transport (speed is relatively expensive), and higher transport-related carbon dioxide (CO_2) emissions per person (speed is relatively polluting).

This overview appears to confirm the existence of a trade-off between transport speed and land use concentration. It appears

77

Table 4.1
Relationships between characteristics of the urban system, and economic and other parameters.

City (by geographical area, with example)	Average speed home to work (km/h)	Modal split home to work			Average distance home to work (km)	Size (million inhabitants)	Density (inhabitants + jobs/ha)	GRP per capita (US $, 1990)	GRP to transport (%)	Total CO$_2$ emissions from transport per capita (kg)
		Car	Public transport	Slow modes						
American cities*										
Average	34.9	86.3	9.0	4.6	15.0	4.8	22.3	26,822	12.5	4,683
Los Angeles	40.3	89.3	6.7	4.0	17.8	8.7	36.3	24,894	12.0	4,476
European cities**										
Average	21.5	42.8	38.8	18.4	10.0	2.5	81.4	31,721	8.1	1,887
Amsterdam	19.8	40.0	25.0	35.0	9.2	0.8	71.0	25,211	7.1	1,475
Wealthy Asian cities***										
Average	15.6	20.1	59.6	20.3	10.0	13.3	240.2	21,331	4.8	1,158
Hong Kong	14.9	9.1	74.0	16.9	10.9	5.5	440.5	14,101	4.1	760

Source: Kenworthy and Laube (1999).
* Boston, Chicago, Denver, Detroit, Houston, Los Angeles, New York, Phoenix, Portland, Sacramento, San Diego, San Francisco and Washington.
** Amsterdam, Brussels, Copenhagen, Frankfurt, Hamburg, London, Munich, Paris, Stockholm, Vienna and Zürich.
*** Hong Kong, Singapore and Tokyo.

to be a case of 'accelerate *or* concentrate', rather than 'accelerate *and* concentrate'. But it also indicates that from a purely economic point of view a range of combinations of these two factors appears to be viable. There are *different* ways (or different combinations of speed and spread) of increasing the effective size of urban markets. The link between the effective size of urban markets and the performance of a local economy, as identified by Prud'homme and Lee (1999), provides a useful reference for urban development efforts. However, such efforts can become much more focused, if this economic goal is combined with other, possibly more discriminating, goals. In line with this conclusion, the design challenge can be formulated as follows:

> **How, within given preconditions derived from non-economic criteria (including environmental sustainability), can the effective size of urban markets be increased through consistent combinations of transport and land use policies?**

The Netherlands and transport performance

The design challenge outlined above was central to research conducted by the University of Amsterdam as part of the 'Transport Performance for the Region' ('VPR' in Dutch) programme initiated by the Netherlands Agency for Energy and the Environment (Bertolini *et al.*, 2002). The objective of VPR is to promote sustainability in regional transport planning. One of the basic assumptions is that within a broader social and political context, environmental sustainability will never be the sole objective but will always have to be weighed up against other goals, including that of encouraging economic competitiveness. The implication is that multi-dimensional solutions, which are able to serve several objectives simultaneously, are often the most feasible and almost always the most promising ones. In addition to environmental sustainability, typical operational goals are associated with transport systems are accessibility, safety and quality of life. In this context, accessibility is of primary importance as it represents, if adequately defined, a direct translation of the policy-design challenge of increasing the effective size of urban markets (and thus contributing to the improvement of regional economic performance). How then can the enhancement of accessibility be combined with environmental sustainability? Before attempting to answer this question, it is necessary to define the two terms more precisely.

Accessibility

Defining *accessibility* requires the introduction of three assumptions, which are well cited in research on human behaviour (see in particular Hägestrand, 1970; Zahavi, 1974; Hupkes, 1982; Downes and Emmerson, 1985; Schafer and Victor, 1997; WBCSD, 2001). These are as follows:

1. People for the large part travel in order to participate in activities
2. They strive to be able to choose between participation in as many and varied a range of activities as possible
3. Possible travel options are restricted not so much by distance but rather by their cost and, in particular, in terms of their duration which can be expressed in the form of fixed daily time budget; for example, acceptable travelling time as a proportion of the total time spent on an activity, or acceptable commuting time

Based upon these assumptions, accessibility can be defined as the number and range of activity locations which can be reached within an acceptable time, particularly from the home and the workplace. This is the same type of definition that Prud'homme and Lee's adopted in their operationalization of the concept of the effective-urban market as number of jobs or workers within a given travel time. The most important determinants of accessibility thus defined are the quality of the urban transport system (relating to the distance covered in a given time period) and the quality of the urban land use system (e.g. the extent to which one can reach employment or services).

Environmental sustainability

Sustainability, in the context of this chapter, is discussed in relation to accessibility and transport. Urban transport, while providing accessibility and other benefits, can produce a number of environmental costs. Direct measures such as energy use, CO_2 emissions, air pollution, traffic noise would be the best indicators of the environmental impact of urban transport. However, these measures are often unavailable, making the *per capita distance travelled by car* the most widely accepted (un)sustainability indicator (Wegener and Fürst, 1999). This indicator, at least in the present technological context, is highly correlated with most of the negative environmental impacts of urban transport (see *inter alia* Wegener and Fürst, 1999; Hall and Pfeiffer, 2000; WBCSD, 2001; Van Wee and Annema, 2002). Whether, and to what extent this will also be true in the future is still a matter for discussion. Some contend that technological progress will continue to put into perspective the present environmental impacts of the private automobile. Cases in point include innovations in engine and fuel technology radically reducing emissions and energy use per kilometre travelled, or advanced travel-demand management systems and intelligent transportation systems which dramatically curb congestion and make more efficient use of infrastructure possible (WBCSD, 2001; Van den Brink, 2002). However, others argue that limiting mobility by car would have to remain part of the solution (Van Wee and Annema, 2002). This is because of the still unresolved technical uncertainties, political controversies and the long-term nature of most technological solutions.

If this latter view is adopted, environmental sustainability in urban transport can be improved primarily by reducing private-car miles as much as possible, and making those driven as 'clean' as possible; in more general terms, by reducing all motorized transport, including public transport, as much as possible and making what remains as 'clean' as possible.

In practice, this comes down to, in order of priority:

1. increasing opportunities to walk or cycle, or even to participate in activities without moving at all as much as possible
2. if walking and cycling, or not moving, are not realistic or desirable options, increasing opportunities to use public transport as much as possible whilst at the same time improving the intrinsic environmental performance and efficiency of public transport
3. if the use of public transport is also not an option, improving the intrinsic environmental performance and efficiency of the car, including a limitation of the average distances travelled

The multi-modal urban region: enhancing both accessibility and sustainability

Based upon the above objectives of accessibility and sustainability, the operational assignment of VPR is worded as follows:

> Create conditions under which as much of the transport used for urban-regional movements as possible is environmentally friendly, whilst maintaining and if possible increasing the number and variety of activity places which are reachable within an acceptable time from homes and workplaces.
>
> Bertolini *et al.* 2002

Such a development is possible if households and companies are within the reach of activity locations either without moving, or on foot, by bicycle or by public transport, or by making more efficient use (e.g. shorter distances, more passengers) of cleaner private cars (e.g. energy efficient, emission poor). A shift in urban mobility patterns of this type has implications for both transport and land use policy, as illustrated in Figure 4.2.

This pattern of thinking has been developed and applied within the VPR programme and is summarized here. The central idea is that the quality of the accessibility of a given location has to be matched by the type of activity located there, exploiting the specificities of *all* transport modes. The idea is thus not so much that of giving priority to the most environmental modes as such, but rather of limiting the number of situations in which the use of the least environmentally friendly modes becomes either a necessity or has unparalleled advantages. At the same time, and most importantly, this has to be obtained without diminishing the opportunities to participate in activities. We define this philosophy as 'multi-modal urban-regional development'. It implies, figuratively, both working horizontally across Figure 4.2 (logically coupling transport and land use interventions) and working vertically (i.e., realizing all the available opportunities to link activities at the 'upper' levels of the scheme before moving on to the 'lower' levels of the scheme).

Figure 4.2
Policy implications of accessible and sustainable urban form.

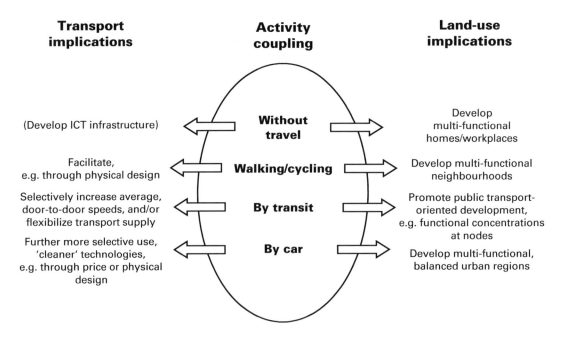

Transport implications	Activity coupling	Land-use implications
(Develop ICT infrastructure)	Without travel	Develop multi-functional homes/workplaces
Facilitate, e.g. through physical design	Walking/cycling	Develop multi-functional neighbourhoods
Selectively increase average, door-to-door speeds, and/or flexibilize transport supply	By transit	Promote public transport-oriented development, e.g. functional concentrations at nodes
Further more selective use, 'cleaner' technologies, e.g. through price or physical design	By car	Develop multi-functional, balanced urban regions

In this perspective, two features of activities are especially important: the *spatial reach* of an activity or function (or its spatial market or 'catchment' area, e.g. expressed in kilometres) and its *intensity* of use (e.g. expressed in inhabitants, workers and/or visitors per unit of space and/or time). Given these two dimensions the features of the available transport modes (e.g. speed, flexibility and capacity) determine the preferred location of an activity, or the most logical coupling between transport and land use, as illustrated in Figure 4.3. For instance, activities should be situated on and around public transport nodes, which have a spatial reach matching the scale of operation (and thus the speed) of the public transport infrastructure and the intensity of use (e.g. concentrations of office, leisure, shopping). Cycling and walking are the most suitable travel modes for activities with a low spatial reach, say within the neighbourhood. Crucially, only activities with middle to high spatial reach and a low intensity of use (i.e. living, working or recreation in low-density areas) are best served by the car. This is because the speed and the flexibility of the car cannot be matched by the alternatives in these cases.

The diagram in Figure 4.3 can be usefully employed to characterize existing urban systems. Los Angeles is for instance a city where most activity and mobility patterns fall into the 'car

Figure 4.3
Principles of multi-modal urban and regional development, conceptual scheme.

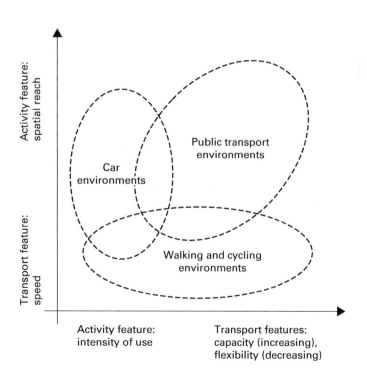

environment' type, Hong Kong can be best characterized as a 'public transport environment', and many European historic city centres still function as 'walking and cycling environments' (as the typically high share of slow modes there testifies). The diagram can however be also used in a more normative way: it is a *combination* of these different 'mobility environments' (Bertolini and Dijst, 2003) exploiting the specificities of each that allows the highest accessibility with the lowest dependence on the car, or 'urban development without [increased] mobility by car'. Where transport modes other than the car are, or can be, competitive methods of linking spatially disjointed activities (and hence providing alternative ways of increasing the effective size of urban markets), transport, land use and other policy measures should enhance rather than frustrate this possibility.

The essential elements of the multi-modal urban and regional are illustrated in Figure 4.4, where a schematic transport infrastructure network determines the location of activities according to their spatial reach and intensity of use. Activities

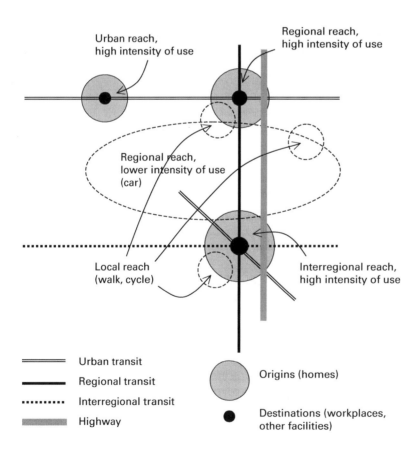

Urban reach, high intensity of use

Regional reach, high intensity of use

Regional reach, lower intensity of use (car)

Local reach (walk, cycle)

Interregional reach, high intensity of use

Urban transit

Regional transit

Interregional transit

Highway

Origins (homes)

Destinations (workplaces, other facilities)

Figure 4.4
Principles of multi-modal urban and regional development, morphological scheme.

with a high spatial reach and high intensity of use are located around transit nodes, activities with low spatial reach are within walking and cycling environments, and activities with middle to high spatial reach and low intensity of use would dependent on car use. In practice, both the spatial pattern of activities and the pattern of the transport infrastructure could be the starting point of development; it should be noted however, that such development would depend on the local context.

Past trends in the Randstad considered

The above conceptual framework was applied to a detailed analysis of development in the Amsterdam region by Bertolini and le Clercq (2003). Here, trends in the Randstad, the highly urbanized west of the Netherlands, will be referred to. These trends are represented in Table 4.2. For the purposes of this chapter, the Randstad has been divided into three area types: large cities, their agglomerations and the rest (see Figure 4.5).

The data in Table 4.2 reveal a marked modal specialization of relationship types. For instance, the car and bicycle dominate mobility 'within' all area types. The train has a significant above average share in large-city-to-large-city relationships and in large-city-to-other-agglomerations relationships. For all other middle and long distance relationships the car is virtually hegemonic. Most intriguing is that in most cases, this specialization of 'mobility environments' has grown between

Table 4.2
Randstad, modal split, all trips
(walking not included).

Type of relationship	As % of all trips		Modal split 1986/1987 (%)				Modal split 1997 (%)			
	1986/1987	1997	Car	Train	BTM	Bicycle	Car	Train	BTM	Bicycle
Within LG	36.7	33.3	49.2	0.5	14.5	35.8	42.6	0.6	11.9	44.9
LG-OWA	6.5	6.8	66.1	4.7	13.8	15.4	66.6	5.1	12.1	16.2
LG-LG	2.2	2.9	67.3	26.6	4.6	1.6	56.0	38.9	3.6	1.6
LG-OTA	1.3	1.8	81.2	10.8	2.2	5.8	74.8	18.2	3.1	3.9
LG-R	8.8	9.1	71.2	9.1	10.1	9.6	71.3	11.7	8.7	8.3
Within A	12.7	12.8	52.9	0.1	2.6	44.1	51.2	0.2	1.9	46.7
A-R	3.8	4.6	80.1	3.0	4.4	12.6	80.5	3.5	3.3	12.6
Within R	27.9	28.6	54.4	0.4	1.7	43.5	55.0	0.6	0.9	43.6
Total	100.0	100.0	56.2	2.3	8.2	33.4	54.2	3.4	6.4	36.0

Source: Goudappel Coffeng (1999).
LG = large city; A = agglomeration; OWA = own agglomeration; OTA = other agglomeration; R = rest of Randstad;
BTM = bus, tram, metro.

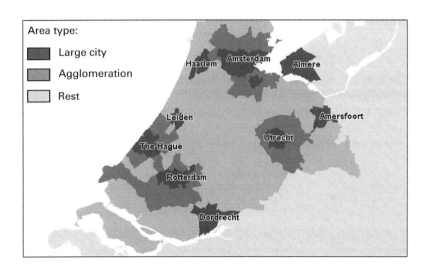

Figure 4.5
Randstad, area types.
(*Source*: redrawn from
Goudappel Coffeng, 1999.)

1986/1987 and 1997. The bicycle has increased its share of trips at the expense of the car and public transport within agglomerations, the rest of the Randstad and above all within large cities, signalling the further consolidation of walking and cycling infrastructures there. Also several car environments seem to be strengthening their profile, albeit less spectacularly, as trends in relationships with and within the rest of the Randstad illustrate. Finally, trends in relationships of large city to other agglomerations document the possible emergence of public transport environments. Each mobility environment documents a different, specific fit between transport and land use characteristics, which need to be understood and built upon (Figure 4.6).

The aggregate result of this increasing specialization is a stable, and relatively sustainable, modal split in the face of a high rate of regional economic growth in the same period: as much as 45% growth in production, 57% growth in added value, and 27% increase in employment between 1985 and 1995 (NEI, 2000). An in-depth discussion of the role of specific policy measures and/or autonomous developments in this evolution, while important, falls outside the scope of this chapter. However, Figure 4.2 can be usefully referred to for some of the main policy elements that have contributed to the trends described above (more detailed discussions are in Bertolini and le Clercq (2003), and le Clercq and Bertolini (2003)). An essential measure of cycling and walking environments has been the widespread development of dedicated infrastructure in terms of transport (most notably for the bicycle), matched by land use

Figure 4.6
Characteristic examples of
emerging, complementary
mobility environments in
the Randstad.

Leidseplein in Amsterdam
as walking and biking
environment.
(*Source*: Luca Bertolini.)

Utrecht central station as public
transport environment.
(*Source*: Luca Bertolini.)

The A2 motorway as
car environment.
(*Source*: Martin Dijst.)

changes including heritage regeneration and the development of new mixed-use neighbourhoods. As far as transit environments are concerned, substantial investment in the upgrading and expanding train and metro infrastructure (such as new train links connecting Schiphol airport to the national railway network and new metro lines in Amsterdam and Rotterdam) are important transport policy elements. Their impact has been positively reinforced by a land use policy seeking to concentrate large-scale offices and regional facilities around public transportation nodes. The most significant policy dealing with the car has been regulation of parking allowances, which has proved to be an invaluable tool in managing the accessibility of urban centres.

As far as the future sustainability of the Randstad transport system is concerned (including average distance travelled) the most important question is probably whether public transport will be able to cater for the continuing growth in the spatial scale of relationships. Alternatively, or rather in combination with this, there is an additional issue as to whether land use policies (such as densification and diversification of uses) will be able to contribute to the goal of limiting the growth of average distance travelled.

Future plans for the Randstad considered

The concept of the multi-modal region introduced in this chapter offers a context within which current policy proposals can be examined. The goal of this exercise is not so much a thorough evaluation of alternatives, as using existing evaluations to illustrate the scope for developing policy within the conceptual framework (illustrated in Figures 4.2 and 4.3). The questions are: to what extent do different plans achieve the objective of maximizing accessibility and minimizing environmental damage? What are the factors behind the different outcomes? And what are implications for the integrated design of transport and land use policies? In this respect, the assessment of the Dutch government's transport and land use plans by the Milieu- en Natuurplanbureau (2001) provides some interesting results. These are summarized in Table 4.3.

This table compares four policy scenarios, each a different combination of transport and land use measures. These scenarios were originally chosen because they were representative of the main options being advanced in political debate in the

Table 4.3
Effects of land use and transport measures in the Netherlands, following four scenarios.

Scenario	Policy measures completion date	Transport	Land use	Mobility (The Netherlands)		CO$_2$ (The Netherlands)	Job accessibility (Randstad)		Total transport
				Car	Public transport		Car	Public	
				(% change from 1995)					
Effects of current policy measures									
1	2020	MIT	Trend	45–50	10–15	5–10	0–5	40–45	0–5
2	2020	MIT + BOR + NVVP car and public transport	Trend	25–30	50–55	–5–10	25–30	85–90	30–35
Effects of extra-public transport policy measures									
3	2030	MIT + BOR + NVVP public transport	Intensify Randstad ring	35–40	50–120	–5–0	0–5	100–110	5–10
4	2030	MIT + BOR + NVVP public transport + Randstad loop	New public transport nodes	35–40	50–130	0–5	0–5	150–160	10–15

Source: Milieu- en Natuurplanbureau (2001).

Key to land use scenarios:
MIT = Infrastructure development in an approved investment programme
MIT + BOR + NVVP car and public transport = Infrastructure development in approved *and* proposed investment programmes, the latter both for car and public transport, with road pricing
MIT + BOR + NVVP public transport = Infrastructure development as in approved *and* proposed investment programmes, the latter for public transport only, without road pricing
MIT + BOR + NVVP public transport + Randstad Loop = As above, with the addition of a high-speed train system connecting the main cities in the Randstad

Key to land use scenarios:
Trend: follows present urbanization trends
Intensify Randstad ring: concentration of new urbanization in corridors between the major cities in the Randstad New public transport nodes: concentration of new urbanization around the nodes of the new high-speed train system

Netherlands at the time. They can be usefully employed to identify relationships between types of policies and types of outcomes. Scenario 1 is a combination of the investments already agreed in Dutch policy as part of the long-term Infrastructure Investment Programme (MIT) with current trends in land use. Scenario 2 involves additional transport-related measures, encompassing a selective increase of road capacity coupled with car-use pricing and a radical improvement of public transport performance (through the development of urban–regional networks, integration of high-speed lines in the intercity network and higher overall frequencies). Scenario 3 adds to this by further increasing public transport capacity in the Randstad and by further concentrating land use in public transport corridors there, but does not include car-related measures. The final Scenario 4 is based upon the creation of an entirely new high-speed public transport system between the major cities of the Randstad, the so-called 'Randstad Loop,' with concentrated land use around the nodes in this new transport system. Particularly relevant are the effects of the different scenarios upon accessibility within the Randstad; in this study defined as the number of jobs that can be reached within a reasonable journey time (of 1 hour).

Perhaps unexpectedly, by far the greatest growth in accessibility is observed in Scenario 2. The total increase is many times greater than that in Scenario 3 or 4. It is also interesting that this growth will primarily be caused by an increase in employment in the Randstad through the concentration of land use, whilst the average speed of the transport system will remain virtually unchanged. Much of this also applies to Scenario 4. Here, accessibility by public transport will increase dramatically partly due to policy measures including a 5% rise in the average speed of the public transport system, but 20–25% of the increase in related accessibility will be accounted for by land use concentration around public transport nodes. As far as growth in car mobility is concerned, the results are also interesting. Such growth appears to be lowest in Scenario 2, due in large part to the pricing of car use. Accordingly, the same applies to CO_2 emissions, which are lower even than in the 'public-transport' Scenarios 3 and 4.

There are two more general implications to be taken into account. In terms of the urban development goal as defined above, maximizing accessibility while minimizing environmental damage, Scenario 2 performs the best. This is primarily because car use is actively incorporated into the solution, most importantly in the form of car-use pricing and technological improvement. Given its dominance, addressing car use appears to be an essential component in combining environmental and economic goals in urban development. With reference to Figures 4.2 and 4.3, this indicates that a spectrum of solutions, including more efficient use of (cleaner) cars and functionally balanced urban regions to shorten distances travelled by car must be taken into account, alongside other 'classic' policies such as 'transport oriented development' which, in isolation, will not be enough to achieve such goals. It has already been established that accessibility has transport and land use dimensions to it. But it is the latter, in the form of spatial concentration, that appears to have the greatest net-positive impact on the Dutch scenarios. As far as transport is concerned, it would appear to be difficult to maintain the current average travel speeds. So consideration of land use measures is, alongside the more traditional consideration of transport measures, an essential aspect of enhancing accessibility.

Conclusion: some research, design and policy challenges

This chapter has introduced a definition and operational form for a central challenge for urban development: that of maximizing accessibility, and indirectly the productivity of the local economy, and minimizing environmental damage. To further facilitate transport and land use, the policy design would require a threefold effort:

1. reinforcement of *fundamental knowledge*
2. the cultivation of *design capacity*
3. the *interactive application* of both of these within the policy process

This concluding section examines these aspects.

The research challenge

More research is required into the links between urban spatial conditions and economic performance to address important questions:

- What is the impact of alternative configurations of the urban spatial system, as a combination of transport and land use characteristics, upon the productivity of regional economies?
- What would be revealed if urban markets other than the labour market, such as the housing market or the mutual interaction between businesses were taken into consideration?

- What would be the results if, instead of productivity as a whole, the productivity of certain strategic business clusters of importance to a specific local economy were to be focused upon?

Furthermore, analyses could be carried out which involve theoretically more rigorous measures of accessibility, which might address distance-reducing functions and the effects of competition between destinations (Geurs and Ritsema van Eck, 2001). Research that might follow on from the Dutch case study could investigate the relationship between the urban spatial system and other characteristics of regional economic performance other than productivity – for example, innovative ability.

The design challenge

More research, fundamental or otherwise, is however not sufficient on its own. The ultimate task is to develop optimum combinations of transport and land use policies. In advanced societies, these may incorporate the adjustment of existing configurations but could also include more radical forms of system innovation. In developing these solutions, the evaluation of the *output* of design processes are necessary but not enough. It is also essential to use knowledge as an *input* into the processes for designing interventions. The core question is: What are the conceivable changes to transportation networks and to land use patterns, given the objective of increasing accessibility *and* the conditions imposed by other goals such as environmental sustainability? Such exploration should be regarded as a form of research and development into the 'multi-modal' fit between the features of new and adapted transport systems and the land use system.

The policy challenge

Finally, both fundamental knowledge and design capacity need to be better incorporated into active policy processes. From the perspective of *actual* urban development, knowledge and capacity without a direct relationship to everyday policy practice – either *reflecting upon* or *applicable to* that practice – is of limited significance. Feedback from real-world policy processes, with the inevitable inherent complexities, is essential in honing the research and design effort described above. The most effective solution is to interactively involve researchers and designers in public or other policy processes as an essential precondition for the successful integration of their knowledge into the practice of urban development.

References

Alonso, W. (1971) The Economics of Urban Size. *Paper of the Regional Science Association*, **26**: 71–83.

Bertolini, L. and Dijst, M. (2003) Mobility Environments and Network Cities. *Journal Urban Design*, **8(1)**: 27–43.

Bertolini, L. and le Clercq, F. (2003) Urban Growth without More Mobility by Car? Learning from Amsterdam, Multimodal Urban Region. *Environment and Planning A*, **35(4)**: 575–589.

Bertolini, L., le Clercq, F. and Levelt, M. (2002) *Naar een Vervoersprestatie Voor de Regio. Eindrapportage Fase 4. Naar een Vernieuwd Werkprotocol*, AME (Commissioned by Netherlands Agency for Energy and the Environment), Amsterdam.

Cervero, R. (2001) Efficient Urbanisation: Economic Performance and the Shape of the Metropolis. *Urban Studies*, **38(10)**: 1651–1671.

Downes, J.D. and Emmerson, P. (1985) *Urban Travel Modelling with Flexible Travel Budgets*, Transport and Road Research Laboratory, Crawthorne.

Geurs, K. and Ritsema van Eck, J. (2001) *Accessibility Measures: Review and Applications*. Rijksinstituut voor Volksgezondheid en Milieu, Bilthoven.

Gordon, I. and McCann, P. (2000) Industrial Clusters: Complexes, Agglomeration and/or Social Networks? *Urban Studies*, **37(3)**: 513–532.

Goudappel Coffeng (1999) *Synthese Personenvervoe: Ruimtelijke Trends*, Connekt, Delft.

Hägestrand, T. (1970) What About People in Regional Science? *Paper of the Regional Science Association*, **24**: 7–21.

Hall, P. and Pfeiffer, U. (2000) *Urban Future 21. A Global Agenda for Twenty-First Century Cities*, Spon, London.

Hupkes, G. (1982) The Law of Constant Travel Time and Trip-rates. *Futures*, **14**: 38–46.

Kenworthy, J. and Laube, F.B. (1999) *An International Sourcebook of Automobile Dependence in Cities 1960–1990*, University Press of Colorado, Boulder.

le Clercq, F. and Bertolini, L. (2003) Achieving Sustainable Accessibility: an Evaluation of Policy Measures in the Amsterdam Area. *Built Environ*, **29(1)**: 36–47.

McCann, J. (1995) Rethinking the Economics of Location and Agglomeration. *Urban Studies*, **32(3)**: 563–579.

Milieu- en Natuurplanbureau (2001) *Who is Afraid of Red, Green and Blue? Toets van de Vijfde Nota Ruimtelijke Ordening op ecologische effecten* (*The ecological effects of the Fifth Memorandum on Land Use tested*). Rijksinstituut voor Volksgezondheid en Milieu, Bilthoven.

Nederlands Economisch Instituut (NEI) (2000) *Atlas ruimtelijke-economische ontwikkeling Nederland* (*Atlas of the Spatial-Economic Development of the Netherlands*). Ministerie van Volkshuisvesting, Ruimtelijke Ordening en Milieubeheer, Den Haag.

Prud'homme, R. and Lee, C. (1999) Size, Sprawl and the Efficiency of Cities. *Urban Studies*, **36(11)**: 1849–1858.

Rietveld, P. and Bruisma, F.R. (1998) *Is Transport Infrastructure Effective? Transport Infrastructure and Accessibility: Impacts on the Space Economy*, Springer Verlag, Berlin.

Schafer, A. and Victor, D. (1997) The Past and Future of Global Mobility. *Scientific American*, October: 36–39.

Van den Brink, R. (2002) Technologie in Verkeer en Vervoer: de Invloed op Milieu, Veiligheid en Bereikbaarheid. In: *Verkeer en Vervoer in Hoofdlijnen* (*Traffic and Transport, Main Lines*) (eds. van Wee, B. and Dijst, M.), Coutinho, Bussum.

Van Wee, B and Annema, J.A. (2002) Verkeer en milieu (*Transport and the Environment*). In: *Verkeer en vervoer in hoofdlijnen* (*Traffic and Transport, Main Lines*) (eds. van Wee, B. and Dijst, M.), Coutinho, Bussum.

Wegener, M. and Fürst, F. (1999) *Land-Use Transport Interaction: State of the Art*. Institut für Raumplanung, Dortmund.

World Business Council for Sustainable Development (WBCSD) (2001) *Mobility 2001 – World Mobility at the End of the Twentieth Century and its Sustainability,* WBCSD, Geneva, (prepared by MIT and Charles River Associates).

Zahavi, Y. (1974) *Traveltime Budgets and Mobility in Urban Areas. Report FHW PL-8183*, US Department of Transportation, Washington DC.

5

Raymond Green

Creating a Sustainable City Region

Introduction

It is 30 years since the Club of Rome published *The Limits to Growth* (Meadows, 1972) warning us of the consequences of continuing to deplete the world's resources at the present rate. That warning was repeated in a sequel report entitled *Beyond the Limits* (Meadows and Randers, 1992) calling upon us again to constrain growth to within the capacity of the world's resources. The threat to the global environment has focused opinion upon both waste in the 'West' and poverty in the 'North' and 'South', as Brandt described the division between the rich and poor nations (1980).

Global conferences in Rio de Janeiro (The Earth Summit) and Johannesburg (e.g. United Nations, 1992) set the agenda of responsibilities that must successfully be met to reduce both the demand for non-renewable resources and levels of pollution. In Europe our cities continue to make unacceptable demands on the natural environment and we are still struggling to find ways in which cities may evolve sustainably.

In Britain the Government, aided and abetted by some environmental groups, architects and planners, believes that the policy of building at least 60% of new housing on re-usable urban land will lead to a more sustainable pattern of settlement. However, without a corresponding policy on better, more strategic location of workplaces and related public transport investment, this housing policy will only lead to increased congestion and, particularly in urban areas, higher emissions of air pollutants. Falling rates of house building and rising prices have contributed to acute shortages of housing at prices that essential workers might afford. The Government has already been forced to build substantially more residential development on open land in Milton Keynes, Stansted and Ashford, only to face inevitable opposition from the rural protection lobby of south-east England (namely CPRE).[1] Some of their claims of the obliteration of beautiful countryside through needless development (CPRE, 2004b) are emotive to say the least. However, the belief that we should be making the city more compact in order to protect the natural environment arguably distorts the debate on how best to cater for increasing numbers of households and their changing lifestyles and livelihoods. The collapse of our traditional industries and the growth of financial and personal services as well as knowledge-based sectors of the economy all point to irrevocable changes in the way people live and what they demand from their living environments.

In this chapter, three key factors in the evolution of British cities will also be examined: the persistence of counter-urban dispersal, the need to regenerate cities and towns, and national environmental sustainability objectives. These three factors will be discussed in detail with reference to two case studies, Bristol and (to a lesser extent) Sheffield within the parameters of a sub-regional plan. Five key stages in the sub-regional plan will be outlined in the former case study, which will deal with the needs of the city and the region as a whole, as like the planning process as it relates to the sub-regional level.

Persistent counter-urban dispersal

In the evolution of our cities and regions there are three strong but conflicting factors. The first is the persistent dispersal of housing, commerce and industry from major urban centres, which has been taking place since the Second World War (Clapson, 1998). There has also been a related shift into central and southern England from the rest of the UK. Two reports from the Town and Country Planning Association (TCPA), *The*

People, Where Will They Work? (Breheny, 1999) and *The People, Where Will They Go?* (Breheny and Hall, 1998) indicate how strong is the pull outwards and southwards from the metropolitan centres. The former ('Work') report concludes that:

> . . . the immediate future will be like the recent past. Cities are likely to continue their relative and absolute declines . . . suburban and non-urban areas will continue to take the lion's share of new jobs in expanding sectors and occupations.
>
> Breheny, 1999, p. 221

Research has shown that given the choice, most investors would prefer to build or buy property (including their homes) outside the major cities. This is reflected in the loss of half a million jobs in 20 of Britain's large cities while the rest of the country has gained 1.7 million jobs, more than three times this amount (Turok and Edge, 1999). The counter-argument that this preference is merely a reaction to the continued deterioration in many parts of the major cities has some validity. Most of the main problems identified by householders with their local area recorded in the Survey of English Housing relate to maintenance, including vandalism, litter and graffiti (cited by the Urban Task Force, 1999). However, the building on every potential urban site is likely to be counter-productive by adding to congestion on already overloaded roads and to already polluted areas.

Arguments against dispersal are also framed around the belief that it adds greatly to commuting, but a study of the central and southern shires in England (Green, 1997) showed that despite the incoming millions of people, long-distance commuting was largely restricted to those working in financial and transport services. Only 7.5% of people regularly travelled out of the shires to work in the metropolitan counties of London, the West Midlands and Avon (or beyond). This research examined 1991 commuting patterns, which indicated that nearly 90% of the total workforce lived within 18 miles of their workplace (and that 70% worked within 7.5 miles of home). Those supporters of concentration within existing urban areas also point out that a very high proportion of additional households will comprise single adults, some elderly surviving partners, others single or separated or divorced (with or without children), some of whom may (or may not) be satisfied by small dwellings in high-density city developments (for further discussion, see Urban Task Force, 1999).

However, advocates of the compact city tend to overlook the social circumstances underlying the movements of population between the metropolitan and rural regions. Recent studies suggest that people satisfied with or seeking city life favour 'the large central cities such as Manchester, Birmingham and Leeds, with their mix of private rented stock (of housing), younger population, upper income groups and vibrant atmospheres' and as the older people 'move out to quieter more family-friendly environments they are replaced by the next wave of youth' (Allinson, 2003, p. 135). Nevertheless, movements out of the metropolitan areas of England and Wales exceeded inward movements by 860,000 persons in the decade 1991–2000, the rate of loss rising from 1.7% in 1991 to 2.1% in 2000. This is further supported by Murdoch who cites attitudinal surveys which indicate that the majority of British people would like to live in rural areas (1998).

It seems that many smaller households demand, and can afford to acquire, larger premises in more open environments. This can also be argued to be the case in urban areas where gentrification occurs, which can lead to social exclusion of some members of society (Carmona *et al.*, 2001). Yet another difficulty in trying to contain dispersal is that the better off are not dependent on new building developments but can outbid locals for existing stock, thereby causing a serious shortfall in affordable housing and stimulation of local dispersed demand.

The need to 'generate' cities and towns

The second factor is the genuine need to regenerate major cities and to revitalize declining industrial towns which may not have sufficient resources to rebuild their economic base. While the term regeneration may evoke ideas of exploiting the industrial past through the creation of museums or theme parks round famous names, or by hosting occasional international events, there is a real need to generate some parts of our towns and cities. This need stems from factors such as the prevalence of poverty in certain neighbourhoods and higher mortality rates and higher unemployment than in other parts of cities, and the country (SEU, 2000). Other factors include the need to improve poor quality of life which can be linked to run-down areas with poor economic performance (DETR, 2000). Many who see little future for themselves or their children move into England's central and southern growth areas, and this movement could well continue until the distribution of population more evenly balances economic opportunity.

Objectives of environmental sustainability

The third conflicting factor relates to the environmental objectives of reducing the demand for and use of non-renewable resources and decreasing the emission of pollutants. In terms of city planning and development these objectives are usually translated into improving the insulation of buildings, increasing the efficiency of heating, and lighting and promoting a shift from private to public transport. Despite some progress (exemplified by the presentation to Parliament in 1990 of an environmental strategy by the Government), the environmental footprint of most British cities is widening and the transport tale is a sorry one in which the carriage of goods by road vehicle is increasing and crime on public transport is a real concern (Crime Concern, 2004). Car ownership and use continues to rise, offsetting the economic and environmental effects of bus and rail subsidies, new tramways and light railways (Clark, 2004), park and ride, and bus-priority schemes. Public transport remains a political nightmare and for the foreseeable future, national resources are likely to be directed in the largest measure at the national road network. As a Minister of State recently inferred, we seem as far as ever from persuading people out of their cars, or to use less gas and electricity; indeed the supply companies urge us to use more as competition reduces the price. Now our consumer demands are met increasingly by cheap imports from countries with low labour costs. Perhaps the resource we are saving most effectively is soil, although the need for land for agricultural production is still, arguably, steadily declining.

These conflicting factors could be turned to positive advantage if the planning canvas is sufficiently enlarged to recognize the city itself as a competitor within a wider economic and geographic region and to plan its regeneration and development within its whole sub-region. This will be illustrated in the details of the two case studies below.

Case study background

Sheffield

Sheffield is situated in West Yorkshire and competes economically with Huddersfield, Bradford and Leeds. Each town had an industrial specialism; Sheffield's (Figure 5.1) being

Figure 5.1
Sheffield centre.
(*Source*: Kevin Gaston.)

steel and cutlery. With the demise of these heavy industries, the city has had to compete for investment which could have been channelled into a wide variety of locations. It has had some success, arguably helped by being close to the attractive Peak District, but hindered by being at the centre of a sub-region still recovering from the closure of coal mines, the decline of engineering and other heavy industries on which its prosperity had partly rested. Between Barnsley, Rotherham, Doncaster and Chesterfield is a complex pattern of old industrial towns and villages served by an old network of railways and a modern network of motorways and trunk roads. Counter-urban dispersal, regeneration and environmental objectives would be more difficult to harness here, where economic growth is limited, than in the more prosperous south.

Bristol

Bristol is also a city with a changing economic base which faces formidable problems of regeneration in some of its inner city areas. But the city lies within the 'Rising Shires', the counties of central and southern England where a high proportion of economic and employment growth is forecast. Bristol (Figure 5.2) is the capital of its region and faces little real competition from within (however Birmingham and Cardiff are close enough to compete economically). The city's sub-region includes

Figure 5.2
Bristol. (*Source*: Morag Lindsay.)

Weston-Super-Mare, a commercially expanding seaside town, the historic city of Bath and a number of smaller towns set in open countryside. Highly prosperous Bristol should be able to exploit the forces of dispersal while achieving regeneration. However, to secure environmental objectives will demand far greater political will and popular support, as will become clear.

Analysis

Sheffield

The Sheffield sub-region was one of the heartlands of industrial Britain, with high proportions of its population working in manufacturing and mining. Its legacy alongside the closed factories and pits is a comprehensive railway network, and in Sheffield a modernized but curtailed tramway system. The sub-region has attracted some inward investment and lies within a region which benefited, in 2001, from £169 million from European Union (EU) structural funds (and an additional sum of about £10 million from UK Government assistance to industry). Today the sub-region is served mainly by road transport and by new motorways providing excellent links with the rest of the region and with the Midlands and the South. Here, the concept of corridors of growth might be applied to the Sheffield sub-region by concentrating growth and redevelopment along a revitalized local rail network, extended to serve some additional settlements and development areas. The network would need to be integrated with regional and national services.

The sub-region is also served by a road system developed during its industrial past and by motorways giving excellent links with the rest of the region and with the Midlands and South. Figure 5.3 shows how high-density corridors could both attract new investment and help regenerate some of the areas in greatest need.

Sheffield City is well known for the open spaces which are situated towards its centre. This facility could be extended and new zones of recreation and landscaping could be defined between the growth corridors. No doubt the scheme would qualify for EU funding but those funds in 2001 met only some 38% of total investment costs, and that proportion might fall as the capital cost rises. Yet without such a plan as that outlined in Figure 5.3 it is difficult to contemplate sustainable economic and physical regeneration. Priming the pump of investment remains a first priority to reduce unemployment, increase

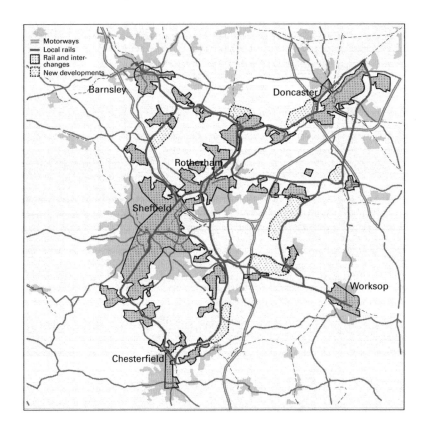

Figure 5.3
High-density corridors in the Sheffield sub-region.

earnings to be nearer the national norm and stimulate a rise in land values and potential betterment. If the Government were to tackle the issue of land value, some of the grossly inflated values of the South would be well transferred northwards to help stabilize the market in both areas.

Strategic planning in South Yorkshire is to be transferred from the Metropolitan Council to the proposed Regional Chamber for Yorkshire and Humberside, whose spatial strategy will replace the County Structure Plan. Even if the Regional Chamber is persuaded that a sub-regional plan based on the corridor development concept will help create sustainable settlements, would such a plan be supported and set in motion by the five councils responsible for transportation and for preparing local development frameworks? The Government claims that their new planning administration will deliver sustainable communities. Sadly, that seems unlikely.

Bristol

In their book *Sociable Cities,* Peter Hall and Colin Ward show how the power of dispersal could be directed into a series of linear expansions in the London region, based on rail transport (1998). They also refer to examples where the opportunity had been taken to drive green wedges between corridors of development. I have applied this concept to the growing Bristol sub-region to show that it can offer wide choices to potential investors, assist in regeneration and achieve a more sustainable form of development than compaction would. In this endeavour, transport would be a key issue.

In Britain it seems that only the largest metropolitan centres are able to afford metros or new light rail or tramways. In France finance is made available for cities as relatively small as Rennes to create an integrated transport system but such a venture is unlikely to be afforded in Bristol while so much remains to be done in the higher-priority fields of health, education, housing and public safety. Thus in Bristol in this study, a pragmatic solution has been sought to the transport problem from within the existing structure of roads and rail – new routes being proposed mainly to serve new development. In particular, parts of the primary road system would be reserved for exclusive use by public transport vehicles. Access to properties by private vehicle would be retained but via restricted road system. The purpose would be to effect a radical modal shift towards a

50 : 50 split between public and private transport. As a new fast, efficient and comfortable public transport service is introduced, so the capacity of the city to carry cars would be reduced. Such an approach implies a degree of certainty in a sub-regional plan and a political will to carry it out. There would be five key professional stages in the preparation of this proposal:

Key stage 1

This is to identify and locate major centres of activity, mainly economic but also large institutions such as hospitals and colleges. Figure 5.4 shows these centres in the Bristol sub-region. They include the commercial centres of Bristol and Bath, and of other smaller towns; major institutions; areas in which relatively large numbers of people are employed in manufacturing and service industries, some with traditional river and rail-side locations, but others in new industrial and trading estates close to motorways or trunk roads. New retail centres are also located close to motorway intersections. A wide range of other activities once centrally located is now situated on the

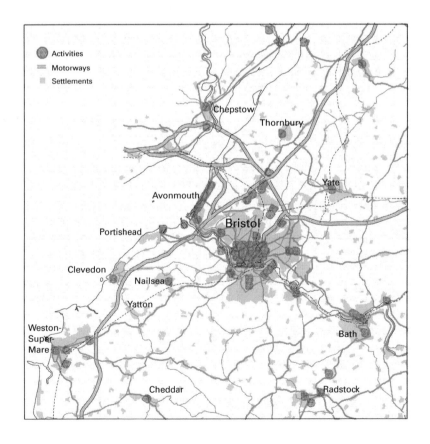

Figure 5.4
Commercial centres in the
Bristol sub-region.

city outskirts or beyond. The old 'tidal wave' of workers and shoppers moving daily into the city centre in the morning and out in the evening has been superseded by a more complex set of movements between a dispersed residential population, and a scatter of workplaces and facilities. This dispersal of activity seems set to continue but will be guided to locations to be served by the new public transport system.

Key stage 2

This stage is to select the routes to be followed by the new public transport service, both existing roads to be given over to the service and new roads to serve areas selected for new development. Figure 5.5 shows how this stage might evolve in the Bristol sub-region. The system utilizes five of the main radial routes from the city centre, a disused rail track and a number of cross town and country roads to link existing activity centres and four major new tracks to be built within the proposed development areas. For this study the assumption is made that new single-decker articulated buses would be used,

Figure 5.5
Proposed public transport routes for the Bristol sub-region.

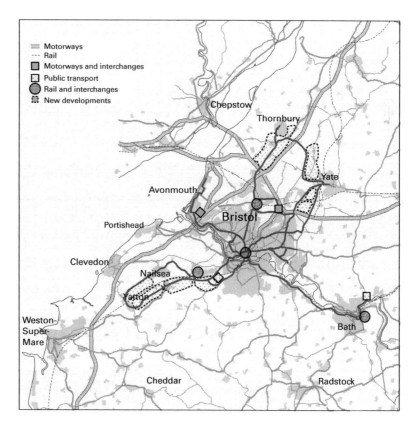

but a light railway could be built if funds were forthcoming. Two difficulties that would need to be resolved are access to properties fronting the roads taken over by the public transport service and the design of junctions where private vehicles must cross the public transport routes. In some sub-regions, small towns might be expanded to meet the demand for development, but in the Bristol sub-region the better prospect seems to be in the form of linear growth towards Weston-Super-Mare and a loop in the north incorporating the towns of Yate and Thornbury and a number of hamlets. This pattern offers locations for housing, industry and commerce served by the new public transport routes via rail and road. The proposals also allow for the expansion of a park and ride service to transfer travellers from the motorways to public transport and also for an interchange with main line and suburban railways to provide easy access by public transport from surrounding towns and from South Wales to all major activity centres.

Key stage 3

This key stage is to define the 'remainder' road system to sustain private access to all residential and business properties. This might prove the most controversial of all the proposals in the sub-region but if it cannot be faced by residents and businesses the prospects for a more sustainable city seem bleak. Testing the proposition in the centre and inner suburbs of Bristol, this stage proved simpler than anticipated and offered the prospect of considerable environmental improvement in most residential areas. The necessary closure of all side roads where they join the public transport routes would reverse traffic flows but would result in large residential areas being divided into smaller, more self-contained neighbourhoods. When fully implemented this stage would result in the road pattern as it appears on Figure 5.6. A preliminary calculation suggests that distributor and radial roads would be reduced to about 60% of their present capacity.

Key stage 4

Key stage 4 would be to develop a system of goods delivery which respects both residential and historic environments. There are three difficult dilemmas facing transport operators, businesses (where home delivery services would need to be much extended) and highway authorities: the routes to be sanctioned, the related size of vehicles and the timing of

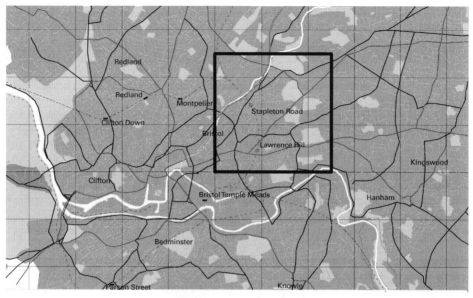

Figure 5.6
Creating a new-road pattern,
showing main and local roads in
Bristol (above) and proposed
closures of local roads to create
self-contained neighbourhoods
(below).

deliveries. Many new activity areas can be serviced directly from motorways and this will continue to stimulate dispersal, but the sub-region is typical in needing deliveries in historic centres and other locations accessible only through residential streets. The question then arises regarding the authorization of goods vehicles along some public transport routes or the restriction of the size of vehicle and the timing of deliveries along residential distributor roads.

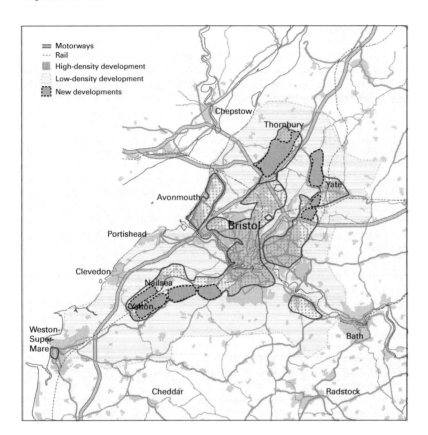

Figure 5.7
Spatial strategy showing zones
of intensive use and green
zones.

Key stage 5

This stage lays down the zones of intensive use following the
public transport routes, with intervening green zones of low-
density use, open space and landscaping.[2] Figure 5.7 defines
such a spatial strategy for the Bristol sub-region. By linking old
and new areas of activity the corridors should stimulate
regeneration and widen social and economic prospects for all
who live within easy reach of public transport routes. Rail and
motorway interchanges will bring city facilities closer to many
people living in the countryside and with the public transport
system will give city dwellers easy access to the facilities in the
green zones in which city farms and forests, leisure centres,
sports arenas and playing fields could be developed.

Bristol: political reality

In the Bristol sub-region there had been the opportunity to plan
sub-regionally but this was not grasped by the now disbanded

Avon County Council, hamstrung by its political composition. Now the sub-region straddles four administrative units for planning and transportation in South Gloucestershire, the city of Bristol, Bath and North-East Somerset and North Somerset. Soon the Government intends to remove the current structure of planning powers from these councils and establish a Regional Chamber to propose a spatial strategy for the whole of south-west England. Comprised of representatives of Government Ministers, the Regional Development Agency, other agencies and local authorities, the Chamber will be instructed to integrate sub-regional issues into its regional strategy. That sub-regional plans might grow from this seed is possible but somewhat unlikely. The regional strategy is to be 'set in motion' by transport plans and through local development frameworks. In the Bristol sub-region there will be four highway planning authorities. Even if the Regional Chamber were to conceive a sub-regional plan of the form envisaged in this study could four different authorities implement it is under question. In my 50 years working in the British political planning system I have found that radical policies and imaginative plans come from a combination of a dedicated professional team and a single-minded political backed by an electorate offered a product worth the cost. The preoccupation with process and the dullness of statutory plans have made the public highly sceptical that planning can deliver sustainable cities and countryside. Whatever else a sustainable community may require, it will need a high level of investment in human and financial resources.

Let us suppose that even through the statutory system, a positive plan for a sustainable city region should emerge, could it be implemented? Using the Bristol study as a guideline, funds would be needed for:

- A radical reorganization of the road structure
- The laying down of new public transport tracks, mostly in newly developing areas, but also in parts of the city and surrounding towns
- The provision of new public transport vehicles
- The construction of 'stations' offering shelter and facilities along the public transport routes and at motorway and rail interchanges and the related parking facilities
- Where necessary the purchase of land for development and redevelopment
- The provision of clinics, schools, and other community and recreation facilities to be programmed with housing and the related construction and replacement of utility services

Without funding, the new public transport system would not materialize.

At present the law allows authorities to seek contributions from developers to meet governmental 'planning obligations' which have arguably been used mainly to fund off-site highway improvements and sometimes other local facilities. The amounts have seldom met more than a small proportion of the impact costs of the development but the result has been to lower land values as the developer tries to deduct his obligation from the price of the land, in effect transforming his obligation into a variable form of betterment charge.

In a government consultation paper aimed at 'Influencing the Size, Type and Affordability of Housing' (ODPM, 2003), it suggests that developers of sites of 0.5 ha and over should help subsidize a proportion of new houses and pass the cost onto the landowner 'via reduced land-sale values' (p. 26). In other words, the Government wishes to secure from betterment a reduction in house prices or rents, to counter the escalation which has arisen in part from planning policies which have reduced the supply of some categories of new homes. The proposal would lessen the possibility of funding sustainable public services (particularly the capital costs of new transport systems), or of alleviating some of the adverse effects of shifts in the location of commerce and industry by transferring back to non-growth areas of low value, the betterment accruing to the inflated value of land in high-growth areas. It remains unclear as to how assurance can be given that funds from accruing betterment values will be channelled into those areas that need it, and will tackle aspects such as counter-urban dispersal, regeneration and environmentally sustainable objectives.

Conclusion

Both the Bristol and Sheffield studies support the assertion that the current, conflicting factors of dispersal, regeneration policy and environmental objectives can be turned to sustainable advantage, but only if certain principles are followed. The city sub-region is adopted as the scale of the plan; the key issues of locating activity, determining the form and routes of transport, deciding the location for new development and regeneration and defining corridors of intensive use are all comprehensively addressed.

I have to conclude that such an approach will continue to be frustrated by a lack of investment in some regions, low levels of funding generally, the failure to confront issues such as development value, the structure of planning administration and by its emphasis on procedure rather than product. Unless the Government abandons its apparent obsession with unselective compaction and containment, there is little hope that the statutory planning system in England will realistically help cities and towns evolve sustainably, which seems to be attributable to a real lack of public support and political will in the English planning system.

Notes

1. CPRE (Campaign to Protect Rural England), who care passionately about our countryside and campaign for it to be protected and enhanced for the benefit of everyone (2004a).

2. *Corridors and green wedges*: The concept of corridors of intensive use separated by green wedges cited in *Sociable Cities* (Hall and Ward, 1998) is at least 75 years old. The MARS group suggested something similar for London in the 1930s and reference has been made to the Finger Plan for Copenhagen in 1948 and to the Markelius Plan for Stockholm in 1952. In the 1960s, Alfie Wood, the then City Planning Officer, proposed linear extensions to Norwich and in 1993, the concept was promoted by the Sustainable Development Study Group of the Town and Country Planning Association (TCPA). Yet there is a marked reluctance to adopt its apparent benefits. The reasons seem to be threefold: the administrative structure of the planning system, its lack of real resources and dependence upon the private sector to implement most parts of most plans, and a preoccupation with the processes of planning rather than the product.

References

Allinson, J. (2003) Counting the Counterurbanisers: Reasons for Continuing Metropolitan Out-Migration in the UK Over the 1990s. *Town and Country Planning*, **4(72)**: 133–135.

Brandt, W. (1980) *North–South Report of the Independent Commission on International Development Issues*, Pan Books, London.

Breheny, M. ed. (1999) *The People: Where Will They Work?*, Town and Country Planning Association, London.

Breheny, M. and Hall, P. (1998) *The People: Where Will They Go?*, Town and Country Planning Association, London.

Campaign to Protect Rural England (CPRE) (2004a) *Our Purpose*, Retrieved on 27 April 2004 from the World Wide Web: http://www. cpre.org.uk/about-us/index.htm

Campaign to Protect Rural England (CPRE) (2004b) *Crunch Time for Gigantic Greenfield Development*, Retrieved on 27 April 2004 from the World Wide Web: http://www.cpre.org.uk/news-releases/news-rel-2004/06-04.htm

Carmona, M., de Magalhaes, C., Edwards, M., Awuor, B. and Aminossehe, S. (2001) *The Value of Urban Design: A Research Project Commissioned by CABE and DETR to Examine the Value Added by Good Urban Design*, Thomas Telford, London.

Clapson, M. (1998) *Invincible Green Suburbs, Brave New Towns: Social Change and Urban Dispersal in Postwar England*, Manchester University Press, Manchester.

Clark, A. (2004) Tram Systems Too Costly and Underused: Excess of Enthusiasm Wastes Millions, Says Watchdog. *The Guardian*, 23 April 2004, 5.

Crime Concern (2004) *Crime and Disorder on Public Transport*, Retrieved on 27 April 2004 from the World Wide Web: http://www.dft.gov.uk/stellent/groups/dft_mobility/documents/page/dft_mobility_503806.hcsp

Department of the Environment, Transport and the Regions (DETR) (2000) *Our Towns and Cities: The Future*, Stationery Office, Norwich.

Green, R.J. (1997) *The Rising Shires: A Study of 26 Counties in Central and Southern England*, Town and Country Planning Association, London.

Hall, P. and Ward, C. (1998) *Sociable Cities*, Wiley, Chichester.

Meadows, D.J. (1972) *The Limits to Growth*, Universe Books, New York.

Meadows, D. and Randers, J. (1992) *Beyond the Limits*, Earthscan, London.

Murdoch, J. (1998) *Counter-Urbanisation and the Countryside: Some Causes and Consequences of Urban to Rural Migration*, Environmental Planning Research Unit, University of Wales College of Cardiff, Cardiff.

Office of the Deputy Prime Minister (ODPM) (2003) *Proposed Change to Planning Policy Guidance Note 3 Housing: Influencing the Size, Type and Affordability of Housing*, Office of the Deputy Prime Minister, London.

Social Exclusion Unit (SEU) (2000) *National Strategy for Neighbourhood Renewal: A Framework for Consultation*, Cabinet Office, London.

Turok, I. and Edge, N. (1999) *The Jobs Gap in Britain's Cities: Employment Loss and Labour Market Consequences*, Policy Press, Bristol.

United Nations (1992) *Johannesburg Conference on Environment and Development,* Regency Press Corporation, London.

Urban Task Force (1999) *Towards an Urban Renaissance*, E & F Spon, London.

Forecasting the Sustainability of Alternative Plans: The Cambridge Futures Experience

Introduction

There is general consensus that sustainability indicators in urban planning should encompass three aspects: economic efficiency, social benefits and environmental sustainability. Like a tripod, the omission of any of the three 'legs' supporting a plan would unbalance a city and affect its long-term sustainability. There is, however, less agreement as to what constitutes the economic, social and environmental aspects of a plan and how they should be measured. Furthermore, even if there were consensus as to what to measure and how to measure it, there would still be a problem of how to combine the three individual measures of sustainability.

This chapter addresses these general issues of what elements of sustainability can be measured and the way in which they can be measured, as well as how they can be meaningfully applied when indicators have been defined. It refers to a case study, the Cambridge Futures experience, which has been influential in shaping the new structural plan adopted recently for the Cambridge sub-region. The approach taken by Cambridge Futures has been to engage stakeholders in the planning process from the outset, outside the statutory process, to fully explore the range of options and opinions available as a way of achieving politically acceptable plans. Once all proposed options were defined by Cambridge Futures, they were tested through a land-use transport model that simulated the behaviour of firms, households and travellers. The outcomes of the model were assessed in relation to the aforementioned sustainability indicators and were presented to the public for consultation and discussion. The most popular options revealed the relative weight that each aspect of sustainability held for the participating population. The survey of the population's preferences and opinions was accompanied by exhibitions displayed in several towns and in the city of Cambridge, which included a video animation that simulated the likely physical outcome of each option.

Cambridge Futures

Cambridge Futures is a group of local business leaders, politicians, government officers, professionals and academics investigating possible planning alternatives for Cambridge and its surrounding area. It is a not-for-profit organization and was established in 1996 due to growing concerns about the future of Cambridge. Cambridge Futures has published two studies: the first (Echenique *et al.*, 1999) focussed on alternative options for the sub-region development and was given the Royal Town Planning Institute Award for Innovation 2000, the results of which are summarized in this chapter. The second study focussed on the transport options to support the development of the region (Echenique and Hargreaves, 2003).

Cambridge sub-region

The sub-region of Cambridge has been defined by the Regional Policy Guidance (DETR, 2000) and adopted by Cambridgeshire County Council following the Cambridge Futures proposal. It is centred on the city of Cambridge and includes the surrounding ring of market towns (Figure 6.1). The area is home to approximately 475,000 inhabitants and encompasses most of the commuter traffic into Cambridge. The sub-region has a buoyant economy based on the so-called knowledge-based industries that have emerged from university research, and has been referred to as the 'Cambridge Phenomenon' (Segal Quince and Wicksteed, 1985), which is a cluster of high-tech industries, constituting a leading European centre for research and innovation.

Figure 6.1
The Cambridge sub-region as
defined by Cambridge Futures.

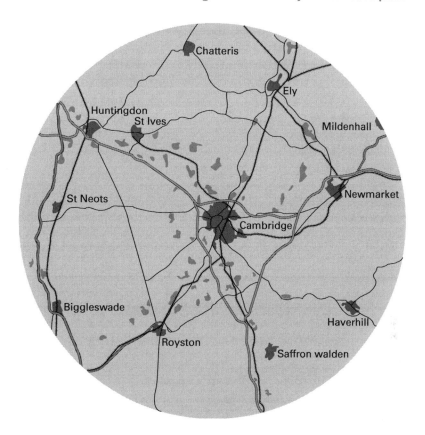

Past policies

During the past 50 years, the growth in the Cambridge area has been restrained. The recommendations in an influential report by Holford and Wright (1950) have been followed in successive structure plans which have sought to maintain Cambridge as a university town within a rural surrounding. The policy was adhered to for the first 20 years of planning, as very limited growth of employment and housing was permitted within the city and surrounding villages. However, it became inconsistent with the arrival of new high-tech firms in the 1970s, which has continued to date. This change of policy was the product of a report by Sir Neville Mott (1969), which permitted the development of Trinity Science Park and the explosion of new firms in and around the city.

It is estimated that today over 30,000 jobs are directly related to firms in the high-tech sector (Segal Quince and Wicksteed, 2000). The deviation from Holford and Wright's report occurred as employment was allowed to increase within the city boundaries and housing was located beyond the Cambridge

115

green belt, generating long-distance car-based commuting from the surrounding market towns and villages. Today commuting and freight vehicles are causing gridlock on the sub-region's trunk road network. Journey to work duration through the radials into Cambridge are considerable and the high property prices and road congestion are driving up the cost of living and of production, which could adversely affect the economic growth of the region.

Option testing

Cambridge Futures estimated that the continued growth of knowledge-based employment between 2001 and 2016 would lead to more than 40,000 additional jobs, which includes service sector growth associated with the increasing population. A similar number of dwellings was factored in for the same time period in defining seven alternative options, which are outlined below. They were then put through the computer simulation model. These are as follows:

Option 1: Minimum Growth

Minimum Growth preserves the city of Cambridge. Surrounding business floor space is allocated to East Cambridgeshire and Huntingdonshire. Critical questions to ask are: If no further development were to be allowed, would rising property prices displace all but the wealthiest residents? How would this affect the area's prosperity? How appropriate would this be in the districts of East Cambridgeshire and Huntingdonshire in terms of environmental sustainability?

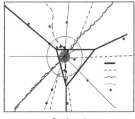
Option 1

Option 2: Densification

Densification simulates maximum development in the city centre where demand is highest. Dwellings and business floor space are allocated predominantly in the city, so higher buildings in a more compact form would be allowed to replace existing low-density development. There are two questions: First whether the environment would deteriorate owing to a lack of private green space? While it might encourage cycling and public transport use, would the increased population lead to higher numbers of cars using the existing road infrastructure, causing more congestion and pollution? The second question is whether there

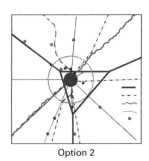
Option 2

is a point at which Densification that results in critical adverse environmental effects, but below which the urban, living environment may be fully acceptable to residents and users.

Option 3: Necklace

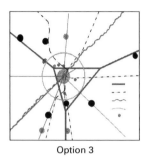

Option 3

Necklace is the continuation of the policy which has existed for the last 50 years: Minimum Growth in the city and green belt, growth in the main market towns and existing villages, and the establishment of new villages such as Bar Hill or Cambourne. This policy would be a compromise between the protection of Cambridge as a university town within a rural setting and the need to provide accommodation within a reasonable distance from the city. However, would this be considered sustainable in terms of a potentially increased demand for commuting? And would the dispersed nature of this development encourage increased car use, congesting the roads and increasing pollution?

Option 4: Green Swap

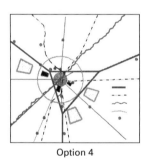

Option 4

Green Swap looks at permitting development in selected areas of the green belt. New dwellings and business floor space are allocated to the peripheral areas of the city, which are of arguably 'less scenic value' and are not available for public use. Developers can provide equivalent or enhanced amenities for the public to use further out of town. An issue to examine here is whether development will allow the quality of the city's environment to be maintained and whether the additional development would be more sustainable because housing is located close to employment.

Option 5: Transport Links

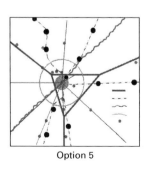

Option 5

Transport Links encourages all further development to be within easy access of a public transport corridor. It includes more intensive use of the existing London King's Cross, Liverpool Street, Ely and Newmarket lines, and the reinstatement of the St Ives-Huntingdon line. This option would require investment for the enhanced public transport system and opening of new stations. The critical issue that needs to be addressed is whether enough people would use the public transport facilities to make them economically viable. Would there be a reduction in the use of cars and thus congestion? Would households and firms actually locate in these corridors? There is also the possibility that potentially harmful traffic flows may emerge, in and out of the corridors.

Option 6: Virtual Highway

Virtual Highway develops a high-capacity electronic communications system that would provide instant business and personal communication for work, education, retail and other services. It is based on a concept of a multi-media super corridor where audio, computer and visual communications are interconnected. It involves investment in a high-capacity communication network for wide-band radio wave transmission connecting residents and workers. Questions raised here are: Would enough people use the system for tele-working, tele-shopping and tele-education to make a significant reduction in transport requirement? Would these facilities provide the necessary infrastructure to disperse the location of jobs, rather than concentrating in the city and surrounding area? Would the increase in the spatial area of interaction generate additional long-distance traffic?

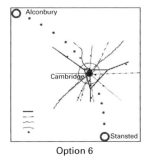

Option 6

Option 7: New Town

New Town concentrates most of the development in a single location. The allocation of dwellings and business floor space is large enough to make the New Town an alternative to Cambridge city centre. It would require investment in new Transport Links to and from the city. The question is would the New Town attract enough firms and households to make a difference in the pressure for development elsewhere? A New Town of any scale is unlikely to be totally self-contained in terms of complete eradication of commuting. Would the interaction with the existing city and other parts of the area be of such a scale as to create large traffic problems? It is also argued that a New Town would be most sustainable in traffic terms below a population of say 50,000 or above 250,000.

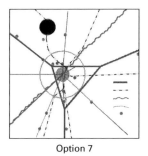

Option 7

Forecasting the impact of the options

Cambridge Futures has made use of two types of models for estimating the likely market responses to the policy options: the

MENTOR land-use model developed by ME&P and the SATURN highway model developed by WS Atkins. MENTOR is a Windows®-based land-use model. Although it is based on an innovative new software product, the model uses tried and tested techniques originally developed as part of the MEPLAN modelling framework (see Webster *et al.*, 1988). It has been designed to use standard census data for the UK and measures of accessibility from transport models. It requires inputs on a study-area scale to start the process of forecasting overall levels of employment and households for the region, and the allocation of dwellings and commercial floor space to zones within the area; this represents the policies to be tested. Given the inputs stated above, the model simulates equilibrium between the demand and supply of land and transport. The equilibrium provides a price (in rent or congestion) for space/land and networks. Figure 6.2 illustrates the main operations in the model: in the land-use model the demand for space and location by firms and households interacts with the supply of business floor space and housing in each location. The result of this interaction is seen through the price (or rent) for the space and land in each location. Once a balance between supply and demand is established, the transport model estimates the demand for travel by mode. The transport demand is modelled with the supply of transport resulting in an equilibrium price (congestion) in each part of the network. The transport model outputs the accessibility of each location, which is one of the determinant factors alongside price, in attracting firms and households in the following time period. The model is run in consecutive 5-year time periods. The seven policy options are

Figure 6.2
Land-use and transport model.

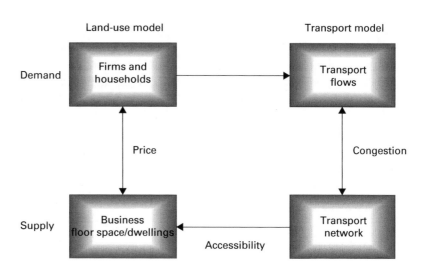

represented by changing the supply of dwellings and business floor space in each location and also by adapting the supply of networks connecting the locations.

Outputs from the model in any particular time period cover the location of households and firms, the price paid for dwellings and floor space of each zone and the transport flows between zones (e.g. journeys to work, to school, etc.). Transport flows are then inputted into a transport model, which estimates the likelihood of a journey being made by various modes of transport.

The output of the multi-modal transport model is subsequently entered into the highway assignment model SATURN, a proprietary traffic model developed for Cambridgeshire County Council. SATURN assigns vehicular traffic to individual roads and calculates delays at junctions due to traffic and congestion. The MENTOR model was calibrated using the 1991 Census (i.e. all parameters governing the relationship between the factors are modelled). It includes a large classification of firms and households. In addition, the model relates firms and households to four buildings types (industrial, office, retail and residential). The results of the model in any particular time period give the monthly rent levels of the buildings in each location. The model thus reacts to policy changes by producing new rent levels in each zone, which in turn affect the cost of living for households and the cost of production for firms. These costs influence the location of households and firms, alter trip patterns and affect levels of road congestion. MENTOR outputs reproduced the values of the 1991 Census and produced an estimate of rent levels for each zone in the study area. Results for 1996 were validated against partial data for that year.

The Cambridge Highway Transport Model is a detailed model that covers the Cambridge sub-region. With the ability to assign matrices (the data associated with origin to destination movements produced by MENTOR), the model is an ideal partner to the land-use modelling undertaken by MENTOR. The network is split into a rural area, where traffic loading relative to the road capacity determines the appropriate speed on the link, and also within the urban area where individual junctions are modelled. In the urban area, delays are calculated based on the traffic at priority, roundabout or traffic-signal control junctions. The validity of the model is verified by comparing the traffic flows predicted by the model against observed traffic counts conducted in the area covered by the model. The counts are conducted annually (such as the counts on all the routes entering Cambridge city) and provide a good source of data, as changes through time can be readily identified.

Results

The result of the options as modelled above illustrate the need for policy modification by present and future administrations. The modelling indicates trends within the defined options and provides a means of comparing the effects of each policy option. Other factors that have not been accounted for, such as taxation, could, of course, significantly affect each modelling prediction, but do not generally undermine the basis of comparison between options. External influences are extremely difficult to predict and would imply a need to review and re-model policy options regularly in future years.

The quantitative results produced by the model were translated into three-dimensional illustrations of the options (see Figure 6.3). The illustrations were animated to represent a view of the area before and after the implementation of each policy. The main results are summarized as follows.

Option 1: Minimum Growth

- Substantial cost of living increases within the city and south Cambridgeshire
- Displacement of traditional jobs in the city by more competitive high-tech and private-service jobs
- Increased imbalance in the social community in the city and south Cambridgeshire (e.g. disparity between wealthy and poor inhabitants)
- Employer's costs rise, putting the competitiveness of the region at risk
- Good protection of the city and green belt at the expense of increased use of greenfield sites elsewhere
- Increased commuting results in a rise in emissions and pollution in the access roads to Cambridge

Option 2: Densification

- Cost of living stabilizes within the city but continues to rise elsewhere
- Improved prospects for employees in traditional jobs in the city, with more socially balanced community

121

Figure 6.3
Green Swap: before and after illustration of development in the green belt (airport site).

- The city becomes more densely populated with a reduction of private and public open space
- Employer's costs stabilize, at least within the city, encouraging the competitiveness of the region
- Good protection of the environment outside the city. Increase in emissions and pollution in the city
- Reduced commuting *into* Cambridge but increased congestion *within* the city

Option 3: Necklace

- Cost of living increases substantially within the city and less so in south Cambridgeshire
- Displacement of traditional jobs in the city by more competitive, high-tech and private-service jobs
- Increased imbalance in the social community in the city (e.g. disparity between wealthy and poor inhabitants)
- Employer's costs rise, putting the competitiveness of the region at risk
- Good protection of the city and green belt, at the expense of the countryside around the Necklace villages

Option 4: Green Swap (Figure 6.3)

- Cost of living increase within the city and south Cambridgeshire
- All job types increase in the city and its fringe, with a more socially balanced community
- Employer's costs stabilize, encouraging the competitiveness of the region
- Reduced need for long-distance commuting
- Protection of the city at the expense of the green belt and overall increase in public green spaces and facilities
- Substantial increases in emissions and pollution in the city from concentration of traffic

Option 5: Transport Links (Figure 6.4)

- Some cost of living increases in the city but rising higher elsewhere in the region
- Imbalance in the social community continues in the city but becomes more balanced elsewhere
- Increasing employer's costs diminish prospects for the competitiveness of the region

123

Figure 6.4
Transport Links: before and after
illustration of the development
in Chesterton sidings of a
new station, housing and
employment.

- Good protection of the environment in the city and the countryside outside the development areas
- Increased public transport reduces private-car commuting but congestion remains high
- More intensive use of land in the transport corridors may raise levels of emissions and pollution

Option 6: Virtual Highway

- Restricted housing supply leads to some increases in the cost of living in the city
- Continued displacement of traditional jobs in the city by high-tech and private-service jobs
- Increased imbalance in the social community in the city and south Cambridgeshire (e.g. disparity between wealthy and poor inhabitants)
- Damage to the region's competitiveness is possible, due to development restrictions where demand is high
- Good protection of the environment in the city and the countryside outside the development areas
- Reduced commuting into Cambridge and its fringe

Option 7: New Town

- Cost of living increases *on average* in all areas, but reduces within the New Town
- Displacement of traditional jobs by high-tech and private-service jobs continues in the city
- Increased imbalance in the social community in the city and south Cambridgeshire (e.g. disparity between wealthy and poor inhabitants)
- Employers' costs increase, putting the competitiveness of the region at risk

- Good protection of the environment in the city and the countryside generally
- Significant congestion between New Town and the city, and high emissions and pollution locally

Assessment of the options

Households and housing costs

The cost of housing by 2016 (i.e. monthly rents, which reflect house prices), varies significantly across both the districts and the seven options which illustrates the differentials between areas. Looking at a broader indicator, equivalent to the cost of living per month for a family (and including elements such as the cost of travel to work), we see a similar pattern which confirms the differentials between areas noted above.

Jobs and cost of production

The variation of job location in each district between options is remarkably small. This is partly due to growth in the city of the tertiary sector (university and high-tech) and public sector (government, health and education). The variation for Cambridge city is about 15,000 jobs, with the Densification and Green Swap options attracting the largest number and the Minimum Growth the lowest. Production cost, measured by cost per employee (including wages, floor space, rent and transport), varies much less across both the districts and the seven options than household costs, due to the apparent freedom that people have to travel wherever employment is offered, which offsets the differentials between zones and areas. Throughout the sub-region area, employers would face an increase in the cost of production over the next 15 years, ranging from 17% in the Densification option to over 45% in the Minimum Growth and New Town options. This would represent an annual rate of increase of between 1% and 3% which, if not compensated for by an equivalent rate of productivity gain, could put economic growth at risk.

Transport

Each of the seven options reflects a slightly different pattern of transport use. However, the predominance of car use is quite remarkable and, with the exception of the Virtual Highway option, ranges from 60% to 67% of all trips. The reason that car travel continues to be so popular could be that it is arguably more flexible and more comfortable than public transport, and for many recreational, social and business journeys, there are few viable substitutes at present. When reliable, rapid public transport is available to all and the pattern of development is served by it, as in the Transport Links and New Towns options, patronage increases from 5% of total, to 9% and 12%, respectively. But the impact on car travel is rather less, reducing by between 3% and 10% only.

Table 6.1 illustrates the impact of each option on road congestion in the Cambridge urban area and in the sub-region area as a whole. It can be observed that apart from the Virtual Highway option which does not add much to congestion in the city or outside it, travel time in all the other options is set to double within Cambridge and increase from 40% to 87% for the sub-region as a whole.

The increase in fuel consumption, and subsequent emissions and pollution will be largest in the Green Swap (+74%) and Densification options (+68%). Due to queuing and stop/start traffic flow, pollution within Cambridge will increase substantially in these options. It may be necessary to implement a high-quality public transport system, such as light rail or similar, to attempt to re-direct the increase in car traffic to public transport. The other options, such as Minimum Growth and Necklace, emerge as the next largest fuel consumers, which increases by 56–60%. These options would also increase emissions from motor vehicles and thus pollution, which would mainly occur around the access roads to Cambridge. The best options, in terms of fuel consumption, excluding the Virtual

Table 6.1
Relative change in road travel in the options in 2016 (1991 = 100).

Options	Cambridge urban area			Cambridge sub-region			
	Travel time	Travel distance	Travel delay	Travel time	Travel distance	Number of trips	Fuel consumption
Average	206	116	317	161	121	136	153
1 Minimum Growth	215	116	338	179	129	142	156
2 Densification	238	120	383	176	124	143	168
3 Necklace	226	116	362	184	128	143	160
4 Green Swap	253	121	417	187	123	143	174
5 Transport Link	197	114	258	141	113	130	148
6 Virtual Highway	112	101	122	105	108	115	107
7 New Town	201	123	257	158	123	137	155

Highway option are Transport Links (48%) and New Town (55%), mainly due to increased rail use.

Economic implications

Exporting firms in the primary, secondary and tertiary sectors would suffer rising costs of varying degrees under each option. Where the rises are steep, firms would find difficulty in competing with products and services from more competitive regions in the rest of the country and beyond. As illustrated in Figure 6.5, the Minimum Growth and New Town options indicate the highest export cost rises to 2016 and beyond. The Densification and Green Swap offer the lowest increase to 2016. In between these two extremes lie the Transport Links, Necklace and Virtual Highway options. The range of annual cost increases faced by exporters would lie between 1% and 3%. The tertiary sector – higher education and high technology – would suffer higher-cost options, which could adversely affect economic growth in the area, to the detriment of the country at large and to research in general.

The export unit cost index has been selected as the indicator to measure the economic sustainability of the options. It

Figure 6.5
Average export unit cost index 1991–2016 for each option.
TEC: total export cost.

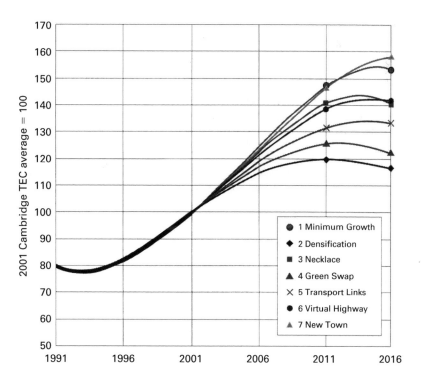

127

encapsulates the final impact of an option on the efficiency of the area. All other economic costs in the model which affect households and firms are passed on through the chain of inputs and outputs to the final demand, which in this case, is represented by the export sectors.

Social implications

The options that have differentially higher costs of living in each district would generate a higher segregation of socio-economic groups. Table 6.2 illustrates the index of segregation that has been adopted to measure social mix.

The table shows a relative social mix of each district. An index of 100 means that at the district level, the mix of socio-economic groups is equivalent to that of the sub-region as a whole. If the index is below 100, it indicates that the district has a higher proportion of high-income socio-economic groups: (1) professional and managerial and (2) clerical and administrative. If the index is above 100 it means that there is a higher proportion of lower-income socio-economic groups: (3) manual and (4) unskilled workers. Although the table does not show any inordinately large changes between the options over the region as a whole, the decrease in the index in Cambridge city indicates a shift towards professional and managerial group households. This happens to a lesser extent in south Cambridgeshire and is reversed in east Cambridgeshire and Huntingdonshire where more manual worker households are located. This trend towards segregation of groups is most marked in Cambridge city in the Minimum Growth and New Town options, and least in the Densification option.

Table 6.2
Relative social mix in the options in 2016 (sub-regional average mix is 100).

Options	Cambridge sub-region standard deviation	Cambridge city	South Cambridgeshire	East Cambridgeshire	Huntingdonshire
Average		**90.4**	**96.4**	**108.5**	**108.6**
1 Minimum Growth	10.1	88.1	95.5	108.7	108.5
2 Densification	7.4	94.7	96.4	107.9	108.6
3 Necklace	9.7	88.6	97.0	108.4	108.4
4 Green Swap	8.3	92.0	97.1	108.3	108.6
5 Transport Link	8.6	91.7	96.3	108.5	108.6
6 Virtual Highway	9.4	89.6	96.5	108.6	108.5
7 New Town	10.2	88.5	95.8	109.0	108.9

Environmental implications

The results obtained by this exercise point towards environmentally quantified impacts, but the values cannot simply be added together to give an unambiguous total. Therefore the aggregate values shown below are essentially subjective. A list of possible environmental criteria can be drawn up which includes:

- Effects upon open space and bio-diversity: this should include the effect on private and public open space, the re-use of brownfield land and the impact on greenfield sites

- Effects upon man-made amenities: this should include the impact upon the historical and cultural value of the built environment and its scale as well as the impact on streets and public spaces

- Effects upon emissions and pollution from transport due to congestion, etc

- Effects upon local safety and security, due to traffic congestion

Table 6.3 attempts to score the environmental impacts of each option under each criterion. Negative numbers (up to -3) indicate a detrimental effect, whilst positive numbers (up to $+3$) indicate positive effects. The value 0 is either used to score a neutral effect or is the result of positive and negative effects that on balance produce a neutral score. The table shows that the Densification option would have the most detrimental environmental effects, followed by the Green Swap option. The Necklace and Minimum Growth options would appear to have the least effect on the environment. In terms of positive effect, the Virtual Highway is most effective, closely followed by Transport Link.

Table 6.3
Environmental impact.
Ranges: -3 (negative),
0 (neutral) and $+3$ (positive)
as weighted by the research
team.

	Open space and bio-diversity	Man-made amenities	Emission and pollution	Local safety and security	Aggregate score
1 Minimum Growth	0	+3	−1	0	+2
2 Densification	−1	−3	−3	−2	−9
3 Necklace	−1	+3	−2	−1	−1
4 Green Swap	0	−1	−3	−2	−6
5 Transport Link	+1	+1	+1	+2	+5
6 Virtual Highway	0	+2	+3	+3	+8
7 New Town	0	+3	+2	+2	+7

	Economic efficiency	Social equity	Environmental quality
1 Minimum Growth	*	*	***
2 Densification	*****	*****	*
3 Necklace	**	*	***
4 Green Swap	****	***	**
5 Transport Link	***	***	****
6 Virtual Highway	**	**	****
7 New Town	*	*	****

Table 6.4
Comparison of benefit factors in the options as weighted by the research team (* = minimum to ***** = maximum).

Summary

Table 6.4 attempts to compare the options using the three criteria: economic efficiency, social mix and environmental impact. While there are objective elements by which to judge the economic and social benefits of each option, the environmental quality score contains a mixture of objective (such as levels of pollution) and subjective elements (such as the research team's assessment of the extent of environmental effects) which renders this score essentially subjective. All three criteria are important, and if an option performs badly against one of them, it may make that option unsustainable in the broader sense. According to this table, the option which best fulfils the criteria set by the research team would be the Densification option, just ahead of the Transport Link option.

Public consultation

The results of the modelling were presented at the University's Senate House, attended by members of the business, local government and academic communities. There was considerable interest from local and national press as well as coverage on all the regional television channels (and, later, national). A highly innovative interactive and paper survey of public reactions was undertaken by Cambridge Architectural Research. In order of preference, the options were rated as follows:

1. **Transport Links**
2. **Virtual Highway (perhaps not properly understood)**
3. **Green Swap**
4. **Densification**
5. **New Town**
6. **Minimum Growth**
7. **Necklace.**

Respondents were also invited to rate statements which included examples relating to matters such as investment in public transport and high-tech growth. Significantly, only 18% agreed that Cambridge and its surroundings should remain the same which may have come as a surprise to local government members!

On a political and practical level, the project has made a significant impact. The Regional Planning Guidance (RPG6) issued by the Department of the Environment, Transport and the Regions has recommended a combination of four of the project's options: Densification, a review of the green belt (Green Swap), the development of sites related to new Transport Links and a New Town. Such an outcome is broadly in line with the project team's predictions although it is important to realize that the reason why the relatively unpopular New Town option is being included is mainly because it will be based on a former Ministry of Defence-owned airfield. The Cambridgeshire County Council, in its Structure Plan, has also taken on board some of the options tested in Cambridge Futures in a combined form, rejecting those that are least successful in terms of economic and social performance (Cambridgeshire County Council, 2002).

Recently, despite the absence of a formal plan, Cambridge has been rapidly adopting a new form (Figure 6.6). Three new 'edge cities' are emerging at various stages of development: at West Cambridge, home to the University and related scientific research laboratories; in the south, at Addenbrooke's, where the hospital and related medical research facilities are situated; and in the north, on the old Chesterton railway sidings near the Science and Business Parks and regional College, where high-tech development and housing are found. A further emerging possibility in the east, first proposed by Cambridge Futures, is an edge city on the site of Cambridge Airport. These edge cities, and in particular those at Addenbrookes and Chesterton, will be linked to new stations on the existing rail system, thus theoretically reducing road traffic for the city as a whole. Beyond the city boundary, there is every indication that 'New Towns' (in reality, large villages) will develop on and around the old airfield sites at Oakington and Waterbeach. The author considers that the construction of the southern relief road connecting the M11 and the A14 to form a complete orbital around Cambridge is the missing link in this evolutionary process is (see Carolin, 2000). Crucially, it is important to ensure that the green spaces ('wedges') that connect the inner city with the countryside will be protected by statutory planning regulation.

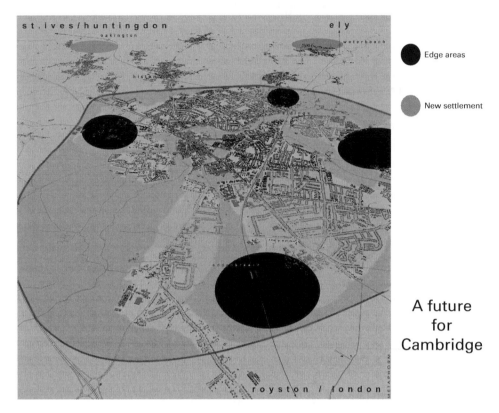

A future
for
Cambridge

Figure 6.6
Emerging Cambridge urban
form.

Conclusion

The Cambridge Futures experience demonstrates that advanced tools and methods exist for measuring the sustainability of different urban plans. This involves the use of sophisticated interaction models that are capable of simulating land use and transport markets. From the outputs of the model an assessment of the three sustainability indicators of economic efficiency, social mix and environmental impact can be made. Stakeholders can then assess the strengths and weaknesses of each option performance. By adopting a public participation framework with the help of sophisticated tools for forecasting and representation, consensus has emerged on the part of all stakeholders on the most suitable combination of options for all stakeholders, which will guide the development of the Cambridge sub-region in the 21st century.

References

Cambridgeshire County Council (2002) *Cambridgeshire and Peterborough Joint Structure Plan Review*, Cambridgeshire County Council, Cambridge.

Carolin, P. (2000) Cambridge Futures in *Cambridge Magazine*, April 2000.

Department of the Environment, Transport and the Regions (DETR) (2000) *Regional Planning Guidance for East Anglia to 2016: Regional Planning Guidance Note*, Stationery Office, London.

Echenique, M. and Hargreaves, T. (2003) *Cambridge Futures 2: What Transport for Cambridge?*, University of Cambridge Department of Architecture, Cambridge.

Echenique, M., *et al.* (1999) *Cambridge Futures Report*, University of Cambridge Department of Architecture, Cambridge.

Holford, W. and Wright, H.M. (1950) *Cambridge Planning Proposals*, Cambridge University Press, Cambridge.

Mott, N. (1969) *Report*, University of Cambridge, Cambridge.

Segal Quince and Wicksteed (1985) *The Cambridge Phenomenon: The Growth of High Technology Industry in a University Town*, SQW Limited, Cambridge.

Segal Quince and Wicksteed (2000) *The Cambridge Phenomenon Revisited: (Parts 1 and 2)*, SQW Limited, Cambridge.

Webster, F.B., Bly, P.J. and Paulley, N.J. (1988) *Urban Land Use and Transport Interaction*, Gower, Aldershot.

Designing for Sustainable Urban Form at High and Lower Densities

7

Justyna Karakiewicz

The City and the Megastructure

Introduction

Are megastructures a form of sustainable development and do they hold any promise as a mode of urban development? It is believed that Fumihiko Maki invented the term in 1960s to describe large projects, even though his own schemes never reached the scale of a megastructure (Bognar, 1996). The nature of a megastructure, however, has not been clearly articulated. 'Megastructures were large buildings of a particular kind, though what kind remains difficult to define with neat verbal precision' (Banham, 1976, p. 7). Maki (1964) suggested a megastructure is a '. . . large frame in which all the functions of the city or part of the city are housed'. He compares megastructures to Italian hill towns, with its frame being the hill on which the towns were built. A large frame (or supporting structure) implies a concentration of functions, similar to those contained by the walls in a medieval city.

Historical examples

An understanding of what makes a development into a megastructure can be gained from a brief historical review. The Romans constructed buildings on a massive scale. With the fall of the Roman Empire some of these vast structures were transformed by their inhabitants into the fabric of their cities.

Good examples are the Roman amphitheatre which has become the core of the city of Arles, and the Diocletian Palace located in Split in Yugoslavia. Diocletian's Palace was built with the typical layout of a Roman military camp, a rectangle surrounded by walls with bisecting axes intersecting at the centre and ending up at the gates (Williams, 1985). Transforming this kind of structure into a city was relatively easy since the form of the structure was similar to that of a city from the outset. Today, the Diocletian Palace still represents about half of Split's historic-city centre. After the fall of the Roman Empire, buildings of this scale ceased to be built in Western Europe, but the idea of the city contained in one structure never really went away. In the 16th century, for example, Pieter Bruegel painted the 'Tower of Babel' (Figure 7.1) (Brown, 1975). The significance of this painting was tremendous. It represented a miniature, a vertical city within a city's walls. Arguably, this powerful image highlights important aspects of city design that have some contemporary relevance.

The Metabolists in Japan were the first to acknowledge the potential of vast structures in addressing aspects of Asia's urbanism, and they were responsible for several megastructure proposals (Kikutake *et al.*, 1960). It is not surprising that projects were conceived in a place like Japan since land there is scarce. The proposals did much more than simply stack dense floor plans on top of each another in order to deal with both the scarcity of land and increasing population densities. The Metabolists believed that cities should be designed to grow and change, and only the underlying structure should be permanent. The other elements, which they called units of the city, should be attached to permanent structures like flowers and leaves are attached to the branch, and should be easily replaceable.

The idea of a permanent supporting structure with temporary interchanging units, which can be plugged in or removed also had a very significant influence on the work of the Archigram group. Where the designs of Metabolists presented themselves as projects to be built, Archigram's work never presented itself as buildable. On the contrary, the Archigram images were designed to shock, to pose questions, and to challenge assumptions of patterns of living (Crompton, 1994). This challenge was reflected in the name 'Archigram', an abbreviation of Architectural Telegram, suggesting that the publication carried an urgent message (Figure 7.2).

Figure 7.1
Building of the Tower of Babel, by Pieter Bruegel the Elder. (*Source:* **Visionary Architecture by C.W. Thomsen, Prestel-Verlag, Munich, 1994.**)

Figure 7.2
Plug-in City by Peter Cook, **Archigram, 1963–1964.** (*Source:* **Banham R. (1976)** *Megastructures of the Recent Past*, **Icon Editions, Harper and Row Publishers, New York.**)

Habraken[1] built further on Archigram's ideas of permanent supporting structures with interchangeable units. In his book *Supports: An Alternative to Mass Housing* (Habraken, 1972) he defined a support structure as a:

> . . . construction which allows the provision of dwellings which can be built, altered and taken down independently of each other. A support structure is quite a different matter from the skeleton construction of a large building. The skeleton is entirely tied to the single project of which it forms part. A support structure is built in knowledge that we cannot predict what is going to happen to it.
>
> Habraken, 1972

Habraken identified that support structures were missing in temporary mass housing projects. His later work argues that a built environment is universally organized by form, place and understanding, three interwoven principles which roughly correspond to physical, biological, and social domains (Habraken, 2000). In many respects his highly influential work shows that ideas espoused by Archigram could be built (Habraken, 2001).

Isozaki's work was probably closer to the Archigram's ideas than to those of his Metabolist colleagues in Japan. His early project, 'City in the Air', designed in 1961, appears to have a basic tree-like structure, but actually looking more like a forest than a tree (Figure 7.3) (Isozaki, 1996). Isozaki continued to challenge the Metabolists' ideas through numerous projects and experimental exhibitions. More recently, Isozaki was commissioned to design

Figure 7.3
City in the Air, by Arata Isozaki, 1962. (*Source*: Thomsen C.W. (1994) Visionary Architecture, Prestel-Verlag, Munich.)

139

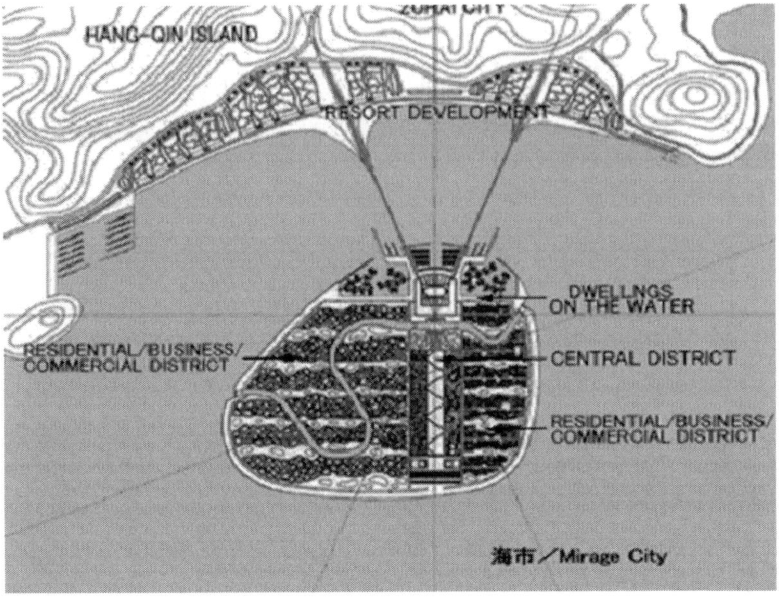

Figure 7.4
Plan of Mirage City, by Arata
Isozaki, 1996. (*Source*:
Catalogue of the Venice
Biennale 1996.)

Mirage City, near Macau (Figure 7.4) (Morioka, 1997). In this project, Isozaki considered the image of a New Utopia, allowing for new perspectives in a time of globalization. To emphasize global connections, Isozaki created a web page with his design and through the Internet-invited international architects and the public to contribute to the design (Tanaka, 1998). The design combined the principles of Feng Shui and geomantic technologies that were intended to reinforce the harmonious connections with nature, and led to a proposed man-made island approximately the size of Venice. In the design process, Isozaki also used a computer-simulation program in order to create various scenarios within the city.

It is clear that Isozaki's work does not belong to Metabolist theory. Where the Metabolists' architectural concepts were grounded in a linear conception of time and growth, Isozaki's work sought to escape from these constraints, entering a more complex labyrinth of time and space, to create more organic systems capable of dynamic and complex growth. Isozaki represents the post-Metabolist movement, which has become known as 'neovitalism',[2] which concentrates on developing more organic systems, capable of dynamic and complex growth (Hanru, 1999).

Although Archigram emerged in Britain, and without a doubt influenced many architects and planners during 1960s and early

Figure 7.5
Byker estate, by Ralph Erskine,
1978. (*Source*: http://www.
greatbuildings.com/
cgi-bin/gbi.cgi/
Byker_Redevelopment.html/
cid_1803148.gbi)

1970s, British 'megastructure' projects could never compare in scale with the Japanese ones. The Byker estate (Figure 7.5) in Newcastle (Erskine, 1982) is one of the biggest; the complex was intended to be one mile long, with one elevation almost blank as a screen from the north winds and the adjacent highway. The other elevation is rich with balconies and windows. Here the megastructure was not just the architect's dream; Erskine invited the tenant's cooperation in designing the project, making the Byker estate an early attempt to create a dialogue between architecture and the community (Sharp, 1990). There are other examples of megastructures in Britain, like the Brunswick Centre in London, designed by Leslie Martin and Patrick Hodgkinson for Camden City Council, but the vision of megastructures as an approach to city design was not well received either in Britain or Europe. It was too often impractical to build structures for large populations in one project, and financing was not sympathetic to such a scale. Above all, population growth and housing shortage in Western Europe is not of the same scale as in South-East Asia.

Megastructures in Hong Kong

Such problems of scale do not exist in Hong Kong. Here, the need to accommodate an ever-increasing number of people, combined with an acute shortage of land, has led to the development of various types of megastructures.[3] Hong Kong's megastructures are not the result of any urban theory. The fundamental force behind these developments is the necessity to provide accommodation for a rapidly increasing population, and so in Hong Kong, high-density, high-rise living became the norm. Most of the population live in high-rise apartments, where living on the 60th floor is less and less uncommon. New middle-class developments are being built with densities of 2000 people per hectare and more. In public housing estates the densities are even higher. These kinds of densities can only be achieved by building housing in form of extremely tall towers, on top of podiums which include clubhouses, leisure and sports facilities, car parking, shops and transportation. There are many different types of these developments, which could be classified as megastructures, the form of which can be categorized into three different types:

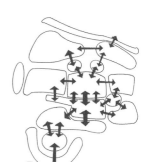

Figure 7.6
Diagrammatic representation of megastructures of type 1.

1. Developments that take the form of an island surrounded by a sea of dilapidated and deteriorating urban structures, fighting for survival, and competing aggressively with businesses in surrounding areas (see Figure 7.6)
2. Developments that take the form of an island which can survive on its own but remain connected to the existing environment (see Figure 7.7)
3. Developments that take the form of a connector, or a magnet that successfully facilitates pedestrian movement, connecting different parts of the city efficiently and making pedestrian movement more pleasant (see Figure 7.8)

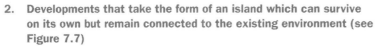
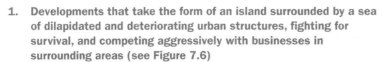
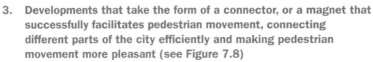

Examples of these three types of megastructures are illustrated below, and analysed to assess their sustainability within the urban environment.

Figure 7.7
Diagrammatic representation of megastructures of type 2.

Olympian City (Figure 7.9)

Olympian City is an example of the first type of megastructure isolated, and in competition with its surroundings it offers expensive housing in an area that is dominated by old-public housing, frequently in poor condition. It offers a lifestyle that is not familiar to the people living in the area. Over-decorated lobbies, resident's clubhouses, and the shiny-shopping centre appear out of place in the area, not only because of the scale and proportion of the development, but also by its functions, which are alien to the local community.

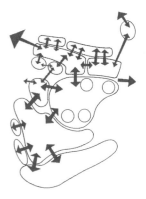

Figure 7.8
Diagrammatic representation of megastructures of type 3.

Figure 7.9
Olympian City.

The project was developed together with Olympic Station, one of the new stations of the mass transit railway (MTR) that runs parallel to Airport-Express northwards through the western side of the Kowloon peninsula. Olympian City occupies 13.1 ha and was developed in three stages:

- **Stage one: the Island Harbour view, has nine 40-storey towers and provides 2314 flats, estimated to accommodate 6942 residents**
- **Stage two: Central Park, has four 50-storey towers and provides 1344 flats for approximately 4032 residents**
- **Stage three: Park Avenue, has five 50-storey towers with 1592 flats for approximately 4776 residents**

In total the project will be able to accommodate around 15,750 residents. Like many other private housing developments, the project has its own clubhouse and two shopping malls and extensive sports facilities. The MTR station is located within the complex, which in theory should encourage people to go through the shopping centre when using the system, to shop before going home. The shopping centre also provides an air-conditioned environment, which in the Hong Kong climate could be very desirable. Unfortunately the shopping complex remains deserted for the most part of the day. It only becomes busy late in the afternoon and during the holidays.

The area around the development remains consistently deserted despite the fact that a great amount of money has been put into developing landscape features, street furniture and the installation of enormous television screens. Nothing seems to attract people or make the place vibrant and lively. The development has nothing to do with the existing city structure. The two towers of office space provide too few customers to support the many restaurants within the complex, which remain empty, despite very favourable prices. From the outside the development appears a defensive structure, isolated and not integrated with the existing environment. Most of the ground floors consist of blank concrete walls with few entry points. The area around the development has less and less chance of survival. The small shops and once thriving-street life has been eroded, and the old grain of the traditional city is disappearing with incredible speed, giving room for yet another isolated development, turning its back on the overall city structure.

The Olympian City was placed on newly reclaimed land, not far from existing old and very dense communities of Yau Ma Tei, and Tai Kok Tsui, and within the walking distance of Mong Kok. These old districts may be overcrowded and run down but they offer a vibrant atmosphere. Mong Kok, one of the densest areas in Hong Kong, is extremely popular with young people. It offers the best shopping in town in terms of the fashion and prices: 75% of young people, when asked what is the most popular destination they visit in their spare time, responded Mong Kok. Yau Ma Tei is also a popular destination and often frequented by tourists, who come for the Night Market, Jade Market or Cinema Complex. Tai Kok Tsui does not have anything special to offer but it has a thriving community and benefits greatly from its location, very close to Mong Kok and Yau Ma Tei. The real worry is that similar isolated islands could in the near future replace these vibrant parts of Hong Kong.

Tai Koo Shing (Figure 7.10)

The second type of megastructure has less of a negative influence over the existing city structure, taking the form of an island which can survive on its own but which remains connected to the existing environment. One such example, and possibly the first real example of a megastructure in Hong Kong, could be said to be the Tai Koo Shing development, at the Eastern end of Hong Kong Island. Tai Koo Shing covers a total area of 21.4 ha. The area was originally used as a dockyard by the Swire conglomerate for the construction and repair of ships but, in 1972, Swire Properties Ltd proposed a redevelopment scheme for new residential community with shopping and entertainment centre. The project was completed in 1984 and consists of 61 residential blocks of various heights from 22 to 30 storeys.

The housing occupies in total $956,000\,m^2$, producing a domestic plot ratio of about 4.5. There are approximately 48,000 people living in 13,800 flats. The overall site density is approximately 2240 people per hectare or 645 flats per hectare. The heart of the development is the City Plaza, a large commercial project, which includes a shopping mall with restaurants, cafes, fast food centre, an ice-skating rink, a bowling alley, a cinema complex and adjoining office blocks. The complex is connected to the MTR below and green

145

Figure 7.10
Tai Koo Shing.

recreational space at the waterfront. Open space is provided ($103,613\,m^2$) which, although very limited by Western standards, is much more than the government requirement of $1\,m^2$ per person. Additionally, the development offers $13,057\,m^2$ of sports facilities. Shops and shopping malls act as connectors to bring all the different parts of the development together. They also link to the MTR station and the underground car parking. Tai Koo Shing has many restaurants, which cater for different tastes and budgets. The development functions as an island, totally independent from the city structure, but at the same time is well connected to the existing city structure. People can live, work, shop and entertain themselves without stepping out from the development. When inside the development, people may be completely unaware of the world outside, the city as such ceases to exist. It could be said, however, that the surrounding areas benefit from the development, in a symbiotic relationship. The nearby neighbourhoods are connected into the development; thus Tai Koo Shing has spread beyond its original boundaries by adding new parts and new connections.

Pacific Place (Figure 7.11)

Pacific Place represents the third type of megastructure development in Hong Kong (which takes the form of a magnet that successfully facilitates pedestrian movement, connecting different parts of the city efficiently) and is probably the most successful. In the early 1980s, the main British army barracks, Victoria Barracks, were decommissioned. The government proposed that the steep-sloping site in the centre of the city should be disposed of in several lots. These lots were later designated for commercial use, one as Pacific Place one for Hong Kong Park, and one for the Supreme Courthouse and office blocks. Today Pacific Place, which was completed in 1990, is one of the largest comprehensive commercial developments.

The development consists of over $490,000\,m^2$ of usable space. It includes a shopping mall of $65,000\,m^2$, three hotels,[4] and a 36-storey high-office tower block. One hotel houses 240 service apartments, while another hotel provides $65,000\,m^2$ of office space. The shopping mall is located on four floors along internal covered streets, with car parking for approximately 650 cars below. The podium level is accessible

147

Figure 7.11
Pacific Place.

by road, which leads up the hill onto the platform with views of the harbour in between the buildings. From this level one can enter the lobbies of all three hotels, and office towers and also the Hong Kong Park. The park provides recreation facilities for office workers, tourists and residents, and acts as a connector to the residential area further up the hill. Pacific Place is also connected at this level to the High Court Building and Terry Farrell's British Consulate and British Council Complex.

The shopping centre is connected by a pedestrian bridge to other commercial areas, namely the Admiralty Centre and United Centre, underneath which there is an MTR station that can also be accessed from Pacific Place by an underground connection. At the ground floor of the Admiralty Centre there is a bus terminus. United Centre is further connected through an elevated pedestrian walking system to a commercial site by the waterfront and a car park underneath a small park. The whole complex facilitates the pedestrian movement through the city, offering short cuts and different experiences. It has a positive effect on the businesses located close by. It encourages people living above Pacific Place to walk through the park instead of using cars or public transport. Thus, the complex connects four different parts of the city that otherwise would have remained isolated and inaccessible.

Conclusion

In Bruegel's painting of the Tower of Babel, he depicts sections of the tower at various stages of completion and other sections already in decay, representing the city as a product that is never finished. This raises a valid question for planners and architects as to whether large-scale design in a city should ever be a final project. Cities never stand still; they are in a continual process of reinvention. Too often, master plans intend to provide proposals that are fully resolved and complete. The megastructure defies such attempts at resolution.

All three examples given above share a common strategy of podium and towers, a model adopted throughout Asia for nearly all new public and private housing developments. Putting housing on top of the podium provides residents with not only shopping, sports, community facilities, restaurants and car parking, but also with badly needed recreational facilities. It is a successful way of dealing with high-density development, and maximizing the site intensity. Unfortunately most of these megastructures in Hong Kong remain isolated island developments, having very little connection to the existing city

149

structure, often disrupting existing areas, contributing to the dilapidation of surrounding neighbourhoods (i.e. type one above). By comparison, Tai Koo Shing is an example of an island development that is very well connected to existing city structure, but this type of megastructure is less common in Hong Kong. Pacific Place is one of the very few successful megastructures in that it acts as a *connector* and not as *isolator*. Unfortunately this type of megastructure, facilitating the movement of people and connecting different parts of Hong Kong which would remain otherwise divided due to its topography and roads structure, is very rare.

How then can a megastructure be sustainable? Being a self-contained community, a defining feature of the megastructure is clearly not enough. Providing high residential densities sufficient to support services and facilities in one structure, as in the context of Hong Kong, cannot be seen as a replacement for the city or of its urban form. A megastructure can only begin to be sustainable if it is a truly interconnected part of the city.

Notes

1. Habraken is the founder of The Dutch Foundation for Architectural Research (SAR), established in 1962.
2. The concept is explained in the philosophy of Giles Deleuze (1994).
3. For the purposes of this chapter, I propose to define a megastructure as *any development in which residential densities are able to support services and facilities essential for the development to become a self-contained community.*
4. Marriott Hotel of 609 rooms, Conrad Hotel of 511 rooms, and Shangri-La Hotel of 566 rooms.

References

Banham, R. (1976) *Megastructure: Urban Futures of the Recent Past*, Thames and Hudson, London.

Bognar, B. (1996) *The Japan Guide*, Princeton University Press, New Jersey.

Brown, C. (1975) *Bruegel: Paintings, Drawings and Prints*, Phaidon, London.

Crompton, D. (1994) *The Guide to Archigram*, Academy Edition, London.

Deleuze, G. (1994) *Difference and Repetition*, Athlone Press, London.

Erskine, R. (1982) Byker Redevelopment: Byker Area of Newcastle upon Tyne, England. In: *Global Architecture* **37**, Tokyo: A.D.A. Edita Tokyo.

Habraken, J. (1972) *Supports: An Alternative to Mass Housing*, Architectural Press, London.

Habraken, J. (2000) *The Structure of the Ordinary: Form and Control in the Built Environment*, MIT Press, Cambridge, Massachusetts.

Habraken, J. (2001) *Housing for the Millions*, NAI Publishers, Rotterdam.

Hanru, H. (1999) *Cities on the Move*, Hatje, Ostfildern-Ruit, Germany.

Isozaki, A. (1996) Arata Isozaki Volume II. In: *GA Architect* **7**, A.D.A. Edita Tokyo.

Kikutake, K., Otaka, M., Maki, F. and Kurokawa, K. (1960) *Metabolism 1960 – A Proposal for New Urbanism*, in the Proceedings of 1960 World Design Conference, Tokyo.

Maki, F. (1964) *Investigation in Collective Form*, Special Publication No. 2, St. Louis School of Architecture, University of Washington, USA.

Morioka, Y. (1997) *The Mirage City: Another Utopia,* NTT Publishing Co., Ltd, Tokyo, Japan.

Sharp, D. (1990) *Twentieth Century Architecture: A Visual History*, Facts on File, New York.

Tanaka, J. (1998) *The Ideology of Virtuality and Auto-Poiesis: On the Mirage City,* University of Tokyo, http://ziggy.c.u-tokyo.ac.jp/files/Mirage.html

Williams, S. (1985) *Diocletian and the Roman Recovery*, Routledge, London.

8

Stephen Lau, Jun Wang, R. Giridharan and
S. Ganesan

High-density, High-rise and Multiple and Intensive Land Use in Hong Kong: A Future City Form for the New Millennium

Introduction

There has been much research on the 'compact city' as an alternative urban form to the urban sprawl endemic in many developed countries (Burgess, 2000). In addition, Dutch researchers have initiated a global study of high-density, mixed-use city growth, introducing the concept of Multiple and Intensive Land Use (MILU).[1] The authors of this chapter suggest that, if the urban experiment of Hong Kong is examined closely, there is a similarity between the principles established for the compact city, and the ideas embodied in MILU research.

The chapter reports on MILU research started in early 2001. The central theme of MILU is to intensify the use of land resources within single sites through high residential densities and mixed land uses, supported by public transport and pedestrian-based facilities. The research was carried out by means of field studies that demonstrate attributes of an effective MILU urban approach in Hong Kong. This depends on intensification and inter-connection of mixed land uses, which generally comprise six uses: residential, commercial, recreational, community, institutional and transportation. It was observed that the intensification of mixed land use was associated with a number of distinguishable features related to compact urban form,

153

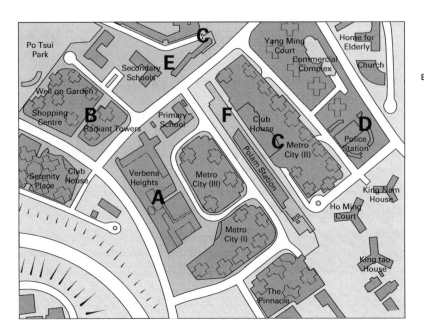

Figure 8.1
To be successful, 'smart' MILU
urban development in Hong
Kong needs to have more than
six uses: A (residential),
B (commercial), C (recreational),
D (community), E (institutional)
and F (transport).

which are: verticality, compactness, convenience and 'sky city' living (Figure 8.1).

Hong Kong: constraints

Problems of land scarcity and increase in population have posed challenges to the urban development of Hong Kong. Only 21% of Hong Kong's land area is build-able, the remaining area is largely mountainous and water bound. Continuous urban migration from Mainland China, which started in the early 1950s, has contributed to a population increase of, on average, 1 million or more people per decade. Of the nearly 7 million people living in Hong Kong, more than 50% live and work in the small inner city centres. As a result, population density reaches 46,000 people per square kilometre, in the densest areas with an average of approximately 6250 plus people per square kilometre overall. The remaining 50% of the population live in new towns shaped by a planned strategy developed since the 1990s, the majority of whom travel to work in the urban centres by means of public transport. These constraints have directly determined Hong Kong's high-rise urban habitat (Hong Kong Government, 2002).

Multiple use of space

Rowley (1998) points out that multiple-use development is to a large extent a relative concept, varying in definition from country to country. He argued that it was important to have mixed-use development not only within a city block or township but also within buildings both vertically and horizontally. However, there are no clear guidelines to differentiate between horizontal and vertical developments, or to indicate the number of uses that are necessary to classify a building or a complex as a multiple-use development. Some planners in the UK argue that any development, over $300\,m^2$ should be host to a mix of uses. Similarly, planners in Germany have stipulated that commercial development should allocate at least 20% of its gross floor area to residential activities (Coupland, 1997). Most researchers agree that properly conceived multiple use development could bring variety, vitality and viability to a place (Jacobs, 1961; Roberts and Lloyd-Jones, 1997; Rowley, 1996). Indeed, a sophisticated mixing of various uses is a precondition for sustainable urban development.

In Hong Kong, the multiple use of space, be it outside or inside a building, is a standard practice. This arises from market forces rather than from a formal planning mechanism. Mixed-use practice found in Hong Kong exhibits almost all the theoretical and practical attributes of a compact city – an urban system with a large population, high density, high floor-to-area ratio (FAR), shared and accessible mixed land use, short travel distances and an efficient public transit system. All of these are essential contributing factors to the concept of convenience, an underlying theme for a compact city (Burgess, 2000). For instance, the average travel time between home and work in Hong Kong is 30 minutes (Figure 8.2), which compares favourably to other cities such as Tokyo, which has an average 90-minute travel to work journey. Clearly, this is an advantage of the compact city that is widely welcomed by its inhabitants.

Vertical intensification

The skyline of Hong Kong is characterized by thousands of high-rise towers, with the majority reaching 200 m in height, no matter whether they are residential apartments or offices. In the past few years the 200 m mark has been surpassed by the latest

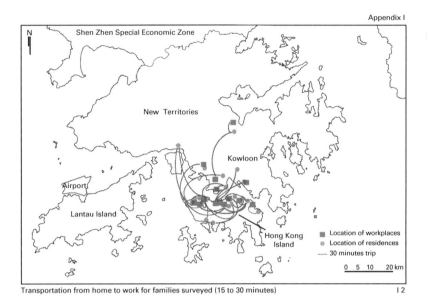

Appendix I

Figure 8.2
Travel time from home to work
in Hong Kong. (*Source*: Lau and
Li, 2001–2002.)

Transportation from home to work for families surveyed (15 to 30 minutes)　　　I 2

generation of super high-rise towers in both office and residential developments that are now rapidly changing the silhouette of the city. The norm in Hong Kong is for 80-storey office buildings or for 60-storey apartments. The continuous increase in building heights is a direct result of the city's provision for an ever-growing population, increase in gross domestic product (GDP), and a shortage of land. A high FAR of a maximum of 8 in the inner urban areas, together with government-controlled restrictions in land supply, produces a vertical concentration in the city's growth. This urban concentration also means convenience and efficiency for city dwellers, with multiple floor levels with different uses and reduced traffic congestion and pedestrian flow by means of vertical stratification. The UN (2000) claims that the vertical urban planning approach of Hong Kong, stacking floors with different usages on top of another, produces one of the most energy efficient urban built forms in the world.

A recent survey[2] of 102 residential households indicated a majority (64%) who liked to live on higher floors for the enjoyment of better views and fresh air, ranking these higher than other factors such as the monetary benefit of being on a higher floor (Figure 8.3). The same survey also investigated concerns over the psychological damage to young children growing up in high-rise apartments. The majority of mothers, asked about the effects on young ones, replied positively (98%), and noted that the artificial ground, which is a common feature

Figure 8.3
Percentage of residents citing
advantages of high-rise living.
(*Source*: Lau and Li, 2001–2002.)

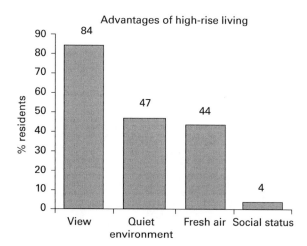

on the roof of most podium decks on which the high-rise residential towers sit, offers a welcome and safe place for their children.

Sky city

In such a 'sky city', events and activities do not just take place at ground level. Pedestrian footbridge networks (or skywalks) are found in both commercial and residential developments. In a dramatic way, numerous double-level web-like all-weather walkways crisscross in and out of buildings, over pavements and roads providing an above-ground connection between different land uses. The multi-layering and segregation of pedestrian movement from vehicular movement stem less from planning theory, and more because there are simply too many people moving around on the narrow pavements at ground level. Today, more than 90 major office buildings under different ownership in Hong Kong's central business district (CBD) were linked to each other or to other public walkway networks by covered walkways. These are accessible 24 hours a day, resulting in an open CBD that is operable at all hours. The network of skywalks, and escalators which climb the hilly topography, enable residents to walk easily to and from work and back home in all weathers. Like their counterparts, the double-decker bus, double-decker ferry and double-decker tram, the double-level pedestrian movement system exemplifies the 'sky city' concept. The intensive use of footbridges and escalators helps to promote the sharing of

157

Figure 8.4
In Hong Kong, human activities
take place on many levels.
(*Source*: Stephen Lau.)

facilities, and most of all, offers easily accessible connections
at all times. However, it should be noted that this does not
preclude street level activities (Figure 8.4). Ground level is as
busy, active and vibrant as the multi-level skywalks. So, it
seems that connectivity at all levels is an important concept for
a 'sky city' to function effectively. A similar idea, for example,
is found in a Japanese proposal to link and connect the
otherwise isolated super block office towers in West-Shinjuku

to intensify commercial interactions in this under-used zone of the city, especially during after work hours.[3]

MILU: a way of spatial planning

Observations from the field study indicate that Hong Kong adopts a compact city planning concept that is frequently applied to a single site combining a number of different uses in a successful way. This form of the compact 'city within a city' approach plays an influential role in the implementation of the MILU concept. Two projects conceived for the new millennium, which represent market preferences that have prevailed since the early 1970s are examined to demonstrate MILU in practice.

Tseng Kwan O New Town, Metro-City residential development

Tseng Kwan O (TKO) is one of 10 satellite towns in Hong Kong. It is separated from the main areas of Hong Kong by an ultra-efficient subway and a public transport system that reaches the CBD within 25 minutes travel time.

The TKO Metro-City development took shape in three phases from May 1997 to April 2000. Phase I contains 2048 households or 6700 residents in six 43-storey towers. Phase II includes 11 towers of 38 storeys and has 3344 households or 13,376 residents. Phase III comprises four towers of 43 storeys that have about 1376 households or 5600 residents. In this 'city within a city', MILU is achieved on a relatively small land parcel with a FAR of 8–10 times the land area, realized by 21 tall towers housing a total population of 25,676 people.

The unique feature of such MILU development is that all of the residential super-high-rise towers are built over a 4-storey podium which covers 100% of the site area. The three phases were developed on three land parcels connected by covered walkways, open 24 hours a day and conveniently connected to the Mass Transit Railway and to neighbouring mixed-use residential developments. On the ground floor there is a terminal for long haul and local commuter buses, maxi-cabs, taxis, and car park entry and exit points. Next to the transport terminal are a post office, food market and supermarket. The podium then includes a two level car park for residents and

159

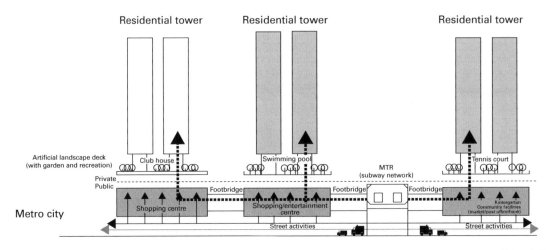

Figure 8.5
Schematic section to
demonstrate the planning
concept at work for a mixed-use
residential development at
Metro-City. (*Source*: Stephen Lau.)

shoppers. Above the car park is a shopping mall, which includes retail, food, entertainment, all kinds of supplies, and community support services. On the podium roof are other land uses, comprising man-made green parks, playgrounds, indoor and outdoor swimming pools, club houses, tennis courts and jogging tracks, for use by residents living in the towers.

The Metro-City case exhibits the interplay of connectivity and intensification of residential-based activities. The Metro-City podium represents hundreds of other similar MILU podiums in Hong Kong. The majority of them are connected with each other by covered walkways, making them in effect an interconnected town, working on different levels (Figure 8.5).

Kowloon Station reclamation site, multiple-use development

The Kowloon Station is a newly designed major transport interchange connecting the new international airport to the existing urban centres by an express train track. The Station belongs to the Mass Transit Railway Corporation (MTRC), a publicly owned company. Prior to the Kowloon Station development, the MTRC had been an excellent practitioner of MILU, successfully combining transportation with commercial and residential activities along its subway station lines in other parts of the city. The Kowloon Station was designed as MTRC's flagship for mixed-use development.[4] Private sector participation was invited and four-joint ventures were created to

Figure 8.6
Typical floor plan showing eight residential units, ranging from 60 to 90 m² in gross area, serviced by a central core of elevators and fire escape stairs. The plan represents local preferences for a way of life: external windows for every room, and emphasis on space efficiency.

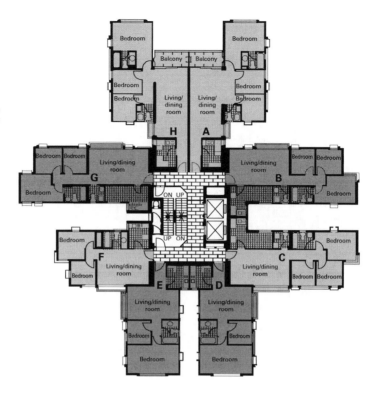

provide investment for homes, jobs, services and facilities. The development accommodates 58,282 families in 16-apartment towers ranging from 30 to 60 storeys in height, with another single 102-storey tower accommodating 231,778 m² of office space and a 330 room business hotel. To add to the dynamism of the development there are two further towers of 64 stories each, one comprising executive serviced apartments and residential accommodation, and the other a 1060-room super-class hotel. All 19 super towers sit on massive podiums with a huge urban park on the roof. As one would expect, the podium includes a shopping centre and also a multi-level car park, which has spaces for 6000 cars. Finally, there is the transport interchange on the station level. Unprecedented, compared to the mixed-use developments primarily for home and leisure such as the Metro-City project, the Kowloon Station represents the most recent urban experiment in high-density mixed use. It is an advanced evolution of MILU that has come about in the pursuit for combined living, working and leisure in a high-quality urban setting, supported by highly efficient transportation and a large urban green space (Figures 8.6 and 8.7).

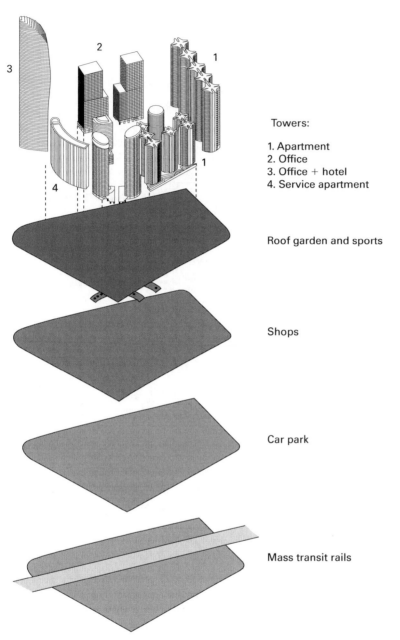

Figure 8.7
Axonometric illustration of the
Kowloon Station comprehensive
development. (*Source*: based on
Terry Farrell and Partners,
1998.)

Towers:

1. Apartment
2. Office
3. Office + hotel
4. Service apartment

Roof garden and sports

Shops

Car park

Mass transit rails

Kowloon station development isometric

Conclusion

Hong Kong is a practical example of an alternative to urban sprawl, and suggests that MILU is a more sustainable urban form. MILU optimizes land resources in a compact urban form realized by intensification (or densification) and mixed land uses, interconnected by an efficient public transportation system. Social acceptance is a significant factor for a compact and high-density urban model such as Hong Kong (Coupland, 1997). Due to the immense pressure from market demand, real estate developers and government planners rely on an empirical approach in the search for a socially and economically viable urban form, in order to guarantee a sustainable way of living that corresponds to local preferences.

The Hong Kong case study reveals the success of the compact urban form based upon the concepts of 'convenience, connectivity, comfort, and artificial ground' (Zaman *et al.*, 2000). The two case studies show the typical form of several towers on top of a podium with green space on its roof, a multi-level car park, shops, or other functions underneath and within. Direct connection can be made to public transportation nodes via a subway station or multi-route bus terminal, to offer connectivity and convenience to residents and visitors. The development of the podium concept is a clear demonstration of MILU, combining a desired way of living, with an effective mechanism for the public and private sector to combine and share community-based facilities.

However, MILU with such high densities poses a unique dichotomy between privacy and communal life. It has led people to seek privacy in their small flats, but to intensive interaction in the neighbourhood and streets, with regular dining out with friends and relatives. Living in a constrained environment could be attributed to Chinese history and culture (Zhang, 2000), so in the case of contemporary Hong Kong, limited space and close proximity to other buildings and people is seen as tolerable. This close proximity has rewarded Hong Kong residents with efficiency as well as economy in the use of time and space (Forrest *et al.*, 2002).

In Hong Kong, the urban space utilization represented by MILU development is closely linked to the culture and lifestyle of the people (Hughes, 1968). The research shows that inhabitants seem to be satisfied with living in small apartments in a high-rise building that offers a high quality of living with views of harbour, natural landscapes and the sea, which are always close by. Hong Kong provides a good quality of urban life, with close proximity to facilities, friends, family, work and shops, and reliable and convenient public transport giving acceptable travel times from home to work. For children, schools are within walkable distance from residential areas. Low crime, low divorce rates and low instances of respiratory diseases are interesting indicators in favour of the acceptability of high-density living found in Hong Kong. However, it would be rash to attribute such factors to high-density lifestyles alone, without further research.

In summary, Hong Kong's high-rise, high-density and mixed-use developments can be characterized by four concepts: compactness, verticality, connectivity and the 'sky city'. The urban form of Hong Kong continues to offer urban dwellers an exciting and comfortable lifestyle that prospers, and most of all appears sustainable.[5] The compact city of Hong Kong, although far from being the perfect solution, has great strengths and advantages, and is an urban form that is becoming more popular in the expanding cities of China and beyond.

Acknowledgements

Thanks are extended to the following: P.Y. Li, K.Y.K. Ip, K.M. Au and F.M. Li for their support. Special thanks are also due to developers of the two case studies: MTRC Limited, and Henderson Development Limited.

Notes

1. This chapter is developed from a series of research publications invited by the HabiForum Research Foundation, The Netherlands, from 2000 to 2002, a project to study MILU in different countries. A preliminary version of this chapter was presented at the International Symposium on Urban Environment organized by Oxford Brookes University in December 2002.

2. The principal author and P.K. Li conducted a 9-month research survey in 2001–2002 on subjective responses of households towards various aspects of high-rise living. A total of 102 families in Hong Kong was interviewed and asked about their opinion towards the advantages and disadvantages of high-rise living. Of the 102 surveyed, 98 households enjoyed high-rise living as an acceptable form of urban living. Mori Building Company sponsored the survey.

3. Shizou Harada, Lecturer of the Waseda University, at a presentation at the Tongji University Shanghai on November 3, 2003, introduced his proposal to the Hyper Building Committee of the Japanese Ministry of Construction to enhance the urban roles of the existing group of high-rise office buildings in the Shinjuku district into a mixed-use sky city – enhancing the impacts of ground level activities with multi-levels of skywalks and skymalls.

4. Terry Farrell and Partners were appointed as Lead Consultants in 1992 to design the station, to create a master plan for the surrounding city and to lead the detailed design team (Terry Farrell and Partners, 1998).

5. It should be noted that as a result of the severe acute respiratory syndrome (SARS) outbreak in March 2003, there is a suspicion that dense urban form might be conducive to the spread of respiratory diseases such as SARS, and such fear has alerted planners and researchers to examine the correlation with environmental health-related issues of high-density cities, in an attempt to improve the performance of high-density developments to satisfy environmental and health concerns in compact cities.

References

Burgess, R. (2000) The Compact City Debate: A Global Perspective. In: *Compact Cities: Sustainable Urban Forms for Developing Countries* (eds. Jenks M. and Burgess R.), Spon Press, London.

Coupland, A., ed. (1997) *Reclaiming the City: Mixed-Use Development*, E & FN Spon, London.

Forrest, R., Grange, A. and Ngai-ming, Y. (2002) *Neighbourhood in a High-Rise and High-Density City: Some Observations on Contemporary Hong Kong*. Retrieved from the World Wide Web: http://www.neighbourhoodcentre.org.uk

Hong Kong Government (2002) *Hong Kong in Figures*, Department of Census and Statistics. Retrieved from the World Wide Web: http://www.info.gov.hk/censtatd/

Hughes, R. (1968) *Hong Kong: Borrowed Place – Borrowed Time*, Andre Deutsch Ltd, London.

Jacobs, J. (1961) *The Death and Life of Great American Cities*, Random House, New York.

Lau, S.S.Y. and Li, P.Y. (2001–2002) *A Survey on Residents' Response to High-Rise Living in Hong Kong*, Report, Centre of Architecture & Urban Design for China and Hong Kong, The University of Hong Kong.

Roberts, M. and Lloyd-Jones, T. (1997) Mixed Uses and Urban Design, in *Reclaiming the City: Mixed-Use Development* (ed. Coupland, A.), E & FN Spon, London.

Rowley, A. (1996) Mixed Use Development: Ambiguous Concept, Simplistic Analysis and Wishful Thinking? *Planning Practice and Research* **11(1)**: 85–98.

Rowley, A. (1998) *Planning Mixed Use Development: Issues and Practice*, Research Report by the Royal Institute of Chartered Surveyors, UK.

Terry Farrell and Partners (1998) *Kowloon: Transport Super City*, Pace Publishing Ltd, Hong Kong.

United Nations (UN) (2000) *United Nations Statistics Year Book of the Year 2000*, United Nations, New York.

Zaman, Q.M.M., Lau, S.S.Y. and So, H.M. (2000) The Compact City of Hong Kong: a Sustainable Model for Asia? In: *Compact Cities: Sustainable Urban Forms for Developing Countries* (eds. Jenks, M. and Burgess, R.), Spon Press, London.

Zhang, X.Q. (2000) High-Rise and High-Density Urban Form. In: *Compact Cities: Sustainable Urban Forms for Developing Countries* (eds. Jenks, M. and Burgess, R.), Spon Press, London.

9

Perry Pei-Ju Yang

From Central Business District to New Downtown: Designing Future Sustainable Urban Forms in Singapore

Introduction

Singapore as a city is known for its downtown skylines, high-quality public housing, green urban landscape and efficient infrastructure system. In the past three decades, the Singapore urban skyline has changed rapidly in the downtown revitalization process. With its astonishing urban changes, clean environment and neat city images, Singapore, as a city-state, has influenced the ways the city has been shaped and managed. This is evident, for example, in the success of controlling traffic growth in the central city area through public transport and advanced management systems like electronic road pricing (ERP). Singapore's approach has become a unique model of urban management in East Asia, where governmental planning plays a fundamental role in the shaping of both economic growth and urban physical environment through long-term urban policies, nimble decision-making, delicate skills of urban design and efficient plan implementation.

However, the achievements of the past may not guarantee its future success. In the late 1990s, a 14 million m² downtown development was proposed on reclaimed land at Marina South, which represented a typical Singapore approach based on governmental initiation and planning. The optimistic scenario of continuous economic growth and city development through building Singapore as a 21st century global business centre is now in question. Development has slowed since the economic downturn in 2001, making the future scenario pessimistic and unpredictable. The issues faced in Singapore downtown (the physical core of the island city and the concentration of capital flows, information exchange and decision-making) can be regarded as the tip of the iceberg of the city's economic future. Through the examination of urban design policies and proposals, this chapter discusses how downtown Singapore has been transformed in a specific historical context of building a modern city-state, and how the future downtown urban forms are envisioned to respond to the recent challenges in global competitiveness and sustainable urban development.

Functional divide: decentralized new towns and the downtown central business district

What shapes Singapore's urban landscape and downtown urban form today? What are the urban concepts behind the planning and downtown urban design policy, which initiated and then constituted the radical urban transformation over 30–40 years? In 1959, Singapore established her own self-government. The 1958 Statutory Master Plan, a colonial product based on the concept of Singapore as a middle-size town surrounded by countryside, was replaced in 1963 by a new vision of decentralized 'ring development', which was drafted by a UN team in a report 'Growth and Urban Renewal' (Abrams et al., 1963) (Figure 9.1). Although the spatial scale is much smaller, some believe that the ring development in the UN team's Singapore Master Plan gained their inspiration from the ring of cities and green heart concepts of Randstad metropolitan area in Holland (see Koolhaas, 1995; Tan, 1999).

The policy of decentralizing population growth through the ring pattern was clearly set in the island-wide concept plan in 1971 (Tan, 1999). The ring pattern decisively influenced the geometry of the urban transport systems such as rapid transit and expressways, and the water resource planning through the protection of the central water catchment's and green areas in the centre of the island. Under the ring development policy, the spatial effects of decentralization and centralized revitalization

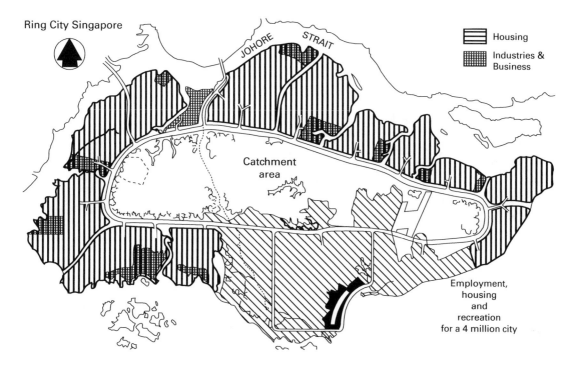

Figure 9.1
The Singapore 'ring
development' plan (after
Abrams et al., 1963).

coexisted. The development of public housing and new towns along the ring corridors and at the outer fringes of the city paralleled the revitalization of the central city area and the relocation of existing inhabitants.

The government through its Housing Development Board (HDB), a public housing planning, design, construction and management entity, determined the urban landscape of decentralized new towns in Singapore. To date, more than 80% of the population inhabit the 20 decentralized new towns, which are 10–15 km away from the city centre and occupy more than 160 km² or a quarter of the land area of the whole island (Singapore URA, 1991; Koolhaas, 1995; Malone-Lee et al., 2001).

Simultaneously, business activities were highly centralized at the nodal centre of the ring city. From the late 1960s, the Singapore central business district (CBD) and financial centre 'Golden Shoe' were rapidly developed along the waterfront and Shenton Way under the urban renewal programme (Figure 9.2). Almost 3 million m² of downtown office space was formed over the subsequent four decades. The CBD became a financial centre where most of the headquarters' offices, major local and international banks, stock brokers' companies, law firms, accountants and management consultants are rooted, including

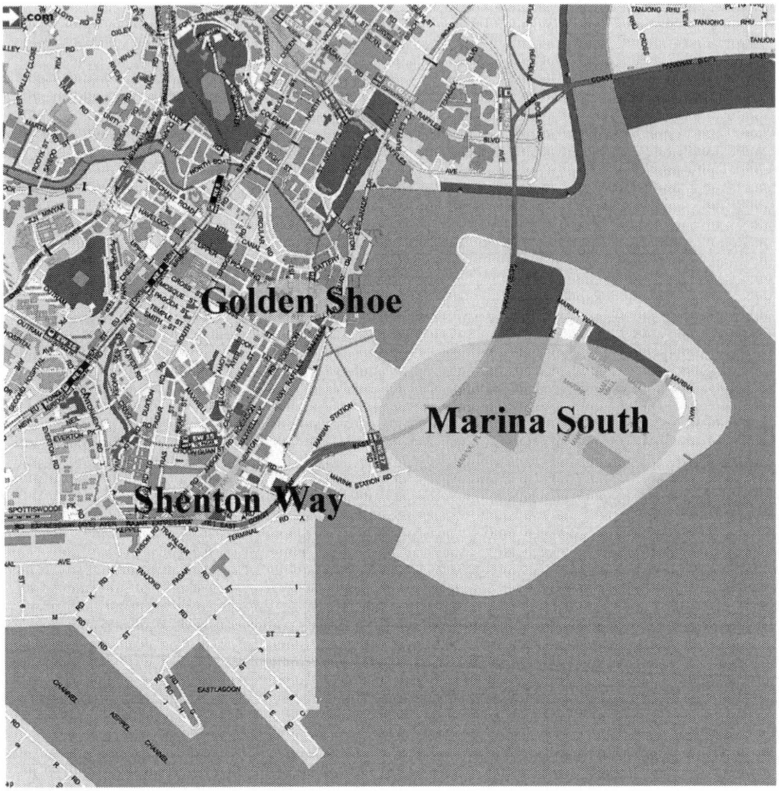

Figure 9.2
Location of the 'Golden Shoe',
Shenton Way and Marina South.

the fourth largest foreign exchange market in the world. The incremental shaping of the towering urban skyline responds to the rising position of Singapore city in the expanding international economy, and its increasingly important role in regional finance, industry and port services (Chua, 1989).

The spatial consequences of the decentralized new towns all over the island, and the concentrated downtown development in the centre, resulted in an almost total functional divide between living and working. The boundaries of the city centre, fringe towns and restricted green areas are clearly demarcated, and spatially divide the way people work, live and play in the city.

From CBD to New Downtown

The office-oriented development of Shenton Way CBD since the late 1960s is a clear example of functional planning, in which profitability, land-use optimization and independently operating institutions and corporations are reflected in a

Figure 9.3
The urban skyline of 'Golden Shoe' CBD in the late 1990s. (*Source*: Pacific productions.)

planning of isolated object-like building design, intensive development and high-rise urban form. The principles of efficient layout, road circulation and parking dominated at the expense of the pedestrian environment. The consequences of this type of functional planning and its high price resulted in a very exclusive CBD (Figure 9.3). After office hours, the downtown areas have become a deserted and dead urban environment.

In 1996, the government proposed a 'New Downtown' to be located on the reclaimed land of Marina South with the policy intention of creating an environment combining work, leisure and living in a single location. Planned as an extension of the existing Shenton Way CBD area, the Singapore New Downtown was planned to provide about 3 million m^2 of office space, which almost doubled the size of the current CBD. The design of New Downtown applied the principle of 'maximum pedestrian traffic, minimum vehicular congestion'. All modes of transportation were planned next to, under or at the edge of the development. Vehicular traffic was stopped or restricted at the edge of the district by interceptor car parks, which were intended to encourage the district-wide pedestrian movements that were to be connected to inward looking and 'all weather comfort' environments at the basement, 2nd storey and 30th interchange floor by multi-level through block links and travellators (Singapore URA, 1996). The concept of Singapore Urban Redevelopment Authority's (URA) New Downtown design was close to that of 'the city as a megablock shopping centre', possibly influenced by Victor Gruen's designs of downtown urban forms generated by the concept of 'simultaneous movement systems' with separated multi-modal pedestrian and transportation circulation (Loukaitou and Banerjee, 1998).

The urban design principles behind the 1996 New Downtown proposal went beyond the traditional form and function of office-oriented development of Shenton Way CBD in many aspects (Figure 9.4). First, the 'live–work–play' mixed-use development included 26,000 new homes with high accessibility to the workplaces and was evenly distributed across the overall area in the waterfront, downtown centre and the surrounding urban parks. Second, the injection of entertainment and recreational facilities was intended to change the nature of working environment. The live–work–play combination was meant to transform the daytime office downtown to a 24-hour 'New Downtown'. Third, some emerging technologies were implemented in infrastructure planning and building design, such as a district cooling system, high-speed lifts with artificial intelligence control systems, central computer-based building automation systems and common services tunnels. These urban design principles aimed to achieve the new objective of the island to create a 'global business hub'. The proposal represented another 'non-stop' government policy initiative to keep track of Singapore's economic progress in the global marketplace.

Figure 9.4
The urban design of Singapore New Downtown, 1996. (*Source:* Singapore URA urban model.)

Reflections on downtown urban form

The transition of Singapore's downtown design concepts from the 1970s Shenton Way to the 1990s New Downtown is significant but also problematic. The New Downtown proposal indicates an innovative form of corporate space intended to integrate living, working and recreational activities. The ideas seem 'too good to be true': the multi-level pedestrian and vehicular movements, parking systems and public transports provide an environment with almost 'zero-friction' circulation. Urban design formulae such as tree-lined boulevards, waterfront promenades, urban parks and plazas are ubiquitous across the whole area, and were illustrated through a few images of Western cities. Although western design formulae aspire to a certain quality of urban life, ironically, the New Downtown design transmits a strong sense of placelessness.

The 1996 New Downtown proposal in fact expresses the ultimate form of functional planning, surprisingly akin to the principles of Shenton Way's downtown urban design of the 1970s. Unlike the mono-functional design of Shenton Way, the New Downtown is designed with multiple uses, but this is not only for corporate profitability, but also for tourism and consumption. Like many precedents in Singapore planning and urban design, the urban environment and experience cut across all boundaries of geography, culture and ideology, where urban form is built without reference to history and geography. It is hard to detect any social differences, cultural distinctions or confrontation points in this new urban vision because they seem to have disappeared or, as Marshall Berman's comments on modernity and the experience of contemporary urban life, 'melted into air' (Berman, 1992).

In 2003, Singapore URA announced a revised New Downtown plan. Based on a similar development projection, 6 million m^2 of floor area, the propositions of the 1996 New Downtown plan were largely followed by the 2003 revised plan: a pedestrian-friendly environment with at, above or below ground level connections, state-of-the-art infrastructure and multi-functional mixed-use design, which aimed for 'a distinctive and global location for business and for living, working and leisure, around-the-clock'.

There were only minor differences between the two downtown plans in terms of physical design (Figure 9.5). A new 75-m wide and 700 m long linear urban park was created and

173

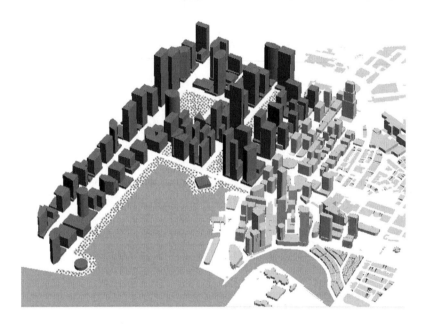

Figure 9.5
The comparison of 1996
(above) and 2003 (below) New
Downtown master plans.

oriented towards the Marina Bay. Within the 100 ha of the New Downtown core area, the open space ratio was increased from 6% to 12%. The average block size was reduced from 1.6 to less than 1 ha. A regular block system provided a spatial framework which would 'allow room for expansion, subdivision and phasing of developments to suit changing market need' (Singapore URA, 2003). The smaller block design and flexible grid system reflected the more conservative position adopted by the 2003 revised plan due to the difficulties faced by the government in attracting real estate investment to the new area.

The critique of the 1996 and 2003 designs gives rise to two fundamental questions. To what extent can the downtown urban space be designed and planned? Beyond the functional aspects, what are the alternative design and development strategies, which could contribute to the particular quality of downtown urban space? The first question seems obvious if we accept Koolhaas's analogy that Singapore is a mega-shopping centre (Chung *et al.*, 2001), or that the city is a huge lounge of Changi International Airport. The issue of 'privatized public space' in Western cities does not exist, because the whole city has in almost all respects privatized public space through government land acquisition, delicate planning and careful management, resulting in neat and organized streets, parks, underground and open spaces in the city centre and at the fringes. As a consequence, the downtown urban space, even the whole city, has become a designable object.

Unexpectedly, the first question in designing downtown is now becoming increasingly difficult to answer. The global economic downturn since 2001 slowed down the speed of development of the New Downtown. It led to uncertainty about how economic growth could be sustained, especially in office and commercial development. If the office development in Shenton Way and the commercial development in Orchard Road could not maintain or guarantee its profitability, 'How could the planning of another 6 million m^2 in New Downtown be viable?' Under these new and unanticipated circumstances, a second question is now timely: What new design and development strategies could help stimulate downtown liveability and sustainability?

An urban design studio

In 2001, Singapore URA (2001b) published a new concept plan. It 'stressed the importance of taking into account the changing global trend in living and working patterns, sustainability and energy-saving strategies, variation in identity of urban neighbourhood and the strong sense of islandness'. The key proposals included a global business centre, high-rise city living, an extensive rail network and focus on identity. The URA appointed an International Panel of Architects and Urban Planners, including Peter Hall and Fumihiko Maki, to review the draft of the 2001 Concept Plan. In the central city area, the panel suggested a strong linkage between the successful commercial boulevard Orchard Road and the historical waterfront Singapore River, where 'the visibility of the developments on both sides of Orchard Road' is to be increased and 'more green relief in public spaces' is to be introduced on the Singapore River (Singapore URA, 2001a).

An urban design team, sponsored by Singapore URA, was established in January 2002 at the Department of Architecture of the National University of Singapore (NUS) through its Master of Architecture programme. The URA-NUS urban design studio aimed to rethink the area in between Orchard Road and Singapore River, and to explore the future form of downtown urban space in a broader urban context. The site covers the eastern part of Orchard Road, the future interchange Dhoby Ghaut, the historically significant Fort Canning with surrounding cultural resources, the six-lane Clemenceau Avenue intersecting the area and part of Clark Quay next to the avenue.

The urban design studio started with a series of questions. During the economic downturn, What would make Singapore continue to be a globally competitive city? How could physical urban quality contribute to this competitiveness? When development slows down and the projections for commercial development and tourism become pessimistic, what are the alternatives to the big sites, big capital and big developers? What alternative modes of development are there to the principles of functional planning which currently dominate the production of urban space through the overall control of development by government? What are the alternative strategies for design and development?

At the beginning of the studio, a 1-week intensive Urban Design Workshop was set in NUS to initiate a rapid response for the Singapore URA sponsored project. A short experimental design charette provided opportunities for students to learn the basic principles and skills in urban analysis, urban form making and development processes over extended spatial and temporal environments. A kilometre-wide downtown area surrounding Fort Canning was selected, which was then divided into six 'quadrants': Museum and Rochor Area, Civic and Cultural District, Singapore River, River Valley, Orchard Road and Dhoby Ghaut (Figure 9.6). Through the analysis of urban context and the fast development of sketch-conceptual design, different design approaches were tested and some critical urban issues were presented and highlighted during the final workshop meeting between NUS tutors, students and URA planners.

Figure 9.6
Site location.

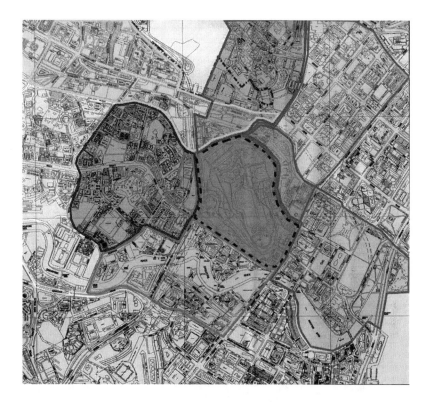

The history of the urban design concepts was traced from 1970s' Shenton Way CBD to the 1990s' New Downtown design. The critical thinking on different downtown urban design approaches stimulated the studio's design question: What will be the next downtown urban form, which could sustain downtown liveability? How could appropriate design and planning interventions initiate a large-scale urban transformation that would respond to the current and future challenges of downtown design and development? This was not an easy task when facing the area with its multiple stakeholders, indeterminate and unpredictable programmes, and complicated spatial arrangements of urban activities and built forms.

Downtown interchange, Campus City and the Boulevard

The 'Sketch Concept Development' immediately followed the workshop. Three experimental concepts were developed during the preliminary design process, which was driven by the critique of the current downtown urban space. The three conceptual designs, Downtown Interchange, Campus City and the Boulevard, were drafted with distinctively strong propositions, arguments and design solutions.

Downtown interchange

The expansion of the existing 93 km of rail lines to about 500 km in the future (Singapore URA, 2001b) will make the downtown transportation problems more complicated and require new spatial solutions. In addition to the existing three mass rapid transit (MRT) interchanges, the NUS Master Plan proposed a concept called 'district interchange' instead of the current 'one single station as an interchange' (Figure 9.7). This included the concept of a ring-shaped downtown infill development as a 'central district interchange'. The proposal

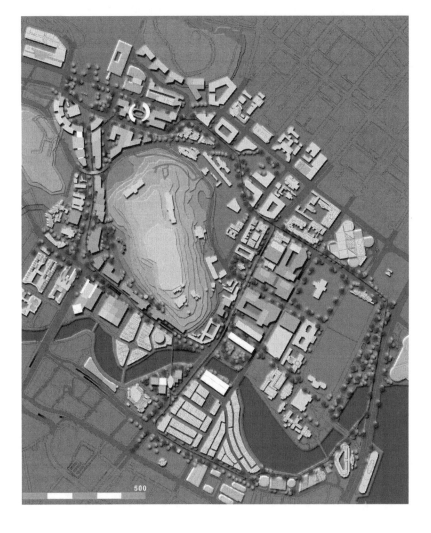

Figure 9.7
The 'Downtown Interchange' concept.

FUTURE FORMS

redesigned the whole district to become a car-restricted zone, with some road sections or lanes strategically reduced and a pedestrian-friendly environment created within this ring to integrate commercial, civic, recreational and cultural activities. To relieve the anticipated problems of future pedestrian flows and vehicle circulation, some emerging technologies of transportation were considered for integrating the mass rapid transit (MRT) system and upgrading the current infrastructure, including personal rapid transit (PRT), intelligent community vehicle system (ICVS), and smart bicycles and vehicles. The multiple choices of transit enables the creation of a car-restricted urban landscape for the future form of downtown. At the same time, the historically significant Fort Canning Park in the centre of the ring is protected by restoring the original tropical forest to maintain its ecological function as a city lung.

Campus City

The economic downturn shows that the tourism may not be able to adequately sustain downtown's commercial and retail development, a situation especially applicable to Singapore's main street Orchard Road. An alternative proposition of downtown urban form was taken: a campus as the downtown space (Figure 9.8). The university campus is an essential element of future downtown, where the interchange of

Figure 9.8
The 'Campus City' concept.

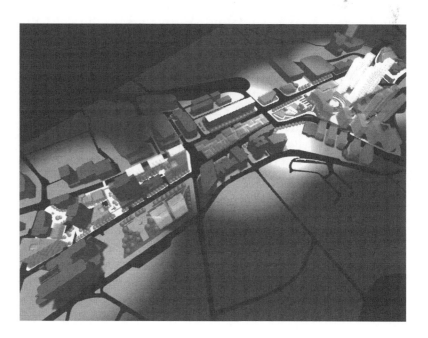

FUTURE FORMS

knowledge is as important as the interchange of capital, services and goods in the physical core of a city. The proposed strategy of designing future downtown form in this area is to intertwine campus and learning institutions with business and commercial development. Unlike the traditional type of university such as the NUS which accommodates academic and research activities in a relatively isolated environment, the proposed Campus City emphasizes meeting the increasing needs of entrepreneurship, focusing on innovation among staff and students, and the interaction and collaboration between university, business and industry. The downtown learning environment will contain thousands of meeting points to nurture creative relationships. The spatial form of the downtown campus is a 'sandwiched' mixed-use pattern, in which the linear learning belt is situated between two sides of mixed uses with commercial, retail, residential, art and cultural activities. The new population generated from the Campus City would not only stimulate the urban activities and economic development of the downtown area, but also provide new facilities for the interchange of ideas, knowledge and business incubation. While tapping resources from the existing urban fabric, the city campus would also provide a research centre for the surrounding developments.

The Boulevard

A boulevard-like urban corridor was proposed by redesigning Clemenceau Avenue and the surroundings through the shrinkage of the original six-lane road to a five-lane boulevard. This would provide a direct physical linkage toward the Istana Park, a piece of tropical green-park in front of Singapore's political centre (the Istana) and a gateway that leads people into the boulevard. With the strong reference and a new landscape strategy to the Istana Park, pedestrians would have been made aware of the significant civic space of the Istana. Using fine-grain and mixed-use patterns as the design strategy, the proposal stimulates the shaping of urban connections through numerous interventions of small-scale development, providing a transitional urban experience where one can move from one destination to another. The planned boulevard embodied a meaningful journey through the introduction of new aspects of urban including an innovative training space, an artistic and cultural space, a marketplace, green-parks and an entertainment belt, which taken together created a series of vibrant places where people can receive information and learn about new

Figure 9.9
The 'Boulevard' concept.

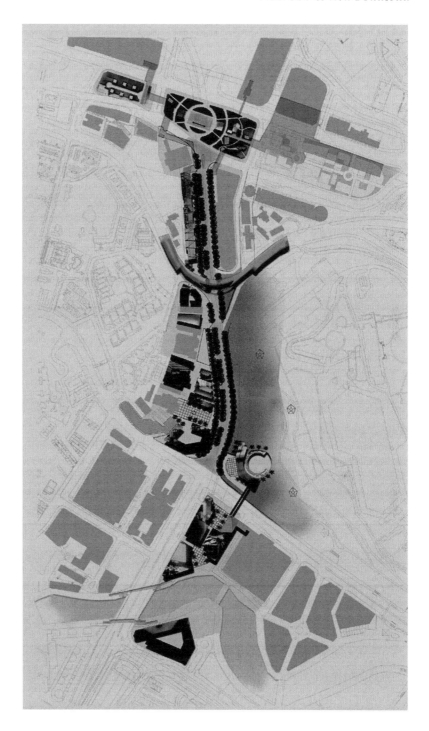

things while at the same time enjoy the green of Fort Canning. The boulevard would serve as a linkage to connect the two disparate zones of Singapore River and Orchard Road to achieve an integrated urban fabric (Figure 9.9). These programmes adopt an incremental mode of development reflecting the ever-evolving and dynamic process of Singapore throughout time.

The concept-driven proposals touch the sustainable aspects of future urban form, the car-restricted zone as the downtown interchange, downtown campus space as the knowledge interchange and a fine-grain boulevard environment as an urban connector. Due to the clarity of the plan, the responses throughout public meetings were meaningful and thoughtful. The three downtown design concepts critically reconsider the planning principles of the existing Singapore CBD development and the New Downtown plan in order to propose some alternative scenarios for future development with different urban characteristics. It also responded to the island-wide Concept Plan 2001, which emphasized the ideas of rail-oriented development, high-rise city living, global business centre and the issues of identity (Singapore URA, 2001b).

From plan clarity to plan effectiveness

The three distinctive urban design proposals, Downtown Interchange, Campus City and the Boulevard tried to seize the attention and imagination of designers and policy makers by their clear urban form, spatial concepts and distinctive visions. At the final stage, a practical approach was adopted by the NUS studio team for making the final urban design scheme more feasible and implementable. The final urban design proposal was prepared based on the following three major urban design components.

Final urban design master plan

By reorganizing the previous three conceptual designs, a final proposal was drafted by coordinating the design and planning principles of the three conceptual schemes. Some of the design concepts were further developed by the NUS studio team, including the encouragement of small-scale enterprises through fine-grain strategies for mixed-land uses, a vertical zoning policy for the downtown campus, the transformation of the retail landscape by injecting new urban form and activities along main routes and by providing the boulevard with new open landscapes. Three final schemes, the City Campus, the City Boulevard and the City River, were proposed which comprise the overall urban design master plan.

Urban design guidelines

Urban design guidelines, in the Singapore context, are a governmental tool for achieving expected performance and spatial quality of possible urban form. By looking at the more detailed block-scale massing study and design, some aspects of urban design quality were achieved by developing a visibility analysis, a built form and streetscape study, connectivity consideration of vehicular and pedestrian access and the implementation strategies for development programmes. The traditional ways to deal with urban design guidelines such as design control plans and sections were applied. New techniques of describing three-dimensional (3D) urban quality, such as 3D massing rendering, were also tested for illustrating the criteria and guidelines of the design area.

Design for strategic urban sites

For the purpose of demonstrating how the urban design guidelines work, more detailed architecture and landscape designs were done in some strategic urban sites in order to show the potential quality of urban space and to test the requirements of the proposed urban design guidelines.

Conclusion

The incredibly fast urban transformation of Singapore's downtown is a good example for rethinking urbanism in an Asian urban context. This provides a different experience from European and North American urbanism in terms of urban form, driving forces and alternative future scenarios. The reflections on Singapore downtown urban design and development have some implications for governmental sponsored urban design studios. A series of questions were raised through the critique of functional planning, which stimulated design thinking during the process. It is a reminder of what might be missing in the contemporary urban life of Singapore. The urban reality contains many conflicting values of old and new, short-term interests and long-term visions, profitability and the public interest, aesthetics and functions, all of which are sometimes hidden in Singapore planning and urban design. An approach towards a more sustainable downtown urban form was proposed by the urban design studio through a few design strategies: the car-restricted zone, campus downtown space, finer-grain urban fabric, small business and small-scale development, a rich mix of land use, the emphasis on streetscape rather than large-scale open space, releasing the control of spaces and the decentralization of ownership, small and incremental development process rather than a one-shot development with big parcel and big money. None of these design ideas can stand alone. A dynamic urban setting, economy and society usually rely on not only the vision and policies from the government, but also through the responsibility and involvement from the public.

References

Abrams, C., Kobe, S. and Koenigsberger, O. (1963) *Growth and Urban Renewal in Singapore: Report Prepared for the Government of Singapore*, United Nations Programme of Technical Assistance, Department of Economic and Social Affairs, New York.

Berman, M. (1992) Modernity and Revolution. In: *A Zone of Engagement* (ed. Anderson, P.), p. 25–55, Verso Press, London.

Chua, B.H. (1989) *The Golden Shoe: Building Singapore's Financial District*, Urban Redevelopment Authority, Singapore.

Chung, C.J., Inaba. J., Koolhaas, R. and Leong, S.T. (2001) *Project on the City 2: Harvard Design School Guide to Shopping*, Taschen, Cambridge, USA.

Koolhaas, R. (1995) Singapore Songlines: Thirty Years of Tabula Rasa. In: *Small, Medium, Large, Extra-Large by OMA* (eds. Koolhaas, R. and Mau, B.), The Monacelli Press, New York.

Loukaitou, A. and Banerjee, T. (1998) *Urban Design Downtown: Poetics and Politics of Form*, University of California Press, Berkely.

Malone-Lee, L.C., Sim, L.L. and Chin, L. (2001) Planning for a More Balanced Home-work Relationship: The Case Study of Singapore. *Cities*, **18(1)**: 51–55.

Singapore URA (1991) *Living the Next Lap: Toward a Tropical City of Excellence*, Urban Redevelopment Authority, Singapore.

Singapore URA (1996) *New Downtown: Ideas for the City of Tomorrow*, Urban Redevelopment Authority, Singapore.

Singapore URA (2001a) *Skylines: Draft Concept Plan 2001*, Urban Redevelopment Authority, Singapore.

Singapore URA (2001b) *The Concept Plan 2001*, Urban Redevelopment Authority, Singapore.

Singapore URA (2003) *Downtown at Marina Bay*, Urban Redevelopment Authority, Singapore.

Tan, S. (1999) *Home, Work, Play*, Urban Redevelopment Authority, Singapore.

Towards a Sustainable City: Rebuilding Lower Manhattan

Introduction

The attack of September 11, 2001 on New York City, killing some 2800 innocent people from 115 countries reverberated around the globe. With New York City being the home to many cultures and a centre of world trade and finance, it seemed like an attack on the modern world. The World Trade Center (WTC), 16 acres covering 12 city blocks, and other buildings in the surrounding area, were destroyed (Figure 10.1). This action had a staggering impact on the lives of people who live and work in Lower Manhattan and on New York City's economy. Thirteen million square feet of office space was demolished and nearly 17 million square feet of office space was damaged. Over 600,000 square feet of retail was lost.

Eighty-three thousand jobs disappeared in Lower Manhattan. Many businesses and residents left the city. Most of those who lost their jobs earned less than $25,000 p.a. There were two entry-level service employees (e.g. restaurant, sales clerks, and maintenance workers), for every one high-income employee. Twelve hundred to two thousand small businesses were ravaged. Sales volumes of the remaining businesses have dropped by up to 80%. Consequently, the surviving retail, service firms, and restaurants are struggling (Alliance for Downtown NY,

Figure 10.1
Aerial photograph of the WTC
site and surrounding area
immediately after the attack
on September 11, 2001.

2002). Stations for three subway lines and the PATH train linking
New York and New Jersey were levelled. These had carried
thousands of workers daily to and from the New York City
boroughs, New Jersey and Connecticut to the WTC area. The
tragic September 11 attack damaged in varying degrees the
physical, economic, and social fabric of Lower Manhattan (Figure
10.2). This provided an opportunity to reconsider how we build
and live in New York City.

Civic response after the disaster

The US mainland had never been attacked before. The anguish
and trauma resulting from the event engendered an intense

Figure 10.2
Assessment of the extent and
type of damage. An area of
2 miles was affected.

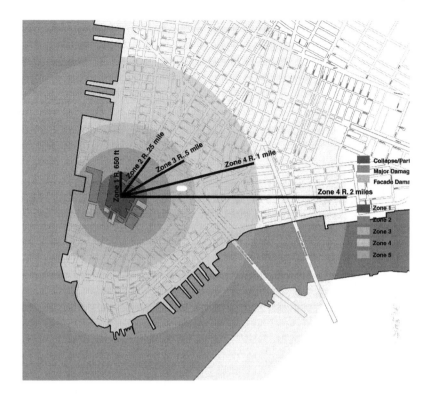

citizen response. Civic organizations voluntarily banded together to formulate public policies that could restore normal living and working conditions in the area and guide the rebuilding. Some had been lobbying for many years for specific city and regional improvements, such as mass transit, housing, parks and public spaces, waterfront development, economic and social justice, and good urban design.

Organized by the author[1] and Susan Szenasy,[2] Rebuild Downtown Our Town (R.Dot) was formed immediately after September 11 to give the Lower Manhattan community a civic voice. R.Dot comprises Lower Manhattan residents, business people and business associations, community advocates, artists, colleges, and academic and design professionals, as well as city officials and public appointees. These participants meet regularly to discuss, research, and develop a collective vision that can shape the new downtown. Through its member groups, R.Dot represents the voices of thousands of people who have been directly affected by the destruction of the WTC. Known as the 'Voice of Lower Manhattan,' it works collaboratively with other major civic groups in New York City, and local, state, and federal government representatives. R.Dot, along with 80 other organizations, formed the umbrella group, the Civic Alliance to

Rebuild Downtown New York, which is administered by the Regional Plan Association.

Context

Lower Manhattan is the historic heart of New York City. During the American Revolution, New Yorkers burned the city to the ground in order to save it from British occupation. At its centre is Wall Street, the historical centre of America's financial world. Designated a special historic district by the city, Lower Manhattan's narrow streets and crooked blocks predate the automobile, and are edged by a mix of many small-scale historic buildings, churches, graveyards, and tall 20th century buildings (Figure 10.3). West Street (a six-lane highway) borders the southern tip of the triangular-shaped district, which includes the historic commercial core of New Amsterdam (New York's original name), Wall Street banking and commercial centre, and the Battery where cannons once protected the harbour.

Figure 10.3
Lower Manhattan.

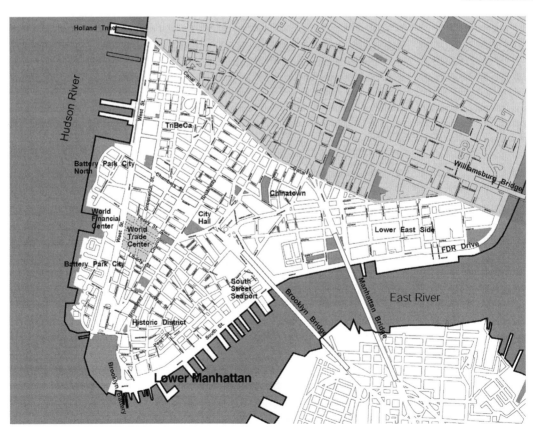

The WTC site is adjacent to this historic district. Across the street is Battery Park City, which was built in the 1980s in the area where ships once docked. Constructed on landfill formed in part by the dirt dug up from the WTC site, it is a major residential, business, and recreation area. North of the WTC site is the city's civic centre and TriBeCa, an affluent family neighbourhood consisting mostly of converted and elegantly rehabilitated warehouses and industrial buildings. To the east are the South Street Seaport (another historic district), and Chinatown.

To form the WTC, 12 historic blocks were bulldozed and combined to form a single super block. Two streets, Washington and Greenwich, running north–south were blocked and three streets, Fulton, Dey and Courtlandt, running from east–west were truncated. The WTC site was an anomaly in both its heartless destruction of historic sites and the audacity of its towering heights. That audacity came to symbolize New York City (and America) as a global centre of business and finance.

As the city expanded north, the size of its streets and blocks became larger and, consequently, so did the mass and size of its buildings. Elegant skyscrapers like the Woolworth Building sprung up in the early 1900s, creating a lively contrast with the older structures. This mixture of height and mass still characterizes Lower Manhattan. It is within the context of these images that we considered the revitalization of Lower Manhattan, the reconstruction of the WTC site and other destroyed buildings.

Economic and societal changes

Downtown Manhattan began to decline as an office centre in the 1920s and 1930s. The WTC was built to reverse that trend, but it was not successful. From the late 1970s to the early 1990s, astute property owners converted many older office buildings to residences. Together with the conversion of the surrounding industrial buildings into artist lofts, family-sized apartments, and the construction of the Battery Park City neighbourhood, a new residential downtown was born alongside and interspersed among Wall Street office buildings. Before September 11, there was a negative impact on the quality of life in this new, emerging 24/7 community due to a lack of civic amenities and integrated transportation. It was a fledgling, mixed-use community caught between urban land uses of the 20th century and the emerging ones of the 21st century.

The overall needs of the 21st century city society differ from those of the late 20th century with economic and social changes due to globalization, the birth of a knowledge-based economy, and the gender equality of the workforce. The global economy requires intellectually skilled and technologically adept service workers. The emergence of service industries as a primary source of wealth production has changed the characteristics of the workforce from task based to knowledge based. Society has become increasing mobile, cutting across barriers of language and culture. Competition for wealth producing talent crosses national and international borders. Approximately 150 different ethnic groups comprise almost half of the population of New York City. Whatever their country of origin, talented people are drawn to New York City, like other global cities, where they find a synergy of common personal and professional interests and complementary skills that allow them to achieve their personal goals.

However, perhaps the most important change from the viewpoint of land use is the percentage of women in the workplace. Women now comprise 46% of the American workforce (Hudson Institute, 1997). Two-wage families total 55%. Women now garner 55% of bachelor degrees, 53% of masters degrees, and nearly 40% of doctorates (Hudson Institute, 1997). Women's ownership of small businesses escalated from 5% in the 1970s to 38% in the 1990s (Small Business Administration, 1998). Approximately 64% of all married women in the workforce today have children of less than 6 years of age (Hudson Institute, 1997). Land-use patterns must fit the needs of today's working women, who still perform most of the household duties in addition to their paid work.

Concurrently, these changes together with other factors, such as a plethora of global unskilled workers and the rapidly widening gap between lower and upper incomes, create and perpetuate an underclass. The city must absorb into its overall fabric the disadvantaged groups spawned by all of these changes. Additionally, other factors are affecting how workers live and work. Many have rejected the 2–4 hours lost in daily commuting and have decided to live in the city near their work. Live and work is now commonplace, if not full-time, at least part-time.

Overall these factors strongly suggest the strengthening of neighbourhood so that all of the elements of daily living (retail services, personal services, schools, playgrounds, health care, etc.) are conveniently located within walking distance and all incomes are intermixed.

Vision for the future

It is worth noting that since 1922, nine master plans have been developed for Manhattan. Seven were developed by civic organizations, some in collaboration with the city's planning department. None has ever been adopted. New York City does not have a master plan. However, the widespread damage of Lower Manhattan below Canal Street has offered an opportunity to create a vision of Lower Manhattan based on humane values and a 21st century lifestyle.

New York City is organically clustered into neighbourhood nodes, each with its own identity.

Lower Manhattan presently comprises several and distinctly different neighbourhoods such as the historic financial centre around Wall Street, the residential area of Battery Park City, TriBeCa, South Street Seaport, and Chinatown. These neighbourhoods need new land uses, changes in urban form, transportation and connections to each other, the region and the world in a sustainable manner. Past and present market-driven forces typically form neighbourhoods. Rebuilding requires an understanding of what motivates people and businesses to create their neighbourhood, for public investment to then shape neighbourhood node development.

The R.Dot coalition's objective is to support an imaginative design that creates the possibility of an inclusive, 24-hour residential and business community. It is necessary that the built environment attracts and serves people who provide the intellectual, entrepreneurial, creative, and technological capabilities that empower New York City's society, its economy and the richness of its multi-cultural life. On behalf of R.Dot, the author developed a set of criteria based on the principles of livability and sustainability expounded in her earlier writings (Artigiani, 2002; Civic Alliance to Rebuild Downtown New York, 2002; Oppenheimer and Willis, 2002; Willis, 2002; Willis and Kossler, 2003; Willis and Raimone, 2003). Further position papers about neighbourhoods and housing, and about sustainability and health are currently scheduled for publication.

A changing identity and diversified employment

Since the 17th century, Lower Manhattan's identity has been based upon trading and banking. In the 20th century, many financial companies moved to the city's midtown, a mixed-use business centre with its newer transportation, easy access to regional locations and up-to-date infrastructure. Occupancy rates of financial companies on Wall Street declined. Reacting to business shutdowns caused by the destruction of September 11, financial companies that were located downtown are dispersing their financial operations to more than one location. Decentralization ensures that if one part of the company is destroyed, the rest of the company can carry on its work. This has further eroded Downtown's office building occupancies.

New York economists Alice Rivlin and Rosemary Scanlon concluded in a study for the Civic Alliance that financial services will continue to be an important component of Lower Manhattan's economy, but their size and functions could change considerably after September 11. They explain that 'the continued diversification of the area into a more mixed-use, economically integrated community is both likely and desirable'. They suggest that the identity of Lower Manhattan's identity may change with a potential expansion of both knowledge-based industries, and from overseas and domestic tourists attracted by its culture. They also argue that 'citywide demand for housing is likely to fuel a continued expansion of Lower Manhattan residential population, but both its rate of growth and composition will depend considerably on housing policies and land-use decisions' for example, to subsidize low- to moderate-income housing to achieve a diversity of income, age, and ethnicity (Civic Alliance to Rebuild Downtown New York, 2002).

Making Lower Manhattan sustainable

Rebuilding means rethinking how Lower Manhattan should physically, economically, and socially function in a 21st century context and how Lower Manhattan could be reshaped in a sustainable manner. Two documents, a Statement of Guiding Principles and an Urban Design Armature for Rebuilding Lower Manhattan, were initially used to explore possibilities (Figures 10.4 and 10.5).

Guiding principles

Self-determination and inclusion The state and the city must commit to a transparent planning processes and to giving civic and community voices from the immediate neighbourhood and adjacent neighbourhoods a meaningful place at the planning table.

Memorialization WTC bears witness to the death of thousands of New Yorkers, residents of other cities and citizens of many other countries, of innocent people of all cultures, ethnic backgrounds and, religious belief. It is also a testament to the surrounding community and the living, near and far, which responded to the tragedy. A fitting memorial will honour the dead and their families, celebrate the human spirit, and communicate the worldwide symbolic meaning of the site.

Livability and balance Develop WTC with fresh eye, inviting those elements – residential, commercial and retail, community places and services – that contribute to a 24-hour mixed use character; and connecting the distinct but related neighbourhoods of TriBeCa, Battery Park City, Chinatown, South Street Seaport, the Financial District, and the Lower East Side.

Arts and culture The arts humanize, give voice, stimulate, educate, socialize, build esteem, attract business and are essential to Downtown's rebirth and economic recovery.

Productivity New York's strength is in the intellectual, technological and creative skills and hard work of its people. Seek out essential new business sectors, individual entrepreneurs, and small businesses, as well as large.

Decentralization Communications technologies now make it possible for many business sectors to disperse without loss of cohesion and make high-density conglomeration less necessary.

Sustainability Build a healthy neighbourhood for our children and us, as a model for other cities. Sustainability has many applications: 'Green' architecture, energy efficiency, air and water quality, construction codes, materials and methods, use of local manufacturing capabilities for reconstruction purposes, utilities, and emergency services, pedestrian and mass transportation, outdoor spaces and our rivers.

Diversity Lower Manhattan's historic character is reflected in today's vibrant ethnic communities, convergence of many cultures in the workforce and the energy of local colleges with their mutli-cultural student bodies poised to inherit an equal share of the future city.

Efficient transportation Recognize that Lower Manhattan is a surface and sub-surface transportation hub of the PATH, LIRR, city subways and buses, water traffic, landscape features, pedestrian connections, deliveries, sanitation and security. Services must be up to supporting future needs without burdening other neighbourhoods.

Pride of place Architecture is public art that is a measure of our values, teaches design, proportion, materials, health, technology, and science – buildings and spaces that encourage visual and social literacy.

Figure 10.4
Guiding principles for rebuilding.

Sept. 16, 2002

Urban design armature for Lower Manhattan	
1. Identity	**Icon** Memorial Museum for Remembrance **Image** Financial Center – Wall Street Historical Center – US and New York City Waterfront access, boating, and water views
2. Social/economic diversity	**Social** Mixed-use (20% low-moderate income housing) Mixed-income Diverse ethnicities Diverse age groups Training the disadvantaged **Economic development strategies** Finance Technology Education (presently three universities and 40,000 students) Health care Bio-tech Small businesses Tourism/hotels Cultural places and events Retail uses at street level Flexibility for future development
3. Access and connections to Manhattan, the other boroughs and tri-state region	**Mass transit connections** Train (PATH) Subways Light rail Ferries **Access and connections – mass transit** Subway entrances and lobbies Ease of pedestrian movement to/from transit Stairway and escalator service standards Connections between transit stops Elimination of multi-fare transfers Ease of transfers
4. Surface transit	**Streets** Managed street use Reimpose street grid at WTC Underground west street (6 lane highway) Preserve historic streets Street surfaces, lights, signage and toilet designs **Access – streets** Sufficient space for vehicles and pedestrains, including sidewalks Security Pedestrian level of service standards Neighbourhood connections Space for buses Waterfront access
5. Urban form	Scale Block size Building massing, configuration, height Street widths Street grid Diverse architectural styles Diverse building style Water view corridors

Figure 10.5
Design armature for use in
developing conceptual urban designs.

6. Open spaces	Playgrounds (open and covered) Networks/connectivity of open space Semi-private courtyards Roof tops Ferry docks Trails Dog Rus
7. Nature and buildings	**Sustainability** **Nature** Construct parkways, trails (jogging, cycling, skating) along waterfront. Connect parks and green spaces. **Siting** Stagger buildings to allow day lighting, use of wind towers, water views and minimize shadows **Communications** (wireless, broadband, broadcast) **Heating and cooling** Solar heating (fuel cells, wind tower, day lighting, subterranean water for heating–cooling, natural ventilation) Building, heavily landscaped buildings and roofs, shadow locations Subterranean water for heating and cooling, water collection for landscaped areas (reuse of gray water) **Waste water disposal** Co-generation within buildings **Buildings** Passive and recyclable materials, sun screening Communication devices (receivers, transmitters)
8. Community services and civic amenities	**Personal services** (food, drugstore, cleaners, etc.) Professional (doctor, dentist, attorney, tutors, counselors, etc.) Restaurants, cafes, bars, etc. Outdoor markets Identity (TriBeCa, Battery Park City, Chinatown, South Street Seaport, etc.) **Schools** Public Private Colleges Schools as mixed-use (e.g. part of office or residential building) **Culture/entertainment** Open and enclosed art and performing spaces Public amenity programming (art, performance, celebration) Museums Movies **Health** Clinics Medical offices Hospitals (teaching)
9. Urban issues	**Automobiles and trucks** Parking Traffic Air-pollution (CO_2 emissions) Noise Road safety
10. Regulations and enforcement	Make existing environmental legislation mandatory. Use Battery Park City Residential and Commercial Green Guidelines Enforce LEED Certification Sustainable development incentives

Figure 10.5
(Continued).

Williams *et al.* (2000) point out that 'a prerequisite to achieving sustainable urban form is knowing what it is'. To realize the 'sustainable city' there has to be a clear and commonly held concept of what it will look like, how it will function and how it will change over time. In a review of several books on the topic of 'sustainability', Steven Moore writing in the *Journal of Architectural Education* (2000) points out that there are substantial differences in the use of the word. Neither, he explains, 'do the terms "eco-tec", "green", "regenerative", "ecological", or "bio-climatic" architecture provide a more precise meaning'. He gives examples of several viewpoints: Catherine Slessor, *Eco-Tech* (1997), argues that the ecological hypothesis is a style. Steele in *Sustainable Architecture* (1997) believes that the ecological hypothesis is a political and economic doctrine. David Lloyd Jones in *Architecture and the Environment* (1998) argues that the ecological hypothesis requires retrieval from the radical fringe. In *The Technology of Ecological Building*, Klaus Daniels (1997) focuses on a set of empirically tested construction practices.

The term sustainability used in this chapter straddles several of the above meanings, and represent the ideas of a group of civic activists, including several well-known urbanists and designers[3] who are lobbying to make Lower Manhattan a more livable place. Concepts of sustainability included people and buildings, pollution, urban form, transport, communication, legislation, and public investment.

Human sustainability

Thousands of people rushed to the destroyed area to help in the rescue attempt and to recover the bodies of the dead. Remains were found of approximately 39% of those who died when the buildings were destroyed. The explosion vaporized bodies, sections of the buildings, furnishings and equipment, mixing all into a fine white dust that penetrated every micro-inch of the surrounding offices, dwellings, and stores. No scientific analysis or regulatory standards exist for mitigating its impact on air quality. The WTC fires continued to burn for almost 3 months after the attack.

Consequently, human sustainability set the public tone, beginning with the recovery efforts in Lower Manhattan. It was paramount in discussions with thousands of rescue workers, residents, employees, and families of the victims. So too were issues like eco-sustainability, carbon dioxide (CO_2) emissions, and stringent environmental guidelines for air pollution caused by transporting the debris during the 9-month-long rescue efforts.

Infrastructure for people

Lower Manhattan is a city within a city. It is the third largest downtown in the USA after Midtown Manhattan and Chicago. Prior to September 11, the residential population was almost 42,000 residents and growing. Consequently, R.Dot defined 'infrastructure' to mean an armature that integrates all of the public parts of the community. The rationale was that *people* are its consumers. The types of infrastructure that are needed in Lower Manhattan must come from the habits and values of those who will use it: residents, employers, employees, visitors, and tourists. Infrastructure must be able to accommodate the needs of the present, while being flexible enough to change with the future needs of the area's neighbourhoods.

This definition stemmed from the belief that the functions of infrastructure are driven by people's activities: eating, sleeping, communicating, interacting, conducting business, pleasurable pursuits, making art, partaking in or watching performances, thinking, playing, sports, travelling or relaxing. People create neighbourhoods, which evolve from their activities, needs, values, and desires. To demonstrate how these activities affect ideas about infrastructure and land use, industrial designer Roland Gebhardt, co-chair of R.Dot's infrastructure committee, created a series of 'experience maps' showing how people in different lines of work used the city's infrastructure (Figure 10.6). This showed that 'cities have to be places where people want to live. Unless cities are perceived as high-quality environments, there is little chance that they will ever be sustainable' (Williams *et al.*, 1996).

Transportation

Lower Manhattan is one of the most concentrated business districts in the world, but its transportation infrastructure has not been substantially upgraded for nearly six decades. However, 80% of all trips to the area are made via public transport. Rivlin and Scanlon (2002) point out that 'transit enhancements will be the most important determinant of the

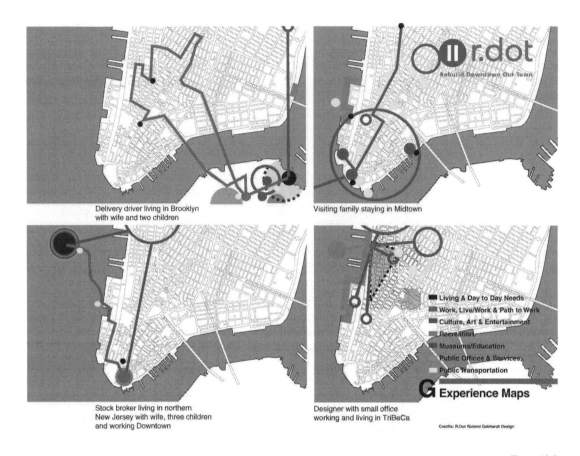

Delivery driver living in Brooklyn
with wife and two children

Visiting family staying in Midtown

Stock broker living in northern
New Jersey with wife, three children
and working Downtown

Designer with small office
working and living in TriBeCa

Living & Day to Day Needs
Work, Live/Work & Path to Work
Culture, Art & Entertainment
Recreation
Museums/Education
Public Offices & Services
Public Transportation

G Experience Maps

Credits: R.Dot Roland Gebhardt Design

Figure 10.6
Maps show how different types of individuals use the downtown area. (Source: R.Dot Roland Gebhardt Design.)

size of Lower Manhattan's employment base and office market. The extent to which this network is restored, improved, and expanded will largely determine how many workers the district can support.' Civic groups also argued that an improved transit infrastructure should be a multi-modal hub with long distance rail lines, subways, buses, water ferries, and airport connections. In addition to rebuilding the damaged subways and the PATH train connection to New Jersey, a rail connection to the city's John F. Kennedy airport should be built. This is considered critical to the future economic success of Lower Manhattan.

An unexpected, positive result of the September 11 destruction was the development of what is now a popular ferryboat fleet. As Manhattan is an island with existing, under-used piers, it was possible to quickly construct ferryboat terminal docking facilities. Now outer boroughs and states, like New Jersey and Connecticut, are a 5–15 minute, non-congested, ride away. The expanded ferry system is carrying a large percentage of passengers who once arrived at the September 11 demolished subways and PATH stations.

New York City is a walking city. Its streets define its character. In Lower Manhattan, the size, congestion, access, and connectivity of the streets determine the urban environment. Streets are critical to an urban quality of life. Foot traffic sets the stage for social interactions: shopping, dwelling, eating, travelling, looking, or pausing for a chat. Lively public activities encourage healthy economic conditions, which have a profound effect on the economic well-being of the city and its ability to provide for personal security, parks, landscaping and flowers, clean streets, and regular garbage collection. The typical Manhattan streetscape consists of walkable, single level, streets lined with retail stores, restaurants, and cafes with very few overpasses or underpasses. R.Dot believes street-level pedestrian vitality must be given the highest priority to encourage residents and businesses to remain in the area and to attract tourists. This also means taking measures to provide road safety (especially for children), reduced noise, air pollution, dirt, and congestion. Within many areas of Lower Manhattan, pedestrians and cars intermingle in the streets, as sidewalks are not wide enough to accommodate pedestrians. Trucks double-park, blocking traffic, as there is little accommodation for off-street parking.

This is why R.Dot argues for managed streets (scheduled automobile use) within the narrow, winding roads of the historic district, coupled with parking garages off of the ring road that circles three edges of Lower Manhattan. New York City attempts to discourage the use of automobiles by limiting parking, charging high parking and toll fees, providing an ample supply of taxicabs, and encouraging mass transit. Missing are alternate forms of surface movement (e.g. small vehicles and pedestrian traffic solutions), which must also be interwoven into overall transport planning.

Urban form and buildings

The attractiveness of Lower Manhattan and its design depends upon the character of its urban form and scale, such as its block sizes, the diversity of building types, and architectural styles. Equally important is public investment in the allocation and design of civic amenities (schools, health, and culture); the character, size, and diversity of parks and grounds; and waterfront access and view corridors that attract private development (housing, offices, retail, and entertainment).

Reconstruction provides an opportunity to rebuild using the best technologies in sustainable planning, building design, and energy efficiency. The question for Lower Manhattan is – does the political will exist to overcome the current state of reluctance by some developers to use such technologies? Most New York City civic groups are committed to lobbying the government for high performance and green building practices that seek to reduce environmental impacts while increasing the well-being of occupants and saving overall life-cycle costs. Projects that design-in optimal building performance, such as investments in energy efficiency, day-lighting, and good indoor air quality, provide human resource returns in terms of occupant health and productivity. This, in turn, increases the long-term value of real estate. To help accomplish this, nature can be used to power buildings and mitigate atmospheric heat. For example, greening buildings, incorporating private green spaces within buildings, such as courtyards, terraces or planted roofs; incorporating power generating technology such as windmills and solar panels; designing site plans that create public spaces at the ground level for parks with areas for heavy planting and grey water-pools, are measures to help reduce temperatures.

Other changes can be made on a larger scale, such as recognizing the importance of Lower Manhattan's waterfront for parks, recreation, and boating; designating the area carbon neutral; and requiring that CO_2 emissions are substantially offset by carbon absorbing planting. High-efficiency centralized systems using co-generation technology can support mixed uses and 24-hour activity. They also can reduce dependence on oil and fossil fuels.

Sustainable legislation

Civic groups argue that the redevelopment of the WTC site must achieve zero-net CO_2 emissions for energy used at the WTC site, and a rating of platinum under the Leadership in Energy and Environmental Design (LEED) programme of the US Green Building Council. Lawmakers have regulatory powers to mandate the application of environmental design guidelines. Today, the *Battery Park City Authority Environmental Design Guidelines* are required for all construction in the Battery Park

City neighbourhood, built across the street from the WTC. Here, the recently built 'Solaire' apartment building (2003) is the nation's first sustainable, residential, high rise, a result of the mandatory guidelines.

Community node organization

Neighbourhood nodes grow organically in large, dense mega-cities, like New York. It is a unique phenomenon of such cities. These nodes tend to grow naturally around the intersection(s) of public transportation. Consequently, they can be planned as part of a combined urban plan and transport strategy. The larger the transportation network, the more populated and diverse the neighbourhood is likely to be. These intersections are the areas that require public investment for civic amenities (Figure 10.7).

A neighbourhood node consists of a population large enough in number to create a self-contained community that is eligible for schools, health care, police, fire protection, postal services, banking, and open spaces for playgrounds and parks. It is small enough for professional and commercial services to be within walking distance and delivery services such as groceries, restaurant food, and laundry to be available.

In Manhattan's vertical urbanism, a neighbourhood node of high- and mid-rise buildings usually includes offices, or apartments, or hotels – all with retail at ground level and with limited parking facilities. Some of these buildings may contain schools and health facilities. Tall buildings result from the desire of many people to live and/or work in the same location. People choose places for a variety of reasons: to mix with people sharing similar work; cultural or entertainment interests; or to live near the woods, mountains, or the beaches; or to enjoy a certain type of climate. Whatever the motivation, towering residential and office buildings are attractive to a large number of people. In conjunction with a willingness to live vertically, people make practical decisions about the quality of urban life and employment, as well as the availability and cost of housing, schools, health care, recreation, and entertainment.

In New York's urban area, it is the small things associated with the quality of life that make life acceptably livable. Trees, plants, and flowers on sidewalks, small parks, and building planting are as essential as secure, clean, well-kept streets.

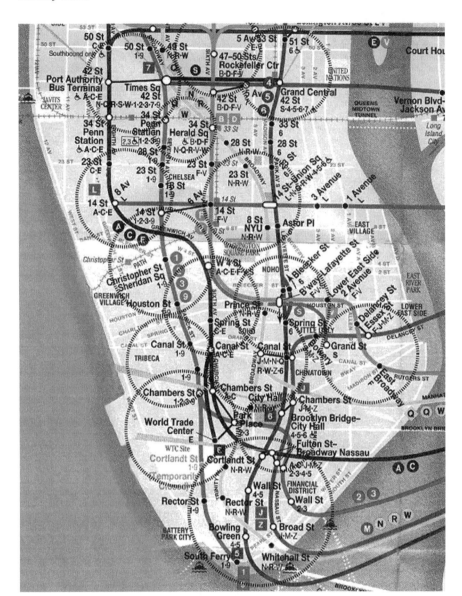

Figure 10.7
Schematic examples
of general locations
of transportation
nodes that encourage
organic community
growth.

New York City is one of the nation's safest cities. Key, personal services should be accessible at a maximum of 10 minutes walk. Mass transportation should provide access to museums, performing centres, sports venues, and government services that may be located cross-town from the neighbourhood node.

Market-driven private investment will organically attach itself to the armature (transit, housing, schools, health services, degree of safety, open space, and water front access) created by public investment and policy. This concept of organic mixed uses differs

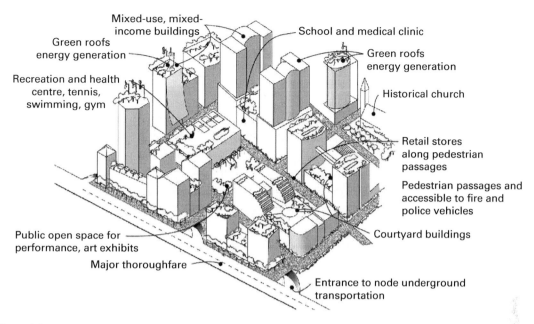

Mixed-use, mixed-income buildings

Green roofs energy generation

Recreation and health centre, tennis, swimming, gym

School and medical clinic

Green roofs energy generation

Historical church

Retail stores along pedestrian passages

Pedestrian passages and accessible to fire and police vehicles

Public open space for performance, art exhibits

Major thoroughfare

Courtyard buildings

Entrance to node underground transportation

Figure 10.8
A conceptual idea of the mixed uses in a self-contained, walkable neighbourhood node.

from the post-war idea of planned multiple uses in one building or complex, as organic uses are intermixed over a several block area (Figure 10.8). Social, economic, and environmental justice depends heavily on mass transportation to incorporate a percentage of low- to moderate-income families into every neighbourhood node. The lesson learned from September 11 is that in cases of disaster and when mass transit is disrupted, moderate- and low-income service people are critically needed. Firefighters, police, health care workers, labourers, and food suppliers must live in close proximity in order to provide immediate help. This interdependency succinctly states the case for mixed-income, diverse neighbourhoods.

Conclusion

Civic action was galvanized to help form public policy (as opposed to simply commenting on the government's proposed plans) and to be involved from the beginning in the revitalization of Lower Manhattan's damaged neighbourhoods. New Yorkers were emotionally, functionally, and financially engulfed in the tragic aftermath of September 11. One of major objectives of R.Dot was to demonstrate that a more democratic, global, creative, socially integrated, and economically productive 21st century Lower Manhattan could grow organically from the ruins. R.Dot has published a number of papers to guide policy makers, which address many of the issues in this chapter.

Epilogue

By 2003, the concepts envisioned within this chapter are all under consideration. There is strong evidence that the concepts of sustainability discussed above will become public policy. The policy-making process is slow and hampered due to the differing objectives of the city's Mayor and the New York State Governor. The Governor, who holds the majority of the decision-making power, has substantially less interest in the city's urban needs. The Mayor and his appointees tend to be sympathetic with the views of the civic groups and R.Dot's papers have been well received. Political and policy decisions that will guide the future development of Lower Manhattan have not yet been finalized. An international, invited design competition resulted in the selection of Daniel Libeskind as the master planner for WTC. A team of architects and engineering specialists in the various elements of the site, together with Libeskind, are developing plans, which should be completed in 2004. The PATH train was scheduled for service in late 2003. Subway services have been restored, but the new subway terminal will not be completed until 2010. The build-out of WTC is estimated to take 10–20 years.

Notes

1. Beverly Willis is President and Director of the Architecture Research Institute, Inc., a think-tank whose mission is livable cities.

2. Susan Szenasy is Editor-in-chief of Metropolis magazine, which publishes articles on well-designed objects, spaces, and buildings with an emphasis on sustainable concepts.

3. Jean Gardner, Professor, Parsons School of Design; Rafael Pelli, Principal, Cesar Pelli & Associates; Ted Liebman, Partner, Liebman-Melting Partnership Architects; and James Biber, Principal, Pentagram.

References

Alliance for Downtown NY (2002) *Downtown Alliance Survey of Lower Manhattan Retail Establishments January 2002*, Alliance for Downtown NY, Inc., New York.

Artigiani, C. (2002) *Youth Council: Building for Future Generations*, Rebuild Downtown Our Town, New York.

Civic Alliance to Rebuild Downtown New York (2002) *A Planning Framework: A Draft Report of the Civic Alliance to Rebuild Downtown New York*, New York: Civic Alliance to Rebuild Downtown.

Daniels, K. (1997) *The Technology of Ecological Building – Basic Principles and Measures, Examples and Ideas*, Translated by Elizabeth Schwaiger. Beirkhauser, Basel and Boston.

Hudson Institute (1997) *Workforce 2020: Work and Workers in the 21st Century*, Hudson Institute, Indianapolis.

Lloyd Jones, D. (1998) *Architecture and the Environment: Bioclimatic Building Design*. Overlook Press, Woodstock, NY.

Moore, S.A. (2000) A Review of the Technology of Ecological Building. *J Architectural Education*, May 2000:246.

Oppenheimer, B. and Willis, B. (2002) *Managed Streets: Street Life Is Crucial to the Revitalization of Lower Manhattan*, Rebuild Downtown Our Town, New York.

Slessor, C. (1997) *Eco-Tech: Sustainable Architecture and High Technology*, Thames and Hudson, London.

Small Business Administration (1998) *New American Evolution: The Role and Impact of Small Firms*, Retrieved from the World Wide Web at http://www.sba.gov/ADVA/stats/eval_pap.html

Steele, J. (1997) *Sustainable Architecture*, McGraw Hill, New York.

Williams, K., Jenks, M. and Burton, E. (1996) Urban Consolidation and the Benefits of Intensification. In: *Compact Cities: Sustainable Urban Development* (eds. de Roo, G. and Miller, D.), Ashgate, Aldershot, UK.

Williams, K., Burton, E. and Jenks, M. (2000) Introduction – Defining Sustainable Urban Form. In: *Achieving Sustainable Urban Form* (eds. Williams, K., Burton, E. and Jenks, M.), E & FN Spon, London.

Willis, B. (2002) *Rebuilding Lower Manhattan and the World Trade Center*, Rebuild Downtown Our Town, New York.

Willis, B. and Kossler, J. (2003) *Strategies for Revitalizing Lower Manhattan Retail*, Rebuild Downtown Our Town, New York.

Willis, B. and Raimone, N. (2003) *Revitalizing Lower Manhattan through Arts and Culture*, Rebuild Downtown Our Town, New York.

11

Ineke Hulshof

Upper City Transformations: A New Strategy for High-density Development

Introduction

This chapter is based on the work of Hulshof Architects.[1] The practice started working in the city of Rotterdam in the beginning of the 1980s when social housing improvement was highly subsidized and organized by the city. Projects were complex, involving a mixture of renovation, restoration and new building, and the process included developing scenarios and a decision-making process in which the current inhabitants played a major role. Indeed, one of the key commitments of the practice is to enable users to take part in the planning process, and to awaken them to their role in the urban environment and a sustainable society.

After a period of significant change in the Dutch housing programme, the improvement of social housing in the big cities stopped after a dramatic policy change in 1992. Today, transforming the cities, in order to increase density and improve the image and quality of poor neighbourhoods, is a major concern (VROM, 2001a). The practice concentrated on urban areas searching for improvement, with a concern for the environment through involvement in special programmes for sustainable development in the city of Rotterdam.

From 1988 the author was involved in an exchange programme on urban renewal and housing development between the cities of Rotterdam and Shanghai. Frequent visits, building with Chinese architects and designing within another culture offered the opportunity to learn a great deal from Shanghai. One of the major lessons was that it is possible to live in a very high-density environment, the success of which depending not so much on volume and floor space but also on the infrastructure, views, privacy and facilities provided.

Ultimately, this experience led to the formation of the Upper City Foundation in Rotterdam, which aims, through an integrated approach to urban areas, to add development space to urban areas without using up more green spaces, and without destroying existing buildings. The major themes are linked to sustainability; increasing density, reuse and reduction of waste, shortening journey distances and improving the existing environment and buildings through urban renewal.

Upper City: *Bovenstad*

Rotterdam was designated Cultural Capital of Europe 2001 (Foundation Rotterdam, 2000), and as part of its cultural programme initiated the idea to explore the roof space of the city. Maik Mager, a sculptor and art teacher at the Willem de Koningh Academy (a part of Rotterdam University) came up with

Figure 11.1
The buildings of Rotterdam University, showing an aerial view of the roof site for 'Bamboo Summit City'.
(*Source*: Hulshof Architects.)

the proposal for a sculpture on the roof of one of its main buildings (Figure 11.1). The concept involved using scaffolding, a very flexible material to make spatial frames and to construct unusual volumes. Together with the practice's experience in transforming existing buildings, and involvement with Shanghai, the concept developed into the idea for a 'Bamboo Summit City' on the University building's roof. Viewing the city from this elevated point, it was clear that the majority of Rotterdam city centre roofs are flat, forming ugly areas scattered with air-conditioning units, chimneys, pipes and services. These flat roofs are not 'designed', yet could potentially be seen to be a fifth facade of a building. There are large areas of such space in the centre of Rotterdam that could offer useful space. Although the idea of using roofs is not new (a proposal was made in the 1970s for an Upper City in Amsterdam (Figure 11.2)), the 'Bamboo Summit City' could be seen as a start.

A fund raising campaign was initiated to realize 'Bamboo Summit City', and to investigate the space on top of the roofs of Rotterdam, and around 500,000 euros were raised. The programme started with a design in the form of a model made by Mager and van der Vlis (Figure 11.3). The practice was in charge of the development process making the design into a building plan and introducing useful spaces like a huge terrace, hall and exhibition room (Figure 11.4). The funding enabled Chinese scaffolders to come from Shanghai to construct the sculpture. The bamboo also came from China as a part of the relationship with

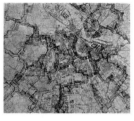

Figure 11.2
Constant's 'New Babylon', a 1970s proposal for an Upper City over the roofs of Amsterdam.

Figure 11.3
Mail Mager and van der Vlis' model for 'Bamboo Summit City'. (*Source*: Hulshof Architects.)

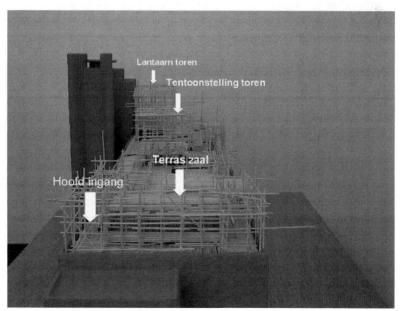

Shanghai. The Dutch Ministry of Housing, Spatial Planning and the Environment (VROM), through the government's architect, also supported the project in order to investigate the space use of the roof and safe public access to it. While it took a year for the project team to complete the project, the actual construction took the Chinese scaffolders only 10 weeks. The construction started with a Chinese ceremony and an opening festival involved Chinese rituals and a dragon ceremony (Figures 11.5 and 11.6).

Before dismantling the 'Bamboo Summit City', the Foundation ended the project with a conference on the subject of 'Air-Bound Building' (as opposed to earth-bound building).[2] This was a new beginning for the Foundation as a society to initiate and stimulate the development of the space in the air. Thus, 'Bamboo Summit City' as a functional sculpture acted as a catalyst to focus attention on the possibilities offered by flat roofs in an increasingly compact urban environment.

Figure 11.5
Building the bamboo structure:
starting ceremony.
(*Source*: Hulshof Architects.)

Figure 11.5
Building the bamboo structure:
starting ceremony.
(*Source*: Hulshof Architects.)

Theoretical survey of opportunities in the Netherlands

Urban development, according to the Dutch programme the fifth National Memorandum (VROM, 2001), is still not decided. Nevertheless VROM point to the possible development of existing urban areas. The national planning programme for neighbourhoods with houses built from 1945 to 1980 includes the following figures:

	Number of houses
Demolish old stock and build new houses	210,000
Transforming and enlarging spaces	85,000
Increase density by adding more houses	155,000
Total	450,000

Figure 11.6
Building the bamboo structure:
the opening dragon ceremony.
(*Source*: Hulshof Architects.)

This programme is planned over a period of 10 years, but it will be very hard to implement. Dealing with residents and existing infrastructure is already causing big delays. Of the existing houses built after the war, around 50% are outdated, which means that there are at least 2 million houses in need of improvement. This is far in excess of the number cited in VROM's policy.

The practice has argued for a transformation programme and the addition of space by developing on top of existing buildings and connecting buildings together 'in the air'. This would offer a significant opportunity, even if only the roofs of the social housing built after the Second World War are considered. This leads to another calculation showing the possibilities of developing on top of the existing buildings with three and four storeys:

	Number of houses	Floor space (m²)
Existing	400,000	32,000,000
New	100,000	10,000,000
	Additional dwellings from roof development 20,000	Total area, with roof development added 42,000,000

The increased area of each existing house was calculated to be an average of $100\,m^2$, to be found within the existing footprint of the housing. This means a real addition of 20,000 houses to the existing stock. Keeping the buildings allows the profit from the new houses to be reinvested in the existing building, so the existing stock can be upgraded and the interiors refurbished. With rising land prices, part of the profit could be invested in the exterior environment of these mostly prefabricated housing blocks.

The city of Rotterdam and Delta Metropolis

Delta Metropolis incorporates the four big cities in the 'Randstad' (Amsterdam, The Hague, Rotterdam and Utrecht) and the towns of Almere and Amersfoort (Deltametropool, 1998; VROM, 2001b). This metropolitan region is economically powerful and the port of Rotterdam is its main gateway, and is crucial for the distribution of goods entering and leaving Europe. However, because of high land and development costs, few houses have been built and there is a small out-migration of population from Rotterdam's city centre. From 1995 to 2002 only 1000 new houses were built in the centre, and the number of inhabitants decreased by 500 persons. To revitalize the centre and encourage more people to live there, density needs to be increased in order to offer a safe and comfortable living environment.

The building programme for the city of Rotterdam planned for the addition of 2250 houses (2000–2004), and a further 3750 between 2005 and 2009 (Figure 11.7). The practice investigated the space offered by the existing buildings, the planning possibilities in open areas, and the replacement of old buildings. Seen in this traditional way, the study showed there was some 300 ha of space available for development in the city centre. However, the study extended to a consideration of the space available if the roof structures were used. It was found that the flat roofs in the centre offered space to develop, in addition to the Rotterdam plan, another 3000–6000 houses depending on their size and, of course, the practicality of gaining access to them.

Precursors for Upper City ideas

Zwarte Madonna in the Hague, a design proposal by Eric Vreedenburgh, is a prominent example of the concept. It envisages a structure with steel frames to make a new complex including a new 'ground' floor with open green playing fields

213

Figure 11.7
Visualizing Rotterdam's planned
expansion and intensification.

Figure 11.8
Zwarte Madonna, an Upper City
proposal for the Hague. (*Source*:
Archipel designers.)

on top of the building and the inner court (Figure 11.8). A real
experiment built on top of the Las Palmas building in
Rotterdam, is a 'Parasite' containing a meeting room. For this
design the architects, Korteknie and Stuhlmacher developed a
lightweight construction system made of wooden panels (Figure
11.9). This system is now being developed for more extensive
use in and on top of existing buildings and built-up areas.

The *Looiershof*, completed in 2002, is a refurbishment project
designed by the practice prior to the Bamboo Summit City
project. It was an integrated approach to the urban environment,
and demonstrates multiple land uses. The site in the harbour

Figure 11.9
The Las Palmas building in
Rotterdam, a roof 'Parasite'.

Figure 11.10
Looiershof, showing the existing building facade, new
extension and roof reuse. (*Source*: Hulshof Architects.)

Figure 11.11
Looiershof showing the interior of the extension.
(*Source*: Hulshof Architects.)

front district of Delfshaven in Rotterdam included a complex of
redundant warehouses and transport areas that were located
on contaminated land. The practice developed four scenarios,
the best of which was to keep the main building, which was of
architectural value, and reuse it completely. The development of
scenarios included the possible use of the top of the roofs.
Before starting the new construction, the contaminated land had
to be treated and removed, which was achieved through a joint
venture between the municipality and the developer.

The completed project has a clear structure, which continues the
5 m × 5 m construction grid found in the old warehouse into the
new extension (Figures 11.10 and 11.11). The column grid is very
flexible and allows for future changes. Underground, the existing
cellar was extended, providing parking for 70 cars and 100

bicycles. The ground floor comprises offices rented by the district government, and four other municipal users. The floors above contain 28 loft apartments, each with a large terrace, the upper ones being on top of the roof (Figure 11.12). All the lower roofs are used for walkways and terraces, and the open area offers space for a clear division between the offices and apartments. Using the roofs in this project added $4500\,\mathrm{m}^2$ to the development.

Upper City Foundation

The Foundation originated from the survey of the space on top of roofs carried out as part of the 'Bamboo Summit City' project. The thinking behind the Foundation stems from the fact that the Netherlands is a compact country with a very high population density and there is an ongoing problem of open space becoming scarce. Dutch cities, even a large, vibrant city such as Amsterdam, are not as densely populated compared, for example, with Paris. The Foundation argues that the development of the 'air' space in the city, developing on top of existing buildings, can solve a part of the problem in a sustainable way. This, it is suggested, can add floor space and value, and generate funds for the upgrading of the existing housing stock.

The aim is to initiate development with an integrated approach that is committed to all parties involved, including users and owners. Thus, the Foundation has partners that represent a wide range of professions.[3] Building companies are called upon to

Figure 11.13
Laurenskwartier, a typical
example of a more traditional
building in Pannakoekstraat, on
top of which the addition of two
storeys under a mansard roof is
planned. (*Source:* Hulshof
Architects.)

invent new ways of construction and the logistics needed when building on top of buildings, as well as being a source of research into the use of steel frames in lightweight construction. The social support for people and neighbourhoods during renewal and redevelopment processes is taken into account through the inclusion of two social housing corporations and a foundation. A research and strategy organization is assisting with the development of scenarios and modelling. Other Dutch architects are involved along with consultants and designers with a sustainable approach. Developers are showing interest in supporting the experiment. The Foundation intends to support pilot projects, to find funding, provide administrative assistance and to support research.

Pilot projects

A number of pilot projects are being undertaken. *Rhijnvis Feith* is a renewal project in the poor area of Delfshaven comprising a housing complex of 18 apartments designed by the practice in 1984. A new building has been designed next to it and the practice is undertaking a pilot project to find out whether the roof can be developed. *Laurenskwartier* is a quarter in the city centre of Rotterdam with a lot of flat roofs. There are also many examples of more traditional architecture with pitched roofs, which is valued but is generally found to be in poor condition (Figure 11.13).

Proposals for this type of building include the addition of an additional two storeys under a Mansard roof. The hope is that Upper City input can generate a shared feeling and understanding that such development increases the value of the area and the buildings, especially if plans are developed together with the communities. Other pilots include *Feyenoord*, a structure on top of existing factory buildings of the former Unilever butter plant (Figure 11.14).

Figure 11.14
Feyenoord, 'De Brug' with a new office structure under construction by DURA-Vermeer.

Figure 11.15
Proposals for an Upper City in part of the 'Laurens' quarter in Rotterdam. (*Source*: Hulshof Architects.)

Conclusion

It has been argued here that Rotterdam needs an addition of 3000–6000 houses to make the city centre survive and constitute a viable, full grown centre with a sufficient number of residents to enable a thriving society to develop. But it is not only design that creates the urban environment: the people who live and work there make it a fully functioning city. The Upper City concept can add to the social structure of urban areas by increasing the number of people living in the areas to be developed, and by ensuring they participate in the development process from the start. The practice has drawn up a scenario for Rotterdam to illustrate a new approach to the development of roofs that could also be used in other Dutch cities (Figure 11.15). It represents a potential opportunity for the Delta Metropolis to increase density and preserve open space through respect for the existing natural environment.

Notes

1. Hulshof Architects is a practice of six architects, with support staff, specializing in housing design, development in urban areas and the refurbishment of old buildings. Throughout the text of this chapter Hulshof Architects will be referred to as 'the practice'.

2. The conference, in Dutch called 'Luchtgebonden Bouwen', was held in September 2001 at Bamboo Summit City and Rotterdam University. The sponsors were 'Stichting *Bovenstad*' (Upper City Foundation), SEV – Stichting Stuurgroep Experimenten Volkshuisvesting (Steering Committee for Housing Experiments), and Stichting Bouwen met Staal. (Foundation for Building with Steel.)

3. The partners involved in the Upper City Foundation include: (i) developers, building companies and housing developers; DURA-Vermeer, Proper Stok, Bouwfonds, ERA, ING Vastgoed (Real Estate). (ii) Social housing consultants and corporations; SBS, WBR. (iii) Local government; OBR (Ontwikkelings Bedrijf Rotterdam), the department for development and land use. (iv) Architects, including Eric Vreedenburgh, Hella Straatman, Cees Reijs, Henk van Schagen, Gert Jan te Velde and the author. (v) Urban design and sustainability consultants; BOOM. (vi) Foundation for intensive and multi-purpose land use; Habiforum.

References

Deltametropool (1998) *Statement Deltametropool*. Retrieved from the World Wide Web at: www.deltametropool.nl

Foundation Rotterdam (2000) *Rotterdam is Many Cities: Rotterdam 2001, Cultural Capital of Europe, Foundation Rotterdam*, Uitgeverji Bis, Amsterdam.

VROM (2001a) *Fifth National Policy Document on Spatial Planning 2000–2020*, Ministry of Housing, Spatial Planning and the Environment (VROM), The Hague, The Netherlands.

VROM (2001b) *Making Space, Sharing Space*, Summary of the Fifth National Policy Document, Ministry of Housing, Spatial Planning and the Environment (VROM), The Hague, The Netherlands.

12

Tom J. Bartuska and Bashir A. Kazimee

Sustainable Cells of Urbanism: Regenerative Theory and Practice

Introduction

The concept of sustainability gives greater meaning to the value of civilization – optimizing our vital human–environmental support systems while providing sustained promise for future generations of all life on earth. While the directions are clear, the process is far less established. Society and the design and planning professions need to continue to determine and agree upon clear definitions of the theoretical aspect of sustainability, and establish this into practice. Sustainable design and planning provides great promise in the search for a regenerative theory and a development process.[1] The defining premise of such a regenerative theory and process is that sustainable programmes require a comprehensive, integrated, and ecological understanding of a community's unique human–environmental resources. By definition, sustainability identifies a process that considers a community's on-site natural land, water, (air), and energy resources as integral aspects of the design (Vieria, 1993). It integrates natural systems with human patterns and celebrates continuity, uniqueness, and place making (Early, 1993).

This chapter will first define its theoretical premise, and will then describe its evolution into a sustainable planning and design process. This process was used to develop the regenerative sustainable community proposal for the city of Pullman.[2] The Pullman regenerative proposal is based upon the above working definitions and related ecological modelling techniques which carefully balance on-site interchanges between the unique human and environmental systems. The amount a development uses renewable human and environmental resources is a useful 'indicator' or measurement of the degree to which sustainability is achieved. The primary ecological or biological variables used in this modelling process were **air, water, food and fibre, energy, and human ecology**. These interchanges became important indicators of sustainable development and define inherent qualities and carrying capacity of the city. This approach allows the Pullman community (as well as others) to model, measure, and programme a series of design strategies for sustainable development as well as to monitor the city's regenerative process over time. The resultant programme and plan was an effort to revitalize the existing community, enhance its sense of place and human, social, economic, and environmental qualities. The critical integrated levels of sustainable, regenerative intervention permeates the qualities of the place at all scales of the hierarchy including the **region, city, neighbourhood, clusters, and dwelling units**. The proposal, its theory, and methodology have created a useful model and method for Pullman (and others) to evaluate the effectiveness of various planning and citizen initiatives as we work towards a sustainable future.

Clustered cells of urbanism: a Tale of Two Cities

Perhaps one of the most challenging issues facing any urban regenerative process, especially in the USA, is to create clustered communities while minimizing auto-driven sprawl. Clustered, transit-oriented developments are critical to sustainable urbanism. The 'Costs of Sprawl' are well documented and highly significant in terms of most human, social, economic, and environmental variables (RERC, 1974; Bartuska, 1979; Kelbaugh, 1993). Fortunately, there are a growing number of successful cells of clustered urbanism and successful regenerative strategies. Unfortunately, there are even more examples of wastelands of auto-dominated sprawl.

One well-known past example of successful clustered planning can be found in the 1944 Greater London Plan (Figure 12.1). London's existing and unique 'internal' villages and focused

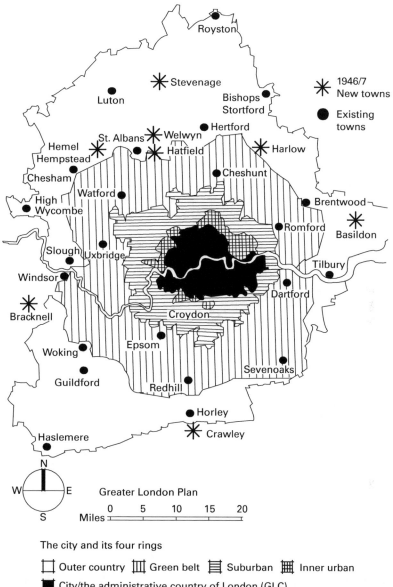

Figure 12.1
London's 1946 GLC regional plan with clustered old and new towns within a greenbelt.

communities of new and old towns surrounding London contained by greenbelts characterized the plan (Figure 12.2) (Forshaw and Abercrombie, 1943; Abercrombie, 1945; Rasmussen, 1983; Hebbert, 1999). This plan and the resultant developments illustrate the nature of a sustainable pattern of small to large clustered communities defined by greenbelts. Unfortunately, there have been regressive changes to these profound planning accomplishments, especially those in the mid 1980s enacted through government policies of deregulation.

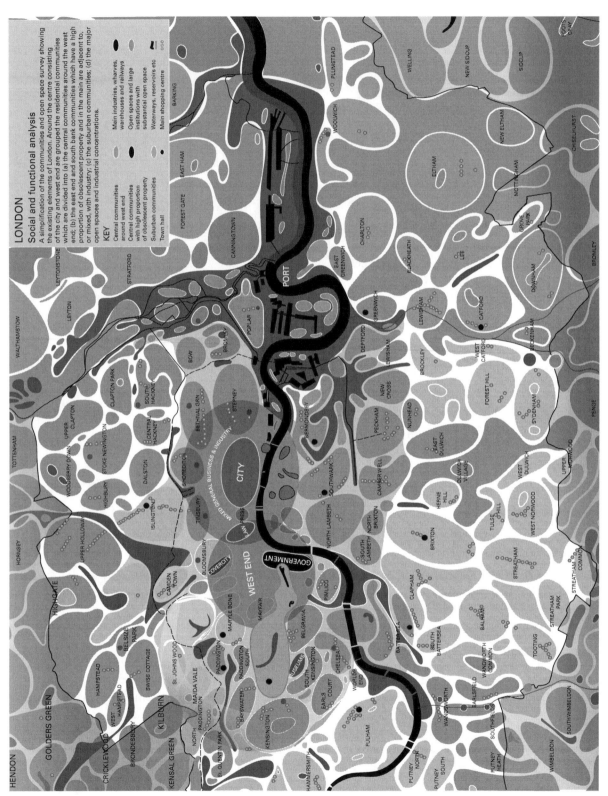

Figure 12.2   London's 1943 CLC Plan of clustered villages defined by transit nodes and green areas.

FUTURE FORMS

Fortunately policy has begun to restore the balance in favour of sustainable development with the introduction of sustainability guidelines (UK Government, 2003).[3]

Fifty years later in the USA, the people of Seattle, Washington have generated a similar alternative to the madness of the free-market, deregulated auto-driven sprawl (Figure 12.3) (PSCOG, 1990). Through an elaborate introspective process, the citizens voted on five urban development alternatives. The citizen's

Figure 12.3
Seattle's Vision 2020 preferred plan of clustered urban development within green areas.

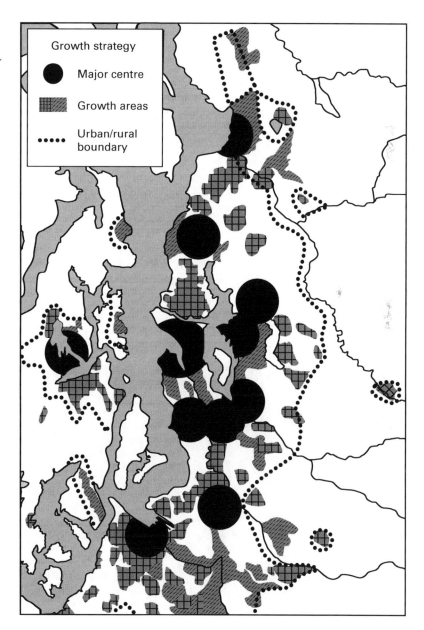

225

'preferred alternative' embodies concepts, which are similar to London's 1946 Greater London Council (GLC) Plan: that is they are clustered, transit-oriented communities of varying sizes surrounded by greenbelts. Like London, similar regressive initiatives and lack of political leadership have compromised this vision and programme for a more sustainable future.

This 'Tale of Two Cities' vividly conveys the 'best and worst of times' (Dickens, 1859; Bartuska, 2002). The principles of this brief tale of two cities are the same: sustainable cells of urbanism require the creation and/or regeneration of clustered, pedestrian, and transit-oriented communities of a variety of sizes (large to small) defined by areas that conserve green or amenity land.

A clustered, sustainable regenerative plan for Pullman: theory and practice

In contrast with Seattle and London, Pullman is a relatively small community of 25,000 people located in the Pacific Northwestern Palouse Region of Eastern Washington (Figure 12.4). It is the size of some of the nested towns and villages in larger metropolitan areas and provides a subset of critical challenges and opportunities for sustainable regenerative development. The regional climate of Pullman has distinct seasons with cold, wet winters and warm, dry summers. The city's economy

Figure 12.4
The Palouse region in eastern Washington, USA.

services the region's agricultural industries and supports a major public university.

Pullman's sustainable community plan was based upon ecological (or biological) modelling techniques, which carefully balance **on-site** interchanges between the human–environmental systems of the city. These interchanges become indicators of sustainable development and define inherent qualities, carrying capacities, and the required ecological footprint of this community. In general, this approach allows communities to effectively model, measure, and programme a series of design strategies for sustainable development. Also, this method allows communities to define and monitor the human–environmental indicators of a regenerative process over time. Sustainable indicators are commonly generated and agreed upon by the community. This study predates the community-generated processes and takes a more theoretical approach based upon fundamental ecological or biological criteria.

The approach was derived from first establishing a working definition of sustainability. There are, of course, many definitions of sustainability. In a review of this term, the **site** or the **human–environmental context** is a critical aspect to most working definitions of sustainability. This emphasis is expressed in the following composite, working definition, which directed the Pullman regenerative study:

> **Sustainable developments are those that fulfill present and future needs while [only] using and not harming renewable resources and human–environmental systems of a site: [air], water, land, energy, and ecology and/or those of other [off-site] sustainable systems. Sustainability integrates natural systems with human patterns and celebrates continuity, uniqueness, and place making (WCED, 1987; Early, 1993; Rosenbaum, 1993; Vieria, 1993).**

The Pullman study models the variables of air, water, land, energy, and human ecology as primary indicators of sustainable community development. These fundamental human–environmental exchanges of the community's 'site' were useful in developing the critical 'input ↔ output' modelling techniques which guide the community's regenerative process. This ecological method illustrates the challenging requirements for programming, measuring, and achieving sustainability. The variables are, of course, interrelated and form the basis for modelling any sustainable community and/or society. The selected variables of the community's human and environmental interrelationships are shown in Figure 12.5.

Figure 12.5
Pullman's ecological systems
diagram.

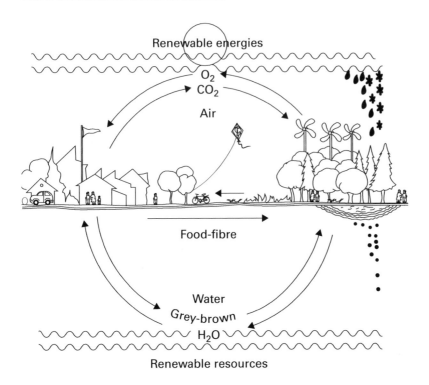

In quantitative terms, the related ecological exchanges between the selected human–environmental systems of air, water, food and fibre (land), and energy for the community are modelled and measured to establish indicators for sustainability (Figure 12.6). For each ecological interchange, the four left-hand rows in the bar graph illustrate the relative quantities of the following:

1. The existing use of each resource
2. The non-renewable and renewable supply of each resource from the site
3–4. The proposed sustainable use and estimated per cent of conservation required to place each human–environmental system in balance

The method demonstrates the interaction of each system and that 40–70% conservation is required to place each variable and its human–environmental exchange in a sustainable balance. Also, the method conveys surprise that air represented by the carbon dioxide to oxygen (CO_2 to O_2) exchange achieved through photosynthesis is one of the most overlooked yet fundamentally critical of all the systems. Without balancing our CO_2 to O_2 cycle, global warming will continue to increase.

Resources and energy variables

Modelling sustainability

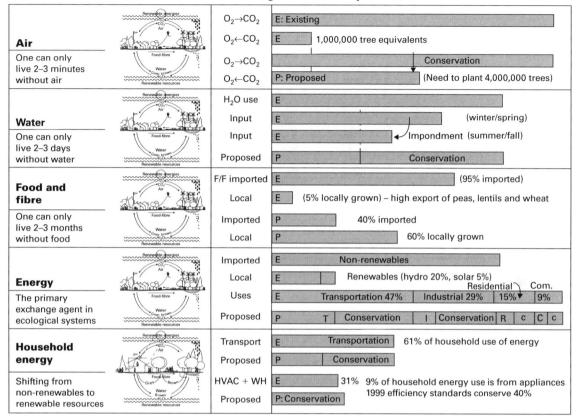

Figure 12.6
Pullman's modelling and analysis of its human–environmental systems. (HVAC = Heating Ventilating and Air-Conditioning; WH = Water Heating.)

The study also demonstrates the integrated use of these modelling methods and sustainable design strategies in the revitalization of this existing community, enhancing its human, economic, social, and environmental quality. A useful ecological organizing technique, 'levels-of-integration,' is used carefully to reanimate Pullman and balance its fundamental human–environmental systems. A summary of these integrated levels of design regeneration (region, city, neighbourhoods, site/clusters, and buildings) is illustrated in the following annotated outline.

A Regional level strategies

Regional level strategies provided a critical opportunity to balance selected human–environmental interchanges. The existing urban

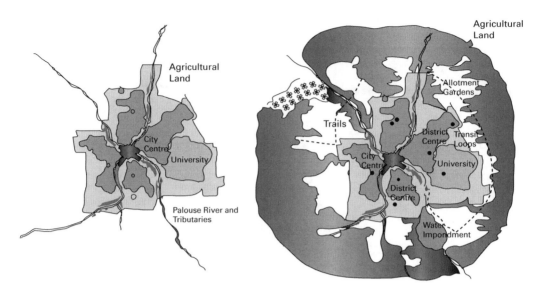

Agricultural Land

Agricultural Land

Allotment Gardens

Trails

District Centre

Transit Loops

City Centre

University

City Centre

University

District Centre

District Centre

Water Impoundment

Palouse River and Tributaries

Figure 12.7
Pullman's Regional plans (existing and proposed) with required green belt and water retention lakes to balance its ecological systems of air and water.

district was too small to be sustainable. Adding a green belt and water impoundment system was necessary to balance air exchanges $(O_2 = CO_2)$; water cycles ((precipitation $= H_2O$) use with conservation, impoundment and reuse of grey water); land and its food/fibre processes (gardens, urban forests, and reducing/reusing/recycling of resources); energy use (conservation and use of renewable resources). Figuratively, the increase in size represents the city's 'Ecologic Footprint' (Wackernagel and Rees, 1996). The existing and proposed regional plans are illustrated in Figure 12.7 and critical **regional design strategies** are summarized below and illustrated in Figures 12.8 and 12.9:

1. Greenbelt and greenways moderate climate extremes and increase recreational opportunities and bio-diversity. These important land banking, green programmes use primarily indigenous landscaping which conserves water, reduces maintenance and celebrates the unique qualities of the region. Family farming is also encouraged in allotment gardens in the greenbelt. A farmer's market fosters local agricultural produce and handicrafts

2. Spring water runoff is impounded and retained in balancing lakes to supplement dry seasons' shortages, to reduce spring flooding, to filter eroded soils, and to improve water quality, fishing and recreation potential

3. The increased costs of non-renewable energy create a positive shift to conservation and renewable resources. The proposed community's sustainable energy budget comes from 50% regional hydropower, 40% solar and photovoltaics, and 10% wind farms in the greenbelt. Wind farms are currently becoming an important renewable energy industry in the region

Figure 12.8
Green belt controlling suburban
sprawl (Boulder, Colorado, USA).

Figure. 12.9
Retention lake/reservoir
(Boulder, Colorado, USA).

B City level strategies

City level strategies provide for a nested hierarchy of central places (city, districts, and neighbourhoods) supported by an effective infrastructure emphasizing pedestrianization, bikeways, and public transit. This more efficient infrastructure is expressed in community greenways and the clustering of activities, which increases pedestrian enjoyment and accessibility. The critical

231

Figure 12.10
Pullman's Main Street Lentil
Festival.

Figure 12.11
Revitalized historic city centre
(Boulder, Colorado, USA).

city design strategies are summarized below and illustrated in Figures 12.10–12.12:

1. The regeneration of the historic city centre is facilitated by its ideal, centralized geographic position. The clustered restructuring of the central city and the 'Main Street Programme' foster

Figure 12.12
Reanimated river system
(Boulder, Colorado, USA).

incentives for economic growth, which reverses its past decline
(a trend experienced by most US city centres due to auto-driven
suburban sprawl and strip development)

2. Design priority is given to pedestrian and public transit systems.
    The clearly defined greenways and transport systems throughout
    the city make a substantial reduction in auto use of non-renewable
    energy. This is the single most important strategy in balancing the
    CO_2–O_2 cycle and improving air quality in the community

3. State building codes increase energy conservation standards,
    currently 50% better than the 1985 buildings, to 70% in the year
    2010. Due to advancements in efficiency, the use of solar design
    strategies, photovoltaics, and wind power many advanced
    buildings can actually contribute to the shared energy grid

4. Resource management (traditionally waste disposal) becomes
    self-sufficient by adopting the state priorities to first reduce, then
    reuse, and recycle. Many families can eliminate their disposal
    service and save their ever-increasing service costs. These
    programmes foster community enterprises based on sustainable
    resource use, reuse, and recycling

C District and neighbourhood strategies

District and neighbourhood strategies encourage a pedestrian
focus and community pride through clarity in bike and pedestrian
greenway connections to activity centres, schools, and parks
creating effective neighbourhood definition and nodes. The
nodes combine transit stops, community information, and focus
as well as convenient recycling stations. The existing and

 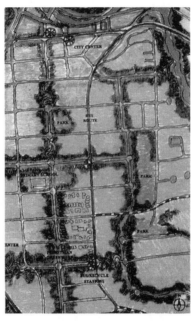

Figure 12.13 Pullman's typical neighbourhood plans (existing and proposed).

Figure 12.14 Pedestrian greenways linking the neighbourhood together (Village Homes, Davis, California, USA). (*Source*: Sandra Satterlee.)

proposed neighbourhood plans are illustrated in Figure 12.13 and critical **district and neighbourhood design strategies** are summarized below and illustrated in Figures 12.14–12.16:

1. Pedestrian priority streets with bikeways and transit networks tie the four prominent neighbourhoods into two districts. Pedestrian accessible middle schools, commercial centres, and related park facilities become the district focus and integrate two pairs of neighbourhoods together into districts

Figure 12.15
Pedestrian greenways and water retention system, 1982 (Village Homes, Davis, California, USA).

Figure 12.16
Pedestrian greenways and water retention system, 1996 (Village Homes, Davis, California, USA).

2. Because of the renewed quality of the neighbourhoods, densification is preferred over low-density sprawl. New low-density patterns have become unpopular because all new developments must provide and pay impact fees for their proportion of greenbelt, trees and infrastructure established by the community's sustainable programmes

3. The green pedestrian street patterns foster walking to neighbourhood facilities, parks, transit stations, recycling and compost centres, and, most importantly, neighbourhood schools. Accessible schools are a critical strategy to enhance each neighbourhood and become active centres during and after school. Their central geographic location is critical to the pedestrian priority concept

4. Water conservation programmes and grey water reuse is implemented throughout the community

5. The successful resource management programmes based on the 3 'Rs' (Reduce, Reuse, and Recycle) are integral parts of the

235

community. The traditional garbage service is now a community
resource recovery process

D Clustering strategies

Clustering strategies for residential developments achieve
increased opportunity for interaction through effective
densification adjacent to community amenities and greenways.
Density is an essential element of community urbanity and
civility. Without reaching a reasonable density in any urban area,
it is difficult to justify the efficient utilization of urban resources
and services. The more people share community facilities, the
more amenities and services can be provided in an economically
and socially justifiable way. Increasing density to 12–18 dwellings
per acre (30–44 per hectare) also creates pedestrianization and
makes public transit more viable. Two of the existing and
proposed clustering plans are illustrated in Figure 12.17 and the
critical **clustering design strategies** for densification are
summarized below:

1. Peripheral infill is achieved in areas where larger side yard
   setbacks occur between the dwellings. In many suburban areas,

Figure 12.17
Pullman's residential cluster
alternative plans (existing and
proposed) showing densification
and pedestrian priority streets.

setback and side yard regulations consume 30–40% of the street frontage. To increase the efficiency on such underdeveloped lots, new infill units and/or greenhouses are provided between and in front of the existing units. Each greenhouse could be commonly shared by the two families or owned by one. This arrangement increases the land use and energy efficiency, and creates a well-defined internal semi-private garden space in the back of the units to be used either collectively or subdivided individually

2. Internal and external block densification is applicable to larger blocks where the combined backyards can internally accommodate new townhouses, apartments, greenhouses and parking. Careful consideration is given to preserve family privacy and territoriality as well as provide spaces for social interaction in the clustered grouping of families

3. External expanded block and communal greenhouses can also occur by utilizing wide or redundant streets between two blocks. This densification can increase efficiency and enriches the communication and social interactions between the clusters. Additional developments could be built between these blocks, including communal playgrounds, gardens, and greenhouse structures

4. Internal unit densification can also accommodate many of the changing domestic needs of the family. In this situation, the house is subdivided internally or expanded to accommodate new members of the family. This is not a new practice. In many regions across the world, families have comfortably lived in one house for generations. Also auxiliary apartments within units are very common in most countries and provide for viable alternatives to increase affordability and the efficiency of residential areas

E Dwelling unit strategies

Dwelling unit strategies (new, infill, and renovated) reach a high level of land and energy conservation, optimizing the use/reuse/recycling of renewable resources of the sun, wind, water (grey and brown), food, and fibre. 'Design Guidelines for Sustainable and Affordable Residential Developments' can be found on our web site (Bartuska and Kazimee, 1999; Kazimee, 2002). The critical **dwelling unit design strategies** are summarized below and illustrated in Figures 12.18 and 12.19:

1. Household cost for energy dramatically decreases due to the shift to renewable energy sources and the following conservation measures:
    (a) Zoning ordinances require the residential plots to be oriented for solar access saving on average 20% of the energy used for heating and cooling
    (b) New state energy standards (quality of construction, higher levels of insulation, and solar benefits) conserve an additional

237

Figure 12.18
Pullman's proposed sustainable
design strategies for a typical
dwelling unit and garden.

Figure 12.19
Solar responsive duplex
(Ecolonia, Holland).

      50–70% of the heating and cooling energy over 1985
      standards

  (c) The improved air quality, cool nighttime temperatures,
      healthy material standards, and natural ventilation strategies
      allow for almost the complete elimination of summer cooling
      loads

2. Families enjoy the beauty of indigenous, low maintenance
   landscapes, and permaculture. The abundance of spring rain is
   impounded in gardens and water cisterns. Most families install
   grey water systems for landscaping/gardening. All brown wastes
   are safely composted by the city and become a valued resource
   for agriculture

3. Many of the families enjoy the development of small vegetable
   gardens adjacent to the home, within the residential clusters or in
   the greenbelt. Greenhouses allow for extended growing seasons

The study concludes with a cost analysis of these sustainable
design strategies, measuring the extent of the resource and

monetary savings for each household, the community, state, and nation. The strategies all have a relatively short 1–7 years payback period and can save the community millions of US dollars. These savings would be retained in the community instead of exported to pay for imported resources and energy. This fosters a sustainable local economy.

Community feedback

The authors of Pullman's *Sustainable Community Regenerative Proposal* (including Michael Owen) have made numerous presentations to the community, including the city and university administration, planners, civic groups, citizens, and students. The presentations allowed for many opportunities for feedback and social–environmental research. Questionnaires were developed to assess the effectiveness of the method, the utility of the ecological variables and to solicit suggestions as to ways the community is and/or could be more sustainable. During this research phase, the community strongly agreed with the modelling method and the appropriateness of the ecological variables used in the study. They also supported the selected strategies used, especially those successfully implemented by other communities (during the presentations, the authors illustrated each strategy with successful examples from other communities). In general, the citizens felt that a great deal of progress was being made by citizen initiative but too little was being advanced by the university and city governance. Further analysis of these town and gown perceptions and developments are summarized in the assessment matrix (Table 12.1).

The results of the above research suggest that although both citizens and town/university governance are very concerned about sustainable strategies, citizen's organizations, and initiatives are far more proactive in implementing successful sustainable projects. Concurrent with all these presentations and dialogue within the community, the city was in the process of updating its comprehensive plan. In the process, the city sponsored numerous workshops where many of the issues of sustainability were discussed. The city generated three future growth alternatives: clustered (higher density), 'business as usual' and diffused (lower density), and sponsored a community voting process. By a significant number, the citizens preferred the clustered alternative. The resulting comprehensive plan, its goals and principles are now based upon clustered,

Table 12.1
Social and environmental assessment matrix (Citizen organizations – PCT: Pullman Civic Trust; CSL: WSU's Community Service Learning Programme; PCEI: Palouse Clearwater Environmental Institute; FOG: Friends of Gladish; MSA: Main Street Association; and GSF: Greystone Foundation). (*Source*: Bartuska, 1997.)

Proposed sustainable strategies by scale:	Citizen initiatives	City governance
A Regional scale strategies:	(14 points)	(3 points)
1. Develop greenbelt to contain sprawl and save agricultural-resources	*	
2. Annexation of land for low-density sprawl	** (against)	(has approved)
3. Extensive tree planting programs (30,000 trees per year)	** (PCT & CSL)	*
4. Water impoundment and flood mediation	** (PCEI)	
5. Artificial wetlands and stream restoration	** (PCEI & CSL)	
6. Pullman-Moscow bike trail (rail banking)	*** (PCT, etc.)	*
7. R/UDAT proposal (Regional/Urban Design Assist Team)	**	*
B City scale strategies:	(15 points)	(9 points)
1. Updating Pullman's Comprehensive Plan	**	**
2. Accessible public transit (free for educational community)	* (PCEI)	**
3. Centrality of community focus	** (PCT & FOG)	(+/−)
4. Downtown improvements committee	** (PCT & MSA)	**
5. Third grader's downtown proposal	**	*
6. Purchasing old high school for a community centre	*** (FOG)	
7. Koppel Farm developments (community gardens)	** (GSF)	
8. Downtown farmers market	*	**
C Neighbourhood and district scale strategies:	(8 points)	(4 points)
1. Accessible neighbourhood parks and schools	*	**
2. Pedestrian/bike priority streets and greenways	*	*
3. Traffic calming strategies	*	
4. Implementation of bike/pedestrian recommendations	**	*
5. WSU Arboretum/greenways development	**	
6. Convenient public transit	(B.3 above)	(B.3 above)
7. Creating neighbourhood planning groups	*	
D Clustering residential strategies:	(2 points)	(3 points)
1. Increased clustering	*	*
2. Increased density	*	**
E Dwelling Unit Strategies:	(9 points)	(3 points)
1. Development of demonstration housing projects	*	
2. Implementing State Energy Code (50% improvements)	*	**
3. Reduction in housing unit and lot size	*	*
4. Implement 'Eco-Team' programme	** (PCEI)	
5. Recycling and compositing versus disposal emphasis	**	(* +/− billing)
6. Water conservation/service billing	**	(* +/− billing)
Assessment totals:	**48 points**	**22 points**

Assessment score card: scale: *acknowledgement; **progress; ***sustainable (1 point per*).

more sustainable growth directives, and marks an important change in the direction for the city. Although there are many past decisions by city governance that support auto-driven sprawl and are not sustainable, there are many others that are being implemented by citizen organizations that are sustainable. The citizen and university student groups denoted in the above assessment matrix have made remarkable sustainability changes to the community. For example, citizen groups are planting some 20–30,000 trees per year, enhancing the waterways, helping to reanimate the historic downtown, have implemented an extensive bike/greenway system along an abandoned railway, sponsored a greenway levy and other programmes to extend these pedestrian pathways throughout the community. A citizens group even purchased an old centrally located high school and converted it into a very active community centre. Internal densification is occurring but unfortunately auto-driven sprawl still outpaces the more sustainable clustered developments.

Conclusion

Pullman's Sustainable Regenerative Proposal is based upon a holistic, ecological model – a critical first step in creating sustainable communities, locally and globally. Modelling human–environmental interchanges was found to be a powerful and useful concept, fundamental to sustainable design and planning processes. Although this methodology is applied to a relatively small community in a rural setting, it is transferable to larger urban places, which are generally composed of sub-units similar to this community. The proposed model is inherently a powerful research, educational, and marketing tool for sustainable community planning and development. It can be used by any city as a guide for developing a comprehensive and sustainable urban regeneration programme. Specific policies and strategies will vary with local conditions, but the methods for demonstrating human–environmental interchanges and benefits are universally applicable.

The continued implementation of these regenerative strategies will require collaboration between government, civic organizations, and private individuals. Pullman's new comprehensive plan reflects many sustainable principles. Sustainable initiatives are being implemented by grassroots efforts from civic organizations and the community continues to be proactive in regards to sustainable development.

The future of the 'Paradise Called the Palouse' looks promising (Austin, 1982). But yes, as Charles Dickens once pronounced, it is still the best and worst of times, it is still an age of wisdom and foolishness; but hopefully Pullman and other communities will continue to nurture successful sustainable cells of urbanism.

Notes

1. Regenerative Theory is an approach to sustainable development which requires carefully analysing, modelling, balancing, and enhancing vital human–environmental variables of an ecological system such as air, water, land, energy and human ecology (generally defined by community indicators). (Bartuska and Kazimee, 1994; Lyle, 1994; Wackernagel and Rees, 1996; Brebbia *et al.*, 2002; SBSE, 2003).

2. The proposal was awarded a gold medal at the UN Habitat Conference in Istanbul, Turkey (IAA, 1996), and probably more importantly, has also increased community concerns for sustainable development. The proposal can be reviewed at the web site www.arch.wsu.edu/sustain.

3. See www.planning.detr.gov.uk/ppg3/5.htm

References

Abercrombie, P. (1945) *Greater London Plan 1944*, HMSO, London.

Austin, B. (1982) A Paradise Called the Palouse. In: *National Geographic*, June.

Bartuska, T. (1979) *A Comparative Study of UK and US Communities*, unpublished cost–benefit study undertaken with 20 graduate and undergraduate students in London and Pullman.

Bartuska, T. (1997) In Search of Sustainable Community, An Assessment of Town and Gown Cooperation, *Green the Campus Conference II Proceedings*, Ball State University.

Bartuska, T. and Kazimee, B. (1994) Modeling Sustainability: Theory and Design, Associated Collegiate Schools of Architecture, *National Conference and Proceedings*, University of Michigan.

Bartuska, T. and Kazimee, B. (1999) Place, Community and Sustainability: Theory and Practice in Creating an Urban Village, *AIA/GBC, Mainstreaming Green Conference*, Chattanooga, TN.

Bartuska, T. (2002) A Comparative Tale of Two Cities in Search of Sustainability: London and Seattle. In: *The Sustainable City II: Urban Regeneration and Sustainability* (eds. Brebbia *et al.*), WIT Press, Billericia, USA.

Brebbia, C., Martin-Duque, J.F. and Wadhwa, L.C., eds. (2002) *The Sustainable City II: Urban Regeneration and Sustainability*, WIT Press, Billericia, USA.

Dickens, C. (1859) *A Tale of Two Cities*, first published as a serial in *All the Year Around*, 30 April to 26 November. London.

Early, D. (1993) What Is Sustainable Design. In: *The Urban Ecologist*, Society of Urban Ecology, Berkeley, Spring.

Forshaw, J. and Abercrombie, P. (1943) *County of London Plan*, Macmillian, London.

Hebbert, M. (1999) *London: More by Fortune than Design*, Wiley and Sons, New York.

IAA (1996) Gold Medal (one of three awarded internationally), International Academy of Architecture Forum, *UN Habitat II Conference*, Istanbul, Turkey, June.

Kelbaugh, D. (1993) The Costs of Sprawl, in *Cascadia Forum*, University of Washington.

Kazimee, B. (2002) Sustainable Urban Design Paradigm: Twenty Five Simple Things to Do to Make an Urban Neighbourhood Sustainable. In: *The Sustainable City II: Urban Regeneration and Sustainability* (eds. Brebbia, C., Martin-Duque, J.F. and Wadhwa, L.C.), WIT Press, Billericia, USA.

Lyle, J. (1994) *Regenerative Design for Sustainable Development*, Wiley, New York.

Puget Sound Council of Governments (PSCOG) (1990) *Region at a Crossroads: The Preferred Choice*, Puget Sound Council of Governments, Puget Sound.

Real Estate Research Corporation (RERC) (1974) *The Cost of Sprawl*, Real Estate Research Corporation, US Government Printing Office.

Rasmussen, S. (1983) *London: The Unique City*, MIT Press, Cambridge, Mass.

Rosenbaum, M. (1993) Sustainable design strategies. In: *Solar Today*, March/April 1993.

Society of Building Science Educators (SBSE) (2003) Regenerative Based Check list for Design and Construction, Society of Building Science Educators. Retrieved from the World Wide Web at http://www.sbse.org/resources

UK Government (2003) Building Sustainable Communities, UK Government Sustainable Development. Retrieved from the World Wide Web at http://www.sustainable-development.gov.uk

Vieria (1993) A Checklist for Sustainable Developments in a Resource Guide for Building Connections: Livable, Sustainable Communities, American Institute of Architects, Washington, DC.

Wackernagel, M. and Rees, W. (1996) *Our Ecological Footprint: Reducing Human Impact on the Earth*, New Society Publishers.

World Commission on Environment and Development (WCED) (1987) *Our Common Future*, World Commission on Environment and Development, Oxford University Press, United Nations.

13

Ferdinand S. Johns

Sustainable Urbanity in a Powerful but Fragile Landscape

The problem defined

Introduction

Mention of the Rocky Mountain region of the American and Canadian West hardly conjures up images of 'urbanity', especially in comparison to densely populated urban regions of Europe and Asia. A vision of cowboys against a background of monumental but empty natural landscape is more likely to come to mind. Western cities of any size and density are, in fact, few and far between, but there is another type of unexpectedly sophisticated urbanity, perhaps more fundamentally American at its heart, to be found throughout the Rocky Mountain region (Figure 13.1), the Great Plains and south-western desert states. It is the unpretentious small-scale urbanity of former railroad towns, centres for commerce and culture, planned as completely as any Greek or Roman colony ever was, ready to offer every urbane amenity attributed to the currently fashionable 'New (sub-) Urbanism'. Some of these towns, which are located away from the stylish active recreational attractions, are dying of neglect, but elsewhere a phenomenal population explosion in the Western states is scattering sprawl around those with easy access to an airport. These towns, including Bozeman, Montana,

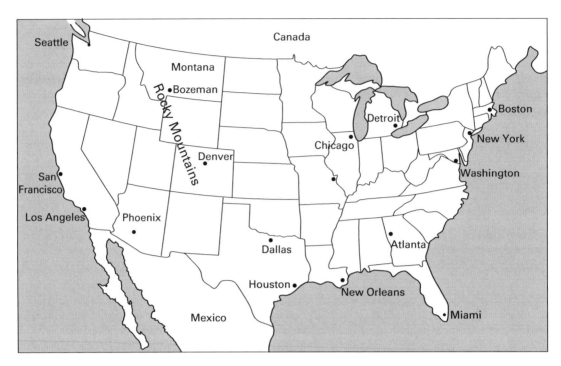

Figure 13.1
The Rocky Mountain region.

are experiencing many of the growing pains typical of the Third World, extremely rapid development without adequate planning or design controls.

A truly sustainable vision for the American West will require difficult but urgent decisions about development patterns in both small urban settlements and the surrounding landscape. This hard-headed approach to sustainability does not envision 21st century homesteaders 'self-sufficiently' populating hitherto unspoiled 'off the grid' areas by using solar and wind energy, but an interdependent community which has resulted from intelligent, logical and forward-thinking decisions as to the best means of utilizing land, water, air and other essential resources to provide human settlement such as transportation, food and water supply, preservation of other species, recreation, viewshed,[1] raw industrial and building materials. Many people currently living in or moving to the West would wholeheartedly agree with such a general and obvious goal statement, but few are actually willing to change their own lifestyle to help achieve it. The following proposals are quite modest, and, in keeping with the principles of American individualism and a consumer-driven market-based system, are designed to appeal to those who wish to enjoy and preserve the lifestyle, as well as the natural and man-made landscape, of the Rocky Mountain West.

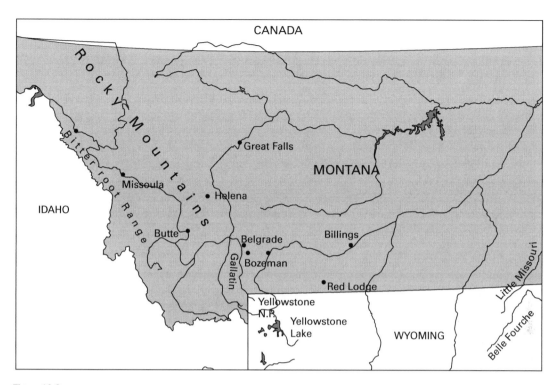

Figure 13.2
Bozeman and the Gallatin Valley.

Population growth and current development

The Rocky Mountain city of Bozeman, Montana, has served as a transportation hub and commercial centre for the nearby mining, timber and agricultural communities for most of its history. It has long been one of the primary 'gateways' to Yellowstone National Park, but the principal employer and dominant presence in town remains Montana State University (Epple, 2001). Bozeman's non-student population increased 21% during the 20-year period from 1970 to 1990 to a total of 22,000 residents (Epple, 2001). It had exploded to over 31,000 residents by the year 2000, an increase of more than 40% in a single decade. It is anticipated that over 46,000 people will live in the city by the year 2020, a further increase of 48% (Epple, 2001). This staggering growth has combined with land-intensive development to consume the rich alluvial soil of the Gallatin River Valley (Figure 13.2) for low-density residential and commercial uses at an unprecedented rate. Over 2000 acres of formerly agricultural land adjacent to Bozeman were annexed into the city between 1990 and 2000, bringing the total acreage within the city limits to 8300, or 13 square miles, surrounded by an additional 25 square miles of planning area in which development is controlled primarily by a utilities expansion plan (Epple, 2001).

39% of the total residential growth in Bozeman between 1990 and 2000 was accommodated in either large or medium-sized lot suburban single-family developments. Another 39% was single-family attached housing, and 20% was in multifamily units. The remaining 2% was accounted for by mobile homes (Epple, 2001). The majority of the truly affordable housing in the area has been concentrated in the nearby town of Belgrade, which has metamorphosed rapidly from a modest but cohesive Western town into a tawdry amorphous dormitory community.

Nearly all of the commercial growth in Bozeman during the past decade has been accommodated in 'strip' centres, 'big box' retail or the rather euphemistically named 'neighbourhood commercial centres' (Epple, 2001). These 'neighbourhood centres' are dispersed throughout suburban areas of the city, and typically include a gas station/convenience store supplemented by adjacent service retail or office space. Most are accessed almost exclusively by automobile, and virtually all serve as detached sections of retail strip development, rather than as authentic pedestrian-oriented centres for their respective neighbourhoods.

Density and 'Living the Myth'

The overall density of Bozeman remains quite low, at a bit less than 2400 people per square mile (927 per km^2), or 3.6 people per acre. The current average household size within the city is 2.3 people, so the overall housing density is 1.6 units per gross acre (3.9 per hectare). The gross average density of the 4405 acres currently zoned 'Residential' within the city limits is about 3 units per acre (7.4 per hectare) (Epple, 2001). So, it would appear that there is plenty of rooms to roam on the range, with 'land, lots of land, and the starry skies above'. The expansive Western lifestyle of hiking, skiing, fly fishing, log cabins and cowboy clothes should still be available to traffic-worn commuter slaves fleeing the cities of the East, the Midwest and even the West Coast to pursue the Rousseaunian myth in Montana, which complete with cell phones, gas-guzzling sports utility vehicles (SUVs) and a fist full of Frequent Flyer tickets, of course. So what could possibly be wrong with this picture?

Ecosystem

The Gallatin Valley, like most Western landscapes, is very powerful yet very fragile. Surrounded and dominated by rugged mountain ranges, the fertile valley is well watered by a network of snow-fed rivers and streams, augmented by a system of engineered irrigation ditches. A short growing season combines with a regular drought cycle to limit vegetation in the valley to native grasses interspersed with occasional trees, which are generally concentrated around the water courses. The lower mountain slopes, where the snowfall is greatest and stays the longest, are covered with sporadically logged coniferous forests, while the valley grassland remains substantially open. The ecosystem is a delicate one, relentlessly subjected to climatic extremes, drought, and wildfire, and now, to generally uncontrolled development.

Political and environmental constraints

The persistent (although myth-based) pioneer mindset which champions personal independence and the ultimate right of total control by the landowner resists any form of governmental restriction, in spite of the West's long history of development by government fiat. The concept of transferring development rights from one site to another is viewed with great alarm, even though it is simply a gentle extension of the long-standing Western concept of separating specific usage rights (such as mineral rights, water rights, access easements) from ownership of the land itself. It is not politic to even mention the American aboriginal concept, which viewed 'land' as a communal resource.

Virtually every Western town or city owes its original master plan to railroad architects and engineers from 'back East', but the reintroduction of responsible physical planning or urban design is currently viewed as a serious abrogation of a God-given right to 'do as I please on my own land', smacking of socialism or even outright communism. Increasingly, however, conflict over the use of limited natural resources in the form of battles over water rights, hunting rights and mineral rights is bringing these complex issues to the fore. Even the most rapacious land developers are beginning to concede that the visual landscape is being despoiled at an unsustainable rate by uncontrolled development, devaluing all other adjacent land economically in the process. Any construction in the valley is immediately visible, even from afar, due to the scarcity of mature trees. Restoration of a disturbed landscape takes a very long time in Montana; the earth heals slowly, and trees mature even slower in the drought-ridden northern climate and rocky soil. Residents have been witness to the fact that a residential subdivision or shopping centre can spring up in a former pasture in a matter of months. Success is rapidly degrading what has been called 'the last best place' in America.

Access and transportation

Montana cities and towns serve as commercial and service centres for very large but thinly populated 'market catchment' areas, which mitigates against establishing an effective mass transit system outside the urban core. Private automobiles, and the roads and parking they require, will therefore remain a significant urban feature for the foreseeable future. Existing rail lines, only one of which is currently used for passenger service in the region, could again be utilized to connect cities and towns, but it is likely that any future mass transit system within the city of Bozeman will rely primarily on buses rather than rails. In any event, there is no mass transitsystem of any kind in operation or even planned at the time of writing.

Loss of agriculture and habitat

Prime agricultural land in close proximity to the urban centre is being rapidly taken out of production in favor of regional shopping and residential subdivision (Epple, 2001). This land was one of the most agriculturally productive in the valley, and it provided expansive open spaces, often populated with cattle or sheep, as environmental 'breathers' and local viewsheds for Bozemanites. Ironically, increasing suburbanization is diminishing production of local agricultural products at the same time as demand for fresh local produce is increasing due to population growth and lifestyle preferences. A net loss of nearby agricultural land will require the conversion of additional land elsewhere to agricultural uses, and make it necessary to import and transport more food into the Gallatin Valley rather than progress toward greater regional self-sufficiency.

A 1990 report from the Ecology and Welfare Subcommittee of the environmental protection agencies (EPA's) Science Advisory Board ranked 'Habitat Alteration and Destruction' as an environmental risk well above 'Oil Spills', 'Groundwater Pollution' and 'Acid Runoff to Surface Waters'. In fact, it was seen as a greater environmental risk than 'Herbicides and Pesticides', 'Airborne Toxins' and 'Acid Deposition' (EPA, 1990). A major reduction in the rate of destruction of natural habitat zones and corridors by development is essential to a sustainable future, as well as to a richer and more enjoyable one.

A partial solution

It is clear that current development trends are consuming the more intangible natural resources of the American West at an unsustainable rate: the wilderness, the productive agricultural land, the open landscape, the laid-back small town urbanity and sense of community. Current patterns of development require us to waste time, energy and non-renewable fossil fuel distributing goods and people. Growth is inevitable; this rapid destruction of our precious resource base is not. New development patterns and building typologies can provide an opportunity to sustain a reasonable amount of growth in existing communities, with no significant adverse effects on lifestyle. Limiting the bulk of future growth to existing settlement areas and reserving the intermediate open landscape for recreation, wildlife, agriculture and viewshed will add value to the entire community. A system which recognizes and embraces the interdependence of urban settlements and the surrounding countryside will ultimately be essential if we are to sustain our ecology and our lifestyle. The following proposals have been explored as a means of demonstrating to the citizens of Bozeman and the Gallatin Valley that appropriately designed new neighbourhoods and buildings in our existing cities and towns can absorb the predicted growth in our region with minimal change in character, landscape and lifestyle potential, while simultaneously improving the potential for continued sustainability of the new Western lifestyle.

Design proposals

Climatic influences

The climate of the Gallatin Valley and Bozeman is not as severe as locally perpetuated myth might suggest. There are relatively rare but admittedly severe Arctic air incursions, sometimes dropping temperatures to as low as −30°F for several days, but typical winter day temperatures range from the teens to the thirties. A typical winter day, although admittedly short at 45°N latitude, provides abundant sunshine and little wind. Spring is an unpredictable and widely varied season, often referred to as 'mud season', as May and June, which account for most of the region's annual rainfall, immediately follow the spring snowmelt runoff. Summers are typically very dry, and pleasantly warm with cool nights; for this season a well-designed building with adequate natural ventilation need not have air conditioning. Fall is also often temperate, although the early onset of winter is not uncommon. Intelligent building design can readily use the natural climatic cycle to great advantage.

Densification potential

Modest densification measures can go a long way towards maintaining the essential character of the community as it grows. The largest city in Montana, Billings, currently has slightly over 100,000 people spread over a very large land area, and the entire state has less than 900,000 people (Epple, 2001). Bozeman and its environs could have absorbed over 200,000 people over the past 40 years with minimal physical impact if the measures recommended in this study had been in place. The resulting scale and physical character of new development would have resembled the much-loved historic district, the city limits could have remained exactly the same as they are today, and no further extension of roads or utilities would have been necessary. It is obviously too late to fully develop the Bozeman area to these target densities, but it is clear that a population of 100,000 could still be comfortably accommodated by establishing growth policies favoring infill development, mixed-use prototypes, adaptive re-use and densification of existing properties, with specific incentives for denser development within the existing city limits. The surrounding valley, foothills and mountainsides which are either undeveloped land, national forest or farmland could be reserved for watershed and aquifer recharge, sustainable agriculture and timber production, viewshed, recreational uses and limited development compatible with those uses.

'Ranchettes' and large plot development: alternatives

Many Montana ranches have been divided into 20 acre plots as a result of a well-intentioned but ill-advised state law initially intended to control the proliferation of rural subdivisions. These tiny 'ranchettes' chop up the expansive Montana landscape into a fenced grid of plots, which ignore topography, ecology and viewshed. New developments closer to town tend to subdivide former valley and foothill ranches into large lots, usually 2–5 acres in size (0.8–2 hectares), which are too big to mow and too small to plough. The area immediately surrounding Bozeman has its share of these wasteful and ecologically disastrous developments.

This study recommends two alternative means of developing the urban periphery and existing highway corridors without continuing to devastate the physical landscape and the ecology. The first is a high-density prototype, which might resemble a large resort ranch, providing up to 80 individual condominium housing units of varying size and cost, on 160 acres of land, achieving the typical large plot subdivision density of 1 unit per 2 acres. Residents would share stables, garages, corrals and other community buildings, which could easily be designed to occupy less than 10% of the total land area, with roads, corrals and garden areas taking up no more than another 10%, thus leaving approximately 130 acres in open range and/or recreational preserve.

A second lower-density prototype would cluster up to eight totally private single-family units, with shared stables and corrals sited sensitively on 160 acres of land, achieving the typical 'ranchette' density of 1 unit per 20 acres, but leaving over 90% of the site in open space. Both of these proposals cluster the buildings compactly on the landscape, offering a far more intelligent approach to ecological/environmental concerns, a protected viewshed, shared resident access to and use of the entire common land area, efficient road and utility maintenance, and a presence in the landscape recalling the traditional ranch clusters which dot the larger Montana landscape.

Single-family development: alternatives

Historical precedents and existing conditions

This next group of low-density prototypes was designed to infill a typical Bozeman city block, or to create new blocks of approximately the same size. The proposals provide alternatives to existing historic typologies, which develop greater densities without a negative impact on neighbourhood scale or character. The typical single-family residential block in the historic district and other older neighbourhoods in Bozeman includes 10 or 12 homes fronting on the original railroad town street grid, each backed up to a mid-block service alley running north/south. This historical pattern results in a net density of 2.8–3.4 units per net acre (6.9–8.4 per hectare), including the alley and a proportional share of the adjacent city streets, but not including other commonly shared public amenities such as parks and schools.

Zero-lot line

The lowest-density configuration proposed in this category is a clustered single-family zero-lot-line prototype (Figure 13.3), which provides each unit with a large private south-facing courtyard space. A double mews arrangement allows 24 units per block with a two-car garage attached to every house (6.7 units/net acre (16.5 per hectare); over twice the typical existing density) with no perceptible change in the scale or character of the neighbourhood. Skilful attention to scale, landscape, opportunities for interaction and other pedestrian-level amenities is always essential to the quality of any residential neighbourhood, but specific stylistic constraints are neither necessary nor desirable.

Figure 13.3
Zero-lot-line (single family)
housing prototype (6.7 units per
net acre; 16.5 units per hectare)
block plan, unit plan, street
elevation.

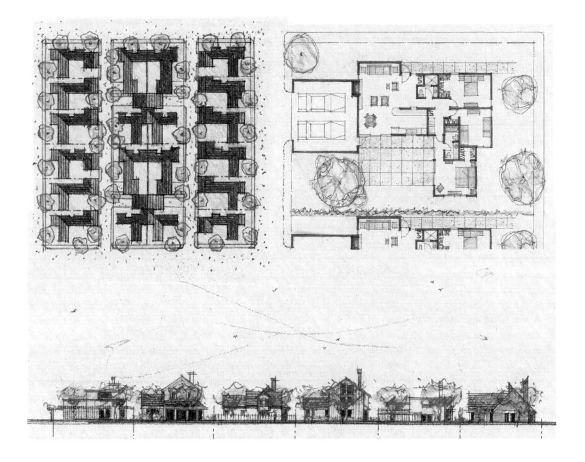

Duplex

The next proposed design places 18 duplex buildings on the same size block for a total of 36 attached single-family units per block (10.1 units per net acre (25 per hectare)), and can also be accomplished with little change in neighbourhood character or scale (Figure 13.4). Shared garages face a single alley, providing covered parking for one car per unit, and each two storey-plus unit has a private walled south-sunlit courtyard as well as a share in the community (block) garden. Windows on three sides of these units will admit light and air, while the direct rays of the low east and west sun are blocked or screened by adjacent units or street trees.

Multifamily courtyard

Figure 13.4
Duplex (two family) housing prototype (10.1 units per net acre; 25 units per hectare) block plan, unit section, street elevation.

The last prototype in this group derives from the courtyard housing popular in Los Angeles in the early 20th century (Figure 13.5). As densities increase, it becomes less feasible to orient all units only to the south, as common wisdom might dictate. Units

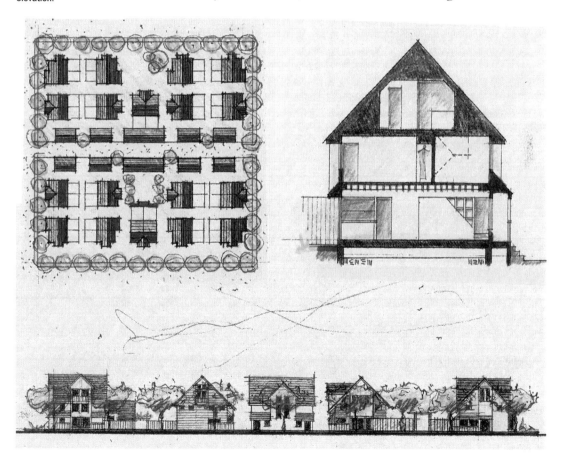

Figure 13.5
Multifamily courtyard housing
prototype (20.2 units per net
acre; 50 units per hectare) full
block first level plan.

organized around a shared south-facing courtyard, however, can provide sunlight and aspect to every room. Careful orientation of openings relative to adjacent buildings and trees will screen or block undesirable low eastern and western sun. Through-ventilation and private outdoor space can be easily achieved, even at the higher densities achieved by this prototype (72 units per block or 20.2 units per net acre (50 per hectare), plus 96 covered off-street parking places). These small-scale multi-family units can easily be designed to respect the scale and character of most single-family neighbourhoods. They are superior in every

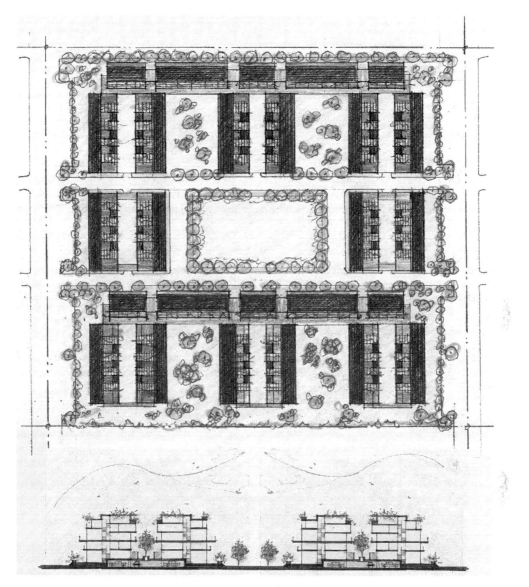

Figure 13.6
Neighbourhood centre housing prototype (43 units per net acre; 106 units per hectare) block plan, partial section.

aspect (including construction costs) to the bulky double-loaded three-story walk-up housing of equivalent (or lesser) density currently being constructed in Bozeman.

Pedestrian-oriented neighbourhood centre: an alternative

This prototype is suggested as an alternative to the drive-in automotive-oriented centres currently being built. It is a genuine mixed-use complex, with buildings containing housing, offices, and retail, and is envisioned as a prototype for neighbourhood centres in new developments (Figure 13.6). The example shown includes up to 400 housing units, over 500 parking spaces, a public square or park, plus 40,000 ft² of commercial space on 9.4 acres, for a net residential density of 43 units per acre (106 per hectare). It will require more sophisticated design and construction technology due to its height and the inclusion of 240 decked-over parking spaces, but offers the convenience and minimum-maintenance lifestyle popular with a growing segment of the residential market. Hydraulic elevators provide accessibility and convenience, but many residents of a more health conscious community will probably choose to walk up the maximum of three flights of stairs. Every unit has been designed for natural through-ventilation, as well as outlooks to the greater landscape beyond the wide south-facing landscaped courts and intimately-scaled elevated pedestrian access 'streets'.

Commercial area infill opportunities

In addition, two opportunities for infill development in existing commercial areas were investigated (Figure 13.7).

Strip centre parking infill

This first proposal fronts the perimeter streets of a typical 'big box' or strip centre parking lot, providing additional ground level

Figure 13.7
Infill typologies: suburban 'strip' retail parking-lot infill site section and downtown full-block infill site section.

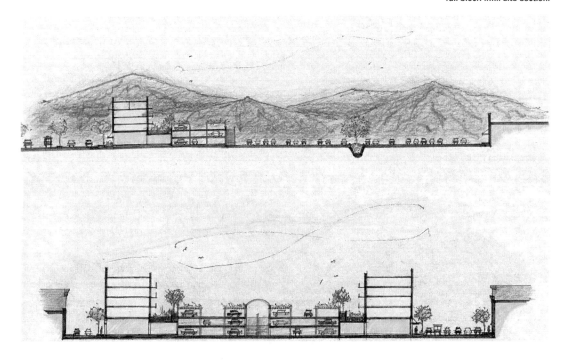

retail topped by several levels of housing, all built on the periphery of the existing parking lot. The typical 'strip centre' or 'big box' parking lot was sized in response to conventional planning wisdom and developer-generated parking ratios of the 1950s; they are seldom full in Western towns. Soaring retail rents suggest that the revenue generated from this additional development would quickly offset the cost of any parking structures required to replace the lost spaces. An asphalt wasteland can become affordable housing, convenient for shopping, creating a far more pleasant streetscape and enlivening a typically unattractive, lifeless, automobile dominated zone of the city.

Traditional downtown block infill

The second diagram suggests a high-density infill development of an entire downtown Bozeman city block. A scale-less office project with minimal street activity and no on-site parking has been proposed for the vacant site formerly occupied by the historic Firestone Building on Main Street. This counterproposal shows four levels of housing over street-front retail and office space, surrounding (and screening) a parking structure buried in the middle of the block. There is increasing interest in Bozeman in providing adequate parking downtown to keep the core alive. This proposal provides adequate parking for all uses without destroying the urban fabric, and contributes to a walk-able residential downtown as well. The uppermost partial level of the parking deck is reserved for the residential units, and is heavily landscaped. This typology would provide 128 residential units on this block with 1.5 dedicated parking spots per unit, plus over $55,000\,\text{ft}^2$ of commercial space with parking at a ratio of 4.5 cars per $1000\,\text{ft}^2$. The net housing density is 35 units per acre (86.5 per hectare) in a mixed-use infill configuration.

A test case

The design prototypes proposed above were applied in a comparative theoretical test comparison with a recent typical suburban development located at the extreme edge of the Bozeman city limits. The existing development consisted of 418 plots of approximately one-third acre, 130 smaller plots and 16 larger multifamily plots, for a total capacity of 932 housing units. The alternative design could have increased local densities enough to produce up to 300 additional housing units while leaving over 50% of the site as dedicated open space. This would have allowed the community to preserve a pre-existing stream, create contiguous wildlife habitat throughout the site, keep large areas of the site in agricultural production, provide a larger and more accessible multiuse public park, and greatly enhance the viewshed and overall environment for neighbourhood residents and the entire Bozeman community.

Proposed design priorities

The following is a summary of the recommended design priorities for future development in Bozeman and environs:

1. Increase overall development density within the city without annexing additional land to create a more compact city, reducing development pressure on surrounding agricultural lands and habitat

2. Increase local densities in exchange for preservation of agriculture or open space within and between perimeter developments, incorporating ecologically sensitive design principles and providing viewsheds and habitat corridors as well

3. Encourage infill and recycling/adaptive reuse of existing structures, the existing urban fabric and even the existing suburban fabric to increase capacity without increasing consumption of new land

4. Require all future projects to respond logically to climate and orientation, depending upon the density of the prototype, by taking full advantage of opportunities to save energy and create a more pleasant living environment suited to the Bozeman lifestyle

5. Initiate policies which will result in walk-able communities, with safe, convenient, esthetically pleasing pedestrian access to services and shopping, designed to take advantage of future mass transit and reduce automobile dependence now and in the future

6. Encourage mixed use community centres, which provide pedestrian-oriented community gathering places, shopping, higher density residential, as well as adequate, but not excessive, parking

7. Encourage the design of primarily low rise buildings of high density, suitable for the widest range of simple, low-tech construction techniques available, in order to keep housing affordable, maintain the scale of the existing context and encourage use of sustainable construction methods and materials as they continue to emerge

8. Encourage the design of compact housing typologies, which maximize utility, convenience, spatial expansiveness, amenity and privacy in interior and individual outdoor spaces, while conserving land, materials and energy

9. Encourage better development prototypes for the ubiquitous surrounding 20 acre and large plot (2+ acre) developments,

which provide greater amenity value for those individual developments, as well as less destruction of the overall natural landscape amenity for the entire community

10. Encourage and enable nearby small towns (Belgrade, Manhattan, Three Forks, Logan, Amsterdam, Livingston) to establish similar development priorities in order to preserve and enhance their long-term environmental quality, character and lifestyle, without losing their revenue base

Conclusion

This study concludes that a sustainable urbanity is an essential factor in the conservation of the wilderness and rural landscape, as well as the lifestyle, of the American West. A number of planning and architectural prototypes have been suggested which can significantly increase density with minimal physical and visual effect on the typical Western town or city. Although the densities envisioned are far less than older Anglo-American, European and Asian cities (or even suburbs), the potential increase in overall population capacity is quite significant.

Western states must find the will to balance their vast undeveloped natural reserves with more dense urban centres, resisting the temptation to focus on short-term gain rather than the long-range future. Urban and suburban development boundaries must be established, accompanied by a realistic system for the allocation and transfer of development rights. These well-proven mechanisms can facilitate responsible local and regional planning for a sustainable future, without abridging or violating individual property rights in the process. Alternative design models appropriate to the relaxed individualistic 'Western lifestyle' may then be used to concentrate development in accordance with those sustainable planning goals. One can only hope that our neighbours, both the newcomer 'wannabes' and those wonderfully independent old-time ranchers, cowboys and Native Americans, will view this as a way to save what they love most about this powerful but fragile landscape.

Note

1. Viewshed is a term that means 'an area bounded peripherally by the extent or range of vision' and is based on a concept similar to the well-known term 'watershed'.

References

Environmental Protection Agency (EPA) (1990) Reducing risk: setting priorities and strategies for environmental protection. *Report of the Science Advisory Board Relative Risk Strategies Committee to the EPA*, USA, November issue.

Epple A. (2001) *Bozeman 2020 Community Plan*, Bozeman City Planning Commission, Bozeman, Montana, USA.

14

Helena Webster and Peter Williams

Envisioning the Future: Sustainable Models for Rural Communities

Envisioning the future: introduction

Arguably, one of the most critical tasks facing the global population today is the creation of a shared vision for a sustainable future within the biophysical constraints of the real world. Towards this end researchers in virtually every discipline have been working hard to define 'sustainability' within the bounds of their particular fields. The resulting plethora of research findings publicised through books, conference papers and journal articles has gradually led to a notional international consensus on the 'core' interrelated aspects of sustainability, social, economic and environmental, and the associated indicators of sustainability (Jenks, 1996). However, when it comes to applying sustainable principles to local conditions, policy-makers at national, regional and local levels have encountered real difficulty in understanding the multi-dimensional dynamics of the existing heterogeneous condition, let alone finding mechanisms to steer change towards integrated sustainable futures. Despite these very real methodological problems the concept of 'sustainability' has become a kind of politically correct 'meta-fix'. Indeed, the word 'sustainable' has become so potent that everyone involved in change has now to declare, whether reality bears this out or not, that they are promoting 'sustainability'. Yet, beneath the rhetorical surface of the sustainability debate, there remains disagreement about even the most basic issues underpinning sustainable development, for example, whether future sustainability lies in moving towards urban densification or urban dispersal (Breheny, 1993). Further, close scrutiny of new urban paradigms which make claims to be integrated sustainable solutions, such as the Urban Villages concept in the UK[1] or New Urbanism in the USA (Calthorpe, 1993), seem to rest their visions of a sustainable future largely on the appeal of the architectural aesthetics of the past with little regard to the contemporary condition or notions of progress, either social, economic or environmental.[2] For the apologists of these paradigms, attaining sustainable futures seems merely a matter of 'choosing where in the past we would like to live in the future' (French, 2000). Despite a growing number of alternative, but as yet largely theoretical, models emanating from Europe and particularly the Netherlands,[3] the current position facing those involved in steering urban change is that both the mechanisms for attaining sustainable development and the future form which sustainable development might take remain ill-defined and contested.

The chapter that follows reports on the methodology and findings of a multi-disciplinary team of graduate students from Massachusetts Institute of Technology (MIT) and Cambridge University who investigated issues surrounding the creation of new sustainable rural communities, in relation to both process and product, through a design case study. The results of the case study project made several contributions to current practice. Firstly, in relation to process, the project team developed the concept of a charitable trust as an innovative development model for new rural communities. It was argued that a charitable trust, made up of local stakeholders charged with a holistic and continuing sustainability remit, would be more likely to produce an ongoing sustainable settlement than the present developer-led models. The team also demonstrated how such a development model would work financially in today's economic climate. Secondly, in relation to urban design, the project team demonstrated how the design of physical infrastructure could make a significant contribution to its lasting environmental sustainability. Additionally, and counter-posed to the paradigms offered by the New Urbanist movement, the case study project also demonstrated how quality infrastructure design can provide a sense of place without constraining the architectural language of individual developments that might take place within it.

The case study context: the future of the Cambridge region

One of the many urban growth scenarios that presents challenges for those who strive towards the realisation of sustainable futures is found in cities and regions around the world, from Silicon Valley in the USA to Silicon Fen in England, that have seen rapid economic success due to the proliferation of 'high-tech' and more recently 'bio-tech' spin-offs from university research laboratories.[4] The economic growth of such regions has resulted in population growth and consequential demands for new housing, office accommodation and transport infrastructure. Well-rehearsed arguments, based on a thorough analysis of these phenomena, suggest that if these regions do not respond to the pressures for physical growth and infrastructure improvements they risk stifling future economic growth (Sainsbury, 1999). Therefore, the pressing question for these regions is how, where and in what form sustainable development might occur?

Silicon Fen, within the Cambridgeshire sub-region, faces all the challenges mentioned above. Over the last 20 years the spiralling success of new industries, mainly in the fields of biotechnology, telecommunications, software development and technology consultancies, which have spun-off from primary research carried out at Cambridge University, have placed enormous pressure on the region's landscape, settlements and infrastructure (Segal Quince, 1985; Segal Quince Wicksteed, 2000). This technology-driven growth and the consequential changes in the production, distribution and marketing of goods have altered both the space and location requirements for firms and their employees, and resulted in huge demands for new types of accommodation (such as offices, laboratories, housing, schools) and more efficient distribution systems (such as roads, public transport systems).[5] Yet, despite the success of the Cambridge region, public policy has found difficulties in responding rapidly enough to the changing needs of the regional economy. A recent evaluation of the situation by the Cambridge-independent economic development and management consultancy Segal Quince Wicksteed (2000) concluded that:

> The private elements (in the region) are evolving well, but they are in many ways let down by the formulae and traditions that determine the current spending and investment by the public sector, whether in the education of children or the provision of roads and public transport . . . Cambridge is suffering from congestion that is in danger of choking the growth dynamic.

With the danger that inertia on the part of the local and regional government may inadvertently stifle the growth of the regional economy, and the consequential loss of economic opportunity for the UK, there is now general agreement among stakeholders that there is an urgent need for strategic action. Hence, the pressing question for Cambridge and many other similar cities and regions is how to achieve 'desirable' expansion, permitting the growth of businesses and employment, without destroying the distinctive Cambridgeshire environment?

Over the past few years the city and the region have started to address these issues; regional and local plans have been developed in accordance with standard planning procedures. However, there have also been complimentary, but arguably more innovative, attempts at steering growth. The Cambridge Futures Project (Cambridge Futures, 2002) brought stakeholders together, including the university, businesses and the public, to identify a number of alternative forms for coping with the physical growth of Cambridge city. More recently, the UK government and industry sponsored Cambridge–MIT Institute (CMI)[6] commissioned a joint 2-year research project from the Department of Architecture, Cambridge University and the School of Urban Planning at MIT, to explore the relationship between innovation, urban design and sustainability. The project brought together multi-disciplinary staff and postgraduate students from the two universities to explore whether innovations in spatial and physical design, and public policy could create sustainable 'enabling' environments that might foster the development of innovatory, knowledge-based enterprises.

The project's multi-disciplinary remit was partly conceived as a response to widespread concerns expressed in government reports (Burton, 1992; Dearing, 1997; Egan, 1998) about the poor standards of multi-professional working in the built environment, a problem thought to be at least partially the result of the autonomous nature of discipline-specific education, and partially as a response to the multi-dimensional nature of the problem. During the academic year 2001–2002 the project team looked at the future of Cambridge as a case study. The work, premised on results of the Cambridge Futures Project, examined different approaches, locations and institutional means to enable Cambridge to foster and accommodate growth. Students worked in multi-disciplinary teams, consisting of architects, planners and land economists. Each team looked at one of the expansion sites identified by the Cambridge Futures Project (Figure 14.1).

Figure 14.1
Cambridge expansion – the four
case study sites (previously
identified by the Cambridge
Futures Project).

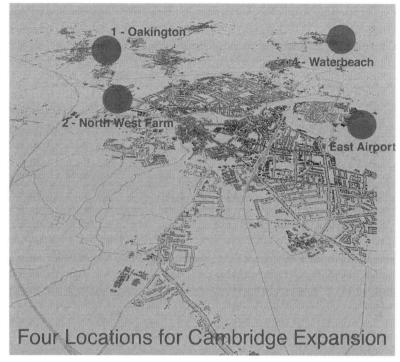

Four Locations for Cambridge Expansion

Taking the existing planning and economic framework as given, the team were asked to work in a multi-disciplinary way to produce a feasible sustainable development framework for the site, with particular reference to:

- exploring new urban and built forms appropriate as hosts to innovation, productivity and competitiveness
- reconciling the requirements for new urban settings with conservation goals for existing settlements and rural areas
- understanding the relationship between environmental and sustainable development, and social development
- understanding and managing large scale, complex urban systems

During the 10 weeks of the project, each team explored a variety of urban forms and implementation mechanisms that would create sustainable settlements and in particular foster synergy and creative collaboration between the university and its setting, while seeking to ensure that such new development helped address current social and economic shortcomings, and sustained the attractive nature of Cambridge and its region.

The case study project: Oakington Barracks

The following describes the working methodology and resulting sustainable development model produced by one of the

Figure 14.2
The disused Oakington Barracks
Development Site in 2002.

multi-disciplinary project teams. The team focused their study on Oakington Barracks, formerly a Ministry of Defence base, to the northwest of Cambridge (Figure 14.2). The Cambridge Futures Project, the Cambridge Structure Plan and South Cambridgeshire District Council had previously identified the 390 hectare site as suitable for future development. The site's suitability was premised on three significant factors. Firstly, the site was largely disused 'brownfield' land, as opposed to agriculturally valuable 'greenfield' agricultural land. Secondly, the site was located in the economically successful Huntington–Cambridge development corridor and thirdly, the site was located on the route of a proposed rapid transit system that would link Cambridge and Huntingdon.[7] Additionally, the site seemed 'topical' because Gallagher Homes had recently published a development proposal for a high-density new town of some 10,000 homes. The challenge to the project team was to produce an alternative development model to the existing Gallagher proposal.

Inter-disciplinary working

The aim of the Oakington design team, consisting of an economist, a planner and an architect, was to work throughout the project in an integrated way towards envisioning a sustainable development proposal for the site. Although individual team members had worked in inter-disciplinary teams, none had worked in multi-disciplinary teams. Recognising the 'new' and 'particular' nature of multi-disciplinary team working, the academic staff inducted the students as part of the project briefing to the theory and practice of successful team working (Stott and Walker, 1995). The key elements of this training included understanding individual roles, team working and decision-making processes and particularly the need to establish team 'ground rules' including:

- shared goals and objectives
- recognition of the contribution of each discipline to the solution
- shared leadership and decision-making
- the need for effective communication

Equipped with the knowledge of successful multi-disciplinary team working, the project team set about employing their newly acquired knowledge to produce a sustainable development proposal for the Oakington site. In effect, the project set the team an ill-defined problem that required the adoption of a 'creative' problem-solving approach. As there was no 'correct' answer, only solutions that were more or less convincing, students were asked to make their own decisions about the bounds of the problem and subsequently to argue the case for their solution on the basis of researched evidence. Within this scenario the role of the academic tutors was framed less as 'master' (transmission model), as is traditional in architectural education, and more as 'liminal expert' (student-centred model) where the tutor helps the students to think critically about their work as well as facilitating their learning processes. At the end of the project each team was asked to produce a report charting their research, design process and solution. Observations and reflective interviews with the Oakington team confirmed that they adopted classic creative problem-solving techniques (divergent thinking, brainstorming, etc.) and moved through the recognised phases of creative problem solving[8] during the process of designing their development model for Oakington. Interestingly, it was apparent that all three members had engaged in creative thought both within their own disciplines and across disciplines, and that creativity was not the sole territory of the architect. Thus, the 10-week project was characterised by seemingly endless cycles of research, design and testing, as ideas were continually informed, generated tested and accepted or rejected, revealing the need for further research of alternative ideas, against the multi-dimensions of sustainability, as translated to the locale. Hence, the Oakington team started their project by researching the problem as they perceived it rather than as defined by the Gallagher development brief (so that the solution was no longer bounded by a narrow definition of the problem). Each specialist, economist, planner and architect, viewed the design problem through his or her

269

Table 14.1
Scope of the multi-disciplinary
project team's research (ranging
from the global to local, and from
the empirical to the theoretical).

Aspects of sustainability:	Global	Regional	Local
Social	Social capital theory		Employment and housing patterns
Economic	Innovation theory	The Silicon Fen innovation cluster	Local growth indicators and projections
	Economic forecasting: The Lowry model	Regional growth indicators	Local house prices, office rentals and building costs
	Economic costing Models for built form, infrastructure and transportation		
Environmental	Urban design theory (the history of garden cities, Dutch urban design theory)	The genius loci of the fens: architecture and landscape	Site Analysis Inc: ecology, water, infrastructure, built form
	Ecological design: urban and built form	Cambridgeshire regional planning and transportation documents	Cambridge structure plan

individual 'specialist' eyes. Their collective research covered all three aspects of sustainability: social, environmental and economic, and ranged from the global to local, and from the quantitative to the qualitative (Table 14.1).[9]

On the basis of the above research the team agreed on a set of objectives for their project towards achieving the general aims of the project brief (the design of a new sustainable settlement) as follows:

- To develop a low-density 'urban–rural' model for sustainable development on the Oakington site
- It should be possible to implement the model in today's planning and economic climate, and flexible enough to respond to future uncertainties
- The design should create a place to foster 'innovation'; economic (predominantly agri-tech, and bio-tech), social and environmental
- The design should retain and build on the rural qualities of the site, its existing ecosystems and the surrounding context (built form and landscape)

After 12 weeks of research, creativity, deliberation and false starts, the design team reached the end of the project. The result was

Figure 14.3
ECO-town Oakington Project
team's development plan.

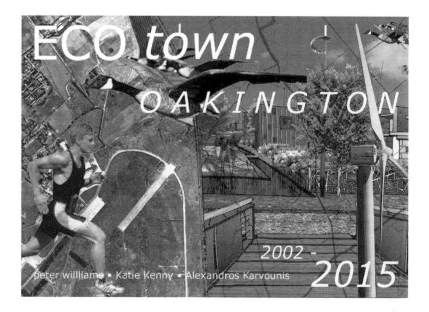

a set of frameworks based around the issues of economic, social and environmental sustainability within the constraints of the market. Their research and proposals were presented in an extensive two-volume report and are summarised below.

The case study design: ECO-town

The project team's proposal, 'ECO-town' (Figure 14.3), was conceived as an urban management framework that would promote and direct the development of a new sustainable low-density town. Departing from conventional single-stakeholder development models, the ECO-town framework proposed that the development would be administered by a specially constituted development trust, made up of multiple stakeholders including representatives of the existing community, which would have not-for-profit status. The remit of the trust would be to promote the development of a largely self-sustaining, socially inclusive town (with a maximum of 6000 dwellings) that could foster the dynamism and prosperity of Cambridge's research and technology-based industries. The trust would work towards providing a full range of infrastructure including roads, parks, transport, services and social facilities to support private housing, commercial and office developments. In all of its promotional and controlling activities the trust would promote the notion of social, economic and environmental innovation, and continually test the emerging development against its own aims and accepted indicators of sustainability.[10]

The urban design framework

Urban design was conceived as having a key role in providing the community with a sense of place and a sustainable infrastructure as well as establishing a physical framework within which private development could be located. The design of the urban framework was premised on the notion of 'working with the landscape'. It conceived the Cambridgeshire Fenland landscape as a dynamic and continually evolving form. Once wet lands and then tamed in the 18th century by ditches and dykes to allow agricultural uses, the Fenland landscape now lies increasingly redundant due to the uncompetitive nature of British agriculture (DEFRA, 2002). So, what next? How could the landscape evolve to accept new uses? The concept for the design of the infrastructure of ECO-town identified the deep underlying two- and three-dimensional patterns, and textures both in the Fenland landscape and in the site itself and used them to provide the formal structuring devices for the development frame-work (Figure 14.4).

Hence the urban framework was characterised by patchworks, watercourses, horizontal planes and hedges. Distinctive existing elements would be, wherever possible, used, enhanced or extrapolated to form the visual character and infrastructure (such as roads, plot divisions, parks, networks of watercourses) for the development. Thus the infrastructure both created the *genius loci* and prepared the ground for future building. This approach conceived the urban environment as being extrapolated from the existing site conditions as a kind of contextual metamorphosis. This notion of metamorphosis meant that the infrastructure could be precise and flexible, anticipatory and indeterminate, at the same time. Through urban management the development could grow and adjust according to shifting local, regional and global conditions. Hence the development would not progress to a predetermined vision or state but could evolve within the loose envelope of the urban design constraints. Thus the infrastructure created a 'directed field' by setting the technical and infrastructure limitations in which different architects and designers could contribute without aesthetic constraint. Such an approach might be contrasted to the predetermined 'architectural vision' approach of the New Urbanists (the generic 'traditional' English village).[11] Whilst the New Urbanist approach promotes the reinstatement of a largely defunct historical urban paradigm, this alternative approach suggested a development model that promoted the transformation of the countryside into something new and

Figure 14.4
ECO-town: the new infrastructure
layout extrapolates the existing
landscape morphology.

relevant through employing sustainable rather than stylistic criteria.

The framework development over time

The ECO-town development framework projected, following the land use demand forecasts generated by the Lowry model (Lowry, 1964),[12] that development would be realised in a series of three notional phases, of varying sizes and programmes, with a fourth contiguous phase relating to the country park which

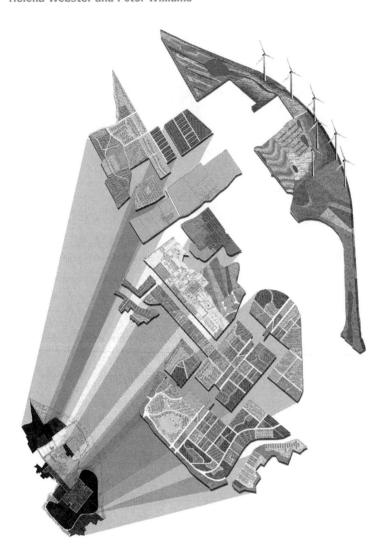

Figure 14.5
ECO-town: an exploded
axonometric of the
development framework
showing the phasing (different
tones) and indicative
morphology for each phase.

would form a green backbone to the site and link the sites ecosystems together to enhance the biodiversity of the site (Figures 14.5 and 14.6; Table 14.2).

The first phase, Phase A, would be the establishment of the 'incubator', housing and social/commercial infrastructure on the site based around the existing infrastructure of the Ministry of Defence base. This phase would also set up the first two rapid transport interchanges, one for the new settlement located in the zone of the existing Ministry of Defence runway and another adjoining the incubator. The first phase was intended as a catalyst development and financed by pump-priming investment raised by the ECO-town Development Trust/Ministry of Defence Partnership (Table 14.3).

The development site

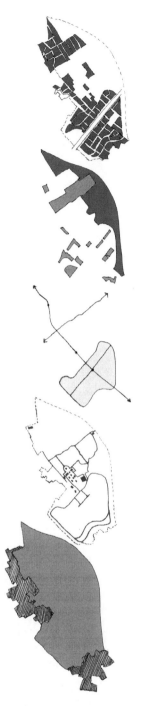

The existing infrastructure:
roads and tracks (re-used in
the new development)

New transport infrastructure
(most importantly: N–S guided
tramway connecting to
Cambridge and St Ives and
E–W new connection to A40
trunk road, and park and ride
to Cambridge)

Green hubs and ECO-park

Land parcels for private
development

The partnership arrangement, in which the Ministry of Defence
shared the profits from the development over the first two phases,
at a ratio of 40:60, made the scheme more viable because it meant
that the trust did not have to raise the large amount of money
to purchase the land. The infrastructure for Phases B and C

Table 14.2
Detailed breakdown of the projected phasing and associated development (it should be noted that planned phasing and uses may vary over time in response to the market or other significant criteria).

Phase	Associated development
Phase A	
Area: 44 ha	
(a) Incubator, mixed-use development and parks	• Development of 23,000 m² of existing space.
	• Permission for expansion to 50,000 m² by the end of Phase B.
	• Employment 2000 by the end of Phase B.
	• New leisure facilities for wider company.
	• Use of existing infrastructure only.
Area: 50 ha	
(b) Housing, mixed-use development and parks	• Development of six land parcels (4.5–6.5 ha each).
	• Densities between 28 and 50 dwellings per hectare.
Phase B	
Total area: 128.5 ha	
Locality I: 80.7 ha adjoining Phase A(b)	• Eleven land parcels between 4.5 and 40.5 ha.
Locality II: 40.2 ha adjoining Phase A(b)	• Densities between 30 and 40 dwellings per hectare.
Locality III: 7.67 ha to the north area of site	
Phase C	
Area: 56.1 ha	
Housing and parks	• Five land parcels between 9.2 and 12.0 ha
	• Densities between 28 and 50 dwellings per hectare.
ECO-park	
Area: 111.5 ha	
Concurrent development	• A concurrent development to the above (including implementation of sustainable energy systems and site water management system).

Table 14.3
ECO-town projected development costs. (The figures demonstrate that the development trust would be able to finance the infrastructure and make profits for re-investing into the community.)

	Cost	Revenue	Net revenue	Development trust revenue	MOD revenue
Phase A	5,088,750	147,000,000	141,911,250	**56,764,500**	85,146,750
Phase B	5,906,515	192,750,000	186,843,485	**74,737,394**	112,106,091
Cumulative	10,995,265	339,750,000	328,754,735	**131,501,894**	197,252,841
Phase C	34,532,600	84,150,000	49,617,400	**49,617,400**	n/a
Cumulative	45,527,865	423,900,000	378,372,135	**181,119,294**	n/a

MOD: Ministry of Defence; n/a: not available.

would be built on demand for the purchase of land parcels, but its design would accord with the development framework plan (Figure 14.5). All development sites would be sold with use, density and embodied energy targets, but no stylistic constraints.

Profit derived from the sale of land would be used to provide quality infrastructure, including the wind turbines[13] and the community facilities necessary for developing identity and social capital. The trust would take special care to ensure a diverse social mix by allocating certain sites for self-build and low-cost housing. By the end of Phase B the level of profit would be sufficient for the trust to subsidise such developments (Table 14.3). The final phase would be the completion of the 100-ha Country Park that would form the backbone of the development and tie all the emergent ecosystems together (water and waste management systems in particular) (Figure 14.7). The Lowry model was used primarily for financial costing and feasibility purposes and required fixed projections. However, the proposal recognised that future development demand was inherently unpredictable and therefore sought to achieve a break even point for the trust as quickly as possible, thereafter allowing the trust to make policy decisions relatively free of loan or debt dependency.

Working within the framework

The second stage of the design was to take a 1-ha case study block, together with the densities and energy targets specified

Figure 14.7
ECO-town country park (tying the development into the existing fenland landscape as well as providing a location for electricity producing wind turbines and reed beds used for water filtration).

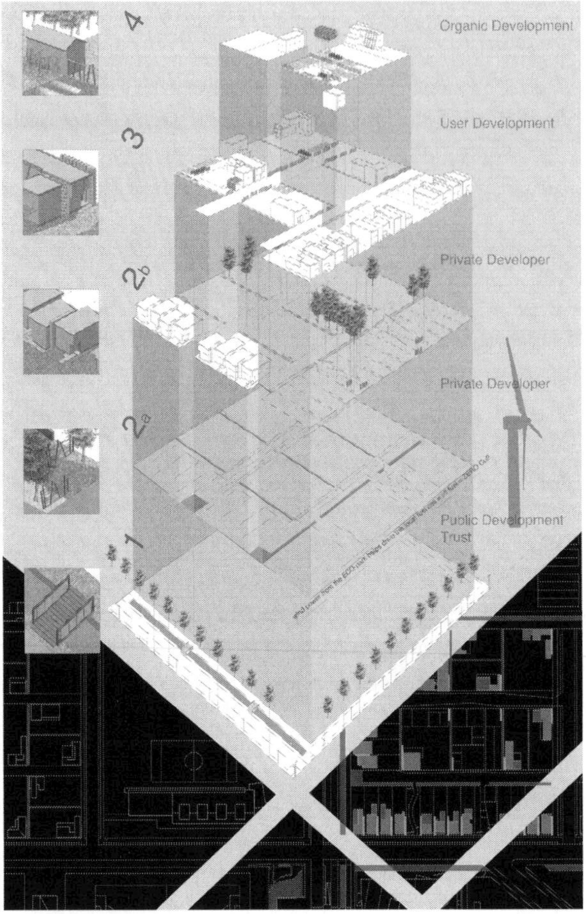

Figure 14.8
Case study block (1 ha):
exploded axonometric showing
one scenario for the layering of
infrastructure and built form.

by the development framework and administered by the development trust, and investigate ways in which a developer might work within the constraints to produce built form.

The axonometric (Figure 14.8) demonstrates the layering of the major infrastructure provided by the trust (grid roads, gravel minor roads and landscaping, including drainage channels, and trunk services), the developer built secondary infrastructure (services to plots), the developer and privately built houses, and finally the more *ad hoc* organic development (e.g. sheds) that would occur over time. The intention was that the development trust infrastructure, carefully designed landscaped avenues and watercourses, would provide the *genius loci*, leaving the designers of individual buildings 'free' to design without stylistic constraints, so long as they met the density and energy codes. In this case the housing block might be purchased by a developer who would then divide it into serviced plots and sell them to builders or individual clients with a requirement to use a

Figure 14.9
Case study block: model of the 1 ha block showing the rich morphology produced by allowing a variety of building types and densities.

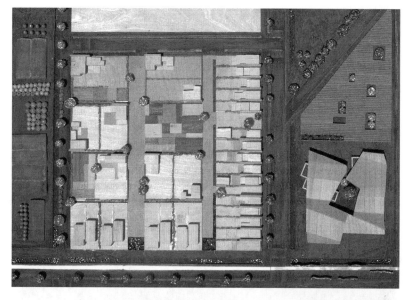

component-build system which met the energy targets specified by the trust (Figure 14.9). The result would be a rich and varied building morphology held together by the aesthetic strength of the infrastructure design.

Envisioning the future: conclusion

This chapter described the process by which multi-disciplinary student teams from Cambridge University and MIT worked together on a case study project towards envisioning sustainable development models for new rural communities. The chapter outlined the working method of one multi-disciplinary team and presented their

Figure 14.10
ECO-town: four collages of
'envisioned' public realm
(the distinctive landscape
infrastructure creates the sense
of place and allows the built
form to be varied in form and
architectural expression).

Figure 14.10
(continued).

development proposal for a case study site, Oakington Barracks, Cambridgeshire. The project results confirmed that (i) students from a variety of disciplines are able, with a little training, to work successfully together; and (ii) multi-disciplinary working increases the likelihood that development proposals address both process and product in an integrated way.

The Oakington project was described fully because of the team's creative approach to both the development process and the urban morphology. The team proposed that the development process for the new community be controlled by a charitable development trust, made up of a number of local stakeholders rather than a single developer, which would be responsible for planning, promoting and monitoring the sustainable development of the new rural community. This radical concept seemed to offer advantages over present development processes for several reasons; it avoided exclusively profit-driven development; it's structure was socially inclusive and it had sustainability at the core of its remit. However, the team realised that the degree to which the development trust would be successful in achieving a sustainable rural development was largely dependent on having usable working tools for planning and/or assessing holistic notions sustainability and that these tools were currently not available. This finding pointed to the urgent need for the development of *usable* working tools for assessing *holistic* notions of sustainability.

In addition to considering the development process the project team investigated how concepts of local sustainability might be objectified into physical form. Through the design of the infrastructure and development guidelines for the case study site the project team demonstrated firstly, that the physical infrastructure design of a new development can be key to its lasting environmental sustainability and secondly, that infrastructure design can establish a distinctive yet dynamic sense of place through the subtle synthesis of the new and the old without having to control the aesthetics of the subsequent architectural form (Figure 14.10). The designs for the Oakington settlement, with its low-density, field-like patchwork morphology, offered a strikingly innovative and refreshingly optimistic image of a future of rural communities compared to the rigid, homogeneous, style-driven masterplans that have become accepted in the UK as paradigms for new settlements.

In conclusion, the findings of the above research project offers three contributions to the sustainable development debate. Firstly, the search for convincing place-specific sustainable solutions requires the adaptation of universal notions of sustainability to the specific conditions and value biases, economic, political and environmental, of the local/regional condition. Secondly, and following on from the first point, the inherently multi-dimensional nature of sustainability requires that multi-disciplinary teams work in truly collaborative ways if they are to produce convincing development models for a sustainable future. Lastly, the lack of evidence to substantiate any necessary link between sustainability and urban or architectural forms of the past provides contemporary designers with a new opportunity to *envision* truly progressive sustainable forms for new rural communities and re-address the challenge posed by Paul Ricoeur of 'how to become modern and return to sources' (Ricoeur, 1981).

Notes

1. The Urban Villages concept has been promoted in the UK since the 1980s by a consortium of house builders backed by Prince Charles. Their publicity insists that a return to 'traditional' medieval English village morphologies and typologies will result in sustainable environments. However, the built examples appear little more than dormitory suburbs that look more like stage sets than real villages. Behind the pastiche facades modern families surf the net. For more details see Aldous, T (1992) *Urban Villages*. London, Urban Villages Group.

2. For commentary on the regressive nature 'the heritage industry', see Robert Hewison's *The Heritage Industry* (1987).

3. The obviously 'constructed' nature of the landscape of the Netherlands together with the pressures for expansion in the 1980s and 1990s made the notion of directing environmental both urgent and exciting for Dutch designers. For examples see *Artificial Landscape* (Ibelings, 2000) and *9 + 1 Young Dutch Landscape Architects* (Van Blerck, 1999).

4. These phenomena are commonly known as 'innovation clusters'.

5. The government acknowledged the pressure for growth in the region in the Regional Planning Guidance Note 6 (PRG6) (2000) by setting housing targets for Cambridgeshire and Peterborough at 80,000 new dwellings by 2016.

6. The CMI's declared mission is 'to undertake education and research designed to improve the UK's competitiveness, productivity and entrepreneurship' (CMI, 2003).

7. The proposal was the result of the Cambridge to Huntingdon Multi-Modal Study (CHUMMS) (DTLR, 2001).

8. According to Steinberg (1999) the recognised phases of creative problem solving begin with finding, recognising, defining or refining the problem, move through seeking possible solutions or ways of making progress towards a solution, and end with evaluating the alternatives, settling on the best of them and then further developing or consolidating the best solution.

9. The research might have taken on a different profile if it had been made up of members from different disciplines. The epistemology of Urban Design is currently very hazy and it is very unclear which disciplines should be part of an urban design team.

10. Many organisations, including the UK Government (DETR, 1999), are developing indicators of sustainability in the hope that they might be used as both a design tool by a project team and as an evaluation tool for planners and others keen to assess the sustainability of a proposed development.

11. Most new developments that align with the New Urbanist thesis use building codes ensure that architects work within an architectural style loosely based on a regional 'pastiche'.

12. The Lowry land use model uses spatial interaction models to build a system that claims to predict population and employment distributions. This model was used by the project research teams firstly to estimate how much employment, and of what type, would be generated by the presence of 6000 houses on the Oakington site, and then to generate the associated land-use mix.

13. Wind energy is increasingly regarded as economically feasible; the cost for electricity production from wind power in the UK was 2.88p per kW in 2002 compared to 2p for coal.

References

Aldous, T. (1992) *Urban Villages*. Urban Villages Group, London.

Breheny, M. (1993) Centralist, Decentralists and Compromisers, In: *The Compact City* (eds. Jenks, M., Burton, E. and Williams, K.), E & FN Spon, London.

Burton, A.R., ed. (1992) *Report of the Steering Group on Architecture*, Royal Institute of British Architects, London.

Calthorpe, P. (1993) *The Next Urban Metropolis*, Princeton University Press, Princeton.

Cambridge Futures (2002) *Cambridge Futures Project*. Retrieved from the World-Wide-Web at http://www.hop.co.uk/cambridgefutures/ on 8 August 2003.

CMI (2003) *CMI mission*. Retrieved from the World Wide Web: http://www.cambridge-mit.org/about on 8 August 2003.

Dearing, R.F. (1997) *Higher Education in a Learning Society*, Her Majesty's Stationery Office (HMSO), London.

Department for Environment, Food and Rural Affairs (DEFRA) (2002) *Rural White Paper: Our Countryside – The Future – A Fair Deal for Rural England*, DEFRA, London.

Department for Environment, Transport and the Regions (DETR) (1999) *Indicators of Sustainable Development*. Retrieved from the World Wide Web: http://www.sustainable-development.gov.uk/indicators/index on 8 August 2003.

Department of Transport, Local Government and the Regions (DTLR) (2001) *Cambridge to Huntingdon Multi-Modal Study (CHUMMS)*, DTLR, London.

Egan, J. Sir (1998) *Rethinking Construction – The Report of the Construction Taskforce*, Department of Trade and Industry (DTI), London.

French, H. (2000) 'The Garden City'. In: *Impossible Worlds* (ed. Stetter, A.), Birkhauser, Basel.

Hewison, R. (1987) *The Heritage Industry*, Methuen, London.

Ibelings, H. (2000) *Artificial Landscape*, Netherlands Architecture Institute, Rotterdam.

Jenks, M., Burton, E. and Williams, K., eds. (1996) *The Compact City: A Sustainable Urban Form?* E & FN Spon, London.

Lowry, I. (1964) *A Model of Metropolis*, The Rand Corporation, Santa Monica, California.

Ricoeur, P., trans. and ed. J.B. Thomson (1981) *Hermeneutics and the Human Sciences: Essays on Language, Action and Interpretation*, Cambridge University Press, Cambridge.

Sainsbury, Lord J. (1999) *Biotechnology Clusters*, Department of Trade and Industry (DTI), London.

Segal Quince (1985) *The Cambridge Phenomenon (Parts 1 and 2)*, Segal Quince, Cambridge.

Segal Quince Wicksteed (2000) *The Cambridge Phenomenon Revisited (Parts 1 and 2)*, Segal Quince Wicksteed, Cambridge.

Steinberg, R.J., ed. (1999) *Handbook of Creativity*, Cambridge University Press, Cambridge.

Stott, K. and Walker, A. (1995) *Teamworking and Teambuilding*, Prentice Hall, London.

Van Blerck, H. (1999) *Landscape: 9 + 1 Young Dutch Landscape Architects*, NAi Publishers, Rotterdam.

Section Three

Aspects of Design for Sustainable Urban Forms

15

Mike Jenks and Nicola Dempsey

The Language and Meaning of Density

Introduction

One of the enduring themes behind the search for more
sustainable urban forms is that of the density of development.
Whether the debate has been about urban forms in general,
or more particular arguments about the compact city, higher
densities are seen as a significant component in achieving
sustainable development (Jenks *et al.*, 1996; Urban Task Force,
1999; Williams *et al.*, 2000). While, in the UK at least, the idea
is embodied in policy (DETR, 2000a, b; 2001), and in practice
for new development (ODPM, 2003), the idea is not as
straightforward, or new, as the many proponents would have
us believe. Breheny (1997) noted rightly that while density is
now top of the list, it is somewhat of a 'lost art'. There are
certainly many questions to resolve. If sustainable development
is so dependent on higher densities, then the question is higher
than what, and what does it mean? Is there any link between
the different physical forms implied by higher densities and
what is claimed to be its benefits? Indeed, is density a
meaningful concept when it comes to suggesting standards for
development, and the form it may take?

This chapter concentrates on the density of housing in the UK,
and the attempts through time to set and maintain density

standards. It considers some of the roots for the ideas behind both lowering and increasing densities, and the claims made for attempts to implement such standards. Delving into the past gives a perspective on the current debate, and shows that little may have changed. There appear to be clear cultural boundaries in the UK that mitigate any radical shift towards the forms of development that might be needed to assure sustainability. The chapter ends with a short speculation about the concept of density in a wider global context.

High density: overcrowding?

Arguably, there is a point in time when density came into the consciousness of politicians and the public in general. During the 19th century, towns and cities in Britain experienced a process of unprecedented rapid urbanisation. By the 1840s London was a huge city of 2½ million people, and the industrial cities of the North – for example, Birmingham, Leeds, Liverpool and Manchester – were growing with astonishing rapidity. The big issue was a combination of overcrowding, unsanitary conditions and poor health amongst the poor. Engels most vividly portrayed the living conditions of the mass of the population of 19th century cities between 1844 and 1845. In London, quoting a local preacher in Bethnal Green he noted that 'it is nothing unusual to find a man, his wife, four or five children, and, sometimes, both grandparents, all in one single room' (Engels, 1892 (1969 edn.) p. 62). Of particular interest here, he highlighted the built forms that were common, specifically housing courts (Figure 15.1) which were enclosed with buildings backing on to each other, and an emerging form of new development, the 'back-to-back' terraces (op. cit. see Figure 15.2). A similar pattern existed in many industrial towns, for example, areas with courts and back to backs in Liverpool resulted in densities of around 700 persons per acre (1730 persons per hectare) (Muthesius, 1982). Although the term density was not explicitly mentioned, the link between numbers of people living in a given area, and the form of residential development, had been implicitly made.

The problems of health, sanitation, water and slums were subject to legislation to ameliorate some of the worst excesses. However, it was the Public Health Act of 1875 that proved a landmark. It had 'three direct influences on building; it gave power to urban authorities to make building by[e]-laws, it established . . . the principle of building lines, and it required

Figure 15.1
A Victorian housing court.
(*Source:* Cadbury Schweppes, 2005.)

Figure 15.2
The back-to-back terrace: a high-density, overcrowded and unhealthy urban form. (*Source:* Engels, 1892 (1969 edn.) p. 89.)

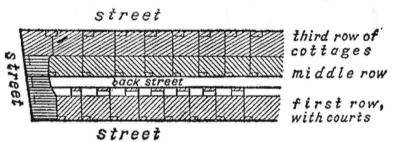

every authority to appoint a surveyor' (Edwards, 1981, p. 67). Effectively the bye-laws controlled the width of streets and prevented development from projecting beyond a building line. It led to a form of development that transformed cities throughout the UK into the early part of the 20th century, with straight streets in a grid pattern with uniform terraced housing (Figure 15.3). Bye-law housing spread rapidly to the suburbs, in a similar form, but with wider streets and slightly more spacious terraced houses. The density of this form of

289

Figure 15.3
Bye-law housing, Wood
Green, London.
(*Source*: Edwards, 1981.)

development in the cities was reckoned on average to be around 31–41 dwellings per acre (76.5–101 dwellings per hectare), but ranged between 60 and 200 persons per acre (150 and 500 persons per hectare), although it is hard to find agreement on, or a common form for the precise figures (Swenarton, 1981; Muthesius, 1982). Although overcrowding was reduced, this ubiquitous form of development was often built to poor standards, and still at reasonably high densities, and was perceived by some as failing to provide a sufficiently healthy and spacious environment for its inhabitants.

At the same time as the explosion of bye-law housing, other ideas were being developed. Philanthropic industrialists were building model villages at Port Sunlight near Liverpool in 1887 (by W.H. Lever, soap manufacturer), and at Bourneville near Birmingham in 1894 (by George Cadbury, chocolate manufacturer). These were developed at low densities of between 5 and 8 dwellings per acre (12 and 20 dwellings per hectare) (Burke, 1971). They gave inspiration and reinforcement to Ebenezer Howard's powerful advocacy for the 'Garden City', published in 1898. He gave no specific figure for housing density, but rather an indicative plot size, which has been interpreted as a density of 14.25 dwellings per acre (35 dwellings per hectare) (Osborn cited in Burke, 1971). In 1903, Howard raised capital to form a public company 'First Garden City Limited' and purchased a site at Letchworth about 55 km north of London. The new garden city was planned at a density of between 6 and 12 dwellings per acre (15 and 30 dwellings per hectare), and the designers were Raymond Unwin and Barry Parker (Figure 15.4).

From the mid-19th century to the first decade of the 20th century, cities expanded apace, with new development occurring at ever-decreasing densities, spreading out into the suburbs (Table 15.1). Even so, by the start of the First World War, living space for the many remained in dense and overcrowded areas, in housing that was in poor condition. Towards the end of the war, the government decided it needed to act to improve the conditions for those returning from the conflict. For the first time, government stepped in to set density standards, and as will be seen, the ideas of Howard and the influence of Unwin won the day. However, a small diversion is needed to understand what might be meant by the many figures used to express density.

Measuring density

It should be apparent from the above that there are difficulties in determining density figures. When looking back in time it is possible to make some approximations, but there are many differences, and this makes comparison problematic. One of the first problems is to clarify whether the density is measured and recorded as a gross or a net figure – as gross densities usually refer to a whole area and include all uses, net densities are solely concerned with residential uses. At the largest of scales gross figures are produced for countries and for cities, and these are normally expressed in persons per km^2 or per 1000 hectares (e.g. World Resources Institute, 1996; UN, 2002). Density

Figure 15.4
Low-density Letchworth garden
city. (*Source*: Edwards, 1981.)

Table 15.1
Densities of housing
1840–1914.[1]

	Approximate dates	Dwellings per hectare	Persons per hectare
Back-to-back housing	Pre-1875	385	1730
Bye-law housing (maximum)	1875–1914	110	500
Bye-law housing (minimum)	1875–1914	33	150
Model villages (maximum)	1887–1900	20	80
Model villages (minimum)	1887–1900	12	48
Garden city (maximum)	1903–1914	30	120
Garden city (minimum)	1903–1914	15	60

comparisons have been made between cities worldwide, and these have been broken down into the central/inner city, metropolitan areas, and metropolitan planning areas (e.g. Lloyd Jones, 2000; Richardson *et al.*, 2000). While of interest and use, there are uncertainties about boundary definitions and therefore accurate comparisons between countries.

However, for this chapter, and in the UK context, the key measurement used will be that of net residential density. Since 1918, a wide range of different measurements have been used including: persons per hectare; dwellings per hectare; habitable rooms per hectare; bed spaces per hectare, and floorspace per hectare (Woodford *et al.*, 1976). Today, three of these measures are still used – dwellings, habitable rooms and bed spaces per hectare – the former being the most common and the latter most rare (Breheny, 1997). The problem is that all these measures are largely incompatible, making it difficult to arrive at an accurate conversion of one set of figures into another. Research for the UK Government (DETR, 1998) recommended that dwellings per hectare become the common unit, and indeed it is the most frequently used by local authorities. This is further reinforced by guidance about net site density that defines what should be included in the measure – access roads, gardens, car parking, incidental open space and children's play areas (DETR, 2000b). Even so, London still uses habitable rooms as its measure, a hangover, it is claimed, from the Greater London Council (Lock, 1998; Llewelyn Davies, 2000),[2] although earlier DETR (1998) research suggested maintaining it.

Even if a measure such as dwellings per hectare is settled on, it still remains controversial. David Lock (1998, p. 323) suggests that density 'can be life-threatening when in the wrong hands'. Using net residential density alone fails to take into account wider issues of land capacity, mixed uses, and gives no guide for assessing aspects such as 'walkability' and the viability of public transport (Rudlin and Falk, 1999). For these issues, it is also necessary to measure gross densities. Another dimension to the measurement of density relates to peoples' perceptions of it and their subjective impressions of when high density is felt to be overcrowding (Alexander, 1993; Churchman, 1999) – an issue that is beyond the scope of this chapter. In other words, density is a bit of a minefield. To give a common base for the following comparisons, net density expressed in dwellings per hectare will be used, and if appropriate, persons per hectare. Inevitably some assumptions will have to be made where density standards are converted from one measure to another.

Government steps in

By the end of the First World War, it was acknowledged that much of the housing stock was in poor condition and that there was an estimated shortfall of 3–400,000 houses. A Parliamentary Select Committee was set up in 1918 under the chairmanship of Sir John Tudor Walters (of which Raymond Unwin was a member). The result was known as the Tudor Walters Report, and it provided the basis for a government housing manual setting out standards for housing development including those for density (Local Government Board, 1918; 1919). In parallel, an act called the Housing and Town Planning Act 1919 provided for subsidies for new housing for the first time, and by 1924 the Housing Act made the guidance on densities statutory (Jenks, 1983). The low-density standard of 12, or 8 houses per acre in rural areas (30, or 20 houses per hectare), became the norm for the inter-war period, and influenced the spread of a uniform suburbia.

The next landmark came towards the end of the Second World War with an influential report in 1944 under the chairmanship of Lord Dudley, the then Minister for Health (Central Housing Advisory Committee, 1944). There was a climate of criticism of the inter-war suburbs being aesthetically and socially monotonous, and the development of ideas that favoured mixed development and 'neighbourhood units' to promote 'social integration' (Burnett, 1978). The Dudley Report was backed up by guidance in Housing Manuals of 1944; 1949 (Ministry of Health, 1944; 1949) in which higher densities were encouraged in urban locations, and a variety of house types with supporting shops and facilities (Jenks, 1983). The density standards were expressed in persons per acre, ranging from 30 in rural areas to 120 in urban areas (approximately between 25 and 100 dwellings per hectare).

Central government continued to produce guidance, promoting standards for higher densities and varied housing forms. A handbook in 1952 (MoHLG, 1952) explored a range of density standards for different types of housing and housing forms, using the measure for habitable rooms per acre. The densities examined for 2-storey houses ranged from 65 to 105 habitable rooms per acre (15 to 30 dwellings per hectare); for

3-storey housing 85 to 135 (20 to 35 dwellings per hectare); and for flats 150 to 200 (40 to 70 dwellings per hectare). The recommendations on densities were complex, and became fairly impenetrable when advice was given about development comprising a mixture of flats and houses. Here a maximum of 90 habitable rooms per acre (25 dwellings per hectare) was suggested, but this could include flats at 180 and houses at 80 habitable rooms per acre, but with a seemingly infinite number of possible combinations. Equally complex guidance was given about gross densities across whole towns, and included standards for open space and provision of facilities.

Ten years later government, in a Planning Bulletin, was advocating even higher standards for urban areas with densities of between 60 and 140 persons per acre (50 and 115 dwellings per hectare) and between 12 and 20 dwellings per acre (30 and 50 dwellings per hectare) for new development elsewhere (MoHLG, 1962). The 1962 Bulletin noted that it was possible to have a good environment at all these densities, but also to have a 'poor environment at any density' (*op. cit.* p. 8). The critical stance against low-density suburbs was not restricted to government, for example, industry promoted studies inspired by Gordon Cullen in *A Town Called Alcan* suggesting densities of between 90 and 125 dwellings per hectare (Alcan, 1964), or polemics such as *Civilia: The End of Sub Urban Man* (de Wolfe, 1971) advocating a high-density city in place of the suburban New Towns of the time. Figure 15.5 shows conceptual ideas for the city centre and some residential areas.

Despite the advocacy and standards, most development occurred at the edge of towns and cities at relatively low densities. During the 1970s many county statutory development plans had density standards of a maximum of 15 dwellings per acre or much less (35 dwellings per hectare) (Jenks, 1983). The structure and local plans of the 1970s and 1980s gave little significance to density (DETR, 1998), and although almost all counties had design guides for housing layout, density appeared to have been dropped from their agenda. Breheny (1997, p. 84) noted that planners had 'not taken densities very seriously for many years'. His survey recorded that local authority plan-based standards averaged out at 28.8 dwellings per hectare, with 10 the lowest in Hartlepool and 68 the highest in Barking. This needs to be set against the average density of 25 dwellings per hectare achieved in the UK in around the year 2000 (DTLR, 2002). Yet again, government has responded, arguing for higher densities, with

Figure 15.5
Civilia – illustrating concepts of
high-density city and living areas
using a collage of developments
current at the time.
(*Source*: de Wolfe, 1971.)

Figure 15.5
(continued)

recommendations between 30 and 50 dwellings per hectare for new development, and certainly no less than 30 dwellings per hectare (HM Government, 2000). Evidence suggests that while most local authorities have responded by increasing density requirements, there has been resistance in some areas. Also, house builders, while feeling they had acted to increase densities, reported many barriers to achieving the change (ODPM, 2003). But for some these increases are not enough. The CPRE (Campaign for the Protection of Rural England) argues that the expansion of London along the Thames Gateway should be developed at an average of 90 dwellings per hectare (CPRE, 2004) – a proposal not too distant from the ideas of Civilia in 1971.

Over a period of more than 80 years, density standards have changed marginally for residential areas, and the reality has

Table 15.2
Density standards (dwellings per
hectare) in the UK, 1918–2000.[3]

Date	Houses		Houses and flats		Flats	
	Minimum	Maximum	Minimum	Maximum	Minimum	Maximum
1918 (Tudor Walters)	20	30				
1944 (Dudley)	25	25	40	60		100
1952 (MoHLG)	15	35			40	70
1962 (MoHLG)	30	75	50	75		115
1970–1980 (Local Authority Development Plans)		35				
1999 (Urban Task Force)	35	40				
2000 (Planning Policy Guidance Note 3 (PPG 3))	30	50				

hardly changed at all from the 1944 Dudley Report. Table 15.2 compares standards over this period (1918–2000), and it can be seen that the new standards for higher densities are in fact rather tame, and certainly not quite as radical as many would have us believe.

Same arguments, different forms?

If the advocacy for standards appeared to have such limited impact, then what was it about the arguments that encouraged government to persist? Today the arguments are well known for increasing the density of development and creating more compact forms, consequently ensuring a mix of uses, the containment of urban 'sprawl' and achieving social and economic diversity and vitality (Jenks *et al.*, 1996; Urban Task Force, 1999). Despite their current currency, the debate is strangely familiar.

Analysis of a selection of relevant UK Government publications since the 1950s shows a consistent trend for the promotion of higher densities, predicated, perhaps, on a modernist anti-suburban agenda. In the 1950s, key guidance on *The Density of Residential Areas* showing increases in density standards was based on the premise of ascertaining 'the least amount of land required to satisfy needs in an urban residential area' (MoHLG, 1952, p. 64). In addition to the concerns over 'losses of agricultural land resulting from urban expansion' (p. 66), appropriate densities should allow for: a variety of dwellings; enough space for amenities; convenience to shops, schools and other facilities and a close relationship to the existing town or city. The standards were related to different contexts from rural

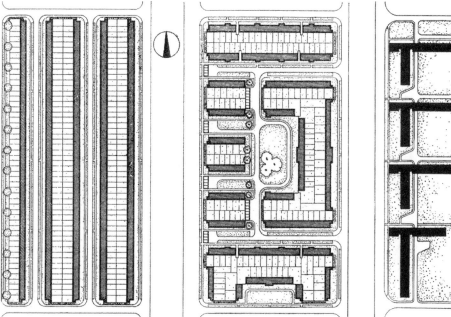

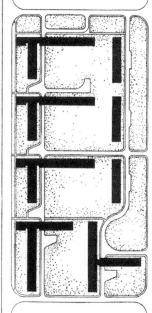

Figure 15.6
1952 – 2-storey houses at 30 and 20 dwellings per hectare, respectively.
(*Source*: MoHLG, 1952.)

Figure 15.7
1952 – flats at 70 dwellings per
hectare. (*Source*: MoHLG, 1952.)

to urban, and different forms of development were illustrated, some representing good practice, some showing limitations. For example, the high-density form of 2-storey terraced housing in streets with little or no open space was seen as excessive and liable to produce monotonous forms. A lower density was preferred with the implication that this was good practice (Figure 15.6). Development of flats was typical of its time (Figure 15.7), but it was the design ideas for mixtures of houses and flats that were given pride of place in the publication (Figure 15.8).

In the next decade similar arguments were reinforced and some were added. Central to the guidance on increased density was 'the preservation of good agricultural land, the prevention of urban sprawl and the protection of the countryside – all of which point to the need for compact development, closely integrated with existing development and making the fullest use of available land' (MoHLG, 1962, p. 8). Again, illustrations were provided to show what government had in mind for higher-density development (Figures 15.9–15.11). By the 1970s it was noted that factors advocating higher densities included 'nearness to the central area, place of work, transport facilities or an open space', and that within an overall density standard

Figure 15.8
1952 – flats (6 storeys) and
houses (3 storeys) at an average
density of 25 dwellings per
hectare. (*Source*: MoHLG, 1952.)

there could be variations within a development (Department of the Environment, 1976). The impact of higher densities on community and social factors was also considered in government research (MoHLG, 1970; Department of the Environment, 1973; 1975).

Effectively, most of the arguments now in vogue had been made decades ago, namely for urban containment, compact forms, efficient use of land, a mix of building types, and proximity to facilities, transport and work. Yet, despite the familiarity, there is something new. The arguments for compact forms and higher density in the 1990s and present decade are promoted in terms of sustainability (see Table 15.3). If the earlier arguments had an anti-suburban bias, the arguments of the 1990s were more likely to have an anti-car slant. The link between higher densities and forms that encouraged a modal shift to more sustainable forms of transport was made (e.g. Jenks *et al.*, 1996; Williams *et al.*, 2000; Schoon, 2001), and was reflected in government publications and policy. The Urban Task Force (2000, p. 64) noted that 'higher densities allow a greater number of public amenities and transport facilities to be located within walking distance, thus reducing the need for the car and contributing to urban sustainability'. Government guidance implemented the ideas to locate development near to transport (DETR, 2001) and for denser development, again related to

Figure 15.9
1962 – 100 dwellings per hectare, Alton Estate, Wandsworth, London. (*Source*: MoHLG, 1962.)

Figure 15.10
1962 – 60 dwellings per hectare, Gleadless Valley Estate, Sheffield. (*Source*: MoHLG, 1962.)

Figure 15.11
1962 – 50 dwellings per hectare,
Highsett, Cambridge. (*Source:*
MoHLG, 1962.)

Table 15.3
Reasons put forward to make
the case for higher densities.

1950s to 1970s	1990s to 2000s
• Preserve agricultural/amenity land	• Preserve agricultural/amenity land
• Contain urban sprawl	• Contain urban sprawl
• Use land efficiently	• Use land efficiently
• Compact forms	• Compact forms
• Mixture of building types	• Mixture of building types **and uses**
• Communities and social issues	• **Sustainable** communities and social issues
• Proximity to facilities, transport and work	• Proximity to facilities, transport and work
	• Sustainability and environmental issues
	• Reduced car dependency and encouragement of walking, cycling and public transport use

transport with strictures to avoid housing development which makes inefficient use of land and provide more intensive housing development in and around existing centres and close to public transport nodes (DETR, 2000b). The strong emphasis on the link to transport was based on the environmental argument of reducing vehicle emissions and thus lessening one of the causes of climate change. These more recent arguments have been associated with much cited examples seen as good practice. Examples of acclaimed developments from 1990s to 2000s are shown in Figures 15.12–15.14.

While the arguments have remained much the same over time, albeit with some distinction in emphasis and standpoint, the difference in the style of development for any given density is quite marked. Indeed, without the illustrations, it could be hard to distinguish one document from another.

How high is high?

The arguments for higher densities over the past 60 years in the UK also have resonance in other parts of the world (Jenks and

Figure 15.12
BedZed, London.
(*Source*: Dawson, 2004.)

Figure 15.13
Greenwich Millennium Village,
London. (*Source*: Dawson,
2004.)

Burgess, 2000). This should be no surprise. In countries such as
the USA, where there is a profligate use of land and widespread
suburban sprawl, arguments for higher-density development
have begun to emerge, and have been embodied in ideas such
as those of the 'New Urbanists' (Duany and Plater-Zyberk,

Figure 15.14
Homes for Change, Manchester.
(*Source*: Dawson, 2004.)

Figure 15.15
Three-storey town houses in
Northern Ireland, thought by
many to be too high a density.
(*Source*: Mike Jenks.)

1994). In other parts of the world, especially Asia where there is rapid urbanisation, similar concerns exist about the containment and sustainability of megacities and huge urban agglomerations. While the arguments may be similar, the concept of 'higher' is entirely relative. The 30–50 dwellings per hectare recommended as an advance in the UK, is particular and mediated by the density of most current developments

Figure 15.16
New development in Hong Kong
at a culturally acceptable
density. (*Source*: Mike Jenks.)

(25 dwellings per hectare), and by an informed judgement as to what densities might be acceptable to future residents. Outside the UK, these standards may represent a threshold that is either unacceptably high to some, or far too low for the cultural expectations of different countries (Figures 15.15 and 15.16).

Table 15.4
Comparative density of selected cities worldwide.[4]

	Inner city	Metropolitan region
Beijing	4.7	1.1
Cairo	4.4	8.0
London	**1**	**1**
Los Angeles	0.4	0.3
Mexico City	1.9	3.6
New York	1.4	0.9
Paris	3.1	1.1
Sydney	0.3	0.1
Tokyo	1.9	1.7

Worldwide there are huge variations in density, and therefore both the form and style of urban development. Table 15.4 gives an indication based on gross-density figures of a selection of cities across the world. The figures show London as the baseline and other cities are compared to show relative densities of the inner city and wider metropolitan region of each. It makes a small point about context and therefore the likely meaning of 'higher' in different locations. There is no 'one size to fit all' – a variety will be needed 'to meet the needs between and within countries, regions and towns' (Churchman, 1999). What is clear is that while the arguments for increases in density may be transferable, density standards and, to an extent forms of development, most definitely are not.

Conclusion

The high level of consensus amongst the arguments for increasing density, and the current link to urban sustainability should not disguise the problem. Density, if considered alone, is problematic and not of itself a solution. A direct link between standards set and the style and particular form a development takes, the level of standards claimed to be high, and what may be acceptable in different locations and cultures has not yet been established. Density may be of use as one instrument amongst others to achieve the efficient use of land and sustainability, but even this has its difficulties. Where net density is used, it only takes residential areas into account, and omits all the other, desirable mixed uses. Gross density takes other land uses into the calculation, but the figure is merely reduced and borders on being meaningless as there is no way of measuring the other uses. Thus it is difficult to assess the intensity of use of an area, how vital it might be or whether it is only active during the day and closes at night.

There is, however, a general relationship between net density and the form residential development might take. It is evident that the higher the density required, the more it will force development to take certain forms, whether all 2- to 3-storey development at relatively low densities, a mixture of houses, flats and maisonettes at medium to high densities, or developments comprising almost all flats and apartments at high density (e.g. MoHLG, 1952; Schoon, 2001, p. 243). And of course, for very high densities such as those in Hong Kong, it forces the construction of very high buildings, and some distinct and different forms (see Chapter 8). Beyond these broad categories, the relationship with density is more one of fashion and style – the illustrations in this chapter indicate how taste has changed over time for developments of similar densities.

Perhaps, if the claimed benefits of higher densities are to be achieved, the key is less the density standard, but more the style and image that such densities might portray – and the level of acceptability of such densities (and styles) in the wider cultural context. In the UK, the lifestyle choice is still largely one of flight from the city to low-density suburbs and the country, but with some counter movement by small numbers back to large cities (Champion, 2004). Setting higher-density standards is unlikely to change peoples' hearts and minds, or for them to suddenly see the benefits of what is claimed to be a more sustainable form in which to live. High densities may only work if what is developed can demonstrate that a good quality of life can be achieved. It has been suggested that high-density living has some 'competitive advantage' in relation to convenience, lifestyle and environmental amenities' (Peirce, 2002). But arguably more important is that the lifestyle choice is seen to be fashionable, and above all desirable.

Acknowledgements

The authors are grateful to Dr Stephen Green, Sheffield Hallam University, for undertaking the initial literature search for this chapter, and for his contribution to the jointly authored presentation of the same name, at the 5th Symposium of the International Urban Planning and Environment Association in Oxford 2002.

Notes

1. The sources include: Burke, Engels, Edwards, Muthesius, Swenarton and Wohl. The figures are all converted from imperial figures. Conversions to and from dwellings per hectare to persons per hectare are based on an average family size of 4.5 in the 19th century, and of 4 in the first 14 years of the 20th century.
2. The use of habitable rooms per acre or hectare derived from the Housing Cost Yardstick introduced in the early 1960s (MoHLG, 1963).
3. Conversions from acres to hectares have been made, rounding figures up or down to the nearest 5 dwellings.
4. The figures are drawn from Richardson (2000) and Lloyd Jones (2000) who gave densities in persons per km^2. The figures are problematic as they differ for the same cities in some cases, and the boundaries and root sources are not clear. Nevertheless, they give a reasonable level of consensus about relative densities. Table 15.4 should therefore be treated with caution, as it is only an indication of differences.

References

Alcan (1964) *A Town Called Alcan*, Alcan Industries Limited, De Montfort Press, Leicester.

Alexander, E. (1993) Density Measures: A Review and Analysis. *Journal of Architectural and Planning Research*, **10(3)**: 181–201.

Breheny, M. (1997) Local Authorities and Residential Densities – An Attitude Problem? *Town and Country Planning*, **63(3)**: 84–90.

Burke, G. (1971) *Towns in the Making*, Edward Arnold (Publishers) Ltd., London.

Burnett, J. (1978) *A Social History of Housing 1815–1970*, David & Charles, Newton Abbot.

Central Housing Advisory Committee (1944) *The Design of Dwellings*, HMSO, London.

Champion, T. (2004) The Census and the Cities. *Town and Country Planning*, **73(1)**: 20–22.

Churchman, A. (1999) Disentangling the Concept of Density. *Journal of Planning Literature*, **13(4)**: 389–411.

CPRE (2004) *Thames Gateway: Making Progress*, CPRE, London.

Dawson, R. (2004) *Towards Good Practice in Sustainable Urban Land Use*, Bristol LA21 Land Use Group and The Architecture Centre, Bristol, Woodside Press, Bristol.

Department of the Environment (1973) *High Density Housing: A Current DOE Development Project*, Housing Development Directorate, London.

Department of the Environment (1975) *The Social Effects of Living Off the Ground*, Housing Development Directorate, London.

Department of the Environment (1976) *Residential Density in Development Briefs*, Development Advice Note 2, HMSO, London.

Department of the Environment, Transport and the Regions (DETR) (1998) *The Use of Density in Urban Planning*, Department of the Environment, Transport and the Regions, HMSO, London.

Department of the Environment, Transport and the Regions (DETR) (2000a) *Our Towns and Cities: The Future – Delivering an Urban Renaissance*, White Paper Cm 4911, HMSO, London.

Department of the Environment, Transport and the Regions (DETR) (2000b) *Planning Policy Guidance Note 3: Housing (PPG3)*, The Stationery Office, London.

Department of the Environment, Transport and the Regions (DETR) (2001) *Planning Policy Guidance Note 13: Transport (PPG13)*, The Stationery Office, London.

Department for Transport, Local Government and the Regions (DTLR) (2002) *Land Use Change in England: Residential Development to 2001*, Statistical Release LUCS-17, London.

de Wolfe, I. (1971) Civilia: The End of Sub Urban Man. *The Architectural Review*, **CXLIX(892)**: 327–408.

Duany, A. and Plater-Zyberk, E. (1994) The Neighbourhood and the District. In: *The New Urbanism: Toward and Architecture of Community* (ed. Katz, P.), McGraw-Hill Inc., New York, xvii–xx.

Edwards, A. (1981) *The Design of Suburbia*, Pembridge Press, London.

Engels, F. (1892 (1969 edition)) *The Condition of the Working Classes in England*, Granada Publishing Limited, St Albans, UK.

HM Government (2000) *The Government's Response to the Environment, Transport and Regional Affairs (Select Committee) Seventeenth Report, Housing: PPG3*, The Stationery Office, London.

Jenks, M. (1983) *The Relationship between Design Guidance and the Layout of Public Sector Housing Estates*, unpublished PhD Thesis, Oxford Polytechnic, Oxford.

Jenks, M., Burton, E. and Williams, K., eds. (1996) *The Compact City: A Sustainable Urban Form?* E & FN Spon, London.

Jenks, M. and Burgess, R. (2000) *Compact Cities: Sustainable Urban Forms for Developing Countries*, Spon Press, London.

Llewelyn Davies (2000) *Sustainable Residential Quality: Exploring the Housing Potential of Large Sites*, London Planning Advisory Committee (LPAC), London.

Lloyd Jones, T. (2000) Compact City Policies for Megacities, In: *Compact Cities: Sustainable Urban Forms for Developing Countries* (eds. Jenks, M. and Burgess, R.), Spon Press, London.

Local Government Board (1918) *Report of the Committee on Building Construction in Connection with the Provision of Dwellings for the Working Classes*, HMSO, London.

Local Government Board (1919) *Housing Manual on the Preparation of State Aided Housing Schemes*, HMSO, London.

Lock, D. (1998) Higher than what? *Town and Country Planning*, **67(10)**: 323.

Ministry of Health (1944) *Housing Manual 1944*, HMSO, London.

Ministry of Health (1949) *Housing Manual 1949*, HMSO, London.

Ministry of Housing and Local Government (MoHLG) (1952) *The Density of Residential Areas*, HMSO, London.

Ministry of Housing and Local Government (MoHLG) (1962) *Residential Areas: Higher Densities*, Planning Bulletin 2, HMSO, London.

Ministry of Housing and Local Government (MoHLG) (1970) *Families Living at High Density*, Design Bulletin 21, HMSO, London.

Muthesius, S. (1982) *The English Terraced House*, Yale University Press, New Haven and London.

Office of the Deputy Prime Minister (ODPM) (2003) *Delivering Planning Policy for Housing: PPG3 Implementation Study*, HMSO, London.

Osborn, F. (1946) *Green-Belt Cities*, Evelyn, Adams & Mackay, London (cited in Burke, 1971).

Peirce, S. (2002) Selling Urban Housing in London: Can High-Density Urban Living be sold to a Sceptical British Public? *European Planning Studies*, **10(8)**: 955–970.

Richardson, H., Bae Chang-Hee, C. and Baxamusa, M. (2000) Compact Cities in Developing Countries: Assessment and Implications. In: *Compact Cities: Sustainable Urban Forms for Developing Countries* (eds. Jenks, M. and Burgess, R.), Spon Press, London.

Rudlin, D. and Falk, N. (1999) *Building the 21st Century Home: The Sustainable Urban Neighbourhood*, Architectural Press, Oxford.

Schoon, N. (2001) *The Chosen City*, Spon Press, London.

Swenarton, M. (1981) *Homes Fit for Heroes*, Heinemann Educational Books, London.

UN, Department of Economic and Social Affairs, Population Division (2002) *World Urbanisation Prospects: The 2001 Revision*, United Nations, New York.

Urban Task Force (1999) *Towards and Urban Renaissance*, E & FN Spon, London.

Williams, K., Burton, E. and Jenks, M., eds. (2000) *Achieving Sustainable Urban Forms*, E & FN Spon, London.

Wohl, A. (1977) *The Eternal Slum: Housing and Social Policy in Victorian London*, Edward Arnold, London.

Woodford, G., Williams, K. and Hill, N. (1976) *The Value of Standards for the External Environment, Department of the Environment*, HMSO, London.

World Resources Institute (1996) *World Resources: A Guide to the Urban Environment*, World Resources Institute, Oxford University Press, Oxford.

Urban Densities, Quality of Life and Local Facility Accessibility in Principal Japanese Cities

Introduction

The compact city is an important urban spatial model that has emerged since the Commission of the European Community published its *Green Paper* on the Urban Environment in 1990 (Frey, 1999). Urban compactness is perceived as one of the essential elements that make up the sustainable city. According to Williams *et al.*, urban forms that are more sustainable than typical traditional forms are 'in the main ... characterized by compactness (in various forms), mixed uses and interconnected street layouts, supported by strong public transport networks, environmental controls and high standards of urban management' (2000, p. 355).

This chapter will examine the relationship that high urban densities of the compact city have in relation to the quality of life of its residents and the levels of accessibility to local facilities in Japanese cities. Firstly, the relationship between urban densities and selected aspects of quality of life in sample cities will be examined, using governmental statistical data. Secondly, the conditions and range of levels of accessibility to local facilities in relation to various urban densities will be investigated, with reference to statistical data relating to the case study. Forty-nine Japanese cities have been investigated in this case study analysis. For the purpose of this study, the cities were divided into five groups: *mega-cities* (Tokyo and Osaka); *semi-mega cities* (including Yokohama and Kyoto); *local cities* (populated by around 1 million inhabitants, including Hiroshima and Nagasaki); and two groups of *smaller, regional-centre cities* (which include Aomori and Nagano, and Nara and Wakayama). The characteristics of each grouping of cities will be discussed, and the methodology behind the categorization of the cities will be described. The intensity of the relationships between density and accessibility in these cities will be analysed by correlation analysis. Finally, conclusions will be presented regarding the implications that high densities have for levels of accessibility and the quality of life of urban residents, as well as some comment offered on the applicability of density as an indicator for accessibility.

The compact city and sustainability

It is generally accepted that high residential density is an essential element of the compact city. According to Burton, 'the so-called compact city … is taken to mean a relatively high-density, mixed-use city' (2000, p. 1969). Burton goes onto argue that high densities, along with a good public transportation infrastructure, which encourages people to walk and cycle rather than to drive their cars, go some way towards realizing aspirations for the sustainable city. These aspirations are based on sustainable urban development, defined in the *Brundtland Report* as meeting 'the needs of the present without compromising the ability of future generations to meet their own needs' (WCED, 1987, p. 43). Elkin *et al.* (1991) list four underlying principles of sustainable urban development: futurity, environment (in that the full environmental costs of all human activities must be taken into account), equity (that there should be equitable access to resources for all) and participation (referring to a democratic process in decision-making that affects the population). It is this third principle, that of equity, which is the primary focus of this chapter. What is the relationship that the high density of the compact city has on accessibility to local facilities?

The compact city and high densities

Travel behaviour which suits urban life, mostly, in the compact city would consist of sustained public transport use, walking and cycling, and minimal car use. A high-density urban form can incorporate such sustainable travel behaviour easily, but may not adequately support the individual car driver. However, many cities suffer from high congestion and air pollution because of the prevalence of the car as the primary mode of transport. A public transport system, which links up with opportunities for walking and cycling, that realistically reflects the needs of its residents and workforce in getting them where they need to go, quickly and efficiently, is an essential and complementary component of the compact city.

It is also well cited that the high-density urban form is favourable to the convenient location of local facilities. The high-density, mixed-use urban model has been strongly advocated in the pursuit of the sustainable city, and is dependent on good local accessibility for residents to the services and facilities that they use on a day-to-day basis. Thomas and Cousins state that the components of compact urban forms which typically consist of a high-density development area 'approximately 5–10 minutes' walk (about 400–600 m) from the centre to edge' up to one mile from the nearest 'central public transport stop' (1996, pp. 328–329). The centre of such a development area should contain services and facilities, such as food shops, schools, a doctor's surgery and public space (Barton *et al.*, 1995). The Town and Country Planning Association (TCPA) in the UK go further than this, asserting that 'accessibility to facilities should be the guiding factor in moving towards more sustainable forms of development rather than density *per se*' (Gossop, 1990, p. 342).

Reducing the need for private transport use is one of the aims of sustainability. By increasing residents' accessibility to services and facilities through situating them locally could reduce transport use. If appropriate local facilities are located within walkable distances from the home, the necessity of owning and using private cars is diminished. It, therefore, follows that the most efficient way in which to make this work, is by ensuring that the densities of urban areas are:

1. high enough to support the services and facilities locally provided (including the transportation and infrastructure)
2. large enough to attract employers to the area to capitalize on the workforce in the area

It is a cyclical process: if people use and support the services in the area, more employers will move into the area further supporting the area, increasing the need for quality public transport, reducing the need for the car, and increasing the range of services and facilities for residents to make use of.

While this theoretical discussion appears convincing on paper, there are many reasons why successful high-density living is currently not the case in the world's cities. These range from an apparent need for large living spaces (often with a garden and/or garage), a desire to live away from the city which was often a result of post-war planning (certainly in the UK, (Clapson, 1998)) and a strong attachment to the car that many urban dwellers will seemingly not give up. In Japan, such phenomena are also occurring: counter-urbanization has persisted since the 1960s; residential densities have fallen and car ownership has risen dramatically.

The compact city in Japan: policy

Recently interest in the concept of 'compact city' has been demonstrated in Japanese planning. Some new policies illustrate a change of direction from urban sprawl towards a more compact urban form. For example, new development in suburban areas has been restricted and urban regeneration zoning has been introduced in metropolitan areas, particularly in Tokyo. There have been many policies introduced for the revitalization of city-centre areas, including the introduction of more pedestrian-oriented urban zones.

Several characteristics of the Japanese planning system should be noted:

- Radical, clear and consistent changes in planning strategies are not decided by central government
- Policies and implementation can have various aims and expectations, for example, economic revitalization, countermeasures against public finance difficulties, regeneration of declining urban centres, reform of confused regional spatial conditions and environmental issues. They are introduced in response to factors such as projections of low population growth and of an overall ageing population

Population change and growing car use in Japan

The rate of population growth in Japan had been consistently high for 100 years until around 1980 when it began to slow down considerably. From the 1960s to around the same time as

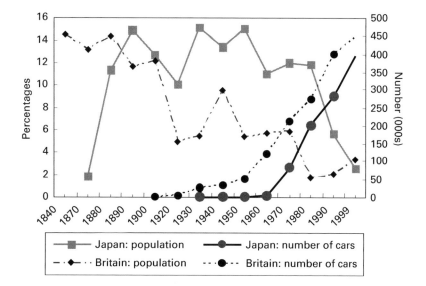

Figure 16.1
Percentage of population change and car ownership in Britain and Japan.

the population decreases, economic growth, large-scale urbanization and motorization occurred. Figure 16.1 shows a comparison of population change and car ownership in Japan and Britain. Both the countries have experienced some population decrease in the last 50 or so years, with Britain's population increasing gradually between 1985 and 1995, and more rapidly to date. Japan, on the other hand, apart from a period of slow growth from 1960 to 1980, has experienced rapid decline. Car ownership has increased significantly in both the countries, which occurred earlier for Britain, around the mid-1950s, and in the mid-1960s in Japan. The urban forms that had been constructed to house such large populations were strongly affected by changes in economic and social conditions. They manifested themselves in transportation growth, planning policies and development control. In addition to these factors, relaxed planning controls encouraged urban sprawl.

Designated land use in Japan

Table 16.1 shows the composition of national land in Japan by designated planning use. Japanese City Planning Areas (CPAs) and Urbanization Promotion Areas (UPAs), cover 25.7% and 3.7% of national land area, respectively, within which a high proportion of the population resides. Densely built-up areas are defined in the Japanese census as Densely Inhabited Districts (DIDs[1]). The percentage of DIDs of the total national area

Designated land planning use	% land area (total: 377,863 km^2)	Densities (persons per hectare)
Densely Inhabited Districts (DIDs)	3.2	66.3
Urbanization Promotion Area (UPA)	3.7	58.4
City Planning Area (CPA)	25.7	11.9
Out of City Planning Area (OCPA)	67.4	3.3

Table 16.1
Composition of Japanese National Land by designated planning use (based on 1995 figures).

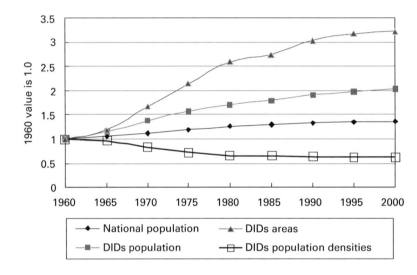

Figure 16.2
Changes in DIDs in Japan, 1960–2000 (over 40 persons per hectare).

stands at 3.2% with the highest residential density of 66.3 persons per hectare. The conclusion to be drawn from this table is that while the DIDs and UPAs constitute a small proportion of Japan's total land area, they can house high densities of people. If the CPAs were to be transformed into UPAs or DIDs, the population capacity would increase at least fivefold.

Although Japanese cities have a wide range of different levels of urban density (illustrated in Table 16.1), the overall average densities in urban areas are generally higher than in Western country cities. As discussed earlier, the Japanese population has been declining since modern urbanization took hold after the 1960s. Figure 16.2 shows the change of population and densities in DIDs; the figure for each measure in 1960 is set at 1. This clearly illustrates that densely inhabited areas have expanded threefold and that urban population densities have fallen by half. This indicates that overall, the popularity of the DIDs (at least in the eyes of the planning authorities) is increasing. The fact that overall densities in DIDs have halved might indicate that the acceptability of high density has been decreasing or that planning practices themselves have been in favour of lower densities. However, Figure 16.4 does show that since the 1980s, the density level has stabilized, which may be a sign of hope for supporters of the compact city in Japan.

Case study: 49 Japanese cities

The cities selected for this case study are the principal cities in Japan (Figure 16.3). *Principal cities* are defined as the large, local capital cities in each prefecture. They are distributed throughout Japan and on the whole, typify the regional characteristics in which they are located. The populations of these cities range from 0.14 million in Yamaguchi city to 7.97 million in Tokyo (special wards). The residential population densities range from 41 to 128 persons per hectare in each city's DIDs. The cities were divided into five groups: *Group A* incorporating the mega cities of Tokyo and Osaka; *Group B*, made up of semi-mega cities including Nagoya and Yokohama; *Group C*, made up of local cities, of populations of around 1 million, including Matuyama and Urawa; and *Groups D and E*, made up of smaller regional-centre cities, which include Aomori and Nagano, and Nara and Wakayama.

Division of case study cities into groups

Case study: densities

Figure 16.4 shows that in 1960, the average residential population density in the selected cities' DIDs was 105.6 people per hectare. Between then and the 1980s, it fell rapidly, down to 68.9 in 1980. Density has continuedto decrease overall, but at a much slower rate than the 20-year period between 1960 and 1980. There have been differences in the densities amongst the cities themselves. The reduction in larger high-density cities was greater than in other, smaller cities. Figure 16.5 shows the population density for Tokyo, which after peaking in 1965, dropped off considerably until the 1980s. After the 1980s, densities in DIDs in most of the cities began to increase, particularly after 1990. In Tokyo, DID densities continued to fall and in the past 5–10 years, have only increased slightly.

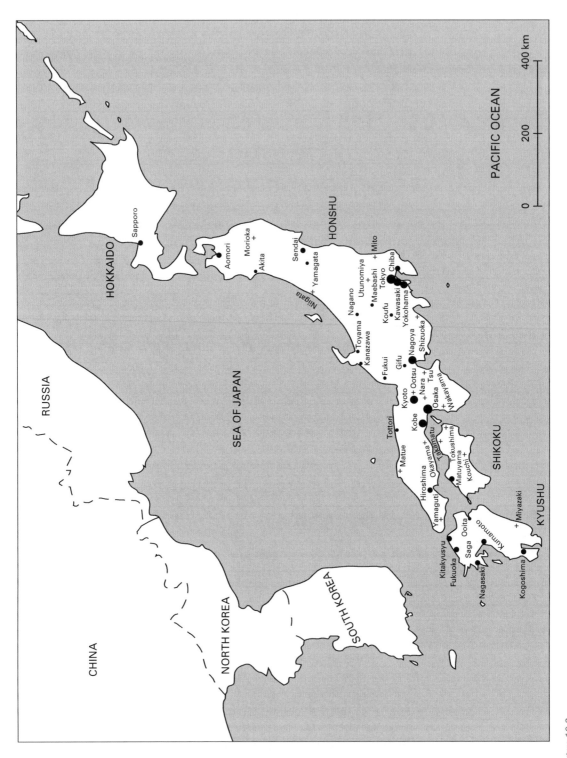

Figure 16.3
Japanese principal cities.

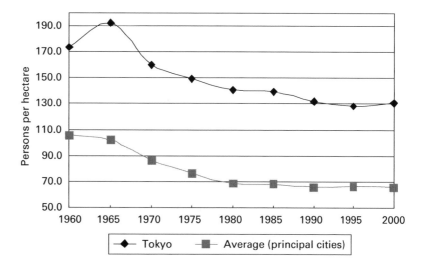

Figure 16.4
DID population densities in Japanese principal cities and Tokyo: 1960–2000.

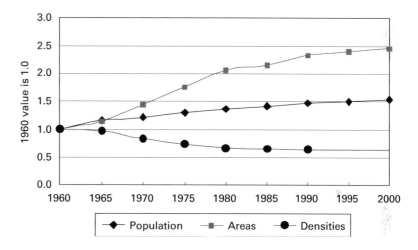

Figure 16.5
Changes in population, area and densities of DIDs.

Figure 16.5 shows the changes in population, area and densities in the DIDs of the principal cities. After 1960, DID's areas in the sample cities had more than doubled, which is lower than the national figure for DIDs which had more than tripled. The population in DIDs increased by a factor of 0.64, which is also lower than the national average for DIDs population which was doubled since 1960. Population density in the principal cities was much the same as the national average.

Rapid urbanization: the case of Kanazawa city

Kanazawa is one of the cities under examination, and in 1960, had a population of about 225,000. Kanazawa was originally a

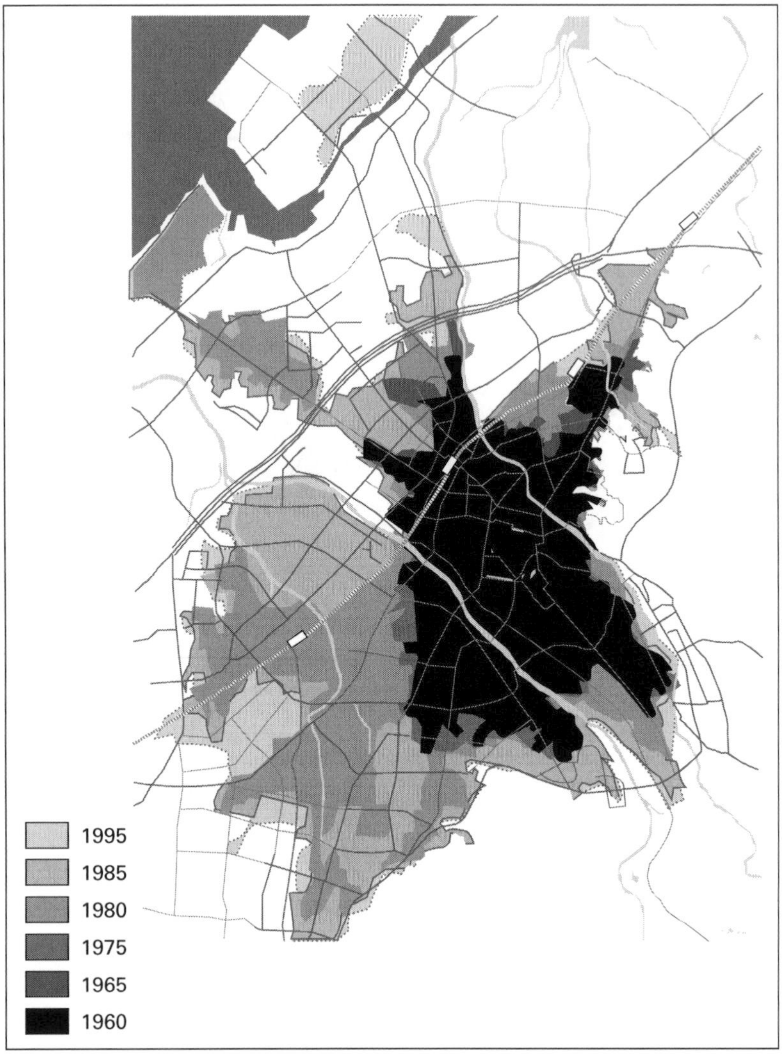

Figure 16.6
Rapid urban sprawl in Kanazawa
city: 1960–1995.

Legend:

- 1995
- 1985
- 1980
- 1975
- 1965
- 1960

castle town in the Edo era from the 17th century to the middle of the 19th century. The size of the city area had not expanded markedly until the 1960s when it began to rapidly increase in size (see Figure 16.6).

Table 16.2 shows the changes in population, area and density in the DID of Kanazawa between 1960 and 1990. While the population has increased consistently since 1960 (to 450,000 in 1995), the population density has markedly decreased. As a consequence, the area of Kanazawa has also increased to accommodate higher populations but at lower densities. The population density has actually increased since the late 1990s (not tabulated here), but only gradually. The distribution of density across Kanazawa's DID is shown in Figure 16.7. Looking at this

Table 16.2
Population, area and population
density of Kanazawa:
1960–1990.

Year	Population	Area in hectares	Population density persons per hectare
1960	225,000	1600	141
1970	251,000	2500	100
1990	370,000	5160	61

Figure 16.7
Population densities in
Kanazawa city's Urbanisation
Promotion Areas in 1995.

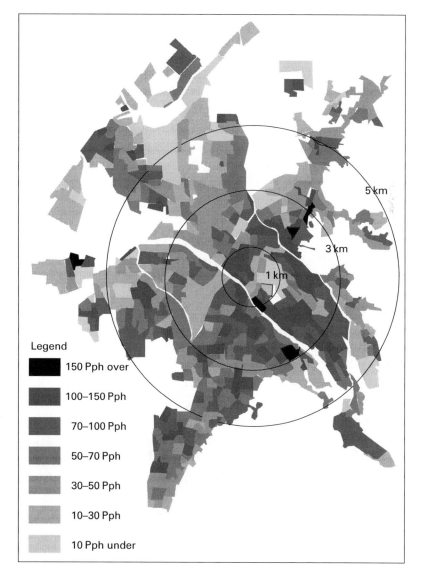

Legend

150 Pph over

100–150 Pph

70–100 Pph

50–70 Pph

30–50 Pph

10–30 Pph

10 Pph under

together with Figure 16.6 (which clearly marks the trunk roads in
the DID), illustrates the way in which higher-density areas have
spread along the trunk roads, indicating the importance of
transport infrastructure. However, the difference here is that the
transport infrastructure is oriented around the individual car use.

Some aspects of quality of life and urban densities

Methods for analysis

Some aspects of quality of life related to urban densities are examined here through statistical data analysis. To examine urban densities and car use, three indicators, namely the rate of car ownership, annual quantities of petrol purchased per household and the ratio of commuting by car, have been selected. To examine the relationship between urban densities and the influence of spatial qualities, two indicators, average house floor space and average land price, have been selected. Five scatter plots show the results of these analyses, by using data from each indicator and DIDs' population densities of each case study city. Approximate curves and the multiple correlation coefficients are also calculated.

Analysis of the indicators

Car ownership (Figure 16.8)

The number of private cars per household in the case study cities ranges from 0.56 to 1.90 and the average is 1.27 per household. A fairly strong negative correlation can be seen between the

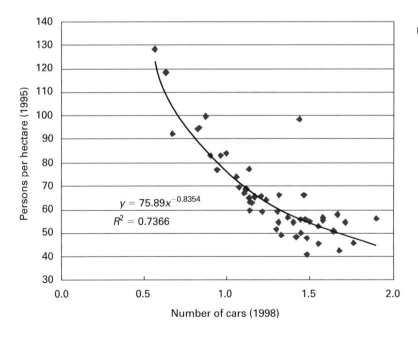

Figure 16.8
DID population densities and car ownership per household in Japanese principal cities.

number of car owners and urban population densities (with a correlation coefficient of 0.7366); as the population density falls, car ownership rises. This shows that living in lower-density built-up areas brings with it the need for private car ownership in households in these case study cities. However, it may also indicate that a lack of adequate, acceptable public transport and car use is the preferred option.

Purchased quantity of petrol (Figure 16.9)

Petrol is consumed mainly for car use in most households. According to government research, the average quantity of petrol purchased per year in the sample cities is 476 litres per household. As to be expected, there is a high-negative correlation between the quantities of purchased petrol and urban population densities (a correlation coefficient of 0.8068); as densities fall, the amount of petrol consumed rises. This would follow from the data in Figure 16.8: lower urban densities favour private car use.

Journey to work (Figure 16.10)

The most popular means of travelling to work is the car, with 45.4% of residents in the case study cities. However, 33.2% of residents used other forms of motorized transport, such as the bus, train or multiple modes; 11.9% of residents cycled to work

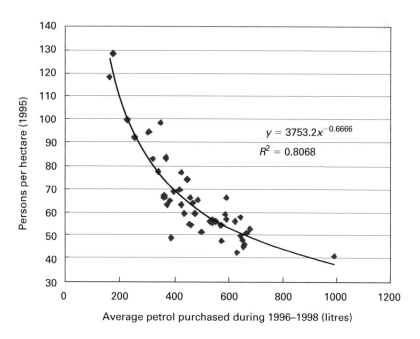

Figure 16.9
DID population densities and petrol purchased per household in Japanese principal cities.

$$y = 3753.2x^{-0.6666}$$
$$R^2 = 0.8068$$

Persons per hectare (1995)

Average petrol purchased during 1996–1998 (litres)

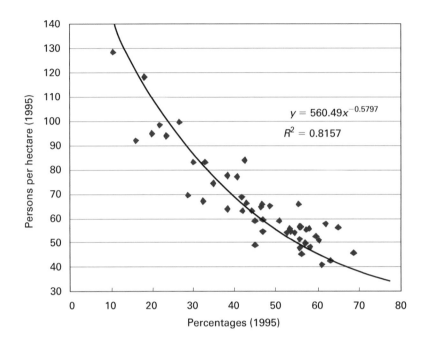

Figure 16.10
DID population densities and
car journeys to work in
Japanese principal cities.

with 9.5% walking. It became clear in the case study analysis that people who live in the cities with lower DID population densities are more likely to drive their car to work. The strong correlation between driving to work and urban population density is illustrated in Figure 16.10.

Floor space of residences (Figure 16.11)

It was found that there is a fairly strong negative correlation between average floor spaces of residence and urban population density. As densities drop, the average floor space increases. It should be borne in mind however, that in Japan, the floor space of a residence is strongly affected by important variables including theclimate, the social way of life and the structure of household. The average overall household floor space in case study cities is $86.4 \, \text{m}^2$, with the average reducing in metropolitan areas, such as Tokyo and Osaka to about $60 \, \text{m}^2$, and increasing in smaller urban areas to about $120 \, \text{m}^2$.

Land prices (Figure 16.12)

Land prices in Japan are very high compared with those in the Western countries. The average land price (regardless of use) in the case study cities is 228,000 yen (approximately £1137 or

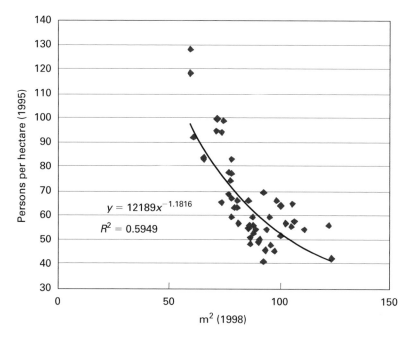

Figure 16.11
DID population densities and average household floor space in Japanese principal cities.

$$y = 12189x^{-1.1816}$$

$$R^2 = 0.5949$$

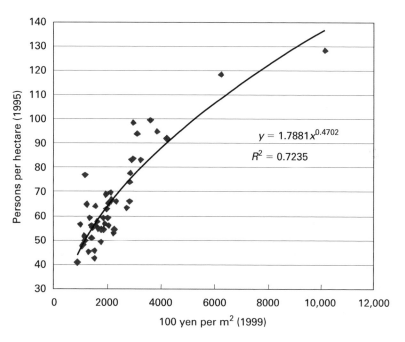

Figure 16.12
DID population densities and average land price in Japanese principal cities.

$$y = 1.7881x^{0.4702}$$

$$R^2 = 0.7235$$

€1670) per m². The average land price in Tokyo, which has the highest population density of all the case study cities, is 1,012,000 yen per m² (approximately £5048 or €7415). Yamaguchi, which has the lowest density, is 90,000 yen per m² (approximately £450 or €660). It can be seen then that there is

Table 16.3
Correlations between DID
population densities and
indicators of quality of life.

Quality of life indicator	Car ownership	Amount of petrol purchased	Using car for journey to work	Average floor space	Land price
Correlation with DID population densities (multiple correlation coefficient, R^2)	0.7366	0.8668	0.8579	0.5973	0.7531
Implication of higher densities (for planning)	Reduced need to own/use car as method of transport (concentration should be on providing public transport/multi-mode transport options)	Reduced quantity of petrol purchased (reduced need to concentrate on road infra-structure)	Reduced need to drive to work (concentration should be on increasing the accessibility of local services and facilities)	Smaller household floor space[a]	Increased land prices[b]

Note: (a) Location is an important consideration to be taken into account, (b) will be affected by location and other factors, such as climate and household structure.

a fairly strong positive correlation between the average land prices and urban population density: as population density falls, so does the land price.

Results: quality of life and urban densities

The results of the above analysis are tabulated together in Table 16.3. Five indicators show fairly strong to strong correlations with DID population densities. The people who live in cities with lower-density DIDs own and use private cars more than in higher-density cities. That higher-density areas have smaller floor space of houses and higher land prices than lower-density areas is not disputed.

Urban density and accessibility to local facilities

Methods of analysis

The condition and diversity of the level of accessibility to local facilities in relation to various urban densities were examined in the case study. The percentage of houses located within 500 m, walkable distance[2] from local facilities, was the measure used to evaluate the level of accessibility. Seven types of local facilities were selected, which include

1. local community centres
2. parks and gardens
3. rail stations
4. hospitals and clinics
5. banking facilities and post offices
6. day-care centres for older people
7. food convenience stores

The data used was based on the 1998 housing and land survey of Japan, which was used to draw up scatter plot graphs. The main conclusions of this data analysis are discussed below.

Analysis of accessibility

Day-care centres

Although the numbers of public and private day-care centres for the elderly are rapidly increasing in Japan, due to its ageing population, they are not yet enough to meet the demand in many regions. The percentage of houses located within 500 m of day-care centres is generally low in the case study cities, with the average at only 13%. Currently, the relationship between the level of accessibility to day-care centres and the densities of DIDs is not strong.

Railway stations

Railway stations represent a small part of the national transport system in most local areas of Japan. Local bus systems are often developed instead of tram or rail systems. The percentage of houses located within 500 m of a railway station is generally low, in fact under 30% in principal cities. The overall average is only 25.7%. The relationship between accessibility to train stations and DID densities is not strong.

Local community centres

Local civic centres are essential for community activities. But there is incongruity in the percentages of houses located within 500 m of them in sample cities. The overall average is 53.9%, but accessibility levels vary widely in each case study city.

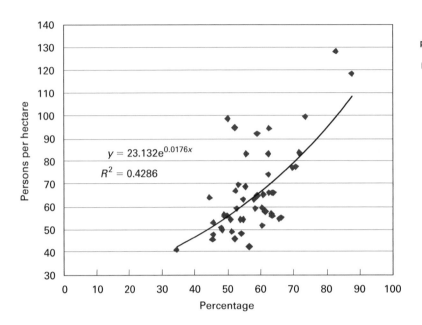

Parks and gardens

Public parks and gardens are generally built and managed by local governments. Their national average area is $8.2\,\text{m}^2$ per inhabitant. The average percentage of houses located within 500 m from them is 58.5%. As with local community centres, the level of accessibility is wide-ranging depending on the city and so the relationship with DID densities is not a strong one.

Banking facilities and post offices (Figure 16.13)

The average number of households per banking facility is 1442 and per post office is 6791. The post offices are managed by central government as a public service that is provided in a given area. The level of accessibility to both post offices and banking facilities does increase (but not considerably) in urbanizing areas. The overall average percentage of households located within 500 m of these facilities is 57.8%, resulting in the conclusion that the relationship with density is relatively weak.

Hospitals and clinics (Figure 16.14)

Hospitals and clinics are managed by a variety of different organizations in Japan. The average percentage of households located within 500 m of hospitals and clinics is 66.4%. This is relatively high as it would include primary health care facilities

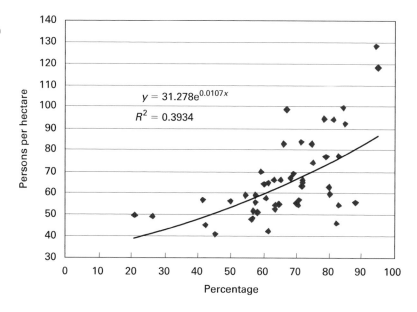

Figure 16.14
DID population densities and
percentage of households within
500 m of a hospital or clinic in
Japanese principal cities.

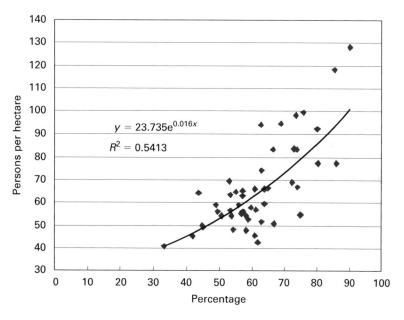

Figure 16.15
DID population densities and
percentage of households within
500 m of a convenience store in
Japanese principal cities.

(general practitioners and health centres). A moderately strong relationship between the percentages and DID's densities is shown in Figure 16.14.

Convenience stores (Figure 16.15)

The first convenience store in Japan appeared in 1974. Nowadays, it is one of the essential local facilities. Convenience stores are wholly managed by the private sector, with their location oriented to maximize profitability. The average percentages of houses located within 500 m is 61.8%. The strength of relationship between the percentages and DID densities is illustrated in Figure 16.15.

Results: urban density and accessibility
(Table 16.4)

The average percentage of households located within 500 m of a number of facilities seem to fall into two groups, depending on the facility in question. The percentages of households within 500 m of a railway station and day-care centres range between 10% and 20%. Far higher are the percentages of households within 500 m of the other five facilities: between 50% and 66%. Furthermore, accessibility to local facilities whose location is influenced by market conditions, (i.e. convenience stores), is clearly affected by DID densities. However, public facilities (i.e. local community centres, and parks or gardens), are not much affected by the density of the DIDs. For the other facilities (i.e. banking facilities, hospitals and clinics, and railway stations), the correlation is moderate.

These results imply that the strength of correlation between urban population density and local facilities depends on

Table 16.4
The relationship between DID population densities and percentages of households within 500 m of local facilities.

Local facilities	Day-care centres for the elderly	Railway stations	Local community centres	Banking facilities/ post offices	Parks and gardens	Conven- ience stores	Hospitals and clinics
Households within 500 m of local facilities: standard deviation (% in brackets)	7.3 (5.9)	15.4 (10.1)	53.8 (27.6)	57.8 (9.7)	58.3 (22.9)	61.8 (12.0)	66.4 (15.3)
Correlation with DID's population densities (multiple correlation coefficient, R^2)	–	0.3316	–	0.4286	–	0.5413	0.3394
Market orientation	Various	Various	None	Strong	None	Strong	Various

'marketability' of the facility and the individual policies of municipalities. Urban densities, as an indicator to demonstrate accessibility, are not sufficient for all kinds of local facilities. Accessibility and arrangement of local facilities are also affected by other local characteristics.

Further case study city analysis

Principal component analysis

Eleven factors were selected for principal component analysis. Three principal components were calculated and their qualities were examined by the size of the eigenvalue of each factor (see Table 16.5). It was decided that the first principal component should relate to the theoretical requirements of the compact city. This can be seen through its relatively strong relationship with aspects such as DID's population densities, land prices and good accessibility to convenience stores, hospitals and clinics and banking facilities. The second principal component shows characteristics of urban diffusion, with the correlation with good access to local community centres and parks, and high car use. The third principal component, which was named urban 'reluctance' is illustrated with good access to railway stations and day-care centres for the elderly as well as increased floor space of residences.

Table 16.5
Results of principal component analysis.

Eigenvalue: Principal components	1: Compact city	2: Urban diffusion	3: Urban 'reluctance'
DID population densities	0.3717	−0.1805	−0.1406
Land prices	0.3439	−0.2133	0.1509
Convenience stores	0.3310	0.0649	−0.3269
Hospitals and clinics	0.3172	0.2157	0.0693
Banking facilities	0.3144	0.2186	0.0353
Local community centres	0.1336	0.6016	−0.0152
Parks and gardens	0.2193	0.5113	−0.2309
Driving to work	−0.3242	0.3436	0.1774
Railway stations	0.2934	−0.2263	0.5347
Day-care centres for the elderly	0.3041	0.0342	0.5233
Household floor space	−0.2915	0.2594	0.4470
Eigenvalue	6.1936	1.5386	0.7323
Proportion	0.5631	0.1399	0.0666
Cumulative	0.5631	0.7029	0.7695

Table 16.6
Group averages by cluster analysis.

Group	DID pop-ulation/ 1000 people	DID pop-ulation density ppha	Car owner-ship per house-hold	Average quantity of petrol (litres)	% of house-holds driving to work	Average house-hold floor space (m²)	Average land price per m² (yen)	Percentage of households within 500 m of local facilities						
								Community centres	Parks and gardens	Railway stations	Hospitals and clinics	Banking facilities and post office	Day-care centre for the elderly	Convenience stores
	1995	1995	1995	1996–1998	1995	1998	1999	1998	1998	1998	1998	1998	1998	1998
A	5284.8	123.3	0.6	167.5	14.3	59.6	8167.5	78.5	84.2	44.7	94.7	85.1	25.7	87.9
B	1837.8	91.6	0.9	284	24.8	70.6	3519.4	44.7	72.7	26.7	82.2	63.7	13.4	73.6
C	773.5	75.1	1.1	401.8	38.1	74.8	2395.8	69.5	71.2	15.3	72.2	60.4	6	69.5
D	231.8	55.2	1.5	555.4	56.9	100.5	1603.6	71.9	66.8	11.2	66.3	58.7	6.8	59.1
E	245.6	55.2	1.4	552.3	50.3	90.1	1709.4	28.4	35.7	12.3	54.8	50.4	4.5	52.5
Avg.	728.3	66.2	1.3	476.6	45.4	86.4	2281.5	53.8	58.3	15.4	66.4	57.8	7.3	61.8

Characteristics of each city group (Table 16.6)

The cities of Group A (the two mega cities, Tokyo and Osaka) are high density (about 123 persons per hectare in DIDs) and have high levels of accessibility to all facilities. The level of car ownership and use are low, and public transport is well developed and used.

The semi-mega cities in Group B (consisting of five cities) have an average population density of about 92 persons per hectare. Accessibility to local facilities is lower than that of Group A but higher than Groups C–E. Car ownership and use are also lower than in Groups C–E.

Group C (made up of 12 cities) have an average population density of about 75 persons per hectare, with a higher level of petrol use, which is to be expected with higher car ownership and use than Groups A and B. Accessibility to community centres is higher than Group B, which may be affected by the particular circumstances of Group C cities.

The two other groups, Groups D (consisting of 13 cities) and E (17 cities) have almost identical average population densities of about 55 persons per hectare, but have varying levels of accessibility to facilities. Group D has much higher levels of accessibility to community centres than Group E (72% of

Figure 16.16
The scatter plot and five groups by cluster analysis.

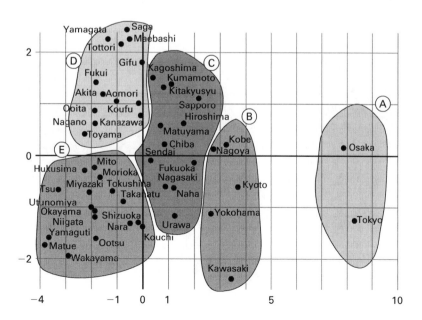

households within 500 m of one against 28%, respectively) and parks and gardens (67% of households within 500 m of one against 36%, respectively). Overall, the accessibility to facilities is higher in Group D than in Group E. It should be noted that the cities of Group D are located in cold regions that get heavy snow and frosts in the winter period. It could be the case that the seasonal influence has dictated the good accessibility of local services (see Figures 16.16 to 16.21).

Figure 16.17
Group A: Tokyo.
(*Source*: Kiyonobu Kaido.)

Figure 16.18
Group B: Yokohama.
(*Source*: Kiyonobu Kaido.)

Figure 16.19
Group C: Hiroshima.
(*Source*: Kiyonobu Kaido.)

Figure 16.20
Group D: Aomori.
(*Source*: Kiyonobu Kaido.)

Figure 16.21
Group E: Nara.
(*Source*: Kiyonobu Kaido.)

Conclusion

This chapter has examined the relationship that the high urban density of the compact city has with some aspects of quality of life, and levels of accessibility to local facilities. It can be concluded that high density does and does not mean increased accessibility. The case study has shown that on the whole, higher population densities do tend to offer higher accessibility to services in urban areas of large populations (over 700,000 inhabitants). However, it is more difficult to determine consistent levels of accessibility with any certainty in the medium-sized cities (those with populations of 200,000–500,000 inhabitants). There are other variables that affect the ssspaccessibility to services, such as climate.

It is also concluded that the urban density as an indicator of good accessibility is not sufficient for all types of local facility, which are dependent on local government's planning policies. It is therefore important for local and central government to undertake efficient planning policies to make an effort to improve local facility accessibility, which has shown to be variable in different city categories. However, it can be concluded that higher densities can feasibly and easily support high levels of accessibility to services and facilities in Japanese urban areas.

Notes

1. DID: Densely Inhabited District. This is defined as an urban area in the Japanese census. Normally, the minimum density is 4000 people per km^2 (which is equal to over 40 people per hectare) and the minimum scale of population is 5000. It was first introduced into the census in 1960, when rapid urbanization began.

2. Walkable distance: 500 m was decided as a 'walkable distance' after a review of literature that included Shokokusya: the Next American Metropolis – Ecology, Community and American Dream by Calthorpe (1994).

References

Barton, H., Davis, G. and Guise, R. (1995) *Sustainable Settlements: A Guide for Planners, Designers and Developers*, University of the West of England and The Local Government Management Board, Bristol.

Burton, E. (2000) The Compact City: Just or Just Compact? A Preliminary Analysis. *Urban Studies*, **37(11)**: 1969–2001.

Calthorpe, P. (1994) *Shokokusya: The Next American Metropolis – Ecology, Community and the American Dream*, Architectural Press, Princeton.

Clapson, M. (1998) *Invincible Green Suburbs, Brave New Towns: Social Change and Urban Dispersal in Postwar England*, Manchester University Press, Manchester.

Elkin, T., McLaren, D. and Hillman, M. (1991) *Reviving the City*, Friends of the Earth, London.

Frey, H. (1999) *Designing the City: Towards a More Sustainable Urban Form*, E & FN Spon, London.

Gossop, C. (1990) The Euro-ideal that sells the city short, *Town and Country Planning*, **59(12)**: 340–342.

Thomas, L. and Cousins, W. (1996) A new compact city form, concept in practice. In: *The Compact City: A Sustainable Urban Form?* (eds. Jenks, M., Burton, E. and Williams, K.), E & FN Spon, London.

Williams, K., Burton, E. and Jenks, M. (eds.) (2000) *Achieving Sustainable Urban Form*, E & FN Spon, London.

World Commission on Environment and Development (WCED) (1987) *Our Common Future*, Oxford University Press, Oxford.

Emerging Work Patterns and Their Implication on the Strategy and Planning of Work Environments

Introduction

This chapter describes two profiles of future work patterns and illustrates the potential implications for the planning of work environments. These two profiles are distinct but inextricably linked. Work environments are changing in terms of boundaries, location and ownership which have implications for city planning. This chapter will explore the drivers behind these profiles and propose solutions, which accommodate the demand for workspace in the modern city. The two proposed work profiles and associated work 'environments' are:

Virtual network: The main criteria determining organisations that would operate across a virtual network are that they tend to be reliant on *virtual communication* within a group, tend to be *outwardly focused*, that is, towards their market or client base and are likely to *be service providers*. The range of environments and tools that together make a virtual workplace will be explored, with reference to the *Sustainable Accommodation for the New Economy* (SANE) space environment model. This model explores the changing relationships between people, place and technology. Challenges facing these groups include corporate identity, connecting communities of people, fostering culture, identity and self-esteem, balancing territories and environments that traverse local and global contexts

Cluster of physical hubs: The main criterion that organisations operating across a cluster of physical hubs must fulfil is to provide inwardly focused *face-to-face interaction* within a group, that is, towards a project or within a discipline, which will often have a *product focus*. This profile concerns knowledge workers who overlap into technical fields such as research and development. These are groups whose work environment may be mobile but is often across *specific locations*. The range of environments and tools that together make a network of physical places for these individuals and organisations will be examined (as before) using the SANE space environment model. Challenges facing these groups are: *understanding the relationship* between physical and virtual space, connecting communities of people, relationship building, the 'office as the city' (Harrison, 2001), and *environments* that traverse local and global contexts

Containing a world of virtual work will impact city design pervasively. There are many established design solutions such as mixed-use '24-hour electronic neighbourhoods' (Mitchell, 1999), Airport Cities (Briggs and Worthington, 2000) and anonymous space for hire that is temporarily branded in order to give it the identity of the user. This temporary and sporadic use of place raises questions related to ownership, management and methods of charging. Virtual settings can be anywhere and do not usually have high demand for space, in terms of quality or quantity. Containing a world of physical hubs will create a demand for larger buildings. These buildings may need to be clustered together and be associated with a particular location. The quality and quantity demands of the space will be higher. In conclusion, this chapter will illustrate a potential future for work environments as might be played out in the modern city and the design elements that have been developed as a response to the changing demands in the city.

The 'New Economy' context

The context within which these profiles are explored is the 'New Economy'. The underlying forces that characterise or define the New Economy used here (see also Gillen and Wheeler, 2001) are summarised as follows:

1. Classical economics focuses on supply, demand and 'the assumption of scarcity'. Resources are assumed to be tangible. With the shift from tangible to intangible factors of production, the underlying premise of economics is increasingly relying on plenitude

2. Rather than viewing physical property simply as a liability, the challenge of the New Economy may be to change how, and to understand where, it adds value for organisations

3. Technology is becoming the cheapest component of work and people the most expensive

4. Organisations will have to create a balance between its own space and the individual's space

5. Managing the work–life balance is one of the central challenges of the New Economy

6. Globalisation is challenging perceptions of identity. Individuals are increasingly concerned with what distinguishes and connects them to other people

7. The emergence of networks is more about linking people to people rather than people to things

8. In New Economy markets (that are not characterised by scarcity), power will be in the hands of consumers

9. The only scarcity is human attention. It is at the level of experience that companies can have the best opportunity to market products, to make them memorable

Emerging work patterns and context

Geographically dispersed teams and work environments are a reality for many global organisations. Workers can find their physical work environment increasingly disconnected from their project team. The connections between these workers are predominantly virtual, with team meetings and interactions through e-mail, telephone and online software such as NetMeeting. A challenge to such geographically dispersed and managed teams is maintaining an effective work environment. The role for managers of these teams is changing to that of a communicator, and the role of the work environment is evolving to have new meanings.

Part of maintaining effective work environments is keeping people connected. Increased access to, and increased quantity of, information makes effective knowledge exchange critical. Workers can no longer work on projects from beginning to end as independent specialists: they must rely on other specialists to handle parts of the process and so are forced to work in teams. Trust and maintaining a sense of belonging in an environment where people need to rely on team members they may not have met, highlights the new role of place in connecting people. Indeed, increased competition has resulted in a renewed emphasis on the role of innovation and creativity in organisations. Many companies are looking to physical places to provide enriched meaning and locations for memorable events, believing that this will help catalyse innovation.

Now that people are in more of a position to choose their location of work, how do organisations decide on the most effective work environments? Some activities are best accommodated through physical places while other activities are most efficiently accommodated through virtual places or through enabling tools. Differentiating between when to use physical or virtual space depends on the type of communication involved. For example, negotiations or initial meetings are often felt to be most effective face to face while more routine weekly team meetings or project updates can perhaps be more efficiently executed by phone.

The city is an important tool in connecting and maintaining relationships. They are major nodes for travellers and provide a rich variety of places to meet and connect with others. The choice of work environment in the city is far broader than simply a range of privately owned locations: public spaces such as hotels, airport lounges and coffee bars are often used as temporary work environments. It will be increasingly important for cities to respond to the nature of this demand in order to provide for it, and to compete effectively with other cities. To understand how the city can respond to these new demands, the two parallel profiles of work that these themes point to are explored.

Profiles of work

The two profiles, the *virtual network* and the *cluster of physical hubs*, are parallel and interdependent. It is unlikely that people would fall exclusively into one or the other but would more likely have one dominant profile with the other in support.

The virtual network

The main criteria determining organisations that would operate across a virtual network are as follows:

- Workers are predominantly reliant on *virtual communication*
- People tend to be *outwardly focused* and likely to be *service providers* not tied to physical production or products. The work environment is mobile and *non-location specific*, that is, workers operate across a variety of places they do not come into work in the same place every day. The mobile nature of this work pattern results in an increasingly intangible environment

- It predominantly concerns *knowledge workers*, as described by Drucker (1993) and Handy (1990)

Significant examples of sectors that would fall into this profile are consultancy groups (management, financial, business), telecommunications organisations and marketing and sales groups. These are groups whose work environment is fluid, non-location specific and increasingly intangible.

The role of the physical place is more important than ever in the light of these challenges. Mobility means that virtual workers have to be close to, or often pass through, major transport hubs in cities. Cities provide the greatest opportunities and physical places to connect such mobile people, the virtual workers.

Cluster of physical hubs

The main criteria for organisations that operate across a cluster of physical hubs are as follows:

- A dominant requirement for *face-to-face interaction*
- Teams tend to be *inwardly focused*, on a project or within a discipline
- There will often be a *product focus*
- The work environment is mobile but often across *specific locations*
- The predominant concern relates to *knowledge workers who overlap into technical fields*

Examples of knowledge workers who overlap into technical fields include pharmaceutical and petrochemical organisations, and research and development groups. This profile also applies to knowledge workers who are reliant on being physically present with like-minded individuals, for example, within the financial service industry on dealing floors.[1] These are groups whose work environment is mobile but often across specific locations. These locations are typically either out-of-town campuses (e.g. in the case of pharmaceuticals and petrochemical organisations), or are major cities (e.g. as in the case of the financial services industry).

The SANE space environment model

The SANE project is an European Commission research project falling under its 5th framework. It was a 5 million euro project, which ran from January 2001 to December 2002. The starting point for the project was the requirement from globalised companies and new mobile communications technologies for new models of workplace, work processes and property management. Traditional approaches to workspace would no longer serve the needs of global networked organisations. DEGW led a multi-disciplinary team of experts in the workplace, technology and human behaviour. Its goal was to develop a unified framework which integrated people, process and place. This involved the creation of sustainable, collaborative workplaces for European knowledge workers, encompassing both virtual and physical spaces.

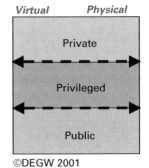

©DEGW 2001

Figure 17.1
Three categories of space (SANE space environment model).

The SANE space environment model has three categories of space, namely private, privileged and public. In addition to this, the model has two 'lenses', called the virtual and the physical (Figure 17.1).

The characteristics of the three categories are as follows:

1. **Private space is characterised by protected access.** Private space can be either physical, for example, the corporate headquarters of a company, or virtual, such as an Intranet. Private does not relate to the activity but rather to the conditions of accessibility of that private space which can be for either individual or group pursuits

2. **Privileged space is characterised by invited access.** Privileged space also refers to both physical space, such as a members' club and virtual space, like an instant messenger service

3. **Public space is characterised by open access.** Public space is also either physical, for example a shopping centre, or virtual such as the Internet

The following sections illustrate the use of this model through exploring tools and spaces against these parallel virtual and physical 'lenses'.

The tools associated with the SANE model

Work tools are taken to mean the virtual settings associated with work that is delivered through technology. Technology ranges in scale from the individual to the group.

1. **Virtual – private:** The primary feature of private space is protected access. The example given in Figure 17.2 is the Hive, a Collaborative Virtual Environment (CVE) created by the

Figure 17.2
The Hive: an example of virtual private space.

Figure 17.3
MSN messenger: an example of virtual privileged space.

petrochemical organisation BP, which uses a 3D 'immersive' environment to bring engineering professions together to exchange information, enabling multi-disciplinary teaming and complex systems to be understood more easily

2. **Virtual – privileged:** The primary feature of privileged space is invited access. An instant messenger service such as that offered by MSN is a good example; others include project Extranets or video conferencing. This can be an effective way of bringing a community of people together to share information, documents or simply for conversation (Figure 17.3)

3. **Virtual – public:** Open access characterises public space. The most obvious virtual example is the worldwide web. Internet sites tend to focus on communities of common interest. Other examples of virtual public space include online databases and public chat rooms (Figure 17.4). This category is effectively the virtual coffee house of the modern city

The increasingly important role of the city in these virtual environments is to provide portals and connection points. The evidence is clear in the explosion of Internet cafes and access points now commonly found in facilities such as gymnasiums, hotels and shopping centres. For those who use these environments the city can be a physical 'pulse point' (Mitchell, 1999) into an increasingly virtual world. The more time people choose to, or have to spend interfacing with a computer, the more important physical experiences will become. The availability of mobile technology means that people now have the capability to work almost anywhere. What will determine their choice will be factors concerning convenience and meaning.

345

Figure 17.4
Public chat room: an example of
virtual public space.

The places associated with the SANE model

1. **Physical – private:** Private space has controlled access
    and covers a wide variety of locations from the home to the office.
    Private space can be for either individual or group activities.
    A private space could be an individual office, a hotel room, a
    car or a whole building (depending on the access conditions)
    (Figure 17.5)

2. **Physical – privileged:** Privileged space has invited access. This
    model has been around for a long time in the form of membership
    clubs. The change is that access to these clubs is now less to do
    with money or status and more to do with networking and
    common interests. These are the sorts of spaces that involve
    communities and membership fees. A good example is 'Baby' in
    Amsterdam, as shown in Figure 17.6. Baby is a club for those
    in the Dutch media industry, to come and work when they are in
    Amsterdam. It is centrally located which is convenient for mobile
    people to drop in between meetings. Most of the members work
    at home or at client sites and they come to Baby to meet like-
    minded individuals. This workspace does not shut at the end of
    the working day but is transformed into a nightclub in the

Figure 17.5
Physical private space.

Figure 17.6
Baby, Amsterdam: an example of physical privileged space.

evening. The primary function of this place is to act as a
community hub. This building is also a converted church, and an
excellent example of the sustainable use of an existing city fabric
responding to new sorts of workers.

3. **Physical – public:** Public space is open to everyone. A good example
of how a city is reinventing its public spaces in response to the
demands of its inhabitants is Manhattan, New York City. There are
over 70 wireless access points planned across parks and public
places. Anyone with a laptop and wireless access card can now
connect to the Internet. Bryant Park in mid-town New York, once a
dangerous area renowned for drugs and crime, is now one of the
best used public spaces in the city. Bryant Park shows free movies
on a large screen in the summer, is a popular lunch location and can
support 500 live users on a wireless network (Figure 17.7).

The following section proposes a system by which people
might decide where to work. With increased mobility and
demands on people and resources, it will be necessary to
choose which sort of space best suits different activities.

Determining which profile fits different work styles

It is not a simple question of choosing between virtual and
physical spaces: virtual space will not completely replace
physical space; both are complementary. Choice of locations

347

Figure 17.7
Bryant Park, New York: an
example of physical public
space.

from which to work has increased, and different (physical) settings will be better suited to different activities. Sustainable cities will need to accommodate these work styles and respond to their needs in order to either keep or attract this demand.

A simple way of characterising virtual and physical space is that virtual space can take on the role of convenience, while physical space becomes more about providing meaning. As virtual space can work well to maintain relationships, physical space can become more symbolic acting as sustenance in an otherwise virtual existence. The growth of conference locations such as castles in rural settings, survival weekends and golf days are indicators of this. The physical attributes of a place, namely views, architecture, history, location, accessibility, can greatly contribute the experience of an event.

In order to determine which profile fits an activity, or to what degree virtual and physical spaces should be used, the critical issues to be considered are: *time, location* and *connectivity*. These issues are important when making decisions, as shown by some of the criteria listed below (Figure 17.8).

These criteria are by no means exhaustive and they show the range of issues that have significance in the two parallel work patterns of the cluster of physical hubs and the virtual network. An organisation or population that tends towards criteria on the left-hand side (see Figure 17.8) will be more suited to a cluster of physical hubs, whereas the needs of those tending towards

Figure 17.8
Decision-making criteria
influenced by issues of time,
location and connectivity.

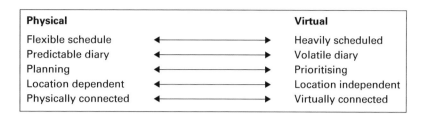

Figure 17.8
Decision-making criteria influenced by issues of time, location and connectivity.

the criteria on the right-hand side will be better accommodated by a virtual network.

Accommodating these profiles in cities

As people and organisations cover wider distances and deal with more information, the need to stay connected becomes more important. Looking at two major cities New York and London, evidence of sectors clustering together is clear. Both cities have a media centre, financial centre and a commercial centre, within which local and international companies cluster together. The area becomes 'branded' for that activity; for example, Soho is known for art, fashion and media in both cities. People are attracted to such areas for reasons including networking, access to labour and access to like-minded individuals. Often these places grow up around transport hubs or from historical conditions, which drives the rental and land value up, especially evident in the financial services industry. The density of these areas increases in order to meet the demand, and so clusters of tower blocks and large buildings appear.

Similar clustering can be seen at a regional level. The Øresund area of Scandinavia has attracted technology-based companies and universities to create a technology hub in northern Europe. New Jersey, between New York and Philadelphia is a major hub for many pharmaceutical companies due to its historical location of the Philadelphia School of Pharmacy and due to the pool of talent clustered in that area.

Cities offer a rich variety of settings for the mobile worker. As both activities and the duration of the working day become less defined, what used to be a business lunch venue might now be a place for escape from the office to do concentrated work in the afternoon. A street café can be the perfect place for a confidential conversation. A playing field in Hyde Park is a great location for a corporate teambuilding exercise. What tied workers to a location was access to information and management systems. Mobile and wireless technology means information can be accessed from where ever the worker is.

Flexible working, irregular hours, less regimented management systems mean that reporting systems are not as linear as they were, and that workers increasingly report into multiple organisations and people rather than a single point of contact.

Studying these evolving work patterns and physical conditions has led to the following design elements being developed as potential solutions for how the city can respond to such demands. These changes should be seen as both a great opportunity and responsibility for the modern city.

Design elements for the city

Breaking down public and private boundaries

Breaking down public and private boundaries concerns accessibility and ownership of spaces. The modern inhabitants of the city no longer fall into neat boxes of separate uses. The city must accommodate a freer flow of people through spaces. Examples of this can be seen in the design of modern office buildings where the ground floor has been allocated to greater public access, with shops and cafés for example. These office buildings may not necessarily be owned by organisations but may be used on a 'pay-as-you-go' basis and managed by private organisations, developers or even the city itself. Just as the city currently provides car parks, libraries and sports facilities, it may in the future provide workspace (e.g. Bryant Park, see Figure 17.7).

Virtual accessibility

Enabling virtual accessibility is about providing high-speed access points. While space owned by organisations or individuals will provide their own networks and access points, the city now has an increasing responsibility to do the same. Priority locations for such access points are places where people pause, gather and have time to connect. These are places such as train stations, airports, hairdressers and coffee shops. Transport hubs currently provide privileged access in the form of business lounges, and it is likely that other public spaces will have to follow suit and provide Internet access points in the same way that cities currently provide park benches and pedestrian crossings.

Physical accessibility

As populations spend more time travelling between home and work or between work locations, it will be necessary to make travel time as efficient as possible. Minimising journey times to destinations through high-speed transport connections from airports to business districts will be a critical determining factor of where large organisations locate. In larger cities like London, where transport systems are already under extreme pressure, and it may be a better solution to look at creating alternative 'destinations'. Locating conference centres near major transport hubs or indeed as part of an airport would make for easier accessibility. Schipol, or 'The Airport City' (Briggs and Worthington, 2000), outside Amsterdam is already accommodating such needs. Schipol and London's Heathrow airport are of a comparable size and have a steady flow of short-term visitors, for whom speed and efficiency are a priority. Schipol Airport now markets itself as a city destination in itself, with a wide variety of shops and restaurants and is also growing as a conference venue (Figure 17.9).

Memorable events and places

In an increasingly dispersed and virtual world, managing relationships and exchanging ideas with others are more important than ever. The majority of people travel in order to meet other people. Spaces for gathering and meeting are increasingly in demand. This is linked with the growing need to create places for special events. Physical space can play an important role in creating memorable events. When organisations or individuals come together, it is often to start or maintain relationships and knowledge exchange. As discussed earlier, there has been a growth in popularity of conference venues as diverse as isolated castles and major global cities. Organisations may follow a circuit of conference venues mirroring where their populations are based. Many organisations may own country houses as part of their real estate portfolio to meet this demand for high quality and memorable places. Cities themselves can also become a physical stage for broadcasting to a virtual audience at meaningful times, global summits or New Year's Eve in Times Square (Mitchell, 1999). There will be increased demand for places with special features that a group of people can take over for short periods of time and use as the setting for an important event.

Figure 17.9
Schipol: a virtual city.

Developing quarters

Mixed-use developments have long been recognised as a sustainable way of planning cities. Planning mixed-use developments at the scale of a city quarter supports the clustering of sectors and like-minded individuals. Communities of common interest can share public space, and proximity to other organisations enables knowledge workers to interact and provides employers with access to a concentrated pool of talent.[2]

Walkable zones

A common feature of a good city quarter is that it is walkable. Mixed-use neighbourhood developments seem to be popular locations and are less reliant on existing transport systems. Vibrant, local areas where people and visitors can work, sleep, eat and relax all within walking distance are highly prized.

Conclusion

The world of work is evolving into something different. Organisations and individuals have demands that can no longer be met within the confines of one organisation's resources. Boundaries of territory, ownership, public and private spaces are being redefined. The most sustainable way to plan for work environments in the future is to be flexible and adapt to such changes in workplaces and practices.

The city has responsibilities to meet these new demands. The city needs to respond in an holistic way with organisations, occupiers of space, developers and city councils. The provision of workspace is no longer the sole responsibility of the employer. Charles Handy predicts 'Portfolio working' (Handy, 1990) where people will increasingly work freelance for a variety of organisations. The design of work environments for portfolio workers is multi-dimensional and highly changeable. Mobile workers of all kinds are a population that cities will want to hold onto and provide appropriately for, because they will provide valuable income and diversity to cities. In return, these cities must provide a valuable base, accessible portals and a network of memorable places to sustain and enrich an increasingly transient and virtual people.

As people and organisations operate across physical and virtual environments, the relationship and interdependency between the two will need to be carefully understood. It will not be a question of virtual environments replacing physical environments – they should be seen as complementary. As virtual spaces are about convenience, physical space should become more meaningful. The city is central to both providing a rich physical environment as well as sustaining a gradually more virtual world.

Increasingly dispersed populations of people, connected together virtually, will have growing needs to come together face to face more easily. The city is central to providing a variety of meeting and gathering spaces and has a responsibility to act as a 'Pulse Point' in the New Economy.

The power of place ... will prevail. As traditional locational imperatives weaken, we will gravitate to settings that offer particular cultural, scenic and climatic attractions ... Sometimes we will network to avoid going places. But sometimes still, we will go places to network (Mitchell, 1999).

Notes

1. It should be noted here that there does not appear to be any technical reason for people on dealing floors to be co-located. Research done by DEGW (2001) indicates that the desire for physical co-location is behavioural.

2. A cautionary note on mixed-use developments is that they should avoid highly specific single sector occupiers with no holdings elsewhere. They should be seen as a network of quarters across which large corporations can operate. Locating all resources in one place can cause security concerns for organisations. The re-development of lower Manhattan after September 11 is suffering from what can happen if, admittedly under extreme circumstances, one sector is driven out. Financial services organisations are being offered huge tax and financial breaks to come back to Lower Manhattan but this currently does not appear to be tempting them away from mid-town areas and New Jersey.

References

Briggs, G. and Worthington, J. (2000) Airport City: Interchange, Gateway and Destination for Conference Entitled *Airports and Regions, New Driving Forces First Roissy* – CDG International Forum, December 14/15, 2000.

DEGW (2001) *London High Rise Strategy: Final Draft Interim Report for the GLA*, DEGW, London.

Drucker, P.F. (1993) *Post-Capitalist Society*, Harper Business, New York.

Gillen, N. and Wheeler, P. (2001) *The New Economy – Changing the Rules*, SANE Project, DEGW, London.

Handy, C. (1990) *The Age of Unreason*, Harvard Business School Press, Boston.

Harrison, A. (2001) *The Initial Space Environment Model, D1,* SANE Project, DEGW, London.

Mitchell, W.J. (1999) *e-topia: Urban Life, Jim – But Not as We Know It*, MIT Press, Cambridge, Massachusetts.

18

Susan Roaf, Manuel Fuentes and Rajat Gupta

Solar Cities: The Oxford Solar Initiative

Introduction

The Third Assessment Report of the Intergovernmental Panel on Climate Change (IPCC, 2001) confirmed that there is compelling evidence that the Earth's climate has undergone a period of rapid warming over the last 50 years as a result of human activity. World-wide in the last decade, there have been increasingly violent storms, floods and droughts, with the UK, Europe and the remaining world experiencing unprecedented rainfall and flooding (DETR, 2000; Smith, 2001; Hulme *et al.*, 2002). The rate of warming is now perceived to be increasing. Climate models indicate that in the coming century, we will live in a progressively warmer, wetter world, with raised sea levels and increased coastal and fluvial flooding, and extreme weather events. Global average temperatures, it is projected, will rise by 1.4–5.8°C (IPCC, 2001; Hulme *et al.*, 2002) (Figure 18.1).

The scientific evidence of the increasing atmospheric concentrations of human-induced greenhouse gases has been well rehearsed (Houghton *et al.*, 1990; IPCC, 1996; Hulme and Jenkins, 1998; DETR, 2000; Graves and Phillipson, 2000; IPCC, 2001). Carbon dioxide (CO_2) appears to be the most important and it is currently responsible for around two-thirds of the global warming effect (Met Office, 1999; UNEP and UNFCCC, 2001).

355

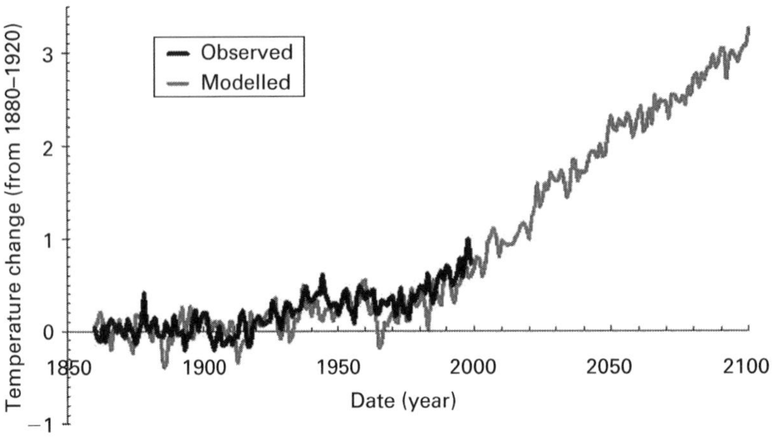

Figure 18.1
Observed and predicted global
temperature change. (*Source*:
IEMA, 2000; DETR, 2000.)

The atmospheric concentration of CO_2 has increased by 31%, since 1750 and has probably not been exceeded in the last 20 million years (IPCC, 2001).

The extent of the CO_2 problem was recognised by the UK Royal Commission on Environmental Pollution, which argued for the need to halt the rise in CO_2 concentrations produced by burning fossil fuels in order to reduce the risks of catastrophic alterations to the climate (RCEP, 2000). For the UK this implies a reduction of 60% of CO_2 emissions by 2050 and 80% by 2100, relative to 1997 levels (RCEP, 2000).

For industrialised countries, the most effective actions to effect reduction of CO_2 emissions lie in the building sector, largely because buildings, in use or construction, are the biggest single indirect source of carbon emissions generated by burning fossil fuels. They account for over 50% of total emissions (Shorrock and Henderson, 1990; Watson *et al.*, 1996; Smith, 2001). The building sector can most realistically accommodate fairly rapid change without pain (Smith, 2001). Studies have demonstrated that, it is not difficult to reduce carbon emissions from houses by 60% or more through energy efficiency measures, but it is only possible to reach the 90% level of reductions required by using renewable energy technologies (Roaf *et al.*, 2001). Even the Government's Interdepartmental Analysts Group (IAG) and Performance and Innovation Unit (PIU) conclude that to achieve a 60% reduction in CO_2 emissions, there is a need for a combination of energy efficiency improvement and carbon-free electricity generation (IAG, 2002; PIU, 2002). The Carbon Trust too believes it is technically possible for the UK to meet the 60% target with a combination of energy efficiency measures and new low-carbon technologies (Carbon Trust, 2001).

In addition, with the relatively short fossil fuel horizons that are predicted (40 years left for oil and 65 years for gas), humanity needs to move rapidly away from the use of greenhouse gas producing fossil fuels towards a greater dependence on clean renewable energy. In fact, reducing carbon intensity (carbon per unit of energy) can occur independently of a reduction in energy intensity (energy per unit of economic activity), for example, through use of renewable energy. Sustainable energy supplies require a reduction in both carbon- and energy-intensity (Shackley *et al.*, 2002).

For these reasons, renewable energy systems (RES) must become the major source of the world's energy supply sooner rather than later, and a shift away from conventional fossil fuel energy systems must begun as soon as possible (Roaf *et al.*, 2004a). It is also recognised that to minimise greenhouse gas emissions during the transition it is important to improve the efficiency of energy use, that is, through the rational use of energy (RUE). In order to achieve such a rapid transformation from fossil fuel to renewable energy powered built environments, the concept of the Solar City has been developed (Droege, 2002).

The concept of a Solar City

A working definition of a Solar City is a city that aims at reducing the level of greenhouse gas emissions through a holistic strategy for the introduction of RES and the RUE to a climate stable and thus sustainable level in the year 2050 (Kates *et al.*, 1998; Droege, 2002).

Some of the stated goals of the emerging Solar Cities concept include:

- Lowering of greenhouse gas emissions by the year 2050 to an amount equal to a city's 1990 population level multiplied by 3.3 tonnes of CO_2 (Kates *et al.*, 1998; Droege, 2002). This target is based on fundamental equity calculations that each person has only an annual 3.3 tonnes emissions 'allowance', in order to allow oceans and forests to neutralise excessive carbon emissions (Byrne *et al.*, 1998)
- Identifying near- and medium-term milestones for greenhouse gas reductions according to a schedule for the years 2005–2050
- Identifying corresponding improvements in the transformation of energy production to solar and other renewable systems, reduced energy consumption, reduced consumption of natural resources, protection and improvement of urban environmental quality, improvement of social equity and improved quality of life

It has been argued (Capello, 1999; Droege, 2002) that a number of scientific and technical objectives of Solar Cities are needed to achieve the overall goals,[1] and that some key activities are needed to ensure that the objectives are met (www. solarcitiesineurope.nu).[2]

Some activities have already been implemented. The use of renewable energy and micro-power systems is already on the rise, but the current speed of change is still too slow to meet the global goals for CO_2 reduction in time to avert the pending serious crises threatened by climate change and fossil fuel depletion (Droege, 2002). Cities and towns are increasingly regarded as settings for co-ordinated policy implementation programmes aimed at global renewable energy technology introduction (Figure 18.2). Against this background a number of 'Solar City' projects and initiatives have been established as global or regional networks in Europe and America.

Figure 18.2
Solar thermal systems –
Kunming City Roofscape in
Yunan Province, China.
(*Source*: Susan Roaf, 2003.)

For example, in Ashland, Oregon, in 1996 the municipal utility supported a net metering law that established a simple grid-interconnection policy that guaranteed the purchase of exported electricity at full retail price of up to 1000 kW of excess electricity per month. On a larger scale San Francisco, spurred on by the power crisis of 2000/2001, plans to place as much as 50 mW of photovoltaic (PV) panels on city rooftops, financed by the sale of revenue bonds agreed by the electorate (www.e-coop.org/news529.cfm). In Europe the strong coalition of Solar Cities, reinforced by European research funding (www.solarcitiesineurope.nu) includes London and Berlin, and also Barcelona, a city where every new building must have a solar hot water system and where the local municipality has invested heavily in PV systems on public buildings. In 2002, a group of local Oxford Councillors, council employees, consultants and academicians put together a team to promote Oxford as a leading Solar City in the UK, and the following sections detail their approach to this challenge.

A community-based approach

Increasingly local authorities are recognising the need for efficiency, demand management and lower-carbon energy (including renewable energy) to go hand-in-hand. The more successful local authorities, for instance in dealing with related issues such as carbon reduction strategies and the mitigation of fuel poverty in the future, are likely to be those that identify the non-carbon benefits (financial, social and developmental) arising from CO_2 reduction initiatives.

Moreover, actions at the local to regional scale are needed to deliver extensive carbon emission reductions, but to date most strategic thinking has focused on national policy (Shackley et al., 2002). There is a great untapped potential for community-driven carbon reduction initiatives at the local to regional scale. The participation of local and regional authorities creates a favourable context for area-based carbon reduction as many of their key priorities have a strong link to carbon emissions (e.g. regeneration, inward investment, renewable energy, transport, new markets, job creation, rural diversification). New strategies should focus on planning and objective setting, although carbon reduction typically extends across the principal sectoral and functional priorities and groupings.

Members of the European coalition of Solar Cities are generating, not only a range of solar scenarios for their own future, but also a range of activities and funding streams to promote and demonstrate how to use buildings to generate the clean energy on which the low carbon economies of the future will be based. Lessons have been taken from other Solar Cities and will be built upon in the Oxford Solar Initiative (OSI).

The Oxford Solar Initiative (OSI)

Focus areas

The OSI emerges from a new generation of research and development that seeks city-wide applications of renewable energies and other means of greenhouse gas emissions reductions and absorption that will be applied in a coherent spatial and social context, as well as within community-wide framework.

The OSI proposes three areas of focus. They have to be advanced simultaneously. These are briefed below.

CO$_2$ reduction focused urban planning strategies

In part, due to restrictions imposed by clients, construction, design, architecture and development firms can, but rarely do, have a major influence over the embedded carbon in new developments. Local authorities, through planning strategies, should reverse this situation.

Targets, baseline studies and scenario development

Ambitious long-term targets for carbon reduction are valuable, but are often at best seen as 'aspirational'. Milestones can be used to monitor and manage the achievement of long-term targets over shorter time scales. The reason for realistic short-term targets is that expectations about reductions in energy use have been raised before, but not met, breeding disappointment and scepticism. The development of tools to evaluate and assess individual initiatives needs to be done with scientific rigour.

Urban energy technologies, industry and business development

This group of actions includes job creation, attracting green industry, creating a new 'green' economic sector, promoting entrepreneurship in the green sector, efficiency improvements that reduce expenses and improve profits (Figure 18.3).

Figure 18.3
Three areas of focus of OSI.

Figure 18.4
Actors involved in OSI.

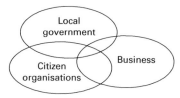

Actors involved

The OSI recognises that its success will depend upon a collaborative approach among all involved parties. In Oxford, there is recognition that it is not enough to tackle such issues only at the global and national level, but that practical, workable solutions are also required based on strong local action. Oxford is fortunate in having an elected local authority that has made a *commitment* to tackling these issues strategically. The main role of the local authority in the initiative will be as a catalyst in the creation of a local 'Oxford Team'. This team will draw together the relevant stakeholders who will in turn develop a co-ordinated approach to energy efficiency and renewable energy solutions (Figure 18.4).

The overall objective of the OSI is to find the best ways to introduce Solar Energy Technologies (SET) and the RUE in Oxford. The initiative contains several clear goals including:

- *Goal One:* 10% of all houses in Oxford will have solar systems by the year 2010
- *Goal Two:* To implement a capacity building programme for local government to provide information, training and other services oriented to CO_2 mitigation strategies
- *Goal Three:* To establish strategic alliances with, and participation of local government, households, business organisations, energy supply companies and community organisations to fulfil Oxford's CO_2 reduction targets
- *Goal Four:* To initiate and implement a solar campaign to support local CO_2 reduction initiatives at every level within the Oxford community from primary school children to business leaders

The feasibility study

The aim of the OSI was to carry out a feasibility study to lay the foundations for the establishment of a Solar Street and a Solar Suburb in Oxford. As part of the feasibility study, a survey of 700 householders was carried out to investigate attitudes towards the installation of PV, solar hot water and/or passive solar features in combination with energy efficiency measures on houses in North Oxford. The results of the survey are shown in Table 18.1.

Table 18.1
Results from the questionnaire survey. (*Source:* Roaf *et al.*, 2003.)

External wall construction		Loft insulation	
Cavity wall/not insulated	4.0%	25 mm (1″)	2.0%
Cavity wall/insulated	3.0%	50 mm (2″)	11.9%
Solid brick/stone (mainly pre-war)	67.4%	75 mm (3″)	10.9%
Do not know	8.9%	100 mm (4″)	15.8%
Other	16.8%	150 mm (6″)	5.9%
		200 mm (8″)	2.0%
		None	4.0%
		Do not know	47.5%
Draught proofing		**Hot water cylinder insulation**	
All	12.9%	Jacket	34.7%
Most	11.9%	Rigid foam	36.6%
None	25.7%	None	28.7%
Some	49.5%		
Low-energy lighting		**Secondary/double glazing**	
All	1.0%	All	25.7%
Half	2.0%	Half	3.0%
Most	9.9%	Most	11.9%
Some	66.3%	Some	40.6%
None	20.8%	None	18.8%
Types of heating		**If standard boiler or combi, year installed**	
Condensing boiler	9.9%	Before 1980	37.0%
Standard boiler	65.4%	1980–1990	29.6%
Standard combi	14.9%	1990–2000	21.0%
Other	9.9%	After 2000	12.4%
Consider applying energy efficiency		**Consider using solar energy**	
Agree	26.7%	No	2.0%
Agree strongly	64.4%	Yes	64.4%
Do not know	8.9%	Do not know	33.7%
Of yes responses, price prepared to pay for solar hot water		**Of yes responses, price prepared to pay for solar PV**	
£1000	37.0%	£1500	44.6%
£1500	26.2%	£2500	18.5%
£2000	9.2%	£5000	6.2%
£3000	3.1%	Do not know	30.8%
Do not know	24.6%		

It appears from the survey that a large percentage of the respondents (68%) have solid brick/stone walls without insulation. 26% do not have any draught proofing on their doors and windows while 50% have some draught proofing. Only 2% of the respondents have 200-mm thick loft insulation while 29% have no hot water cylinder insulation. The results showed that there is a considerable scope for improvement in terms of fabric insulation. And since only 10% of the respondents had condensing boilers, there was potential for improving heating systems also. Importantly, 91% of the respondents agree or agree strongly that they would consider applying energy efficiency measures. 65% of them also agree to consider using solar energy. And among these, 41% agree to pay £1000–1500 for solar hot water systems and £1500–2500 for solar PV systems (Roaf *et al.*, 2003). A Geographical Information System (GIS) map of the local area of North Oxford was developed to identify location of survey areas and to map the information gathered in the residents' surveys. This is shown in Figure 18.5.

The survey has demonstrated that there is a high demand for energy efficiency measures and solar advice; properties were typically in poor condition and therefore offered a high potential for improvement; the buildings services offer an additional opportunity for emission reductions. The older boilers are now ready for replacement and could be replaced

Figure 18.5
GIS map of the local area of North Oxford showing location of survey areas based on number of responses.

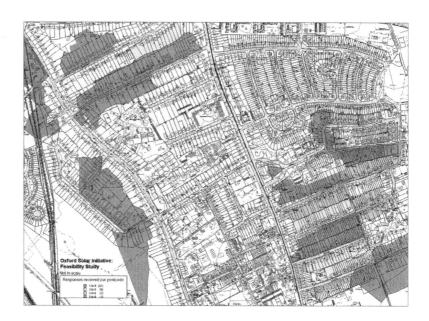

with gas condensing boilers; and solar hot water systems are a popular choice and people are willing to install them installed, if they perceive them to be reasonably priced. Furthermore, the survey confirmed that there is an excellent opportunity to pursue the implementation phase of the project, and that it made sense to prioritise energy efficiency measures before solar hot water systems and consider PV as a final (and not inexpensive) addition in the Low-Carbon Homes package.

At a city level, the project offers a huge potential for not only carbon reductions from the building stock but for providing the foundation of an affordable and effective strategy for the implementation of the Decent Homes standards, required by 2010, throughout the city (ODPM, 2001). Under the Decent Homes standard, a home is classified as decent if it is above the current statutory minimum standard for housing (the fitness standard) and in a reasonable state of repair, has reasonably modern facilities and provides a reasonable degree of thermal comfort; that is, it has effective insulation and efficient heating (DTLR, 2002; ODPM, 2003). While the original feasibility study was on private sector homes, there are many council houses in the area that are well below Decent Homes standards and could, at a minimal cost, be brought up to the required standard. There is also a great deal of interest, from Housing Associations, who see the potential for adding value to their housing stock by taking advantage of the 50% cost reductions in energy efficiency measures offered by the scheme.

Implementation of OSI

The implementation plan for the OSI is being carried forward through the following strategy.

The Oxford Solar partnership

Strategic alliances have been established with the participation, of the local government, household, business organisations, energy supply companies and community organisations advocated to implement Oxford's CO_2 reduction targets. A core group has been established with the participation of Oxford Brookes University, elected Oxford Council, the local authority and leading UK consultants specialised on RUE and SET.

The OSI team have held two public open events; one with stalls set up one Saturday on a busy city thoroughfare in Stroud.[4] The second was a successful Solar Fair in Oxford Town Hall where over 400 members of the public visited and saw a wide range of displays of solar hot water systems. The public even tried making their own solar systems and discussed their own homes and plans for the installation of energy efficiency measures and solar technologies.

Oxford Solar scenarios

The project includes scenario development using models and visualisations that can provide input into planning and strategy development, and influence research and urban development policy. This involves tailoring the relevant tools and processes for urban planning, urban and industrial strategy development to produce a range of scenarios to evaluate the optimum routes for the introduction of solar systems and RUE in Oxford. The relevant scenario development tools include back-casting techniques, exploratory scenarios and the use of scenario workshops.

Back-casting is a technique that helps people create a clear vision of a preferred future, and to devise strategies to make it happen. The outcome of a back-casting event is a timeline with specific events and quantifiable goals needed to make the vision a reality. The procedure for arriving at this is a meeting at which the lead participants, through a visioning exercise, develop a robust image of the team's preferred future. A vision is an image of an ideal future, one that most participants would like to see happen.[3] Scenarios are plausible descriptions of how things may change in the future, built to reflect what is possible, not what is preferred, desirable or undesirable. They are meant to be politically and morally neutral constructs (Roaf *et al.*, 2004b). This component is currently under way by a research team at Oxford Brookes University.

Pilot projects

There are two pilot projects under development. The first is to be a street or small area of houses equipped with PV and single point of connection to grid, sized to qualify for a Renewable Obligation Certificate. The second is the implementation of a Solar Suburb.

Working in conjunction with the Councillor member of the Core Group, the local authority, the university and consultants are promoting and developing a basic package for energy efficiency – a solar hot water and PV system. This package is linked to one of the two different economic models: selling energy to the grid through as a single energy producer (by using the Renewable Obligation Contribution), or installing individual systems by using a local CO_2 programme funding (by using national funds). The public reaction towards these two different options will be tested.

The Oxford Solar dissemination

Outreach to the public will show what Oxford can look like as a Solar City, how it can function, and why it is important. Dialogue will be entered into with citizens on the demand for different scenarios in order to build public support for processes of change towards a sustainable energy future.

Conclusion

The OSI has been designed to use a community-based approach to develop Oxford as a pioneering Solar City. The ultimate aim of the project is to build local partnerships to implement actions to reduce CO_2 emissions from the buildings of the city, by up to 90%. The project aims in turn to stimulate local industry and to ensure that the citizens of Oxford are future-proofed, in safe and comfortable homes, against the twin challenges of climate change and increasingly expensive fossil fuels. To date, the first phase of the project has demonstrated that energy efficiency measures are more popular among householders, being cheaper and better understood technologies. The householders are however, also very keen to have solar hot water systems installed, and many of them would like (eventually) to have solar PV panels on their roofs. It is estimated that with time, the take-up rate for solar systems will increase as the technology becomes more familiar.

Notes

1. The scientific and technical objectives include:

   • To better understand the energy needs of cities for different energy qualities, and the potential of different forms of RES and RUE in cities

- To identify or develop optimal strategies for rapid integration of RES and RUE in the energy systems of cities, best suited for different categories of urban areas and different city surface uses
- To optimise the performance of RES and RUE for city application
- To find ways of improving the adoption of RES and RUE technology by small- and medium-sized enterprises (SMEs)
- To identify the different actors in a community and identify their needs, possibilities and limitations

2. Key activities include:

- The collection, evaluation (analysis and assessment) and re-dissemination of information on best available techniques, successful strategies and policies, and best practices for the introduction of RES and the RUE in cities, towns and urban regions
- The evaluation and development of tools and processes for exploring how Solar Cities can function in the future and what they could look like. This includes scenario work (simple models and visualisations) that can provide input into planning and strategy development, and influence research and urban development policy. Included in this component action can be work on defining the criteria and/or targets for a city to be a Solar City within different time frames
- The evaluation and development of tools and processes for urban planning as well as city and industry strategy development. This will be an efficient way of rapidly introducing RES and the RUE in Solar Cities. This includes back-casting techniques and the use of alternative scenarios, the use of external exploratory scenarios and the use of scenario workshops
- The support for research and development of technologies for RES and the RUE with the clear aim of moving products to large-scale markets in Solar Cities
- Research on how to further increase the development of industries for RES and the RUE, with particular emphasis on the take-up of new technologies by SMEs in Solar Cities
- The implementation of a number of demonstration projects to prepare for rapid large-scale implementation of technologies for RES and the RUE in Solar Cities
- Outreach to the public to show what Solar Cities can look like and how they can function. Dialogue with citizens on the need for different scenarios in order to build public support for processes of change towards a sustainable energy future

3. Stalls were set up with the help of the Green Shop in Stroud, Chris Jardine and the Blue Planet Solar School Demonstration team.

4. For more details, see www.prospectiva.net/docs/BackcastingMaking%20it%20Happen.pdf

References

Byrne, J., Wang, Y.-D., Lee, H. and Kim, J.D. (1998) An Equity- and Sustainability-Based Policy Response to Global Climate Change. *Energy Policy*, **26(4)**: 335–343.

Capello, R., Nijkamp, P., Pepping, G. and Bithas, K. (1999) *Sustainable Cities and Energy Policies*, Springer, Berlin.

Carbon Trust (2001) *The Carbon Trust: Leading the Way to a Low Carbon Economy*, The Carbon Trust. Retrieved on 4 June 2002 from the World Wide Web: http://www.thecarbontrust.co.uk/template.cfm?name=objectives

Department for Environment, Transport and the Regions (DETR) (2000) *Climate Change: The UK Programme*, The Stationery Office Limited, London.

Department of Transport, Local Government and the Regions (DTLR) (2002) *Decent Homes: Capturing the Standard at the Local Level*, Department for Transport, Local Government and the Regions, London.

Droege, P. (2002) *Solar City*, Retrieved on 30 May 2003 from the World Wide Web: http://www.solarcity.org/solarcity/contents.htm

Graves, H.M. and Phillipson, M.C. (2000) *Potential Implications of Climate Change in the Built Environment*, Foundation for the Built Environment, London.

Houghton, J., Jenkins, G. and Ephraums, J., eds. (1990) *Climate Change: The IPCC Scientific Assessment*, Cambridge University Press, Cambridge.

Hulme, M. and Jenkins, G. (1998) *Climate Change Scenarios for the United Kingdom: Scientific Report*, UKCIP Technical Report No. 1, Climate Research Unit, Norwich.

Hulme, M., Jenkins, G., Lu, X., Turnpenny, J., Mitchell, T., Jones, R., Lowe, J., Murphy, J., Hassell, D., Boorman, P., McDonald, R. and Hill, S. (2002) *Climate Change Scenarios for the United Kingdom: The UKCIP02 Scientific Report*, Tyndall Centre for Climate Change Research, School of Environmental Sciences, University of East Anglia, Norwich.

Institute of Environmental Management and Assessment (IEMA) (2000) *Managing Climate Change: A Business Guide*, Institute of Environmental Management and Assessment, London.

Inter-departmental Analysts Group (IAG) (2002) *Long-term Reductions in Greenhouse Gas Emissions in the UK*, Report of an Inter-departmental Analysts Group, London.

Intergovernmental Panel on Climate Change (IPCC) (1996) *Climate Change 1995: The Science of Climate Change: Contribution of Working Group I to the Second Assessment Report of the Intergovernmental Panel on Climate Change*, Cambridge University Press, Cambridge, UK and New York, USA.

Intergovernmental Panel on Climate Change (IPCC) (2001) *Climate Change 2001: The Scientific Basis: Contribution of Working Group I to the Third Assessment Report of the Intergovernmental Panel on Climate Change*. Cambridge University Press, Cambridge.

Kates, R., Mayfield, M.W., Torrie, R.D. and Witcher, B. (1998) Methods for Estimating Greenhouse Gases from Local Places. *Local Environ*, **3(3)**: 279–298.

Met Office (1999) *The Greenhouse Effect and Climate Change: A Briefing from the Hadley Centre*, Meteorological Office Communications, Bracknell.

Office of the Deputy Prime Minister (ODPM) (2001) *Quality and Choice: A Decent Home for All: The Way Forward for Housing*, Office of the Deputy Prime Minister, London.

Office of the Deputy Prime Minister (ODPM) (2003) *The Decent Homes Target Implementation Plan*, Office of the Deputy Prime Minister, London.

Performance and Innovation Unit (PIU) (2002) *The Energy Review*, Performance and Innovation Unit, Cabinet Office, London.

Roaf, S., Fuentes, M. and Thomas, S. (2001) *Ecohouse: A Design Guide*, Architectural Press, Oxford.

Roaf, S., Fuentes, M. and Gupta, R. (2003) *Feasibility Study Report on the Oxford Solar Initiative*, Submitted to the Energy Saving Trust, Department of Architecture, Oxford Brookes University, Oxford.

Roaf, S., Crichton, D. and Nicol, F. (2004a) *Adapting Buildings and Cities to a Changing Climate*, RIBA Publications Ltd., London.

Roaf, S., Horsley, A. and Gupta, R. (2004b) *Closing the Loop: Benchmarks for Sustainable Buildings*, RIBA Publications Ltd., London.

Royal Commission on Environmental Pollution (RCEP) (2000) *Energy – the Changing Climate: Summary of the Royal Commission on Environmental Pollution's Report*, HMSO, London.

Shackley, S., Fleming, P. and Bulkeley, H. (June 2002) *Low Carbon Spaces Area-based Carbon Emission Reduction: A Scoping Study*, A report to the Sustainable Development Commission prepared by the Tyndall Centre for Climate Change Research, Norwich.

Shorrock, L. and Henderson, G. (1990) *Energy Use in Buildings and Carbon Dioxide Emissions*, Building Research Establishment, Watford.

Smith, P. (2001) *Architecture in a Climate of Change: A Guide to Sustainable Design*, Architectural Press, Oxford.

UNEP and UNFCCC (2001) *Climate Change Information Kit*, United Nations Environment Programme's Information Unit for Conventions, Geneva.

Watson, T., Zinyowera, M. and Moss, H. (1996) *Technologies, Policies and Measures for Mitigating Climate Change*, IPCC Technical Paper 1, Geneva.

Quantification of Urban Solar Access

The concept of solar access is an abstraction generalized from particular observations. The natural world appears to abound with examples of arrangements based in some measure on exposure to the sun. More to the point, observations of the modern built world reveal that we have not usually followed nature's example in this regard. Our cities are non-directional. Our buildings are undifferentiated by orientation to the sun. They stand static, unresponsive to the rhythms of their surroundings.

Ralph L. Knowles (1981)

Introduction

The interaction between buildings and light from the sun and sky is a defining characteristic of the urban environment. Daylight is by its very nature a dynamic phenomenon. The urban form, in particular its vertical extent, serves to amplify the dynamic character of daylight through the casting and progression of shadows by tall buildings. Planners and architects have long appreciated, at least qualitatively, that the perception of the urban environment is directly related to the prevailing daylight conditions, or as it is often called, the *solar access*. A characteristic feature of urban environments is the large gradient in solar access over small spatial scales. An office or apartment perceived as brightly daylit may be one that, a few storeys below, is quite shaded. A pedestrian in the city is likely to

371

experience both well- and poorly-daylit areas during the shortest of walks. It is of course quite natural for people to associate a wide range of subjective environmental and social factors with the perceived solar access. Offices or apartments where the main windows see little of the sky may be considered gloomy and unattractive. Streets or zones with very restricted solar access may be perceived as squalid or dismal. In public spaces, poor solar access may even be associated with criminal and anti-social behaviour, such as muggings or vandalism. Whatever the realities of the situation, the perceived amenity of living or working spaces and the use that people make of the public spaces will depend in part on the perceptions that are related to solar access. This presents a formidable problem to planners and architects: How can the constantly changing daylight in urban environments be assessed in terms of some meaningful measure of solar access? In the sections that follow, the traditional methods used to estimate solar access are described and their shortcomings identified. A new schema to quantify urban solar access is proposed and the means to compute it are outlined. A series of examples demonstrating application of the new schema are presented.

Imagining solar access

A (non-exhaustive) list of factors relating to commonly perceived notions of solar access might read as follows:

- *Overall perception of the space (internal or external)*; Is the space 'bright/open' or 'gloomy/squalid'?
- *Direct exposure to sunlight*; Can the sun be 'seen', and, if so, for how long?
- *Availability of daylight*; How 'much' of the sky is visible? Is there a greater 'view' of sky for some directions than others, for example to the north or south?

Efforts to systematize these perceptions into a schema that can be applied to the evaluation of building designs or urban plans has not resulted in a consensus view: solar access means different things to different people. Two very different analytical techniques are commonly employed in an attempt to make some measure of solar access in urban environments. One of these is based on shadow patterns cast by the sun at various times of the year; for example, on the summer solstice. For this, a sequence of images is produced using either scale models with a heliodon

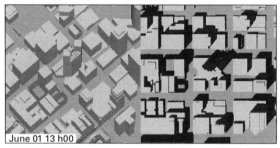

June 01 11 h00

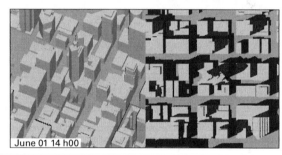

June 01 12 h00

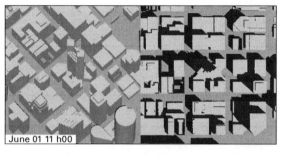

June 01 13 h00

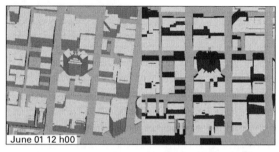

June 01 14 h00

Figure 19.1
Shading patterns for
San Francisco 3D model.

or by computer rendering (Figure 19.1). This approach is essentially qualitative: the brightness of the sun plays no part and the light from the sky is not considered. The other method is based on the illumination provided by a single (i.e. unchanging) standard overcast sky without sun. The brightness of the standard overcast sky increases gradually with altitude from the horizon to the zenith, but it does not vary with azimuth. In other words, the illumination received at any surface will not change if the building model is rotated about the vertical axis.[1] Although quantitative, the second approach is highly idealized because only one sky condition is considered: no account whatsoever is made of the sun or non-overcast skies (Figure 19.2). It may be that both methods are employed together. However it is not at all clear how, in an analysis, it is possible to weigh one (or more) shadow patterns against a measure of the illumination from a (sunless) overcast sky.

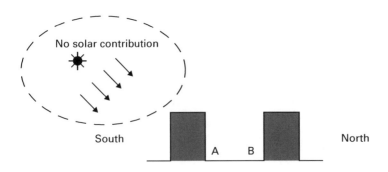

Figure 19.2
Overcast sky approach.

Where attempts have been made to recommend (usually) minimum levels of solar access, the definitions vary and are largely incompatible. For example, in San Jose (USA) solar access is defined as the unobstructed availability of direct sunlight at solar noon on December 21; the winter solstice. Whereas in Boulder (Colorado, USA) an ordinance was enacted to guarantee unobstructed sunlight availability between 10 a.m. and 2 p.m. on December 21. These could be tested using the shadow pattern technique. Other definitions make a less specific measure of solar access, for example, the solar envelope (Knowles, 1981).

The current situation with the evaluation of solar access has arisen because the fundamentals of the two most commonly used approaches have changed little over the past 50 years. Indeed, they are now part of the mental landscape of the majority of practitioners and researchers, be they planners, architects or engineers. Computer modelling may be used nowadays in preference to scale models to generate shadow patterns and predict illuminance under standard overcast sky conditions. This however gives only the illusion of progress because the fundamental limitations are an intrinsic part of the methodology itself, not the means by which it is carried out.

The reality of our everyday experience of the daylit luminous environment differs markedly from what the two most commonly used assessment methods can tell us. Light from the sun and the sky (overcast, clear, etc.), both directly and indirectly, illuminates the urban environment. And, of course, the sun and sky act *together* to provide illumination. Direct sunlight accounts, overall, for about half of the available daylight energy. The remainder comes from the sky and is usually referred to as *diffuse light*. Of the diffuse (sky) light, less than half of that, depending on locale, is due to conditions that approximate standard overcast. It is evident therefore that the

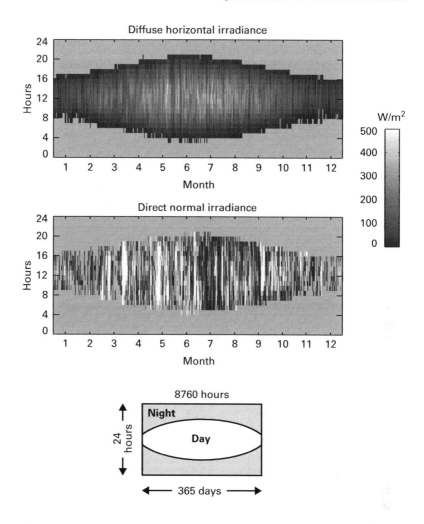

Figure 19.3
Visualization of meteorological
data.

shadow casting and overcast sky methods, either independently or together, provide only a very limited insight into solar access. To advance our perception of solar access, indeed to make some measure of it that is closer to our experience of the daylit environment, we first need to examine the underlying meteorological conditions.

And the forecast is ...

The quantity and character of light from the sun and sky are subject to regular daily and seasonal patterns of variation together with irregular events governed by local meteorological conditions. An illustration of the dynamic nature of sky and sun conditions is given in Figure 19.3. Hourly values of diffuse horizontal irradiance and direct normal irradiance over a period of a full year are shown as (tiny) shaded rectangles arranged in a 365 (days of the year) by 24 (hours of the day) matrix. The diffuse horizontal irradiance is the energy from the sky that is incident on an unobstructed horizontal surface. The direct normal irradiance is the energy from the sun and circumsolar region incident on a surface that is normal to the direction of the sun. The shading in Figure 19.3 represents the magnitude of the irradiation with zero values shaded light-gray. Presented in this way it is easy to appreciate both the prevailing patterns in either quantity and their short-term variability. Most obvious is the daily/seasonal pattern for both irradiances: short periods of daylight in the winter months and longer in summer. The hour-by-hour variation in the direct normal irradiance is clearly visible, though it is also present to a lesser degree in the diffuse horizontal irradiance (i.e. from the sky). Of course, both diffuse and direct irradiances will, in reality, vary over periods shorter than an hour. However, the hourly datasets are the most generally available and they do exhibit much of the variation in conditions that might be expected (e.g. in the absolute magnitudes of the two quantities, the occurring sun positions, etc.). Furthermore, these standard datasets provide definitive yardstick quantities for modelling purposes.[2]

It is relatively a straightforward matter to generate sky and sun conditions from, respectively, the diffuse horizontal and the direct normal irradiance quantities. It is understood that it is impossible to recreate an actually occurring sky brightness pattern from a measurement of diffuse horizontal irradiance because a real sky will exhibit unique brightness configurations resulting from cloud patterns and so on. However, it is possible to achieve reasonable approximations to actually occurring conditions using theoretical sky models that generate idealized sky brightness patterns from the basic irradiance quantities found in climate datasets. The character of the sky brightness pattern (e.g. overcast, intermediate or clear) can be inferred from the relative values in the diffuse horizontal and the direct normal irradiances, and the sun position is calculated from the 'time-stamp'.

To recap, the theoretical models and the basic meteorological data exist to generate hour-by-hour descriptions for the sky and sun that are representative of actual conditions for the majority of locales in the developed world. Then how might we make use of these to assess solar access? One possibility is to make a quantitative measure of illumination for an urban setting at one or more times of the year using sky and sun conditions generated from the meteorological data. Unfortunately, this approach will give only a 'snapshot' of solar access, as indicated by the resulting illumination, for the times examined.

Whilst it can be informative to determine, say, a monthly average for a scalar quantity such as temperature, illumination is strongly dependent on the directional character of the incident light. Associated with every data value in Figure 19.3 are the solar altitude and azimuth which, of course, vary from hour to hour.[3] In terms of providing a basis for predicting solar access, the notion of 'average' days is less than useful because an 'average' sun position would give entirely misleading patterns of illumination. In fact, simple averages could result in sun positions that never occur in reality, for example sun position due south and at a lower altitude than that for the winter solstice. Illumination parameters, therefore, are generally not suited to manipulations such as averaging. Sub-sampling the meteorological dataset (e.g. taking only the first day of each month) will reduce the number of hours to consider. However, the action will inevitably introduce biases because equally valid but most likely quite different sky and sun conditions/positions would be excluded. Indeed, it seems that the only way to avoid the pitfalls of averaging or sub-sampling is to consider the meteorological dataset in its *entirety*. That is, all the hourly sky and sun conditions for a period of a full year. Only this can capture the full range of both the short- and long-term variations in the sky and sun conditions. A schema to evaluate solar access based on a full year's meteorological data is described in the next section.

The new schema

There are essentially two ways to base an evaluation of solar access on the illumination provided by all of the hourly meteorological conditions that can be generated from a Test Reference Year (TRY) dataset. One is to examine the time series of illumination, hour by hour, that results from all of the unique sky and sun conditions. Necessarily, this would involve the manipulation and analysis of large amounts of data, approximately 4000 values (i.e. daylight hours) for every location evaluated. The other, much more straightforward method, is to base the measure of solar access itself on the *cumulative* effect of the illumination that results from *all* of the unique sky and sun conditions. In other words, on a measure of all the light energy from the sun and sky that is incident on a surface over a period of a full year. It is proposed that this second method offers a true measure of solar access because it accounts for the totality of illumination (light from the sun and the sky over a period of a full year) and presents it as a definite, numerical value.

The cumulative light energy over a period of a full year is called the *total annual irradiation* which has units of Watt-hours per m^2 (per year). It has a visual equivalent called the total annual illumination which has units of lux-hours (per year). Equating solar access with total annual irradiation (or illumination) is consistent with the prevailing experience of daylight where the sky and sun together interact with the urban form to create the luminous environment. Daylight, as noted, is subject to enormous variation, and 'snapshot' evaluations (i.e. shading patterns on particular day) reveal little about the prevailing conditions. Thus a period of a full year is needed to account for the hour-by-hour, day-by-day and seasonal variability that sky and sun conditions are subject to. Any shorter period would introduce biases and be unrepresentative.

How then can we begin to investigate solar access (defined as total annual irradiation) in urban settings? In principle, it would be a straightforward matter to measure the total annual irradiation (or illumination) at an actual location by recording the incident irradiance (or illuminance) over a complete 12-month period. The total (annual) irradiation is simply the integral over time of all the measured irradiances. Of course, in practice maintaining a single recording instrument over a full year would be a costly as well as lengthy exercise. Also, a large number of locations would need to be measured to gain any insight into how the solar access is related to the urban form. Furthermore, it is preferable to have the predictions of total annual irradiation founded on reference meteorological datasets, which would allow for meaningful comparison between examples. At first sight, physical modelling using one of the latest generation sky simulator domes (SSDs) seems capable of delivering predictions of total annual illumination. Here, a scale model of an urban setting could be 'wired-up' with illuminance metres and the brightness pattern of the SSD could be generated from a reference meteorological dataset. The 4000 or so daylight hours of the year could, in principle, be modelled fairly swiftly using 'accelerated days'. However, SSDs were discovered to be inherently subject to parallax errors (Mardaljevic, 2002a) and the rapid changing of lamp output to mimic 'accelerated days' is considered problematic due to calibration and stability issues. Physical modelling is therefore not considered a practical method for predicting total annual irradiation. Computer simulation offers a far more effective, reliable and consistent approach to predict and investigate total annual irradiation than physical measurements in either real or scale model settings. A computer-based method to predict total annual irradiation in arbitrarily complex urban settings has recently been developed by the author (Mardaljevic and Rylatt, 2003). The design goals for the new approach are as follows:

- To accurately predict the total annual incident irradiation/ illumination on surfaces (e.g. ground, building) based on hourly meteorological data. To provide facility to compute any temporal or source component of total annual irradiation, for example seasonal, direct sun only
- To include the contributions of realistic sky patterns as well as radiation from the sun
- To account for shading of and inter-reflections between buildings
- To present results as images
- To extract geometrical information from the images to allow for quantitative assessment of the surface area associated with each pixel

These aims have been realised in a simulation approach that uses the state-of-the-art rendering and data visualization techniques. The new approach is called *Irradiation mapping for Complex Urban Environments* or ICUE.[4] The ICUE approach is currently implemented in software on a UNIX workstation as an 'expert-user' tool for proof-of-concept, demonstration and research. The ICUE simulation system is a suite of programs and scripts to initiate, process and view irradiation images. The underlying numerical 'engine' for ICUE is the rigorously validated (UNIX) *Radiance* lighting simulation system (Ward, 1998). The theoretical basis for ICUE is derived from the work carried out by the author on lighting simulation, validation and data analysis/visualization (Mardaljevic, 1995; 1997; 2001; 2002b).

The data requirements for the ICUE simulation are a three-dimensional (3D) model of the urban setting (i.e. building geometry and surface reflectivities) and a meteorological dataset for that locale. If the surface reflectivities are not known, then typical values for building materials should be assumed. A series of example results using the ICUE approach are given in the next section. For the remainder of this chapter, solar access will be taken to mean either the total annual irradiation or the total annual illumination depending on the context.

Solar access made visible

The possible application areas for ICUE are illustrated here using a series of demonstration examples.

San Francisco: a dense urban setting

The first scene that was irradiation mapped using ICUE was a computer-aided design (CAD) model of the De Montfort University Campus in Leicester. Although it was instructive to visualize for the first time the solar access and how it relates to a particular built form, the De Montfort campus buildings are fairly low rise with only moderate overshadowing. It was decided therefore to apply the technique next to a dense urban setting with many high-rise buildings where it might be expected that complex patterns in the solar access would be revealed. This was indeed the case for the San Francisco city model (used earlier for the shading example), as can be seen from the five views of the 'target area' shown in Figure 19.4. The total annual irradiation (or illumination) is shown using colour (see legend in Figure 19.4). The image in the middle shows the view from the zenith of the 'target area'. The surrounding images show the views from the four mid-compass directions (e.g. north–east, south–east, etc.). Most readily apparent is the difference in the total annual irradiation between the two views from the north and those from the south. On closer inspection, the large gradients in total annual irradiation across many of the building facades becomes evident.[5]

These images are first and foremost representations of quantitative data the result of exacting computations. However, their significance can be readily appreciated by non-engineers: planners and architects who have seen the approach have understood immediately the significance of the data. This is in large part because the approach is image based. Each 600×600 pixel image is comparable to a visualization of the annual total of hourly data collected by 360,000 irradiance metres arranged over the building facades, ground, etc. Therein lies one of the key advantages of an image-based approach over a points-based calculation: the new technique makes visible, literally, the solar access in complex urban settings.[6] The individual pixel values can be read interactively on-screen using the ICUE display software.

The San Francisco city model was chosen because it was, at the time, the most detailed 3D model freely available on the World

N

kWh/m²		kLuxh
1400		1.7E5
1000		1.2E5
600		7E4
200		2.4E4
Total energy		Visible part

Figure 19.4
Solar access images for
San Francisco.

Wide Web.[7] ICUE predicts total annual irradiation based on hourly meteorological data. Therefore, a time series of basic irradiance quantities for San Francisco was needed, that is hourly values of global horizontal irradiance and diffuse horizontal irradiance for a full year. The climate dataset, Typical Meteorological Year (TMY) for San Francisco, was downloaded from the Renewable Resource Data Centre in the USA. Hourly sun and sky conditions for San Francisco were derived from the meteorological data and used in the simulations. An unexpected feature of using San Francisco was that the total annual irradiation on unshaded east-facing surfaces was predicted to be a little lower than on unshaded west-facing surfaces. This was puzzling as weather files for other locations did not show this effect. Further investigation revealed that this is in fact a consequence of the San Francisco morning fog. The fog occurs so regularly throughout the year that its effect is present in the weather file: irradiation from the sun in the morning (in the east) is slightly attenuated compared to irradiation in the afternoon (in the west) when the fog has lifted. It is noteworthy that this subtle aspect of the locale should be discernable in the visualizations of the solar access. The use of the San Francisco model was also important to demonstrate the inherent scaleability of ICUE: the system does not contain any practical limits on the complexity of the model and it can be equally applied to small-scale architectural features as to large-scale city models.

Harvesting solar energy: building integrated photovoltaics

Of the renewable technologies that have been proposed to reduce the carbon emissions associated with the energy consumption of buildings, *in situ* generation of electricity by photovoltaics (PVs) is considered one of the most promising (IEA, 1998). PV devices at present are based on silicon in various formulations. New materials and novel approaches to PV fabrication are under vigorous investigation. Whatever the type of the PV module, the potential for exploitation of building integrated photovoltaic (BIPV) installations depends primarily on the available solar irradiation. A recent report by the Department of Trade and Industry gave details of 16 typical BIPV projects (DTI, 2000). For these demonstration projects recently completed, planned or speculative, shading issues were largely avoided by choosing open sites with minimal nearby obstructions. However, in the medium- to long-term BIPV in dense urban environments will need to be considered since this is where the majority of energy use takes place. The wider adoption of BIPV will depend on sound demonstrations of its economic viability. Foremost in the evaluation of PV economics is the calculation of the available solar energy. The ICUE images allow rapid identification of candidate facade and roof areas where the total annual irradiation is sufficient to warrant consideration as a site for BIPV. The ICUE images given in this chapter show cumulative totals of irradiation.

The performance of a BIPV installation is degraded by transient-shading effects, which are not revealed by cumulative totals. Therefore, detailed analysis of these effects would be required once a candidate site has been identified.[8]

Strategic irradiation mapping of city models

One of the conceivable uses for the ICUE system is the large-scale quantification of building facade areas, graded for total annual irradiation. This provides information on the potential for wide-scale deployment of various solar-dependent facade technologies (e.g. BIPV, electrochromic (EC) glazing, solar control glazing). Economic models for the wide-scale deployment of emerging facade technologies have often been based on estimates of the total facade area. However, the effectiveness of these technologies is critically dependent on the magnitude of the exposure to total annual irradiation. Thus, the true potential market for wide-scale deployment of these emerging technologies is more reliably determined from the quantified solar access. How this would be achieved in practice is as follows.[9] The building facade area, graded for total annual irradiation, was determined for the entirety of the 3D model. To gain further insight into this parameter (and to demonstrate the processing capabilities of ICUE), a two-dimensional (2D) grading was used. The facade area was sorted into bands of total annual irradiation and height above ground. The results are shown in Table 19.1. The total area for vertical and slightly sloping facades was determined to be $1.18 \times 10^6 \, \mathrm{m}^2$. The target area was set to include the entire model (to remove the need for incremental steps) and the usual five views were generated. The irradiation

Table 19.1
Facade area (m²) graded for total annual irradiation and height above the ground level for the San Francisco model.

Height range (m)	Total annual irradiation (Wh/m²)			
	4E5–6E5	6E5–8E5	8E5–1.0E6	>1.0E6
3–25	1.04E+05	4.96E+04	3.73E+04	1.92E+04
25–50	1.03E+05	7.68E+04	4.78E+04	1.66E+04
50–75	6.96E+04	9.08E+04	5.71E+04	1.68E+04
75–100	3.54E+04	6.91E+04	6.31E+04	1.64E+04
100–125	1.85E+04	3.86E+04	4.94E+04	1.84E+04
125–150	7.47E+03	2.51E+04	3.52E+04	2.17E+04
150–175	6.44E+03	1.44E+04	2.11E+04	1.74E+04
175–200	2.68E+03	3.82E+03	6.80E+03	4.08E+03
>200	2.13E+03	3.36E+03	7.01E+03	3.17E+03

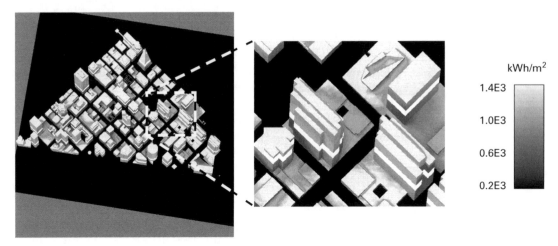

kWh/m²

1.4E3

1.0E3

0.6E3

0.2E3

Figure 19.5
Solar access images for San
Francisco. Facade areas in
the height range 50–75 m are
highlighted white.

map for one view is given in Figure 19.5. The data given in Table 19.1 are unprecedented both in scale and resolution.[10] ICUE can therefore be rightly described as a *strategic modelling tool*.

An architectural masterplan

The ICUE approach was used to assess a 500-m² section of a masterplan design for solar access at ground level (Figure 19.6). The accommodation blocks have varying height, spacing and roof slope. This produces marked variation in solar access at ground level; the region marked A has much higher exposure to daylight than region B. Whilst this could be inferred qualitatively from a 3D physical or computer model, the ICUE simulation gives a precise figure: the overall daylight exposure at B is only 15% of that at A. The colour scale shows units of total annual daylight energy (kWh/m²) and the visible component (kLuxh).

Assessment of massing schemes

The 3D CAD modelling is now commonly used in the early stages of design to investigate massing schemes. Several of the commercial CAD packages offer rudimentary shading of 3D models.[11] Some of the packages include shadow casting to reveal patterns of shading around buildings at various times of the day or year (see Figure 19.1). In contrast, a single image showing the total annual irradiation provides an immediate insight into the solar access and how it relates to the built form. Consider the example of a group of equally sized tower blocks

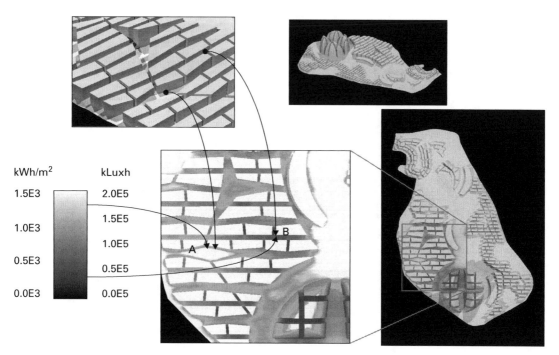

kWh/m² kLuxh

1.5E3   2.0E5

        1.5E5

1.0E3   1.0E5

0.5E3   0.5E5

0.0E3   0.0E5

Figure 19.6
Quantification of solar access for
masterplan scheme (Singapore).

with progressively increased spacing (Figure 19.7.1). The
ground-level solar access viewed from above is shown in Figure
19.7.2. Here the data were processed to show the solar access
as the percentage of total annual irradiation incident on an
unobstructed horizontal surface.[12] The relation between the solar
access and the spacing between the blocks is evident as is the
difference in solar access to the north and to the south sides of
the tower blocks. Notice that there is a 90% contour south of the
tower blocks as well as to the north. This is mainly due to partial
obstruction of northern sky from points on the ground that are
to the south of the tower blocks. Several planners and architects
who have seen these and other ICUE images have remarked
that, not only are the ICUE graphics highly informative, but also
it is actually *quicker* to comprehend an ICUE image than it is to
unpick the significance of a sequence of shadow pattern images.

Changing cities: changing solar access

The cost and financing of a BIPV installation is usually based
on an effective electricity producing lifetime of 20 or more
years. Cities can change dramatically over these timescales with

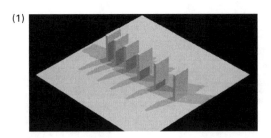

(1)

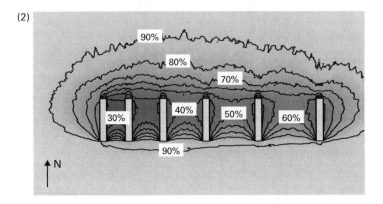

(2)

↑N

Figures 19.7
Ground level solar access
around variously spaced tower
blocks.

new-build creating or adding to the overshadowing of existing BIPV arrays. Any introduction of, or increase in, overshadowing will reduce the power output from a BIPV array. The degree of injury to a BIPV array caused by overshadowing will be closely related to the decrease in total annual irradiation. The ICUE approach can compute this decrease using a simple technique called '*difference mapping*'. Here the ICUE simulations are carried out for the scene both *without* and *with* the proposed building: viewpoints showing the 'at-risk' facades would be chosen. The total annual irradiation image with the proposed building in place is subtracted from that of the original scene. Thus it is possible to visualize, and indeed quantify, the impact of the proposed building in terms of the reduction in the incident total annual irradiation on the existing buildings. This can then form the basis for a measure of financial injury resulting from reduced power output.

The financial injury due to overshadowing on a BIPV array is a relatively straightforward quantity to estimate. Putting a price on injury due to reduced solar access at a window, however, is considerably more problematic because, unlike electricity, units of daylight (e.g. the Luxh) do not have a tangible monetary value. In part, this is because effective daylighting for buildings needs artificial lighting controls that respond to varying levels of daylight illumination. Recent field trials in San Francisco have shown that daylight responsive lighting control systems can 'bring about sustainable reductions of 30–41% in electrical energy for an outermost row of lights in a perimeter zone, and 16–22% for the second row of lights' (Rubinstein *et al.*, 1999). The field trials should be repeated for other settings and locales. However, it is clear that there is considerable potential to reduce the electricity demand for lighting. Thus it should be possible to place a monetary value on daylight. However, as noted in the previous section, solar gain and the resulting cooling also figure in the estimation of overall energy consumption. It may be that additional overshadowing could *reduce* the energy consumption of the 'injured' building if the reduction in cooling exceeds the increase in electric lighting consumption.[13] These interactions are complex, but it is conceivable that the irradiation mapping could be enhanced to include some representation of the energy flows across the building perimeter. Then it would be possible to carry out fairly detailed energy modelling of the facade and perimeter zone of the building using only the building envelope and a 'virtual construct' for the internal spaces. The theoretical basis for an enhanced version of ICUE is currently being formulated.

Solar access responsive facade configurations

The building facade is a key determining factor for the lighting and cooling requirements of a building. Use of daylight can displace electric lighting for long periods of the year. However, a facade that brings in ample daylight may also admit high solar gains, leading to electric cooling requirements that could outweigh the savings in displaced electric lighting. An 'optimum' facade design would be one that maximizes the energy-saving potential of daylight against the solar cooling load. Although the precise relation is complex, the ideal transmission properties for an energy-saving facade depend in some way on the solar access. Evidently, the largest degree of solar control is needed where the solar access is the greatest. In urban settings, the total annual irradiation can vary by an order of magnitude or more across just one facade of a tall building. The degree of variation is greater still when all of the facade orientations are taken into account. Although there is work to be done to calibrate the facade transmission properties for energy performance with respect to total annual irradiation, the ICUE images provide an indication of how building facades

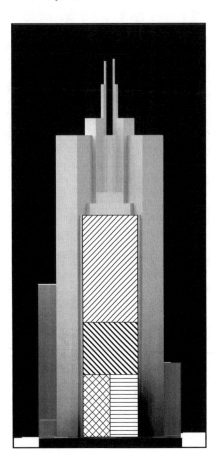

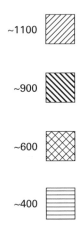

~1100

~900

~600

~400

Figure 19.8
Solar access responsive façade
configurations.

could be configured to be *responsive* to the local solar access. The example in Figure 19.8 shows how a facade might be apportioned into regions of broadly similar solar access. The notion of 'inhomogeneous' facade configurations may not be immediately welcomed by some in the, traditionally conservative, construction industry. Here perhaps, the lead could be taken by those architects that are attracted by new design possibilities. A facade design that is responsive to the local solar access should be seen as *enriching* architectural possibilities as well as providing a more energy-efficient building.

Components of solar access

In addition to total annual irradiation (or illumination), ICUE can produce images showing components of the total which can further inform our understanding of solar access. For example, images can be generated to show any of the following: the maximum possible number of sun hours; the irradiation (or illumination) resulting from sky only; the irradiation (or illumination) due to inter-reflection between buildings, and so forth. Furthermore, seasonal or monthly images can be generated in addition to annual totals. The simulation data can also be processed to generate a time series of irradiation (or illumination) data for any point, or collection of points, in the image.

The prevailing temporal aspect of solar access could be investigated by comparing images processed to show the total annual irradiation for the before-noon and after-noon hours separately. The subtle effects of inter-reflection between buildings can be revealed by different mapping images created using building models with different reflective properties.

Government agencies have responded to calls from various quarters to promote 'green' spaces in the cities. The amenity aspects of green spaces are usually the foremost in these discussions. However, in dense urban environments a key consideration is the availability of daylight to support plant growth and survival. Plant species for shaded 'green' areas could be selected on the basis of the predicted levels of the photosynthetic component of total annual irradiation. Here perhaps knowledge of the seasonal components would be helpful too. Assessments of the available area and prevailing illumination for planting could be carried out at a city-wide scale (see Figure 19.5).

Conclusion

The notion of 'solar architecture' has existed since the dawn of architecture itself. In 400BC, Socrates is believed to have considered solar design principles in house construction (Butti and Perlin, 1980). For low-rise domestic and small dwellings, it is true that Socrates' observations still have relevance today. However, it is also true that the evaluation paradigm for solar architecture has changed little since the Socrates' time; it is still essentially qualitative and woefully inadequate for the design and evaluation of buildings in urban settings. Knowle's observations bear repeating: '*Our cities are non-directional. Our buildings are undifferentiated by orientation to the sun. They stand static, unresponsive to the rhythms of their surroundings.*' Design principles that are heedless of the character and quantity of solar access in urban settings will not produce buildings that maximize energy efficiency. By equating solar access with total annual irradiation we give it a definite meaning. Thus we create a much needed criterion with which to evaluate solar architecture on a quantitative basis. The new schema presented here offers a powerful insight into urban solar access. More significantly, it paves the way for the formulation of urban design principles where the morphology and fabric of buildings are fashioned in response to the local solar access to maximize their energy-saving potential; one of the goals of urban sustainability.

Notes

1. Standard overcast sky brightness patterns can be mimicked in artificial skies for physical modelling or reproduced exactly for computer simulation studies.

2. These hourly time series are known variously as Test Reference Year (TRY) or Typical Meteorological Year (TMY) datasets. They are readily available for many locales across the developed world and are ordinarily used for dynamic thermal modelling.

3. As well as specifying the position of the sun, the altitude and azimuth also fix the position of the circumsolar region for non-overcast skies.

4. Pronounced IQ.

5. The images are best appreciated in colour. A set of 'online' colour figures for this Chapter are available from the author.

6. A points-based calculation is one that produces a prediction for one or points in list form. As the list of numbers is not directly associated with the scene geometry, it is impossible to understand the form and variation of solar access in a way that is comparable to the ICUE image-based approach.

7. As is common with 3D models on the web, the San Francisco model was in Virtual Reality Markup Language (VRML) format. The VRML format was designed to be converted to and not from. Thus, there were difficulties in converting it to a form needed for the simulations, and a few polygons were lost in the process (missing roof tops in Figure 19.4). The VRML itself would have been generated from CAD formats such as DXF of 3D Studio. The city model would have imported into the simulation intact had these formats been available.

8. There exists in ICUE a capability to generate time-series irradiation data for selected pixels as well as cumulative totals. The possibility of generating an image representing some summary of the degree of occurrence of transient effects is currently being investigated.

9. The San Francisco Financial District is used once again because it was the most complex city model available to the author at the time.

10. The algorithms that compute the total facade area are not exact and the degree of imprecision will depend on the building form. In particular, facades on re-entrant building surfaces may be partially accounted for. However, these usually make up only a small percentage of the total facade area. This is a minor imprecision in the context of the wealth of previously unobtainable data and insight delivered by the ICUE system.

11. That is, not a physically correct lighting simulation.

12. The 'jaggies' in the contour lines result from sampling the continuous motion of the sun at discrete intervals. Here, the sampling is equivalent to a sun position sampled at intervals of less than 1 hour throughout the year. The 'jaggies' can never be entirely eliminated, but they can be reduced with greater computational effort (i.e. more frequent sampling).

13. There are believed to be instances where a new building with a highly reflective facade causes 'injury' on neighbouring buildings by reflecting solar radiation onto them and increasing their cooling load.

References

Butti, K. and Perlin, J. (1980) *A Golden Thread: 2500 Years of Solar Architecture and Technology*, Van Nostrand Reinhold, New York.

Department of Trade and Industry (DTI) (2000) *Photovoltaics in Buildings: BIPV Projects* ETSU S/P2/00328/REP, London.

International Energy Agency (IEA) (1998) *Photovoltaic Power Systems Programme – Strategy Document 1998–2002*, International Energy Agency, London.

Knowles, R. (1981) *Sun Rhythm Form* Cambridge, MIT Press, Massachusetts and London.

Mardaljevic, J. (1995) Validation of a Lighting Simulation Program under Real Sky Conditions. *Lighting Research and Technology* **27(4)**: 181–188.

Mardaljevic, J. (1997) *Validation of Lighting Simulation Program: A Study Using Measured Sky Brightness Distributions*, Lux Europa 97, Amsterdam, Proc. 555–56.

Mardaljevic, J. (2001) The BRE-IDMP Dataset: A New Benchmark for the Validation of Illuminance Prediction Techniques. *Lighting Research and Technology* **33(2)**:117–136.

Mardaljevic, J. (2002) Quantification of Parallax Errors in Sky Simulator Domes for Clear Sky Conditions. *Lighting Research and Technology* **34(4)**: 313–332.

Mardaljevic, J. (2002) Shadowlands. *The Architects' Journal*, **215 (9 May)**: 44–46.

Mardaljevic, J. and Rylatt, M. (2003) Irradiation Mapping of Complex Urban Environments: An Image-Based Approach. *Energy and Buildings* **35 (2003)**: 27–35.

Rubinstein, F.D., Jennings, J., Avery, D., and Blanc, S. (1999) Preliminary results from an advanced lighting controls testbed. *IESNA 1998 Annual Conference*, San Antonio, TX, 10–12 August 1998, and published in *Journal of the Illuminating Engineering Society*.

Ward Larson, G. and Shakespeare, R. (1998) *Rendering with Radiance: The Art and Science of Lighting Visualization,* Morgan Kaufmann, San Francisco.

20

Alex Amato, Richard Frewer and
Steven Humphrey

A Comparative Sustainability Assessment and Indication of Future Housing Trends in Hong Kong

Introduction

This chapter reports on research that assesses the environmental and economic sustainability of current public and private sector housing blocks and a proposed speculative development, The Integer Concept Tower, in Hong Kong. Comparisons are made between each of the housing types using the following indicators: capital cost and costs in use; embodied and operational energy and carbon dioxide (CO_2); and construction waste. As the relative values of the environmental and economic impacts of each housing type are shown, indications emerge of where to concentrate the industry's efforts in reducing or mitigating negative impacts on sustainability.

The research has drawn on a range of work including studies that have shown the potential benefits of the extensive reuse of construction products in terms of the reduction of embodied impacts (Amato, 1999) and that has assessed the market barriers to the wide-scale adoption of reusing construction elements and components (HKUST *et al.*, 1999). The research also builds on work recently carried out by Davis Langdon and Seah (DLS) Management Ltd. that compared the cost of the main structure in standard public and private housing blocks, and work carried out in the UK by the Steel Construction Institute (Amato, 1996; HKUST *et al.*, 1999).

This research has progressed into the development of an internationally recognized methodology to undertake comparative assessments of the relative 'sustainability' of buildings and civil engineering projects. The methodology is specifically tailored to Hong Kong's Construction Industry, and the intention thereafter is to make it applicable to the broader South-East Asia Region. Construction and development of Hong Kong and the South China region are strongly driven by costs so, in this context, it is important life-cycle costing (LCC) is included in any assessment, together with life-cycle assessment (LCA). In the research, two of the three recognized environmental aspects of sustainability are measured: economics and environment. The third, the social impact, has been excluded because of a current lack of data, the difficulty in setting the scope of such a study, and setting recognized and appropriate 'yardsticks' within Hong Kong to measure social indicators. The intention is to focus on social indicators in future work.

The work demonstrates to key construction industry representatives and 'stake holders' the implementation of the methodology by undertaking a comparative assessment of archetypical residential towers in Hong Kong. The assessment was less to do with highlighting differences between the buildings, but more to demonstrate how the methodology can be used as:

- A means to inform the debate on a macro-scale about how comparative construction methods and housing types might evolve in the light of LCA/LCC data
- A useful tool for client bodies to analyse their property portfolio, for design teams on projects, and for manufacturers on improving their products

The study compared the environmental and cost performance of the following three 40-storey residential tower types:

- A housing authority 'standard' harmony block (Figure 20.1)
- A private sector housing block (Figure 20.2)
- The Integer Concept Tower[1] (Figure 20.3)

Regional background

Following the pattern of Hong Kong of some 20 years ago, China has a 'high-skilled–low-labour-cost' economy that is

Figure 20.1
A housing authority 'standard'
harmony block.

driven both by internal external and demands from its relatively newfound ability to manufacture high-quality goods very competitively (Reuters, 2002). As a consequence, China has substantially higher-growth forecasts when compared with other regional centres, and is considered by some economic forecasters to become the future 'workshop of the world' (Peoples National Congress, 2001). Indeed, it is calculated that the Guangdong province (directly north of Hong Kong) alone produces 34% of the national industrial output (Ming Pao, 2002).

Over the last few years the majority of industrial production in Hong Kong has moved over the border to the special economic zone of Shenzhen, and beyond, where labour costs are much lower. In addition, a significant proportion of the property and industrial development in China is financed by Hong Kong capital (70% of total contracted amount of

Figure 20.2
A private sector housing block.

Guangdong investment) (Hong Kong Trade Development Council, 2002). Similarly, international manufacturing organizations are looking to source materials and products from around the world, where costs are substantially lower (Hang Seng Bank, 1998). Moreover, this trend is exacerbated by the continued rise of environmental standards set by governments in mature developed economies like the European Union, the consequence of which is now forcing manufacturers to either clean up their manufacturing operations or to look for new manufacturing bases elsewhere with lower labour costs and less-stringent environmental standards.

At present, China still lacks an adequately robust system to regulate the environmental burdens caused by its manufacturing industries, and this continues to allow serious pollution to

Figure 20.3
The Integer Concept Tower.

occur (Dasgupta *et al.*, 1995). However China is taking environmental issues very seriously, as evidenced by China's ratification of the Kyoto Protocol at the Earth Summit in South Africa in September 2002. Nevertheless the size of the country and its population, together with the need to balance economic growth and social stability with environmental improvement means that time is required before significant results can be achieved (China Council for the Promotion of International Trade, 2000).

The situation in Hong Kong, although a little different, leads to a similar conclusion. Hong Kong has operated under a strictly '*laissez faire*' system and remains one of the most (if not the most) competitive economies in the world (Country Reports Organisation, 2002). Again the desire to reduce environmental burdens without clearly demonstrating the economic implications of any mooted 'greener' construction practice is regarded as 'dreaming'.

Ultimately the route to understanding how improvement in the sustainability performance of Hong Kong's buildings can be achieved is through the identification of the economic and environmental profiles of the buildings designs. It is at this stage where the commitment is made to use certain materials, construction elements and components, to the method of construction and the operational systems, and the lifespan of the buildings (Hong Kong Housing Authority, 2002). It is therefore at this point that suitable economic and environmental information must be delivered to the client and design team.

The best method of establishing such information is through the comprehensive life-cycle mapping of construction materials in terms of cost and environmental burdens of the existing building designs. This is not as difficult as at first it might appear. Hong Kong, unlike most other country's construction sectors, is dominated by a relatively standard design approach, called the use of reinforced concrete (Burnett, 1998). Equally Hong Kong has a substantial number of high-rise residential towers, of which the housing authority accounts for 48% of the total market supply (Census and Statistics Department, 2001). Therefore, studying this particular housing solution, that is one of just a few housing block archetypes, will be representative of Hong Kong's residential construction sector which in turn is a considerable proportion of the industry's total output.

Thus any move towards a more sustainable construction industry in the region needs to be sufficiently sophisticated enough to reconcile both economic and environmental impacts (Xu, 2000). It is for this reason that a unified methodology that includes both LCC and LCA is essential to discern 'real' and acceptable improvement strategies. The next section outlines the four stages of the methodology, which include: data collection, the creation of life-cycle models, comparative analysis and the development of improvement strategies.

Methodology

Regional data and selection of performance indicators

Carrying out a comparative LCA/LCC assessment throughout the full life cycle of each building type requires a comprehensive database of the costs and environmental impacts. These impacts result from the manufacture and delivery of all the major construction materials, elements and components. Initial investigation showed that much published environmental material data had been generated in Europe or Australia. However, validated regional data was considered important, so it was decided to restrict the European data on embodied energy of construction materials data to a range of key construction materials considered to be applicable for use in Hong Kong (Chen *et al.*, 2000).

However, good local data on the operational energy consumption per building (the energy consumed during the operational life of the building: e.g. cooling, ventilation and lifts) were available, as were reasonable local data on the material consumed in the repair and maintenance regimes. Good local data were also available for waste and together with the above data, it was then possible to create a reasonably good life-cycle model.

Finally, very good local cost data were available throughout the building life cycle and thus the study was able to create building life-cycle models for each building type. Thus the assessment took into account the full life cycle of all the buildings, from the manufacture of the building components and elements from raw materials, through the construction and operational life of the buildings and finally to the end of the buildings lives. Assumptions had to be made of course about the maintenance regime of the Integer Tower. The performance of each building type was then compared in terms of the following indicators:

- *Energy both embodied and operational*: because energy is a robust indicator of environmental impact, and crudely assesses impacts to the biosphere. It measures global impacts in the sense that it is a resource that is being depleted. Moreover, data are available

- *CO_2 both embodied and operational*: because it is an indicator of greenhouse gas emissions and data are available

- *Waste*: differentiating between that going to landfill and that recycled or reused. This is a local issue, which means the consumption of very scarce land. Nevertheless, it is considered important as estimations indicate that the quantity of waste annually produced in Hong Kong is predicted to rise rapidly. Very accurate data has emerged from the inventory analysis proposed (Koenig *et al.*, 2001)

- *Cost*: because not only it is the basis of many, if not most, construction decisions in Hong Kong, but also is a key economic indicator, and goes much of the way to satisfying the assessment of economic sustainability

Creating the models

The basic model for the selected housing blocks is established with reference to both published and historical quantity data obtained from DLS Management's database of projects. Sub-elements and specific material components are extrapolated from this data to generate the complete material mass model.[2] Upon completion of the building material mapping, the individual material quantities can then be separated and converted into their physical masses by using published and accepted conversion factors.

The material masses included within the models are based on generic building designs. In the case of the housing authority blocks, this is a standard specification, whilst the private sector version is a typical representation of the building design most commonly adopted. The material masses within the models include standard foundations design allowances and building services installations for each of the building types. In the case of foundation design, whilst ground conditions vary, as a result of both the building location and loading, it has been possible to produce what can be regarded as a 'typical foundation design'. This type of design is considered to be applicable for a significant proportion of housing blocks constructed in Hong Kong.

The models are also expanded to include repair and refurbishment regimes for each of the studied building types over their respective notional lives. The major 'cost in use' materials and refurbishment cycles have been identified, using historical records available from DLS databases. This approach allows the generation of a realistic life-cycle model. Each of these individual material groupings are then further analysed to create detailed repair and maintenance 'mass' models suitable for application to the housing block types. In the case of refurbishment, typical churn rates[3] for the different blocks have been considered. Importantly, the residential profile is different, with the housing authority blocks being public rental housing, whilst the private sector blocks are split between owner-occupier and rental units on a ratio of 75:25. For the purposes of this study, the rental profile, in terms of refurbishment rates, of the private and housing authority blocks are considered to be comparable, whilst the owner-occupier churn factors are different and reflect the longer gaps between refurbishment. It is worth noting that in Hong Kong the churn rate within residential blocks in the private sector is generally high, when compared with other countries.

The resulting collation of all the material masses identified at the construction, repair and maintenance stages form the total material life-cycle mass for the different housing block types. This presents for the first time a true material-usage full-term life profile for a residential building in Hong Kong and is the most in-depth analysis available. Having developed this whole-life mass profile for one block type, results can be benchmarked against different residential buildings on a floor area basis. This mass profile forms the underlying source of the calculation of the energy, environmental and waste models for the different blocks.

The development of the waste model, although primarily driven by the mass model, requires the inclusion and assessment of the quantities of materials 'wasted' at each stage of the construction and maintenance process. The identification of which materials are currently recyclable and which materials could potentially be recycled is another factor influencing the format of the waste model. Generally, the construction waste quantities are derived from established and accepted allowances used in the construction industry (Architectural Services Department, 1982). Recycled materials are identified from information already published in the public domain, supplied by manufacturers and extracted from related reports and studies, information that is considered adequate for the current model.

The development of the energy and CO_2 models for the different materials is established using conversion factors derived from recognized international sources and then applied to the mass values for each stage of the building's life. Creating an operational energy consumption and CO_2 emissions 'profile' for each building type has been achieved by resorting to recorded data already in the public realm. The utility organizations within Hong Kong have published some general data on this issue, but some adjustment is required to make allowance for the different resident lifestyle profiles between the public and private sector residential blocks.

The final segment of the model is the cost element, which is derived from benchmarked construction costs for the selected building types and then broken down to the different building elements, and then further to material categories wherever possible. The repair and maintenance models are also costed using data sourced from past DLS projects and these have been included as typical snap-shots of the whole-life expenditure profile. In the case of the operational costs of the building, these have been generated from historical consumption records from different clients and information on utility pricing in the public domain. The other key operational cost included within the overall whole-life assessment has been the administration and management costs for the different building types. Here actual records for selected buildings have been examined and since Hong Kong generally adopts an outsourcing model the identification of these costs, from the housing authority's property services contracts and private sector building management companies, is relatively easy. The inclusion of this information is considered necessary to ensure that the true whole-life cost of the building is presented and allows future comparative analysis to be made and placed in the context of the whole-building cost and not just a segment of the building cost profile.

All of the indicators selected for measurement in this study are capable of division into the different stages of the building life, namely initial, repair and maintenance, and end of life. In the case of the operational stage, the only indicator not measured here is waste. The models created in this study allow complete life profiles for each of the indicators measured to be presented in numerical and graphical form, and together produce a detailed inventory of the building throughout its whole life.

Comparative analysis

Having derived models and subsequent data, a series of comparative analyses were carried out including an overall embodied life-cycle analysis, an analysis of operational energy, and construction costs.

An overall embodied life-cycle comparison (omitting operational energy/CO_2) was carried out on the selected building types. Assessments were made at key points during the buildings' life cycles and differences that emerged were analysed on an element-by-element basis. There will be further careful scrutiny of the different repair and refurbishment regimes to ascertain if they lead to any expected difference in the notional building life of each housing type. The sensitivity of this data will be examined to determine whether the quality of the data will influence the overall results. This is considered to be important since all of the building types being studied are less than their planned design lives, making historical information for older building unavailable. Clearly if the repair and maintenance data is sensitive in the overall model, then the impact of variations in the regimes adopted in older buildings may have an impact on the overall whole-life assessment results.

Operational energy/CO_2 was also assessed and although differences emerged between the two existing housing types due to the varying occupant lifestyles, a breakdown of the data indicates areas where comparisons in construction material usage are valid. However, the main purpose for the inclusion of operational energy/CO_2 is to set the embodied impacts and capital cost in the context of the block as a whole. This is important in discovering the best ways of reducing the environmental impacts of constructing and operating for all the housing types. Moreover, attempts to reduce operational impacts are often dependent on changing or improving the building construction in some way (e.g. additional insulation). Construction methods almost certainly have an impact on the cost and embodied energy/CO_2 content of the building; usually (but not always) increasing them. A cost–benefit assessment of each suggested 'improvement' will therefore be undertaken to ensure that it is worthwhile both in terms of environmental benefit and capital cost.

Construction waste produced by each building type was compared in the construction phase, in the repair and refurbishment regime, and in the demolition phase. During these phases, specific detailed analysis was carried out using three assumptions that:

1. no materials are recovered for recycling/reuse
2. easily recoverable or valuable materials are recovered for recycling and/or reuse
3. all possible recyclable and/or reusable materials are recovered for recycling and reuse

Development of improvement strategies

From the detailed analysis carried out above, it should become evident where improvements can be made. For example, if the life-cycle energy and CO_2 impacts are found to dominate the operational phase and especially in the growth of air-conditioning, strategies will focus on improving fabric insulation, renewable energy sources like photovoltaic cladding, passive cooling and dehumidification. Once specific improvements have been identified, the best strategy can be selected to reduce environmental impact per unit cost.

Results

The results shown in Table 20.1 are a sample of the comparative data obtained from the modelling process. Comparative figures were obtained for energy and these showed that the Integer Concept Tower was very sensitive to the material-embodied energy for steel and to the overall flexibility of the building, in other words to check whether the building would actually last for 50 or 75 years (25 years longer was one of the primary assumptions put forward by the designers of the Integer Concept Tower). When considering the results it must be remembered that the Integer Concept Tower is just that, a concept, not a real building while the other two blocks are. Furthermore, the housing authority block is the end result of an evolutionary process of considerable refinement and there is no doubt that it is extremely cost and material efficient.

Table 20.1
Embodied energy for various life-cycle stages.

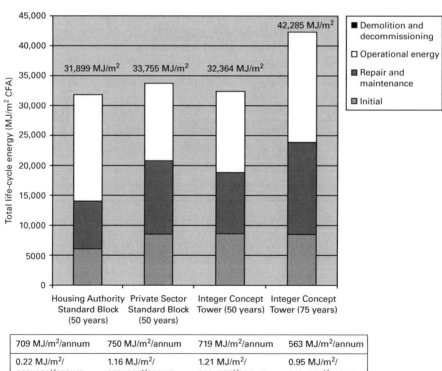

| 709 MJ/m²/annum | 750 MJ/m²/annum | 719 MJ/m²/annum | 563 MJ/m²/annum |
| 0.22 MJ/m²/ occupant/annum | 1.16 MJ/m²/ occupant/annum | 1.21 MJ/m²/ occupant/annum | 0.95 MJ/m²/ occupant/annum |

Nevertheless, the overall energy performance of the Integer Concept Tower lies between the housing authority block and the private sector block and when amortized over the 75-year life, its rate per annum is best. However, the initial embodied energy of the Integer Concept Tower emerges as the worst of the three.[4] The other noteworthy point is the significance of the operational energy figures, in relation to the initial and repair-and-maintenance figures; it is about equal to the total of both the construction of the building in the first place and repairing the building fabric during its life.

However, it would seem that the repair and maintenance regime of all the housing blocks is considerable. It is over 30% more than the construction of the building in the first place for the housing authority block, and while repair and maintenance for the Integer Concept Tower is only approximately 25% of the initial figure, interestingly it is almost 50% more for the private sector block. The question that emerges is why the repair and maintenance values should be so high in comparison with the initial values. This, and the explanations of why the figures should also vary considerably (from 25% to 50%) over the range of building types will be analysed comparatively with other international work in the future.

Finally, the buildings have very different occupancies and so at the end of each parameter the *annual rate per occupant* is shown. Clearly, the housing authority block emerges as being extremely efficient in this respect and the housing authority can take some pride in this achievement. However this does provoke a long-term concern about people's aspirations towards future standards and whether the desire for greater space and consumption standards will inexorably drive the occupants to demand a 'consumption level' that is more comparable to those enjoyed in the private sector. If this view is taken the Integer Concept Tower, over 75 years, does seem to offer the best long-term solution.

Similar results were obtained for waste (Table 20.2), where again the quantity of steel was significant, as this time the steel frame was recycled and reduced the total quantity of waste going to landfill. It should be remembered that at present, the waste figures are calculated by volume and not by mass, and greater differences might emerge between the Integer Concept Tower and the existing concrete housing blocks as steel has a greater mass than concrete.

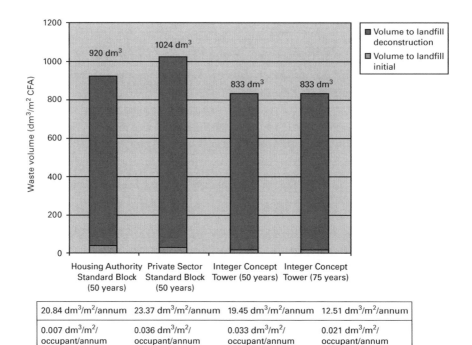

Table 20.2
Waste volume figures for various life-cycle stages.

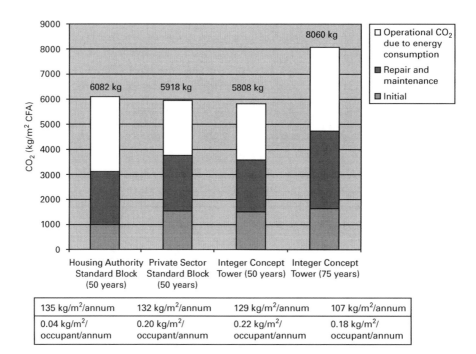

Table 20.3
Quantities of CO_2 at various life-cycle stages.

It appears that the best-performing building type for the waste indicator is the Integer Concept Tower, over both the 50- and 75-year life. It has been assumed that all the metals for all the buildings will be recycled and because there is a considerably greater tonnage of metals (structural steel) in the Integer Concept Tower, this boosts the amount recycled, and thus reduces the amount of waste going to landfill. In addition, the effect of amortizing the building by an additional 50% considerably reduces the rate per annum.

CO_2 values were unable to be reliably calculated for the demolition process, as the energy consumption and fuel mix attributable to the transport of waste material to disposal sites were found to be extremely variable for the examples investigated (Table 20.3). However, CO_2 emissions resulting from the demolition process are likely to be of a similar order as those for energy; that is, very much smaller when compared with the initial and overall life-cycle totals.

Here again the figures presented in Table 20.3 show the Integer Concept Tower is the overall best-performing building but the most striking aspect of the above results is the high level of operational CO_2 emissions.

Table 20.4
Cost figures for various life-cycle stages.

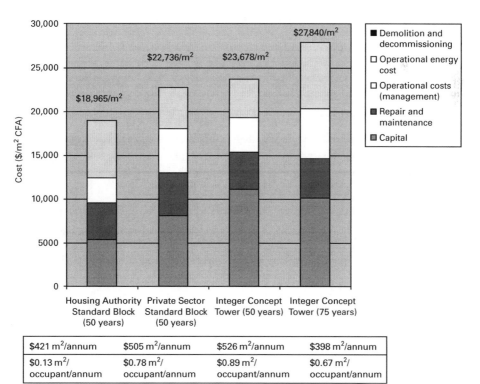

Interestingly the cost indicator, as shown in Table 20.4, appears to mirror the energy results.

Conclusion

Longevity is important. The Integer Concept Tower is the best performer over all the indicators in the 75-year life assessment. The presumption is that it will have this long life because of the intrinsic flexibility of its frame construction. Whether this same flexibility and thus extension of overall building life can also be achieved in reality by the other two standard blocks is outside the scope of this study. Moreover, redundancy is seldom caused by the basic constructional materials losing their functional integrity and nearly always to do with the economics of flexibility. As Hong Kong's gross domestic product (GDP) increases it is very likely that tenants, once content with space-standards that would be considered in many other countries to be small, may well demand greater habitable floor area. If this cannot be achieved by the refurbishment of buildings due to the inherent inflexibility of, say load bearing cross-wall type construction, then building design should be changed to facilitate flexibility. It is also worth mentioning that the demographics of Hong Kong are changing in a way similar to many first world countries. In Hong Kong a move towards smaller nuclear families is predicted. This, together with a reduction in couples having children and an overall population decrease, will result in a greater need for smaller housing units, (one or two person units) and this shift in demand is already affecting the Hong Kong Housing Authority (HKHA).

Clearly, both changing demographics and the growth in personal aspirations with rising GDP will lead to an assessment of how the existing housing stock can accommodate these increasing requirements. A judgement will have to be made whether adaptation and refurbishment, or demolition and rebuilding, is the correct course. The answer is likely to vary with the circumstances of each housing block or estate. However it is worth considering the following points that largely come down on the side of demolition and rebuilding:

- The operational regime is significant for all the buildings and energy efficiency is clearly important. Strategies to reduce energy demand and supply with energy generated renewably should be examined. However, the application of insulation is perhaps the most cost-effective solution although this might be difficult to achieve on a number of the existing standard housing block designs

- The repair and maintenance regime is also significant. This indicates that improving building construction in order to minimize maintenance and running costs could considerably reduce the overall life-cycle impacts

- The inherent inflexibility of the traditional *in situ* cross-wall construction together with the standard H-plan form makes conversion and reconfiguration relatively difficult

- Recently after the severe acute respiratory syndrome (SARS) outbreak last year there has been increasing concern about the spreading of both pollutants and pathogens and that the spread of contagious diseases and poor air quality are exacerbated by the standard housing block plan form. It is possible that refurbishment could contribute to improving or eliminating this situation

The question posed for the HKHA is, by using the modelling process, how can the choice between refurbishment and redevelopment be optimized in terms of environmental and economic impacts? This now requires a series of different refurbishment and redevelopment alternatives to be assessed using the model methodology outlined above. In this respect, the Integer Concept Tower is definitely worthy of further investigation as a possible new build alternative.

This should go hand in hand with the development of the model to extend to cover a substantial part of Hong Kong's building stock. The extent of relatively standard building archetypes in Hong Kong makes this process relatively straightforward and about 20 building archetypes have already been identified that represent over 90% of the building stock. A process of benchmarking the complete range of Hong Kong's building types should be undertaken so that best practice standards can become design targets.

The models described above can now be tested to review a whole series of design questions. For example, at what point would the inclusion of a photovoltaic façade cladding be cost effective or conversely, how much would the price of energy have to rise for its inclusion to be effectively paid for in say 10 years? A similar question could be posed for insulation. And, if the layout (plan form) of the buildings was rationalized, what would be the consequence? Perhaps the largest question to be raised in Hong Kong's construction sector at present relates to the extent and potential of the use of precast elements. Here a range of alternatives can be explored and the proposals optimized. This research has resulted in the development of models that can be already used, and further work is now underway to refine them.[5]

Notes

1. The Integer Hong Kong partners are: Gammonskanska, CLP Power, Swire Properties, the HKSAR Government, the UK Government, Integer UK, Hong Kong Housing Society and Hong Kong Housing Authority (HKHA). The patron is the HKJC Charities Trust, who have sponsored an exhibition and the construction of the Integer Pavilion, which over 20,000 school children have now visited. The construction of the Integer Pavilion and the mounting of the exhibition have also initiated a construction industry research and development group that focuses on construction-related sustainability issues. The group is composed of representatives from the Integer partners as well as leading university department involved in construction, interested in advancing sustainable construction.

2. 'Material mass' is the mass of any material expressed in kilograms or tonnes.

3. 'Churn rates', – the rate at which tenants vacate their flats, and are replaced with new tenants (e.g. every 5 years). The rate has a considerable impact on repair and refurbishment, which in turn affects the energy and material inputs in the model.

4. It rises to 11,650 MJ/m² CFA when 32 GJ/ton is the input figure used for structural steel and not the 13.5 GJ/ton figure used above for all the other steel items. A range from 32 GJ/ton (primary raw materials) to 9.8 GJ/ton was analysed; finally, a life-cycle figure of 13.58 GJ/ton was used in the figures shown above. This methodology is in accordance with the sensitivity analysis established by previous work (Amato, 1996).

5. A second study has been initiated that focuses on the New Harmony Block for the HKHA. The outcome is a combined LCA/LCC decision-making tool especially for assessment of the New Harmony Block. The LCA/LCC decision-making tool measures and quantifies the following 10 environmental impacts for each life-cycle stage: energy (GJ); resource depletion (tonnes); water consumption (m³); waste (tonnes); climate change (ton CO_2 equivalent); acid rain (kg SO_2 equivalent); photochemical smog (kg ethane equivalent); ozone depletion (kg CFC-11 equivalent); toxicity to humans (kg toxicity equivalent); toxicity to ecosystems (kg toxicity equivalent).

References

Amato, A. (1996) *A Comparative Environmental Appraisal of Alternative Framing Systems for Offices*, unpublished PhD, Oxford Brookes University, UK.

Amato, A. (1999) Appraising the Impacts on the Construction Sector of Adopting a Quantitative Methodology for Assessing Recyclable and Reusable Construction Products. *Italian National Steel Construction Conference*, Naples (October).

Architectural Services Department (1982) *SDQS Technical Instruction*, Technical Report No. 8, Hong Kong.

Burnett, J. (1998) *Conventional Approaches Which Improve the Environmental Performance of Large Buildings*, Department of Building Services Engineering, Hong Kong Polytechnic University, Hong Kong.

Census and Statistics Department of Hong Kong (2001) *Hong Kong Annual Digest of Statistics 2001 Edition*, Census and Statistics Department, Hong Kong.

Chen, T., Burnett, J. and Chau, K. (2000) *Analysis of Embodied Energy Use in the Residential Buildings of Hong Kong*, Elsevier Science Ltd, New York.

China Council for the Promotion of International Trade: Guangdong Subcouncil. (2000) *Guangdong Survey: General Survey*. Retrieved from the World Wide Web http://www.getgd.net/gd_surv/gd_cur1.html

Country Reports Organisation (2002) *Hong Kong*. Retrieved from the World Wide Web http://www.countryreports.org/content/hongkong.htm

Dasgupta, S., Mody, A., Roy, S. and Wheeler, D. (1995) *Environmental Regulation and Development: A Cross Country Empirical Analysis* (World Bank Policy Research Working Paper No. 1448), World Bank, New York.

Hang Seng Bank (1998) The Changing Dynamics of the Hong Kong Economy, *Hang Seng Economic Monthly* (December).

HKUST, Davis Langsdon and Seah Hong Kong Ltd. (1999) *Cost Efficiency of Structural Designs of Standard Domestic Blocks*, Presented to the Hong Kong Housing Authority, July 1999.

Hong Kong Housing Authority (2002). *Management of List: Components and Materials Team*. Retrieved from the World Wide Web http://www.housingauthority.gov.hk/dc/applist/manage6.htm

Hong Kong Trade Development Council (2002) *Market Profiles on Chinese Cities and Provinces: Guangdong Province*, Hong Kong.

Koenig, A., Kwan, A., Lee, P. and Liu, W. (2001) Building Waste in Hong Kong: Generation and Potential Reuse. In: *One Day Seminar on Environmentally Friendly Structures*, Hong Kong Institute of Engineers (Structural Division) and the Institution of Structural Engineers (Hong Kong Division), Hong Kong.

Ming Pao (2002) Hong Kong–Guangdong Economic Integration. *Ming Pao*, 27 August.

Peoples National Congress (2001) Peoples Republic of China Central Government Growth Projections from 5 Year Plan Endorsed by People National Congress.

Reuters (2002) Analysis – Rivers Envy Chinese Mix of High Tech, Cheap Labour. *Reuters Company News* 21 August.

Xu, J. (2000) *China's Paper Industry: Growth and Environmental Policy during Economic Reform*, International Development Research Centre, Ottawa, Canada.

Conclusion

Future Forms for City Living?

Nicola Dempsey and Mike Jenks

Conclusion: Future Forms for City Living?

Achieving sustainable urban development is no easy task. The complexities of the scale and variety of urban forms, and the intimate interweaving of environmental, social and economic issues, could all too easily suggest that, as everywhere is so different, consistently meaningful action is almost impossible. However, the research in this book suggests that there are many pathways to achieving sustainability. There is certainly no 'one size fits all' solution, but there are strategies and actions that have some commonality within particular urban contexts. So what are the future forms for city living?

At the regional and city scale the concept of polycentric development, linked closely with transport infrastructure, appears to have potential. Both Okabe and Bertolini cite the Randstad, an urban region comprising four major cities, linked by an excellent public transport system. This has a clear polycentric structure, but Okabe goes further and suggests that Tokyo also has a similar, although 'hidden', spatial structure. Green's characterization of Bristol with surrounding centres of economic activity, and his proposals for new transport links again suggest a polycentric structure as a sustainable form. These forms suggest intensification around sub-centres and transport routes, and an intention to protect green spaces. However, there are potential problems. Bertolini notes a relationship between speed of transport and spread of the urban development – a point pertinent in Japan where the ultra-fast 'bullet train' links the two mega-cities of Tokyo and Osaka into a virtual urban agglomeration of some 40 million people. Yet in smaller-scale rural environments, as Echenique shows, a polycentric form (necklace of villages) appears to have negative transport consequences and is not a popular option.

As expected, any attractive 'solution' needs to be treated with caution. In the cities of the West, where population growth is low, much of the pressure for development comes from the increase in household numbers. Existing cities are often older, high-quality environments, with well-established surroundings. Protecting these assets is likely to be a priority. The concentration of development around existing centres and transport appears to be a feasible way forward. Certainly the integrated planning in the Netherlands of the Randstad and Deltametropool demonstrate that polycentric development is a worthwhile model to consider. In countries, particularly in Asia where populations are growing and there is mass migration into cities, there is a compelling need to control urban sprawl. There is certainly a growing interest in this region in ideas of the 'compact city', and polycentric development, with investment in modern public transport systems. In areas of such aggressive urban growth, polycentric forms, with intensification around transport interchanges, including transit development zones might be one of the few spatial options to achieve urban forms that are a little more sustainable than at present.

One of the most common nostrums about achieving sustainable urban form is that densities should be higher. Jenks and Dempsey demonstrate that 'higher density' is a relative and culturally determined term. Clearly, what is acceptable in Hong Kong and other already dense cities, would not be appropriate to the historic cities of Europe or the small towns and cities of the middle of the USA. The forms and densities considered by Karakiewicz, Lau *et al.* and Yang (Hong Kong and Singapore), Willis (the centre of New York), and Hulshof (dense parts of Rotterdam), are very different from the denser forms suggested by Bartuska and Kazimee, and Johns (Pullman and Bozeman), or the more radical suggestions by Webster and Williams in a rural context. However, these are mediated by what degree of intensification or change might be acceptable to populations used to living at very high or very low densities. In principle there is no difference. All are advocating relatively high-density, mixed-use environments. What changes is the degree to which this can happen in the particular urban context and culture concerned. The way forward here depends upon a clear understanding of the existing environment, the people who live there, and thus the type of development or intensification that would be acceptable.

Spatial strategies at the regional and neighbourhood levels are complex and fraught with difficulties, but any benefits of manipulating urban form would be outweighed if the buildings themselves were unsustainable. It is not within the scope of this book to detail the range of solutions for sustainable building, but it touches upon issues that impact on urban form. The configuration of cities tends to be very long-lived and difficult to change, but the buildings within them, while lasting for a long time, may be replaced more frequently. Thus their sustainability throughout their life cycle should be an important consideration, and can be predicted, as Amato *et al.* show. The promotion of high-density development has consequences such as the loss of open space and overshadowing from closely packed buildings. The design and layout of buildings needs to be carefully considered to allow sunlight to penetrate, and Mardaljevic's model shows how this might be achieved. At the same time, taking advantage of the large areas of roofs in urban areas as collectors for solar energy is shown to have potential by Roaf *et al*. There is a complex dynamic, with spatial planning leading to forms that will, for the very long term, affect transport and consequent carbon emissions, and buildings which will relatively frequently adapt and change, and be renewed, but which need in themselves to be sustainably designed.

But it is behaviour, lifestyles and peoples' aspirations that are at the heart of achieving a sustainable environment. The form of urban areas, and buildings within them, do not determine sustainable behaviour, but they might provide the right setting for it. For example, ideas drawn from the 'compact city' concept suggest that high densities lead to better access to facilities, and therefore are socially desirable. Kaido shows that density is not the key determinant, but rather that behavioural and policy issues may be more significant. The effects of information technology and new forms of communication, as noted by Briggs and Gillen, have an impact on the way cities are used, and maybe as a result, impact on their form. Participation and the involvement of local communities, as Willis shows, can regenerate and support sustainable communities, even *in extremis*. Ultimately, it is whether a more sustainable city can offer a good quality of life, which brings us back to the suggestion by Giddings *et al*. that it is 'urban spirit' which really matters.

It is always a great comfort to find that there is a ready-made, easy solution to a problem. This book, and the issue of future forms for sustainable cities, gives no such comfort. What has been presented is a range of ideas and solutions that research has shown either to work, or have the potential to work in a number of different urban environments. Underlying all of the ideas in the chapters is a deeper understanding of aspects of sustainability, a clearer definition of problems to tackle, as well as ideas and designs that are sustainable.

In conclusion it can be suggested with some confidence that future urban forms for city living will include: polycentric urban forms, closely linked to good public transportations systems; development that is directly related to transport; culturally appropriate increases in the density of development, that is responsive to the urban context; urban forms and buildings that take advantage of solar energy, and that take account of the life cycle of the development; forms that interact with new technology; developments which enable accessibility and sustainable behaviour and involve the people who live there.

The book ends with a review of a number of projects that give practical insight into some of the issues raised in the chapters above, and which also have innovative approaches to sustainable development. The examples are not intended to give a comprehensive view, and the choice, with some justification, could be seen as a little eclectic. However, each contains a wealth of ideas, and most importantly, key references and links are given, so ideas in this book, and on the projects below can be explored in more depth. The review is divided into sections reflecting the scale of the projects and the structure of the book, namely: sustainable regional development; transit-related development; sustainability through urban regeneration; sustainable buildings and energy efficiency; and, greening the city.

Sustainable regional development

Øresund Region

The project

The Øresund Region comprises Zealand, Lolland-Falster, Møn and Bornholm in Eastern Denmark and Skåne in Southern Sweden, covering an area of 20,859 km². The region (Figure C.1) is home to businesses specializing in foodstuffs, life sciences, environmental engineering and information technology. There is also a strong tradition of social and environmental awareness, and according to Øresund Network, many international businesses have chosen to locate their operations in the Øresund Region.

Over 3.5 million people live in the region: approximately 2.4 million in the Danish region (total Danish population: 5.4 million) and 1.1 million in the Swedish region (total Swedish population: approximately 9 million), with a collective workforce of around 1.9 million people.

Economically this region produces approximately 20% of the regions' Gross Domestic Product (GDP). The improvements in the infrastructure were in an effort to compete economically with Stockholm.

Sustainability features

The aim to link two countries physically into an integrated economic region is innovative. This has been achieved through improvements to the transport infrastructure with the addition of the 16 km long road and metro rail link, comprising the 8 km long Øresund Bridge, 4 km long (Figure C.2) man-made island and 4 km tunnel between Malmö and Copenhagen. There have also been recent underground rail links in Copenhagen to the Bridge and Kastrup airport, and the forthcoming City Tunnel between Malmö station and the Bridge. Västra Hamnen, the much acclaimed sustainable settlement, is also located in the region. The rail system has been a success while the volume of cars has been lower than anticipated, perhaps due to the steep toll charges (SKr500 – approx £38 or $70 for a return journey).

Because the region crosses two countries, people are concerned about being taxed twice if they live in one country and work in the other. For the idea to succeed, communicating the tax breaks is of real significance for the governments concerned.

References and links

Copenhagen Capacity (2002) *Cooperation Strengthens the IT Trade in the Øresund Region.* Retrieved from the World Wide Web http://www.oresund.com/oresund/newsframeset.asp? content=newseng252 on 24 August.

Copenhagen Capacity (2004) *Traffic Across the Øresund Bridge Still Increasing.* Retrieved from the World Wide Web http://www.oresund.com/oresund/newsframeset.asp?content=newseng252 on 24 August 2004.

Elghamry, N. (2003) Bridge to Prosperity. *Estates Gazette,* **0324**: 64–65.

Roberts, A. (2003) A Midsummer Night's Dream. *The Economist,* **367(8328)**: 3–16.

Helgadottir, B. (1998) Spanning the Cash Gap. *Public Finance,* 20–26 March 1998: 14–15.

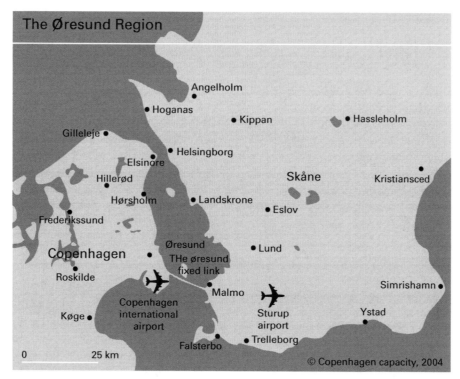

Figure C.1
The Øresund Region.

Figure C.2
The Øresund Bridge linking Denmark and Sweden into one economic region.
(*Source*: Image: http://encyclopedia.thefreedictionary.com/Oresund%20Bridge)

Thames Gateway

The project

The area of land currently houses approximately 1.6 million people and measures approximately 80,000 hectares (ODPM, no date) and falls into the counties of Essex, Kent and London. The Thames gateway (Figure C.3) is a UK national priority for regeneration and growth. The redevelopment of this area could reduce pressure for greenfield housing and industrial development, as well as helping to mitigate the urban out migration from London (CPRE, 2004). The Gateway has the potential for providing at least 128,500 new homes and over 200,000 new jobs in the area by 2016.

Sustainability features

Development includes:

Inner Gateway: ongoing development in the finance and business district of Canary Wharf; recent regeneration project at the Greenwich Millennium Village (Figure C.4) and the Greenwich Peninsula.

Outer London Riverside: advanced manufacturing and engineering at Dagenham; high-density riverside settlement at Barking Reach; housing expansion at Thamesmead; regeneration of Woolwich town centre.

Central Gateway: new residential development at Thurrock to integrate with existing commercial development and urban areas at Grays and Lakeside; mixed-use development at North Dagenham; major business and residential development at Ebbsfleet (Figure C.5) with high-speed transport link to central London and Europe.

South-east Essex: regeneration of Basildon town centre; establishment of a regional centre for culture, leisure and education, which will incorporate the University of Essex.

Medway Estuary: town expansion of Sittingbourne, which will incorporate high-tech industry at the Sittingbourne Research Centre; waterfront regeneration and residential development at Medway.

While the aim is to provide sustainable settlements, and much needed homes in the south-east, there have been some concerns. It is feared that there will be inadequate investment in transport infrastructure, and the reliance on 'planning gain' for the provision of social housing. Doubts are also expressed at the absence of skills needed to plan and design sustainable communities (Gardiner, 2004).

References and links

Campaign to Protect Rural England (CPRE) (2004) *Thames Gateway: Making Progress*, CPRE, London.

East of England Regional Assembly, the Mayor of London and the South East England Regional Assembly (2004) *Growth and Regeneration in the Gateway:Interregional Planning Statement by the Thames Gateway Regional Planning Bodies*, Office of the Deputy Prime Minister, London.

English Partnerships (no date) Greenwich Peninsula: investing in the 21st Century, Sector Light Design.

Gardiner, J. (2004) Concrete Bungle? *Housing Today*, No. **38**, pp. 24–26.

Office of the Deputy Prime Minister (2003) *Sustainable Communities: Building for The Future*, Office of the Deputy Prime Minister, London.

Office of the Deputy Prime Minister (no date) *Overview of the Thames Gateway*. Retrieved from the World Wide Web 22nd August 2004 http://www.odpm.gov.uk/stellent/groups/odpm_communities/documents/pdf/odpm_comm_pdf_030604.pdf

Figure C.3
Planned expansion along the River Thames estuary. (*Source*: after ODPM, 2003.)

Figure C.4
Greenwich Millennium Village, a flagship sustainable settlement.
(*Source*: English Partnerships)

Figure C.5
Plans for Ebbsfleet sustainable urban extension. (*Source*: TBA.)

Transit-related development

Slateford Green, Edinburgh: car-free housing

The project

The project covers 1.6 hectares on the site of a former railway goods yard in the inner suburb of Gorgie, west Edinburgh, Scotland (Scheurer, 2001). The development consists of 120 'ecologically friendly' flats (Dawson, 2004) in a development which takes the form of a traditional Edinburgh tenement with a landscaped central communal space. There is no parking permitted on-site, except for disabled drivers (Figures C.6 and C.7).

Sustainability features

The development is located close to prioritized bus routes. There is a car club which gives access to cars without ownership, and 74% of residents have opted not to own a car. There is good provision for pedestrian and cycle routes. Energy efficient appliances are installed in the flats. Good use is made of recycled materials: for example, material made from recycled newspaper provides super-insulation for flats. Apart from the aluminium roofs, all building materials are low in embodied energy, are from recycled or sustainable sources, and can themselves be recycled. Natural surveillance has been created through the design of the development and there is virtually no crime (Dawson, 2004).

References and links

Dawson, R. (2004) *Towards Good Practice in Sustainable Urban Land Use*, Bristol LA21.

Land Use Group and The Architecture Centre, Bristol, Woodside Press, Bristol.

Scheurer, J. (2001) *Urban Ecology, Innovations in Housing Policy and the Future of Cities: Towards Sustainability in Neighbourhood Communities*, unpublished PhD thesis, Institute for Sustainability and Technology Policy, Murdoch University, Perth, Western Australia. Retrieved from the World Wide Web 22nd August 2004 http://wwwistp. murdoch.edu.au/publications/projects/jan/

Figures C.6
Slateford Green, Edinburgh. (*Source*: http://www.canmore-housing.org. uk/pdf%20forms/sg_review.pdf)

Figures C.7
Car-free housing. (*Source*: http://www.canmore-housing.org. uk/pdf%20forms/sg_review.pdf)

Vancouver SkyTrain extension

The project

The SkyTrain was first installed in 1986 and has since been upgraded with trains reaching 90 km/hr each with the capacity to carry 260 people. It was created in response to calls for an improved transit route within the city, providing users with a quick, reliable alternative to the car (RTP 2000, no date). There are two train lines, the Millennium Line, which is due for completion in 2005, and the existing Expo Line.

Sustainability features

This is an energy efficient transportation system that minimizes ground level infrastructure through the use of elevated concrete sections. It runs on electricity and produces no emissions, and produces less noise than a diesel bus. The transit system promotes compact development, the results of which can be seen in the mixed-use districts of Metrotown, Burnaby and the New Westminster Quay (GVRD, 2003).

References and links

Greater Vancouver Regional District (GVRD) (2003) *Regional Town Centre Profiles: Metrotown (Burnaby)*. Retrieved from the World Wide Web 22nd August 2004
http://www.gvrd.bc.ca/livablecentres/metrotown.htm

Rapid Transit Project 2000 Ltd (RTP 2000) (no date) *Background – Why SkyTrain?* Retrieved from the World Wide Web 22nd August 2004
http://www.rapidtransit.bc.ca/

Railway Technology (2004) *Vancouver SkyTrain Light Rail Network, Canada*. Retrieved from the World Wide Web 22nd August 2004
http://www.railway-technology.com/projects/vancouver/ index.html#vancouver4

Figure C.8
Brentwood Rapid Transit SkyTrain station. (*Source*: http://canada.archiseek.com/news/2004/000124/brentwoodskytrain.html)

Kowloon Station, Hong Kong

The project

The brief for the masterplan, as well as for the Kowloon railway station, required extensive mixed uses (1.1 million sq. ft) including residential, office, retail and hotel accommodation as well as public spaces, recreation areas and 22 towers (Seex and Erickson, 2001). The premise behind the development was the establishment of a high-quality connected area, both locally through pedestrian bridges, nationally via the train station and globally via the airport (Terry Farrell and Partners, 1998). By 2010, this transport interchange would be 'contained within a new town to sustain a population of 50,000' (op. cit., p. 59). It forms part of a dense new city district instigated in 1989 by Hong Kong's government to replace its congested airport at Kai Tak with a new £12 billion airport on the man-made island of Chek Lap Kok (Figure C.8) (Seex and Erickson, 2001).

Sustainability features

Lau et al.'s chapter about Multiple and Intensive Land Use (MILU) highlights the sustainability of the urban form and strategic planning. In addition, the efficiency of the transportation itself makes a significant contribution to the overall sustainability of the project. Along the rail axis, 34 escalators and 71 staircases descend 14 metres, through a grand escalator hall, from ground level to the Tung Chung mass transit railway (MTR) Line platforms at the station's lowest level. This will be the most intensively used space, with 43,500 passengers arriving and departing from the platforms at peak hours. This project demonstrates how a very high-density transit (Figure C.9) development zone can be achieved.

References and links

Seex, D. and Erickson, B. (2001) Case studies. In: *Approaching Urban Design: The Design Process* (eds. Roberts, M. and Greed, C.), Pearson Education Limited, Harlow.

Terry Farrell and Partners (1998) *Kowloon: Transport Super City*, Pace Publishing Limited, Hong Kong.

Terry Farrell and Partners (no date) *Kowloon Station and Masterplan, Hong Kong*. Retrieved from the World Wide Web 1st August 2004. http://www.terryfarrell.co.uk/projects/masterplanning/mp_kowloon.html

Figure C.9
The multi-level city. (*Source*: Terry Farrell and Partners, 1998.)

Pudong, Shanghai, China

The project

Pudong, with an area of 533.44 km², is located on the east bank of the Huangpu River that runs through Shanghai. Shanghai's population is 13.3 million, of which Pudong is home to 1.68 million people. The development objective of Pudong was to create a 'multi-functional, export-oriented and cosmopolitanized new urban area of Shanghai' (PNAA, 2000). The complete redevelopment of the Pudong area, including infrastructure installation, had a significant focus on transportation to and from the wider Shanghai area (Zhao *et al.*, 2003).

Sustainability features

While much of Pudong's development is far from sustainable (it has included the displacement of local communities, and aggressive urban growth with unsustainable buildings), the transportation system is leading edge, and well worthy of note. The development includes the Pudong International Airport, the Pudong International Deep Water Harbour, a light transit railway, a river crossing project which includes the automated Lujiazui Pedestrian Tunnel carrying people between Pudong and West Shanghai. It also includes the Maglev, the world's first commercial magnetic elevated railway which uses highly efficient electromagnetic systems forces to uplift trains and propel them. Built from German technology at a cost of $1.2 billion, the Maglev train (Figure C.10) links the new Shanghai Pudong International airport to the centre of Pudong. The system has a length of about 30 kilometres with a maximum speed of about 440 km/hr. It takes about 8 minutes to go from one end to the other, making it the fastest urban transit system in the world.

References and links

Pudong New Area Administration (PNAA) (2000) *Geographic Location*. Retrieved from the World Wide Web on 25th August 2004. http://pudong.shanghaichina.org/basi.html

http://people.hofstra.edu/geotrans/eng/ch3en/app l3en/ ch3a2en.html

Zhao, B., Nobukazu, N., Chen, J. and Kong, L. (2003) The Impact of Urban Planning on Land Use and Land Cover in Pudong of Shanghai, China. *Journal of Environmental Sciences*, **15(2)**: 205–214.

Figure C.10
The ultra-efficient Maglev. (*Source:* http://people.hofstra.edu/geotrans/eng/ch1en/conc1en/maglevshanghai.html)

Sustainability through urban regeneration

Homes for Change

The project

The development, on a 0.63 hectare site, formed part of the regeneration efforts in Hulme and Moss Side, Manchester. The Hulme estate, which was knocked down to make way for the Homes for Change development, was 'one of the highest-crime estates in the country' (Shaftoe, 2000). Tenants got together in 1990 to form the cooperative when the demolition and redevelopment of their homes were confirmed. The tenants wanted a mixed-use, green development with a unique sense of place and identity reflecting the needs of the cooperative members (CABE, 2002).

The aims of the cooperative included: creating a supportive mixed community in which Hulme residents could afford to live, and choose to continue to live; incorporating green design and sustainable building technology in designs to reduce costs and environmental damage (Figures C.11 and C.12); adopting a highly participative approach in controlling the design, construction (through self-build), ownership and management of the development (Dawson, 2004).

Sustainability features

The 75 residential flats in the development have been constructed at a density of 119 dwellings per hectare. The 16,450 sq. ft of workspace is managed by the sister initiative, Work for Change, providing affordable workspace and contributing to the local economy. Leaseholders must adhere to a list of 'ethical principles for social and environmental responsibility' (Dawson, 2004).

Environmental targets were set, including the reduction of space heating costs to £1 per week which would reduce carbon dioxide (CO_2) emissions to 50% of a typical house (Rudlin and Falk, 1995). There were also other targets set pertaining to sustainable materials, waste and infrastructure (*op. cit.*).

References and links

CABE (2002) *Homes and Work for Change, Manchester.* Retrieved from the World Wide Web 3rd August 2004. http://www.cabe.ord.uk/library/casestydy.asp?id=47&show= analysis&PARAMS

Dawson, R. (2004) *Towards Good Practice in Sustainable Urban Land Use*, Bristol City Council, Bristol.

Rudlin, D. and Falk, N. (1995) *21st Century Homes: Building to Last: A Report for the Joseph Rowntree Foundation*, Urban and Economic Development Group (URBED), London.

Shaftoe, H (2000) Community Safety and Actual Neighbourhoods. In: *Sustainable Communities: The Potential for Eco-Neighbourhoods* (ed. Barton, H.), Earthscan, London.

Figures C.11 and C.12
Homes for Change – a high-density mixed-use regeneration scheme. (*Sources:*
http://www.lookingatbuildings.org.uk/default.asp?Document= 3.T.2.5&Image=231
http://www.designforhomes.org/hda/1997/schemes/homesfor/hommain.html)

Figures C.13 and C.14
Greenwich Millennium Village combining highly sustainable building design with urban regeneration.
(*Source:* http://www.stacey.peak-media.co.uk/Docklands/ GreenwichPeninsula/GreenwichPeninsula.htm)

Figures C.15 and C.16
Sainsburys, a sustainable supermarket design. (*Sources:* www.gold.ac.uk/world/millen/planning/sainsburys.html
www.cabe.org.uk/library/casestudy.asp?id=176)

427

Greenwich Millennium Village

The project

Located at the Greenwich peninsula, London, the project currently consists of 220 dwellings, at a density of 95 dwellings per hectare, with another 1157 planned. This is a mixed-use development, with a primary school (Figure C.13), health centre, cinema, hotel and park. The Peninsula is home to other commercial development, including a supermarket, a DIY shop, an electrical goods retailer and a yacht club. Greenwich (Figure C.14) is part of the UK Government's Millennium Villages Initiative and is held as a model for the creation of new communities. The objectives behind the Millennium Village are to encourage sustainable building technology innovation, to achieve high urban design standards and to focus closely on sustainable measures in terms of energy and conservation (ODPM, 2000). The land on the site of this Millennium Village was previously the site of a gas works, was heavily contaminated and an extensive clean up was required.

Sustainability features

Computer-led building techniques, monitoring and off-site pre-fabrication is used to reduce building costs and time, as well as construction waste and energy by 50% (Allen, 2001). The development uses a combined heat and power system, providing the development with central heating, hot water and electricity. The development also integrates water-saving devices such as water efficient taps, toilets and washing machines to achieve its aim of reducing water demand by up to 30%. Of the planned total number of 1377 homes, 172 will be rented, 94 shared ownership and 40 on a flexible tenure basis (Dawson, 2004). Greenwich Peninsula is home to the UK's first low-energy food store which makes use of natural light and high levels of insulation, which contribute to it being 50% more efficient than standard supermarkets (Figures C.15 and C.16).

References and links

Allen, I. (2001) Village Green. *Architect's Journal*, **213** 1 February 2001: 26–35.

Dawson, R. (2004) *Towards Good Practice in Sustainable Urban Land Use*, Bristol LA21, Land Use Group and The Architecture Centre, Bristol, Woodside Press, Bristol.

Office of the Deputy Prime Minister (ODPM) (2000) *Millennium Villages and Sustainable Communities*, Department of the Environment, Transport and the Regions, London.

Crown Street, Glasgow

The project

Situated in the Gorbals, Glasgow, its construction will be completed in 2005 and will comprise a total of 1708 dwellings, at a density of 73 dwellings per hectare with a mixture of tenures – 1200 owner occupied, 300 social rented and 208 student flats (Dawson, 2004). The mixed-use development has local shops, retail space, a partly refurbished church, theatre, local police station as well as a range of gardens and open public spaces. The development has a primary aim of physical, social and economic integration with the existing community in the Gorbals area.

Sustainability features

In addition to its mixture of uses and high density, it is supported by good transport links (Figure C.17) by bus and train and as it is located close to the city centre, their need to travel is reduced. In an attempt to reduce car ownership, car parking provision is just over one per household (*ibid.*, 2004).

References and links

Dawson, R. (2004) *Towards Good Practice in Sustainable Urban Land Use*, Bristol LA21, Land Use Group and The Architecture Centre, Bristol, Woodside Press, Bristol.

Figure C.17
Crown Street: urban regeneration of the Gorbals.
(*Source*: http://www.glasgowarchitecture.co.uk/crown_street_gorbals.htm)

Sustainable buildings and energy efficiency

Västra Hamnen, Malmö

The project

Västra Hamnen, the regenerated brownfield site, is now home to a densely populated mixed-use neighbourhood of 600 apartments with integrated commercial activities. It is located on a 30-hectare site and is intended as an international flagship of dense urban development. Public funds were used for land reclamation, environmental improvements, infrastructure and green transport. The private sector developers funded the housing and commercial development. Västra Hamnen is also home to the Turning Torso (Figure C.18), the mixed-use high-rise tower designed by Santiago Calatrava.

Sustainability features

Its ecology is enhanced by designing in green space, planting, 'green roofs', and fast growing trees for harvesting and use as biofuel. 100% of the energy used in the district is from renewable sources, including wind power and photovoltaics, biogas from processed waste and sewage, heat pumps and solar collectors – there is zero importation of energy. Rainwater run-off is controlled, collected and processed centrally. The sewage system is designed to extract nutrients and heavy metals for re-use, while significant amounts of organic waste is transformed into biogas. The streets are car-free with limited parking (one space per dwelling) and a shared pool of electric cars. Priority on streets is given to pedestrians, cyclists (Figures C.19 and C.20) and gas-fuelled buses. To help residents achieve a more sustainable lifestyle there are good communications, in particular a neighbourhood broadband network giving environmental advice, bus times, and monitoring energy and water use.

References and links

City of Malmö (2002) *Västra Hamnen The Bo01-area: A City for People and the Environment.* Retrieved from the World Wide Web on 27th July 2004. http://www.ekostaden.com/pdf/vhfolder_malmostad_0308_ eng.pdf

City of Malmö (2002) *Bo01 – An Ecological City of Tomorrow in the Western Harbour, Malmö.* Retrieved from the World Wide Web on 27th July 2004.

http://www.ekostaden.com/information/ekostaden_tmpl_01.
aspx?pageID=93&parentID=176&sectionID=4&level=4&introID=146

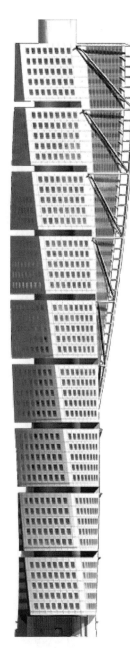

Figure C.19
Modern and sustainable design making use of car-free streets.
(*Source*: Nicholas Low.)

Figure C.18
High rise is not necessarily unsustainable – the Turning Torso.
(*Source*: http://www.turningtorso.com/e_fakta.asp)

Figure C.20
Ecological care of the new environment. (*Source*: Nicholas Low.)

Beddington Zero-Energy Development

The project

Beddington Zero-Energy Development (BedZED), Sutton, London, is a high-density mixed-use urban village on the site of a former sewage works developed for the Peabody Trust. The 82 dwellings are built to a density of 75 dwellings per hectare. It has a mixture of housing types (flats, maisonettes and town houses), uses (residential, commercial, community, open space) and tenures. It is well served by local transport which connects the project to the centre of London (Figure C.21).

Sustainability features

The underlying objective of Bill Dunster's Zed projects is to reduce the environmental impact, give residents the ability to live sustainably without decreasing their quality of life of residents (Bill Dunster Architects, 2003; Dawson, 2004). This is translated into sustainable practices that are based on being carbon neutral, increasing energy efficiency in the home, linking to a sustainable transport network and on getting food direct from 'farm to plate' (BedZED, no date). These include the use of reclaimed building materials, 135 kw wood fuelled combined heat and power generator, building orientation (Figures C.22–C.24) to maximize solar gain, on-site water treatment and grey-water recycling, promoting sustainable alternatives to the car (including photovoltaic power to charge up electric cars) and the siting of community facilities within the residential development. Bill Dunster has extended the principles to even higher densities in a proposal for a sustainable high-rise form, 'SkyZed' (Figure C.24), which is built around a wind turbine and photovoltaics to generate the energy needed for the scheme.

References and links

BedZED (no date) *About BedZED*. Retrieved from the World Wide Web on 28th July 2004 http://www.bedzed.org.uk/main.html

Bill Dunster Architects (2003) *From A to ZED: Realising Zero (fossil) Energy Developments*, Bill Dunster Architects ZEDfactory Ltd, Wallington, UK.

Bill Dunster Architects (no date) *Zero Emissions Development Web Site*, Retrieved from the World Wide Web on 28th July 2004 http://www.zedfactory.com/home.html

Bill Dunster Architects (no date) *BedZED*. Retrieved from the World Wide Web on 28th July 2004 http://www.zedfactory.com/bedzed/bedzed.html

Dawson, R. (2004) *Towards Good Practice in Sustainable Urban Land Use*, Bristol LA21 Land Use Group and The Architecture Centre, Bristol, Woodside Press, Bristol.

Figure C.21
A variety of house types, and an integration between living and work units.
(*Source*: www.zedfactory.com)

Figure C.22
Orientation and design to take advantage of passive
solar gain.
(*Source*: www.zedfactory.com)

Figure C.23
Using the roofs to give private gardens in a high-density
development.
(*Source*: www.zedfactory.com)

Figure C.24
SkyZed, a sustainable high-rise solution.
(*Source*: www.zedfactory.com)

Waterfront House and Ecological Design in the Tropics

The project

The architect, Ken Yeang, is an active proponent of the 'green' skyscraper (Hamzah Yeang, no date). He has proposed and developed ideas for the 'green skyscraper' (Figure C.25), and early designs included a sustainable design for the EDITT (Ecological Design In The Tropics) tower (Yeang, 1999; Hamzah and Yeang, 2000). The concept is to reduce the environmental impact of tall buildings. Design includes the use of 'vertical' landscaping using local vegetation, facades that allow for natural ventilation and passive use of energy, water recycling, flexible floor space design, and the use of photovoltaics to generate electricity. The Waterfront House proposal in Kuala Lumpur represents a new development of the green skyscraper idea.

Sustainability features

In Waterfront House, light pipes will be used to deliver natural light (sunlight and diffuse sunlight) to the deep recesses of the building, using laser- cut panel light deflectors (Hansen *et al.*, 2002), in principle saving up to 50% of electricity

costs. Yeang is not directly following the solar access theory in terms of providing all users access to direct daylight and sunlight, but is rather delivering the light to users. The design is reported to be relatively inexpensive, and so could be used in the refurbishment of poorly sunlit older buildings as well as in new construction (Jayasankaran, 2004). It is unclear at this stage how this design would fare in a tall building as the pipe size is currently very large at 20 m (l) $\times$ 0.8 m (h) $\times$ 2 m (w) (Jayasankaran, 2004).

References and links

Hamzah, T.R. and Yeang, K. (2000) 3 Projects. *Quaderns, d'architctura I urbanisme*, ARCE, Barcelona.

Jayasankaran, S. (2004) Light for life. *Far Eastern Econom Rev (FEER)*. Retrieved from the World Wide Web on 19 May 2004 http://www. feer. com/articles/2003/0311_06/free/p044innov.html.

Hamzah Yeang, T.R. (no date) *Profile*. Retrieved from the World Wide Web on 01 August 2004 http:// www.trhamzahyeang.com/ profile/company.html

Yeang, K. (1999) *The Green Skyscraper: The Basis for Designing Sustainable Intensive Buildings*, Prestel Verlag, Munich.

Figure C.25
The 'green skyscraper.' (*Source*: Yeang, 1999; http://www.trhamzahyeang.com/project/ skyscrapers/ waterfront01.html)

Bank of America Tower, New York

The project

The focus of much sustainable building design has been on domestic architecture, neglecting other forms of building. The Bank of America Tower (Figure C.26) is an interesting departure, demonstrating how commercial buildings can be more environmentally friendly. Upon its completion, this tower will be the world's most environmentally responsible high-rise office building and also the first to aim for the US Green Building Council's Leadership in Energy and Environmental Design (LEED) Platinum rating (Smart Communities Network, no date; The Durst Organisation, 2004).

Sustainability features

The tower project incorporates sustainability measures and high-performance technologies to provide an energy efficient, water efficient building with a high-quality indoor environment (with regard to natural light and fresh air). The Tower will be constructed from mainly recycled and recyclable building materials, and will feature a range of advanced environmental technologies, such as filtered under floor displacement air ventilation, translucent insulating glass windows which allow maximum daylight and an on-site 4.6-megawatt cogeneration plant, which will provide power, cleanly and efficiently. Daylight dimming and light-emitting diode (LED) lights will be used to reduce usage, and CO_2 monitors will automatically introduce fresh air as and when necessary. There will be also planted roofs which will contribute to reducing the urban heat island effect, and a grey-water system in place to capture and reuse all water (Smart Communities Network, no date).

References and links

Smart Communities Network (no date) *Groundbreaking Held for World's Most Environmentally Responsible High Rise*. Retrieved from the World Wide Web on 01 August 2004 http://www.sustainable.doe.gov/management/geninfo.shtml

The Durst Organisation (2004) *One Bryant Park*. Retrieved from the World Wide Web on 01 August 2004 http://www.durst.org/i_bpl_news.asp

Figure C.26
Commercial, but sustainable.
(*Source*: http://www.durst.org/i_bpl_news.asp)

Greening the city

Oslo's Green Heart

The project

Oslo was awarded the European Sustainable City award 2003. The City Government has established and approved a 'Green Belt Boundary' to ensure that forests are not cleared to make way for urban development. The Government also has a plan to conserve existing areas of biological diversity such as wetlands and ponds (City of Oslo City Government, 2002 p. 33). Enhancing the accessibility to green spaces is also part of this sustainable strategy, in an attempt to increase the level of use and interest in Oslo's biological diversity (Figures C.27 and C.28).

Sustainability features

A Municipal Master Plan has been drawn up which states that housing and business developments take place through urban intensification, which will target brownfield sites and strategically situate new housing in relation to employment (City of Oslo City Government, 2002). Alongside this, Oslo has embarked on an Urban Ecology Programme for the period 2002–2014, which targets behaviour: an environmentally efficient public transport system will be established, using renewable energy sources, and environmentally friendly behaviour will be promoted through partnerships with citizens and businesses.

References and links

City of Oslo City Government (2002) *Strategy for Sustainable Development: Environment and Sustainability Status 2002 Urban Ecology Programme 2002–2014*, Department of Transport and Environmental Affairs, Oslo.

Figure C.27
The Oslo Fjord. (*Source*: Samfoto for City of Oslo City Government, 2002.)

Figure C.28
Well-maintained parks can enhance interest in Oslo's biological diversity. (*Source*: http://www.oslo.kommune.no/the_city_of_oslo/about_oslo/)

Île-de-France

The project

Planning in the Île-de-France city region is a strong catalyst for the integration of green spaces into the existing urban fabric. The Loi Solidarité et Renouvellement Urbain (Solidarity and Urban Renewal law), passed in 2000, requires city-region planning to proceed with revised land use plans, taking into account issues such as social mix and housing as a revision to existing planning tools (COST C11, 2001; Bordes-Pagès, 2002).

Sustainability features

Examples of this green space enhancement includes the creation of 'green arteries' connecting services and facilities to green spaces at Levallois-Perret, building height restrictions to protect views and to maximize natural sunlight at Nogent-sur-Marne and the creation of a mixed-use urban park at Plessis-Trévise (Figure C.29). This is one example of the preference for the provision of green spaces by authorities as opposed to delineating open countryside and urban areas (see also Urban Green Spaces Taskforce, 2002; VROM, no date).

References and links

Bordes-Pagès, E. (2002) *CAHIERS 133–134 Public Living and City Spaces: Public Spaces and Green Space Plans: An Avant-Garde Combination.* Retrieved from the World Wide Web http://www.iaurif. org/en/doc/studies/cahiers/ cahiers_133/ uk_PARTIE%20II_C133.134_MIDM. pdf on 25 May 2004.

COST C11 (2001) *Greenstructures and Urban Planning: Spatial Planning in France.* Retrieved from the World Wide Web http://www.map21ltd. com/COSTC11/france.htm on 25 May 2004.

Urban Green Spaces Taskforce (2002) *Green Spaces, Better Places: Final Report of The Urban Green Spaces Taskforce,* DTLR, London.

VROM (Netherlands Ministry of Spatial Planning, Housing and the Environment) (no date) *Urban Regeneration.* Retrieved from the World Wide Web http://www.vrom.nl/international/ on 26 May 2004.

Figure C.29
Green arteries in a mixed-use development, Parc Emile Loubet, in Plessis-Trévise, Île de France. (*Source:* http://www.iaurif.org/en/doc/studies/cahiers/cahiers_133/ uk_PARTIE%20II_C133.134_MIDM.pdf)

Green roofs, Tokyo

The project

Dense cities, such as Tokyo, suffer from the heat island effect, with ambient temperatures considerably higher than the surrounding countryside. The Tokyo government passed regulations in 2002 to 'green' buildings with trees, plants and grass. The regulations require '20% of every new, large private building and 30% of all public buildings' to be covered in greenery (McCurry, 2004). One such example is at Roppongi Hills, a new project by the Mori Corporation – which is also claimed to be Tokyo's (Figure C.30) example of compact city development (Yabe *et al.*, 2003).

Sustainability features

Green roofs, it is suggested, have numerous sustainability benefits. In addition to reducing the heat island effect,

they help to conserve energy and fuel because of their insulation value, and ameliorate storm water run-off through absorption. They enhance biodiversity and wildlife, and provide additional green space in crowded urban areas (Anon, 2004). Roppongi Hills provides 1300 m² of roof garden space. However, such 'sky gardens' tend to be for private use, and the public benefit may be slight.

References and links

Anon. (2004) Green Roofs. *Sustain*, **5(5)** pp. 25–27.

McCurry, J. (2004) Sweltering Tokyo tries to go Green. *The Guardian*, 24 July 2004, p. 19.

Yabe, T., Terada, M., Yamagishi, K. and Yokoyama, Y. (2003) *Roppongi Hills Opening Exhibition Catalogue: The Global City*, Mori Building Co., Ltd, Tokyo.

Mori Building Co., Ltd. (no date) *Roppongi Hills*, Mori Building Co., Ltd, Tokyo.

Figure C.30
A 'sky garden' at Roppongi Hills, Tokyo. (*Source*: Mori Building Co., Ltd.)

Index

accessibility 80
  intelligent city indicator 48
adaptability 3
  Darwinian concept 40–41
Archigram 138
architectural vision 272

back-casting 365
Bamboo Summit City 209–210
Battery Park City 189
blue banana 59
bohemian index 50
boulevard 180–182
Bovenstad, upper city 208–211
Bristol
  political reality 108–110
    Regional Chamber 109
  public transport system, funds
    109–110
brownfield 69, 129, 238, 430, 436
Brundtland Report 312
bubble economy, Japan 63
building integrated photovoltaic
  (BIPV) 382
  overshadowing 386
bye-law housing 289, 290

Cambridge
  past policies 115–118
  public consultation 130–132
  sub-region 114
    knowledge-based industries 114
    Silicon Fen 265

transport links 117–118
  virtual highway 118
Cambridge Futures Project 266
Cambridge Futures 114
  alternative options
    assessment 125–130
    densification 116–117
    green swap 117
    impact 118–121
    minimum growth 116
    necklace 117
    new town 118
    results 121–125
    transport links 117–118
    virtual highway 118
Cambridge Highway Transport
  Model 120
Cambridge Phenomenon 114
Cambridge region, future 265–267
Cambridge sub-region
  knowledge-based industries 114
Campaign of the Protection of Rural
  England 297
Campus City 179–180
carbon dioxide (CO_2) 355–356
  reduction 360
carbon emission 356, 357, 359
central business district (CBD)
  Singapore, functional divide
    168–170
charitable trust 264
China 395
  environmental issue 397

cities 14, 15
  air space, development 216
  changing character 14
  changing form 15–16
  changing 385
  commodifying 19–24
  countryside 26
  design elements
    developing quarters 352
    memorable events, places 351
    physical accessibility 351
    public and private boundaries
      350
    virtual accessibility 350
    walkable zones 352–353
  digital infrastructure 39
  diversity indices 50
  efficiency 76
  fundamental role 35, 38
  greening
    Green roofs, Tokyo 438
    Île-de-France 437
    Oslo's Green Heart 436
  hinterlands 41–42
  intensification 44
  in Japan 314, 316
  physical hub 19
  policy aim 20
  size 75
  social role 14–15
  strengthening 26
  sustaining 24–28
    citizen participation 26–28

cities (*contd*)
  transformation to urban sprawl
    16–19
  well-functioning 74
  workforce mobility 45
cities and towns, need to generate
    98
city authorities, role 20
city identity 45
city intelligence 32, 40
  see also intelligent city
city level strategies 231–233
city living, future form 415–417
city models
  strategic irradiation mapping 383
city-centre housing 23
city-region
  blue banana 59
  as framework 59
  Japanese Pacific Belt 59
  spatial sustainability of 55–69
  towards sustainability 65–69
civitas 14
clustering strategies 236–237
community feedback 239–241
compact city 155
  high densities 312–314
  in Japan 314
  principle components 331
  public transport system 313
  sustainability 312
composite diversity index 50
computer-simulation program 140
Costs of Sprawl 222
counter-urban, persistent dispersal
    96–98
counter-urbanization 58
cycling and walking environment
    86

Darwinian concept 40–41
daylight 371, 378
Decent Homes standards 364
Delta Metropolis 68, 213
demolition and rebuilding 408–409
Densely Inhibited Districts (DIDs)
    315–317, 319, 336n
densification potential 252
density
  arguments 298–302
  different measurements 293
  government steps 294–298
  gross 291
  house builders 297
  language and meaning 287
  local authorities 296, 297
  measuring 291–294
  net 291

standards 294–295
  Tudor Walters Report 294
depopulation 65
difference mapping 386
diffuse horizontal irradiance 376
diffuse light 374
direct normal irradiance 376
Downtown Interchange 178–179
Dudley Report 294, 298
duplex 255
dwelling unit strategies 237–239

economic efficiency 130
economy 25
  driving forces 43
  intelligent city indicator 48
ECO-town 271
  Fenland landscape 272
  urban design framework 272–273
    development 273–277
    working within 277–279
effective labour market 75
environment, intelligent city
    indicator 48
environmental quality 130
environmental sustainability 24, 80–81
  objective 99

facade 387–388
Feyenoord 218
flat development 299
foreign born index 50
fossil fuel 356, 357, 358
fragile landscape
  sustainable urbanity 245
functional planning, Shenton Way
    CBD 170–171
Future City Form 153
future, envisioning 263–264, 279–282
  Cambridge region 265–267
  Oaking Barracks 267–271

Garden City 291
gay index 50
gentrification 22, 98
global cities, potential 57
global environment, threat 95
Golden Shoe 169, 170
Greater London Council (GLC) 226
greenfield 121, 129, 268, 420
gross density figures
  inner city 291
  metropolitan region 291

high density 299, 302–306
  compact city 312–314
  development, new strategy 207
  overcrowding 288–291

hinterlands 41–42
Hong Kong
  building type, performance
    indicator 398, 399
  constraints 154
  future housing trends
    methodology 398
  housing authority block 400,
    405
  Integer Concept Tower 404–405
  Kowloon Station 160–162
  MILU 159
  private sector block 400, 405
  regional background 394–398
  sky city 157–159
  skyline 155
  space, multiple use 155
  sustainability, improvement
    methodology 398
    comparative analysis 402–403
    creating 400–402
    data collection 398–399
    development 403–404
  Tseng Kwan O 159–160
  vertical intensification 155–157
Hulshof Architects 207, 219n
human sustainability 196–197
humane environment
  intelligent city, ubiquitous
    network 31

illumination 376, 377
Integer Concept Tower 404–405
intelligent building 32–33
intelligent city 31
  achieving 45–46
  adaptability 47
  concept 33–34
  diversity 40
  indicators 48, 49
  physical fabric 19, 39
  planning policy 46–47
  planning system, focus of 47
  policy 47
  redefining 35–40
  social sustainability 45–46
  sustainability 40–42
inter-war suburbs 294
irradiation mapping for complex
    urban environments (ICUE)
    379
San Francisco 380–382

Japan
  accessibility
    analysis methods 326–327
    banking facilities 328
    convenience stores 329–330

day-care centres 327
hospitals and clinics 328–329
local community centers 327
parks and gardens 328
post offices 328
railway stations 327
car ownership 315, 322
cities, division 317–321
compact cities 314
principle component analysis
331–336
Densely Inhibited Districts (DIDs)
315–317, 336n
designated land use 315–317
planning system, characteristics
314
population growth 314–315
principle cities 317
quality of life
car ownership 322–323
floor space of residences 324
journey to work 323–324
land prices 324–326
petrol, purchased quantity 323
Japanese Pacific Belt 59

Keynesian economics 20, 43
Kanazawa 319–320
urbanization, rapid 319–321
knowledge economy 42–45

land use
in Hong Kong
compact city 155
multiple and intensive 153
sky city 157–159
vertical intensification 155–157
in Japan 315–317
land-use management 55
Laurenskwartier 217
local area, householder problems 97
local facility, accessibility 311, 313,
327
urban density 326–330
Looiershof 214
Lower Manhattan 188
Battery Park City 189
changes, economic and societal
189–191
community node organization
201–203
context 188–189
decentralization 192
diversified employment 192
future, vision for 191
human sustainability 196–197
identity 192
infrastructure 197

making sustainable 192–196
Rebuild Downtown Our Town
(R.Dot) 187–188
rebuilding 185
guiding principles 193
urban design armature
194–195
Solaire 201
sustainable legislation 200–201
transportation 197–199
urban form and buildings 199–200
vertical urbanism 201
World Trade Center (WTC) 189
civic groups 200
Lowry model 273–277, 283n

measuring change 47–49
mega-cities 14
megastructure, city 137
historical examples 137–141
Archigram 138
City in the Air 139
Diocletian Palace 138
Mirage City 140
Roman amphitheatre 138
in Hong Kong 141–149
Olympian City 142–145
Pacific Place 147–149
Tai Koo Shing 145–147
memorable events, places 351
MENTOR land-use model 119–120
methodology, sustainability
comparative analysis 402–403
creating
cost element 401
energy and CO_2, development
model 401
material masses 400, 401
operational cost 402
waste model 401
data collection 398–399
improvement strategies,
development 403–404
metro-city development, MILU
159–160
MILU 155
city within a city 159
metro-city development 159–160
multiple-use development
160–162
mixed land uses 153
mixed-use development 155
mobility environment 85–86
modernization 18
mud season 252
multifamily courtyard 255–257
multiple-use development, MILU
160–162

neighbourhood center
pedestrian-oriented
alternative 257–258
neighbourhood nodes 201
neighbourhood strategies 233–236
neo-liberalism 20, 22, 26
economic trends 22
neovitalism 140
net density 291
the Netherlands
national planning programme
211–212
transport performance 79
New Downtown 171–172
New Economy 42
business requirements 44
context 340–341
classical economies 347
new town, decentralized
Singapore
functional divide 168–170
New Urbanist 264, 272, 283, 303

Oakington Barracks 267–271
design team
key elements 269
objectives 270
inter-disciplinary working 268–271
Olympian City 142–145
option testing, Cambridge Futures
assessment
cost of production 125
economic implication 127–128
environmental implications 129
housing cost 125
jobs 125
social implication 128
transport 125–127
densification 116
green swap 117
impact, forecasting 118–121
minimum growth 116
necklace 117
new town 118
public consultation 130–131
results 121–125
transport links 117–118
virtual highway 118
overshadowing 386, 387
Oxford Solar Initiative (OSI) 360–361
CO_2 reduction 360
feasibility study 362–364
focus area 360
implementation
Oxford solar dissemination 366
Oxford solar partnership 364–365
Oxford solar scenarios 365
pilot projects 365–366

Oxford Solar Initiative (OSI) (*contd*)
 Oxford Team 361
 targets 360
 urban energy technologies 360
Oxford Solar scenarios 365
 back-casting 365

Pacific Place 147–149
Pearl River Delta, agglomeration 57
photovoltaic devices 382
physical accessibility 351
physical hubs, cluster of 340, 343
 private spaces 346
 privileged spaces 346–347
 public spaces 347
plan clarity 182
plan effectiveness 182
polycentric urban-regions 60, 61
population migration 17, 154, 416
principle cities 317
principle component analysis
 331–336
private spaces 344
privileged space 344
profile fit, work styles 347–350
property, intelligent city indicator 48
public and private boundaries 350
public consultation 130–132
public spaces 344
Pullman 226
 community feedback 239–241
 future growth alternatives 239
 regeneration design, integrated
  level strategies
  city 231–233
  clustering 236–237
  district and neighbour
   233–236
  dwelling unit 237–239
  regional 229–231
 sustainable community plan 227

quality of life 311
 urban density, analysis
  indicator 322–326
  methods 322
quality, focus on 50–51
quarters 352

Randstad 56, 60–62
 Delta Metropolis 68, 213
 green city 61, 62, 68
 polycentric urban system 61
 Randstad Loop 90
 transport system
  future sustainability 88
  policy scenarios, land use
   measures 88–91

Rebuild Downtown Our Town
 (R.Dot) 187–188
 objective 191
regenerative plan, Pullman
 theory and practice
  city level strategies 231–233
  clustering strategies 236–237
  district and neighbourhood
   strategies 233–236
  dwelling unit strategies 237–239
  regional level strategies
   229–231
regenerative theory 242n
regional level strategies 229–231
reurbanization 58
Rhijnvis Feith 217
Rotterdam
 Bamboo Summit City 209–210
 building programme 213
 Delfshaven 215
 Feeyenoord 218
 Hulshof Architects 207
 Laurenskwartier 217
 pilot projects 217–218
 Rhijnvis Feith 217
 Upper City Foundation 208,
  216–217
rural communities, sustainable
 models 263

SANE
 space environment model 343–347
  places 345–347
  space, categories 344
  tools 344–345
SATURN highway model 120
shadow pattern 372, 373–374
Shenton Way CBD 170
 live–work–play 172
 New Downtown 171
 work environment 172
Silicon Fen 265
Singapore 167
 boulevard 180–182
 Campus City 179–180
 Downtown Interchange 178–179
  Fort Canning Park 179
 downtown urban form, reflections
  on 173–175
 functional divide 168–170
 New Downtown 171
 ring development 168
 sustainable urban form 167
 urban design
  guidelines 183
  master plan 182
  studio 175–177
  team 176

Urban Redevelopment Authority's
 (URA) 171–172
 International Panel of Architects
  and Urban Planners 175–176
single-family development
 duplex 255
 historic typologies 253–254
 multifamily courtyard 255–257
 zero-lot line 254
sky city 157–159
social equity 130
social sustainability 45–46
solar access 371
 architectural masterplan 384
 changing cities 385–387
 components 388–389
 definitions 374
 dense urban setting, San Francisco
  380–382
 field trails 387
 forecast 375–377
 illumination, quantitative measure
  376–377
 imagining 372–375
 massing schemes, assessment
  384–385
 new schema 377–380
 responsive facade configurations
  387–388
 solar energy, harvesting 382–383
solar architecture 389
solar cities 355
 community-based approach
  359–360
 concept of 357–359
solar energy, harvesting 382–383
 photovoltaics 382
space
 multiple use 155
 physical 348
 virtual 348, 349
spatial configuration
 of Randstad 60–62
  green heart 61, 62, 68
 of Tokyo 62–64
spatial planning, MILU 159
spatial sustainability 55
strategic irradiation mapping
 city models 383–384
suburban sprawl 19
supporting structure 137, 138, 139
sustainability features
 Bank of America Tower 435
 Beddington Zero-Energy
  Development 432
 Crown Street, Glasgow 429
 Green roofs, Tokyo 438
 Greenwich Millennium Village 428

Homes for Change 426
Île-de-France 437
Kowloon station, Hong Kong 424
Øresund region 418
Oslo's Green Heart 436
Pudong, China 425
Slateford Green, Edinburgh 422
Thames Gateway 420
Vancouver SkyTrain extension 423
Västra Hamnen 430
Waterfront House 434
sustainability 221, 263–264
  alternative plans, forecasting 113
  assessment, comparative 393, 394
    life-cycle assessment (LCA) 394
    life-cycle costing (LCC) 394
  compact city 312
  dimensions 24
  environmental 80
  human–environmental context 227
  site context 227
  through urban regeneration
    Crown Street, Glasgow 429
    Greenwich Millennium Village
      428
    Homes for Change 426
Sustainable Accommodation for the
  New Economy
  see SANE
sustainable buildings
  energy efficiency
    Bank of America Tower 435
    Beddington Zero-Energy
      Development 432
    V‰ostra Hamnen 430
    Waterfront House 434
sustainable cells
  clustered cells, urbanism 222–226
  regenerative theory and practice
    221
sustainable city
  Lower Manhattan 185
    changing identity, diversified
      employment 192
    civil response 186–188
    community node organization
      201–203
    human sustainability 196–197
    infrastructure for people 197
    sustainable legislation 200–201
    transportation 197
    urban form and building
      199–200
  realization 196
sustainable city region, creating 95
  analysis
    Bristol 103–104
    Sheffield 101–102

case study
  Bristol 100–101
  Sheffield 99–100
sustainable regional development 418
  Øresund region 418
  Thames Gateway 420
sustainable urban form, future
  CBD to New Downtown 170–172
  designing 167
  urban design studio 175–177
sustainable urbanity 245
  design proposal
    climate influences 251–252
    densification potential 252
    development, alternatives
      252–257
  infill opportunities
    commercial areas 258
    downtown block infill 259
    parking infill 258–259
  problem defined
    access, transportation 250
    agriculture, loss of 250
    ecosystem 248–249
    habitat, loss of 250–251
    living the myth, density 248
    New Urbanism 245
    political and environmental 249
    population growth, current
      development 247–248
    solution, partial 251

Tai Koo Shing 145–147
tale of two cities
  urbanism
    London 222–225
    Washington 225–226
Test Reference Year (TRY) dataset
  377
theoretical survey
  upper city transformation
    in the Netherlands 211–213
Tokyo 56
  depopulation 65
  dormitory-towns 62, 63
  dormitory-towns 62, 63
  polycentric structure, policy to
    reinforce 64
  regeneration programme 67
  renovation programme 65, 66
  urban functions, over-
    concentration 64
total annual illumination
  see total annual irradiation
total annual irradiation 378
  difference mapping 386
  prediction, computer-based 379
Tower of Babel 138

traditional city 31
  sustainability 41
transit environment 88
transit-related development
  Kowloon station, Hong Kong 424
  Pudong, China 425
  Slateford Green, Edinburgh 422
  Vancouver SkyTrain extension 423
transportation
  Bristol
    analysis 103–104
    background 100–101
    key stages 104–108
    design challenge 92
    policy challenge 92
    land use
    research challenge 91–92
  Sheffield
    analysis 101–103
    background 99–100
Tudor Walters Report 294

ubiquitous network, humane
  environment 31
upper city
  Bovenstad 208–211
  ideas, precursors 213–216
  Looiershof 214
  Zwarte Madonna 213
  transformations 207
  opportunities, in the
    Netherlands 211–213
Upper City Foundation 216–217
urban area
  densities 313
urban density 24, 311
  local facilities, accessibility 326–330
  quality of life 322–326
urban design
  framework 272
  guidelines 183
  master plan 182
  strategic sites 183
urban design studio 175–177
urban development 55
  sustainable, principles 312
urban form
  economic performance
    empirical analysis 75–77
    theoretical background 74–75
urban functions 58
urban intelligence 40, 46
  sustainability 40–42
urban markets, spatial enlargement 74
urban planning
  debates 55
  strategies, CO_2 reduction 360
  sustainability indicators 113

urban regeneration policy, Japan 67
urban region, multi-modal 73
  accessibility and sustainability,
    enhancing 81–85
  development 82
  environmental and economic
    goals 73
    design challenge 92
    policy challenge 92
    research challenge 91–92
  in Randstad
    future plans 88–91
    past trends 85–88
urban solar access, quantification 371
urban space 15
urban sprawl 58
urban success 48
urban sustainability
  achieving 25–26
  changing form 15–16
  cities to urban sprawl 16–19
  citizen participation 26–28
  city, changing character 14
  commodifying cities 19–24
  future 28–29
  social role 14
  sustaining cities 24–28
  see also cities
urban system
  key characteristics 77–79

urban transport, sustainability 80
Urban Villages 282n
urbanism
  clustered cells
    London 222–222–225
    Washington 225–226
  spatial phenomena
    economic activities 43
    knowledge workers 43
  sustainable cells 221
urbanity
  design priorities 260–261
  large plot development,
    Ranchettes
    alternatives 252–253
  pedestrian-oriented
    alternative 257–258
  single-family development
    duplex 255
    existing conditions 253–254
    historical precedence 253–254
    multifamily courtyard 255–257
    zero-lot line 254
  sustainable 245
urbanization 28
  process 58
  Kanazawa 319–321

vertical intensification 155–157
virtual accessibility 350

virtual network 339, 342
  private spaces 344–345
  privileged spaces 345
  public spaces 345

walkable distance 327, 336n
walkable zones 352–353
work environment 339
work pattern
  emerging 341–342
  profiles
    accommodating 349–350
    cluster of physical hub 343
    determining 347–349
    New Economy 340–341
    virtual network 342–343
  work environment 339
work profiles
  accommodating 349–350
  physical hubs, cluster of 343
  virtual network 342–343
World Trade Center (WTC) 185–186,
  189
  disaster, civic response
    186–188

zero-lot line 254
Zwarte Madonna 213

Contents

Note on the Revised Edition   v

Introduction   vi

Topic and skills map for English Language AS and A2   x

Module 1: Introduction to the Study of Language   **1**

What this module is all about   **1**

Starting to explore   **2**

The 'science' of language study   2

A question of language   3

Language all around us   4

Keeping a language glossary   5

You and your language: idiolect   6

Your language history and experience   6

Fitting in: language as a membership card   8

Language varieties: describing and classifying   **9**

Problems with classification   13

Collecting your own data   16

Genres   17

The formality spectrum: register   19

Speech and writing   20

Standard English, slang and dialect   26

Preparing for the examination: Task 1, classification   27

Describing language in detail: stylistic analysis   **32**

Using frameworks   33

Language framework: discourse structure   35

Language framework: layout, form and grammar   38

Language framework: the grammar of the   40

Word formations: morphology   43

Language framework: words and phrases (lexis)   45

Language framework: sounds and spelling   48

Language framework: semantics and pragmatics   51

Putting it all together   55

Analysis of conversation   58

Preparing for the examination: Task 2, stylistic analysis   60

Do you know your language terms?   61

Commentaries   **64**

Module 2 Language and Social Contexts   **79**

What this module is all about   **79**

Links with Module 1   79

What's new about Module 2?   80

Starting to explore   **82**

Language and power   **86**

Language and power in action: analysing conversation   88

Analysing talk: summary   92

Power in practice: classroom language   93

Power in practice: other conversational contexts   94

Language and the professions 95
Language and politics 97
Persuasion and rhetoric 100
The language of power in the media 102
Language and gender **102**
Language and representation 103
Language usage 108
Further reading: some key texts on language and gender 111
Accents and dialects of the British Isles **111**
Accents of English 112
Accent and social class 114
Regional dialects and Standard English 115
The origins of Standard English and regional dialects 120
Representations of accents and dialects 122
Preparing for the examination **123**
Commentaries **124**

Module 3 **Original Writing** **134**
What this module is all about **134**
Producing your texts 137
'Primary purposes' of texts 137
Writing to inform **139**
Choosing an assignment 147
Preparing to produce a text 150
Using facts and statistical information 152
Writing for audio 153
Writing to instruct **154**
Writing to entertain **159**
Autobiographical writing 160
Biographical writing and 'ghosting' 163
Dramatic monologues 165
Prose fiction 170
Fiction for younger readers 172
Choosing your assignment 177
Writing to persuade **178**
Appealing to heads or hearts 179
The structure of arguments 182
Possible topics 183
Preparing your submission for assessment **185**
Selecting your final pieces 185
A note on 'originality' and pastiche 185
Drafting and re-drafting 185
The commentary 187
Practicalities: assembling your file 188
Commentaries **189**

Glossary **194**

English Language

for AQA  B

Ron Norman

Consultant: Tim Shortis

www.heinemann.co.uk
✓ Free online support
✓ Useful weblinks
✓ 24 hour online ordering

01865 888058

Heinemann

Inspiring generations

Heinemann Educational Publishers,
Halley Court, Jordan Hill, Oxford OX2 8EJ
Part of Harcourt Education Ltd

Heinemann is the registered trademark of Harcourt Education Ltd

First edition published 2000
Revised edition published 2003

2007 2006 2005
10 9 8 7 6 5 4

ISBN 0 435 10984 7

Acknowledgements

The publishers would like to thank the following for permission to use copyright material:
Penguin Books UK for an extract from *Sociolinguistics: An Introduction* by Peter Trudgill, Penguin Books 1974, Fourth edition 2000. Copyright Peter Trudgill 1974, 1995, 2000; Penguin Books UK for an extract from *Essential Computers: Creating Presentations*, Dorling Kindersley 2000. Copyright © Dorling Kindersley 2000; The Random House Group Limited for an illustration by Quentin Blake, from *The BFG* by Roald Dahl, published by Jonathan Cape; David Higham Associates Limited for an extract from *The BFG* by Roald Dahl, published by Jonathan Cape and Penguin Books; Pollinger Limited and the Estate of Frieda Lawrence Ravagli for an extract from *Sons and Lovers* by D. H. Lawrence, published by Cambridge University Press; Atlantic Syndication for the recipe and photo 'Macaroni with wild mushrooms' from *YOU Magazine*, 24th November 2002; Methuen Publishing Limited for an extract from *Monty Python 's Flying Circus – Just the Words* (volume one) by Graham Chapman, John Cleese, Terry Gilliam, Eric Idle, Terry Jones and Michael Palin, published by Methuen Publishing; BBC Radio 5 Live and the BBC for transcript of England v New Zealand, Rugby Union commentary, from BBC Radio 5 Live, Saturday afternoon, 9th November 2002; The Royal Institute of Chartered Surveyors for a short extract of text from *Home Buyer's Survey & Valuation*. Copyright © The Royal Institute of Chartered Surveyors, August 1993; Yorkshire Dialect Society for a short extract 'Au'd George: A Methody Pioneer' by A. Stanley Umpleby, from *A Century of Yorkshire Dialect* published by Smith Settle in 1997; The Guardian for an extract from 'Lovers jailed for stabbing murder' by Helen Carter, The Guardian, 9th November 2002. Copyright © The Guardian 2002; Peters Fraser & Dunlop on behalf of Kingsmarkham Enterprises Limited for an extract from *The Veiled One* by Ruth Rendell, published by Hutchinson/Arrow. Copyright © Ruth Rendell; Oxford University Press for an extract from *Floppy The Hero* by Roderick Hunt, published by OUP; Pressdram Limited for three examples from 'Colemanballs 10' Private Eye Productions 2000. Copyright © Pressdram Limited 2002; extract from speech by Nelson Mandela, made on 10th May 1994; D C Thomson & Co Ltd for an extract from *The Call of the Glen* by Helen Stewart, from The People's Friend No 473. Copyright © D C Thomson & Co Ltd, 1941; Leo Burnett for Seicento text. Brand: Fiat Seicento. Campaign Title: Seicento 2tune. Date published: February 2002. Agency: D'Arcy London. Written by: Angus Macadam and Paul Jordan; The Times Educational Supplement for 'Estuary English' from The Times Educational Supplement, October 1984; The *Guardian* for 'Children use geatt words' by David Gow from The *Guardian*, April 1998. Copyright © The *Guardian*, 1998; The Observer for 'Language buffs launch new sos...' by Vanessa Thorpe, The Observer, 31st October, 1999. Copyright © The Observer 1999; Dr Clive Upton for two maps from *Word Maps: A Dialect Atlas of England*; Cambridge University Press for a map from *The Cambridge Encyclopaedia of the English Language* published by Cambridge University Press, 1995; Longman Publishing for an extract from *Women, Men and Language* by Jennifer Coates, published by Longman; The British Council for an extract of text and illustrations from '10 Ways to Fill The Gap' produced by Central Bureau for Educational Visits and Exchanges. (This is an old leaflet which is no longer produced. The Central Bureau no longer exists and most of their work is now carried out by The British Council.); IPC Syndications for 'N is for No More Albums' from NME, January 4th 2003. Copyright © Peter Robinson/NME/IPC Syndication; National Magazine Company for 'The real price of shop lifting' by Erin Kelly, from CosmoGirl! January 2003. Courtesy of CosmoGirl! Magazine © National Magazine Company; Kidscape for 'You can beat bullying! A Guide for Young People' from 'You Can Beat Bullying' a leaflet produced by Kidscape. www.kidscape.org.uk; Penguin Books UK for an extract from *Happy Days With The Naked Chef by* Jamie Oliver (Michael Joseph, 2001) Copyright © Jamie Oliver, 2001; Pamela Coleman for an interview with Jennie Bond, BBC Royal Correspondent in the series 'My Best Teacher' by Pamela Coleman, The Times Educational Supplement, December 6th 2002; The Observer for 'Shaken not stirred' by Franziska Thomas, The Observer, 8th December 2002. Copyright © Franziska Thomas 2002; Atlantic Syndication for 'The day I became Marilyn' by Sarah Wise, from *YOU Magazine*, 24th November 2002; *Chat* Magazine for text and photos in 'Just a bit of fun' by Sarah Phillips, *Chat* Summer Special 2003; Marion Naylor for extracts from 'Stepping In' by Marion Naylor in BELLA, 31st December 2002; Penguin Books UK for an extract of text and one illustration from *Shrek!* by William Steig (Puffin by arrangement with Farrar, Straus and Giroux LLC 2001) Copyright © William Steig, 1990; Egmont Books for an extract of text and one illustration from *Percy the Small Engine*. Britt Allcrofts Thomas the Tank Engine and Friends. Based on The Railway Series by The Rev W. Awdry. © Britt Allcroft (Thomas) Limited 2000. Photographs © Britt Allcroft (Thomas) Limited 2000. THOMAS THE TANK ENGINE & FRIENDS AND THOMAS & FRIENDS are trademarks of Britt Allcroft Inc in the USA, Mexico and Canada and Britt Allcroft (Thomas) Limited in the rest of the world. THE BRITT ALLCROFT COMPANY is a trademark of The Britt Allcroft Company Plc. Published by Egmont Books; John Rawson, freelance copywriter for Shelter for an extract from a Shelter campaign letter; The Observer for 'Your £10 can help...' by Amelia Hill, The Observer, 8th December 2002. Copyright © The Observer, 2002; *When Saturday Comes* Magazine for an extract from the editorial of *When Saturday Comes*, pg 4, January 2003, Issue 191.

Photographs: Seicento; Corbis; Alamy

The publishers have made every effort to trace the copyright holders, but if they have inadvertently overlooked any, they will be pleased to make the necessary arrangements at the first opportunity.

The author would like to thank the students and English staff of Ashton-under-Lyne Sixth Form College; Mr James Martin; Geraldine Norman for additional research and suggestions; Tim Shortis for many perceptive and productive suggestions.

Typeset by TechType, Abingdon, Oxon

Printed and bound by CPI Bath in the UK

Note on the Revised Edition

Ann Watkiss and I wrote the first edition of this book as the new specifications for AS courses were emerging prior to the introduction of the new A Level curriculum in 2000. The previous English Language A Level syllabus cast a long shadow and the new modular structure still had to encounter its first set of real students taking real exams. In the two years since its introduction, teachers and students have contributed hugely to the development of this course, and there have now been several 'sittings' of the new style of examination papers.

The specification has now 'bedded down' and continues to evolve. This revised edition reflects the experiences of teaching, learning and preparing for each of the modules. Much of the most successful material from the first edition has been retained, but the significant changes include:

- more guidance and practice activities in preparing for the Unit 1 examination (Introduction to the Study of Language), with specific reference to the amended rubric introduced from January 2003

- greater use of facsimile material to reflect the style of the examination papers

- the replacement of material relating to 'occupational varieties' in Module 2, Language and Social Contexts, to reflect changing options within the specification from 2003

- a more exam-focused treatment of the other Module 2 topic areas of 'language and gender', 'language and power' and 'accents and dialects of the British Isles'

- a completely new section for Module 3, Original Writing

- suggestions of suitable titles for extended study in Module 2.

Introduction

We hope that this book will support you as you embark on your AS English Language course, and that it may help you discover how fascinating and challenging the study of language at this level can be. If you are following the AQA English Language B specification, you will see that we follow the structure and module titles of that course – though we also hope the book will be of value if you are taking one of the other specifications.

Like all AS courses, English Language AS consists of three modules, or programmes of study. You may be taught and then tested on these one after another; alternatively, your teachers may decide to present elements of all three throughout the year and enter you for all three together. These exams are known as 'unit tests'. For example, although Original Writing is presented here as the third module (ENB 3), many original writing opportunities will arise from the work covered in the other two modules, and you are likely to be working on your Original Writing coursework portfolio in parallel with the rest of your work. However, you will probably find it best to start by working through Module 1, Introduction to the Study of Language, as it establishes the basis for many of the ideas and linguistic terms that arise in the other two modules.

For the sake of clarity, this book covers the three modules in separate parts, but where you see one of these symbols

there is a link to work covered in one of the other modules.

You will also see signposts that highlight links to elements of the A2 course. Although you will meet some new topics and approaches during the second year, in many other ways the A2 course builds on what you learn during your first year, so these links may prove useful later. When you have completed the first three modules and taken the AS unit tests, many of you will opt to continue your English Language studies by moving on to that course.

Using this book

We hope that this book will provide a sound basis for much of the work you do on your AS course – but a book of this size cannot claim to provide everything that you need to be successful on an Advanced Level course. Therefore, at various points in the text you will find recommendations for additional reading and research. These are indicated by the following symbol:

The book uses several different types of text:

- *teaching text* that introduces ideas and approaches, and explains and comments on linguistic material; study these sections before embarking on any of the activities

- *data and extracts* composed of passages, excerpts and other examples of language in use; these form the raw material of your study, so read and respond to them carefully

- *instructions or suggestions for activities*, which are usually one of the following: data gathering or research, group discussion or individual work

- *commentaries* and answers to the activities for you to compare with the outcomes of your own work; try to resist reading these before completing the activities for yourself, and remember that the commentary is not necessarily the only 'correct' response or analysis – differences between your suggestions and these may provoke fruitful discussion.

Linguistic terminology

As you work through this book you will be introduced to a number of specialist linguistic terms; you should gradually become more comfortable with using these in your discussions and analysis of language. The first time these terms appear they are printed in **bold** text. Sometimes they are first presented in the commentaries rather than in the teaching text, because we have introduced technical terminology only when linguistic explorations demand it.

These terms also appear in the **Glossary** at the end of the book, but you are strongly advised to develop your own personal glossary in a notebook (see pages 5–6), along with your own definition and some personal examples for each term. These will then serve as a useful revision source when you prepare for the unit examinations.

Assessment Objectives

Whichever English language specification you are following, the course has been designed to enable students to meet the same set of **Assessment Objectives**. These define the skills and knowledge that you must demonstrate to the examiners in your assessments. .

The specification says you have to . . .	In other words, . . .
AO1 communicate clearly the knowledge, understanding and insight appropriate to the study of language, using appropriate terminology and accurate and coherent written expression	whatever you write should be clearly expressed, with a high standard of accuracy in spelling and grammar, and you should make use of **specialist technical terms** where this helps to define ideas and features of language precisely
AO2 demonstrate expertise and accuracy in writing for a variety of specific purposes and audiences, drawing on knowledge of linguistic features to explain and comment on choices made	you must show that you can choose to write in different styles, according to the needs of different purposes and readerships, and that you can explain how and why you have deliberately adjusted your use of language to suit the people and context you are writing for
AO3 know and use key features of frameworks for the systematic study of spoken and written English	in your analysis of texts you must put into practice some of the theoretical models and ideas about language that you learn at different points in the course. This means more than simply using a 'common sense' approach
AO4 understand, discuss and explore concepts and issues relating to language in use	as in the previous objective, you must show that you understand some important ideas about language and the factors that influence how it is used
AO5 distinguish, describe and interpret variation in the meanings and forms of spoken and written language according to context	you must show that you understand how language is influenced by aspects of the situation in which it is produced

At the start of each module you will see how varying numbers of marks are attached to the different Assessment Objectives, so during your preparation it is important that you know which objectives you must meet.

Key Skills

The activities suggested in the AS modules offer numerous opportunities to produce evidence of the attainment of most of the Key Skills: data gathering work may allow for work in Application of Number as well as ICT, the various types of group work suggested give scope for 'Working with others', and as you monitor, review and develop your own progress you may generate evidence for 'Improving own learning and performance'. However, we confine ourselves in the text to flagging up the many opportunities for Communication-related activities at Level 3.

Key Skills Communication: level 3	
C3.1a	Contribute to a group discussion about a complex subject
C3.1b	Make a presentation about a complex subject, using at least one image to illustrate complex points
C3.2	Read and synthesise information from two extended documents about a complex subject. One of these documents should include at least one image
C3.3	Write two different types of documents about complex subjects. One piece of writing should be an extended document and include at least one image

Where such opportunities arise, we indicate this with the Key Skills symbol e.g.

C3.1a

Topic and Skills Map: English Language AS and A2

This map indicates which topics or skills either receive coverage or are applied in each module. Units ENB 1–3 are covered in English Language AS; Units ENB 4–6 are covered in English Language A2.

	ENB1: Introduction to the study of language	ENB2: Language and social contexts	ENB3: Original writing and commentary	ENB4: Investigating language	ENB5: Editorial writing and commentary	ENB6: Language development
Classifying and describing language	✓	✓	✓ Commentary	✓	✓ Commentary	✓
Studying variation in audience, register and purposes	✓	✓	✓	✓	✓	✓
Writing for different purposes and audiences	✓		✓	✓	✓	
Writing a commentary on your own work	✓		✓		✓	
Using levels of linguistic description, or **frameworks**, to analyse data and texts	✓	✓	✓ Commentary	✓	✓ Commentary	✓
Phonology: the sounds of English	✓	✓		✓		✓
Orthography: the spelling of English	✓			✓		✓
Morphology: the structure of words	✓			✓		✓
Etymology: the study of the origins and development of words and meanings				✓ (possibly)		✓
Lexis: looking at word classes	✓		✓ Commentary	✓		✓
Semantics: the study of meaning	✓	✓	✓	✓		✓
Syntax: the grammar of sentences and word order	✓	✓	✓ Commentary	✓	✓ Commentary	✓
Discourse: the structure of different kinds of spoken and written texts	✓		✓ Commentary	✓	✓ Commentary	✓
(includes the study of cohesion and coherence)	✓	✓	✓	✓	✓	✓
Pragmatics: the study of the meanings of language in specific social contexts	✓	✓		✓		✓
Comparing spoken and written language	✓			✓		✓
Analysis of conversation	✓	✓		✓		✓
Language and gender		✓		✓ (possibly)		✓
Language and power		✓		✓ (possibly)		
Dialects of the British Isles		✓		✓ (possibly)		✓
Social class and language		✓		✓ (possibly)		
Language and thought		✓		✓ (possibly)		
Historical change in language				✓ (possibly)		✓
Contemporary language change				✓ (possibly)		✓
Child language acquisition				✓ (possibly)		✓
Learning to read and write				✓ (possibly)		✓
Carrying out independent research and investigation of data	✓	✓	✓	✓		✓

MODULE ① Introduction to the Study of Language

This unit counts for **35%** of the AS qualification, or **$17\frac{1}{2}$%** of the total A Level marks.

ASSESSMENT OBJECTIVES

The skills and knowledge you develop in this module, which will be tested in the examination you take at the end of it, are defined by the examination board's Assessment Objectives. These require that you:

- **AO1:** communicate clearly the knowledge, understanding and insight appropriate to the study of language, using appropriate terminology and accurate and coherent written expression
(10 out of the 35 marks for the Unit; 10% of the final AS mark; 5% of the final A Level mark)

- **AO3:** know and use key features of frameworks for the systematic study of spoken and written English
(10 out of the 35 marks for the Unit; 10% of the final AS mark; 5% of the final A Level mark)

- **AO4:** understand, discuss and explore concepts and issues relating to language in use
(5 out of the 35 marks for the Unit; 5% of the final AS mark; $2\frac{1}{2}$% of the final A Level mark)

- **AO5:** distinguish, describe and interpret variation in the meanings and forms of spoken and written language according to context
(10 out of the 35 marks for the Unit; 10% of the final AS mark; 5% of the final A Level mark)

What this module is all about

The aim of this module is quite straightforward: it is designed to lay the foundations for the study of English Language at Advanced Level. At first, this may seem odd; after all, you have studied something called 'English' or even 'English Language' throughout your school career, and English is probably your own mother tongue which you use confidently in a wide range of situations.

However, it is unlikely that the work you have done as part of your GCSE course has taken you very far towards the really careful, systematic study of your own language that is involved at A Level. For one thing, the range of language you study as an A Level student is much wider; although you study very little traditional 'literature', you do spend a lot of time looking closely at a great *variety* of written texts, and also begin to examine different kinds of *spoken* language in ways that may be new. Your GCSE English course will certainly have helped you become a proficient *user* of the language, but the emphasis of your A Level course is on turning you into a careful *student* of it.

The first AS module introduces you to ways of thinking about and discussing language that you may not have met before. The unit test will assess how effectively you have begun to apply these new ideas about language. It does this by presenting you with a range of examples of English in use, representing the huge variety of everyday language use, and by inviting you to discuss them in some depth.

Everything you subsequently do on your course is based, in one way or another, on these vital foundations.

Starting to explore

English is the language that you grew up with, and you have become skilled at using it in many situations. What's more, if you have committed yourself to studying it on your AS/A Level course, you've also probably proved to a GCSE examiner that you are rather good at reading, writing, speaking and listening.

The remarkable thing is just how automatic all of this has been. When composing that special letter of application for a job, or a tricky English assignment, we may be conscious of choosing our words carefully, but as native speakers we normally don't have to think very hard about the language we are using – there isn't time!

It's rather like learning to drive a car. At first, you'll probably find that it's difficult to co-ordinate the actions of steering, signalling, checking mirrors, changing gears, reading road signs and so on, but you soon stop thinking consciously about the complicated series of actions needed to get the car from A to B. What's more, most people become drivers without having to learn about the mechanics of the engine, or the intricacies of gearbox and transmission, or the fuel-injection system.

However, during your AS/A Level English Language course, as well as becoming a better 'driver' – developing your own skills as a user of English – you will investigate the workings of the language itself. You will become aware of the unconscious processes that are going on all the time when we use language, as we 'lift the bonnet' and examine just what makes language 'go'.

The 'science' of language study

You may not think of English as a very scientific subject, but in many ways A Level language work is rather like 'language science'. If you are taking a science subject, you will be familiar with certain methods of study such as:

- collecting and examining data (observing experiments, collecting specimens)

- describing, classifying and analysing data using diagrams, measurements and calculations

- testing different ideas about how things work.

These same activities are the basis of your English Language studies. The **data** can be found anywhere and everywhere – wherever the spoken or written word is used. You will learn how to describe language precisely and to classify it in many different ways, developing an appropriate terminology for the purpose. As in science, you will also consider possible explanations for your discoveries – even if you cannot expect to achieve absolute certainty or agreement in your answers.

The aim of your English Language course – and this book – is to help you develop an informed understanding of our language and to become an increasingly accomplished user of it. To achieve this, you need to become something of a linguistic investigator.

A question of language

ACTIVITY 1   C3.1a

Let's start by looking at the kinds of question that will drive our linguistic explorations forwards. The issues you begin to explore here underpin much of the work that you will do throughout your AS/A Level course.

The following language notes and queries arose from a series of interviews with English students. Read the queries and share with your classmates your first reactions to each one. Then, through discussion, try to reach agreement about an answer within your group.

After you have reported back to the class, compare your responses with the brief commentaries offered on page 64.

A ANN, 17

Why do people's accents, and even the words and phrases they use, vary so much – and is it true that some kinds of English are 'better' than others?

B MICHAEL, 19

Which came first, speech or writing – and which is more important?

C AYUMI, 16

When I'm at work I have to watch what I say and talk to customers in the way I've been trained to do. Out with my friends, it's different – we have our own set of words which we use all the time and if you didn't know them you probably wouldn't understand what we were on about half the time. Is this normal?

D GEORGE, 25

I saw a science fiction film in which instead of checking fingerprints, a computer could identify any human being just by analysing the way they talked. So, is it true that we have a sort of linguistic fingerprint – and would this also work with an extract of something which we wrote?

E KIBRIA, 22

What I don't understand when I look at Shakespeare's language, or even hear clips from old radio and TV shows, is why English has changed so much – and who makes it happen?

F JANET, 30

I always hated languages at school – we had to do French and German – and I always struggled with them. Now I've got kids of my own, I'm amazed by how easily they pick up English without really seeming to try! Why is my 4-year-old so much better at language than me?

Language all around us

The scope of English Language study at A Level is extremely wide. As explorers and students of language, you can start by making yourself aware of the sheer variety of the language that we consume or produce as a matter of routine. This variety will be the raw material for our investigations and explorations.

ACTIVITY 2   C3.1a

(a) Consider the four linguistic activities of listening, speaking, reading and writing. Using a large sheet of sugar paper, allocate each of them to one quarter of a circle, as in the figure:

In each quadrant, list as many examples as you can of different kinds of language activity in which you participate in a typical week. Aim to include at least half-a-dozen different activities in each quadrant.

For example, under 'Speaking' you might start by listing:

- on the phone to friends

- explaining the school/college day to parents

- social chat over lunch.

(b) Once you have listed your examples on the quadrants, **classify** them in any way you think is helpful. For example, you might describe both 'on the phone to friends' and 'social chat over lunch' as 'informal chat'. Here are some possible categories – but feel free to suggest your own:

Informal chat	Persuading someone to do something
Asking for information	The media – radio, TV, etc.
Using slang with friends	Making excuses or apologies
Listening to instructions	Being persuaded
Reading for facts	Using mobile phone and texting
Being amused or entertained	Making notes to remember work in class
Telling amusing stories to entertain	Making arrangements

After briefly presenting your findings to the rest of the class, compare your results with the commentary on page 65.

Keeping a language glossary

If you were embarking on a course designed to train you as an engineer, you would expect to learn a great deal of technical 'jargon'. Equally, A Level physicists or sociologists will acquire a working vocabulary of specialist terms unique to those disciplines.

The study of language has its own specialist vocabulary – a language for talking about language, you could say. Such a language is called a **metalanguage**. Throughout this book, you will be introduced to – and encouraged to use – the terminology needed for the precise description of different aspects of language. Remember, the Assessment Objectives require you to use 'appropriate terminology', so you need to make a point of learning and using this metalanguage as you go along. At the end of the book is a Glossary of most of the technical terms introduced – but it is a good idea to build up a personal language glossary of your own.

ACTIVITY 3

Even before you started your AS studies, you had a working vocabulary of the language we use to talk about language. Basic terms such as 'word', 'sentence' and 'paragraph' are all part of this vocabulary.

Take an exercise book and allow a couple of pages for each letter of the alphabet. List under each letter any language terms (such as 'word', 'sentence', 'full stop') that you already know. You'll probably be able to list many terms already.

As the course develops, add new terms, definitions and examples to each page as and when they arise.

You and your language: idiolect

One of our initial language queries raised the question of individual 'linguistic fingerprints' (see page 4). Indeed, our everyday experience suggests that individuals often have distinctive ways of using language, and the discipline of 'forensic linguistics' allows the positive identification of an individual (e.g. someone accused of a crime) by analysing closely a sample of his or her speech or writing. The term **idiolect** is used to define those features of language use which are unique to an individual. In this section we will try to define what makes up your own idiolect.

Of course, as your response to Activity 2 will have revealed, we all have the ability to vary our uses of language according to context. We can refer to this range of styles as our **language repertoire**.

Your language history and experience

As you look around your classroom, and listen to different members of the class speaking, you rapidly become aware that we all have our own, distinctive style of speech. So what has influenced and shaped this idiolect, this individual linguistic fingerprint which each of us reveals as soon as we open our mouths or put pen to paper?

ACTIVITY 4   C3.1a

(a) Look at the diagram on page 7. It represents some of the most important influences that are likely to have shaped your identity and your idiolect. In groups, try to agree on the order of importance of these influences, from 1 (the most influential) down to 8 (the least).

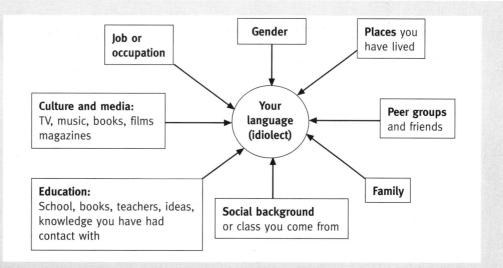

(b) For each of the possible sources of influence shown in the table, try to suggest the *specific* ways in which they have affected your personal language development.

As you consider each one, think about how it might have influenced:

- your accent

- your choice of words, phrases and slang

- your ideas about what is acceptable or 'good' English.

You should also think about how the *extent* of each influence may change as you get older.

Record your responses on a table similar to the one below:

Source of influence	Rank order	Nature of influence/ Changing influence
Your family		
Places you have lived		
Your education (Your school experiences, and the influence of teachers and what you have learned)		
Cultural influences (e.g. books, films, music, magazines and television)		
Your gender		
Peer groups (the various friendship groups you belong to)		

Source of influence	Rank order	Nature of influence/ Changing influence
Social background (the nature of your background, or the social class you come from)		
Employment (any influences from your part-time work experience)		

(c) Compare your own experiences with those of other members of the group, and then compare your group's response with the commentary on page 65.

Fitting in: language as a membership card

As we have noted, an important influence on the ways we use language is the social group or network we belong to. Of course, we all belong to many different groupings, so we develop different styles of language to suit the group we are with at any one time. All kinds of groupings — family, friends, workmates, football supporters, doctors, fans of a particular pop band — may develop distinctive uses of language that come to characterise them and indicate their identity. To join one of these groups we may have to learn its language — in other words, acquire its **sociolect**.

ACTIVITY 5

Start by listing the various social groups you belong to at different times. For example your family, your immediate group of friends, people who live in your town or region, people who share an interest with you, go to the same school or college, come from the same social background . . . Add some of your own.

Then ask yourself: *what is distinctive about the ways in which this particular group uses language?* The distinguishing features could include certain routines, rituals or patterns of interaction; a particular kind of vocabulary, 'buzz words' or slang; a particular accent or style of pronunciation.

Record your suggestions, then read the commentary on page 67.

Inclusion and exclusion

In many ways, a sociolect can act as a membership badge which proclaims the fact that you belong to, and identify with, a particular social group. If we go to live and work in a foreign country, to be fully accepted as a member of that community we expect to have to learn the language, customs and traditions. On a smaller scale, 'outsiders' who wish to join and be accepted by social groups may need to learn and adopt language features that characterise the group in order to fit in. This could mean a slight change in their accent, using a particular kind of vocabulary, or observing certain linguistic rituals.

However, we may be members of a group that doesn't want outsiders to join or to understand the meanings we are communicating to each other. In this case, the group may develop a language that almost becomes a code – a shared language that excludes those not 'in the know'.

ACTIVITY 6 | C3.1a

Suggest how the distinctive **slang** or **jargon** associated with the following groups and activities has the effect of excluding those not 'in the know':

1 drugs slang used between dealers and buyers

2 medical terminology used between doctors as they discuss your condition

3 computer jargon

4 technical terms used by garage mechanics when they explain to you what has gone wrong with your car.

Language varieties: describing and classifying

Having reminded ourselves of the huge variety of language all around us, we now need to look more closely at a range of examples of language in use. Throughout your English Language course, you will be encouraged to collect and describe **data** – that is, specimens of speech and writing – and to explore ways in which these specimens can be compared with or distinguished from each other. We can compare this to the way a scientist – a zoologist, for example – might observe and collect specimens and classify them as mammals, fish, reptiles, etc.

In the examination for this unit you are presented with a collection of such language data or 'specimens', and asked to write in some detail about the different ways in which we can classify and describe them. The texts and activities in this section introduce you to the process of description and classification.

The word **text** is used throughout this book to describe any piece of language in either written or spoken form. Several of the texts are representations of spoken language. When a recording is made of speech and a faithful written representation of this recording is produced, the term for the resulting text is a **transcript**. This differs from a **script**, which is the term used for a piece of writing that is pre-written in order to be spoken, for example on a television programme.

Spoken language can be very different from writing, so when making a transcript it is usual not to use standard punctuation. Throughout this book the following **conventions** are used for transcripts:

- lower case is used throughout, except for names and the pronoun 'I'

- conventional punctuation marks such as full stops, commas, etc. are *not* used (we will consider the reasons for this when we look in detail at the nature of spoken language on page 20 below)

- short pauses for breath are shown as (.)

- longer pauses are shown by a number in brackets, e.g. (2), indicating the number of seconds the pause lasts

- a vertical line (/) indicates where two or more speakers speak at once

- square brackets and words in italics [*like this*] indicate actions or gestures

- underlining is sometimes used for stressed syllables, and CAPITALS for high volume

- [inaud] is used where speech is inaudible.

ACTIVITY 7   C3.1a, C3.1b

On the next page there are ten texts, A–J. In groups, agree how to organise the texts into groups of two or more, linking them by identifying some aspect that they have in common. You should suggest at least four or five groupings – more, if possible.

- Give each of your groupings a title that reflects what the texts have in common. You cannot use 'miscellaneous' or 'other' as a title.

- Include every text in at least one of your groupings.

- You may include the same text in two or more of the groupings.

Record your findings in the form of a table with these headings:

Linked texts	Group title	Features in common

Present and explain your findings to the class, then compare them with the commentary on page 67. This also provides details about the source of each text.

TEXT A

Right (.) you have a sheet in front of you (.) wait a minute I'll get you one (.) on it (.) have a look now please (.) on it (.) there's a list of the characters we looked at on Friday (.) look at the paragraph underneath (.) look at the paragraph underneath (2) what I want you to do please (.) is to ensure that you have a pen or pencil available to you (2) and that as we learn anything about any of the characters (.) you add any relevant information onto the sheet

TEXT B

There were times (.) if you felt in good fettle (I) we used to see who could hoy a ball furthest (3) it was a nice canny game an all but sometimes (2) windows used to get brocken (3) and another thing (.) in them days people were lucky if they had indoor netties (I) and it was bloody murder if you wanted to gan to the toilet in the middle of the neet

TEXT C

We joined the ship on Wednesday morning, the 10th of April, and had boat drill and proceeded at 12 o'clock. We called at Cherbourg and Queenstown. On Sunday it came in rather cold, Sunday afternoon. On Sunday night at about a quarter to 12, I was on the watch below and turned in, when there was suddenly a noise like cable running out, like a ship dropping anchor. There was not any shock at all.

TEXT D

Come live with me and be my love,
And we will all the pleasures prove,
That hills and valleys, dale and fields,
And all the craggy mountains yields.

TEXT E

LAUNCHING POWERPOINT

To run PowerPoint 2000, switch on your PC and go into Windows – in most cases this should happen automatically.

Microsoft PowerPoint 2000 will work happily with Windows 95, Windows 98, and Windows NT.

THE POWERPOINT DIALOG BOX
● Click on the **Start** button on the Task bar.
● From the pop-up menu, point to **Program**.
● From the drop-down menu, click on **Microsoft PowerPoint**.
● If you can't find PowerPoint in the **Program** folder, then it probably means that the software has not been installed. PowerPoint 2000 is generally acquired as a part of the Microsoft Office 2000 suite of programs. If you have a problem, go back to the original CDs – or, better still, get someone more experienced to do it for you.
● Each time you launch PowerPoint 2000, the first screen that you come into contact with is a PowerPoint dialog box. This provides you with four options before you finally get to see the main **PowerPoint** window ⬒.

 The PowerPoint Window

TEXT F

A: Tanya from West Shields on line 2 (.) hi Tanya

T: hi Alan

A: hello the best and the worst from you

T: the best for me was going to Canada (.) em (.) 4 years ago to see an adopted sister / I'd never met before

A: / right (.) which (.) which lump of Canada was it

T: er (.) Toronto and then I flew on to Winnipeg

A: oh great (.) I mean what's (.) you always get the impression that Canada's like just massive (.) this immense country / what's it actually like

T: / it is yeah

TEXT G

They went to sea in a Sieve, they did,
    In a Sieve they went to sea:
    In spite of all their friends could say,
On a winter's morn, on a stormy day,

    In a Sieve they went to sea!
And when the Sieve turned round and round,
And everyone cried, 'You'll all be drowned!'
They called aloud, 'Our Sieve ain't big,
'But we don't care a button! we don't care a fig!
    'In a Sieve we'll go to sea!'

TEXT H

From the beginning all men by nature were created alike, and our bondage or servitude came in by the unjust oppression of naughty men. And therefore I exhort you to consider that now the time is come, appointed to us by God, in which ye may (if ye will) cast off the yoke of bondage, and recover liberty. I counsel you therefore to bethink yourselves, and take good hearts unto you, that after the manner of a good husband that tilleth his ground, and riddeth out thereof such evil weeds as choke and destroy the good corn, you may destroy first the great lords of the realm, and after, the judges and lawyers, and questmongers, and all others who have undertaken to be against the common.

TEXT I

'Why, look yer 'ere,' said the miner, showing the shoulders of his singlet. 'It's a bit dry now, but it's wet as a clout with sweat even yet. Feel it.'

'Goodness!' cried Mrs Morel. 'Mr Heaton doesn't want to feel your nasty singlet.'

The clergyman put out his hand gingerly.

'No, perhaps he doesn't,' said Morel; 'but it's all come out of me, whether or not. An' iv'ry day alike my singlet's wringin' wet. 'Aven't you got a drink, Missis, for a man when he comes home barkled up from the pit?'

TEXT J

'You is not loving it?' the BFG asked innocently, rubbing his head.

'Loving it!' yelled the Bloodbottler. 'That is the most disgusterous taste that is ever touching my teeth! You must be buggles to be swalloping slutch like that! Every night you could be galloping off happy as a hamburger and gobbling juicy human beans!'

'Eating human beans is wrong and evil,' the BFG said.

Problems with classification

Although it is useful to try to categorise language in the ways suggested in Activity 7, as soon as we start to do so we encounter some problems. Perhaps you already found this when looking at the texts for the activity. Many of these texts are surprisingly complex, and it is important not to ignore these complications by fitting language into an over-simplified model.

The Unit 1 examination sets out to assess your ability to recognise and discuss some of these complicating factors. In the next activities we will explore some of them.

Mode – speech or writing?

It is not always easy to define a particular user of language as belonging exclusively to either of these categories. Some types of language may have elements of both modes in them. Text H from Activity 7, for instance, is part of a script which was pre-written in order to be spoken, whereas text I is an extract from a piece of writing – a novel – which tries to create the *illusion* of realistic speech by using accent and dialect features in its dialogue. Text D is clearly a written text, but *pretends* to be the poet 'speaking' to his lover.

We will investigate the distinctive characteristics of spoken and written language in more detail below (see page 20).

ACTIVITY 8

For each of the following examples (some from Activity 7), suggest ways in which they include elements of both spoken and written language. Compare your results with the table in the commentary on page 69.

Text	Problematic aspects
Text C: written record of testimony given to the *Titanic* enquiry	
Text J: extract from *The BFG*	
A politician's speech	
A job interview	
An episode of *EastEnders*	
A series of postings in an Internet chatroom	

What register?

One text may include several different styles of language, and so be impossible to define as being entirely 'formal' or 'informal' – it may have a 'mixed register'. Text G in Activity 7, for instance, features both reasonably formal, literary language such as 'On a winter's morn, on a stormy day' alongside the more informal 'Our Sieve ain't big . . . we don't care a fig!'

We will also see below (see page 19) that we need to think not just in terms of 'formal' or 'informal' language, but of a wide spectrum of styles.

Which audience(s)?

Texts may have more than one set of listeners/readers, and these different audiences may respond very differently to them. For example, the speaker of text B in Activity 7 (a Tyneside speaker reminiscing about his childhood) was talking only to his granddaughter – but he was also aware that she was taping the conversation for possible use in a language textbook, whose readers would be more interested in his dialect speech than in the content of the stories he was telling.

ACTIVITY 9

For each of the following examples (some from Activity 7), identify the possible multiple audiences and the different aspects of the text they may be interested in:

Text	Multiple audiences	Different meanings
Text D: 17th-century poem		
Text F: transcript of a radio phone-in		
Text J: extract from *The BFG*		
A women's magazine such as *Cosmopolitan*		

Compare your results with the table in the commentary on page 70.

Multi-purpose?

It is sometimes convenient to imagine that there are just a few basic 'purposes' for our many and varied uses of language. Indeed, for the purposes of your Original Writing work for Module 3 (see pages 134–89) we consider just four of these:

- language used to exchange **information**

- language used to **amuse** or **entertain**

- language used to **influence, advise** or **persuade**

- language used to give or receive **instructions**.

However, it would be a misleading over-simplification to suggest that all uses of language can easily be slotted into one or other of these categories.

ACTIVITY 10

For each of the language uses listed below (some from Activity 7), identify which (if any) of the above purposes apply. Where you think a text has more than one purpose, try to distinguish between **primary** and **secondary** purposes:

Text/language use	Purposes
Text B: transcript of Tyneside speaker	
Text D: poem	
Text F: radio phone-in	
Text J: *The BFG*	
A casual conversation with your friends	
A TV documentary about wildlife	
A tabloid news report about politics	

Compare your results with the table in the commentary on page 71.

Collecting your own data

ACTIVITY 11

C3.1a, C3.1b

Go back to the four headings you used to classify examples of language use on page 4: listening, speaking, reading and writing. For any one of these, collect your own examples of five or six of the uses of language you suggested there.

For reading and writing, you should be able to find examples of texts easily; for speaking and listening, you can start by making brief recordings of broadcast media. For examples of 'real' conversational speech you need to make tape recordings – but always follow the guidelines below:

Guidelines for recording and writing down 'live' speech:

- Seek permission from any participants before arranging to record conversations.
- Offer to wipe or destroy your tape if the participants object to the content afterwards.
- Let your recorder run for long enough to allow people to become less self-conscious about being recorded.
- Transcribe a short but accurate extract of what is on the tape.
- Don't censor or correct the speech – represent any pauses, hesitations and 'bad' language.

See page 10 for transcript conventions. Also use the examples on pages 10–13 as models for your transcripts.

Re-visit the commentary to Activity 7 on page 67, which introduces some important linguistic ideas and terminology. Then, for your five or six texts, repeat the linking/grouping exercise, copying onto A3 paper a table like the one below and using as many of the suggested categories as you can.

Use the table to explain:

- what your linked texts have in common
- how your linked texts in each category differ from each other
- any problems you have encountered in trying to categorise your texts.

Survey and classification of texts: reading/writing/speaking/listening				
Category	Texts	What the texts have in common	How they differ	Problems of classification
Purpose				
Audience				
Mode				
Register				
Variety				
Graphology				
Period				

Present your table and explain your findings to the class.

Genres

Genre is the term for each specific kind of text – either spoken or written – that seems to follow a distinctive pattern or set of conventions which become an agreed 'norm'. Some examples are offerered below:

Written genres		Spoken genres	
Fairy tales	Letters	Lessons	Jokes
Recipes	News reports	Phone calls	Apologies
Memos	Essays	'Chat-up' conversations	Consultations with
Advertisements	Horoscopes	Formal interviews	a doctor
E-mails	Horror stories	Shopping transactions	Answer-phone
Poems		Radio phone-ins	messages

ACTIVITY 12

C3.3

(a) As an example of a genre, let us consider the following recipe. As you examine it, tick off the genre conventions which apply:

Genre conventions: recipes

- ☐ usually have list of ingredients, itemised and quantified
- ☐ set out steps in a process, separated into short sentences/ paragraphs
- ☐ steps are itemised either with bullet points or numbers
- ☐ may sometimes miss out words and use an abbreviated note form
- ☐ may include some semi-technical vocabulary related to cooking
- ☐ sentences will usually consist of direct instructions
- ☐ sentences will include precise information about timings/ temperatures.

Macaroni with wild mushrooms

This dish packs a punch with a robust sauce of tomato and wild mushrooms. Some slivers of parma ham would also go well. You'll need a chunky macaroni, more like penne in size. You can find tomato salsina or sugocasa in Sainsbury's, but if this is unavailable, give some chopped tomatoes in juice a brief blitz in the food processor.

SERVES 4
40g/1½oz unsalted butter
1 tbsp groundnut oil
3 leeks, trimmed and thinly sliced
sea salt, black pepper
200g/7oz wild mushrooms, picked over, trimmed and sliced if necessary
100ml/3½fl oz white wine
150ml/5fl oz tomato salsina or sugocasa
1 small dried red chilli, finely chopped
200g/7oz chunky macaroni
chopped flat-leaf parsley and freshly grated parmesan, to serve

BRING A LARGE PAN of salted water to the boil for the pasta. Heat 25g/1oz of the butter and the oil in a large frying pan over a medium heat. Add the leeks, season them and fry for 5-8 min, stirring frequently until soft and touched with colour at the edges. Remove them to a bowl, squeezing them with the back of a spoon to leave the fat behind.

MELT THE REMAINING BUTTER in the pan, add the mushrooms and fry, stirring frequently, until soft. Season them when cooked. If any liquid is given out, continue to cook until they're dry. Return the leeks to the frying pan with the mushrooms, add the wine and cook until well reduced. Now add the tomato salsina and the chilli and simmer for a min or two longer.

ADD THE PASTA to the boiling water when you are halfway through cooking the sauce. Give the pasta a stir to separate the tubes and cook until just tender. Drain into a sieve, leaving a little water clinging to the macaroni. Add to the frying pan and toss with the sauce.

TASTE FOR SEASONING and serve scattered with chopped parsley. Hand the freshly grated parmesan round separately.

(b) Choose half-a-dozen more genres from the table and collect/observe some examples of your own. Use a table with the headings shown below to present your summary of the distinctive features, or **genre conventions**, you find:

Genre	Examples/specimens	Genre conventions

(c) Experiment with your own writing by changing texts from one genre to another, referring closely to the genre conventions you have identified. Try one of these:

- Turn a recipe into a passage from a horror novel *or* a fairy story *or* the script for a TV cookery programme *or* an interview with the chef.

- Turn a news report into an apology *or* a poem *or* a fairy tale *or* a recipe.

Write a brief **commentary** in which you explain which genre conventions you have tried to adopt in your new text. See 'The commentary' in Module 3, Original Writing, on page 187.

The formality spectrum: register

If you looked in most people's wardrobes, you would probably find a wide variety of clothing suitable for different occasions: t-shirts and jeans for lounging around, rather smarter shirts, skirts and trousers for college or work, perhaps some overalls or other specific work-clothes, and the odd formal suit or evening dress for smart occasions.

We can compare our choice of language style to our choice of clothes – different levels of formality are appropriate for different situations, and we choose the style or **register** accordingly. If we get our selection wrong, the results may be comical or embarrassing!

ACTIVITY 13   C3.1a

Consider the following versions of the same basic request and order them from the least formal (1) to the most formal (10). Try to identify the elements of each utterance that help define its level of formality, and note these.

- I was hoping you could let me borrow some money.
- I wonder if you might be so kind as to consider making me a small loan?
- Can I borrow a fiver?
- Could I perhaps borrow some money?
- Just gimme some bloody dosh!
- Please can I borrow some money?
- Lend us a fiver, can you?
- Could you possibly lend me some money?
- Gimme some cash, will ya!
- Would it by any chance be possible that you might be so good as to be of temporary financial assistance?

The results of the previous activity should suggest that we cannot speak just of 'formal' and 'informal' registers of English; it is much more useful to think of a *spectrum* of possibilities, as illustrated by the diagram below:

The formality spectrum

INFORMAL   **FORMAL**

1 taboo   2 vulgarism   3 slang   4 non-standard dialect   5 colloquialism   6 informal SE   7 neutral SE   8 formal SE   9 very formal SE

NON-STANDARD ENGLISH   **STANDARD ENGLISH**

1 **Taboo** language – swear words, or words that are generally considered to be deeply offensive and unacceptable.

2 **Vulgarism** – language which falls short of taboo but is nevertheless rather coarse and not normally used in 'polite' society.

3 **Slang** – a very broad term for many different uses of language which are not considered to be 'proper' or Standard English, but may be fairly widespread.

4 **Non-standard (regional) dialect** – words and grammatical constructions not considered to be 'good' or 'correct' Standard English, but which are confined to specific regions of the country. 'Fag' is a slang term widely used in the UK for a cigarette (although in the US it has a completely different usage). 'Tab' may be described as a dialect word, because its use for 'cigarette' is mainly restricted to parts of the north of England.

5 **Colloquialism** – another rather loose term, which literally means 'language as it is spoken'. This may be applied to some kinds of slang, or to the most informal language accepted as Standard English.

6–9 **Standard English** – informal, neutral, formal and very formal. Standard English (SE) is the term used for the vocabulary and grammatical constructions generally accepted as 'correct' English, but even here there is a spectrum ranging from informal (fairly casual language that stops short of slang or dialect), to neutral (the colourless, unremarkable language of 'normal' usage) to the formal and highly formal (such as legal language, for example).

ACTIVITY 14

Write an account of what you did on an ordinary day recently. Bearing the diagram and definitions above in mind, write three different versions of the same day using three different registers, as follows:

Version 1: Use a fair proportion of vulgarisms, slang, dialect (or even an occasional taboo word) to create a highly informal version of the account.

Version 2: Use informal and mainly neutral Standard English terms to produce a 'middling' account.

Version 3: Use formal and highly formal constructions to create an official-sounding version of events.

Write a brief commentary in which you identify some specific details which are different in the three versions, and which contribute to its overall register.

Speech and writing

An understanding of the relationship between spoken and written language is central to much of the work you will do in this course, and is also a key element of this module. Here are some of the questions we need to ask about speech and writing:

- Is writing just speech written down?

- Is writing more 'grammatical' than speech?

- When is it better to use one rather than the other?

To begin to answer these questions, look at some parallel pieces of data in the activity below.

ACTIVITY 15
C3.3

(a) Collect your own data by tape recording and transcribing a spoken response to one or more of the following situations. Also collect a considered, written response.

- Ask a partner to give you directions from your school/college to the town centre.

- Give a short account of how you spent your last summer holiday.

- Make a request to a friend to borrow an item or a sum of money.

- Persuade a reluctant friend to come with you to see a particular film (you could try doing this as a text message, also).

When you have collected your data, work through the following questions:

- What aspects of the spoken version are missing from the transcript you created, and what would they have contributed to the meanings the speaker was trying to convey?

- Is any of the content of the spoken account absent from the written statement? If so, what is missing, and why do you think it was omitted?

- Look at the ways the sentences are formed in both versions. What differences do you notice?

- Does the spoken version include unspecified references to people and places, using words such as *this*, *that*, *he*, *she*, *those*, *here* and *there*? If these are made more explicit in the written account, why do you think this is?

- How does the description of people, actions and events differ in the accounts?

- In general terms, what seems to be the difference between the style and register of the two versions, and what might account for this?

(b) Compare your findings with the following pieces of data. The first is a transcript of an oral account given by a witness to an accident, and the second is the written statement she subsequently produced. Apply the same questions to these and compare your analysis with the commentary on page 72.

Speech (transcript)	Writing (statement)
A: Did you see what happened B: Well (.) not really (.) er (.) I was just walking the dog like (.) you know (.) it was not long turned dark (.) and we'd been down the alley there and back (1) and (.) um (.) then then this car comes racing down here (.) bloody flying he was (.) so as I turned round there was this bloody great crash (.) you know tyres screeching and everything (.) so I turn around and there's black smoke pouring out where it had crashed like A: Could you see if anyone was hurt? B: Well (.) I was standing just over there (.) at the far end of them shops (.) and (.) and like I say (.) it was dark and there was all that smoke (.) and I just thought (.) he must have had it (.) had it like (.) you know	At approximately 8.30 last night I witnessed an accident involving a blue Ford Sierra on Abbey Road, Barrow. I heard the sound of a car approaching, apparently at some speed, before it braked suddenly and subsequently crashed into the wall near the junction with Dalton Road. Black smoke immediately began to pour from the vehicle, and I assumed that the driver must have been seriously hurt.

Characteristics and functions of speaking and writing

ACTIVITY 16   C3.1a

The previous activities revealed that there are some important differences between speech and writing, and the most important of these are summarised in the first column of the table below. These differences have implications for the ways in which we use language, either spoken or written, in a range of situations. The questions in the second column ask you to consider some of these.

However, as with other ways of classifying language, we also need to beware of over-simplifying the differences, and the third column invites you to question some of these distinctions more closely.

When you have worked through the questions, compare your responses with the commentary on page 73.

Differences between speaking and writing	Questions	Problems
1 Speech conveys meanings using sounds which we combine into words, phrases and sentences, whereas writing uses visual signs and symbols (letters and punctuation) to represent these words.	Look again at a transcript of 'real' speech that you have recorded (or the ones on page 10 above). What happens if you try to 'punctuate' this	Our idea of what we mean by 'a sentence' tends to be based on what we have been taught about writing. So trying to describe speech in terms of 'sentences' can be tricky.

Differences between speaking and writing	Questions	Problems
The 'sentences' we speak are much less easy to define than the ones we are taught to punctuate with capital letters and full stops at school.	speech using the usual conventions of full stops, commas, etc?	However, it is *not* true to say that speech is 'less grammatical' than writing. If this were true, we wouldn't be able to understand each other!
2 Speech is an ability which seems to be acquired 'naturally', and without very much direct teaching; writing, on the other hand, has to be taught and learned. In the past many people who could communicate perfectly well in speech were unable to read or write.	Which aspects of the English writing system do you think are most difficult for someone who can already speak the language reasonably well?	As you will see in Module 6, Language Development (A2), this also can be something of a simplification of a controversial subject. In some important ways parents do seem to assist their children's spoken language development.
3 Much of what is communicated in speech comes from **paralinguistic** and **prosodic** features, and is closely linked to the immediate **context** in which it takes place (it is **context-bound**). Writing depends entirely on the words on the page, and is usually meaningful even to people who do not share the immediate context in which it was produced (it is **context-free**).	Which of speech or writing is most likely to reveal dishonesty or insincerity? Which would you prefer to use if you needed to deceive someone?	The **context** includes not just the time and place that the language is used, but also all the things the writer or speaker can assume about the people to whom he or she is talking or writing. With this is mind, perhaps you can suggest how even writing must always be 'context-bound' to some degree?
4 Speech is unplanned, and may include slips and mistakes of all kinds. Writing can be re-drafted: mistakes can be removed before the final version is seen.	When might it be desirable to use writing to avoid making unplanned slips?	When might spoken language be planned, semi-planned or even rehearsed? Which kinds of writing are spontaneous, and may include unedited slips and errors?

Differences between speaking and writing	Questions	Problems
5 Speech is momentary, unless taped, whereas writing offers a permanent record.	In what circumstances might you need to keep a record of a communication?	Writing can offer permanence, of course, but many kinds of writing are not designed to be preserved for long. These texts are sometimes called **ephemera**. Equally, some spoken language is intended to be recorded and preserved. Can you think of some examples?

A C T I V I T Y   1 7

Consider the following texts in the light of the suggested 'over-simplified' comments about speech and writing offered below. Discuss or write about how the examples illustrate problems with those comments.

Text description	Data	Over-simplification
Note left for builders working in a house while the owners are at work	Hi you two! Help yourself to the usual. Please leave key in the usual place when you've finished.	'Writing is always context-free, whereas speech is context-bound.'
(a) Recorded message left on a telephone answering machine (b) Note left in the kitchen	(a) We're sorry that no-one is available to take your call right now. If you'd like to leave a message, please do so after the tone, and we'll try to get back to you as soon as possible. Thanks for calling. (b) Just nipped out for a paper – back in 5. Tea in oven. xxxx	'Speech is informal, and writing is formal.'

Text description	Data	Over-simplification
Exchange between MPs in the House of Commons as recorded in *Hansard*, the official parliamentary record	**Mr Dennis Skinner (Bolsover):** Will my Right Hon. Friend ignore the bleating of the Liberal Democrats, who have been Euro-fanatics from the very beginning? Will he ignore the rants of the Shadow Chancellor of the Exchequer, who condemned the current Leader of the Opposition when they were uniting and dying over Maastricht? Will my Right Hon. Friend also keep finding excuses for not going into the euro? He has managed that for five years—good luck to him. **Mr Brown:** We will publish the assessment that we are making of the five economic tests. It is serious, detailed and rigorous, and the most comprehensive piece of work that the Treasury has done. It will look at all the relevant issues, as the five tests make absolutely clear, and the House of Commons will have the fullest chance to debate these issues.	'Speech is generally informal and temporary.'
Postings on an Internet chatroom site	‹**alice in wonderland**› i see token has gone what a loser ‹**girl_thing**› hi all ‹**pipster**› NE girls wanna chat? ‹**lee1**› final score bolton 1-1 west brom ‹**IceColdEyeingUpAlexandra**› I hate this feeling I'm turning into Ally McBeal ‹**topdogg**› alice pm please ‹**furred_paw**› ello girl thing ‹**IceColdEyeingUpAlexandra**› its unseemly for a bloke ‹**alice in wonderland**› ok topdogg	'Speech and writing are separate systems and very different from each other. Texts are either one thing or the other.'

As you will see from the last example in the table above, new technology text types often have the properties of both speech and writing.

Standard English, slang and dialect

The extracts we considered at the beginning of this module included some examples of English that were clearly different from the 'standard' version we usually encounter in print. For example, in D. H. Lawrence's *Sons and Lovers* (text I on page 13), the speech of Mr Morel is represented in such a way as to suggest his broad Nottinghamshire accent and dialect. This is, of course, a piece of fiction. But what are Britain's regional varieties really like?

Let's hear a little more from the Sunderland man, aged 60, whose reminiscence about life when he was a child featured as text B on page 10. Some attempt has been made to reflect the more interesting pronunciations by using non-standard spellings.

when I was a bairn (.) many years ago (.) does tha want to know (.) grandma (.) that's mi mother (.) used to play bloody waar (.) when we used to come in on a night (.) and we'd all been plodgin (.) down in the bourn (.) that's a stream which is down near the beck (2) all our clathes were up the eyes in clarts (2) and mi ma used to say (.) you cannot ave any more money for any more ket this week (2) so (.) me and mi mates used to gan and clean pigeon crees out for the men who used to fly pigeons (.) when they come back they used to hoy them mebbies down in Bradford (2) they used to flee back (.) and we used to clean the cree out and he used to give us some money (.) to buy our own ket (4) what else does tha want to know (.) tha disn'y know when you're weel off you people (2) does tha want to know what we used to do for holidays (.) we used to get on a bus (.) and gan down to Seaborne about 7 mile away (2) nay Blackpools (.) nay Majorcas (.) nay bloody Ibizas (.) or bloody Tenerifes (.) we never had nowt like that (.) never thout on.

ACTIVITY 18

C3.1a, C3.3

Discuss and/or write an analysis of the Sunderland man's speech in which you identify the ways in which his language differs from Standard English. Then compare your findings with the commentary on page 74.

You might find it helpful to distinguish between *pronunciation* (as far as you can tell from the spellings), *vocabulary* and *grammar*.

Attitudes to accents and dialects

As you worked on Activity 18 you were beginning to make a distinction between two terms that are often confused. When focusing on the aspects of the speaker's pronunciation, you were looking at **accent**, whereas the vocabulary and grammar of a variety of language define which **dialect** it belongs to. The distinctive, educated and regionally neutral accent we associate with BBC is known as **Received Pronunciation** (or **RP**), whereas the vocabulary and grammar of 'correct', acceptable English is called **Standard English (SE)**. Both SE and RP are rather special because they enjoy the prestige of being regarded as 'correct', 'good' or 'proper' English, and they are not native to any one region.

Attitudes towards other accents and dialects vary considerably. Some accents – often those such as Glasgow and Birmingham, associated with large urban areas – prove consistently unpopular and unglamorous, whereas others – such as the rural accents of the south-west of England or East Anglia – are perceived as 'quaint'. A third group of regional accents is highly regarded because the accents seem to combine friendliness with intelligence, which makes them ideal for companies seeking staff for large call centres. Attitudes towards dialects are equally mixed: many people are intrigued and charmed by the non-standard words of our regions, and fearful that we may be losing many of them, whereas others assume that speakers of dialects are either stupid or poorly educated.

 This topic is covered in more detail in Module 2, Language and Social Contexts.

Preparing for the examination: Task 1, classification

In the Unit 1 examination you will be presented with a selection of data or texts and asked to examine them closely before carrying out two tasks. Each of the tasks carries an equal number of marks, and should take about half of the total examination time of $1\frac{1}{2}$ hours, i.e. 45 minutes.

Here we will focus on the first of those tasks, which asks you to explore some of the many possible ways of comparing, linking, distinguishing and classifying different examples of language in use. The task is to 'discuss various ways in which those texts can be grouped, giving reasons for your choices'.

ACTIVITY 19   C3.3

Presented below is a set of texts similar to the range of texts you may find on the examination paper. Examine the texts carefully. Then work through the questions on page 31.

TEXT A

Nonsense Stories and Alphabets by Edward Lear

474   NONSENSE STORIES AND ALPHABETS

TO MAKE GOSKY PATTIES

TAKE a Pig, three or four years of age, and tie him by the off hind leg to a post. Place 5 pounds of currants, 3 of sugar, 2 pecks of peas, 18 roast chestnuts, a candle, and 6 bushels of turnips, within his reach; if he eats these, constantly provide him with more.

Then procure some cream, some slices of Cheshire cheese, four quires of foolscap paper, and a packet of black pins. Work the whole into a paste, and spread it out to dry on a sheet of clean brown waterproof linen.

When the paste is perfectly dry, but not before, proceed to beat the Pig violently, with the handle of a large broom. If he squeals, beat him again.

Visit the paste and beat the Pig alternately for some days, and ascertain if at the end of that period the whole is about to turn into Gosky Patties.

If it does not then, it never will; and in that case the Pig may be let loose, and the whole process may be considered as finished.

Text B

Transcript of an interview between a teacher (T) and her female student aged 17 (S), recorded in a sixth-form college in 2002:

T: right Gemma (.) let's have a look (.) how far have you actually got

S: well (.) I understood all about (.) you know (.) what we did in class

T: you mean the analysis we did of the speech

S: yeah (.) but (.) but I can't seem to do it with the homework

T: OK (2) have you got the framework (.) you know the questions we were using

S: yeah (5)

T: so first you need to read the whole of the passage OK

S: yeah

T: then start to ask yourself some (.) the questions on the sheet

Text C

The script of the opening of an episode of *Monty Python's Flying Circus*, first performed and broadcast on BBC TV in 1970, published by Methuen in 1989 in *Just the Words*.

A man in evening dress, sitting in a cage at the zoo.

Man *[John]*: And now for something completely different.

Pan to show 'It's' man in next cage.

It's Man *[Michael]*: It's

Animated titles.

Cut to studio: interviewer in chair.

[Superimposed caption: 'Face the Press']

Interviewer *[Eric]*: Hello. Tonight on 'Face the Press' we're going to examine two different views of contemporary things. On my left is the Minister for Home Affairs *[cut to minister completely in drag and a moustache]* who is wearing a striking organza dress in pink tulle, with matching pearls and a diamanté collar necklace. *[soft fashion-parade music starts to play in background]* The shoes are in brushed pigskin with gold clasps, by Maxwell of Bond Street. The hair is by Roger, and the whole ensemble is crowned by a spectacular display of Christmas orchids. And on my right – putting the case against the Government – is a small patch of brown liquid . . . *[cut to patch of liquid on seat of chair]* which could be creosote or some extract used in industrial varnishing. *[cut back to interviewer]* Good evening Minister, may I put the first question to you? In your plan, 'A

Better Britain for Us', you claimed that you would build 88,000 million, billion houses a year in the Greater London area alone. In fact, you've built only three in the last fifteen years. Are you a bit disappointed with this result?

Minister *[Graham]*: No, no. I'd like to answer this question if I may in two ways. Firstly in my normal voice and then in a kind of silly high-pitched whine.

TEXT D

Advertisement published in an American newspaper, the *St Louis Dispatch*, in 1912:

WOMEN'S $5.00 TO $7.50
Spring Skirts
For $2.65

There are 700 Skirts included in this wonderful offering & the prices quoted would not pay for the materials alone that have been put into them. We secured them at an absurdly low price from a maker who had odd bolts & half pieces of materials which he desired to dispose of—we had them made up into 30 of this Spring's most sought models. Some have high waist lines, panels in front & back, some with foot plaits—all exceedingly well tailored. The materials include serges, chiffon Panamas & novelty fabrics—in the newest grays, tans, browns, blues also black—skirts well worth $5.00 to $7.50 —Wednesday, while they last, choice of any for $2.65.

TEXT E

Transcript of a commentary on a rugby union match between England and New Zealand, recorded from BBC Radio 5 in 2002:

Commentator A: A great attacking position for England now (.) Dawson gets the ball spins it out (.) to Wilkinson (.) missed pass out to Greenwood (.) and he tries he beats the first tackle he's held up five metres from the line (.) England drive over the white jerseys are all there (.) out to Cohen who's on the right wing although he's the left wing (.) he's held up one metre from the line now the ball comes back (.) Dawson from the (.) right touchline out to Wilkinson swinging across (.) Grewcock in midfield drives (.) England'll get a penalty at worst anyway the referee (.) blows the whistle awards the penalty to England (.) back by the touchline (.) and good play indeed (.) by the English forwards

Commentator B: yes they're certainly taking an upper hand in this area they got that line out right Matt Dawson was so (.) he I don't think he'll oh he will take /

Commentator A: / oh he takes a short kick and oh he (.) th (.) Lomu touches it down but there was a body check there

TEXT F

HOME BUYERS'
Survey and Valuation

C7 Garage(s) and outbuildings
(Comment is restricted to important defects, likely to have a material affect on value. Inspection of leisure facilities, etc., is excluded.)

STONE BUILT LEAN TO CONSTRUCTION DETACHED SINGLE CAR GARAGE WITH CORRUGATED ASBESTOS SHEET ROOF - IT IS ADVISABLE THAT THE ASBESTOS BE REPLACED WITH SOME OTHER MATERIAL

C8 The site
(Only significant visible defects in boundary fences, walls, retaining walls, paths and drives are reported. Reference to potential hazards such as flooding and tree roots is included where these are readily apparent.)

AS NO PLAN OF THIS FAIRLY LARGE SITE WAS SUPPLIED BY SELLING AGENTS, WE HAVE ASSUMED BOUNDARIES AS PER THE ATTACHED COLOURED SECTION O.S. PLAN. ON THE SOUTHERN BOUNDARY IS A TIMBER PLANK FENCE WITH SQUARE TIMBER SUPPORTS WHICH WERE ORIGINALLY CEMENTED INTO THE GROUND THESE ARE ALL NOW LOOSE AND NEED RE-CEMENTING.
MOST OF STONE WALL ON EAST SIDE OF GARDEN AND TO REAR WEST COURTYARD SIDE IS COVERED IN IVY AND SHRUBS BUT AREAS NEED RE-POINTING. AREA OF DRY STONE BASE WALL IN PARKING AREA TO LEFT OF GARAGE IS IN POOR CONDITION
(Inspection covers within the boundaries have been lifted where visible and possible [except

---

TEXT G

The Boardwalk at Canary Wharf
★ ★ ★ ★ ★

Luxurious Serviced Apartments in London

More style, more space, more facilities, more independence and a great place to stay for one night or more

If you are visiting London, for business or pleasure, and you are tired of standard hotel accommodation, then take a look at our superb Boardwalk Suites. These stylish two bedroomed, fully serviced, luxury waterfront apartments are located in the fashionable Canary Wharf area and within 15 minutes of the new ExCel Exhibition Centre and London City Airport. Each apartment will sleep up to 5 adults in comfort, and is available for one night or more. Complete with terrific views across the marina to the Millennium Dome, the living room offers you the space to entertain guests in style. And with a well equipped kitchen, you can even eat in if you choose. But the truly amazing feature is the price, which is far less than the cost of similar hotel accommodation.

Special Offer
£189*
per night for
2 bedroom
Marina Apartment which will
sleep 5 people

*Minimum 2 nights stay or 3 nights for Easter and Bank Holidays. Subject to availability. Offer must be booked & occupied by May 31st 2001. Please quote LW2

So if you are planning a visit, on your own or with friends, give us a call and find out about our unbeatable value. We know we can exceed your expectations. Call now on:
020 7517 4777

LONDON MILLENNIUM SUITES
The Boardwalk at Canary Wharf

258-286 Boardwalk Place, Trafalgar Way,
London, E14 5SH, England.
Tel: +44 (0) 20 7517 4777 Fax: +44 (0) 20 7517 4778
E-mail: info@millenniumsuites.com
Web: www.millenniumsuites.com

TEXT H

A review of a book about text messaging, *Text Me*, in *Craccum Magazine online*, 2002

4 thse of U wndrng wht 2 bi yr mble owng M8s/BF/GF 4 thr BDay, U hv fnd wht U R lkng 4 in a gr8 Pngwn bk clld TXT ME. Accrdng 2 th bk cvr it has 'al U need 2 knw re: txt mssgng'.

It tlls U hw 2 txt emotns _ hi-lites Nclude DLG n CLAB. U cn fite it out wth YR BF/GF via txt mssgs... LMA! MYOB! [:-(:@(Dnt wrry tho, U cn mke up by snding a VH or a @-,-´Ñ- Whn yr out U can qikly chck whr ppl R by txtng W@? and snd YR m8s an ETA if U'L B L8.

TEXT I

An extract from an article 'Au'd George: A Methody Pioneer' by A. Stanley Umpleby.

Au'd George war yan o'them strang-heeaded, rough an' riddy sooart o'men at wi used ti knaw up i't'deeals when we war lads, bud which seeam ti be dyin' oot fast. He hed neea eddication mich an' Ah sud doot if he ivver went ti skeeal aboon a twelvemonth. When he did gan t'skeealmaster used ti tell him he owt ti fetch a few hens wiv 'im ti gether t'cooarn up'at he scattered o't'fleear under his desk.

Here are some questions about the texts and the connections between them to get you started. Remember, as you explore the links between texts, it is important to cover *all* the texts, and use at least four different ways of linking texts together.

- Texts A and B might both seem to share the same **purpose** – giving instructions – but what is the *real* purpose behind text A? Which conventions of the **genre** of recipes is it using to create humour?

- Texts A and D both belong to an earlier **period** of history. In what ways do they reflect changes which have taken place in society and/or in language between then and now?

- Texts B and D both appear to be directed at a gender-specific **audience** – but in which of these is the gender aspect more significant?

- Several of the texts may have **multiple audiences** – which?

- Texts A and C are both designed to be **humorous** in the way they exploit recognisable conventions of specific **genres**. Which aspects of recipes and political interviews do they exploit for humorous effect?

- Several of the texts are written using a semi-specialised **register** which includes vocabulary appropriate to a particular topic. Which?

- Texts D and G are both adverts, and both therefore aim to persuade or influence. What similarities and differences do they have in the way they address their respective audiences?

- If you tried to define the texts by **mode** as belonging to either **speech or writing**, which texts would be most difficult to classify, and why?

- Texts H and I both differ from conventional Standard English. How would you describe and contrast the different **varieties** of English they represent?

- Jot down some more ways in which you can link or group the texts together.

You don't have long in the exam room to write up your ideas, so it may be useful to make a chart such as the one above as a starting point. You may also find it useful to use **Venn diagrams,** for example, to illustrate the ways some classifications overlap. The example below shows that you consider texts A and C to be purely informative, texts D and E to be purely entertaining, and texts B and F to have elements of both.

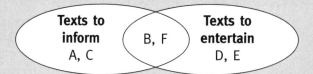

Whatever notes you use, it is vital that you communicate in clear, fluent English to the examiner these things:

- You are aware that language use can be classified in many different ways.

- You can apply this knowledge effectively to the specific texts in front of you. Don't just generalise: discuss the texts specifically and precisely, using the appropriate linguistic terminology.

- You are aware that the danger of classification is over-simplification. The paper is likely to include texts which are not easy to categorise in a straightforward way. You need to discuss these along the lines of the exercises above (see pages 22–25).

It is unlikely that you can do all of this in an answer of less than two or three pages.

Now have a go at writing your answer to this exercise, in about 45 minutes. Then compare your attempt with the sample answer in the commentaries (see page 74).

Describing language in detail: stylistic analysis

So far in this module, we have concentrated on ways of comparing, contrasting and classifying texts. The previous section has introduced some essential ideas and terms used in language studies, and the first task of the Unit 1 examination tests your ability to apply these ideas flexibly and sensitively by making links and distinctions between texts.

This section examines how we **analyse** in detail the ways language is used in a text, and how we explain why or how the **contexts** of these texts have contributed to their distinctive styles. This is what the second part of the Unit 1 examination paper is about. In it, you have to carry out a more detailed study of three of the texts (including one of the transcripts of spoken texts). This kind of activity is known as **stylistic analysis.**

Using frameworks

In stylistic analysis we cannot rely on being able to spot key features by chance. As linguistic scientists and investigators, we need to look systematically at language, asking a methodical series of questions as we investigate it.

This is what is referred to in the Assessment Objective 'know and use key features of frameworks for the systematic study of spoken and written English'.

When we consider why, and how, a particular piece of language has come to be written or spoken the way it has, there are two sets of questions to answer:

- What has influenced the writer or speaker to produce the text?

- How can we describe the distinctive style of this particular text?

Our work so far means that we have already begun to answer the first question. To answer the second question, we need to think of language in terms of different 'levels' or 'frameworks'. At each level (or within each framework) there are a number of questions we can ask – and try to answer – about the style of language in a particular text. In the remainder of this module, we will explore each of these more fully.

ACTIVITY 20   C3.3

The table below sets out some of these key questions and adds a 'key terms' column to flag up important linguistic terminology for later reference. Make yourself familiar with this framework and its key questions; it is the basis of much of the work that follows in this module. Later sections and activities explore it more fully. Once you are familiar with it, you can use it to define the key stylistic features of any text you come across.

(a) Study the examples drawn from text D (page 11), 'Come live with me and me my love'.

(b) Choose any of the other short texts we have considered in this module so far. Try to answer the key questions for your chosen text and write up your responses as a short essay.

Key question	In other words . . .	Example: Text D	Key terms for future study
How is the text organised?	Does it have a clear beginning/middle/end? Is it a list? Is it a series of steps?	Starts with an invitation . . . will lead to the promised result – pleasures.	discourse structure

Key question	In other words . . .	Example: Text D	Key terms for future study
What does it look like on the page?	Is it set out in columns? Paragraphs? Verses? Are its sections numbered or titled? Does it include panels of text or diagrams? Does it use different typefaces, type sizes?	A verse of short, regular lines.	form; layout; graphology
What kinds of sentences does it use, and how are they constructed?	How many sentences are statements? Questions? Commands? Exclamations? Are the sentences long, short or a mixture? Does their construction seem basic or complicated? Does the text use complete, 'correct' sentences or some abbreviated ones? Are there examples of unusual word order?	A command, followed by a promise or prediction. Mainly 'normal', but some unusual word order ('we will all the pleasures prove').	sentence function/ length/ structure
What kinds of vocabulary and phrases does it use?	What proportion of the words convey facts or opinions? Is the language emotional or detached? Does it seem personal or impersonal, simple or sophisticated, formal/neutral/informal? Does it include words that belong to a particular subject or theme? Or words that are specialist, technical, literary or old-fashioned? Are there any non-standard or regional expressions? Is language being used in its literal sense – or does it use similes and/or metaphors and other expressions?	Personal words ('you' and 'we'). Quite simple words ('come') with parts of the country landscape ('hills', 'dales', etc.). 'Prove' used in a different, old-fashioned sense.	colloquialism; slang; archaism; jargon; dialect; metaphor; figurative language; idioms; register; semantic fields; word classes

Key question	In other words . . .	Example: Text D	Key terms for future study
What is distinctive about the spellings or sounds used?	Is the text generally orthodox, or are there examples of unusual spellings or punctuation? Does the speech have a non-regional ('BBC'), 'posh' or regional accent? Are there any noticeable patterns in the sounds/spellings?	Rhyme at the ends of lines. Regular rhythm.	orthography; received pronunciation (RP); rhythm; alliteration; assonance
What meanings does the text have? Does it mean what it says? How can it be interpreted?	What is the actual meaning? Is there an implied or 'hidden' meaning?	Does the writer wish to marry his intended lover? What does he mean by 'pleasures'? Has the meaning of the word 'prove' changed since the poem was written?	semantics; pragmatics; denotation; connotation

Language framework: discourse structure

What do we mean by the *structure* of a piece of language? After all, we can usually recognise what holds everyday objects together: a building, for example, generally consists of a set of foundations, and an interconnecting series of load-bearing walls, beams and girders. Well, just as different buildings – houses, churches, stadiums – have different structures, so uses of language have their own distinctive structures.

This means looking at these key questions:

- How does it start?

- How does it finish?

- What is the sequence of sections involved in the middle?

There are many different ways in which texts and speech can be organised and constructed, but some common structures do occur frequently. You will certainly be able to recognise and identify examples of these. Let's begin by looking at some examples of spoken texts.

Discourse structure in speech

Although we may not be aware of it at the time, how we use spoken language in familiar everyday situations is also structured in particular ways. When we participate in these situations, it is as if we have learned to expect that they will follow a predictable but unwritten 'script'.

For example, many phone calls may follow a similar pattern to the one analysed below:

Example	Structural element
A: 324667. B: Oh hello. Is that Mr Jim Harrison? A: Yeah, speaking. B: This is Hayley Jones – you may remember we met some time ago. A: Yes, of course.	*Exchange of identification of parties*
B: How are you? I hope I'm not calling at an inconvenient time. A: No, no, not at all. I'm fine. How are you? B: Oh, pretty good. I'll tell you why I'm calling. Its about those books you ordered a while ago.	*Small talk, leading to identification of purpose of call*
B: We were just wondering if you'd received our invoice for the goods, and when we might expect to receive your payment? A: Ah yes. I have it in front of me, actually. Thanks for that. You should be receiving our cheque over the next couple of days.	*Main business of call*
B: Oh that's good, Mr Harrison. We'll look forward to hearing from you then. Thanks for your help. A: Not at all. If you'll excuse me, I've got someone waiting on the other line.	*Winding up, perhaps including a summary of what has been said, and a reason to close the conversation*
B: Of course. Goodbye now. A: Bye. Talk to you soon.	*Exchange of goodbyes*

ACTIVITY 21

For each of the following speech situations, describe the stages the conversation is likely to go through – in other words, its typical discourse structure. Keep asking how such discourse typically begins, develops and concludes.

- Making a confession/admission.
- Asking for a favour.
- A doctor's appointment.
- Chatting someone up.

We will consider other important aspects of the structure of conversation later (see 'Analysis of conversation', page 58 below).

Discourse structure in writing

> ### ACTIVITY 22
>
> There are many different kinds of written texts, but many of them may follow one or other of the set of discourse structures suggested below. Add your own examples to the ones given.
>
> | Structure | Examples | Your examples |
> |---|---|---|
> | Non-sequenced **lists**

Stepped or sequenced **lists** | Shopping lists

Instructions | |
> | Logical **arguments** (Because of A, this leads to B, and the conclusion C) | Persuasive articles or newspaper editorials | |
> | **Problem/anxiety–solution** structures | Adverts may establish a problem – spots – and go on to provide the solution – a brand of skin cleanser | |
> | **Desire–fulfilment** structures | Similarly, advertisers (or politicians) may invoke a desire before offering to provide its fulfilment in the shape of their product or party | |
> | **Analysis** and explanation (**X** has happened: what follows works out why and how it did so) | Essays and formal reports | |
> | **Narrative** accounts | News reports; short stories | |

Telling stories: narrative structures

Of course, stories, or narratives, are not confined to written texts; we tell many different kinds of stories in various situations, whether we're gossiping with friends about what happened at the weekend, telling a joke, reading a bedtime story or writing a report of a scientific experiment. However, when we start to look for the structure of stories, some common patterns begin to emerge.

Many stories establish a situation, introduce an element of disequilibrium, reach a crisis and finally resolve the problem, returning to a position of stability. Some, like news reports, give all the essential details first then elaborate on them. Others, like detective stories, withold the key details until the last page.

ACTIVITY 23

Think about the examples of narratives suggested below. For each of them, try to define what their structure is.

- Joke: Three prisoners are captured in the war, and are about to be executed. They are asked what they wish to have for their last meal. The first asks for a pepperoni pizza, which he is served and then taken away. The second requests a filet mignon, which he is served and then also taken away. The third man requests a plate of strawberries. The captors are surprised: '*Strawberries*?' 'Yes, strawberries.' 'But they are out of season!' 'I'll wait . . .'

- Personal anecdote: you tell your friends about something that happened to you at the weekend.

- Excuse provided to teacher about non-completion of homework. Do you give the ending – 'I haven't done it' – at the start, or do you make it your punch line?

- A fairy story or nursery rhyme.

- A typical episode of *EastEnders*.

Language framework: layout, form and graphology

At the level of discourse structure, we are concerned with the inner construction of discourse in different contexts. By contrast, at the level of form and layout, we are interested in those features that contribute to the shape and (in writing) appearance of a written text. Such features are collectively referred to as the **graphology** of a text.

The following questions all relate to the total impact of a text on the page:

- Is it arranged in columns, paragraphs, blocks or continuous text?

- Does it feature diagrams, pictures or other visual elements?

- What typefaces, type sizes and styles (such as *italic* or **bold**) does it use?

- What impressions do any of these features create, for example about the tone or structure of the text?

- How does the **context** of the text (where, when and why the piece was produced) help explain these distinctive features?

ACTIVITY 24

(a) Look again at texts D, F, and G from the set of texts on pages 29–30. Use the questions above to compare and contrast the graphology of these texts.

(b) Find a typical example of each of the following kinds of texts, and then answer the questions above to define their graphological features:

- message in a greetings card

- tabloid newspaper report

- formal business letter from a company

- informative leaflet for the general public

- magazine aimed at an early teens readership.

(c) Now consider the following versions of the same summons to appear at a magistrates' court to answer a criminal charge. What different 'messages' are being conveyed by the different typefaces? Which are the most and least appropriate typefaces?

1

You are hereby summoned to appear at Newtown Magistrates' Court on Tuesday, February 13th at 10.30 am to answer charges that on November 14th, 2002, you did wilfully commit an act of disorderly conduct.

2

You are hereby summoned to appear at Newtown Magistrates' Court on Tuesday, February 13th at 10.30 am to answer charges that on November 14th, 2002, you did wilfully commit an act of disorderly conduct.

3

You are hereby summoned to appear at Newtown Magistrates' Court on Tuesday, February 13th at 10.30 am to answer charges that on November 14th, 2002, you did wilfully commit an act of disorderly conduct.

4

You are hereby summoned to appear at Newtown Magistrates' Court on Tuesday, February 13th at 10.30 am to answer charges that on November 14th, 2002, you did wilfully commit an act of disorderly conduct.

The forms of spoken discourse

At first the 'forms' of spoken discourse may be less obvious. What we mean by the 'form' of a spoken text can be summed up in a few simple questions:

- Who typically are the participants?

- What are their roles in relation to each other?

- In what circumstances does the conversation usually take place?

- What kinds of thing do the speakers usually say to each other?

- Are there any 'rules' which seem to limit what can and cannot be said or done in this situation?

ACTIVITY 25

Let's try applying these questions to some common types of spoken language. Complete the missing sections in the table to describe the forms of these examples:

Question/ discourse type	Job interview	Classroom lesson	Live TV football commentary	Formal meeting
Who takes part?	One or more employers and an interviewee		Main commentator and an 'expert' adviser	
What are the usual circumstances and context?	An office or other room on business premises	A classroom in a school or college		A committee room or similar, with members sitting round a desk/table
What are the roles of the speakers? What kinds of thing do they say?		Teacher leads, asking questions, evaluating answers, giving instructions and explanations, and maintaining discipline		Chair manages the meeting, taking it through the agenda, and maintains orderly discussion

Language framework: the grammar of the text

Sentences: length, construction and function

When we start to break down language into smaller units than the whole of the text, at the level of the sentence we begin to look at those aspects of language that people think of when they use the word **grammar**. This includes areas of language study known as **morphology** (see page 43 below) and **syntax**. The term **syntax** is used when discussing the ways sentences are put together by placing words in a particular order.

Length

However, perhaps the first and easiest way of distinguishing how sentences are used in a particular text is to comment on their *length*.

Some texts may use predominantly short sentences – like this children's story, *Floppy the Hero*, by Roderick Hunt:

> A fire engine went by. There was a fire. Everyone ran to see. 'Get back,' said a fireman. A barn was on fire.

It is not only writers for children who deliberately keep their sentences short. Writers of instruction manuals, such as text E (page 11) may break down their information into small units, as in:

> * Click on the Start button on the task bar

Construction

Very short sentences are also, by definition, simply constructed. For this reason it is easy to confuse length and complexity. In fact, even longer sentences can still be relatively simple. Consider these two sentences, of identical length (48 words):

> **A** It was a nice canny game an all but sometimes windows used to get brocken and another thing in them days people were lucky if they had indoor netties and it was bloody murder if you wanted to gan to the toilet in the middle of the neet.
>
> ---
>
> **B** Not having had prior knowledge of the events which were about to unfold, and being possessed of the mistaken assumption that his way in the world was to be one of unimpeded progress, Michael was ill prepared for the news with which he would be greeted that morning.

Although of identical length, the sentence in text A strikes us as *simpler* than that in text B because of the ways in which it joins together its various parts (mainly using 'and' and 'but' to string them together). Text B, in contrast, uses more grammatically complex ways of linking the sentence elements together ('not having had', 'with which he would be'. . .).

The stylistics framework also reminds us to ask whether a text is written using complete, 'correct' sentences, and whether it uses any examples of unusual word order. Our usual notion of what constitutes a 'complete' sentence is based on written language; in speech, utterances like 'Hi Alan' and 'It is', which are technically not 'complete sentences', are very common. Such sentences are sometimes called **minor sentences**. Some written texts may also use an abbreviated or note form in the interests of economy.

As for word order, we may often find unusual examples in poems. Look back at pages 10–13, and in particular text D on page 11, 'The Passionate Shepherd to his Love' – the poet writes 'we will all the pleasures prove' rather than 'we will prove all the pleasures' – and text G on page 12, 'The Jumblies' ('In a Sieve they went to sea' following the more usual 'They went to sea in a Sieve'). Writers – and speakers too – may choose to vary the usual word order for many reasons.

We shall investigate sentence structures and syntax in more detail in *A2 English Language*: Module 4 Language Investigation, and Module 6 Language Development.

Function

Another relatively simple way of describing the kinds of sentences used in any piece of discourse is to ask what job or function they are most commonly carrying out. Here is one framework that identifies four sentence functions:

- The most common sentence type is the statement or **declarative**. This can be a statement of fact, an event, a feeling, an opinion or a prediction.

- Another type of sentence is the question or **interrogative**.

- A third type is the direct command, or **imperative**.

- The **exclamation** is a rarer type of sentence. Exclamations can include very short utterances, such as 'Great goal!'.

ACTIVITY 26

(a) Go back to any of texts we looked at earlier (see pages 27–31). For any of these, count the instances of each sentence type occurring in the extract, then use a pie chart or bar chart to record your findings. For example, text A (the teacher's instructions) consists of a mixture of declaratives and imperatives:

Declaratives	Imperatives
You have a sheet in front of you	Wait a minute I'll get you one
There's a list of the characters we looked at on Friday	Have a look now please
*What I want you do is to . . .	Look at the paragraph underneath
	. . . ensure that you have a pen or pencil available
	. . . add any relevant information

*This is debatable. This utterance is in some ways an imperative, but by putting 'what I want you to do is . . .' at the start, in effect the teacher turns it into a long declarative.

The resulting pie chart might look something like this:

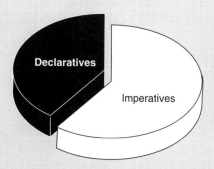

(b) For any of the following types of text, try to predict the proportions in which you will find the four kinds of sentence:

- a manual for a piece of computer software

- a TV advertisement

- an interview with a celebrity in a magazine.

Now find some examples of these kinds of texts and count the numbers of each sentence type to test your prediction.

(c) Finally, try to explain *why* the texts should have more of one type of sentence than another. Think about the purpose and subject matter of the texts, their **context**.

Word formations: morphology

Grammar is not just about word order, or syntax; it is also about the way we change the forms of individual words according to the job they are doing in a sentence. This aspect of grammar is known as **morphology.**

Many words in English are made up of two or more meaningful elements.

For example, in the sentence above, *words* = *word* + *s* (more than one), *meaningful* = *meaning* + *ful* (turns the noun *meaning* into the adjective *meaningful*). These units of meaning are known as **morphemes**.

Many words take on a different from, or grammatical function, by changing one or more of their morphemes. *Happy* can become *unhappy*, or *happiness*, and *cipher* can become *decipher*, *deciphers*, *deciphering* or even *undecipherable*. Some other words may change their form completely – *sing/sang*, *woman/women*, or *is/was*, for instance.

It is the rules of grammar, or morphology, that decide how and where we make these changes to words. For example, with **verbs**, whether we use *is*, *are*, *be*, *was* and *were*, or *talk*, *talks*, *talked* or *talking*, depends on:

The **person** it refers to	I am/we are I talk/we talk	1st person singular/plural
	You are You talk	2nd person singular and plural
	She is/they are He talks/they talk	3rd person singular/plural
The **tense** that is needed	I am, I was, I will be I talk, I am talking, I talked, I will talk	**Present, past or future**

One of the ways in which dialects differ from Standard English is in the patterns of these variations. A speaker of one dialect may say *I were* and *you was* rather than *I was* and *you were*.

Nouns usually change to show whether they are singular or plural (*box/boxes*, *child/children*) but there are exceptions – *sheep* and *deer* do not change.

The forms of words may also change according to their meaning and **word class** (see below), as in *consume*, *consumer*, *consuming*, *consumption*, or their position in a sentence (*She likes me*, *I like her*).

ACTIVITY 27

Look again at text J, the extract from *The BFG*, on page 13. This text includes some examples of unusual morphology, where the giants seem to be getting their grammar and words mixed up.

For each one, try to explain how it differs from Standard English:

Example	Comment
You is not loving it?	
The most disgusterous taste . . .	
. . . that is ever touching my teeth	

Compare your comments with the commentary on page 76.

Language framework: words and phrases (lexis)

The **vocabulary** of a language includes all the words available in it. **Lexis** is the term used for the vocabulary chosen for a text. As the number of questions included in the stylistics framework (see pages 33–35) suggests, at this level there is always a lot to observe.

It is useful here to be able to describe accurately different kinds of words and the jobs they do in a sentence, as well as their meanings. **Word classes** provide one traditional framework for doing this.

Let's look again at the eye-witness testimony from the *Titanic* (Text C, page 11). The following words from the extract have something in common:

We (x2)	morning	Cherbourg	it	I	cable
ship (x2)	April	Queenstown	afternoon	watch	anchor
Wednesday	drill	Sunday (x3)	night	noise	shock

All of these words are involved in various kinds of naming. As such, they all belong to the word class of **nouns**. We can subdivide this class like this:

Word class description	Function	Examples
proper nouns	names of specific places, months, days, people	Cherbourg, Queenstown, April, Sunday
concrete nouns	names of objects	ship, cable, anchor
abstract nouns	names of feelings or ideas	shock
pronouns	substitutes for names of people and things	we, it

Let's look now at these words from text E, 'Launching PowerPoint' (page 11):

run	switch	should happen	click
point	can't find	means	Is

These are words belong to the class **verbs**. This class is sometimes misleadingly referred to as 'doing words', but this is unhelpful; the most frequently used verbs in English are *be/is* and *have/has*, which do not describe actions of any kind. Other verbs define states or feelings (e.g. *I love you*).

Now consider the function of these words from text I, *Sons and Lovers* (page 13):

dry   wet   nasty

These words all add descriptive information about the noun to which they refer. So Morel's *singlet* (a concrete noun) is variously referred to as *dry, wet* and *nasty*. This places these words in the class of **adjectives**, which qualify or provide additional information about a noun.

Now look at the word *gingerly* from the same passage. This is also descriptive, but it does not describe an object – it describes the action of putting out a hand. It therefore belongs to the class of **adverbs**, which provide information about a verb (usually how, where or when it occurs).

These major word classes are the ones likely to be most useful in stylistic 'finger-printing'. They are listed along with **prepositions** and **conjunctions** in the table below.

Principal word classes

Word class	Function	Subclasses	Examples
Nouns	name specific people, places, times; things; feelings, ideas	proper; concrete; abstract	London, Tony Blair, Christmas; jelly, rocks, anorak; happiness, equality
Pronouns	substitute for or refer to nouns	personal; impersonal possessive	I, me, you, s/he, it, we, they; my, mine, your, his, hers, its, yours theirs
Adjectives	provide additional information about nouns	factual; opinionative	blue, steel, six; awful, excellent
Adverbs	provide additional information about verbs	manner (how); time (when); place (where)	quickly, unpleasantly; then, now; here, everywhere
Conjunctions	join phrases together within a sentence	co-ordinating; subordinating (these terms are explored in *English Language A2*)	and, but, so; because, although, despite
Prepositions	define positions and relationships		in, on, between, against, over, under

ACTIVITY 28 — C3.1a

Look back at some of the short texts you collected for Activity 11 on page 16. For any of these texts, identify and highlight examples of each principal word class. Make a list of these items on separate pieces of paper – one each for nouns, verbs, adjectives, adverbs, conjunctions and prepositions – in the order in which they appear in the text.

Give the lists one at a time to a partner, and for each one invite them to predict the nature of the text on the basis of the listed words. At the end, discuss which word class enabled your partner(s) to identify the type of text most easily, and why this might be.

Using word classes within the stylistics framework

If we return to the key questions listed in the table on pages 33–35, we can now use word classes systematically as a means of investigating some important aspects of language use. The table below indicates how the study of word classes in a text can help answer these questions:

Key question	Word class investigation
How much of the text conveys facts and how much conveys opinions? Is the language emotional or detached?	1 The most obvious words to look at are the adjectives and adverbs. Ask whether they convey factual or emotional or opinionative details about the noun or verb they describe. 2 However, nouns and verbs can be just as revealing. Compare, for example: (a) 'The soldier moved away' (b) 'The deserter fled' and (c) 'The hero retreated'.
Does the text seem personal or impersonal?	We can usually answer this question by looking at the pronouns. There are three aspects to consider: 1 Does the writer or speaker draw attention to himself or herself by using 'I' (the first person singular)? 2 Does the writer or speaker use the first person plural ('we', 'our'), and if so, who does it include or refer to? 3 Does the speaker or writer use 'you' (the second person) to address readers or listeners directly? If the answer to all three of these questions is 'no', then we can safely describe the language as impersonal.
Is the text formal/neutral/informal? Is it simple or sophisticated? Does it include words that belong	Here we are considering the register of a text. Nouns and verbs are likely to be central, but consider adjectives and adverbs too. Even

Key question	Word class investigation
to a particular subject or theme, or that are specialist, technical, literary or old-fashioned?	conjunctions and prepositions (such as 'therefore', 'hitherto') can help mark out a text as rather formal.
Are there any non-standard or regional expressions?	This is a matter of the dialect of a text. Most written English is in Standard English, though some writers (like D. H. Lawrence in text I, from *Sons and Lovers*) may try to capture regional speech on paper. Spoken discourse is much more likely to include dialectal variations, which may use alternative nouns and verbs for everyday items and actions. And there may be other differences from Standard English – such as unusual plurals ('childer' for 'children', etc.) or different present and past tenses (such as 'I were', 'you was'). See the section on slang and dialects in this module (page 26).
Is language being used in its literal sense – or does it use similes and/or metaphors and other figurative expressions?	Although single words may be metaphorical – 'You're such an angel!' (noun), or 'I've got to scoot!' (verb), for example – we often need to consider whole phrases here. English makes deliberate use of similes, metaphors and other expressions to convey meanings more vividly, but bear in mind that the language also contains many everyday words and phrases that are idiomatic (their meanings cannot be guessed from their literal sense).

Language framework: sounds and spelling

The study of sounds is called **phonology**; the term for spelling is **orthography**. As we began to see earlier (see 'Speech and writing', pages 20–25), the relationship between the sounds of spoken English and the way we write the language is complex. There are only about 44 basic sounds in English; these basic building bricks, from which everything in our language is ultimately constructed, are called **phonemes**. Unfortunately, we have only 26 letters in our alphabet to represent these – so our spelling system can never be entirely straightforward.

By using pairs of letters (or **digraphs**) such as *sh-* and *ch-* to represent single phonemes, a standard spelling system has evolved over several centuries which makes the 26 letters of the alphabet capable of expressing many sounds, but we are all too aware of many inconsistencies – think of *rough*, *bough* and *cough*, *no* and *know*, or *cyclists* and *psychologists*. Some phonemes in English do correspond fairly reliably with the written alphabet: the letter 'd', for instance, does usually express the sound *d* – though even here the letter may be used singly ('dog') or in a pair ('ladder') to represent the same sound.

Another oddity is that the most common vowel sound in English does not have a letter associated with it, and is expressed using a huge variety of spelling combinations. Say aloud the vowel sound represented by the letters in bold in each of the words below:

> **banana** undeni**able** n**a**tural rubb**er** cust**ar**d

In each case, depending on your regional accent, you will probably be making a short rather abrupt sound, something like 'uh'. This surprising little vowel is, in fact, the phoneme linguists call **schwa**.

Standard and non-standard spellings

Some texts may include non-standard spellings for various reasons. For example, historical texts may include unusual spellings of otherwise familiar words that reflect changes in language over time; and a flick through your local Yellow Pages can also reveal how some organisations (such as Kwik-Fit) deliberately alter spellings to grab our attention. This is also a favourite technique among pop and rock bands.

ACTIVITY 29

(a) For each of the categories in the table below, collect six additional examples of variant spellings. Try to suggest exactly how the alternative spelling affects the way you respond to the name of the company or group.

Cafés and restaurants	Card shops	Groups and bands
The Koffee Kup Brewers' Fayre Donut Magik	Cards 'r' Us Kelly's Kards Wishing U Well	The Beatles Boyzone

(b) Now look again at text I in Activity 19, 'Au'd George: A Methody Pioneer' (see page 31). Here the writer has deliberately departed from Standard English spelling to capture the Yorkshire accent. Read the text aloud, then 'translate' the text into Standard English/Received Pronunciation, noting which features of the Yorkshire accent it is designed to capture, and any differences from Standard English grammar.

An example is provided on page 50.

Non-standard spelling	Feature of Yorkshire accent
Au'd George war yan o' them	Old George were (SE = was) one of them (SE = those) This indicates different vowel sounds from the RP 'old' and 'were' and the absence of 'l' and 'f' in the forms of *old* and *of*
rough an' riddy sooart o' men	
up i't'deeals	
dyin' oot fast	
Ah sud doot	

Phonology in writing

Although it may seem like a contradiction in terms, we can sometimes observe noticeable patterns in the way particular sounds are used in written texts. This may be because such texts are actually designed to be heard, or read aloud, or simply because of the effect they produce as we 'hear' them inside our heads when we read.

These **phonological** patterns may include:

- rhythm

- rhyme

- **alliteration** (*Peter Piper picked a peck of pickled peppers*)

- **onomatopoeia** (*pop, sizzle, splash*).

Of these, perhaps the most difficult to write about is **rhythm**. We can see how rhythm works at its simplest by looking again at text G (page 12), 'The Jumblies'. Musicians are used to talking about the beats in a passage of music; similarly, with verse we can usually feel where the natural 'beat' of the language falls.

ACTIVITY 30

Work through the activities suggested alongside 'The Jumblies' in the table.

Text	Activity/commentary
They **went** to **sea** in a **Sieve**, they **did**,	1 Read these lines aloud and note how the 'beat' falls on the syllables

Text	Activity/commentary
In a **Sieve** they **went** to **sea**: In **spite** of **all** their **friends** could **say**, On a **win**ter's **morn**, on a **storm**y **day**, In a **Sieve** they **went** to **sea**!	in bold. These beats are usually referred to as **stresses** in verse. What sort of pattern begins to emerge? 2 You'll see that there seems to be a pattern of 4-3-4-4-3 stresses in the lines, but that the 'three-beat' lines seem to have an invisible pause built in. Just as in music, where silent beats are marked with a rest, in rhythmical verse the pauses are built into the rhythm.

ACTIVITY 31

Gather some samples of the types of texts shown in the table below. Identify the specific linguistic sound effects used and write them in the second column. In each case, try to explain how the effect makes the text achieve its purpose for the intended audience.

Data/texts	Sound effects used (alliteration, rhyme, rhythm, onomatopoeia, etc.)
Advertising slogans/jingles	
Children's verse	
Tabloid news headlines	

Language framework: semantics and pragmatics

The study of how meanings are created is called **semantics**. Here, we will briskly consider some of the main areas for exploration within this framework and suggest some related activities.

One way of thinking about how the vocabulary of English is organised is to group related words into **semantic fields**. This is, in effect, what a thesaurus does. Some examples follow:

Semantic field	Examples
happiness	joy, pleasure, delight, ecstasy, contentment
red	crimson, vermilion, scarlet, burgundy, cherry
motor vehicles	car, bus, truck, lorry, motorbike, moped, scooter
drinking vessels	cup, mug, glass, beaker, tumbler

Within each semantic field, some words may appear to be very close in meaning – they share a similar **denotation**. However, they may differ in subtle ways; some may have a more positive or negative feeling about them, for instance, or have different associations, or be used in different contexts or registers. Another way of saying this is that they have different **connotations**. This is why it is sometimes said that there is no such thing in English as a perfect pair of **synonyms** (words identical in meaning).

ACTIVITY 32

Explain the differences in the following sets of near synonyms, in terms of their differing connotations:

Sets of synonyms	Differences
my house/my home/my pad/my place	
fat/plump/big-boned/obese	
cheap/inexpensive/bargain/economical	

Use a thesaurus to examine other similar sets, and to make your own distinctions between individual words within them.

Euphemisms and dysphemisms

In many areas of meaning, the semantic field includes items which allow us either to avoid stating precisely what we mean, or the reverse – to put it extremely bluntly. Consider these various ways of telling you that you've lost your job:

You're sacked	You've been made redundant	We're downsizing	You're being shown the door
You're fired	You've got the chop	We're releasing you	You are surplus to requirements
I'm letting you go	You're being given your cards	Your services are no longer required	You're being thrown on the scrapheap

Some of these seem to avoid facing the unpleasant reality – 'we're downsizing' or 'we're letting you go' (as if you really wanted to leave anyway!). Such polite or evasive words and phrases are known as **euphemisms**. On the other hand, phrases such as 'being thrown on the scrapheap' or 'got the chop' seem to be designed to maximise the brutality and emotional shock. Such terms are known as **dysphemisms**.

Literal and figurative language

As the previous exercise has revealed, euphemisms and dysphemisms seldom use language literally, and often include colourful figures of speech and metaphors. So it is not just poets and writers of English literature who use similes and metaphors. On the contrary, ordinary everyday speech – and not just euphemisms or dysphemisms – is full of expressions which are not intended to be taken literally and which are based on metaphors. For example, some of the most common expressions to be heard at the moment include sayings derived from football, such as 'a level playing field', and 'moving the goalposts'.

The closer you look at everyday speech, the more of this metaphorical, or **figurative**, language you find.

ACTIVITY 33

(a) Many common expressions in everyday use are based on metaphors, but they are so familiar that we take them for granted. List – and look out for – examples of these two:

- using something 'high' to represent good, and something 'low' for bad – such as 'I'm on cloud nine', 'She's down in the dumps'

- representing life is a journey – such as 'You're on the right track', 'He's gone off the rails', 'What's the next step?'.

(b) Sometimes the use or accidental misuse of literal and figurative senses can be comical. Here, for example, are some quotations attributed to sports commentators in the collection of gaffes known as *Colemanballs*.

For each of them, explain how the humour arises in terms of literal and figurative meanings.

'Colemanball'	Comment
'He says he'll walk away from the game when his legs go.' (Anon)	
'And Seaman, just like a falling oak, manages to change direction.' (Attributed to John Motson)	
'Dean Headley has left the field with a back injury . . . more news on that as soon as it breaks.' (Attributed to Pat Murphy)	

What we really mean: pragmatics

We have begun to see that the meanings people attitubute to language are not always predictable from looking at the surface meaning of words. We have also seen that there may be many different ways of conveying similar meanings. What's more, even relatively innocent-seeming conversations about the weather, or your favourite music, or what you did at the weekend, may have a 'hidden agenda', or as actors and drama students might call it, a **sub-text**. The study of the meanings people actually intend and understand is called **pragmatics**.

ACTIVITY 34

(a) Let's look again at the transcript of the interview between teacher and student which we met on page 28. Alongside the text below are some prompt questions relating to the possible sub-text, or pragmatic meanings, implied by the situation. Answer the questions, and try re-creating the scene according to the answers you suggest.

Text	Possible sub-text
T: right Gemma (.) let's have a look (.) how far have you actually got	Could the teacher be implying some criticism of the student here with her question and the word 'actually'?
S: well (.) I understood all about (.) you know (.) what we did in class T: you mean the analysis we did of the speech	Does the student answer the question directly? If not, why not? Could she be anxious not to appear 'thick'?

Text	Possible sub-text
S: yeah (.) but (.) but I <u>can't seem to do it</u> with the homework	Why doesn't she just say 'I can't do it'? Or could the student just be using 'can't seem to' as an excuse for not having done the work?
T: OK (2) have you got the framework (.) you know the questions we were using S: yeah (5)	Does the teacher accept that the student has a problem? Or could she suspect this is just an excuse? Would this be reflected in how she says this?
T: so first you need to read the whole of the passage OK S: yeah T: then start to ask yourself some (.) the questions on the sheet	How patient is the teacher? How far will her paralinguistic and prosodic features convey her real feelings about the student and the situation?

(b) To observe pragmatics in action, try role-playing the following situation in groups of three, with A and B as participants and C an observer.

Student A: You had an argument with Student B yesterday, and you wish to make up. You want to be friends again, and you believe that the argument was just a 'blip'. You see Student B working and decide to use the excuse of wishing to borrow a set of notes for a lesson you missed, in order to make contact.

Student B: You had an argument yesterday with Student A, whom you have always privately disliked. As you see him/her approach, your stomach churns – you just don't want to know. You will be reasonably polite.

Both A and B: You must not refer directly to the argument you had, or to any aspect of your relationship. Confine yourself to discussing the question of the lesson missed, and the borrowing of notes.

Student C: Observe to see how the sub-text, or pragmatic meanings, of this apparently ordinary interaction are shown.

Putting it all together
Stylistic analysis of texts

In the Unit 1 examination, the second task on the paper asks you to analyse in some detail the use of language in three of the texts you are given. The question is usually phrased in such a way as to ensure that one of these texts will always be a piece of spoken language.

This task requires you to apply the linguistic knowledge you have gained so far to the analysis of the texts by:

- **selecting** their distinctive features for discussion – you won't have time to discuss every detail of the texts

- applying **some** of the language frameworks to each text – not all the language frameworks will be relevant or useful to any one text

- using the appropriate linguistic **terminology**

- relating the stylistic features of the texts to their **contexts** (where, why and when they were produced).

The basic question is, as always:

How does this text use language and how is this related to the context in which it was produced?

ACTIVITY 35   C3.3

This is an approach which you should be able to apply to most of the short texts you are likely to meet in the exam. We will use text C (*Monty Python's Flying Circus*) from Activity 19 (see page 28) as an example.

Step	Example
First reading: During your first reading of the text, try to answer these basic questions, jotting down your responses in rough: • Who is its audience? • What is the text saying to its audience? • What is the text doing to its audience? • What, in general terms, do you think is the intended impact of the text on its audience?	This text has several audiences. At first, the audience was the actors and director who would enact it as a performance. Then its audience included all the original viewers of the programme. Now, in published script form, its audience may be people simply reading it as a text. The text is clearly designed to entertain and amuse the viewers/readers, but some parts of it are designed to instruct the technical director where to point the camera.
Select and apply the frameworks: How does this text use language? Decide which of the frameworks is most useful for this text: Discourse? Pragmatics? Grammar? Phonology? Lexis? Semantics?	On the page there are two types of text – dialogue and stage directions. It may be useful to comment on how these are distinguished lexically, graphologically and grammatically. Most of the humour results from the style of language used (register, lexis) and the plays on words and meanings (semantics and pragmatics). It is a parody of a certain kind of discourse (TV political programme).

Writing your analysis: now write up your analysis. It's good to start with a very brief summary of your answers to the 'what?' questions. You can comment on the text bit by bit as you go along, but it may be better to use the framework as a way of organising your analysis into five sections.

Remember: keep relating the features you describe to the **context** of the text.

See the commentary on page 76.

Analysing spoken texts

One of the texts you analyse in the second part of the Unit 1 examination will be the transcript of an example of speech. You can apply a similar approach to the analysis of transcripts, provided you also remember to apply, where relevant, the discoveries you have made about the nature of spoken language.

ACTIVITY 36

Let's consider text E, the rugby commentary, which we first looked at on page 29. Use the prompts below to start to focus on how language is used in this extract, before writing up your analysis as in activity 35.

Context:

- What are the functions of this kind of radio commentary?

- How might it differ from a TV equivalent?

- What can the speaker take for granted in his audience?

- In what ways would prosodic features be important in the delivery of this commentary?

Commentator A: A great attacking position for England now (.) Dawson gets the ball spins it out (.) to Wilkinson (.) missed pass out to Greenwood (.) and he tries he beats the first tackle he's held up five metres from the line (.) England drive over the white jerseys are all there (.) out to Cohen who's on the right wing although he's the left wing (.) he's held up one metre from the line now the ball comes back (.) Dawson from the (.) right touchline out to Wilkinson swinging across (.) Grewcock in midfield drives (.) England'll get a penalty at worst

What kind of 'sentences' are these?

List the verbs used. How often? How fast? Which tense? Which semantic field?

How does he avoid repeating 'England'?

Overall, which lexical items seem to assume that listeners have at least a basic understanding of rugby?

How often does the speaker pause at sentence boundaries?

anyway the referee (.) blows the whistle awards the penalty to England (.) back by the touchline (.) and good play indeed (.) by the English forwards

Commentator B: Yes they're certainly taking an upper hand in this area they got that line out right Matt Dawson was so (.) he I don't think he'll oh he will take /

Commentator A: / oh he takes a short kick and oh he (.) th (.) Lomu touches it down but there was a body check there

→ At what points in a sentence *does* he pause?

What proportion of the text consists of proper nouns? Relate this to the text's context and function.

→ Here we move from description/ narration to evaluation. How does the brief break in play affect the kinds of thing the commentator(s) can say?

→ What seems to be the function of Commentator B?

Why does A feel he needs to interrupt?

Analysis of conversation

The most interesting thing about talk is how we interact as social beings. After all, we use language not just to exchange information but also to negotiate our social relationships.

We have already explored ways in which the **discourse structures** of certain conversational situations typically follow a recognisable pattern. For instance, an encounter with friends may start with a greeting and some small talk, move to anecdotes about what you've each been doing, and end with excuses for leave-taking ('Well, must be going . . .', etc.) followed by repeated 'bye', 'see you', 'take care', 'be in touch', or other similar phrases (see page 36 above).

| **ACTIVITY 37** | **C3.1a** |

We need also to consider the factors that determine the ways people talk to each other in a particular situation. In groups, discuss how each of the following factors might influence the part you play in a conversation, and the vocabulary, expressions, tone of voice and accent you use. Take into account the cultural expectations that would apply to each:

- the **place** where a conversation occurs (at home, in class, at a party, in church, at the workplace . . .)

- who else is present (friends, family, teachers, workmates, boss . . .) and your **relationship** with them

- the **purpose** of the conversation (social chat, job interview, buying/selling, asking a favour . . .)

Now compare your responses with the commentary on page 77.

A framework for analysing talk

We have already applied a systematic method to the stylistic analysis of a written text (see pages 33–35). Now let's try something similar for speech, but starting from a slightly different set of questions:

Key question	Explanation
Who seems to lead the talk?	This means looking closely at how the talk moves on as each speaker takes their turn. These alternating turns are referred to as **adjacency pairs**. In some situations, the pattern may be obvious – a teacher or a police officer may ask all the questions, for example.
Who says what gets talked about?	The ability to influence the subject or **agenda** of a conversation is usually a sign of personal status or dominance. In formal talk, the agenda and who controls it (or **topic management**, as this aspect of talk is known) may be obvious; in informal situations, where may topics may be covered, we need to look more closely at whose subjects get talked about and whose don't.
Who talks most?	Always a key question, but the answer to this question will not always lead us to the dominant speaker. Sometimes, the most powerful person needs to say very little.
Who interrupts? Who backs down?	This is usually an interesting question. If someone is easily interrupted this may be a sign of low status, whereas the right to speak uninterrupted is often an indicator of conversational dominance.
Who gets to comment on what people say?	In classrooms, teachers routinely say in response to students 'Good answer', 'Well done', or 'That's right' (or their opposites). However, when a teacher asks a particularly searching question, students seldom say 'Good question, sir/miss'. The right to make judgements about what other people say is often a sign of status or power.
What are people trying to do to other speakers? . . . Or, what do people really mean?	As we have seen (see 'Semantics and pragmatics', pages 51–55 above), we do not always say exactly what we mean, or

Key question	Explanation
	mean exactly what we say. What seem to be the actual meanings either intended, or understood, by the participants in the conversation? What is being implied? What is the **sub-text**?

ACTIVITY 38

(a) To put this framework for analysing conversations into practice, we'll look closely at the piece of spontaneous speech we saw earlier as text F (page 12). It was recorded from a late-night radio phone-in.

Re-read the transcript with this first, basic question in mind: *What do you notice about the way this conversation works and the language used by each speaker?*

Then re-read the data, applying each of the questions in our framework.

(b) Compare your notes with those made by a student, reprinted in the commentary on page 77.

(c) Now try analysing text B, the conversation between a teacher and her student printed on page 28, in a similar way.

We will return to more analysis of talk and pragmatics in Module 2, Language and Social Contexts (see page 79).

Preparing for the examination: Task 2, stylistic analysis

Having spent half of your time on the grouping and classifying task (Task 1) you will have just 45 minutes left to demonstrate your skills of stylistics analysis. In that time you have to choose **three** of the given extracts (one of which must be a spoken text) and write a brief but detailed analysis of them, identifying their distinctive linguistic features and relating these to the contexts of their production and reception.

Here are some key points to remember:

- Judge your time carefully. You can afford to spend only about 15 minutes on each text.

- Write clear, precise English and use the appropriate linguistic terminology to define precisely the language features in front of you. This fulfils Assessment Objective AO1.

- **Don't** just note features mechanically. **Always** try to relate the specific stylistic feature to some aspect of its context (who, why, where and when).

- **Don't** make negative points (e.g. 'there are no questions in this text') unless there is something really unusual about them.

- **Don't** try to apply every framework (discourse, grammar, lexis, etc.) to every text. There isn't time and not all the frameworks are always relevant. Select the most interesting aspects of language to discuss in each case.

- For higher grades, **do** make sure you discuss some of the more 'difficult' frameworks – discourse structure, grammar or pragmatics – in relation to at least one of your texts. Answers which are limited to lexical and grammatical features tend not to receive the highest marks.

Do you know your language terms?

ACTIVITY 39

Test your knowledge of some of the basic linguistic concepts and terms introduced in this module by completing the following passage, inserting the appropriate words. Check your answers on page 78.

We began by exploring the varieties of language all around us. One way of classifying these is by purpose: for the purposes of the Original Writing part of the course we considered four of these – to entertain, to inform, to instruct and to [1] _____. We discovered, of course, that many kinds of writing and speech do not fit easily into this simple categorisation.

There are many other ways of classifying language use. One is to define whether the text is in the spoken or written [2] _____, but even here, some kinds of language (like texting, or chatrooms) embody characteristics of both. Some uses of language can be distinguished in terms of their formality. Of course, we have to be careful not just to assume that language is either 'formal' or 'informal'. There is a whole spectrum of formality, moving from the most vulgar language considered to be unacceptable or forbidden ([3] _____), through to the kind of unofficial, colourful language which is used throughout the country but is not regarded as 'proper' English ([4] _____), to the variety of English vocabulary and grammar accepted as 'correct' ([5] _____) in its 'neutral', formal and highly formal forms. In this way we can define what we call the [6] _____ of a text. This may also refer to the words, or [7] _____, which relate to a specific topic area or subject. We may also come across the language varieties of different regions of the country. We distinguish between the pronunciation that is part of regional speech by calling it an [8] _____, whereas the words and

grammar which distinguish this from Standard English we define as
[9] _____. It is often interesting to consider texts as examples of
distinctive kinds of language use which have recognisable features or
conventions ([10] _____), and it is always important to bear in mind the
readers or listeners for whom the text is being produced – in other words, the
[11] _____.

When we start to analyse precisely the distinctive style of a text, we need to
consider a number of different aspects of language, and use a number of
different [12] _____. We can consider, for example, the way a piece of
language is organised and constructed; how it begins and ends, and what
happens in the middle. Here we are analysing text at the level of
[13] _____. Then, for written language, there is the physical presentation
of the text on the page, or [14] _____.

The study of grammar usually consists of two areas; the way that sentences are
constructed and words arranged in a particular order is covered by
[15] _____, and the way that words are formed, and the changes we
make to them according to their job in a particular sentence, is a matter of
[16] _____.

For example, we say 'I write' but 'she writes' according to whether we use the
[17] _____ or [18] _____ person of the verb. We can also think
about the kinds of sentences used. One way of classifying different sentences
is to define their function. Some sentences ask questions ([19] _____),
others give commands ([20] _____), others simply present statements
([21] _____), while some are outbursts or comments ([22] _____).
Some sentences, in fact, are not really sentences at all by the usual definition,
but may consist of only one or two words. Such sentences are called
[23] _____. sentences. Different kinds of texts may have different
proportions of each type of sentences.

In the past, people used to talk about 'parts of speech', whereas nowadays we
refer to word classes. Words like *pen, grass, automobile, disagreement* and
David Beckham are all [24] _____. We can subdivide this big class: *pen,
grass* and *automobile* are all objects in the real world, so they are known as
[25] _____. *David Beckham* is the name given to a well-known person, so
this is a [26] _____, whereas *disagreement* is an idea or feeling – in other
words, an [27] _____. Then there are so called 'describing words', which
are usually attached to these to provide different kinds of information. These may
describe colours, or qualities, or factual details – they are all [28] _____.

Traditionally, the definition of a [29] _____ is a 'doing' word. However, this is misleading; the most common one is 'is' or 'be', followed by 'have', and many of these words describe states or feelings rather than actions. Extra information about these words is given by [30] _____, which will tell us something about how, where or when this is going on. These, then, are the four principal word classes, but of course there are others: words like *I, you, he, him* and *she* ([31] _____), words like *with, and, but, because* and *so* ([32] _____) and words like *on, in, under, beyond* and *after* ([33] _____).

Breaking language down even further can lead us to think about the sounds of English – this is the study of [34] _____. English is made of 44 basic vowel and consonant sounds called [35] _____. However, when we talk we usually don't just depend on these, as our gestures, eye contact and body language (or [36] _____ features) and our intonation, speed of speaking and the ways we stress our words ([37] _____ features), all play an important part in communication. This is why so much speech seems to be less meaningful if you are not present when and where it is spoken – in other words, it tends to be [38] _____ – _____.

We have also looked at how words themselves convey meanings. The study of this aspect of language is called [39] _____. The meanings of words are complex; two words in a similar [40] _____ field may appear to have similar meanings or be [41] _____ of each other, but the chances are that even though they may share a similar denotation (*house* and *home* can both refer to the building in which you live), they clearly have different feelings and ideas associated with them – in other words, they have different [42] _____. One of the most interesting topics here is the difference between language that means exactly what it says, used literally, and language that works like a kind of metaphor – in other words [43] _____ language. We don't always say exactly what we mean in English; we might sometimes say we are going to powder our nose when we mean something else (that is, use a [44] _____). At other times, we might create coarse humour by being more blunt than is usually polite, which is a [45] _____. Indeed, in many contexts, the meanings we intend, or the meanings people understand, may not be immediately obvious just by looking at the words they use. There may sometimes be a hidden meaning or intention – what drama students and actors might call a sub-text – to the most innocent uses of language. The study of this area of language is known as [46] _____.

Commentaries

Activity 1

A: There are many reasons why there is so much variation in English. If we go back over a thousand years or more, 'English' was not a single language but included a number of related German dialects brought to this country by invaders from the region of present-day Germany (you will study this aspect of English next year, for Module 6, Language Development). These ancient differences produced many local variations, and until the twentieth century many local communities and their **dialects** remained relatively isolated. Even today, communities may take pride in retaining distinctive voices that express their character and identity – this is the subject of one of the sections in Module 2, Language and Social Contexts ('Dialects of the British Isles'). It is true that the version of English used in the media and taught in schools (**Standard English**) is often seen as 'correct', but this can be a controversial issue, as we'll discover later.

B: Speech certainly comes before writing in children's language learning, as it has throughout the history of human society. Spoken language is fundamental to our personal and social lives, yet in our society it often seems to be valued less (by our educational and examination systems, for example) than writing. However, although traditional English courses have often been based on the study of literature and the printed word, your AS/A level English Language course pays at least equal attention to the various forms of talk. You will study speech and writing throughout the course, and the relationship between the two is an important aspect of Module 1, Introduction to the Study of Language.

C & D: The situation described by Ayumi in text C is one that we all recognise. Each social situation we find ourselves in tends to produce its own distinctive forms of language. As we move from one place to another and assume different roles, we adopt the language of the particular social group to which we belong.

Nevertheless, as individuals we may still retain our personal linguistic 'fingerprints', so the science fiction scenario suggested in text D is really not as far-fetched as you might imagine. Although skilled performers like Rory Bremner can produce striking impressions of individuals' voices, the precise combination of tone, pitch, volume and expression that make up an individual's speech can be as distinctive as a fingerprint (see the discussion of **idiolect** on page 6). Furthermore, we have individually distinctive features in our writing, too. The science of **forensic linguistics** has enabled the identity of texts to be established in law, leading to confirmation of the authorship of anonymous letters or poems, and even to the conviction of criminals on the basis of their writing.

E: There is no doubt that every language continually changes, just as the people and the societies that use it continue to evolve. It is easy to see how such changes – for example the development of technology – can bring about changes in vocabulary, but English has developed in many other ways too. As Kibria's question indicates, when we look at old written texts we notice all the *thee's*, *thou's* and strange word order, and see that the **grammar** of English has changed in some ways; and when you hear old BBC news broadcasts or the soundtracks of old films you know that even pronunciation seems to have changed. This kind of change does not happen as a result of someone making a decree or passing a law; however, people who have influence, power or authority in society may be more likely to affect the process of language change. This topic is one of the two major areas covered by Module 6, Language Development.

F: Janet's experience of learning languages is certainly not unusual; most of us find learning a second language far more difficult than acquiring our own mother tongue. This is because we are seldom in the position of infants, totally immersed in the language; neither do we have the same motivation to learn. As children, learning to communicate is vital to our every need. Besides, many British people are deterred from learning a second language by the widespread use of English across the world. It also seems to be true that our receptiveness to new languages and our ability to learn them decline as we grow older. You will study language acquisition in depth as part of Module 6, Language Development.

Activity 2

You will probably have recorded a wide variety of language usage under each of the four quadrants. In practice, of course, speaking and listening tend to overlap in many situations, but you should still have been able to identify plenty of different contexts for each of the four language activities. Of course, there is no single best way of classifying language in use. In this exercise, you may have decided to categorise according to the purpose or **function** of language in a given situation (exchanging information, asking questions . . .), the nature of the situation itself (formal or informal, family/school/workplace . . .) or the language **medium** (phone, Internet . . .). You might also have considered the **style** of language you would actually use (for example slang, polite, etc.). These are just some of the many valid ways of classifying language – we will go on to consider others, and to collect these types of classifications systematically.

Activity 4

Your parents – or anyone else closely involved in your upbringing – were your earliest and, for much of your pre-school life, your main influences. They provided you with much of the 'data' on which you based your earliest guesses at how English works. You probably imitated not just the words and phrases you heard them use, but also their **intonation** patterns and accents. At an early stage, you may also have learned notions of what was acceptable or unacceptable usage in terms of 'good' or 'bad' English, or swear-words considered **taboo**. However, once you started going to school, the linguistic influence of your parents and family probably diminished steadily as they competed with many other and increasingly powerful factors in your life. In your A2 course, you will go on to study in some detail the processes of early language acquisition and the role that parents have in this.

More controversial is the question of how your general **social background** or **class** may have affected your language. There does seem to be a relationship between your social class and some aspects of language use (e.g. accent), and in the past some researchers have suggested that pupils from poorer backgrounds have more restricted language use. However, this is a highly controversial area. Similarly, the question of **gender** has been the subject of much recent interest, with some research indicating differences between the way men and women use language. These are topics which you will study in more depth in Module 2, Language and Social Contexts.

Your education will certainly have had a major influence on your language development, introducing you to many new words and encouraging you to develop your language skills throughout your educational career. Teachers may also have been strong influences in developing your sense of what is 'correct' or 'acceptable' English – though despite years of such influence, outside the classroom you probably still use language in ways they may disapprove of! More generally, your encounters with different subjects and ideas will certainly have contributed hugely to the expansion of your language.

However, in school, the linguistic influence of groups of **friends** is soon likely to outstrip that of either parents or teachers. Your need to be accepted by your peers is likely to have led you to use similar speech to the friends you most wish to be like – so your accent may have become more like your friends' than your parents', and your speech may have begun to include the playground **slang** or swear-words that parents and teachers tried in vain to discourage. Some groups may develop slang words unique to them, or share particular catch-phrases which become 'buzz words'.

The **places** where you lived may have influenced you in ways that you were entirely unaware of at the time. The most obvious aspect of your speech, one that may reveal your geographical origins, is your **accent**; this term is used to describe the way you pronounce the sounds of English, and the distinctive **intonation** patterns that accompany your speech. You may also use words, phrases and unusual grammatical constructions characteristic of a region, collectively known as **dialect.** If you have moved from one place to another you may have adjusted your speech, consciously or unconsciously, to fit in with your new surroundings and, as a result, significantly changed your accent/dialect.

TV, music and other **media** no doubt became an increasing influence as you got older. Phrases adopted from the Australian English of *Neighbours*, or the street slang of 'gangsta rap', may have started to feature in the vocabulary of you and your friends. This is likely to affect accent and grammar, too; phrases borrowed from such sources may include non-standard constructions and pronunciations.

As you grow older, you encounter a new set of linguistic influences when you enter the world of **work**. The way you are obliged to use language when serving burgers, selling shoes or talking with fellow workers on a building site may involve you with a kind of **jargon**, a different kind of slang, or speaking in an accent slightly different from your usual one. To start with, this influence may not extend far beyond your workplace, but as adult life progresses it is likely to have an increasingly strong effect on your individual language use.

Activity 5

Your **family** may well have some words which are used in ways that outsiders might not recognise, perhaps because they arose from incidents in the past or other aspects of family life. Many families have rituals that involve certain phrases being said at certain times (such as birthdays and Christmas). Everyone's examples will be different.

Your immediate group of **friends** may have certain favourite 'buzz words' or slang, or use swear-words in particular ways. You may be influenced by catch-phrases from favourite films, TV programmes or music, which you subsequently introduce into your conversation. There may even be a favoured accent – and newcomers to the group may end up altering their speech in this direction in order to fit in.

People who live in your **town or region** will share some aspects of accent and pronunciation, as well as some dialect vocabulary and non-standard English grammatical constructions. People who share a particular interest and people who do the same job are most likely to share a specialist vocabulary or technical **jargon** that is specific to the interest or job.

People from the same **social background** may also share some linguistic features. The relationship between the **social class** we belong to and the accent, dialect and style of our speech is a complex and often controversial one which is covered in more detail in Module 2, Language and Social Contexts. In general, people from working-class backgrounds do tend to use a higher proportion of regional accent/dialect features than those from professional or middle-class backgrounds.

People who like the same kind of **music** may also share a common language, not only because of references to the bands and music itself but because different styles of music (dance, metal, indie, etc.) are part of a wider **subculture** characterised by distinctive uses of language. Even people who support the same **sports team** often form close-knit groups; the language they use, such as the banter and chanting of a football crowd or the written language of fanzines, helps to cement this tribal solidarity.

Activity 7

The extracts are:

A: Transcript of a recording made during an English lesson in a secondary school.

B: Transcript of a Tyneside speaker reminiscing about his childhood in conversation with his granddaughter of 17.

C: The evidence of an eye witness given to the US enquiry into the sinking of the *Titanic* in 1912.

D: Extract from 'The Passionate Shepherd to his Love', a poem by Christopher Marlowe, written in the late sixteenth century.

E: Extract from T. Burrows, *Creating Presentations*, published by Dorling Kindersley.

F: Transcript of a radio phone-in programme.

G: Extract from 'The Jumblies' by Edward Lear, 1871.

H: Quoted from a speech attributed to John Ball, co-leader of the Peasants' Revolt, 1381.

I: Quoted from *Sons and Lovers* by D. H. Lawrence, 1913.

J: Extract from *The BFG* by Roald Dahl, 1982.

How you decided to group sets of texts will have depended on which aspects you chose to focus on – and of course, there are many possible ways of doing this. The table below exemplifies some of these; note especially the **key concepts and terms** used to define each category.

Linked texts	Group title	Features in common	Key concept /term
C & G	Disastrous sea voyages	Both texts are about sea voyages which end badly! Here we are thinking about the subject matter or **topic** of the texts	**topic**
A & E	Instructions	Both of these texts are designed to convey sets of instructions.	**purpose**
D & H	Persuasion	These texts, on the other hand, are designed to be persuasive. In both cases, we are focusing on the **purpose** or function of the texts to define them.	
D, G & H	Previous centuries	Although separated by roughly 500 years, you might still have linked these texts as belonging to an earlier **period** in the development of English as they include examples of language use not commonly found today.	**period**
A, B & F	Spontaneous speech	These texts are clearly transcripts of spontaneous spoken language.	**mode**
H, I & J	Scripted or fictional speech	These texts include either scripted or fictional representations of speech.	
C, D, E & G	Written texts	On the other hand, these texts seem to be examples of written language. In all three cases, we are focusing on whether the text is in speech, or writing – this is the **mode** of the text.	
A, B, G & J	Young audience	These texts seem to be directed at 'young', i.e. non-adult listeners or readers.	**audience**

Linked texts	Group title	Features in common	Key concept /term
		These texts seem to be directed at significant gatherings of people.	
A & H	Addressing a group of people	These are examples of one-to-one conversations.	
B & F	One-to-ones	In each case we are thinking here about the **audience** of the texts.	
B, G, I & J	Non-standard /regional language	These texts all include examples of language (either **slang** or **dialect**) which is not regarded as 'correct' Standard English. This is a question of the **variety** of English involved.	**variety**
C, D & H	Formal language	These texts all use language with quite a high level of formality – a matter of the **register** of the texts.	**register**
B, C, G, I & J	Stories/ narratives	These texts all tell stories of one sort or another.	**genre**
D & G	Verse/poetry	These texts are written in verse. Here we are classifying the texts according to their **genre**.	
E & J	Illustrations	These texts both use illustrations as well as words to communicate. In other words, we are looking at their lay-out and physical presentation on the page, or **graphology**.	**graphology**

Activity 8

Text	Problematic aspects
Text C: written record of testimony given to the *Titanic* enquiry	This is a record of witness testimony. The witness will obviously have spoken this but it is likely to have been planned, rehearsed or even written first. Then it has been recorded and written down as the official court record.
Text J: Extract from *The BFG*	Like text I, this is a written text which includes the representation of fictitious speech. As a story intended for children, it may also be received by some children as a story read aloud.

Text	Problematic aspects
A politician's speech	Few politicians will risk speaking 'off the cuff' without planning or preparation. Many speeches will be written – possibly by someone else! – and delivered via a script or an autocue.
A job interview	This is an apparently spontaneous conversation – but the questions posed by the interviewer are likely to have been planned and written down beforehand, and the answers by the interviewee may have been rehearsed.
An episode of *EastEnders*	Although we experience this as 'natural' speech, this is, of course, an illusion: these are actors who have memorised the words written down by scriptwriters.
A series of postings in an Internet chatroom	In one sense, this is writing – we communicate using written words – but in another, we behave as if it is speech and conversation.

Activity 9

Text	Multiple audiences and different meanings
Text D: 17th-century poem	Is the poem *really* intended to be for the poet's lover? If so, its other readers – us, and anyone else interested in poetry – are cast as eavesdroppers on an intimate moment. Of course, 21st-century readers may not have been in the poet's mind when he wrote the poem, but 17th-century ones probably were.
Text F: Transcript of a radio phone-in	Tanya was speaking to the DJ – but would also have been aware of the much wider audience listening to the show. This may have made her rather nervous, or certainly limited the kinds of thing she felt she could say.
Text J: Extract from *The BFG*	The audience for the story appears to be primarily children – but it is their parents who may initially skim through, select and buy the book, which they might not do if they considered it unsuitable. It may also be the adults who read the book to, or with, the child, and they may respond to it in a different way.
A women's magazine such as *Cosmopolitan*	Supposedly aimed at a female audience, many women's magazines attract casual male readers, whose interests and responses to what they read may be very different from the primary audience.

Activity 10

Text/language use	Purpose
Text B: transcript of Tyneside speaker	The speaker may be trying to amuse, or even educate (give information to) his granddaughter, though in the context of a language textbook, the purpose of the text may be to give an example of a specific regional dialect.
Text D: poem	On the face of it, the poem is persuading the poet's lover to be his 'love', but this may be a fiction, like a pop song; it is primarily to amuse or entertain its readers.
Text F: radio phone-in	The purposes of the different speakers are different; Tanya is presumably trying to amuse or entertain the DJ, while the DJ is hoping to use Tanya to entertain the audience. Perhaps Tanya is also giving information, but in the hope of some reward or a prize.
Text J: extract from *The BFG*	Stories like this are primarily to entertain and amuse children, but with many children's stories there may be a less obvious, more educational purpose or 'moral' behind the story.
A casual conversation with your friends	Do any of our four purposes really fit here? To 'amuse' is certainly one of the intentions, but perhaps the primary purpose is not covered by the purposes suggested – that is, simply to reinforce social relationships. As we shall see in Module 2, Language and Social Contexts, this is a vital function of language.
A TV documentary about wildlife	There may be several things going on here. Perhaps the primary purpose of the programme makers is to inform, but they know that if it is not also entertaining, few viewers will watch it. There may also be an underlying persuasive intent, if programme makers hope that viewers will be more likely to support animal charities or be sympathetic to animal welfare causes after watching the programme.
A tabloid news report about politics	It is debatable whether many tabloid news stories are primarily to inform or to entertain. Clearly they try to do both, but some types of story (e.g. politics) may have more of an informative content than others (e.g. scandal/showbiz stories). However, there may also be a subtle persuasive element, as the political bias of many papers is often reflected in the way they report political stories.

Activity 15

(b)

- Some features missing from the transcript are the speaker's facial expressions, hand gestures and body language (these physical aspects, which contribute to the meanings of speech, are called **paralinguistic features**). Also missing are the actual sound and tone of her voice (this includes the way her voice moves up and down as she speaks – the **intonation**), the stress placed on particular words, and the tempo of the speech. These aspects of the way our voices and manner of speaking add to our meanings are referred to as **prosodic features**. Their absence makes it difficult to judge the speaker's mood, attitude and feelings about the events she describes.

- The elements of the spoken account most obviously missing from the written statement are the hesitations and **fillers** that occur in spontaneous speech. These may be verbal ('you know', 'like') or non-verbal ('er', 'um'). The written statement also avoids the digressions (the witness's dog-walking) that appear in the spoken version.

- The spoken version seems to consist of long continuous sentences that include breath pauses and the words 'and' and 'so'. These are called **compound sentences**. Sentence boundaries are generally less clear in speech – it is not always easy to say when one sentence stops and the next starts – so it is usual to indicate pauses in transcriptions using (.) instead of conventional punctuation.

- The inexplicit or **deictic references** work in speech because the speaker and the listener both have knowledge of the places referred to. This is often a significant aspect of speech – many of its meanings are closely tied up with the context in which the words are spoken. Thus we refer to meanings which are **context-bound**. In writing we cannot expect our readers to share the same context, so our meanings need to be explicit and **context-free**.

- In her spoken account, the speaker tends to sensationalise events, describing the car as 'racing' and the smoke as 'pouring'. At some points, the speaker uses the present tense – 'this car comes racing down', 'so I turn around and there's black smoke pouring out' – even though the events are in the past. This is a common feature of spoken narratives – it is as if the speaker is bringing events alive by re-enacting them in the present.

- The spoken version contains an example of regional, non-standard grammar ('them shops') and several colloquial expressions like 'bloody great crash' which have been replaced in the written version, making it generally more formal and precise.

Activity 16

1 You might be able to apply some kinds of punctuation quite easily – such as marking questions with a question mark. You may decide to use commas to mark some of the pauses in your speech, but these do not necessarily occur at the places you would normally use commas in writing (between clauses). The major problem is likely to be deciding where sentences begin and end (**sentence boundaries**). In speech, we may produce either long, rambling sentences loosely connected by 'and', but', 'so', etc., or very short utterances which don't constitute sentences at all.

2 You may identify the English spelling system as an obvious source of difficulty because it is not a consistent representation of the sounds of the language. As adult writers, you may also take lots of things for granted which you once had to learn – such as the alternative forms of upper and lower case letters, and the fact that we write from left to right and top to bottom. It also follows from the discussion above that learning to construct acceptable sentences and punctuate them is a major challenge.

3 *Question:* Most people report that it is easier to be deceptive in writing, because you can control everything you put down on paper. Speaking face-to-face, too many of those tell-tale paralinguistic features seem to be beyond your control – avoidance of eye-contact, nervous fidgeting or sweating palms may give you away.

Problem: All writers make some assumptions about their readers. A note you leave for the milkman – 'None today please' – may mean very little if transplanted from the doorstep where you left it, and the meanings of texts written in the past may be so rooted in the times they were produced that they have little meaning for us today.

4 *Question*: In situations where they are nervous, or where their words are likely to be given extreme attention – a speech at a friend's wedding, for example – many people prefer to have the security of a written script, which they have prepared and edited.

Problem: Even when you cannot easily have a script with you, it may be that you have mentally 'rehearsed' what you are going to say – when making an apology, or a difficult request, or breaking some bad news, for example. On the other hand, many people seem to be much less careful about checking text messages and e-mails for errors, treating them almost like a form of spontaneous speech.

5 *Question*: There are many different contexts in which we need to keep records – notes in a class, details of financial transactions, and so on. In these situations writing is vital. Writing also enables us to pass on knowledge to others, preventing us from having to re-invent and re-discover things every generation!

Problem: Many texts such as tickets, wrappers and packaging, text messages and even e-mails are not designed to be kept for long; on the other hand, anyone who has to make a speech or be interviewed in the presence of a journalist or a tape recorder may be aware that their spoken words may achieve some kind of permanence.

Activity 18

Pronunciation. It is difficult to tell from a transcript exactly how a speaker sounds. On the basis of the imperfect information presented here, you would probably note the shortened *mi* for 'my' and some extended vowel sounds (*waar* for 'war' and *weel* for 'well'). He also pronounces 'no' more like the Scottish 'nae'.

Vocabulary. The speaker's vocabulary includes a number of words we do not recognise as Standard English. Amongst these, 'bairn' is commonly used in the north of England and in Scotland for child; 'clarts' to mean mud is rather less common, and is restricted mainly to the north-east of England. 'Bourn' and 'beck' are two alternatives for small streams, while 'ket' in the north and east can refer to snacks or sweets. Oddly, the same word can also mean rubbish in parts of Cumbria and Yorkshire! 'Gan' for go is common throughout the north-east, whereas 'hoy' is rather more limited to the Tyne and Wear region. (*Source*: Upton, Sanderson and Widdowson, *Word Maps: A Dialect Atlas of England*, Croom Helm, 1987.)

Grammar. As far as grammar is concerned, you may have been surprised to find that the speaker generally uses Standard English constructions. The exceptions mainly concern the verb 'do' and its use in the formation of the question 'does tha want to know' (Standard English 'do you want to know') and the negative statement 'tha disn'y know'. There is also an example of what linguists call a **double negative** construction in the phrase 'we never had nowt' (Standard English 'we didn't have/never had anything') – a feature of many regional dialects – and a non-standard prepositional phrase in 'on a night' (Standard English 'at night').

Activity 19

One way of grouping the texts is according to their purpose or function. For example, text A and the teacher in B both appear, at first glance, to be giving instructions. Texts C, E, F, H and I seem to be giving or exchanging information, whereas texts D and G are both primarily persuasive. However, if we look more closely, this method of classifying the texts becomes problematic. For example, texts A and C may resemble instructive or informative texts but in fact are designed to create amusement and to entertain. Text E (the sports commentary) may be designed equally to entertain and to inform, just as the book review (text H) may be designed to influence, and therefore persuade, its readers.

Another way of looking at the texts is according to the time they were produced. Texts A and D are from the 19th/early 20th century, and this is reflected in several ways. We no longer measure foods by 'pecks' or 'bushels', and modern sensitivities may prevent people finding the references to the beating of a pig particularly funny. Fashions, too, have changed, and the style of the corset advert is very different from lingerie adverts of today.

We can also consider the audiences of the texts. Texts B and D are both directed specifically at a female audience, but whereas B is a one-to-one consultation, D is published in a newspaper and is thus aimed at a much wider readership.

Some other texts seem to assume that their audience understands the semi-specialised register which they use. For example:

A (cooking)
E (rugby union)
F (houses)
H (text messages).

However, some of the texts may have multiple audiences, each of which will respond differently to them. Text A, for example, may have been written originally to amuse Victorian children, but may now be read by adults curious about the work of the writer, Edward Lear. Text C was originally a script, intended first for actors to perform, then for a TV audience to see, and only later published for a different set of readers to read on the page.

The texts represent a wide variety of different genres. We have two adverts (D and G) but these are very different in terms of their contexts, intended audience and style. Texts B, C and E all seem to involve dialogues of two or more people, but they are also quite different. B and E are transcripts of spontaneous speech, though a commentary on national radio is clearly a very different genre from a private discussion between a teacher and student. Text C appears to be a dialogue but is, of course, a script written for performance. Something texts A and C have in common is that they both exploit recognisable conventions of their specific genres – recipes and political interviews – for comic effect.

Another way of linking the texts is acording to their mode. Obviously, in the form in which we see them now, all of them are written down. However, texts B and E are transcripts of spontaneous speech, the meanings of which would have depended not just on the words transcribed but also on prosodic, paralinguistic and contextual factors for their full impact on their listeners. Texts A, D, F and G on the other hand were designed and produced as written texts, with D, F and G including important graphological elements (either in terms of illustrations or layout) to help them convey their meanings. Other texts are more problematic; as already noted, C is a written text produced to be enacted as speech, whereas text I uses non-conventional spellings to create the illusion of the sounds of Yorkshire dialect, as if it were being spoken rather than written.

In terms of the varieties of English used, most of the texts use Standard English, though as we have already seen, texts A and D include words which may no longer be as commonly used as they once were. Texts H and I both differ from conventional Standard English. Text H is a new form of abbreviated language which emerged with the introduction of text-messaging technologies, whereas I represents a much older dialectal form of English that is rooted in the past. It may even be the case that text-messaging is a form used mainly by younger mobile phone users, whereas some regional dialect use is more confined to older speakers.

Activity 27

Example	Comment
You is not loving it?	In Standard English we would say 'Don't you love it?' or perhaps 'You don't like it'. The giant is not changing the word order to make the statement into a question, and is using an inappropriate tense – the present tense ending in –ing (the present continuous, or **progressive** tense) would not be used with the verb love here.
The most disgusterous taste . . .	He means 'disgusting', but instead of using the ending –ing to form the adjective, he uses –erous. A similar ending is sometimes used for this purpose, of course, as in disastrous, numerous and dangerous.
. . . that is ever touching my teeth	Here, as in the first example, he uses the present continuous tense where in Standard English we would say has ever touched, a tense called the **present perfect**.

Activity 35

This text has several audiences. At first, the audience was the actors and director who would enact it as a performance. Then its audience included all the original viewers of the programme. Now, in published script form, its audience may be people reading it as a text. The text is clearly designed to entertain and amuse the viewers/readers, but some parts of it are designed to instruct the technical director where to point the camera. Overall, there may be another intention to mock politicians or the kinds of political discussion programmes on which they appear.

TV viewers will probably recognise the conventions of another type of TV programme, with its predictable format, title sequence and 'talking head' introducing the piece to camera. This is the typical discourse structure of serious political discussion programmes. The piece is funny because all of this looks and sounds serious, but what follows is not.

The words of the dialogue are distinguished graphologically from stage directions as they are presented in different styles of type (mainly italics), and also distinguished grammatically, as they are not in complete sentences (e.g. Cut to studio). They also include technical lexis which the director/cameraman would understand (cut, pan, etc.) but which the more general audience for the programme may not.

The humour of the piece partly comes from the register of one context – a fashion show – being used in an entirely different context – a serious political interview. Both of these registers are fairly formal, with their own specialised vocabulary. It is the juxtaposition of these two registers that is funny. We have 'Minister for Home Affairs' and 'views on contemporary things' clashing with 'a striking organza dress in pink tulle'. Both registers include fairly technical lexis (e.g. tulle) specific to their topic. The 'fashion' register uses many descriptive adjectives – striking, organza, brushed, gold, etc.

Much of the humour in the text can be discussed in terms of pragmatics and semantics. First, there is the huge contrast between the 88,000 million, billion houses promised and the three actually built; then the interviewer's polite question, 'Are you a bit disappointed?' seems to be very mild, as the intention of such a question would obviously be to completely ridicule the minister. Finally, the joke at the end of the text depends on the double-meaning of 'two ways'. Usually we expect that it means 'looking at it from two points of view' but it turns out that the minister means it literally, by changing his style of speaking.

Activity 37

Some **places** certainly seem to limit the range of roles you can take and the things you can say. You may have discussed the differences between the way you act in your own home and when visiting someone else's. As a 'host' in your own home, you may assume more of a leader's role with a group of friends; in church you are unlikely to feel it appropriate to tell a certain type of joke to the person next to you; at work, especially if you are involved with the public, you are likely to behave with more attention and respect towards complete strangers than you would in other situations.

However, when the question of where you are is combined with who you are with, and your **relationship** to those people, the limitations become even clearer. You may have thought about **gender** – how an all-male, all-female, or mixed company influences the way you talk. Equally interesting is the question of relative **status** – whether, in any particular situation, you seem to enjoy a dominant role (with younger brothers and sisters, or with friends, perhaps), whether you are more or less equal to your conversational partner, or whether the situation places you in a subordinate role (say, in the classroom, with parents or at work). In each case, the different role you play determines whether you ask questions, crack jokes, use formal or colloquial language, or make an effort to soften your natural regional accent in the interests of formality.

Where the **purpose** of talk is very clearly defined – for example, a customer buying a CD from a music shop – the exchange becomes very predictable. Interviewers ask questions to find the best person for the job, stand-up comedians tell jokes to make us laugh, and doctors ask us questions to diagnose an illness. We would be surprised if any of these people digressed from the style of language that their situation requires.

Activity 38

Student's notes

The talk begins with the DJ cueing in the caller. This places him 'in charge' of the interview. He also uses her first name, assuming some familiarity and informality, and an informal greeting. Tanya replies, using the same informal greeting, but allows the DJ to continue to take the lead with what sounds like a catch-phrase but is also her next cue. Tanya replies, echoing the DJ's words, coming straight to the point but with some hesitation – perhaps as a result of nervousness?

The DJ attempts to interrupt – a bit rude? Broadcasters often try to do this. But Tanya carries on. When she has finished, the DJ now succeeds in getting in his question. Humorous, informal use of 'lump'. Repeats 'Canada'.

Again, some hesitation from Tanya, before a straight reply. The 'lead' in the talk is the DJ. The DJ offers a comment on Tanya's answer – makes her feel good? Like a teacher? False start – personal comment to suggest has shared interest. Phrases next question.

Tanya offers agreement – supportive – but slightly overlaps, forcing the DJ to repeat part of question.

Activity 39

1	persuade	12	frameworks	24	nouns	36	paralinguistic
2	mode	13	discourse	25	concrete	37	prosodic
3	taboo	14	graphology	26	proper noun	38	context-bound/ dependent
4	slang	15	syntax	27	abstract noun	39	semantics
5	Standard English	16	morphology	28	adjectives	40	semantic
6	register	17	first	29	verb	41	synonyms
7	lexis	18	third	30	adverbs	42	connotations
8	accent	19	interrogatives	31	pronouns	43	figurative
9	dialect	20	imperatives	32	conjunctions	44	euphemism
10	genre	21	declaratives	33	prepositions	45	dysphemism
11	audience	22	exclamations	34	phonology	46	pragmatics
		23	minor	35	phonemes		

MODULE 2 Language and Social Contexts

This module counts for **35%** of the AS qualification, or **17$\frac{1}{2}$%** of the total A Level marks.

ASSESSMENT OBJECTIVES

The skills and knowledge you develop in this module, which will be tested in the examination you take at the end of it, are defined by the examination board's Assessment Objectives. These require that you:

- **AO1**: communicate clearly the knowledge, understanding and insight appropriate to the study of language, using appropriate terminology and accurate and coherent written expression
  (5 out of the 35 marks for the Unit; 5% of the final AS mark; 2$\frac{1}{2}$% of the final A Level mark)

- **AO3**: know and use key features of frameworks for the systematic study of spoken and written English
  (10 out of the 35 marks for the Unit; 10% of the final AS mark; 5% of the final A Level mark)

- **AO4**: understand, discuss and explore concepts and issues relating to language in use
  (10 out of the 35 marks for the Unit; 10% of the final AS mark; 5% of the final A Level mark)

- **AO5**: distinguish, describe and interpret variation in the meanings and forms of spoken and written language according to context
  (10 out of the 35 marks for the Unit; 10% of the final AS mark; 5% of the final A Level mark)

What this module is all about

Links with Module 1

In the previous unit, you started to understand the variations in the ways that English is used all around us. You also learned that there are different ways of describing and analysing language use, and began to apply a number of analytical frameworks to this task. These methods of analysis are the basic tools which you will continue to use as you extend your explorations of language throughout both the AS and A2 English Language courses.

As you study this module you will often need to review the relevant material first covered in Module 1, as indicated by the symbol

In particular, we will continue to use the following key concepts and frameworks to explore how social context affects language use:

graphology: all aspects of the visual appearance and presentation of written texts

discourse: the ways in which the content of a text is structured and organised

lexis: the range of vocabulary available to speakers of a language

grammar: all aspects of the structures and functions of a language

phonology: the vocal aspects of language, such as intonation, rhythm, pace, volume and stress in spoken English

semantics: the ways in which meanings are communicated in language

pragmatics: the ways in which social messages/relations and implied meanings are conveyed in language.

What's new about Module 2?

Social contexts

The emphasis in Module 2 is even more strongly on the social contexts of language – how our uses of language are related to the way we live our lives and develop relationships with others. To look more closely at this relationship, we will focus on a number of specific themes prescribed by the examination board; in each case, you will still be developing your skills of linguistic analysis and description of individual texts (both spoken and written), but you will be doing so in relation to the ideas and research about language that already exist.

The main theme of Module 2 is that the meanings of a spoken or written text can be understood only by fully considering the social contexts in which it is produced. This means thinking about:

- *who* produces it – in terms of identity, role, status and position in society

- *why* it has been produced – in terms of the intended (and sometimes unintended) meanings it has, and the purpose(s) the writers/speakers bring to the text

- the *relationship* between the author/producer and the receiver/audience, their relative status and power, and their attitudes towards each other

- the *place and time* in which it was produced.

In this area of language studies we try to answer a basic but far-reaching question: how does our use of language reflect the way we live in our society?

Ideas from language study, investigation and research

If you look closely at the weighting of the different Assessment Objectives for Modules 1 and 2, you will see that Ao4 – 'understand, discuss and explore concepts and issues relating to language in use' – carries more weight in this module. In order to fulfil this objective in this module you will need to:

- explore a variety of language data in the light of existing ideas and research

- recognise some of the difficulties and limitations in language research

- become familiar with some of the most important ideas involved in this research and carry out some small research projects of your own

- be open-minded in applying these ideas and theories to new data.

We have already introduced the idea of becoming a kind of language *scientist*: that is to say, gathering 'specimens' of data, examining them closely, and trying to explain how they 'work'. But scientists do not work at random, or in a vacuum; they usually set out to answer a specific question, or test a theory which other scientists have proposed. They do this by taking care to collect appropriate samples of data and carry out analysis. Sometimes their findings confirm what others have thought, and sometimes scientists make a discovery that appears to contradict the established theories. In either case, they approach their data with an open mind.

A note on using ideas from language study and research

The questions on the Unit 2 examination paper will present you with texts/data for analysis, and may ask you to 'refer to any ideas from language study and research'. 'Research' comes in two varieties:

- *Primary* research includes the systematic gathering and analysis of language data by yourself and your fellow students.

- *Secondary* research means looking at the research and theories of others, especially that which is published in text books or on the Internet.

It is important, throughout this module, to bear these points in mind:

- Approach published research with caution: much of it may be based on old research, in contexts very different from your own.

- Apply the appropriate analytical frameworks accurately – this remains a key Assessment Objective (AO3).

- Little credit is given in the exam for simply reproducing material from notes or text books.

- Credit *is* given for making relevant connections between the data in front of you, the ideas about language you have developed on the course and other investigations/research you have carried out or are aware of (AO4).

- Never try to make the data 'fit' any ideas you bring to it; always be open-minded.

The activities and material suggested in this module will help get you started; however, it is important that you pursue your studies well beyond the limits of this book – please note the suggestions for further research and reading.

After exploring some of the broad issues involved in this module, we will focus on three of the topics which are set (up to 2005) for the Unit 2 examination. You will be asked to answer questions on **two** of these topics in the unit examination:

- Language and Power • Language and Gender • Dialects of the British Isles.

Starting to explore

The next two Activities help you begin to ask the kinds of question you will be investigating later in the module.

ACTIVITY 1

We all vary our language according to the social context we are in at any one time. We can call this variation in an individual's use of language his or her **language repertoire**.

(a) Read the following brief pen portrait of Charlotte Johnson, aged 34.

Charlotte was brought up on the outskirts of Manchester and attended her local comprehensive school before studying Business at Birmingham University. Her parents have lived their lives in the north of England; her father was a factory worker, her mother a shop assistant. Eight years ago Charlotte married Ray, an accountant from Essex whom she met at University, and they now live in London with their twins Emma and Jack, aged seven. She is the Personnel Manager at a local retail computer and software store, which involves being part of the store management team and dealing with staff recruitment, training and appraisal. In her spare time she enjoys playing squash, and occasionally she manages to meet up with a couple of her old school friends who also live and work in London.

Discuss your responses to the following questions:

- How might the way Charlotte uses language (both speaking and writing) vary in the course of a typical week, according to context: at work, with her friends, with her parents, at home?

- What factors might influence these variations?

Compare your responses with the commentary on pages 124–5.

(b) Now let's consider how some data demonstrates the influence of social contexts on language in use.

First, remind yourself of the questions we used in Module 1 (pages 59–60) for analysing talk. Now apply these questions to the following transcript of a conversation. The caller (C), a 40-year-old male, is ringing the Customer Services department of a large company and, after being cut off once and then put on 'hold', has been put through to an employee (A) at the call centre.

Develop your analysis by suggesting the ways in which the following contextual factors may be influencing the way the two speakers are using language:

- the fact that it is a telephone, rather than face-to-face, conversation

- the role that A will have been trained to perform by the company

- the fact that C has already made several attempts to call the company

- the fact that both speakers are male

- the different accents they speak with

- the different underlying pragmatic intentions and meanings of the two speakers.

A: [Edinburgh accent] good morning (.) you're through to XX Customer Service and my name's Adam (.) how may I help you

C: [RP accent] ah, hello (.) it's about a redirection request that seems to be causing a few problems

A: I see sir (.) could I take your customer reference number please

C: yeah (3) it's 543 (.) 986 (.) 674 (.) PY

A: (4) that's (.) Mr Brown

C: that's correct

A: of 57 Jackson Avenue

C: that's it

A: and what seems to be the problem sir

C: well to be honest I'm getting a bit fed up having to explain the same thing over and over again (.) I've tried three times now to get this sorted out but // it seems to be impossible to arrange a simple

A: // oh

C: redirection without (.) // well (.) spending hours and hours trying to get through

A: // mm

A: I'm very sorry to hear that sir (.) can I just confirm a few details and I'm sure I'll be able to sort things // out for you

C: // I've already given my name, number and shoe size to the last person I spoke to before getting cut off

Compare the results of your analysis with the commentary on page 125.

ACTIVITY 2

Another productive approach is to look at the variety of different kinds of discourse which take place even within a specific organisation, such as a college. The following set of data was recorded/collected in a number of different circumstances within a college in the course of a typical week.

(a) For each of the extracts/transcripts, identify examples of ways in which the social factors listed might have influenced the language used within each language framework. You could use a table such as the one below to record your findings for each piece of data.

Data _____   **Context** _____

Social frameworks	Language frameworks					
	Discourse Structure; turn-taking patterns	**Grammar** Standard or non-standard English Variations in sentence construction and word order (syntax)	**Semantics and pragmatics** Literal or figurative meanings Any pragmatic meanings implied	**Lexis** Degree of lexical formality/ informality Non-standard English or technical words	**Graphology** Layout, font type, graphic design	**Phonology** Accent Prosodic features: tone, timbre, tempo and intonation
Situation: Where and when						
Who: identity, status, role or position						
Relationships: Relative status, power and attitudes						
Intentions: Purposes which writers/ speakers bring to the context						

TEXT A

Transcript of answering-machine message on the main college switchboard:

Voice: [female, bright and friendly sounding, RP with hints of local (North West) accent]

thank you for calling Newton Sixth Form College (.) if you know the extension number you require please dial it now (.) for adult education enquiries please dial two six o (.) to leave a message on the answerphone please stay on the line

TEXT B

Extract from transcript of an internal telephone conversation between a teacher (A) and a technician (B):

A: hi is that Dave

B: yeah speaking

A: oh hi (.) it's Paul over in the LRC room (.) sorry to bother you er it's just that I seem to have a problem with my e-mail account

B: yeah

A: it's telling me it doesn't recognise my log-on ID

B: oh yeah (.) you're not the first [laughter] we've got one or two problems on the network // at the minute

A: // oh right

B: and we're on the case (.) are you on Outlook or just the web-based e-mail

A: just the er web-based (.) you know the ordinary one

B: have you got Outlook

A: um I I don't think so (.) I mean I usually just // you know I don't actually use it that much

B: // OK you you might have to come out of e-mail and try from another machine (.) or you could try to re-boot

TEXT C

Teacher's comments on a student's English Literature assignment:

A pleasing effort, Julie, which covers a good range of relevant details. The discussion of IVii hints at some awareness of the dramatic potential of the scene – remember your AOs! – but still needs more detailed examples. Some improvement here in the general standard of expression (AO1!) but do watch your punctuation. Keep up the good work – well done!

Compare your findings with the commentary on page 126.

(b) Carry out your own data-gathering exercise, either in your own educational institution or more interestingly in another type of institution to which you have access, collecting a range of different spoken and written texts, and perform a similar analysis.

> **Remember:**
>
> If recording conversations for language investigation, *always* gain the permission of all the participants beforehand. It is best to draft a standard letter which outlines the circumstances and purposes of the recording you wish to make, and ask all participants to sign it.

As you have seen already, there are many questions to ask about how our use of language is related to social factors and contexts. These questions often overlap, but for the purposes of this module, we can sum them up under three headings:

- How does language in use reflect the status/position of individuals/groups in society and their attempts to influence, persuade or direct others?

We mainly consider this question under the heading 'Language and power' (below).

- How might any differences between men's and women's roles in society, and our attitudes towards them, be reflected in language use?

We consider this question under the heading 'Language and gender' (page 102).

- How are regional variations in English represented and perceived?

  We consider this question under the heading, 'Accents and dialects of the British Isles' (page 111).

Language and power

Whenever groups of people gather together, create organisations or interact, we quickly become aware that some people are able to exercise more influence and authority than others. Indeed, a great deal of 'ordinary' interaction and language use seems to be concerned with trying to exercise influence over others – getting them to do things, to think things, and to feel things. In situations or organisations where we are aware of clear differences in status, such as in the family or at work, we may take for granted these inequalities in influence and authority and the various uses of language they produce. However, even among groups of apparently 'equal' friends or workmates, the language we use may also reflect the constant negotiation for position and influence which is the stuff of so much social interaction.

ACTIVITY 3

Let's consider how far this is true for some of the groups you belong to. For each of the groups listed below – or any others you belong to – order the members of the group in terms of their status or influence within it:

- your family

- the group of friends you socialise with most

- the people at your place of work.

Power and influence may be enjoyed by certain individuals (the Prime Minister, your mother or father, the head teacher, a media boss such as Rupert Murdoch), by groups of people (a trade union, a pressure group, the police), or even by entire nations (the United States, Russia).

ACTIVITY 4 | C3.1A

(a) In a group, try to agree on a list of the five most powerful individuals and groups of people in Britain. Then try to agree which of the following enjoy more power and influence in our society in general terms:

- white people, or people belonging to other ethnic groups

- men, or women

- business managers, or those working for them

- people who help run the media (TV and newspapers), or people who buy or subscribe to media products

- people in the north of Britain, or people in the south.

Explain your views to your class before comparing the outcomes of your discussion with the commentary on page 126.

(b) It is worth distinguishing between the terms power, status, authority and influence. Try to define the differences between these – use the prompts below to develop your ideas:

- Which of these derive(s) from the professional or official position a person holds in society?

- Which of these arise(s) from the personal respect given to them by other people?

- Is it possible for a powerful person to have low status – and vice versa?

Whatever conclusions you reached in Activity 4, you will have started to ask where power (and authority, status, etc.) comes from. You may have considered the relative importance of:

- individual strength of personality: such as that possessed by the extrovert 'leader' of a group of friends

- profession or occupation: a police officer has power because of the uniform, not because of who she or he is

- social class or background: how far might someone from a well-off family or with a good education have some advantages?

- gender: men may still have more influence than women in many areas

- ethnic origins: white British people may still enjoy more power than people from Asian, Caribbean and other non-white backgrounds

- wealth and economic power: rich people may be able exert their power in all sorts of ways

- political power: politicians clearly enjoy the power to shape policies and pass laws.

With all this in mind, we must now turn to the raw material of our study – language – and begin to explore the ways in which these inequalities of power and influence are reflected in the English we use. In general, we can observe this working in two ways; the use of language by powerful individuals or groups to enforce their authority (known as **instrumental power**) and the use of language to exert influence and persuasion (or **influential power**).

Language and power in action: analysing conversation

 It will be helpful first to review the material covered in Module 1 on 'Analysing talk' – see pages 59–60 – and 'Pragmatics' (page 54).

Talking to each other seems so natural that we could easily assume that conversation is a random, unstructured business. However, we have already seen in Module 1 that different kinds of conversations follow different patterns, and that what we can say in different situations is limited by context, purpose and audience.

Perhaps the most obvious structural feature of everyday speech is that we usually take turns to talk. Of course, there are occasions when someone interrupts, or is cut short, or starts to talk at the same time as someone else, but on the whole talking is a fairly orderly business. Even when disagreement is being expressed and tempers are frayed, we tend to observe this basic rule of conversation: *turn-taking*.

The most basic unit of conversation is the **adjacency pair**. This is when one utterance –'Have you been drinking?' – is immediately followed by an appropriate response – 'Certainly not, officer'. Although we are not consciously aware of them, there seem to be rules that limit the kinds of response that we can make to any utterance, depending on the situation. In some contexts (e.g. a social chat) the question 'Have you been drinking?' may be an innocent enquiry; in others (e.g. having been stopped in a car by a police patrol) it could be seen as an accusation. In this case, it could be followed by a denial (as above) or a confession – 'Yes, I'm afraid I have' – or, if you were feeling bold, a counter-question or accusation – 'What makes you say that?' Other responses are possible, but these are potentially provocative – 'What if I have?' (challenge); 'Get lost!' (insult/command) – or just impossible or insane: 'Yellow', 'One hundred and sixty', or 'That's my hamster'.

Some utterance types					
Greeting	Enquiry	Request	Instruction	Challenge	Accusation
Confession	Denial	Excuse	Insult	Answer	Valediction *(saying goodbye)*
Agreement	Disagreement	Declaration	Apology	Acknowledgement	Information

ACTIVITY 5

For each of the following openings, suggest the kinds of response that are most likely to complete the adjacency pair. The first one is provided as an example:

- 'That's a nice top' (observation)

Possible responses: 'Thanks! (acknowledgement); 'I got it in the sales' (information); 'Yes it is, isn't it?' (agreement); 'Do you think so?' (disagreement)

- 'Can I have a word with you?'

- 'Can I help you?'

- 'Leave me alone!'

- 'How do you plead? Guilty, or not guilty?'

Of course, most conversations consist of a *series* of many adjacency pairs in which the response to one pair becomes the start of the next:

'How are you?'

'Fine thanks. And you?'   1st pair: Greeting/enquiry and response

'Been better . . .'   2nd pair: Return enquiry and response

In extended talk, we move from turn to turn with little conscious effort – but we take our cues to speak from a number of clues provided by the current speaker. We then take our turn – or 'seize the floor' – until the next person's turn.

ACTIVITY 6

In groups, try to identify the types of cue that enable us to seize the floor. Think about:

- visual cues (does a speaker give us a sign?)

- **phonological** cues (does something happen to the speaker's voice?)

- **syntactic** clues (can we tell from a speaker's sentences when she or he is coming to an end?).

Compare your suggestions with those in the commentary on page 127.

In conversation, as well as recognising when we can take a turn, we must also choose what *kind* of utterance it is appropriate to make at any given time – it is clear that underlying 'rules' operate here, too. The way these rules might work in practice is likely to vary according to social contexts and relationships. One way of understanding this is to think of everything we say as having both a surface meaning and a social (pragmatic) function. Take this simple exchange:

A: How are you doing?
B: Not bad, thanks. Yourself?
A: Ay, not bad. Bit nippy out, though.

The surface meaning of A's first utterance is clear enough – it seems to be an enquiry about B's health or well-being. However, in many situations – as in this example, which occurred in the corner shop where B regularly stopped to buy sweets and newspapers – the social function of the utterance is to establish a pleasant, social relationship and to create an opportunity for some informal interaction. B's reply similarly has a meaning and a function; the meaning is vague and non-committal, but at least by replying appropriately B signals a willingness to develop the relationship. If B had stopped with 'Not bad, thanks', failing to initiate the next adjacency pair and leaving A to ask the next question, the pragmatic meaning might have been: 'I'm happy to respond to your friendliness and I'm not going to be rude, but I have no particular wish to converse as I'm in a bit of a hurry'. However, the 'Yourself?' that B adds has the effect of putting the ball back in A's court, equalising the conversation in terms of the willingness to participate.

This kind of small talk is sometimes called **phatic talk**; its function is mainly social rather than to carry out a particular transaction. In many informal and social situations, much of a conversation may be phatic, but in other situations this may not be the case. We often discover that running beneath the surface of our conversations is a whole set of functions and intentions that may be quite different from the surface meanings of our utterances. These underlying meanings may reveal as much about power and status relationships as the surface meanings of the dialogue. In drama and theatre, actors call this aspect of conversation the **sub-text**; in linguistics, the study of these underlying meanings and social functions is called **pragmatics**.

ACTIVITY 7

(a) Think of a typical visit to a GP's surgery. If the doctor greets you with the words 'How are you?', how might the meaning and function of this question differ from the casual enquiry of the corner shopkeeper?

(b) Now consider another familiar situation, in which the conversation goes like this:

A: I was just wondering if you fancied coming over tonight (.) you know (.) for a drink and that

B: (3) well (.) I'd like to but (.) I've really got to stay in tonight (.) I've got that history essay to hand in tomorrow

A's surface and pragmatic meanings are both reasonably clear – to ask the question 'Do you want to come over?', and to explore the extent to which B is interested in him or her. Suggest why A does not simply *say* 'Do you want to come over?', or even 'Do you fancy me?'

B's reply is very revealing. The meaning is clear: the answer is 'no', and for a good reason. What do you think is the function of the pauses, the hesitant 'well', and the excuse offered?

Compare your interpretation with the commentary on page 127.

The linguist H. P. Grice tried to define the various guiding principles, or **maxims,** that control how we respond to each other and construct conversations by moving from turn to turn. He maintained that when a conversation is working normally, we tend to assume that:

- what we say will have something to do with what has just been said (the maxim of *relevance*)
- what we say will be neither too long nor too short (the maxim of *quantity*)
- what we say is likely to be true (the maxim of *quality*)
- what we say is likely to be clear and meaningful (the maxim of *manner*).

Of course, these maxims can be broken, and often are – people lie or ramble on, people can be unco-operative, unclear or obscure. But when this happens, according to Grice, we become aware that there is something 'abnormal' about the conversation.

Analysing talk: summary

When examining conversational data, it is helpful to use a systematic framework that reminds you of the different questions to ask at different linguistic levels. This approach will also help you to achieve one of the Assessment Objectives: to 'know and use key features of frameworks for the systematic study of spoken and written English.'

Conversation: applying an analytical framework

Element	Key question	Discuss in terms of
Pragmatic framework	How does the dialogue reflect social relationships and implied meanings?	Turn-taking patterns, agenda and topic management, speakers' forms of address to each other, politeness strategies, phatic talk and implied meaning. Focus especially on the social function of utterances rather than surface meaning.
Grammatical framework	What grammatical structures does each speaker use, and with what effects?	Sentence types, lengths and structure; use of Standard English or non-standard features; non-fluency features such as slips, false starts and repetitions.
Semantic framework	What kinds of meaning does each speaker contribute?	The most frequent utterance type of each speaker – question, command, joke, confession, etc.
Lexical framework	What kinds of vocabulary does each speaker use?	Register; degrees of formality, colloquiality, topic specificity; factual or emotional content; personal or impersonal style; literal or figurative expressions; status and discourse.
Phonetic/ phonological framework	What are the vocal characteristics of speakers and what are the effects of those characteristics?	Intonation, stress, tempo, rhythm and pauses (if this information is available).

Power in practice: classroom language

The classroom is a good place in which to start to examine the pragmatics of everyday conversational discourse, and the ways in which power is reflected in language use. In a classroom, the powerful position of the teacher is reflected in the unique set of rules that seem to control the kinds of conversations taking place. In most schools, these conversations tend to follow clearly defined patterns, and reflect the purpose of the interaction (education/instruction), the context (pupils in a class with a teacher) and power relationships (the teacher has more power than the students).

Many teacher/student interactions may follow a pattern such as the one below:

Example of classroom discourse	Commentary
T: First let's recap a few points from yesterday. What are the various social contextual factors that we thought influenced the way we use language? **S1:** The situation. **T:** Yes, of course, the situation – but what does that mean? Can you unpack that a little for us, John? **S2:** The place and the time. **T:** Good – let's take them one at a time. How might the physical location we're in affect language?	Teacher starts by announcing the agenda and then initiating the talk with a question. The question may be open (inviting a wide range of responses) or closed (allowing only a limited set of possible answers). In either case, the question is designed to test/extend/challenge the students, and is therefore different from the majority of questions we may ask in other contexts. The students respond with an answer. If no response follows, the teacher may re-phrase the original question. The teacher will usually give some evaluative feedback on the response, reinforcing it by repeating it or re-phrasing it in his or her own words. The teacher will then try to move things on, either by pressing the student(s) to provide more detail, or by asking the next question. The teacher has the power to nominate individual students, or allow voluntary responses. This will usually be by first name; by contrast, students are usually expected to address the teacher by 'sir', 'miss', 'madam' or title. The unequal (or asymmetrical) power relationship is also reflected in: • the differences between the kinds of question teacher and students are allowed to ask (could a student challenge a late teacher with 'where have you been?') • the power of the teacher to remind students of the rules of discourse ('stop talking/don't answer back!') • the right to expect to be listened to, sometimes for quite lengthy 'turns' • the control of the agenda – by cutting short any distractions or interruptions • the possible use of irony, sarcasm and humour to make a point.

There are many ways in which you could study classroom language; a few possibilities are offered below. They all involve gaining permission to tape-record part of a lesson and transcribing a section. You may be able to refer to the outcomes of your investigation (and those of your fellow students) in the Unit 2 examination.

- Compare the techniques used by two different teachers to manage the same class.

- Compare the way the same teacher manages classes of different age groups.

- Focus specifically on the way different teachers get a lesson started, phrase questions or evaluate student responses.

- Compare the frequency with which different teachers nominate or accept answers from male or female pupils, and/or examine the forms of address used towards them.

- Focus on how pupils/students try to exercise power for themselves by infringing the normal 'rules'.

Power in practice: other conversational contexts

ACTIVITY 8

(a) Consider a typical family conversation around the meal table. Suggest how the status/power of a family member is reflected in the amount of talking he or she is permitted to do before being interrupted or told to be quiet.

(b) In many social contexts, the right to ask questions and expect truthful answers is an indicator of power. Suggest some examples.

(c) In the following two situations, the respondents' refusal to give a meaningful answer (to a question to which they know the answer) is potentially provocative. Suggest why, referring to Grice's maxims (see page 91) as appropriate.

Teacher: 'What's your name?'
Pupil: 'Why?'

Policeman: 'What's your name?'
Young man: 'Mickey Mouse.'

(d) The right to pass judgment on other people's utterances is another sign of power or status. If you ask a stranger for directions, listen encouragingly, and then respond with 'Very clear directions. Well done!', you may provoke an unpleasant reaction. Suggest why.

(e) Conversational patterns are affected not only by differences of social status and power, but also by differences in the personal status of participants. To explore this idea, let's look at a conversation recorded during an evening meal at a house where a group of middle-aged friends have gathered. Use the framework of questions introduced on page 92 to analyse the conversational relationship of participants A and B:

A: this head (.)

B: oh (2)

A: heads have to be able to understand (.) // the kids that they're dealing with

B: // mm

A: don't they (.)

B: yeah

A: I mean if they're going to do a good job they have to be able to understand the background (.) the problems that the kids they're dealing with have got and //

B: // yeah

A: and (2) being (2) prejudging this bloke // it seems

B: // well that's all we can do because he didn't give anything of himself did he

A: (.) he didn't (3) it wasn't (1) I think what they should have done the day before was they should what they did with the em when the candidates came in for the em (1)

B: // deputy's job

A: // yeah they should have they should have had a programme of people for them to talk to

B: mm absolutely

Now compare your analysis with the commentary on page 128.

Language and the professions

It is sometimes said that one group of people who have power in society is professional people. In different ways, members of the legal, medical, financial and other professions tend to command a certain respect from the rest of us, and they exercise considerable power in their specialist areas. The ways in which these groups use language help to preserve and apply their power over non-specialists.

- They use shared specialist language or technical jargon. This can function as a kind of code which excludes those outside the profession.

- They deliberately or incidentally intimidate non-specialists by the use of such language.

- They tend to patronise non-specialists to preserve the 'mystique' of group membership.

The variety of the written language in which the law of the land is communicated and enforced is, in one sense, the most powerful kind there is. Yet for many people, it can seem an impenetrable and alien variety of English. However, it can also be argued that the peculiar characteristics of legal language can be explained by its peculiar context, history and function.

ACTIVITY 9

After studying the following text, which is the introductory page of a life assurance policy, identify your own examples of each of the features given in the table below.

Whereas the Person Assured named in the schedule hereto has effected the assurance herein described with **The Standard Life Assurance Company** hereinafter called the Company and whereas the Person Assured has delivered to the Company as the basis of this assurance the proposal and declaration referred to in the schedule:

Now this policy witnesseth that in consideration of the payment to the Company of the first and all subsequent premiums as provided herein the Company will pay the benefits stated in the said schedule to the Person Assured or to the executors, administrators or assigns of the Person Assured or as otherwise stated in the said schedule upon proof satisfactory to the Directors of the Company of:

(1) the happening of the event or events on which the benefits are to become payable as specified in the said schedule,

(2) the title of the claimant or claimants, and

(3) the correctness of the date of birth of the Life Assured stated in the said proposal and declaration unless previously admitted by the Company:

And it is hereby declared that the Person Assured is a member of the Company in accordance with and subject to the regulations of the Company and that this policy is subject to any conditions and provisions endorsed or written on this and any following page of this policy.

In witness thereof and by the authority of the Board of Directors of the Company these presents are executed at Edinburgh on the date of signing shown on the said schedule.

Language feature	Contextual explanation
Includes many lexical features with a specialist meaning, including terms derived from French or Latin.	Legal documents are not intended for general readership, but as communications from one expert to another. The presence of French- and Latin-derived terms reflects the historical importance of those languages in law.
Sentences tend to be long, with many qualifying clauses and relatively little punctuation.	Ambiguity must be avoided at all costs. There must be no room for different interpretations.

Language feature	Contextual explanation
Pronouns tend to be avoided in favour of repeated reference to specific names. Terms used to refer to people and organisations are precisely defined.	Again, there must be no doubt about who or what is being referred to at any given point.
May include abbreviated references to articles of law or relevant 'precedents'.	Again, documents are intended to be shared between professionals who share the same legal knowledge, rather than by lay people
Includes some words from a highly formal register (e.g. hereinafter, thereof) which are now seldom found outside the legal context. Similarly, some grammatical forms (third-person singular verb endings in –eth) are used which are not Standard English.	Legal documents have been written to an established formula over several centuries. As such, they have become almost immune to the changes which have taken place in language outside the legal context.

Language and politics

Politics is also an area where language is used to exert power and influence. We will consider below (see page 100) how politicians can use a range of techniques to make their speeches effective; it is also interesting to examine what happens when a politician, intent on getting his or her message across, confronts a political interviewer whose job is to challenge and attack. Here are some suggestions for investigations you can carry out in the field of political discourse.

- Tape and transcribe your own selection of political interviews on programmes like BBC2's *Newsnight* and Radio 4's *Today* programme. Analyse the techniques of the interviewers and the ways that politicians try to deal with them.

- Tape a TV discussion programme such as BBC 1's *Question Time*. Examine how the chair keeps control of the discourse, and how panel members and members of the audience all try to exert influence and power in the discussions.

ACTIVITY 10

This role-play activity provides an opportunity to test some of your discoveries about language and power in practice. You will first need to transfer the 'Situation' and 'Power' cards shown below to plain cards.

(a) In pairs, pick one of the Situation cards. Each describes a situation involving two people in a potentially asymmetrical power relationship.

(b) Agree who will play each of the two roles described on the card.

(c) Each player now draws a Power card without disclosing its contents. This card allocates a power level from 1 (the most powerful) to 4 (the least powerful). Note the types of language use appropriate to your role.

(d) Enact the role play accordingly.

(e) Show the role play to the rest of your class or group. They should try to identify the power rating of each player and support their judgments by referring to characteristics of the language used.

Child/teenager asking a parent for permission to stay out late at a party	Police officer interrogating suspect about a burglary	Boss congratulating employee on good work as part of an annual appraisal interview
Employer interviewing candidate for a job as a waiter	Teacher telling off a student for recent poor behaviour	Customer complaining to shop assistant about faulty goods recently purchased
Barrister in court cross-examining witness in a trial	Judge on *Pop Idol* evaluating a contestant's performance	Teacher praising student for good work

Power cards

Power 1	Power 2
Use formal Standard English but with an RP-ish accent	Use fairly formal Standard English but with a soft local accent
Speak in a deep tone of voice	Speak with a fairly low pitch
Talk slowly, pausing before and sometimes during each sentence	Talk quite slowly, sometimes pausing before speaking.
Use technical, educated or sophisticated vocabulary	Use some technical, educated or sophisticated vocabulary
Lead the conversation– choose and change the topic	Lead the conversation – choose and change the topic
Interrupt frequently. Don't allow your partner to finish sentences	Interrupt your partner once or twice
Comment often on the quality of your partner's responses	Make an occasional comment on the quality of your partner's responses
Ask direct questions abruptly and aggressively	Ask direct questions quite abruptly
Never use hedges if giving instructions/asking questions	Use minimal hedges if giving instructions/ asking questions
Avoid politeness strategies	Use basic politeness markers such as *please* and *thank you*

Power 3	Power 4
Use Standard English but use your natural regional accent	Use quite a lot of non-standard dialect and accent features
Use a middling pitch	Speak in a higher voice than normal
Talk at a moderate speed	Talk rapidly
Treat your partner as an equal – if you wish to use first names check with them first that this is acceptable.	Address your partner formally, using their full title or sir/miss/madam
Avoid technical and highly sophisticated vocabulary	Use lots of vague, non-technical language and verbal fillers like *sort of, like* and *you know*
Use some hedges, apologies/other politeness strategies	Use lots of hedges, apologies/other politeness strategies
Qualify your opinions with phrases like 'I might be wrong'	Always qualify your opinions with phrases like 'I might be wrong' or 'I'm really not sure about this'
Interrupt once or twice but apologise for doing so	Don't interrupt and wait until invited to speak
Allow your partner to lead the conversation sometimes	Give way straight away if someone interrupts you
Only give way sometimes if interrupted	Give lots of supportive feedback when the other person is talking
Give some supportive feedback when the other person is talking	Wait your turn – and say as little as possible without ever appearing rude or uncooperative
Use some hedges when giving instructions or asking questions ('Would you mind …')	

Persuasion and rhetoric

Another important aspect of our exploration of language and power is how it can be used to persuade, influence, convince, inspire – and even intimidate. In this section we ask what makes a particular text powerful in any of these senses, an area of language study which is sometimes referred to as **rhetoric**.

It is perhaps in public speeches made by politicians and others that the characteristic features of rhetoric are at their most obvious. We'll start by looking at a speech made by one of the most influential politicians of the twentieth century, Nelson Mandela. In Activity 11 is an extract from his inaugural address as President of South Africa, which he delivered to a huge crowd on 10 May 1994 (reproduced in B. McArthur (ed.), *The Penguin Book of Historic Speeches*). Mandela's speech is a moving and apparently simple piece of public speaking, yet it conceals considerable artistry and linguistic control. It is an example of the art of powerful public speaking – **oratory** – and also illustrates many of the techniques widely used by speakers and writers seeking to exercise power over an audience. You may find it helpful to refer to this summary of common rhetorical techniques. They are listed here according to the categories in the stylistics framework.

The power of language: some common techniques

Discourse structures	*Problem-solution:* the speaker convinces the audience that they have a problem, then provides a solution *Desire-need-fulfilment:* the speaker convinces the audience that there is something they need or desire, then promises they can have it if . . .
Sentence structures	*Lists and repetition:* Groups of three Parallelism – repeating sentences with similar structures ('Let there be . . . Let there be . . . Let there be . . .') Contrasts and opposites Rhetorical questions
Lexical choice	Pronoun use Direct address (second person: you) Personal authority (first-person singular: I) Unity and bonding (first-person plural: we) Figurative language (metaphor, simile, personification) Emotive language Humorous language Factual support and authority, or citation of other authorities
Sounds and spellings	Alliteration Rhythmic patterns and repetitions

ACTIVITY 11

Try to define those features of the following speech by Nelson Mandela that contribute to its power and impact on the listeners. Look in particular for any *patterns* (such as different kinds of repetition or contrast) used to express and shape the ideas effectively. It will be helpful to review the framework for stylistic analysis outlined in Module 1 (pages 33–35), and some of the linguistic terminology introduced there.

Today, all of us do, by our presence here, and by our celebrations in other parts of our country and the world, confer glory and hope to newborn liberty. Out of the experience of an extraordinary human disaster that lasted too long, must be born a society of which all humanity will be proud. Our daily deeds as ordinary South Africans must produce an actual South African reality that will reinforce humanity's belief in justice, strengthen its confidence in the nobility of the human soul and sustain all our hopes for a glorious life for all.

The time for the healing of the wounds has come. The moment to bridge the chasms that divide us has come. The time to build is upon us. We pledge ourselves to liberate all our people from the continuing bondage of poverty, deprivation, suffering, gender and other discrimination. We are both humbled and elevated by the honour and privilege that you, the people of South Africa, have bestowed on us, as the first president of a united, democratic, non-racial and non-sexist South Africa, to lead our country out of the valley of darkness.

We understand it still that there is no easy road to freedom. We know it well that none of us acting alone can achieve success. We must therefore act together as a united people, for national reconciliation, for nation building, for the birth of a new world. Let there be justice for all. Let there be peace for all. Let there be work, bread, water and salt for all. Never, never and never again shall it be that this beautiful land will again experience the oppression of one by another and suffer the indignity of being the skunk of the world. Let freedom reign. The sun shall never set on so glorious a human achievement! God bless Africa! Thank you.

Nelson Mandela, 10 May 1994.

Now compare your analysis with the commentary on pages 128–9.

In Module 3 you will find more examples of persuasive writing, together with suggestions for your own writing activities that will allow you to try putting some of these techniques into practice.

The language of power in the media

Many of the techniques use by politicians are equally evident in other forms of persuasion with which we are more familiar. In the media, for example, we are bombarded by advertisements, publicity campaigns, news bulletins, articles, editorials and letters which, in different ways, use language to persuade us of their authority and truth.

As part of your preparations for the Unit 2 examination, you should carry out some detailed investigations of these kinds of texts.

ACTIVITY 12 | **C3.1b, C3.3**

Here are some suggestions for possible investigations of the power of persuasion in practice. Each involves gathering some data, analysing it closely, and writing up or presenting your findings to your class.

(a) Gather a selection of advertisements for a variety of rival products, and compare them in terms of their use of powerful or persuasive language. (Remember to check your analysis against the stylistics framework.) Make a presentation of your findings to the class.

(b) Compare the language techniques used by advertisers.

(c) Compare adverts for comparable products (e.g. toiletries or cosmetics) aimed at male and female audiences. This links usefully to some of the issues raised in the 'Language and gender' section below.

(d) Collect two editorial pieces from different newspapers on the same topic and the same day. Carry out a stylistic analysis of the texts, examining closely how they each use language to persuade and influence readers.

(e) Collect some examples of letters written to the correspondence page of your local newspaper. Examine the ways in which writers have attempted to make their language powerful.

Language and gender

In recent years there has been a great deal of interest in the relationship between gender and language use. This reflects a more general concern with the changing roles of men and women in society, and the social trends of the past 30 years or so in which many traditional assumptions about gender roles have been challenged.

Two main issues are implied in an investigation of language and gender:

- Does vocabulary that is used to refer to men and women reflect a kind of institutionalised sexism in our language – and if so, what can be done about it ? This is a question of *language and representation*.

- What differences are there in the ways men and women use language? This is an issue of *language usage*.

Language and representation

It is clear from the way we use English that we think gender is significant. When we refer to people, we usually specify the gender of the person concerned even when it is not particularly relevant. We talk about a 'boy' or a 'girl' more often than a 'child', a 'father' or 'mother' more often than a 'parent', and 'brother' or 'sister' rather than 'sibling'. There is no word in English for 'aunt' or 'uncle' that is not gender specific, and the overwhelming majority of first names immediately identify their bearer's gender. So, if we routinely represent people in terms of their gender, are there any differences in the ways males and females are referred to? We don't need to think very long before coming up with the answer.

Let's start by looking at the titles that we give or are given when identifying ourselves. Unless we have an inherited or other special title, there are two traditional alternatives for men and two for women. If you are male, you have the choice of either Mr or Master. If you are female, you might be Mrs or Miss. On the face of it, these two pairs of titles look as if they are equivalents of each other – Mr/Mrs and Miss/Master. In fact their use and meanings are very different.

ACTIVITY 13

(a) Define the differences between the uses and meanings of 'Master' and 'Miss'.

(b) Explain the differences between the titles available to adult men and women, and suggest what these differences reveal about different attitudes towards men and women.

(c) What reasons do you think 1960s feminist groups may have given for popularising the term 'Ms'? Describe your attitude towards its use.

(d) Brainstorm a list of the terms of abuse most commonly used about people of either gender. Sum up the differences you find, and try to account for them.

(e) The following titles or jobs are listed in male/female pairs. For each pair, decide whether the terms are true equivalents, and describe any differences between them:

- manager/manageress
- father/mother
- author/authoress
- lord/lady
- master/mistress.

Now compare all your responses with the commentary on pages 129–30.

Gender and semantics: marked and unmarked categories

As we have just seen, one feature of our English vocabulary is a tendency for the female form of a title to be more obviously 'marked' than the male form. This can often reflect a particular 'mindset', in which we assume that certain roles or occupations are inevitably assigned to a particular gender.

ACTIVITY 14

The following extract from a careers bulletin mentions a number of professional people.

(a) Supply the words which you think are most likely to fill the numbered gaps in the text.

(b) What do you think these choices reveal about language and gender?

Compare your answers with the commentary on page 130.

CAREERS BULLETIN

Next week as part of our Careers programme a number of specialist professionals will be visiting the college. An engineer will talk about careers in the mechanical and electrical engineering industries. (1) — will meet any interested students in Room 12. A nurse will also be available to discuss career routes into nursing, and (2) — will be in Room 20. Meanwhile Dr Hibbert from the Cambridge Road Medical Practice will speak to potential medical students in Room 14, where (3) — will also show a video entitled 'Careers in Medicine'.

One small step: generic man

One example of our gender-related use of language is the word 'man' itself. When Neil Armstrong stepped onto the moon in 1969 he delivered a carefully scripted epigram. In fact, he slightly misquoted his own lines. He intended to say: 'That's one small step for a man, one giant leap for mankind'. Armstrong omitted the 'a', saying instead: 'That's one small step for man . . .'.

The 'correct' version uses two different senses of the idea 'man'. Had he used this version, Armstrong would have referred to himself as 'a man'. This can mean both an adult male and a member of the human species (as in 'man evolved from apes'). We can call this second meaning of the term the generic use. But which meaning did Armstrong intend? In the event of the first person to land being female, would we have referred to her as the first 'woman' on the moon, and would she have said, 'That's one small step for a woman . . .'? Of course, the epigram works by contrasting the first reference to 'man' with the unmistakably generic 'mankind'. However, in the version that Armstrong actually spoke, 'man' without the 'a' sounds as if it is generic too, thus lessening the effectiveness of the saying.

This illustrates a problem with 'man'. It is ambiguous, being used as both a generic and a gender-specific term. In practice, this can lead to problems: it is quite possible to say 'all men [generic] should live in peace' and intend to include women; but we can hardly say 'the man [generic] next door has just become a mother'! In the second example, where a specific person is identified, the word must refer to gender.

Some people object to the generic use of 'man' because it ignores or devalues the role of women. So should we change our use of English to reflect modern ideas about gender roles and equality of opportunity?

ACTIVITY 15

Below are several examples of commonly used expressions involving the generic 'man'. Add any more you can think of, then provide reasoned objections to the use of the term as it stands. Suggest an alternative that is free of any gender reference.

- The chairman is expected to address the shareholders this morning.

- Sam the fireman put on his shiny new jacket.

- Report to the site foreman at 9.00 am.

- There's a new postman on our route.

- We'll have to reduce manning levels in every department.

Compare your notes with the commentary on page 130.

In recent years there has been considerable controversy over the issue of so-called 'political correctness' in language. Traditional uses of language embody inequalities and discriminatory attitudes which we no longer see as acceptable or desirable, so a number of questions arise:

- Does the 'sexist' use of language do active harm in reinforcing unhelpful stereotypes and attitudes?

- Should we consciously try to change the language – as in some of the examples discussed above – or will our language eventually change 'of its own accord' and catch up with the new social realities?

- This is all part of an even bigger debate – the question of how far the words of our language shape and construct the ways we think about the world. In its most extreme form, made famous by the linguists Sapir and Whorf in the 1930s, the concept of **linguistic relativism** suggests that our language imposes on us the mental categories with which we organise and make sense of our perceptions of the world. This would, of course, imply that speakers of different languages actually *think* differently too.

ACTIVITY 16

C3.1a

Imagine that your school or college has decided to devote one section of its equal opportunities policy to the question of language. In groups, try to agree on the outline of a language policy for your school/college in respect of gender.

Representations of gender

One important area for investigation is the question of how males and females are represented in different kinds of texts. This goes further than the problems of inherent semantic asymmetries, lexical gaps, gender-marked terms and semantic pejoration which we have already noted; it is a question of the ways in which whole texts – news articles, narratives, advertisements, and others – represent gender. How far, if at all, does the linguistic representation of gender reinforce stereotypes and prejudices?

ACTIVITY 17

(a) Read the extract below, which is the ending of *The Call of the Glen*, a story by Helen Stewart published by *The People's Friend*. Some changes have been made to the original text. What do you think they are?

Tom said nothing, only looked up at Virginia as she stood beside him, dark against the sky. All the sounds he loved were caught up and held there in her voice; all the peace and strong, sweet steadfastness of the fields and hills and moorlands which he loved, were caught up and held in her.

She stood beside him, but her eyes were fixed on the hills across the valley, and they glittered darkly in the level sun rays . . . There was silence for a moment and then she said, 'There's something I have to say to you, Tom. I've been meaning to say it since that morning at Craigdhu, but – it's difficult . . .'

He laid a hand on her arm to silence her.

'No,' he said, and his voice was a little unsteady. 'Oh, Virginia! You, too! You think I was – in love with her? Why?'

She shrugged. 'Because of the way you looked, the way you spoke, the tone of your voice and the light of your eyes. I know I'm not mistaken, Tom; you are in love.'

He said nothing to that, and she looked down and went on in a low voice, 'I know the signs, you see, for I'm in the same sad way myself. I didn't mean to tell you, but there it is. I've known for a long time that I love you, but there was Rosy, and though it's better this way, it's hard on you. I thought – Tom, you're crying!'

'Yes.' He looked up at her. 'I'm crying because I'm happier than I've ever been before. I've read about people crying because they were happy but I never believed it. But it's true!'

She put a hand on his shoulder, disbelief, hope, joy, struggling in her face. Then she shook him gently.

'You mean – you love me?'

'So much – so much!' he whispered.

And then he was in her arms.

For a long moment everything was forgotten. Earth, sky, the evening light about them and the night to come were lost, forgotten incidents in some far shadowy world. Only this was real in all eternity.

At last she let him go.

'Fools that we were!' she said softly. 'A pair of proud stiff-necked fools!'

They strolled down the hill side by side. At the gate of the cottage he stopped.

'Don't come any farther, Virginia. I want to go in alone.'

They faced each other, their eyes shining with the clear light of a love that was sure, complete and steadfast.

When she had gone he stood still until the sound of her footsteps died away, then turned to the cottage.

The moon was rising, a slim silver crescent behind the Roman's Hill. A late partridge was calling in the stubble. He could smell wet bracken and the clean scent of dewy grass.

Moon and hill, scent and silence took on a deeper beauty as he thought of her.

A deep, sweet contentment flowed over him, and kissing his hand to the hills and to the sky and to the road where she had been, he walked into the cottage and shut the door.

Compare your ideas with the commentary on page 130.

(b) In what ways did the version of the story printed above strike you as odd? If you can answer this question, you can begin to identify some of the gender stereotypes implicit in its representation of men and women. Use the table below to investigate some specific linguistic features of the text *as it originally appeared*. After listing more examples in the different categories, comment on the differences in the way the two characters are represented, and how this might be typical of gender stereotyping.

	Actions attributed (verbs, adverbs)	Qualities attributed (adjectives)	Speech attributed
Tom	Stood beside her Eyes were fixed on the hills (Eyes) glittered darkly	Dark against the sky Strong, sweet steadfastness	'There's something I have to say . . .'
Virginia	Said nothing Looked up at Tom		'No,' she said, and her voice was a little unsteady

(c) Study the text below, from a recent car advert. In what ways do you think it reflects gender stereotypes in targeting its intended audience/market?

Kinky Boots

Try on the special edition Seicento 2Tone and turn a few heads next time you're in town. Designed with exquisite details like electric front windows, Sony CD player, metallic paint, matching interior trim and body colour co-ordinated features such as bumpers and door mirrors.

In fact, there's a whole range of extras available on any Seicento including driver's airbag, electronic power steering and engine immobiliser. Look drop-dead-gorgeous for just £6,199. Go on, treat yourself. Call 0800 71 7000 or visit us at our website.

Listed below are some suggestions for text-based investigations which will allow you to research some of the gender-related issues raised so far. A framework of possible questions is suggested which you could apply to whichever type of text you choose to investigate.

Key issues	Linguistic focus	Text types
How are males and females identified and referred to? How are they described? What actions are attributed to males and females? How far do your texts exhibit other forms of implicit sexism?	Collate the **nouns** and **titles** which are used to identify people referred to in your texts. *How often are women described as the wife partner mistress/ girlfriend of a male?* Collate the words and phrases (mainly **adjectives**) used to provide additional information about males and females. *How often are men/women described in terms of appearance as opposed to profession/ skills? What kinds of positive and negative judgments are implied by the terms used?* Collate the **verbs** and **adverbs** used to describe males and females. *Are males represented as active, dynamic? Are females represented as passive, having things done* to *or* for *them rather than doing?*	News reports in tabloid and broadsheet newspapers Advertisements Personal ads placed by men and women Children's books – past and present Romantic fiction (e.g. *Mills and Boon* novels)

Language usage

The second part of our investigation concerns the ways in which men and women use language themselves. The questions that researchers have been asking over the past 20 years or so include:

- Do men and women use different vocabularies?

- Do men and women behave differently in conversational contexts?

- Are there differences between the use of non-standard accents and dialects between men and women?

- What are the explanations for, and implications of, these differences?

Gender and conversation

When we examined conversation earlier in this module, we found that the status, power and influence of speakers are reflected in the way people interact and converse. As women have traditionally been associated with less powerful positions in society, and are stereotypically associated with subordinate roles, could it be that men and women behave differently in conversation?

ACTIVITY 18 | C3.1a

In investigating this area, most researchers have tended to focus one or more of the following orthodox ideas. For each of these:

(a) Hold a discussion in your group and suggest whether you think your own experience and observation supports the idea.

(b) Design a piece of research which would enable you test it. Identify the type of data you would need to collect, and how you would need to analyse it.

- In single-sex groups women tend to be very supportive and co-operative whereas men tend to be more competitive.

- Women tend to listen more actively and supportively, giving plenty of supportive feedback with minimal responses ('mm', 'yes', 'did you') during another speaker's turn to indicate interest and agreement.

- Men may delay their minimal responses and thus convey impatience or lack of interest.

- Men are more likely to compete for the floor, interrupt, and use aggressive forms of language such as insults, raised voices, threats and swearing.

- In mixed-sex groups, men dominate women.

- Women tend to spend longer on **phatic** talk; men's talk is functional.

- Women tend to swear less than men.

- Some lexical items are used more by women than men.

- Women are better at articulating emotions.

- Women tend to be more tentative and use more **hedges** and **question tags**.

- In general, women tend towards co-operation, men towards competition.

One often-quoted study set out to test some of these suppositions. In 1975, two academics (Zimmerman and West) published an account of the research they had carried out at the University of California. They taped conversations between pairs of males and females and examined the way they took turns in same-sex and mixed conversations. They noted the frequency with which speakers of each gender overlapped (started speaking just before the previous one had finished) or interrupted (cut off the previous speaker, preventing him or her from finishing).

Their findings can be summarised as follows:

- *Same sex*: in 20 conversations, there were 22 overlaps and 7 interruptions.

- *Mixed sex*: in 11 conversations, there were 9 overlaps by men and 0 by women, and 46 interruptions by men and 2 by women.

ACTIVITY 19

(a) Write down any conclusions you think can be drawn from Zimmerman and West's findings. Also note down your reactions: are you surprised or alarmed, for example? Offer some explanations for the differences in behaviour that these findings seem to reveal.

(b) Compare your notes with the analysis offered by Jennifer Coates in *Women, Men and Language*, as quoted in the commentary on page 131.

(c) Suggest any reasons you can think of to challenge the validity of Zimmerman and West's data. Consider the sample size, where the study was carried out, and any other aspects of the experiment which might limit its wider applicability.

More recently, some people have questioned the validity of some research in this area. Sometimes research (such as that of Zimmerman and West) based on a very small and not very representative sample of speakers has been used to support sweeping generalisations about men and women in a range of situations. Besides, times are changing; perhaps modern female speakers are tending to adopt more traditionally 'masculine' discourse features. It is time to try out some of these ideas by collecting and analysing data of your own.

ACTIVITY 20 C3.3

Design and carry out an investigation in your own school/college to test the ideas and findings of Zimmerman and West. Arrange to make a recording of either a mixed-sex conversation or two similar conversations involving only males or only females. These may be taken from the broadcast media but will preferably be a live conversation. (If you tape live speech, remember always to follow the guidelines given on page 16.) Transcribe a section of the tape, making sure you indicate where interruptions or overlapping occur. Examine the data closely to test the ideas discussed above.

- Count and compare examples of interruptions/overlaps, questions, minimal responses, hedges and question tags.

- Comment closely on these examples.

- Apply the conversational analysis framework (see page 92).

- Present your findings in a report.

Further reading: some key texts on language and gender

Coates, Jennifer, *Women, Men and Language: A Sociolinguistic Account of Gender Differences in Language* (Studies in Language and Linguistics), Longman (14 June, 1993) ISBN: 0582074924

Grey, Clive, *Overview of Work on Language and Gender Variation* [link to this webpage through www.heinemann.co.uk/hotlinks]

Tannen, Deborah, *You Just Don't Understand: Women and Men in Conversation*, Virago Press (26 March, 1992) ISBN: 1853814717

Goddard, Angela, *Language and Gender*, Routledge, an imprint of Taylor & Francis Books Ltd (17 February, 2000) ISBN: 0415201772

Accents and dialects of the British Isles

First, you would find it useful to review the work on this topic covered in Module 1. This included:

- examples of a literary representation (in D. H. Lawrence's *Sons and Lovers*) and an accurate transcription of regional speech (the Sunderland speaker)

- the terms **Received Pronunciation** and **Standard English**

- some ways in which the lexis and grammar of regional speech differ from Standard English

- a review of some attitudes towards Standard English and regional varieties

- the fact that the dialect we call Standard English has come to be regarded as the model of 'correct' English, and that the non-regional accent known as Received Pronunciation (RP) enjoys prestige as the 'proper' way to talk.

As the prestige form of English, SE dominates the printed word, the education system and our public and professional life – but there remain some colourful regional variations which continue to express the distinct local character of the towns, cities and counties of Britain. The study of these regional varieties is sometimes referred to as **dialectology**.

It would take a very thick book indeed to discuss all of these regional varieties in any detail; as with the other sections of this module, the activities and examples included here should be used to provide the basis for extended explorations and investigations of your own.

Accents of English

As we have seen, people tend to have different attitudes towards RP and the regional accents of English. An accent can trigger a whole stereotype of a city or region, and can be the means by which we continue to reinforce unhelpful prejudices.

ACTIVITY 21

(a) Read the following article. It originally appeared in the early 1990s in the *Northern Echo*, a regional newspaper published in the north-east of England.

PUTTING THE ACCENT ON A NORTH MOUTH DIVIDE

The voice on the television advert persuading you to buy bread, beer or crisps probably sounds familiar.

For market researchers associate these products with the North-East accent and qualities of being friendly, down-to-earth – and undynamic.

But the man selling flash cars, holidays or pension schemes is likely to have a southern accent because advert makers say it denotes ambition, authority and intelligence.

Now speech coaches say many Northern businessmen are trying to change the way they speak because they feel they are not taken seriously enough.

As one (southern-based) national newspaper summed it up: 'Northerners are rushing to prove they are not as thick as the accent that marks them out.'

It is just the latest example of an increasing North Mouth Divide which is threatening to stifle strong regional accents.

And language experts argued that the trend should be strongly resisted.

York University lecturer Dr John Local said: 'The media use accents all the time in subtle ways. But it is hard to say with this kind of thing whether the media lead or follow.'

(b) Carry out your own survey of accents in TV advertisements during an evening's viewing, and present your findings to the class. Your investigation should ask:

- What kinds of products are advertised by using different regional accents?

- What kinds of products are advertised using mainly RP accents? Is it true that these tend to be 'high prestige' products?

- How do some adverts use both regional and RP speech? Consider, for example, how often RP voices provide the voice-over or the last word in an advert that uses regional speakers on-screen.

(c) The article's closing sentence raises the question of how far the media are to blame for the perpetuation of these stereotypes. In the light of your findings, try to decide which of the following statements most accurately describes the role of the media in the use of regional accents:

- the media simply reflect stereotypes that already exist in society

- the media help reinforce and strengthen social stereotypes

- the media create and spread stereotypes.

In considering these issues, you may like refer to the following review of a book by Dr J. Honey, *Does Accent Matter?* In this extract, reviewer D. J. Enright summarises some of the research findings reported in Honey's book:

Experimental research shows that RP heads the prestige league (its speakers are even reckoned to be handsomer, taller, cleaner), followed by Scottish (Edinburgh), Welsh and Irish (kept within bounds), while cockney, Scouse, Glaswegian, West Midlands and Belfast come bottom. Yorkshire is relatively well thought of, as the language of farmers and cricketers, and so are rustic accents, a fact ascribed here to the nineteenth-century worship of the countryside. Unattributed theories put Scouse down to the prevalence of adenoids and Glaswegian to ill-fitting false teeth.

We can extend our study of accents in the media to include news broadcasts, so often seen as the benchmark for 'proper English'. National newsreaders almost invariably speak using an RP accent, and even readers of the local news tend to have only the gentlest hint of a regional accent in their speech. Why is this? The following may help you answer this question. It is an account of a much-quoted experiment carried out in the 1970s by the researcher Howard Giles:

In the 1970s a team of researchers led by Howard Giles carried out a number of research experiments called matched guise experiments, designed to test people's responses to different accents. In one of these, Giles delivered two identical presentations on a controversial topic to different groups of Midlands sixth-form students using RP with one group and the local regional accent with the other. Afterwards, he surveyed his audiences for their opinions of his intelligence and knowledge. The students who had heard the presentation in RP rated his intelligence and authoritativeness considerably higher than those he had addressed in the regional accent.

ACTIVITY 22

Bear in mind the results of Giles's experiment as you consider which of the following statements offers the most likely explanation for the universal use of RP among newsreaders. Place them in order of importance, then compare your findings with the commentary on page 131.

- All newsreaders went to similar kinds of schools and had a similar education, so they all have a similar accent.

- Not everyone would be able to understand the broadcasts if they used regional accents.

- People would find the news less believable and take it less seriously if it were spoken in a regional accent.

Accent and social class

The accent of English we seem to respect the most happens to be the one that is used principally by middle-class, usually university-educated people working in professional occupations. In other words, RP's unique status is largely due to its being the accent of the powerful. RP has what linguists sometimes describe as **overt prestige** – an 'official' status of which most speakers seem to be consciously aware.

ACTIVITY 23

(a) The relationship between our accent and our social background is complex. Some researchers (e.g. Peter Trudgill in *Sociolinguistics*, 1974) have carried out surveys to explore the complex relationship between our regional speech and our social class. Use your library to track down some of this research.

(b) Some recent research suggests that the association of RP speech with education, authority and power may be slipping. Other accents, such as the so-called Estuary English, may be gaining ground, as reported in the article below from *The Times Educational Supplement* in October 1984.

After reading the article, answer the following questions:

- What are some of the distinctive features of Estuary English?

- What social reasons are suggested for its growing popularity?

ESTUARY ENGLISH

It seems . . . that the pronunciation of British English is changing quite rapidly. What I have chosen to term Estuary English may now and for the foreseeable future be the strongest native influence upon RP. 'Estuary English' is a variety of modified regional speech. It is a mixture of non-regional and local south-eastern English pronunciation and intonation. If one imagines a continuum with RP and London speech at either end, 'Estuary English' speakers are to be found grouped in the middle ground.

The heartland of this variety lies by the banks of the Thames and its estuary, but it seems to be the most influential accent in the south-east of England. It is to be heard on the front and back benches of the House of Commons and is used by some members of the Lords, whether life or hereditary peers. It is well established in the City, business circles, the Civil Service, local government, the media, advertising as well as the medical and teaching professions in the south-east. 'Estuary English' is in a strong position to exert influence on the pronunciation of the future.

On the level of individual sounds, or phonemes, 'Estuary English' is a mixture of 'London' and General RP forms. Although there are individual differences resulting from the speech background and choices of pronunciation made by the speaker, there is a general pattern. An example of this is the use of 'w' where RP uses 'l' in the final position or in a final consonant cluster. An 'Estuary English' speaker might use an articulation like a 'w' instead of the RP 'l' as many as four times in the utterance: 'Bill will build the wall.'

Non-Londoners often comment on what they see as the jerkiness of the speech of the capital. This is because of the use of a glottal stop in the place of the 't' or 'd' found in RP, as in the stage Cockney phrase: 'A li'le bi' of breab wiv a bi' of bu'er on i'.' This process seems to be analogous to the loss of the 't' in such words as 'Sco'land', 'ga'eway', 'Ga'wick', 'sta'ement', 'sea'-belt', 'trea'ment', and 'ne'work'. Not all RP speakers would sound these 't's. As would be expected, an 'Estuary English' speaker uses fewer glottal stops for 't' or 'd' than a 'London' speaker, but more than an RP speaker.

. . . Because it obscures sociolinguistic origins, 'Estuary English' is attractive to many. The motivation, often unconscious, of those who are rising and falling socio-economically is to fit into their new environments by compromising but not losing their original linguistic identity. Again, often unconsciously, those RP speakers who wish to hold on to what they have got are often aware that General RP is no longer perceived as a neutral accent in many circles. They are also aware that 'Conservative' and more so 'Advanced' RP can arouse hostility. What for many starts as an adaptation first to school and then working life, can lead to progressive adoption of 'Estuary English' into private life as well. Complicated as this may sound to a foreign user of English, these developments may be seen as a linguistic reflection of the changes in class barriers in Britain.

For many, RP has long served to disguise origins. 'Estuary English' may now be taking over this function. For large and influential sections of the young, the new model for general imitation may already be 'Estuary English', which may become the RP of the future.

Regional dialects and Standard English

In discussing accents we are concerned with variations in pronunciation (**phonology**); when we widen the enquiry to look at dialectal variation we consider differences in vocabulary and grammatical constructions. Some of the issues here become even more controversial, especially when they centre on the importance of Standard English, the notion of correctness and the relative status of regional dialects.

ACTIVITY 24

First we need to ask the question: why is it necessary for us to have a 'standard' vocabulary and grammar of English for all speakers? In groups, discuss this issue; try to suggest at least **five** reasons. List your responses and present them to the class, then compare your list with the commentary on pages 131–2.

For most of us, **Standard English** means the vocabulary laid down in good dictionaries, and the grammar of 'correct' English as taught in schools, used in books and broadcast by news media. However, only a relatively small number of us use Standard English exclusively; many of us also include in our speech words, expressions and grammatical constructions that are part of our regional dialects, as the following *Guardian* article from April 1998 makes clear.

CHILDREN USING GEATT WORDS INSTEAD OF STANDARD ENGLISH 'IS DEAD WRONG'

Children may choose not to speak properly even when they have a clear knowledge of standard English, a report for the Government's main curriculum quango said yesterday.

Tape recordings made of 11- and 15-year-olds in four regions of England revealed that many speakers used phrases such as 'They have fell out of the picture' or 'It could have came in the window' at the same time as Standard English.

The most common wrong usage was of 'there is' followed by a plural. In the south-west, children used 'them books' or 'they books', when they meant 'those books'.

On Merseyside, 'dead' meant 'very' as in 'dead good', on Tyneside 'geatt' was a versatile alternative to 'really', as in 'do it up geatt tight' or 'it's a geatt 20 miles'.

Richard Hudson, of University College, London, who analysed the speech of more than 350 children taped in class eight years ago, found that a third used no non-standard English at all, and that girls used fewer non-standard forms.

'Our evidence may indicate that mere exposure is not sufficient, and that some kind of direct teaching or encouragement is needed', Professor Hudson said.

ACTIVITY 25

Discuss and consider the following issues raised by the article, writing down your findings before comparing your ideas with the commentary on page 132:

- What reasons might children have for deliberately avoiding Standard English forms?

- What reasons are there to be either concerned or unconcerned that children are not using Standard English?

On the other hand, some people have expressed concern that some traditional dialectal forms are in the process of disappearing. Re-printed on page 117 is an article from *The Observer* which appeared in 1999.

ACTIVITY 26

Read the *Observer* article carefully. Make a note of the evidence and explanations it offers for the claim that dialect lexis is disappearing. What appears to be the writer's attitude to this development? What do you think will be lost if our dialectal vocabulary disappears?

OUR DISAPPEARING DIALECTS

Britain's rich fund of slang is fast dwindling. Terms such as 'cow-pawed' or 'thwart-eyed' – insults meaning left-handed or cross-eyed which were once commonplace in their native communities – are not thought likely to make it far into the next century.

Many regional forms of invective are already extinct, and the trend is set to continue.

The English spoken in Britain appears to be shedding its quirks comparatively faster than languages spoken in surrounding Western countries.

'The power of standard English seems to be a stronger force here than elsewhere', explained Leeds University lecturer Dr Clive Upton.

The decrease in the use of words such as 'urchin' for a hedgehog and 'lop' for a flea is the result of increased mobility in the population. In the past 50 years people's need to deal with others over a wider geographical area has put a premium on clear communication.

Dialects: lexical variation

To varying extents, each region or major town/city in the UK has its own dialectal vocabulary which differs from Standard English. Many of these dialect words have a very long history, and survive as relics of different dialects first brought to Britain by various Anglo-Saxon and Viking invaders. Dr Clive Upton, the researcher mentioned in the *Observer* article, helped to compile a linguistic atlas of Britain and has produced maps that show the geographical distribution of hundreds of dialect terms (*Word Maps: A Dialect Atlas of England*). For example, if we return to our Sunderland speaker's use of 'bairn' and 'clarts' (see Module 1), the maps indicate that 'bairn' is retreating northwards as the Standard English form 'child' becomes increasingly universal, and that 'clarts' is only one of many alternatives to the Standard English 'mud' spread throughout the country.

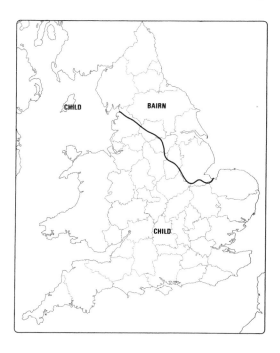

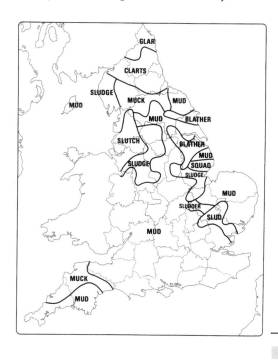

ACTIVITY 27

Find examples of your region's dialect. Carry out interviews with members of your family or neighbours, especially more elderly ones – it would be interesting to interview older people who were brought up in different parts of the country. One useful approach is to ask your interviewees to suggest alternative words for terms that often show marked regional variations. Some suggestions are:

- cold (adjective)

- a narrow alleyway running between houses

- a blister or blemish on the skin

- a gooseberry

- a silly or stupid person

- a splinter (of wood)

- a small bread bun

- a scarecrow.

Dialects: grammatical variation

Although people are often interested in and sympathetic to regional **lexis**, attitudes towards the distinctive **grammar** of regional dialects are often more hostile. Dialectal grammar tends to differ from Standard English in one or more of the following ways.

Subject verb agreement: verbs 'to be', 'to do'	Past tense forms may vary: 'we was', 'you was', 'I were'
	Present tense variations may include 'it do'
Other verb tense formations	The past tense of verbs 'do' and 'see' may become 'I done' or 'I seen'
Negative verb constructions	Forms such as 'ain't'
	Multiple negation as in 'I ain't done nothing' is common in many non-standard dialects
Reflexive pronouns ('myself', 'yourself')	Many variations include 'hissel', 'hissen', 'theirselves'

ACTIVITY 28

(a) Identify any examples of your own regional dialect grammar which correspond to the categories in the table above.

(b) Consider the following examples of dialect grammar, which are quoted from Peter Trudgill's *The Dialects of England* (1990). For each of these examples, decide whether or not you consider it to be 'good' grammar, and suggest a Standard English equivalent.

- Them books there.
- She sings nice.
- I don't want no trouble.
- Are any of youse coming?
- I never seed he.
- I sees the dentist tomorrow.
- He ain't coming.
- Give us a kiss.

Now compare your responses with the commentary on page 132.

(c) How did we come to have a number of non-standard and generally low-prestige dialectal varieties alongside the standard version of English? In groups, try to agree which of these statements you think offers the best explanation of how such varieties have arisen:

- Dialect speakers are simply making mistakes as a result of their faulty education, laziness or lack of intelligence.

- Dialects are derived from, and therefore corrupted versions of, the standard, correct version of English that we started off with.

- Other dialects of English have always existed alongside Standard English, but gradually lost respectability as Standard English became more important.

Compare your findings with the commentary on pages 132–3.

Dialects, Standard English and correctness

It is all too easy to see the grammar of regional dialects as a simplified or corrupted form of the language. This way of looking at non-standard varieties of the language is sometimes called a **deficit model**, and is based on a view that there is a preferred variety of English (Standard English) the rules of which can be laid down, or prescribed. For this reason, such a view of language is described as **prescriptive**.

Accent, dialect and gender

Some researchers have asked the question: Do men and women differ in their use of regional speech features? They have reported some significant findings.

ACTIVITY 29

From your own experience and observation, what difference, if any, would you expect to find between men and women of a similar social class in their use of regional speech? Think in terms of the 'strength' of accents and the use of non-standard dialectal grammar. Compare your findings with the commentary on page 133.

In 1982, the researcher Jenny Cheshire set out to find some answers by investigating the speech of some young speakers in Reading. Her findings are shown in the table.

Use of non-standard grammar by adolescent boys and girls in Reading

Example of non-standard form used	Boys	Girls
'I don't want nothing' (double negative)	100	75
'That ain't working' (non-standard negative 'to be')	74	42
'That's what I does' (non-standard first person 'do')	71	50

ACTIVITY 30

C3.3

(a) Examine Cheshire's data carefully. Note down any conclusions that can reasonably be drawn from her findings, and suggest possible explanations for the apparent trend that they reveal. Compare your notes with the commentary on page 133.

(b) Design an investigation that will allow you to survey use of non-standard lexis and grammar among students of similar backgrounds in your own school/college.

The origins of Standard English and regional dialects

Earlier, we considered the social and technological factors that made a 'standard' version of the language necessary (see page 114). However, if we retrace our steps to a time before electronic communications (the Internet, TV, telephones, radio), fast and convenient transport (aircraft, cars, railways), and widespread literacy with the availability of written texts, we arrive at a time when a standard was not really necessary. Such a time was the fifteenth century – at least until a single technological invention signalled the beginning of the process that would eventually lead to the Standard English we take for granted today. That invention was, of course, the printing press, developed and introduced to England by William Caxton in the 1470s.

Until then, manuscripts were all handwritten and literacy was the preserve of a small, privileged minority. In the two or three centuries after the invention of the press, books began to appear in large numbers, and we were on our way to becoming a print-based literate culture. However, for Caxton and the authors and printers who came after him, there was a problem: which dialect should they use?

ACTIVITY 31

Study the map below, which shows the approximate linguistic geography of fifteenth-century England, together with its principal dialect divisions. In the

centuries after Caxton, the development of a print industry accelerated the pressures for a version of the language that could be recognised as 'standard'. In groups, try to agree on which of the dialects indicated on the map you would back as the most likely candidate. As you make your judgement, consider the following factors:

- the centre of political power in England was London, where the monarch and the court were based

- the church – a very powerful institution during this period – was also based in London, though the universities of Oxford and Cambridge were important seats of learning and centres for the training of priests, who would come from different parts of the kingdom to study there

- commercial printing was based in London

- there seems to have been considerable migration of people from the east and central Midlands to London during the fourteenth century.

Now compare your suggestion with the commentary on page 133.

The outcome of this process of standardisation might have been very different if the distribution of power and influence had been otherwise. If, say, Newcastle upon Tyne had been the seat of government and the cathedral city of Durham exercised greater power than Oxford and Cambridge, this book might well have been written in the variety of English we now know as 'Geordie'.

Representations of accents and dialects

As you have already seen, transcribing regional speech presents some problems (see texts B and I in Module 1, pages 10 and 13). It is unusual to see regional lexis or grammar in texts, unless it is being quoted. We also tend to associate the conventional spelling of Standard English with RP pronunciation, so if we wish readers to 'hear' a particular accent it is necessary to depart from accepted usage. Broadly speaking, there are two ways of doing this, each with their advantages and disadvantages.

(1) Academic linguists have devised an alternative way of representing speech sounds: a set of symbols different from the usual English alphabet. This is the International Phonetic Alphabet, or IPA, which represents the individual phonemes used by speakers, and has a complex set of marks and symbols to indicate stress and intonation patterns. This system allows for a comprehensive and accurate representation of accent, but it is extremely complex, involves learning a new 'alphabet', and is only really comprehensible by other linguists.

(2) Writers often attempt a kind of 'phonetic' writing which remains based on Standard English but indicates some of the distinctive features of an accent by using alternative spellings. This is sometimes known as **eye-dialect**. It is usually easy to understand and can help most readers re-construct or 'hear' some accent features, but it is inevitably highly selective in the features it represents, and it uses a spelling system which is not an agreed and reliable representation of sounds.

ACTIVITY 32 — C3.3

(a) An example of Method (2) above is reproduced below. It is part of a poem designed to represent the accent of a speaker from Wigan in Lancashire, alongside a 'translation' in Standard English. When you have studied both versions of the poem, work through the following questions:

- Identify the distinctive **lexis** and **grammar** of the Wigan dialect represented in the poem.

- Identify the distinctive **phonological** (accent) features represented by the eye-dialect of the poem.

- Identify the specific devices used (the non-standard **orthography**) to represent these accent features.

(b) Try to write a short text – perhaps a short account of your day, or a meeting you have had – to reflect your own regional speech, and accompany it with a commentary in which you explain how you have used non-standard lexis, grammar and orthography to convey selected features of your local speech.

Faythers Day Eawt	Father's Day Out (Translation)
Eeh, owd cock, tha looks smart in yon jackit.	Old man, you look smart in that jacket.
Them britches thi fit thi reet weel.	Those trousers, they fit you very well.
Just wait till tha's geet thi new cap on.	Just wait till you've got your new hat on.
That collar, eaw does it feel?	That collar, how does it feel?
Come here, al tuck thi shart lap in.	Come here, I'll tuck your shirt tail in.
Un them draws tha's geet on, are they clen?	Those underpants you've got on, are they clean?
Un dust know that thi flies on thi pants are undone?	And do you know that the flies on your trousers are undone?
But tha'l at butt'n them up thi sen.	But you'll have to button those up yourself.

Take your studies further by making use of your school/college library. Here are some useful titles:

Chambers, J K & Trudgill P, *Dialectology*, CUP (2nd – 1998) ISBN 0521596467 (An established introductory undergraduate text.)

Honey, J, *Does Accent Matter?*, Faber & Faber (1991) ISBN 0571144446

Hughes, A & Trudgill P, *English Accents and Dialects*, Arnold (3rd – 1996) ISBN 0340614455 [An audiocassette of regional speakers can be purchased to accompany the book.]

Milroy, J & Milroy L (ed.), *Real English: The Grammar of English Dialects in The British Isles*, Longman (1993) ISBN 0582081769

Rampton, B, *Crossing: Language and Ethnicity among Adolescents*, Longman (1995) ISBN 0582217911

Sebba, M, *London Jamaican*, Longman (1993) ISBN 0582080959

Trudgill, P, *The Dialects of England*, Blackwell (2nd - 1999) ISBN 0631218157

Upton, C & Widdowson, J D A, *An Atlas of English Dialects*, OUP (1996) ISBN 0198692749

Preparing for the examination

The unit examination for this module lasts **1¹/₂ hours**. In that time you have to:

- study a selection of short spoken and written extracts illustrating aspects of the topics Language and Power, Language and Gender, Dialects of the British Isles and (from 2005) Language and Technology

- answer **two** questions based on these extracts, dividing your time equally between them.

In order to satisfy the **Assessment Objectives** in your answers you will need to:

(AO1) Write accurate, coherent analysis using appropriate terminology	Revise and learn the linguistic terminology you will need. Remember to revise the ideas and terms in both modules 1 and 2 – use your personal glossary, and the one at the back of this book, to help.
(AO3) Demonstrate your skills of linguistic analysis by applying the relevant frameworks	The exam involves analysis of samples of data. Your analysis should always be the primary aspect of your answer. Don't try to make it fit into the 'theories' or conclusions of the research you have studied; be open-minded, and always start from the data.
(AO4) Show you know, understand and can apply relevant ideas from language study to your analysis of data	You will be asked to analyse individual texts, but also to show that you can bring to your analysis a wider knowledge and experience of linguistic matters. You will need to be able to refer to the findings of different kinds of investigation and research. This can include your own, those carried out in class and by other students, and those published in academic text books. Revise for the exam by summarising some of these. **Remember**: start with the analysis of the data in front of you
(AO5) Show you understand how different aspects of social context influence specific features of language use	For each linguistic detail you discuss – graphological, lexical, grammatical, etc. – try to identify a specific social factor which has directly influenced it. Avoid simply 'feature spotting'; straightforward identification of linguistic features is not sufficient for this unit.

Commentaries

Activity 1

(a) Charlotte is fairly typical of many people these days, in that she has moved both geographically (from Manchester to Birmingham and now London) and socially (her parents had occupations that might traditionally be regarded as working class, but she is now in a professional, middle-class occupation). She also plays many different roles in the course of her week, so her correspondingly wide language repertoire makes her a particularly interesting linguistic subject.

The issues that you discussed may have included:

- How much of a Manchester **accent** did she grow up with, and does she still have it? Will she have lost it at university or afterwards? What might have caused her to do so – or not?

- In formal management meetings at work, would she adopt rather formal language styles and an accent closer to RP? As a manager, what sort of language does she use to give instructions to staff and exert her authority? Does she use terminology or **jargon** that is specific to the technology with which her company deals?

- What happens when she meets with her parents or friends from the North? Perhaps her original accent resurfaces as she re-establishes her bonds with her school friends. Does the same thing happen when she visits her parents? How would they react if she spoke to them in the same way as she speaks to her colleagues at work?

- No doubt Charlotte's language at home is different again; as a mother, she uses language to convey affection, encouragement and authority, as needs arise, and to discuss family issues.

- You may have also have identified gender as a factor in Charlotte's use of language; perhaps the way she talks with her female friends is different from the way she talks to men, or it may be that as a woman she uses language differently from men.

(b) Telephones have been around since the early twentieth century but the nature of the technology makes for conversations somewhat different from those conducted face to face. As illustrated in this example, we have developed specific routines for initiating, greeting and identification, and the absence of visual contexts and paralinguistic cues may affect the degree of explicitness, the way turn-taking is managed, and the need for greater-than-usual clarity.

Of course, in the context of this conversation, the way the interaction develops is determined by the fact that the customer expects a response to his concerns, whereas the role of the adviser is to represent the company and do what he can to satisfy the customer. In terms of status, the relationship is clearly an unequal one – the adviser addresses the caller politely, as 'Mr Brown' and 'sir', while identifying himself as Adam. The adviser speaks only when it is clearly his turn, whereas at the end of the extract the customer cuts in and interrupts him. Advisers are trained to handle calls like this in a particular way – whatever they might personally feel about the caller, they have to enact a particular role and use language in the ways required by their employers. Underpinning the dialogue there are two distinct **pragmatic** meanings – (1) the customer wishes to express his annoyance with the company, and (2) the employee wishes to retain his business and goodwill. Therefore the adviser uses polite phrases such as 'How may I help you?', whereas the customer is blunt and casual ('I'm getting a bit fed up') and even resorts to sarcasm ('name, number and shoe size'). The adviser skilfully combines his requests for information with expressions of concern ('I'm very sorry') and reassurance ('I'm sure I'll be able to sort things out') to calm the customer's irritation. He also makes sympathetic noises as the customer starts to explain the problem ('mm', 'oh').

Whether the conversation would be any different if it was a male/female, female/male, or female/female interaction is highly debatable, though some evidence and intuition suggests this might be the case. Our reaction to different accents does seem to be significant; call centres are often staffed by speakers with accents which surveys have suggested are perceived as 'friendly', whereas an RP accent is often seen as carrying authority.

Activity 2

(a) Text **A** is an example of an institutional switchboard message, and the nature of the technology (telephone) involved in the situation clearly determines many aspects of the data. The need for clarity, and absence of visual clues, imposes obvious **phonological** requirements, and the importance of greeting callers with an appropriate blend of friendliness and professionalism influences the choice of voice (RP for professional authority, with a hint of local accent for approachability) and lexis (formal in so far as it prefers 'require' to 'want', but very polite in its use of 'please' and 'thank you'). The **pragmatic** intent is presumably to create a favourable impression of friendly, polite efficiency. The choice of a female voice raises the question of gender; do callers perceive a female voice as more 'friendly' than a male voice? Might male and female callers respond differently?

In the conversation in text **B**, the symmetrical terms of address (first names) suggests an approximate equality of status although the relationship is complex; caller A, as a teacher, is notionally of a higher status than the technician B, but B's superior knowledge in this area almost reverses this, and in seeking assistance A is careful to use a range of politeness features ('sorry to bother you . . .') more usually associated with lower status speakers. The influence of technology here is significant; not only is it a telephone conversation but the subject matter refers to the ICT system, and the speakers share – to some extent – a knowledge of the technical lexis associated with it.

In text **C** the teacher's comments typify the way superior power or status is expressed in the right to evaluate the language of others. The text is a genre which is specific to a given context – evaluation of an academic assignment – and the writer's intention is to help the student improve without harming her self-confidence. This is directly reflected in the typical text structure: (1) positive point (2) things to improve (3) reassuring summary. The text is personalised by the use of the student's first name, but it is unlikely that the student would be able to reciprocate. The shared educational context enables the teacher to use several abbreviated references ('AOs').

Activity 4

(a) *Powerful individuals*: It would be surprising if you hadn't at least considered the Prime Minister and perhaps the Chancellor of the Exchequer as powerful individuals. You may have thought about the Queen, and then thought again – how much power does she really have these days? On the other hand, media giants such as Rupert Murdoch (owner of Sky and News International, which controls *The Times*, the *Sun* and the *News of the World*) clearly have tremendous influence, as does someone like Bill Gates, the owner of Microsoft, or leaders of big business and industry. You may also have decided that individual scientists, artists or even sporting figures exercise considerable power too, although the influence of some of these – especially in the realms of popular culture – may be rather short-lived.

Powerful groups: The answers to these questions may at first seem obvious. People from non-white backgrounds are generally under-represented in professions where power and influence are to be found (politics, the law, business management, the media), as are women, despite some advances in their position in the past 30 years. On the face of it, the people who control large businesses (managers, directors) would seem to have more power than those who work in them, and people who work in key positions in the media may have more influence than those who merely consume their products. In the north/south debate, northerners often complain that people closest to the southern centres of political and economic power enjoy greater wealth and influence.

However, in all of these cases, you may have thought of some contexts where these 'official' power structures are reversed. In some contexts, women may have more power, or at least more influence; well-organised groups of workers may, in some circumstances, appear to have more power than their bosses; and it might be argued that consumers exert ultimate power over big business by being able to decide whether or not to buy their products. Some figures may have huge influence even though they are 'only' pop stars or footballers, and within a group of apparently 'equal' friends and peers, there may be one individual who enjoys more status and respect because he or she is more witty, attractive, confident, rebellious, or whatever. In other words, some kinds of power are 'official' or obvious (overt) and others more 'unofficial' or less obvious ('covert').

Activity 6

Research suggests that we recognise a number of signs that a speaker is coming to the end of what she or he wants to say:

- **Paralinguistic** cues: the speaker's gestures, posture and eye contact may help us. For example, he or she may start to lean back in the seat, or sustain prolonged eye contact. Where this happens, it is likely that the person who receives the gaze will be the next speaker.

- **Phonetic** and prosodic cues: the speaker may pause, or intonation may indicate that he or she is approaching the end of an utterance. Undue hesitancy or non-fluency can therefore act as a turn-taking opportunity.

- **Syntactic** cues: we may recognise the approach of the end of a speaker's sentence.

- Nomination and direction: a speaker may explicitly identify the next speaker, as in 'Don't you think, Brian?'

Activity 7

(b) A's invitation includes some built-in protection in case of rejection. A suggests it is not a thing of huge importance – 'I was just wondering . . .' – so can save face if the answer is 'no'. A also creates a trivial social pretext (having a drink) for the proposed date. The pause before B's reply is awkward. Long pauses are not easily tolerated in English speech – we experience tension and embarrassment when they occur. Here the pause has the effect of suggesting that B is desperately trying to come up with an excuse. Why not just say 'no', or even 'look, I just don't fancy you'? Because we negotiate many situations involving proposal and acceptance/rejection in such a way as to protect the feelings of those involved. This is one aspect of what is sometimes called the 'politeness principle'.

Activity 8

(e) A starts by leading this part of the conversation, and at first B doesn't make a serious attempt to seize the floor or attempt to change the topic. B's first comments – 'oh', 'mm' and 'yeah' – are typical **minimal responses**, brief utterances that signal sympathetic encouragement and assure A that B is listening. However, A's speech shows some signs of non-fluency with two 2-second pauses and the breakdown of grammatical sense ('and (2) being (2) prejudging this bloke'), which prompts B to 'help out' by providing the supportive 'well that's all we can do'. However, by ending this turn with 'did he', a question tag, B in effect yields the floor back to A. A similar pattern can be seen in the next pair of turns. A pauses twice, but B refrains from interrupting, waiting instead until A seems to stumble over a phrase ('deputy's job'), which B helpfully suggests before giving way again. A is allowed to finish, and B adds the supportive agreement 'absolutely'. So B is certainly behaving in a very co-operative and helpful way, granting the floor and topic control to A, providing supportive minimal responses and even completing A's utterances when A seems to be stumbling.

Activity 11

At the start, Mandela uses the pronoun 'us' (a use of the first person that he sustains) to unite himself with his audience, creating the sense of unity that is one of the key themes of the speech. It is a tremendously emotional and optimistically forward-looking speech, as it anticipates 'liberty' which he personifies as a newly born infant. He also uses a pair of words that are often found together – 'hope' and 'glory' – and repeats this idea later. In the third sentence he lists three aims to try to inspire his listeners – 'ordinary South Africans' – to share the responsibilities for the future: to reinforce humanity's belief in justice, to strengthen its confidence in nobility etc., and to sustain all our hopes for a glorious life. Groups of three are oddly powerful in language, and are often to be found in persuasive texts.

As the speech moves on, his use of language becomes increasingly figurative, referring to South Africa as a body whose wounds are now to be healed, marred by chasms that need to be bridged and the bondage of poverty, deprivation, etc. As usual, the metaphors provide concrete images that express abstract ideas more vividly than the abstractions on their own, and when he talks of leading the country out of the 'valley of darkness', many of his listeners will be aware of the religious register of his language (and a reference to the Psalms of the Old Testament, in particular). The 'road' metaphor is frequently used, and compares the developments of an individual or country to a journey.

The speech builds to a climax with a series of repetitions that become very rhythmical. There are several 'let there be' statements (another echo from the Old Testament, here reminding listeners of another account of the creation of a 'new world' – in the story of Genesis, God says 'Let there be light'). This repetition of phrase or sentence structures is known as **parallelism**. Then there is the repeated 'never' – three times, once again – and the startling contrast between the image of the 'beautiful land' and the 'skunk' to which he compares a South Africa that was for many years shunned by the international community (skunks are shunned because of the vile smell they emit). The climax of the speech works through its simplicity and the shortness of its phrases, as well as the religious reference ('God bless Africa') and the final note of humility with which Mandela thanks his audience.

Activity 13

(a) As a title, 'Master' is relatively rare, being confined to rather formal use when applied to young boys. It has a rather old-fashioned upper-class connotation too, as it might have been used by a domestic servant when addressing the young man of a wealthy household. It may have struck you that in its other forms – to 'master an art', or to 'achieve mastery', or to 'be masterful', it implies command and authority. 'Miss', on the other hand, applies not just to young girls but to women who are unmarried. Even mature women may be described as 'Miss', but not always with positive connotations. So although we have a pair of words that appear to be symmetrical, in fact their usage and connotations are quite different. We call such a difference **semantic asymmetry**.

(b) and **(c)** The title taken by adult women ('Miss' or 'Mrs') reveals their marital status, something that men do not reveal when entitling themselves 'Mr'. Women are thus defined in terms of their relationship to a man, reflecting their lack of social, economic or personal independence in former times. For this reason, the term 'Ms' was coined as an optional equivalent to the male 'Mr'. However, it is by no means universally used or accepted, and is derided by some as the choice of adult women with feminist inclinations.

(d) No doubt you know that English offers a rich source of unpleasant insults to be applied to women – many of which attack them for suggestions of sexual impropriety ('slag', 'slut', 'slapper' etc). Few such terms are available for abusing promiscuous men, though some, such as 'tart', are beginning to be applied to males in an ironic way. The absence of words to insult promiscuous men is an example of what is called a lexical gap – an area of experience or meaning for which the language does not seem to supply a suitable word.

(e) While 'manager' and 'manageress' appear to describe the same job, in practice there are differences. Would we expect the female boss of a major international company to be called the manageress? Probably not. Actually, the term 'manageress' seems to be reserved for lower-status managerial positions, reflecting an expectation that women would not occupy the very top jobs. The morpheme '-ess' also draws our attention to the gender of the person in an explicit way, which the term 'manager' does not, as is the case with 'author' and 'authoress'. Another way of putting this is to say that the female is the marked form.

'Father' and 'mother' seem unproblematic enough as nouns, but when we think about their use as verbs ('he fathered three children' and 'she mothered him somewhat'), we discover very different connotations. Fathering is a rather proud act of reproduction which ends with conception. Mothering begins after the birth, and can have connotations of unhealthy protectiveness and smothering.

'Lord' and 'Lady' also reveal an asymmetry in their wider use. 'To lord it' over someone implies authority, status and assertiveness, reflecting the original social and economic power that a 'lord' enjoyed; however, we cannot say 'to lady it' over someone – 'ladies' don't assert or enforce power; to be 'ladylike' implies a quiet gentility that is in keeping with traditional stereotypes of gracious feminine behaviour. 'Master' we have already touched on; the apparently opposite term 'mistress' has very different connotations, of course. A married man involved in an extra-marital affair may have a mistress, but a married woman in a similar situation is not said to have 'taken a master'.

Activity 14

When this test was given to a group of Year 11 school students, the most common choices were 'he' for numbers 1 and 3 and 'she' for 2. Some students spotted the trick, of course, and suggested 'he or she' or 's/he', but the majority assumption was clear. The term 'engineer' is apparently a gender-free term – there is no single word meaning 'female engineer' – but it seems to contain an invisible male marking. 'Nurse' works in the opposite way, so much so that the term 'male nurse' is often used in the same way as people can sometimes be heard referring to a 'lady doctor'; the term 'doctor' is felt to imply maleness. In fact the term 'doctoress' was in use until the nineteenth century. So it seems that our language often encodes historical assumptions about gender roles and the occupations that men and women follow.

Activity 15

The 'chairman' issue is still unresolved. Although its use is generic, as with the other examples in the list the word nevertheless encodes an assumption that the person in question – here, the most powerful person on a committee – must be male. Nowadays, if the chairman is a woman, we may feel this to be a contradiction. Nevertheless, 'chairwoman' is not widely used as it uses a female-marked gender form and thus seems to draw attention to the gender of the person in a way that 'chairman' does not. 'Chairperson' is unwieldy, and as with other cases where 'person' has been substituted for 'man', has been the butt of jokes about 'political correctness'. 'Chair' may be the best alternative as it already exists as a verb ('to chair a meeting'), but its use is by no means universal.

Similar objections apply to many of the other examples. 'Fireman' has now been replaced by the generic 'firefighter' as a job title, 'foreman' is just as likely to be 'supervisor', and 'manning' is just as easily referred to as 'staffing'.

Activity 17

(a) Throughout the text, the genders have been reversed; that is, all of Tom's actions, speech and thoughts have been attributed to Virginia, and vice versa. To restore the original text, simply substitute 'Tom' for 'Virginia' (and vice versa) and reverse all the he/him she/her references. ('Rosy' was originally 'Ross'.)

Activity 19

(b) Jennifer Coates writes in her book *Women, Men and Language*:

> What effects do such violations of normal turn-taking in conversation have? It seems that after overlaps and especially after interruptions, speakers tend to fall silent. Since most interruptions are produced by men in mixed-sex conversations, the speaker who falls silent is usually a woman. Silence is often a sign of malfunction in conversation. These silences resulted not just from interruptions and overlaps, but also from delayed minimal responses. In mixed-sex conversations male speakers often delayed their minimal responses, signalling a lack of interest in the speaker's topic.
>
> When talking with women, men seem to use interruptions and delayed minimal responses to deny women the right to control the topic of conversation. Men disobey the normal turn-taking rules in order to control topics.

However, many researchers would now take issue both with the methods used in this experiment and Coates's rather simplistic conclusions – see part (c) of the Activity.

Activity 22

While it may be true that most newsreaders are university educated, it is unlikely that they all grew up speaking RP, so the 'schools' explanation is likely to be the least significant one. The 'understanding' explanation seems more attractive: after all, RP is widely used and understood, and is associated with clarity of delivery. However, programmes such as *EastEnders* and *Coronation Street* regularly top the popularity ratings, and even the weather reports that precede or follow news bulletins are often delivered by speakers with regional accents. Does this mean that we spend our time watching soap operas and weather forecasts that we can barely understand? No; rather, as Giles's study suggests, it is because RP is associated in our culture with intelligence, authority and education. We are more likely to believe that the news is truthful and to be taken seriously if it is delivered in RP than if it were spoken in, say, a Liverpudlian accent. Ultimately, this is linked to the stereotypes commonly associated with people from different regions and different social backgrounds. The weather is a different matter, as it is less 'serious' than the news, and soap operas are, of course, fictional.

Activity 24

Among the many possible reasons, perhaps you included these:

- the mass media (TV, press) are produced for national and international consumption

- printed texts have to be written for universal understanding and consumption – it would be impractical to produce different versions of the same books in different dialects

- electronic communications reach not just across the UK but (via the Internet) the world

- we now belong to a very mobile community of English speakers – many of us travel frequently for business and pleasure

- English is a world language and foreign learners need to have one version to learn.

Activity 25

Perhaps you suggested that it was important to the children to use the language of their friends and fit in with them, rather than use the standard forms – an example of the **covert prestige** of non-standard forms in action. Turning to the second question, children need to be able to use Standard English to gain qualifications and function effectively in a print-orientated society. Even in speech, non-standard English is often seen as 'poor' or 'incorrect' and may present an unfavourable impression if used in formal or professional contexts. The counter-argument is that children can understand the need to use Standard English when necessary, but should not be discouraged from using regional speech in informal contexts where it is perfectly acceptable. Besides, it is impossible for schools to tell children how to speak in the playground or among friends.

Activity 28

(b) It would not be surprising if you decided that none of these expressions were 'good' grammar; by definition, none of them belongs to the grammatical structures of Standard English and therefore, in many people's eyes, they are not correct or proper English. Whereas people seem happy to accept that dialects preserve an interesting lexical diversity, the view has taken root that dialect grammar is a corruption of 'proper' English grammar, and that thousands of people in a particular region must somehow be making grammatical 'mistakes' whenever they speak.

However, this is a misguided view. No less than its lexis, a dialect's grammatical system is rooted in that dialect's history – and far from being incorrect or corrupt versions of what we now know as Standard English, dialects have enjoyed a parallel development to the prestige variety of the language. As you will learn in your A2 course, the notion of Standard English that emerged gradually from the fifteenth to the eighteenth centuries was based largely on the speech of those who happened to enjoy some education, influence and power in the south-east of England. By the eighteenth century a clear notion of 'correctness' established itself, with the effect that other dialects were increasingly castigated as inferior or uneducated.

(c) All speakers sometimes make mistakes in their language use – slips of the tongue, minor grammatical errors, sentences getting muddled up, and so on – but it would be remarkable if thousands of speakers were simultaneously and consistently making the same mistakes, which is what statement (1) seems to imply. The examples given are themselves part of the grammatical system of the local dialect, rather than 'mistakes'. Neither is it true to say that non-standard varieties are all derived from a superior, standard version of the language. Many of the dialects we now speak can be traced back to the centuries before the Norman conquest, when Anglo-Saxon and Norse tribes first arrived in Britain from different parts of Germany and Scandinavia. Many distinctive Yorkshire and north-eastern dialect expressions, for example, owe their origins to the presence of the Vikings. So statement (3) offers the most accurate description here.

Activity 29

There seems to be a marked difference between male and female speakers, especially within the lower middle class. Researchers have reported that more than a quarter of males use a particular accent feature, whereas only a tiny minority of females do so. Of course, what you expected to find would depend on your individual observations and speculation. Many people do report, however, an anecdotal perception that boys and men are more likely to talk with a stronger, more pronounced regional accent than their female counterparts. There is considerable speculation and disagreement about the reasons for this. One argument is that local accents tend to be associated with working-class life, which is also identified with 'tough' masculine qualities. Female speakers are therefore less likely to identify with such values; a male speaker with a strong accent may be described as 'tough', whereas men may describe a woman with a similar accent as 'rough' or unfeminine. Another theory is that traditional working-class social networks based on the workplace serve to 'bond' men more closely than women, and that regional speech becomes one of the ways in which men signal the fact that they belong to this group. Other explanations focus on women's alleged sensitivity to the importance of social mobility and a greater anxiety to make a favourable social impression. Needless to say, many of these speculations have proved highly controversial.

Activity 30

(a) The figures from Cheshire's study seem to confirm that males are more likely to prefer the non-standard, lower prestige form than females within the same social class. Interestingly, the researcher tried to relate individuals' use of these dialect forms to their perceived toughness in the eyes of their peers. Sure enough, the boys who used most of the dialectal forms also emerged as those with a high 'toughness' rating. We might conclude that the covert prestige of the dialect seems to be strongest among male speakers because of its association with desirable masculine attributes such as toughness, aggression and even rebelliousness.

Activity 31

You were probably correct in your deduction – it was indeed the East Midlands dialect, spoken in the area including Oxford and Cambridge as well as London, that became the model. After all, this was the dialect used by anyone with power and influence – the court, the church and the printing industry. The dialect we now respectfully see as 'correct' English became so not because it was in any sense a 'purer' or 'better' version of English, but simply because it was the language of power.

This module counts for **30%** of the AS qualification, or **15%** of the total A level marks.

ASSESSMENT OBJECTIVES

The skills and knowledge that you develop in this module, and which you will be required to demonstrate in your coursework folder, are defined by the examination board's Assessment Objectives. These require that you:

- **AO1**: communicate clearly the knowledge, understanding and insight appropriate to the study of language, using appropriate terminology and accurate and coherent written expression
  (5 out of the 30 marks for the Unit; 5% of the final AS mark; $2\frac{1}{2}$% of the final A Level mark)

- **AO2**: demonstrate expertise and accuracy in writing for a variety of specific purposes and audiences, drawing on knowledge of linguistic features to explain and comment on choices made
  (20 out of the 30 marks for the Unit; 20% of the final AS mark; 10% of the final A Level mark)

- **AO4**: understand, discuss and explore concepts and issues relating to language in use
  (5 out of the 30 marks for the Unit; 5% of the final AS mark; $2\frac{1}{2}$% of the final A Level mark)

What this module is all about

In this module, you have the opportunity to apply your growing knowledge about and understanding of texts to some writing of your own. As this is a coursework module, it also allows you to develop pieces of writing over a period of time, redrafting and refining them until they are as good as you can make them.

The **basic requirements** for your coursework folder are as follows:

- Two pieces of your own writing totalling between 1500 and 3000 words. The choice of subject matter of the pieces is entirely open.

- The two pieces should be for distinctly **different** primary purposes.

- The pieces should also achieve a variety in their intended audiences and **genres**.

- The two pieces need to be accompanied by **commentaries** of up to 1500 words in which you explain, justify and evaluate your own writing.

Some aspects of this work may appear familiar from the kinds of writing you did as part of your GCSE coursework; in some important respects, however, Original

Writing presents you with a different kind of challenge from GCSE. It is designed to lay the foundations for Module 5, Editorial Writing, which is part of the A2 English Language course.

In addition, this module provides opportunities to meet several of the requirements for Key Skills Communication Level 3, as it involves reading and synthesising (C3.2) and the production of two documents, at least one of which will be 'extended' (C3.3). If you decide to produce the script for a talk or presentation, you can also satisfy the requirement for C3.1b.

ACTIVITY 1

Some of the key features of Original Writing are summed up in the following table. Answer the questions in the third column, either through discussion or in writing.

Key concept	Explanation	Discussion issue
Produce **real** texts for **real** purposes	You are aiming to produce texts that could fulfil a purpose and find a market in the world beyond the classroom. This means writing material that 'real' people – not just your teacher – would either need or want to read or hear. The texts you write must be much more than mere writing exercises.	How far was this true of the writing assignments in your GCSE English course? Suggest examples of assignments which either met, or did not meet, this condition.
Aim for **professional and publishable** standards	Your aim should be to produce texts which would be worthy of serious consideration for publication. This means that the control of expression, tone, style and technical accuracy should be of a significantly higher standard than at GCSE. 'Publication' may, of course, include local outlets such as student magazines, local newspapers, fanzines and websites, as well as more ambitious media like national newspapers and magazines.	Find out if anyone you know has had writing published in any form. How did they go about it? What was involved in the process?
Writing should be underpinned by **key language concepts** from Modules 1 and 2	You should consciously make links between your writing and the knowledge about language you have gained in Modules 1 and 2. This is your chance to apply theories about language in use to your own practical writing. There may even be opportunities to turn a piece work carried out as part of your work on Modules 1 and 2 into an Original Writing submission.	Brainstorm any 10 ways in which the work you have done so far on Modules 1 and 2 might relate to your own work as a producer of texts.

Key concept	Explanation	Discussion issue
Writing should be a **developmental** process	You should expect to draft and re-draft your work several times, taking on board the editorial advice of your teacher and fellow students and testing the piece on 'guinea pig' readers typical of your target audience.	Suggest 5 reasons why this process is going to be necessary.
Commentaries should be self-critical and **reflective**	The process of writing involves **making choices** of structure and style, and as you work on your writing and apply your growing understanding of language, you should become increasingly reflective, and analytical about your own work. This is where the **commentaries** come in; in fact, these count for one-third of the total marks for this module. Watch out for the **'Commentary tips'** throughout this module; they will flag up many of the writing issues you should discuss.	Start by defining for yourself your strengths and weaknesses as a writer.
Research and **study** model texts	Nobody produces texts in a vacuum. If you are aiming to write a particular type of text, it makes sense first of all to carry out a study of texts of a similar type to understand the usual conventions and expectations of the genre. You can then try to make your text use these creatively. Such examples are known as **style models**.	Consider these two points together. How far do they contradict one other?
Writing should be **original**	The pieces you submit are not likely to be the same as that of other students in your class – the best work usually arises not from class exercises set by the teacher but from individual writing projects which reflect your own interests. To some extent, your own work should have a distinctive style and voice. *Important note*: It is essential that the work you submit *is* your own; material which is reproduced from other sources (such as the Internet) could cause you to be disqualified.	
Not all writing is **'literary'**	You may like to include some 'literary' writing – a genre of fiction, drama, or even poetry – as part of your submission, but the emphasis on the course as a whole is *not* on the kinds of writing you would study as part of an English Literature course.	List some genres of writing which might be described as non-literary.

Producing your texts

Much of your work in Module 1 focused on the various influences which help determine what texts are like, and how these contextual factors – especially **audience, purpose, genre** and **medium** – shape the way language is used in a given situation. In particular the **structure, register, tone** and **style** of the text are influenced by these factors.

As you create your own pieces of writing, you need to ask the same questions, and eventually answer these questions in the accompanying commentaries.

'Primary purposes' of texts

A cautionary note: in this module we will organise our investigation of Original Writing according to the four primary purposes introduced in Module 1 (see page 15):

- to inform

- to instruct

- to entertain

- to persuade.

However, as you have already discovered in Module 1, it is important to remember many texts have multiple purposes and that it is not always easy to define which one is primary. The important issue when you eventually choose your two pieces to submit is that they are significantly different in purpose from each other – but any one piece may have two or more purposes, as the following examples illustrate.

ACTIVITY 2

Listed below are several types of text which may be attractive options for individual Original Writing tasks. Use a table like this one to note how far they fulfil the different purposes indicated, and decide which of the purposes is *primary*.

Text	Purposes	Comment
A review of a concert or film	Inform, entertain or persuade?	
A guide to a particular town or holiday resort	Inform or persuade?	
An article about a musician or a footballer in a lifestyle magazine	Entertain or inform?	

Text	Purposes	Comment
A story written for children	Entertain or persuade?	
A website devoted to a musician or celebrity	Entertain, inform, persuade or instruct?	
The script for a TV 'food and drink' programme, including recipes	Instruct or entertain?	
An audio guide given to visitors to an exhibition or historic site	Instruct, inform or entertain?	
The script of a satirical TV/radio show, such as Alistair McGowan's *Big Impression*	Entertain or persuade?	

Commentary tip

When reflecting on your writing, acknowledge and explain that it may have primary and secondary purposes. Go on to discuss how these are reflected in the language you have used.

As you work through this module, you will have the opportunity of attempting several different pieces of writing before finally choosing two pieces which you will develop fully as your own individual writing submission. Whatever kinds of writing you attempt, here are some hints which may help you to become a better writer.

Good writing practice

- To be a good writer you need to be a **reader** – so make sure you read plenty of different kinds of writing in newspapers, magazines and the media generally.

- Good writing is anything that communicates effectively with its intended audience – so as you read, consider the different ways in which writers of different texts communicate (e.g. *The Guardian*, *NME*, *Just 17*, Radio 1, Radio 4).

- As you browse and read, you may come across items of particular interest which may be the seed of a writing idea. Keep a **scrapbook** for such items.

- You might want to keep a separate notebook or **writer's log** – paper-based or electronic – or use the back of your scrapbook for scribbling down ideas for pieces of writing. These may strike you at any time, so keep your log handy!

- Writing is a skill you can improve only through regular practice – so try to **write frequently**. Use your notebook to scribble down reflections, observations or accounts of experiences. Use it as a diary if you like – and don't discard or delete anything! It may come in useful one day – especially for writing your commentaries (see pages 187–8 below).

Writing to inform

There are many different kinds of texts in different media whose primary purpose is to inform, even though there may well also be elements of entertainment, instruction and persuasion involved.

In every case, for the informative writing to be successful, there needs to be:

- something a group of people need or want to know

- a writer able to fill this gap by providing the relevant information

- an appropriate form or medium which enables the writer to reach his or her audience

- a shared language which the writer can use so as to make the information accessible to the audience.

ACTIVITY 3

(a) For each of the contexts given here, complete the missing details by considering either **who** needs to know (target audience), **what** they need to know (subject/information) or via which **media** they can best be reached.

(b) Collect or make a note of texts similar in kind to those listed.

Context *Where/when?*	Target audience *Who needs to know?*	Subject/information *What do they need to know?*	Media/genres *How can the audience best be reached?*
Your school or college	Students in the institution	How to choose and apply to a university	Tutorial presentation Pamphlet/handouts Intranet site
School	Year 11s thinking of studying A levels	What studying A level English Language is like	
Teenage girls' magazine	Girls aged 12-16		Magazine article
Tourist information	Visitors to your area		
Current affairs magazine	Adult non-scientists with a general interest	How cloning works	

Context *Where/when?*	Target audience *Who needs to know?*	Subject/information *What do they need to know?*	Media/genres *How can the audience best be reached?*
Local museum/ exhibition	Visitors to the museum	The subject of the exhibition; background information to explain the items displayed	
Local Health Authority campaign		How to be protected against flu this winter	

(c) Collect and add to the table your own list of informative texts, both spoken and written. These may include:

- news/sports reports and articles in various kinds of newspapers and magazines and on radio

- pamphlets, leaflets and hand-outs

- text books

- CD ROMs

- radio/tape reports

- different kinds of talks and presentations

- websites

- popular encyclopaedias (e.g. David Crystal's *Cambridge Encyclopaedia of the English Language*, CUP)

- 'part works' (weekly or monthly instalment-based reference magazines on a variety of subjects; those launched in 2003 included one series devoted entirely to miniature teapots!)

- posters and wall charts

- factual books aimed at younger readers (e.g. *Horrible Histories*, published by Eaglemoss Publications).

As you begin to look closely at your examples of informative writing, the most important question to ask is: How does each text bridge the **'information gap'** in a way that suits the intended audience?

ACTIVITY 4

To investigate how informative writing works, you will need to carry out a detailed survey of a number of different kinds of texts, both spoken and written. The texts shown on the next few pages should get you started – if you are working in groups, each group could concentrate on one and share findings later. The commentary on pages 189–91 refers to these in some detail. However, you should also extend your survey by looking at additional examples. Look at the ways in which:

- factual material is presented to younger readers in the *Horrible Histories* series

- travel writers/journalists describe their experiences of holiday destinations in the travel sections of newspapers

- technical or scientific material is presented to a non-specialist audience in newspaper supplements such as *Guardian Education*.

For each of the texts you survey, try to answer the following questions:

Key question
1   How does the writer 'hook' the audience and convince them that they need or ought to be interested in what follows?
2   How is the information organised and structured, and how easy is it for the reader/listener to follow? Look out for the use of section headings, panels, boxes, bullet points and sub-headings in written texts.
3   For audio texts, what use is made of different voices, music and sound effects (SFX), and how are the listeners made aware of the structure of the text (the equivalent of headings and sub-headings)?
4   What does the writer of the text seem to assume about the audience and their interest in or knowledge of the topic? How can you tell?
5   How does the writer refer to people, places, films, TV programmes, etc, and what does this say about the assumptions made about the audience? For example, if an article refers to 'Paris', does it simply say 'Paris', or 'Paris, the capital of France', or 'a city in France called Paris', or even 'a big city in a country called France'?
6   Identify any specialist or technical terms introduced. How, if at all, are they explained?
7   Consider the following types of information that might appear in an informative text. What are the proportions of each in the texts you are examining?   • Facts and figures.   • Diagrams, images and charts.

Key question

- Stories or anecdotes about individual people and their experiences.
- Detailed and factual explanations.
- Amusing or light-hearted comments.

8	In general, what level of formality or seriousness is maintained?
9	If images or diagrams are used, how does the writer help the reader make sense of them?
10	Does the text directly address the reader or listener using the second-person pronoun ('you'), and if so with what effect?
11	Does the text use either the first-person singular 'I', or the plural 'we'? This is rare in information texts. What might be the reasons for these choices?
12	How far does the text also fulfil an instructive, entertaining or persuasive function?

TEXT A

CASH IN HAND

First things first - let's earn some money! Your year could start at home, working round the clock, saving like mad to finance any travel planned for later on. Alternatively, you can combine job & adventure by working abroad.

Follow the French *vendange* as the grapes ripen, work the winter season as a waiter in a Swiss ski resort; spend the summer as a courier on the Spanish coast . . .

Elizabeth worked in hotels in Germany, Switzerland and France, interspersed with travel around Europe and Canada: *My year out financed itself completely, with money to do some travelling I couldn't otherwise have done.*

Iain worked in Curry's in order to finance a trip to Australia; Jacci stacked shelves for 7 months at Tesco to pay for an expedition to Indonesia. Both feel that it was more than worth it. Rachel was doing hotel work when her luck was in one Saturday; her £10,000 share of a lottery win went to fund voluntary work and some travel.

If you see the gap as a chance to gain work experience, perhaps leading to sponsorship or a future career, then you could apply for an industrial or commercial placement, where you'll do real work for a real salary. Henry spent most of his year on a feasibility study for Shell: *It was meaningful and relevant work, and valuable experience for someone about to start a degree in engineering.*

☼ **Where to find out more** (see *Resources*)
📖 *Working Holidays*: short-term/seasonal work
📖 *A Year Between*: work placements and more
📖 *Workplace*: work experience options

TEN WAYS TO FILL THE GAP

CREATIVE OPTIONS FOR TAKING A YEAR OUT

Gain new skills, develop existing ones, broaden horizons. The gap year is a rare chance to stand back, assess where life has brought you so far, and seize the freedom to take on a different challenge.

VOLUNTEER!

Maybe you would like to contribute something to society by working as a volunteer, though this demands commitment, not just an urge to see the world with a bit of work thrown in. There are thousands of projects to choose from; most gap year placements are in Europe or America, rather than the Third World. Development projects need those with specialist skills and experience, though there are openings helping less privileged members of your own society. Overseas placements are an educational experience as well as a period of service; you may have to pay a fee and cover your own travel expenses to offset any costs to the host community.

Jo worked on a project building village health centres in Tanzania: *Definitely a beneficial experience, working in a team, getting first-hand experience of life in a developing country. I learned Swahili, saw the way of life in rural Africa and came back with greater awareness and self-confidence.*

Jayne volunteered for 6 months at a hostel for homeless people: *I found myself in an environment that was often challenging, frequently confronted with new situations. I'd recommend voluntary service as a way of discovering your expectations and uncovering problems that exist in society.*

☼ **Where to find out more** (see *Resources*)
📖 *Working Holidays*: short-term projects
📖 *A Year Between*: volunteering in a year out
📖 *Volunteer Work*: for those with experience

(continued)

GLOBE TROTTING

Travel to far flung corners on a Round-The-World (RTW) ticket, stop off for an overland trek, a spot of river-rafting or lazy days on the beach. Take a tour round Europe: sample sunlit Italy or explore Scandinavia. RTW air tickets can be tailor-made; route combinations are endless, restricted only by the time and money you have available. Keep going in the same direction; backtracking puts up the price. Pick your final destination, say Sydney, then places to visit en route: New York on the way out, Bangkok and Vienna on your way home. An open ticket means you can enter and leave a country or continent by different airports - ideal for overland trekkers.

Planning a grand tour? Inter-Rail passes allow up to a month's rail travel through Europe and around the Med. Eurotrain tickets, valid for 2 months, allow you to plan your route and stop off along the way. Obtainable at student travel agencies; Inter-Rail and other passes from major railway stations. On a tight budget? The cheapest way round Europe is by coach; stow your luggage in the boot and forget about it till you get there. Eurolines offers coach services to over 400 destinations. Bookings can be made through student travel agencies.

☼ **Where to find out more**
- Campus Travel: offices on student campuses nationwide (in London ✆ 0171-730 8111)
- STA Travel: offices in London (✆ 0171-361 6166) and throughout the UK
- USIT: office in Belfast (✆ 01232 324073)

ADVENTURE & DISCOVERY

A variety of operators specialise in adventure packages: overland tours/treks across Asia, Africa or Latin America; student travel agencies can make bookings. Expedition and exploration programmes are great for developing self-confidence, teamwork, maturity and leadership skills.

They'll teach you survival in an Arctic climate or jungle terrain and will involve an aspect of community service, conservation or environmental research to challenge decision-making and problem-solving abilities. You'll need to raise money to take part - all part of the challenge, testing your resourcefulness and imagination. Sponsored events can be good ways to raise funds - the wackier the better. Try bungee jumping, racing rubber ducks down the river, or cleaning someone's car with a toothbrush!

Clare took part in an expedition to Indonesia working on a turtle project: *Definitely the most brilliant and valuable experience of my life so far. I learnt a great deal about the Indonesian way of life, the jungle, how to cope with people 24 hours a day, how to help each other through thick and thin, and how to cope with hardship. I made friends for life.*

☼ **Where to find out more** (see *Resources*)
- *A Year Between:* expeditions offering the opportunity to increase understanding of the environment, people and cultures
- Expedition Advisory Centre can advise on planning expeditions

LEARN A NEW LINGO

A year out offers a brilliant chance to learn or brush up on another language, perhaps by spending time studying abroad. In today's workplace, most employers expect an international outlook with foreign language fluency. Your future university course may involve work or study abroad. Get a head start by getting to grips with the language. Options range from 2 week intensive courses, through 1-2 month summer schools, right up to an academic year.

Miranda took an intensive Spanish course in Barcelona: *I was almost a complete beginner, but 3 weeks saw a real improvement. I'm now doing beginner's Spanish at university, where a high level has to be reached after one year. The course in Barcelona has definitely been an advantage in all aspects. As well as teaching me something about Spanish life, it has given me the confidence to participate in class. Overall my gap year improved my confidence, gave me independence and helped me organise things for myself. It's been the best year of my life and has contributed to having a fantastic time at university.*

☼ **Where to find out more** (see *Resources*)
- *A Year Between:* gap year courses
- *Home From Home:* language learning through homestays and exchanges

Over the page Exchange Cultures; At the Chalkface; Eco-Logic; Expand your Mind; Stay at Home! *and* Resources.

TEN WAYS TO FILL THE GAP is one of a series of leaflets published by the Central Bureau for Educational Visits & Exchanges, 10 Spring Gardens, London SW1A 2BN. For further information ✆ 0171-389 4886 Fax 0171-389 4426

TEXT B

N IS FOR NO MORE ALBUMS (OR SINGLES)

Thanks to internet piracy and CD burning, the way bands release their material is set to change forever

TEXT: PETER ROBINSON

Since the invention of the CD player and its marvellous skip facility, our listening habits have changed. We're now much less likely to wade through duff tracks by listening to albums end to end. Still, it's (kind of) nice to know that they're there. But if the events threatening to unfold during 2003 reach their logical conclusion, those few tracks we listen to most will actually be the only ones we ever hear. During the next 12 months, the music industry will make its first, lumbering steps towards a business model that will spell the end not just of the album – but of album tracks, too. Oh, and it's all our own fault.

2002 was the year the global music industry lost control, of its product and of its consumers. Sales were down – seven per cent year on year, according to one report from the Recording Industry Association of America (RIAA). Blame was laid squarely (and unfairly) at the door of internet piracy and CD burning. As the RIAA shut down file-sharing networks like Audiogalaxy and Muchmusic, so others sprang up with services more sophisticated but just as illegal, providing more than enough material to fill the 2.2 billion blank CDs sold last year . . .

The music industry should have seen the internet as its friend more than half a decade ago but, finally, it's decided to harness the evil and offer tracks for legitimate download. Microsoft's MSN network have already introduced such a service, and HMV are minimising the future damage to their high street sales by offering another. At a price, naturally, with different payment tiers depending on whether you want to stream a song, download it for a limited period, or download it and burn to disc . . .

Time for a comparison test, then: MSN's legal service vs WinMX's illegal peer-to-peer network. On MSN's service, only one in every seven of our searches found us an artist whose label had given permission for their artists to be included. (It's likely most indie labels haven't even been approached.) So: no Ladytron on MSN, though WinMX returns over 100 different files. No Streets (WinMX gave us the album, all the B-sides and mixes, and a couple of live recordings we hadn't come across), no Radiohead (we stopped counting when WinMX got to 3,000 files). No White Stripes, no Libertines. No Oasis, even though MSN's co-branded BT Broadband promotion uses a picture of Liam Gallagher. Oh, and MSN's nearest offering for The Smiths is 'String Quartet Op.11, Molto Adagio pt3' by the Smithsonian Chamber Players.

© Peter Robinson/NME/IPC Syndication

TEXT C

IF YOU'RE THINKING HOW EASY IT WOULD BE TO MAKE LIKE LIGHT-FINGERED STAR WINONA, THINK AGAIN. A GROWING NUMBER OF SHOPLIFTING TEENS ARE PAYING A HUGE PRICE FOR THEIR CRIME. ERIN KELLY REPORTS

THE *REAL* PRICE OF SHOPLIFTING

I t's Saturday afternoon. You're checking out the make-up in a store, when you realise just how easy it would be to slip the lip balm into your bag. So you do. Your heart is pounding as you walk out on to the street. And then you feel it – a firm hand on your shoulder, asking if you can just step back inside and show them what's in your bag.

Scary stuff – but that's the kind of stupid thing you'd never do, right? Don't be so sure. Britain is currently in the grip

of a shoplifting epidemic – 31% of people accused of the crime in 2000 in the UK were under 18. And girls overtook boys – 7,528 girls aged 13-15 were caught, compared with 6,370 boys.

JUST FOR KICKS

As more and more girls from middle-class backgrounds turn to the crime, it looks like peer pressure, bullying and seeking a 'buzz', are the real reasons behind the current shoplifting craze.

According to Harry Kauffer, chairman of Crisis Counselling for Alleged Shoplifters, 50% of the shoplifters his charity sees come from affluent families. "Girls often start with cosmetics but they graduate to trainers, CDs and radios. Many see it as a safe and 'victimless' crime because they're stealing from a big shop, not an individual," says Harry Kauffer. But when stock is stolen, shops have to make their money back – and they do this by putting up prices. So in the end, all of us pay.

IT HAPPENED TO ME

Two CG! readers share their shoplifting confessions

"I WISH I'D NEVER DONE IT NOW"

Lucy Metcalfe*, 16, from Sheffield, has lived to regret her shoplifting past – she now has a criminal record.

"There was a lot going on in my life when I started shoplifting. I was having a rough time at home, which meant I was getting into trouble at school and I was eventually expelled when I was 13. I got into all sorts of trouble in the year after that. Looking back, I was trying to kick out, rebel and get some attention from all the people who didn't understand me – teachers, parents and social workers. It was a cry for help.

LOCKED AWAY

I was 13, out of school, and too young to get a job, so the only way I could get things I wanted was to steal them. And I had loads of time to practise. I used to go on my own: I think you're less suspicious that way. I'd go into Sheffield town centre because it's so busy. I thought, 'Who's gonna notice me?' I'd go into clothes shops and stuff things in my bag or inside my jacket. I never got caught because I wasn't nervous. I guess because I didn't care. I was best at taking alcohol from supermarkets. I used to get away with huge bottles of Bacardi, which I would sell on or drink on my own. It seemed so easy.

Then, one day, a security guard from the supermarket followed me down the street. He waited until I took the bottle out of my jacket and that's when he nicked me. I went to the police station and was put in a cell. They took my phone off me, which they do so you've got no sense of time – I could have been inside three minutes or three hours. There were prostitutes and crackheads in there and I thought, 'If I don't stop this, this could be me in four years' time'.

Eventually, I was taken to an interview room and interviewed by a WPC, with a social worker present. They weren't horrible to me, which in a way was worse. It left me thinking about what I'd done, and I realised I didn't want my life to turn out like that of the other women in the cell. I've enrolled in SCAPE, a youth programme, and I tell other teens my story so

> ## "I was taken to the police station and put in a cell with prostitutes and crackheads"

> ## "You get outside and think you've got away with it – then they grab you"

they don't make the same mistake. I'm studying music and I'm going on a business studies course next year. I'm finally getting my education. I just wish I hadn't wasted it all in the first place. I'd tell anyone who's thinking of shoplifting – it's not worth it! You might think it's a solution to your problems but it's only going to make things worse."

"WHAT STARTED AS FUN TURNED INTO MY WORST NIGHTMARE"

Janine Dobby*, 16, from Oldham, hasn't stolen anything since the day she was caught by a store detective.

"I started shoplifting as a laugh with my mates. It was just because we were bored. We started off with little things, make-up, sweets, anything you can fit up a sleeve. There were usually four of us, and three would stand around giggling to take the attention away from the one stealing.

But the more you get away with it, the more confident you get and before long we were going to Manchester for the day and nicking from clothes shops. You just found a top without a tag on it and then wore it under your clothes to walk out of the shop. I got loads of compliments on my new clothes – although I had to hide them from my mum! I always made sure I never stole anything from a little corner shop or anything like that. It was always a big chain store where they could afford to lose it."

SCARED AND CRYING

"The day I got caught was the only day I went shoplifting on my own. I put some shampoo in my bag, but then I lost my nerve and walked around the shop for about 15 minutes trying to pluck up the courage to leave. When I did it was just like your worst nightmare. They wait until you're outside and then they place their hands on your shoulder just as you think you've got away with it.

They took me to a little back room in the shop and I was crying so much they couldn't get any sense out of me. They said I could either go to the police or ring my mum. I didn't want to call home but I did because I thought getting a caution might have stopped me getting a Saturday job. My mum went mental. She found all my 'secret' clothes in the bottom of my wardrobe and made me give them to charity. I'll never do it again." *CG!*

* NAMES AND IDENTIFYING DETAILS IN THIS STORY HAVE BEEN CHANGED. THANKS TO RPS RAINER, A NATIONAL VOLUNTARY ORGANISATION WORKING WITH YOUNG PEOPLE AGED 10–25 YEARS. VISIT RPSRAINER.ORG.UK. SOURCES: CCAS, THE PORTIA CAMPAIGN, THE BRITISH RETAIL CONSORTIUM, SCAPE, RPS RAINER, THAMES VALLEY POLICE

snip out and slip in your purse ✂

Caught in the act!

If you are caught shoplifting, Inspector Gordon Sinclair of the Thames Valley Police can tell you what to expect

1 A police car will pick you up from the shop where you were caught and you'll be arrested.

2 The police will take you back to the station, where they'll remove all your personal belongings.

3 Most people are out within a couple of hours, but the police can hold you for up to 24 hours.

4 Mates won't cover for you and they'll usually squeal if they think it'll get them off the hook.

5 If you're under 17, the police have to let your parents know you're being held for questionning.

6 If it's your first offence, you'll get a caution. It stays on your record for five years and if you go for a job that requires a police check, it shows up.

7 If you're a repeat offender and you go to court, you'll have a criminal record for life.

8 Most shops ban teens who are caught shoplifing. If you're caught in your local mall, you can be banned from the entire shopping centre.

Who to ask for help & advice

- For information on shoplifting, the law and you, go online to thamesvalley police.uk/tvp4kids.

- If you're worried about shoplifting you can contact Harry Kauffer at Crisis Counselling for Alleged Shoplifters on 020 8954 8987 between 9am-5pm, Monday-Friday and 9.30am-5.30pm, Saturday-Sunday.

JANUARY 2003 CosmoGIRL!

TEXT D

Transcript of a Radio 5 Live sports report:

> **Commentator**: And at the Rec an important win for Bath as they try and pull away from the bottom of the table. They beat Harlequins 23 points to 9. Alistair Hignell.
>
> **Hignell**: No happy return to big match action for Harlequins wing Dan Luger. The England and Lions pace man playing his first game for eight months was always eager for work but was restricted to a watching role as Bath took early control and thanks to a Kevin Maggs try and three penalties from Ollie Barclay established a comfortable 16-3 lead at half time. And the ball didn't run Luger's way even when Bath went off the boil at the beginning of the second half, allowing Paul Burke to kick his second and third penalties. Ian Bolshaw, another on the comeback trail, was far more involved in both attack and defence for Bath, but he was only a decoy runner as Mike Tyndall scored the try that sank Quins, their late onslaught failing to yield a desperately needed bonus point.

Commentary tip

When you write your informative text, you will have to think about the questions given in Activity 4 from a writer's point of view. Your comments about some of them should be included in your final commentary.

Choosing an assignment

Once you have studied a good range of informative texts, it is time to choose an assignment for yourself. The following activity should help you do so.

ACTIVITY 5

First, remind yourself of the basic guidelines on Original Writing on pages 135–6 above. Remember: the task needs to be **realistic**, **practical** and **original**.

When you write your informative piece, you will need to feel confident that you are something of an 'expert' in the area you are writing about. So it makes sense to choose a subject which you already know quite a lot about, or on which you can easily carry out the required research. This will usually mean starting from something close to home.

Working in pairs, your task is to suggest some possible writing tasks for a partner with this in mind. Interview your partner to find out what kinds of knowledge or information he or she already has. Use the prompts and suggestions below – but of course, there are many other questions you could ask!

Prompt question	Who might like/need to learn about this?	In what medium/genre?
What school/college subjects are you studying?	Year 11 students contemplating taking any of these subjects, and their parents, might welcome information on what the course is like from a student's perspective.	A **short pamphlet**, or an **illustrated presentation** to be given 'live' at an Open Evening.
	If you have carried out some research as part of your work for Module 2, Language and Social Contexts, other language students may want to read about it.	An in-house **English Language magazine** for articles of linguistic interest.
What kinds of part-time work have you done?	Anyone taking on a part-time job might like to know the best way of getting a job in the first place, how to get the application right, how to survive the interview, and then how to cope with the demands of the job.	An **article** in a local or student news-sheet, or a **leaflet** for the Careers Area.
How well do you know the area where you live?	Visitors – perhaps students moving to the area to go to college/university – might welcome a guide to the region, its shops, sporting facilities, restaurants, pubs and clubs.	An **article** in a students magazine, or local paper, a **pamphlet** for the local Tourist Information office, an item for your **local radio** station, or a contribution to your town's official **website**.
Where else have you travelled to?	If you know a holiday destination very well, it may be that you can provide a more realistic and up-to-date guide than the ones commercially available.	Look at **travel guides** like *The Rough Guides,* or the *Time Out* series, for possible formats. Also, travel sections can be found in weekend newspapers.
What do you do with your spare time? Do you: • enjoy going out? • play sports? • take part in music/drama/arts? • spend time on computing/games/ICT?	People less familiar with your area may well need to know about its cinemas, and sporting and leisure facilities. If you follow your local team(s), there is always a market for well-written information about them and their players, and some people might like to know about how to get started in a particular sport that you enjoy. Similarly, the inside story of a music or drama production might be of interest to many readers. Perhaps your reviews of new CDs, gigs or films would be of interest.	Many **local radio** stations, **newspapers and magazines** have *What's On* programmes/sections and may also include reviews. Some **websites** also invite contributions. A **radio documentary** or feature article could describe your school team's cup run, your

Prompt question	Who might like/need to learn about this?	In what medium/genre?
• have other special interests/ hobbies/ expertise?	Games enthusiasts may be able to share tips and hints about how to climb up the higher levels of the latest game, and there is always a market for well-informed coverage of the latest technological developments. Perhaps you have a special interest, expertise or experience – from work experience to learning to ski, from stamp-collecting to bereavement – which someone, somewhere would like to hear about.	drama production or concert. Your local sports team may have a **fanzine** – or start one of your own. A general interest or specialist **magazine** could be an outlet for articles on hobbies and interests.

As you make your choice of writing assignment, you may find it helpful to submit to your supervising teacher a 'Proposal/Pre-commentary' form like the one below. Be prepared to take on board the advice of your teacher.

Proposal/Pre-commentary: Writing to inform

Key point	Explanation	Your ideas	Teacher comments
Content/subject matter	What is the information content you are going to include?		
Your research	How much do you already know about the subject, and how will you go about becoming an 'expert'?		
Target audience	Which group(s) of people are you hoping to reach?		
Why do they need/want to know the information? How much or how little do they already know?	Identify the 'information gap' and be clear about what you think you can assume about your audience's prior knowledge.		
Which aspects of the information will they be least/most interested in?	Think carefully about the kinds of information to include and omit.		
Which medium/genre do you intend to use to reach your audience?	Define as precisely as you can your intended medium. Don't just say 'a magazine', but decide which specific title.		
What style models do you intend to study?	Note the titles of similar texts, aimed at a similar audience but *not* on the same topic.		

Commentary tip

Write these key details of your assignment on a separate sheet of paper called a 'Pre-commentary'.

You can briefly discuss your reasons for choosing your assignment in the first part of your final commentary.

Preparing to produce a text

Once you decide on a writing assignment, the next step is to collect the **information** you need for your text. The principal sources are likely to be:

- yourself – choose a subject you already know something about and brainstorm the topic thoroughly

- reference sources – text books, encyclopaedias, reference books, etc.

- printed media – newspapers, magazines, etc.

- the Internet

- personal interviews with relevant people.

Remember:

- Always keep a record and copy of the resources you use; you will need to submit these and refer to them in your commentary and bibliography.

- You must not simply reproduce the words or methods of presentation used in your sources without acknowledgement – this is plagiarism and will be penalised.

When you feel you have as much information as you – or your readers or listeners – need, organise it by dividing it into sub-sections, and then start to make some decisions about what to include, and in what order.

ACTIVITY 6   C3.1a

Imagine that you have decided to write a piece about the health risks involved in smoking, and that you have already gathered a fair amount of possible source material. You have sorted this material into a number of categories, as listed below:

A A picture of a diseased lung.

B Statistics comparing the numbers of deaths each year from heart disease and lung cancer among smokers and non-smokers.

C The personal story of someone who is dying of lung cancer, having smoked for many years.

D Technical and scientific data about the nicotine, carbon monoxide and tar emissions produced by different kinds of cigarettes.

E Biological/scientific explanations of how tobacco by-products are associated with cancer development, heart disease and other circulatory problems.

F Taped interviews with two teenagers about why they started smoking.

G Advice on how to give up smoking.

H The legal position regarding sales of tobacco products to young people.

(a) The first major choice you face is how much of these different types of material you should include or leave out. The answer to this question will, as always, depend on your purpose, medium and audience.

Listed below are six different possible texts on this topic. For each of them, your first task is to order the material **A–H** above, according to the amount of each type you would use in each assignment; use 1 to represent the most, and 8 little or nothing. If possible, discuss this in small groups before deciding on your order, and then compare your solution with those of other students.

- A health education pamphlet for teenagers.

- A health education leaflet for general use in a GP's surgery.

- An article in a medical journal, read mainly by health professionals.

- An article in a Sunday newspaper supplement with a family audience.

- A student's presentation on an AVCE Health & Social Care course.

- A Radio 1 news item about trends in teenage smoking.

(b) As well as deciding how much of each type of ingredient to put into the mix for your particular text, you also need to choose the best sequence and structure in which to arrange it. Where should you start? What path should you follow?

For the same set of six possible 'smoking' texts, your task is now to decide the best arrangement and sequence of the material, numbering the material from 1 (use at the start) to 8 (use at the end).

There is, of course, no single 'correct' solution to this problem. However, your discussions should raise the kinds of questions about selection and structure which apply to all kinds of informative writing.

Commentary tip

In your final commentary you should refer to the different sources of information you used and the different types of information you decided to include in your text. Explain why you decided to include more of some, and less of another type of material.

You should explain the choices you made about structure and sequence, and your reasons for them.

Using facts and statistical information

It is likely that at some stage in your text you will present your readers or listeners with some factual or statistical information. As your survey of different informative texts will have revealed, there are many ways of doing this. How will you achieve maximum impact and the desired effect?

ACTIVITY 7

Imagine you have decided to write a piece about food and drink, and in particular, about the growing popularity of pasta in the UK. Here are some alternative ways of conveying in words the basic facts of spaghetti consumption:

A Every year in the UK we consume 100,000 tons of spaghetti.

B Each UK household consumes an average of 4 kilos of spaghetti a year.

C If all the spaghetti consumed in the UK this year were tied end to end it would circle the earth three times.

D More than 60% of us eat spaghetti at least once a month.

E Nearly two in three people eat spaghetti once a month.

F Over a third of us eat spaghetti only rarely.

(a) Explain which version of the above information you would use, and why, if you were:

- writing for a non-specialist audience and wanted to emphasise the importance of spaghetti

- writing a more formal, specialised piece for people in the food industry

- trying to minimise the importance of spaghetti.

(b) In what non-verbal ways might you convey this information? Try expressing these facts using:

- a pie chart

- a cartoon or diagram.

Commentary tip

In your final commentary, you should discuss the ways you have decided to convey factual or statistical information, including any diagrams, pie charts, etc. you decide to use.

Writing for audio

At some point in your Original Writing course, it is a good idea to try writing for a listening audience; although it is not a requirement of the AS specification, the A2 Unit 5 examination (Editorial Writing) frequently includes writing for audio, so it makes sense to gain some experience of this skill on your AS course. This genre includes:

- 'live' talks and presentations

- speech radio broadcasts (either local or national radio, especially Radio 4)

- audio tapes

- audio guides, often available at museums, exhibitions and historic sites.

There may be a real opportunity to produce a script for a substantial presentation, either as part of your English Language studies (perhaps as a means of sharing the results of some research into gender, power or technology) or as part of your study of other subjects. If you deliver the talk to a real audience, this will allow you to generate relevant evidence for your Key Skills Communication portfolio.

ACTIVITY 8
C3.1b

Practise the skills involved in writing for audio by producing the script for short talks, tapes or programmes on one or more of the following subjects:

- choosing your AS subjects

- leisure facilities in your area

- student facilities in your school/college.

Writing for audio

Set out your script in three columns as shown: use the left column to specify speaker/voice, the centre column for the dialogue, and the right column to specify SFX (sound effects), visual aids (if part of a presentation) and music.

Voice/speaker	Dialogue	SFX/VA
M, 30s, unmarked RP	Good morning. Welcome to 'On the line' with Jenny Smith	

- Specify gender, age and accent for any speaker.

- Consider using more than one speaker.

- Identify speakers by name regularly.

- Use SFX or music to establish a mood or theme, e.g. short snatches of popular songs which refer to the topic of the text.

- Announce *regularly* what is coming next. Listeners can't look ahead or see headings or lists of contents.

- Speak the text aloud as you write.

- Make a recording of your text to see if it works.

- Don't try to script 'spontaneous' interviews.

Commentary tip

When writing your commentary, explain your choice of speakers and voices, perhaps by referring to relevant Unit 2 issues connected with gender, dialect or power.

Writing to instruct

There is a very grey area where 'informative' and 'instructive' types of writing overlap; instructions will, by definition, always include some information, and many of the informative texts you considered may well have contained elements of instruction, or at least advice. Here we will look briefly at some texts that are primarily instructive and/or advisory.

Remember:

If you decide to submit both an informative and an instructive text for your coursework, you should ensure that the two texts are significantly different in purpose, genre, audience and approach, and that they allow you to demonstrate a genuine variety of writing skills.

Many instructive texts – such as recipes, or 'how to do it' pamphlets associated with practical skills and activities, may appear relatively straightforward to write. But as with all your Original Writing choices, it is important that you attempt a task that is sufficiently challenging. Some 'instructions' may take the form of feature articles ('How to cope with leaving home/bereavement/divorce/multiple sclerosis . . .') which offer advice and tackle difficult or sensitive issues, and these may provide a greater challenge. Beware, however, of writing *impractical* instructions for practical activities, for which a set of written instructions is not very useful (e.g. 'How to salsa').

As with informative writing, you will need to study a range of suitable style models. Sometimes it is tempting to limit the notion of 'instruction' to the predictable kinds of pamphlets and leaflets we associate with this purpose, but it is important to include more imaginative ways in which writers convey instructions.

ACTIVITY 9

Below are two examples of instructional/advisory texts; the first is a conventional set of instructions, whereas the second is an example of a more imaginative approach which uses techniques more associated with other kinds of writing, such as writing to entertain.

For each of the texts you study, produce a short report on the methods they use to present their instructions/advice to their intended audience. Use the following prompt questions to structure your analysis:

- How does the introduction contribute to the effectiveness of the leaflet in text A?

- How do these texts address and establish a relationship with their target audience(s)?

- What use is made of bullets, headings and other graphological devices?

- What seem to be the 'rules' for using bullets effectively? (Look at the kinds of sentences/phrases that follow each bullet.)

- Are instructions/advice given with direct imperatives, or are they softened, for example by using modal verbs such as 'should', 'ought', 'could'?

- How do the texts give reassurance and confidence to their readers?

- How and when is the first person used, if at all?

- In what ways is the language tailored to its target audience?

- In what ways – if any – do the texts depart from the conventions of instructional texts?

Compare the findings of your investigation with the commentary on page 192.

TEXT A

You can beat bullying!
A Guide for Young People – Kidscape

Introduction
. . . It is surprising that all sorts of people who are now very successful adults were bullied when they were young. It is encouraging to know that it is possible to succeed in spite of being tormented at school. All of these well-known people were bullied at school: Phil Collins (singer), Harrison Ford (actor), Mel Gibson (actor), Daryl Hannah (actor), Tom Cruise (actor), Michelle Pfeiffer (actor), Dudley Moore (actor) . . .

CONTENTS
This booklet has three main sections: Bullies, Victims and Self-assertiveness Techniques. Bullies and victims sometimes have similar problems so you might find helpful suggestions in all the sections.

WHAT CAN I DO IF I AM BEING BULLIED?
Your school may already have a way of dealing with bullying.

For example, some schools:

- have anti-bullying guidelines and procedures for dealing with incidents

- encourage anyone who is being bullied or who witnesses bullying to tell about it

- have 'bully boxes' where students put in a note about what is happening

- have student meetings, circle time or 'courts' where problems like bullying are discussed and dealt with

- have specially trained students to help each other or teachers who are assigned to help.

If your school has an anti-bullying system, use it to get help. If you're not sure how it works, talk to your teacher or Year Head.

If your school ignores bullying, *don't become resigned to being a victim.* **You can still help yourself and you can ask others to help you.**

- **Tell a friend what is happening.** Ask him/her to help you. It will be harder for the bully to pick on you if you have a friend with you for support.

- **Try to ignore the bullying or say 'No' really firmly, then turn and walk away.** Don't worry if people think you're running away. Remember, it is very hard for the bully to go on bullying someone who won't stand still to listen.

- **Try not to show that you are upset or angry.** Bullies love to get a reaction – it's 'fun'. If you can keep calm and hide your emotions, they might get bored and leave you alone. As one teenager said, 'They can't bully you if you don't care'.

- **Don't fight back, if you can help it.** Most bullies are stronger or bigger than their victims. If you fight back, you could make the situation worse, get hurt or be blamed for starting the trouble.

TEXT B

The Easiest Sexiest Salad (from Jamie Oliver, *Happy Days with the Naked Chef*)

I love this salad. Apart from being a great combination, it always seems unbelievably effortless, which is the kind of recipe I like. The constant success of this is due to the common-sense marriage of salty Parma ham, milky buffalo mozzarella and sweet figs, which obviously need to be of good quality. The best figs to use are Italian and the best time to buy them is June to August when they are in season. Greek figs are a good second best and are in season from September to November. The best figs always seem to be those that are about to split their skins. Use green or black figs – it doesn't really matter.

One thing I do is to criss-cross the figs but not quite to the bottom – 1 fig per person is always a good start. Then, using your thumbs and forefingers, squeeze the base of the fig to expose the inside. At this point you'll think, 'Oooh, that looks nice, I'm quite clever . . .' or at least I do. More importantly, it allows your dressing to go right into the middle of the fig. All these little things really help to make a salad special. Simply place the figs in a dish, weave around 1 slice of Parma ham or prosciutto per fig, throw in some slices of buffalo mozzarella, rip over some green or purple basil and drizzle everything with the honey and lemon juice dressing. As far as salads go it's pretty damn sexy.

PS: it's a good idea to have some spare bread on the table to mop up the juices – always a treat.

Commentary tip

When reflecting on your own instructional writing, apply the questions given in Activity 9 to your text and write your answers in some detail.

ACTIVITY 10

For this activity you will need to collect a wide variety of instructional/advisory leaflets. They are not hard to find; you can start by collecting them from your own school or college (perhaps your English department has handouts instructing you how to go about your coursework!), local library, health centre, Social Services department, GP's surgery/clinic, and other public information outlets.

Study the range of leaflets carefully. Then design and draft your own leaflet, aimed at other A Level English Language students, on the subject of 'The Art of Writing Effective Leaflets'. This will be useful not only as part of your preparations for Original Writing, but also for A2 Module 5, Editorial Writing.

As you make your choice of writing assignment, you may find it helpful to submit to your supervising teacher a 'Proposal/Pre-commentary' form like the one used for informative writing above (page 149). The key points are somewhat different – use the ones given below. Add to them your own specific ideas for your writing task, and leave room for your teacher to comment.

Proposal/Pre-commentary: Writing to instruct

Key point	Explanation
Content/subject matter	What are the instructions/advice you aim to give?
Target audience	Which group(s) of people are you hoping to reach?
Why do they need/want the instructions/advice you are going to give? How much or how little do they already know?	Identify your audience's needs precisely, and be clear about the assumptions you are making about their prior knowledge and experience.
Which aspects of the information will they be least/most interested in?	Think carefully about the kinds of information to include or omit.
Which medium/genre do you intend to use to reach your audience?	Define as precisely as you can your intended medium. Don't just say 'a magazine', but decide which specific title
Which style models do you intend to study?	Note the titles of similar texts, aimed at a similar audience but *not* on the same topic.

Writing to entertain

This primary purpose is extremely broad and includes a multitude of possibilities. Sometimes the term 'entertainment' is used lightly to describe material which is trivial and undemanding. However, we can be 'entertained' in many ways; we can have our feelings and emotions engaged, we can be made to laugh or cry, and we can have our minds stimulated to think and reflect on different aspects of experience.

You need to keep in mind the full range of possibilities when planning a piece of coursework; while some kinds of light, undemanding material may be relatively easy to imitate, you may be more likely to achieve the highest standards of work – and marks – by tackling something a little more challenging.

ACTIVITY 11

Some possible interpretations of the term 'entertainment' are given below. Suggest two or three examples of specific texts you have encountered (spoken and/or written) which might fall into these categories:

- passes the time pleasantly

- causes amusement

- makes us think and reflect

- frightens us

- moves or touches us emotionally

- allows us to escape from the reality of our lives

- confronts us with the reality of our own or other people's lives.

In general, the range of possible texts for study and writing tasks might include:

- narrative fiction for different audiences (such as teenage, or younger) in various genres (romance, crime, sci-fi, fantasy, etc.)

- scripts for stage, radio, TV or film

- feature articles for magazines and newspapers

- autobiographical and biographical writing (including 'ghost' writing)

- humorous writing such as comic books, satirical sketches and observational comedy (either journalism or for 'stand-up' performances)

- verse or song lyrics.

In this book, we can consider briefly only a few examples of these; however, if you decide to attempt a form of writing not covered here, your approach is likely to be similar to that for other primary purposes:

1   Decide on a form and a topic for your writing.

2   Decide who you are going to entertain.

3   Study some varied examples (style models) of the genre you are attempting.

4   Attempt a first draft. Try not to just imitate the obvious features and conventions of the form you have chosen, but inject a little of your own voice and style.

Autobiographical writing

For many writers, the easiest place to start writing is from their personal experience. However, although it may be easy enough for you to write your life story, it does not necessarily follow that someone else will be interested in reading about it! Unless you have already achieved a degree of fame (or infamy) for your accomplishments, it is unlikely that there will be a market for a straightforward autobiography.

However, several newspapers and magazines *do* run columns in which relatively 'ordinary' people create a snapshot of their lives within a specified format. For example, the *Sunday Times* used to run a feature called 'A Day in the Life', in which subjects wrote about a typical day, but also used this as a vehicle for expressing their views on life generally and revealing their likes, dislikes, hopes and fears. For the purposes of your Original Writing submission, it is better to shape your writing to fit a format such as this than to launch into a full-scale story of your life, which would not find a realistic market.

Good autobiographical writing which might be published is not just a narrative of events and reminiscences; it will also include:

- some reflection on the importance and impact of your experiences

- some revelation of your values and preferences

- lively portraits of friends and families

- a glimpse of your whole approach to life.

ACTIVITY 12

(a) The *Times Educational Supplement*, a weekly journal aimed at education professionals, runs a feature entitled 'My Best Teacher' in which well-known personalities write a short autobiographical piece about their school experiences. As the title suggests, each piece focuses on a single teacher who has been a particularly strong influence on the person concerned, but the piece also allows writers to reflect more broadly on their educational experience and the ways in which it helped shape the person they became.

Read the example that follows, which is based on the experiences of Jennie Bond, the BBC TV journalist; then try to draft your own article of approximately 800 words. Be sure to include some of the features listed above.

MY BEST TEACHER

JENNIE BOND

I spent all my school life at St Francis' college, Letchworth, where I was a day girl. I remember my schooldays as happy, but my 12-year-old daughter was recently reading my old diaries and tells me I had written how much I hated school. I remember that the workload was great and I was very conscientious, working fantastically hard. I didn't like being told off, so was hideously well behaved. It is a matter of embarrassment to me that I never got a detention or a conduct mark.

Most of the teachers were nuns so it was very refreshing when I got to O-levels to have a lay English teacher who dressed rather sexily. Mrs Cherry had hennaed hair and a gravely, smoky voice, and we could see her legs under her gown. She was of the school of thought that I came across later at university: that books are fine, but are a means of making you think. But the most illuminating thing I remember her saying was that we'd know when we were really in love with a man because we wouldn't mind sharing his toothbrush . . .

Miss Wilson, the maths mistress, was a tiny lady who shouted a lot. I never enjoyed maths. I found the subject difficult and I don't think her method of teaching was helpful.

But Mrs English, who taught French, was delightful. She was gentle and interested in us and in our lives, and had a relaxed way of teaching. She inspired me and made me enjoy speaking the language. I liked working on pronunciation and enunciation. I thought I'd probably become a French teacher myself. English and French were my best subjects.

I went to Warwick University to read French and European literature, planning to teach, and as a part of the course was sent to France to work as an *assistante* for a year. My placement was at a lycée in Juan-les-Pins in the south of France, where I taught senior children conversational English. I only had to work eight or nine hours a week, but I was hopeless and soon learned that I could never be a teacher . . .

When a couple of my friends went into journalism, I thought it seemed like fun, and I got a job as a cub reporter on the *Richmond Herald*. I had no idea I would end up as the BBC's royal correspondent. I wasn't particularly interested in the royal family as a girl. My family had a middle-class respect for the monarchy, but life didn't stop for the Queen's Christmas message.

BBC royal correspondent Jennie Bond was talking to **Pamela Coleman**

(b) Another autobiographical format which has been used in the media is the **video diary,** where relatively 'ordinary' and unknown people make recordings over a period of time in which they talk about their lives in much the same ways as was once common with written diaries. Try drafting the script for your own video diary, aiming to write one minute of air time for each of four or five entries over a period of a couple of weeks.

(c) Perhaps there has been a particular aspect of your life that sets you apart from many other people of your age – a particular achievement, a disability or illness or some sort, or the need to care for a friend or relative. An example of such a piece of writing is the text which follows ('Shaken not stirred'), which is an extract from a 15-year-old student's account of coming to terms with epilepsy. It was published in *OM* Magazine, a supplement of the *Observer* newspaper.

After reading the article, consider whether you might be able to write a similar piece about yourself.

SHAKEN NOT STIRRED

BLACK EYES, BRUISED RIBS, A BROKEN NOSE . . . EPILEPSY LEAVES YOU WITH MUCH TO LEARN AT THE SCHOOL OF HARD KNOCKS. BY **FRANZISKA THOMAS**

I've have a bad month. I've had 13 seizures in four weeks, five of them over one weekend. Two weeks ago during the fourth week of my *Observer* internship, I had a fit (seizure) and woke up under the Sports desk. The next day I was asked if I might write an article about what it is like to live life as a 'practising epileptic' (as I tend to refer to it). I've got used to fits landing me in unusual positions over the years, both literally and figuratively speaking, but getting a job because of one has to be the most unusual to date.

I developed epilepsy four months and three days shy of my 16th birthday. Doctors have concluded that my case was most likely brought on by a febrile convulsion I experienced at 18 months, and while many who develop epilepsy in childhood grow out of it in later life, I apparently grew into mine.

Epilepsy is the tendency to have recurrent fits and is caused by abnormal bursts of chaotic electrical activity in the brain. Anyone can develop the condition at any time, although it is more usual to develop it before the age of 20 or after 60. The easiest way to visualise a fit is if you can imagine your brain as a computer. A surge in electricity will cause the computer to crash in much the same way as an excess of electrical activity will

cause the brain to fit . . . I fall unconscious to the ground, often in mid-sentence and then twitch, chew my tongue and make screeching noises, which friends say sound like I am in excruciating pain. This can last up to 10 minutes, after which I wake up dazed and confused, invariably bruised and battered, muttering incoherent half-sentences. Within 15 minutes, however, I am fully conscious and able to continue the conversation where I left off . . .

Witnessing someone having a fit must be very disturbing; I have never actually seen one. In my mind's eye I have an image that has been conjured up by Dostoyevky's depiction of a fit in *The Idiot* and by a continuing narrative of all the quirky things I do and say when I regain consciousness or as I hit the floor.

I have built up a very personal relationship with the floor over the years. It's a strange sensation repeatedly waking up on the floor, your eyes level with chair legs, shoe soles and dirt. The average person walks into a bar, looks around and orders a drink. I walk into a bar, look at the floor and try to imagine how much it would hurt to fall on it. My stories from holidays abroad frequently involve a description of ambulances, pavements and the differences in medical care.

Biographical writing and 'ghosting'

It may be that you are attracted to the idea of writing about the life of someone else rather than your own. There is always a demand for well-written profiles of individuals whose experiences or expertise make them worthy of interest to a particular audience.

What's more, some writing that appears to be 'autobiographical' is in fact written by a journalist on behalf of the person whose life it documents. Such writing is known as 'ghost' writing.

In both cases, this writing task involves the following stages:

Choose a subject, medium and possible style model	**Don't** go for someone famous. Enough has already been written about them and it will be hard for you to do anything original. **Do** choose someone you know; this could be: <ul><li>a relative who has had an interesting experience (fought in a war/lived abroad/set up a new business/worked in an interesting job/overcome an illness/gained an award or qualification)</li><li>a fellow student who is doing or has achieved something notable (represented the town/county/country, won a scholarship, gained an award, an unusual hobby/skill, played in a band)</li><li>someone you have worked for (their career, how they became a manager, other jobs they have had)</li><li>someone in your community (business person, sports person, doctor, religious leader, politician, councillor, head teacher).</li></ul> You could write an article for a local newspaper or magazine, or script a feature for your local radio station.
Do some homework	Do some research about your subject's achievements before you talk to him or her.
Interview your subject	Contact your subject and explain what you are doing – and gain permission to use him or her as a subject for your writing assignment. Think in advance about what you want to find out about your subject – have some questions prepared, but don't stick to them rigidly, and go with the flow of the conversation. Use a tape recorder to record your interview – but gain permission first. Alternatively, take detailed notes.
Re-work your raw material	Your finished piece – whether article, radio feature or contribution to a website – will be completely different from the interview. Look for an 'angle' on your subject with which you will 'hook' your audience in your opening few sentences, and adopt a suitable format and style from your style models. If you wish to write an article, why not take a couple of photographs of your subject? When ghost writing, the same steps apply – but write in the first person, as if you were the person concerned.

Commentary tip

When writing about your biographical piece, refer in detail to the raw material you gained in your interview and explain how you chose to re-write and re-arrange it – and why.

Quote both from your final text and your notes/tape recording to show this.

ACTIVITY 13

Reprinted below is the opening of an article which appeared in *You* magazine (the supplement of the *Mail on Sunday* newspaper). It focuses on the life and achievements of a person its readers are unlikely to have heard of before.

(a) Study the piece and identify the 'angle' or 'hook' which the journalist has used to make the subject sound interesting.

(b) Suggest a subject known to you and an 'angle' on his or her life which you could use as a way to shape a piece about him or her. It could be someone you work with or who lives near you, who has reached some kind of milestone in life; or it could be a fellow student whose achievements might interest the readership of a local newspaper or college magazine.

(c) Attempt a first draft of this piece.

THE DAY I BECAME MARILYN

UNA PEARL WAS A 20-YEAR-OLD FILM EXTRA FROM CROYDON WHEN SHE LANDED THE PART OF MARILYN MONROE'S BODY DOUBLE. HERE SHE TELLS SARAH WISE HOW IT FELT TO POSE AS THE ULTIMATE SCREEN GODDESS

As jobs go, it must be one of the strangest – standing for ten hours a day under blazing hot lamps, caked in heavy make-up and wearing a tight, unyielding dress, pretending to be Marilyn Monroe. But for 20-year-old film extra Pearl King, who had adopted the stage name Una Pearl, being Marilyn's stand-in for the 1957 film *The Prince and the Showgirl* 'was one of the happiest times of my life. I loved every minute of it, no matter how exhausted I felt – and we were all exhausted at the end of that shoot.'

It was certainly tiring work being a 1950s body double.

In the days without the computer technology that allows directors to alter skin colour and body shape post-shooting, body doubles were used to dummy-run scenes, testing out hundreds of postures and positions for the lights and cameras.

Today, Una is a glamorous 60-something mother of two grown-up daughters, with a sweep of platinum hair and a peaches-and-cream complexion, living in contented obscurity in Epping Forest. She gave up acting in 1963, when she married her husband, John, a Lloyd's underwriter, and started a

family; but several boxes in her attic contain well-preserved mementos of her time as a shadow of the stars. Una 'was' Brigitte Bardot for a parachute jump in the 1959 film *Babette Goes to War*; in Stanley Kubrik's *Lolita* (1962), she stood in for 15-year-old actress Sue Lyon (who thought Una had been sent on set to take her entire role), and she body-doubled perfect Englishwoman Deborah Kerr in the 1960 drawing-room farce *The Grass is Greener*, alongside romantic leads Cary Grant and Robert Mitchum.

Dramatic monologues

One form of writing which often produces interesting work is the **dramatic monologue**. In this, you create a character who tells a story directly, as if speaking aloud to a friend or confidante. These pieces can work particularly well on radio, as little visual action is usually involved, but they can be equally effective for the stage or TV. If you are also studying Drama or Performing Arts, you may have a ready-made outlet for your script.

Dramatic monologues have many uses – even museums may personalise the information they present by putting words into the mouths of actors representing historical characters, who guide visitors around exhibitions. They have sometimes featured in the writing assignments set for Module 5, Editorial Writing.

Dramatic monologues also allow you to apply many aspects of your AS English Language studies – and to discuss these in your commentary. For example, you can use your understanding of the nature of spoken language to make your character talk realistically; you can establish aspects of his or her character by including regional elements of language, and you could even draw on aspects of your work on language and gender by employing 'typically' gendered speech.

Many of the most interesting monologues are much more than mere stories; the narrator is likely to spend as much time giving us opinions and observations as mere narration, and thus he or she reveals aspects of character to us. We may also gradually realise that the character telling the story may not be 'seeing' things quite straight; perhaps he or she is a child, or has only limited understanding, or is subject to a particular prejudice or 'blind spot'.

ACTIVITY 14

Perhaps the most well-known examples of this genre produced in recent years are the two series of *Talking Heads* by Alan Bennett. It is likely that you will find a copy in your school/college library. Read and study at least one of the monologues, and as you do so, answer the following questions:

- What is the approximate balance (in percentage terms) between narrative and reflection or observation?

- Which **idiolectal** features of the narrator's language help establish personality or character?

- Are there any hints to the reader or listener that the narrator's judgment or understanding of things may not be 100 per cent reliable?

ACTIVITY 15

Before you can start writing your own monologue, you will need to decide a number of things about your central narrator character. It is best to choose the kind of person you understand well – perhaps someone in your own age group. Use this prompt sheet to help you – the final question should provide you with the initial spark for the story he or she is going to tell.

- What gender is your character?

- How old is he or she?

- If in education, what does your character study, and where?

- If in work, what is his or her job?

- Who is the most important person in your character's life?

- List three things or people your character likes and dislikes.

- Does your character speak with a regional accent or RP?

- Does he or she use a regional dialect or Standard English vocabulary and grammar?

- List five other distinctive characteristics of the way your character talks (aspects of his or her idiolect).

- In what way is your character's narrative going to be slightly distorted, unreliable or biased? Is he or she prejudiced? Naïve? Slightly 'disturbed'?

- Think of something that happened to your character today that he or she wants to talk about. Avoid deaths and disasters – something apparently trivial is fine to get you started.

Commentary tip

If you write a monologue, make links in your commentary with Module 2 work by writing about:

- how you have incorporated idiolectal features to create your character

- any accent/dialect or general speech features you have included to establish your character

- any aspect of language and gender that you have consciously applied to your monologue.

Writing to entertain is not limited to fiction, and it isn't necessary to have a particularly vivid imagination to turn the material of 'real life' into highly engaging text. The kinds of 'true life' feature articles that appear in many magazines, for example, may have an informative (or even instructive) dimension to them, but they are usually read recreationally, even when they deal with relatively serious subjects, as with the following example.

ACTIVITY 16

(a) As you study the following article, closely consider how it engages the interest and emotional sympathy of its readers. Although it is based on fact, there are several strongly narrative elements in the piece which we might also find in fictional stories. These are listed in the table below; find examples in the text.

Narrative elements	Examples
A central character with whom the readers of the magazine can identify and/or sympathise	In what ways is this true of the 1st person narrator of the story?
The representation of other characters	Who are they, and what is their role in the story (friend, supporter, adviser, etc.)?
The action springs from a significant event in the character's life	In what ways did the events of the story change life for Sarah?
Several dramatic incidents/episodes	How is language used to convey these?
Dialogue used to bring these alive	Note how selectively this is done.
Dramatic language to bring home the 'action' in the story	Suggest some examples.
An ending which resolves the issues of the narrative in a satisfying way	How does it do so?
A 'moral' or implied meaning/message	What 'meanings' emerge by the end of the piece?

(b) Collect two or three more examples of this kind of 'real life' story feature from popular magazines (e.g. *J17, Cosmopolitan, Bella, Best, New Woman, More!* and *Chat*) and survey them, applying the same set of questions.

(c) Perhaps you have had an experience which you can exploit for a piece such as this – though, of course, it could be for a very different audience. If so, sketch an outline of the article before attempting a first draft, and try to include some of the elements included in the table above.

(d) It is likely that this article was at least partly 'ghost' written (see page 163 above) by a journalist who had interviewed Sarah Phillips, the subject of the story. Someone you know may have had an experience that would make an interesting read – an unusual encounter or experience, a triumph or disaster, an achievement or a disappointment.

Interview your subject following the same procedure as for biographical writing (see page 163 above) and tailor your piece to the 'house style' of an appropriate magazine or other suitable medium.

Just a bit

Should I..? Yeah! Well, you're _meant_ to let your hair down on holiday...

By Sarah Phillips, 19, from Herne Bay, Kent

Now boarding the 7.05 flight to Ibiza,' boomed the voice over the loudspeaker. I smiled at my mates Jenny and Emmie. It was finally here – the holiday we'd been planning for months.

I was 17 and it was the first time I'd been abroad without Mum and Dad. I loved clubbing, so Ibiza seemed the perfect choice.

We were staying in a resort called Figueretes, which was pretty quiet. So on the third night, we decided to head for San Antonio – we'd heard the nightlife there was amazing.

Emmie had gone out with some other mates she'd met, but me and Jenny couldn't wait for our first big night out in Ibiza.

'Come on, Jen,' I sighed, slumped on the bed in our apartment as she put on a third coat of mascara. She always took ages to get ready. Me, I'm one of those girls who's ready in 10 minutes.

We couldn't have looked any different – her dressed up to the nines in a silver slinky number and strappy sandals, and me – my hair all scruffy and trainers on. But we were great mates. Jenny and Emmie were both older – Jenny 29 and Emmie 28. And they were quite protective with me.

We jumped on a bus to San Antonio and got there at about 8pm.

'Sex on the beach?' laughed Jen, as we pushed our way through the crowd to the first bar. The cocktail had become our favourite holiday tipple, and it was always a laugh to order it.

A few cocktails later, we headed for the dance floor. One of my favourite DJs,

Dave Pearce, was playing, and I was desperate to get a photo with him.

'Just do it,' said Jenny. So I did, walked right up and introduced myself. I couldn't believe I was there chatting to him.

'Are you coming to Eden tonight?' he asked.

But it'd cost an extra £50 and we didn't have enough money. None of us were that well off – we all worked on the tills in Safeway.

'No worries, girls, I'll get you on the guest list,' said Dave. Wow! I felt a bit like a celeb. Dave headed off, and me and Jen went to another bar. We got chatting to these blokes, Wayne* and Stewart*, from Birmingham and we really hit it off. But we weren't looking for anything romantic. I was seeing Dave* back home. And anyway, this was a girly holiday – we weren't interested in lads.

'I'm horny, horny horny horny…' Jenny started singing when our favourite holiday song came on.

We were all dancing, but Wayne took me to one side. 'Have you ever taken drugs?' he asked, and I nodded, a little embarrassed.

'Just the once – at a club in Kent.'

He asked me if I wanted to share an ecstasy pill. I knew it was risky, but the last time had been great – it'd given

me loads of confidence – and anyway, I was on my hols. It was only half an E. Where was the harm?

As the night wore on, I couldn't even tell I'd taken anything.

'That wasn't very good,' I shouted to Wayne over the music, but he was too drunk to care.

I headed to the bar. 'Agua por favor!' I yelled. From now on, I'd stick to water.

We left the club about 2am – it was weird, last time I took ecstasy, it kept me up all night, but this time I was exhausted.

'Hungover?' said Jenny, coming in to my room in her PJs the next

All I wanted was to go home to my mum

morning. She buried herself in my pillows.

'I feel like someone's beaten me over the head with a hammer.'

I felt awful, too, but I hadn't been drunk. I'd only drunk water when I was

SARAH'S NOT-SO-ECSTATIC TRUE STORY

of fun

at Eden – I never drink alcohol when I'm out clubbing.

Must be the heat, I thought, as I clutched my stomach in pain. Either that or I'd swallowed some water when I'd been scuba diving the other day. Whatever it was, it got worse. A few days later, I couldn't leave the apartment. I felt sick all the time and I had the runs. But that's normal when you're abroad, isn't it?

Emmie went home early – she broke her foot and then her little girl had an accident at home. The holiday was turning into a nightmare. My first time abroad and I was on the phone to my mum every day. But I still had another week out here.

'I want to come home, too,' I'd cry, but I couldn't really leave, I felt too bad about Jenny. At least she

was having a good time.

Eventually, the two weeks were up, and we headed home. Emmie and her fella Paul picked us up from the airport. I walked through the barrier and Emmie looked at me in horror. I'd turned yellow.

'It looks like jaundice. You could have something wrong with your liver,' she said. Her mate had had liver problems, so she knew the signs.

I was back and forth to the hospital. The doctors thought I had hepatitis. They told me to stay off work for a couple of months – *it must be serious.*

I felt rough for a while, but gradually, my liver seemed to repair itself. I felt loads better.

'I think it's time you had a night out,' said my mate Claire. I'd been cooped up for long enough.

So, the next week we went to our favourite club – Amadeus in Kent. Had a few too many vodka and Cokes.

The next morning, I had a killer hangover. I couldn't shake it. A week later, I started to feel sick. I was going yellow again with jaundice.

Gradually I got worse. I was texting my boyfriend Dave one day and didn't know what I was writing. My sister Tracey tried to take my

mobile off me, but I went mad. Mum phoned my dad and asked him to come round. She thought I was drugged up. Dad took me to the hospital. By then I was out of it and I was hysterical – locked myself in the toilet, screamed and ranted like a loony.

The doctors put me on a ventilator and a dialysis machine. It didn't work. I slipped into a coma and needed a liver transplant.

One of the doctors asked Dave if he knew if I'd ever taken drugs.

'She's taken ecstasy once or twice,' he said, and the doctors looked at me.

'Why didn't she tell us this before?'

Truth was, I'd worried it might have been the drugs that had made me ill. But I thought Mum would go mad if she found out, so I hadn't said anything.

We found out later that the toxins from the E I'd taken on holiday had been poisoning my body. Of course, I was out of it, didn't know how ill I was. But Mum told me later that I'd nearly died.

'It's really not looking good. Her body is very weak,' the doctor had told Mum. 'She's probably only got another 72 hours.'

Mum stayed with me, holding my hand, hoping

against hope for a miracle.

And she got one – the doctors found a liver. A transplant might just save my life.

When I came out of theatre, I was babbling. 'Where's my baby?' I asked. I don't have any kids. I was hallucinating, but Mum just laughed, tears of joy streaming down her face. I was alive. That's what mattered

It took me another three months before I was completely better. I'd been through hell, put my family through it, too, all because I'd wanted a laugh.

People think that's what ecstasy is – just a bit of fun. But it kills people.

I even split up with Dave over it. He took a few Es after I came out of hospital. He lied to me about it because he knew i disapproved, but I caught him at it when we were out clubbing one night.

He chose drugs over me, and we split up. I won't be around people who do drugs now.

I met a lad in a club a few months ago, and realised he was off his face.

'You're on E, aren't you? You mad, or what? It nearly killed me.' Then I showed him the scar from my transplant. He looked like he was going to throw up. He couldn't get away fast enough. I hope it made him think twice before he took it again.

I don't even smoke fags or drink any more – I can't because of my liver, but I wouldn't anyway. I'm lucky to be alive. I got a second chance at life and I'm not going to do anything to mess it up.

> *I thought Mum would go mad if she found out, so I hadn't said anything*

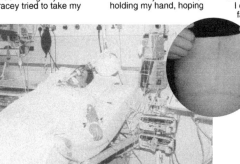

I hope what happened to me puts others off

'Wayne', 'Stewart' and 'Dave' are not their real names.

27

Prose fiction

Writing good prose fiction is difficult – and unless you are a regular reader of fiction yourself it is often unwise to attempt this for your Original Writing coursework. Moreover, on an A Level course you will not have time to develop a narrative of anything like the length or complexity of a novel, and however popular it is as a school writing exercise, there is only a limited market for the short story.

But it may be that you have a particular interest in fiction of a certain type or **genre**, and that there is a particular medium in which short examples (up to 1500 words) of the genre do appear. Such genres might include:

- crime/detective fiction

- romantic fiction

- action/adventure

- science fiction/fantasy

- horror/thriller.

Many genres of fiction have shared characteristics which writers adopt with varying degrees of originality. For your chosen genre, you will need to read widely within the genre and carry out an investigation of the following:

- Story titles and characters names. (Would 'Mist in the Morning' be a more appropriate title for a crime thriller or a romantic story? What might we predict about a tale that has 'Lex Zoldark' as its central character?)

- Settings and locations. (For which genres of story would a crumbling mansion adjacent to a graveyard be a suitable setting?)

- Typical storylines. (Boy meets girl, they overcome problems and live happily ever after.)

- Common stylistic features (Many dynamic verbs are used in action/adventure stories, and adjectives/adverbs in descriptions for horror stories.)

As you investigate any genre, as with other kinds of Original Writing, you should spend time studying good examples, or style models. Whatever genre of fiction you study, the questions to ask of your style models will be similar:

- What does the writer establish about characters and setting?

- How many characters are involved, and of what kind?

- What use does the writer make of narration, dialogue, description and reflection?

- Is the story narrated using the first or third person – and whose point of view does the narrative primarily present?

- What is the 'crisis' of the narrative, and how is it resolved?

- How does the writer achieve an effective ending?

ACTIVITY 17

Here, we will look at the opening of a story, 'Stepping In', which appeared in *Bella* magazine's popular 'Tales with a Twist' series of family-orientated if somewhat formulaic short stories.

(a) Answer as many of the questions above as you can for the extract given.

(b) Now provide your own ending to the story in a style that is consistent with the first part of the tale. Remember to try to achieve some sort of 'twist' at the end.

Compare your study of the first part of the story with the commentary on page 192.

STEPPING IN

JAN COULDN'T GET EXCITED ABOUT CHRISTMAS – HAD THE MAGIC GONE FOREVER?

Jan glowered at the tree. 'I hate Christmas!' she said. Tim had brought the tree home, grumbling at its price, and it stood in the corner, bare and dismal, waiting for her to decorate it. Any time now it would start shedding its needles all over the carpet and making more work.

Her mother frowned. 'Don't say that. It's the season of goodwill.'

'Huh!' Jan poked about in the box of decorations. A tawdry looking lot they were, too. 'It'd be better scrapped.'

'You don't mean that,' Mum protested. 'You loved it, once.'

'Of course I did, once. Christmas is for kids. Santa Claus, Away In a Manger, Little Donkey . . . I go along with it because I don't want our children to miss out. But what's in it for adults? Mothers, especially. Hard labour and an empty purse.'

The presents – modest though they were – had cost the earth. Then there were the drinks you had to lay on for anybody who dropped in, the cards, the stamps, food for the regulation blow-out, and all the things you'd forgotten to budget for, like marzipan for the cake and chocolate liqueur.

Not to mention crackers. All silver stars on the outside and nothing inside but a paper hat and a silly plastic toy.

'You're tired,' Mum said.

You could say that again, Jan thought. Especially this year, what with just recovering from flu and the worry about Tim's job, besides the usual 1001 things that had to be done.

Mum was bringing round old Mrs Bates for Christmas dinner, and there'd be Tim's Uncle Frank with his endless 'Did I tell you about the time when . . .'

In Module 2 you may have studied the ways that characters of different gender, class or region are represented in fiction. Perhaps in your story you have followed the pattern and deliberately worked with the stereotypes that you think the genre demands. More interestingly, you may have decided to defy these expectations. Either way, discuss these issues, and make the link to your Module 2 work.

Fiction for younger readers

It may be that you wish to try your hand at a piece of fiction for children. It is however, a lot more difficult than may at first appear to capture the interest and imagination of children; a good idea for characters and storyline needs to be matched by a controlled yet imaginative use of language.

What makes a successful piece of children's fiction? The only way to find out is to look at a variety of texts aimed at children of all ages – and to talk to children themselves!

ACTIVITY 18

Below is a list of some characteristics of successful children's fiction as suggested by a group of students. This is followed by two extracts from contrasting examples. *Shrek* is the source of the successful animated film, and *Percy the Small Engine* is an example from a previous generation of writing for children – part of the Rev. W. Awdry's popular series of which 'Thomas the Tank Engine' is the best-known character.

As far as you can judge from these short extracts, and using any additional examples you can find, suggest how far – if at all – each of the following characteristics applies:

- central character(s) with whom younger readers can identify – these may be children, animals, mythical creatures or even humanised inanimate objects
- a fast-moving series of adventures/episodes
- the story at some level reflects issues which do arise in children's lives
- a clear sense of 'good', 'bad, 'right' or 'wrong'
- an underlying 'moral' or message
- some playful uses of language
- language may be limited in complexity (e.g. in terms of syntax, abstraction and lexical range) but does stimulate and enrich the readers' linguistic experience
- the ending 'rewards' the central character in some way.

Compare your discussions of these extracts with the commentary on page 193.

TEXT A **SHREK**

His mother was ugly and his father was ugly, but Shrek was uglier than the two of them put together. By the time he toddled, Shrek could spit flame a full ninety-nine yards and vent smoke from either ear. With just a look he cowed the reptiles in the swamp. Any snake dumb enough to bite him instantly got convulsions and died.

One day Shrek's parents hissed things over and decided it was about time their little darling was out in the world doing his share of damage. So they kicked him goodbye and Shrek left the black hole in which he'd been hatched.

Shrek went slogging along the road, giving off his awful fumes. It delighted him to see the flowers bend aside and the trees lean away to let him go by.

In a shady copse he came across a witch. She was busy boiling bats in turpentine and turtle juice, and as she stirred she crooned . . .

'What a lovely stench!' Shrek cackled. The witch specialized in horrors, but one single look at Shrek make her woozy.

When she recovered her senses Shrek said, 'Tell my fortune, madam, and I'll let you have a few of my rare lice.'

'Splendid!' crowed the witch. 'Here's your fortune.

> 'Otchky-potchky, itchky-pitch,
>
> Pay attention to this witch.
>
> A donkey takes you to a knight –
>
> Him you conquer in a fight.
>
> Then you wed a princess who
>
> Is even uglier than you.
>
> Ha ha ha and cockadoodle,
>
> The magic words are "Apple Strudel".'

'A princess!' Shrek cried. 'I'm on my way!'

Soon he came upon a peasant singing and scything. 'You there, yokel,' said Shrek. 'Why so blithe?'

The peasant mumbled this reply:

> 'I'm happy scything in the rye,
>
> I never stop to wonder why.
>
> I'll hone and scythe until I die.
>
> But now I'm busy. So goodbye.'

'Yokel,' Shrek snapped. 'What have you in that pouch of yours.'

'Just some cold pheasant.'

'Pheasant, peasant? What a pleasant present!'

The last thing the peasant saw before he fainted was Shrek's glare warming up his dinner. Shrek ate and moved on.

Wherever Shrek went, every living creature fled. How it tickled him to be so repulsive!

TEXT B PERCY THE SMALL ENGINE

Percy is a little green tank-engine who works in the Yard at the Big Station. He is a funny little engine, and loves playing jokes. These jokes sometimes get him into trouble.

'Peep peep!' he whistled one morning. 'Hurry up Gordon! the train's ready.'

Gordon thought he was late and came puffing out.

'Ha ha!' laughed Percy, and showed him a train of dirty coal trucks.

Gordon didn't go back to the shed.

He stayed on a siding thinking how to pay Percy out.

'Stay in the shed today,' squeaked Percy to James. 'The Fat Controller will come and see you.'

James was a conceited engine. 'Ah!' he thought, 'the Fat Controller knows I'm a fine engine, ready for anything. He wants me to pull a Special Train.'

So James stayed where he was, and nothing his Driver and Fireman could do would make him move.

But the Fat Controller never came, and the other engines grumbled dreadfully.

They had to do James' work as well as their own.

At last an Inspector came. 'Show a wheel, James,' he said crossly. 'You can't stay here all day.'

'The Fat Controller told me to stay here,' answered James sulkily. 'He sent a message this morning.'

'He did not,' retorted the Inspector. 'How could he? He's away for a week.'

'Oh!' said James. 'Oh!' and he came quickly out of the shed. 'Where's Percy?' Percy had wisely disappeared!

When the Fat Controller came back, he did see James, and Percy too. Both engines wished he hadn't!

James and Gordon wanted to pay Percy out; but Percy kept out of their way. One morning, however, he was so excited that he forgot to be careful.

'I say you engines,' he bubbled, 'I'm to take some trucks to Thomas' Junction. The Fat Controller chose me specially. He must know I'm a Really Useful Engine.'

'More likely he wants you out of the way,' grunted James.

But Gordon gave James a wink . . . Like this.

'Ah yes,' said James, 'just so . . . You were saying Gordon . . .?'

Now is your chance to create a piece of fiction of your own. As you develop your ideas you may wish to think about the kinds of illustrations you would use. They are important in helping to contextualise unfamiliar language – but you do not need to produce these for yourself. Make sure you test your work on some 'guinea pig' readers of the age group you are aiming at, and ask them for their honest opinions.

Commentary tip

If you attempt a piece of children's fiction, there will be plenty of issues to discuss in your commentary:

- your choice of central character and storyline

- how you have controlled the syntactic complexity of your language

- how you have made the language interesting and challenging, as well as accessible

- how you provided sufficient contextual information to allow readers to guess the meaning of unfamiliar language.

Choosing your assignment

As you make your choice of writing assignment, you may find it helpful to submit your proposal to your supervising teacher; as with previous assignments, make sure you cover the following key points:

Proposal/Pre-commentary: Writing to entertain

Key point	Explanation
Content/subject matter	What/who are you going to write about?
Genre/medium	What kind of text are you going to write, and where might it appear? Be as specific as you can. Is this different from your other pieces?
Target audience	Which group(s) of people are you hoping to reach? Is this a distinctly different audience from your other pieces?
What style models do you intend to study?	Note the titles of similar texts, aimed at a similar audience, but *not* on the same topic.

Writing to persuade

The primary purpose of persuasion includes not only texts which set out to persuade us to do something – give money, buy a product, vote for a political party – but also any piece of writing that seeks to influence us, or change our opinions, or challenge our beliefs and assumptions. Some obvious examples include:

- advertising and marketing campaigns

- letters to newspapers, magazines, MPs, etc. on controversial topics

- newspaper or magazine articles putting forward a particular point of view or argument

- flyers and leaflets on a controversial subject

- reviews of films, CDs and other consumer products and services

- political pamphlets, speeches and election addresses

- other speeches and presentations.

Many forms of writing have a persuasive element, and you could argue that for some of the examples listed here (such as reviews) the informative function is equally important. As always, it is important to be alert to the ways in which these purposes overlap and help shape the distinctive nature of texts.

There are strong links between the study of writing to persuade, and the study of Language and Power for Module 2 (see pages 86–102 Module 2 above). It may be a good idea to study these two parts of the course in tandem. As part of your study of Language and Power, you will be examining the power of rhetoric and investigating what it is that makes language influential, impressive and powerful – the very things you need to do when producing a persuasive text of your own.

Commentary tip

Refer to the section in Language and Power on rhetoric and persuasive language (page 100 Module 2) – and identify some specific examples in your own writing of any of these techniques.

Appealing to heads or hearts

What makes a piece of language persuasive or influential? One way of starting to answer this question is to think of it in terms of three key elements – the **who**, the **what**, and the **how**. The framework below can be applied to persuasive texts:

Key element	Explanation	Some language features to consider
Who is addressing us?	What is our relationship with the author/source? How much should we trust/respect him or her?	At what points – if at all – does the author/speaker use 'I' or 'we' – and with what effect? How does the author establish or claim authority or expertise on the topic? What sort of relationship does the author establish with his or her readers/listeners?
What exactly is he or she telling us?	How strong is the case or argument being put forward? Does the logic stand up to analysis? Does it convince us *intellectually* about the truth of what is being said?	What is the main conclusion the text tends towards? What does it want us to think/believe/do as a result of reading/hearing the text? What are the main arguments? What facts or other pieces of evidence are given in support of these? How clearly does the logic lead to the conclusion? (Look for words such as 'so', 'therefore', 'because', 'however'.) Does the text deal with any possible objections or counter-arguments to the case it is making?
How does he or she convey ideas to us?	How effective is the delivery or presentation of the message? Does it create an *emotional*, as well as an intellectual, response?	How does the text convey opinions and subjective judgements? (Look, for example, at the kinds of adjectives used to make evaluative comments.) How does the text make us care about the issue? At which points is the choice of language particularly emotive? Which rhetorical/persuasive techniques give the text its particular impact?

ACTIVITY 19

Apply the sets of questions in the table on page 179 to the examples below – and supplement these with additional texts of your own. For example, study some examples of film, music and other reviews in popular magazines and newspapers.

Compare your responses with the commentary on page 193.

TEXT A

SHELTER

Dear Friend

Forgive me if I sound angry. But hearing the stories I hear every day, and knowing how badly many homeless families are treated in Britain today, I find it hard to be cool and unemotional about it.

Ours is supposed to be a civilised society – and yet the conditions in which many homeless families are living are nothing short of scandalous. The latest figures show that in England alone, a total of 81,270 households are living in temporary accommodation – the highest number ever. Of these, 12,000 households, including thousands of children, are living in bed and breakfast accommodation – the worst and most insecure form of temporary housing. Often whole families are crammed together in a single room for several months at a time.

Every day Shelter hears from people living in overcrowded conditions where they are forced to share basic amenities with several other families. We hear about people being placed in houses with dangerous stairs, poor ventilation, defective gas fires, unsafe wiring, filthy kitchens and stinking toilets. We hear about children suffering from bronchitis, asthma and stomach aches because of their disgusting living conditions. We hear of parents sinking into depression as they struggle to cope.

We can't let this go on. It's degrading, inhuman and plain **wrong.** That is why I want to ask you to share our anger and concern – and to turn it into **practical action** by pledging £2 a month to help us win a better deal for Britain's homeless people.

If you are wondering how £2 can help, let me give you an example – among thousands I could choose – of how Shelter works to help people in housing need.

Louise is a mum with two young children, who was made homeless when her landlord sold the flat she rented. Her local council placed her in bed and breakfast accommodation, where for six long, dreadful months she had to endure the sheer hell of bringing up her children in one cramped room . . .

This is where Shelter's work is vital. We are Britain's leading charity working with homeless and badly housed people. Our housing aid centres and our free national 24-hour housing helpline, Shelterline, give advice, information and practical help to well over 100,000 people every year. **But as a charity we struggle to raise the money to keep these services going – and there is so much more we need to do.** That is why your £2 a month really is important to us. It will help us raise the regular income we need to be here for families like Louise's, 24 hours a day, 365 days a year.

. . . **Please help us to make it happen by using the form enclosed to pledge £2 a month,** or as much as you can spare. Thank you.

Yours sincerely

Christine Parrish

Director of Housing Services

TEXT B

YOUR £10 CAN HELP TO CHANGE THESE YOUNGSTERS' LIVES

Amelia Hill visits Fairbridge, a group that unlocks the potential of teenagers crushed by inner-city deprivation.

Fairbridge doesn't assist sufferers of a particular disease. It can't produce figures showing how many people it has helped to achieve a concrete goal. Instead, it targets teenagers suffering from inner-city deprivation.

Fairbridge works quietly and efficiently from 12 bases across the country to catch youngsters aged from 13 to 25 who have slipped through all society's safety nets.

These are people who have been crushed by life; victims of physical and emotional abuse, and long-term sufferers of drug and alcohol addiction. They are typically homeless, have little – if any – education and are angry, aggressive and abusive to those who reach out to them . . .

Fairbridge enabled 241 young people last year to develop the self-confidence to take part in team activities for probably the first time in their lives; learning to make and keep commitments, turn up on time and trust both themselves and others.

. . . 'We offer these young people a good deal,' said Tony Maybery, manager of the Southampton centre. 'They take part in activities they enjoy on an entirely voluntary basis. All they have to do is commit to explore their behaviour and attitudes.'

The group receives financial donations from a range of bodies, including AOL and Barclays, as well as support from a range of businesses such as Waitrose and members of the Guild of Food Writers, who regularly visit centres to help teach the youngsters how to cook.

Just over half its annual funding of £340,000 comes from statutory grants but Fairbridge is determined to make up financial shortfalls with trust money and public donations.

. . . 'By making a donation to Fairbridge, the public can give young people someone to believe in and that's when they start to believe in themselves,' said Allan.

'We're the last opportunity for many of these children to put their lives back together.'

The Observer

The structure of arguments

When constructing your persuasive text it is important to be clear about the points you wish to make, and the conclusion you want your readers to reach. Whether you can persuade someone to accept this conclusion who did not already do so will largely depend on the reasons you give in support, and how you lead your reader/listener logically from one reason to another until you reach your conclusion.

ACTIVITY 20

In this Activity you will examine an example of an 'argument' and the way in which different reasons are assembled to lead to the conclusion. The text is an extract from an editorial in *When Saturday Comes*, a weekly football magazine.

After reading the piece, below, answer the following questions:

- What is the conclusion of the text?

- List the principal reasons given in the text which lead to this conclusion.

- How does the writer acknowledge – and then counter – the reasons given for the proposal in the first place?

- What words/phrases are used – often at the beginnings of paragraphs – to build the argument from one point to the next?

IF THE CAP FITS

Both the Canterbury Bulldogs (one of the top rugby league clubs in Sydney) and the Australian Rules club Carlton (something like the equivalent of Arsenal in Melbourne) were plunged into crisis by the application of the salary cap, the very mechanism proposed as a solution to the problems of European football both by the ever-active imaginations of the G14 group and some Nationwide League chairmen.

Carlton were fined £330,000 and subjected to heavy penalties in the AFL's draft system, for making under-the-counter payments to several players in order to evade the salary cap rules . . . The Bulldogs were docked 38 points near the end of this season for similar breaches of the league cap, dumping them firmly at the bottom of the table and making a farce of the whole campaign . . .

The arguments over salary caps (and the draft systems that go with them in many American and Australian sport) tend to divide people along unusual ideological lines. On the one hand, the stated aim is to keep competitions balanced and not allow a few clubs to become far richer than the others for an indefinite length of time . . .

On the other hand, salary caps are generally resisted by players' unions, for obvious reasons, and by the restrictive practices zealots of the European Union, who see them as a blatant restraint of trade. While a more equal league and a reduction in the percentage of turnover spent by clubs on wages are both desirable goals, the current proposals for salary caps are likely to prove not only ineffective in achieving them, but also disingenuous in their motivation.

The first objection is that salary caps simply do not work . . . Examples from other countries and the experience of our maximum wage until its abolition suggest that clubs will always try to find a way around the caps. What's more, if they are caught, the consequences make a joke of the competition and are deeply unfair to fans who have invested time and money in following the league in good faith . . .

The second objection is that neither the G14 nor the Nationwide League chairmen (led by the most profligate of the First Division spenders) are in any position to demand a salary cap. On the most basic level, the idea that any cap should be based on a percentage of turnover (rather than an absolute sum) would serve not so much to iron out inequalities as to institutionalise them.

More iniquitous still is the idea that the G14 (now comprising 18 clubs) is entitled to dictate how other clubs should organise their finances. Their proposals on the salary cap . . . are in fact simply their latest ploy to gain legitimacy at the expense of the game's governing bodies.

As in many other areas of industry, this plea for a certain kind of regulation is essentially a smokescreen designed to cover up gross mismanagement. The proposals are likely to prove unworkable, unfair and illegal. But history suggests that is not likely to stop football charging enthusiastically towards an apparently neat solution to its problems.

Possible topics

The range of possible subjects for persuasive writing is enormous – and your topic doesn't have to be a matter of huge national or philosophical importance. There is already a great deal of material related to the more popular topics such as hunting, smoking, drugs, abortion and even euthanasia, so why not go for something a little different, possibly a little closer to home?

ACTIVITY 21

What follows is the beginning of a list of some possibilities, moving from very local topics right through to major philosophical questions. Use the various sections of the table as a framework to interview a partner and find out what he or she feels strongly about.

Domestic or personal issues	School or college-based issues	Neighbourhood issues	Town/regional issues	National issues	International political/ scientific issues
Should smacking of children be allowed? Do kids watch too much TV? Should children get more/less pocket money, or do more/less homework? Should people be encouraged to eat a healthier diet?	Dress code Recreational facilities – access and quality The value of Key Skills/ General Studies/other compulsory courses Access to IT facilities Homework/ coursework policy Student Charter issues	Community facilities for young people Litter, graffiti, vandalism Transport	Crime, drugs Unemploy-ment Transport, education, health services Sports team Charity campaigns	AS exams Student fees Drugs policy Religious/ single-faith schools Race/gender issues Censorship – sex and violence on TV The Euro Transport policy The NHS	Third World poverty Environment/ pollution GM foods War, terrorism The Middle East Cloning

As you make your choice of writing assignment, you should submit your proposal to your supervising teacher – covering the key points suggested below:

Proposal/Pre-commentary: Writing to persuade

Key point	Explanation
Content/subject matter	What are you going to persuade your readers/listeners to do, think or believe?
Target audience	Which group(s) of people are you hoping to reach? Is this a distinctly different audience from your other pieces?
Genre/medium	How are you going to reach them? What kind of text are you going to write, and where might it appear? Be as specific as you can. Is this different from your other pieces?
Your argument	What information are you going to include/need to collect? Outline in brief the structure of your argument. How will you appeal to heads and hearts?
What style models do you intend to study?	Note the titles of similar texts, aimed at a similar audience but *not* on the same topic.

Preparing your submission for assessment

Selecting your final pieces

On your AS course, you may have had the opportunity to attempt several potential coursework pieces in draft form; if so, you will now need to choose two pieces which you will develop to completion for your submission. As you do so, remember the requirements for the folder and the key words in the table on pages 135–6. You should also bear in mind the following guidelines:

- Choose two pieces which show a strong contrast of purpose, audience, genre and style. You are aiming to demonstrate your versatility as a writer.

- Choose pieces which reflect your own individual interests.

- Make sure that the pieces provide enough challenge; some types of writing – such as writing basic sets of instructions, or writing for very young children, may not allow you to demonstrate sufficiently high-level skills to achieve the higher mark bands.

- Find one or two examples of texts written for the same purpose/medium/genre as your chosen task, but on different topics. Study these style models closely – applying the same kinds of detailed questions to them as if they were texts for analysis on the Unit 1 paper.

A note on 'originality' and pastiche

After thoroughly researching the genre and style models of the kinds of writing you intend to produce, there is a danger that you could end up merely producing acceptable imitations of established kinds of text, or **pastiches**. Pastiches can easily topple over into **parodies**, where a writer deliberately exaggerates some of the distinctive features of a genre in order to mock them.

The principal challenge facing any writer is to work within the established expectation of a genre while doing something just a little different. If you disregard all the conventions and expectations of the genre, your work is unlikely to be published; on the other hand, you should be doing more than just slavishly copying a list of characteristic features and cloning existing texts.

For example, the film *The Blair Witch Project* used many of the rather clichéd expectations of the horror genre, while at the same time offering a different kind of experience for the viewers. Effective work for Original Writing will be of this kind – clearly rooted in a study of the appropriate genres and style models, but demonstrating your individuality in the way you work with these conventions. It can be a difficult balance to strike.

Drafting and re-drafting

It is likely that your final pieces will need to go through at least two or three drafts before you are completely happy with them. Make sure that you know the **internal deadlines** which your school or college sets for submission, and allow time for this process to take place. Each draft should represent your best attempt at the task; once you have completed a draft, you should seek feedback from the following groups of people:

- Yourself. It is important to become increasingly critical of your own work. Put your writing aside for a couple of days after you have finished a draft, and then return to it as objectively and critically as you can. It is a good idea to read your text aloud. This is particularly important for scripts and other texts intended to be heard, but it can also help you spot problems of expression with all kinds of writing.

- Your fellow Language students. Try a 'workshop' approach where you and your classmates offer helpful, critical comments on each other's work.

- Your teacher. He or she will act as your advisor or editor and offer constructive advice and criticism. Your teacher will *not* be able to correct errors or details, but will be able to offer quite substantial guidance on what you need to do to improve the piece.

- Your readers. You need to select a number of 'guinea pigs' who are typical of the kind of readers you are trying to reach with your pieces, and try out your writing on them. For their feedback to be useful, you might like to give them a short questionnaire which invites them to comment (anonymously) on some specific aspects of the piece – otherwise, they are likely to offer rather bland approval, out of friendship or kindness.

- A 'real' editor. For some kinds of writing it may be possible to submit a well-developed draft to an editor of the kind of medium you are aiming for – such as a student magazine, local newspaper, or a website – and invite comment. However, don't be too disappointed if you receive either no response, or only a flat rejection.

It is very important that you keep a copy or record of each draft of your piece. If you are working with a word processor, save each successive draft with a different file name; you will need to submit *each* draft in your folder and to discuss the changes you have made in your commentary.

Commentary tip

One alternative way of saving versions of your work is to make use of the 'track changes' function in a program such as Microsoft Word, which enables you to highlight changes you make to a draft. You can then discuss in detail your reasons for some of the more significant alterations you make.

Your teacher will also require you to keep any notes he or she gives you on the drafts, as well as any other feedback you receive from other sources.

ACTIVITY 22

As you revisit a draft of your work, ask questions such as the following. Make a note of your answers in your notebook and refer to these later when writing your commentaries.

- Is it well organised – is there a logical structure and is it easy to follow?

- In particular, does the opening sentence and paragraph do the job it needs to?

- How does it compare with the style models you have studied?

- What kind of relationship have you tried to achieve with your reader? Are your choices about whether to address readers directly using the second person, and whether to use the first person, all appropriate?

- What **register**(s) have you chosen to use, and are these suitable for your audience? Have you achieved the right level of formality/seriousness?

- Are your sentences well-constructed and accurately punctuated? Reading aloud will help you to judge.

- How accurate is your spelling? A high standard of technical accuracy is expected at A Level.

The commentary

When you are satisfied that you have completed the final drafts of your pieces, you should turn to writing the final version of your commentaries. If you have taken the advice offered earlier by writing ongoing commentaries on your work and keeping a working notebook, you will already have a lot of the raw material. Look back, too, at the 'Commentary tips' offered throughout this module.

Remember, the commentaries account for one-third of the total marks in this module. Here are some guidelines to help you to gain as many of these marks as possible:

Key point	Comments
Explain your **aim**	This is your chance to show that you have addressed complex and subtle language points. Don't spend too long giving a long narrative account of how you came to develop the idea, but do give a brief explanation of your aims, ideas and intentions. Briefly outline your aim, then discuss how the web of requirements of audience, purpose and genre made your task complex and demanding.

Key point	Comments
Reflect on the **choices** you have made and select the most significant ones to discuss	As a writer of texts you have made hundreds of choices within each language framework. These include: **Content (selection)**: what to include and what to leave out **Structure (discourse)**: how to begin, how to end, and how to get from one to the other **Form/lay-out (graphology)**: how to present your text on the page **Register (grammar/lexis)**: the level of formality/technicality to use **Tone and style (grammar, lexis, semantics, pragmatics)**: the degree of lightness/seriousness to adopt, how to address your readers/listeners, and how to use language to achieve your desired effect. In about 750 words per commentary, you cannot possibly explain every detail of these choices, but do pick out some of the most significant ones and include at least some detailed analysis of linguistic details from your text. Remember to quote relevant extracts from your work to illustrate your points.
Analyse the changes you have made	In the course of re-drafting your work it has probably changed significantly. Explain why you have made some of the revisions to your texts, and refer specifically to some changes in the drafts included in your folder.
Refer to **style models**	In explaining your choices of language and approach, refer specifically to any style models you have used.
Refer to **sources**	Make it clear exactly how you have used information from other sources, and demonstrate how you have changed and re-presented it by referring specifically to the sources you include in your folder.
Evaluate the results	Arrive at an objective judgment on your pieces. How successful are they? What do you think might still need to be revised if you had more time?
Keep to **word limits**	You'll probably need most of the 1500 words allowed for both commentaries to do justice to the task, but don't go beyond this; the best commentaries are brisk and selective, not leisurely and encyclopaedic!

Practicalities: assembling your file

When it comes to submitting your folder, your school/college will advise you about the practicalities of how to present your work. The file you submit should include the following key elements.

Key element	Comments
Contents page	Use a single sheet of A4 to list the contents of your file.
A short **'pre-commentary'** for each of the two pieces, simply stating the intended audience, purpose, genre and medium of each.	This can be a single sheet of A4 at the front of your folder. Do not include this in your word counts.
The **final version** of both pieces, free from all annotations and presented as professionally as possible.	It is good to make the pieces appear in the format in which they are intended to be published. However, no real credit is given for artwork and graphic design, so concentrate on the text rather than spending hours formatting and laying it out.
Bibliographies.	Include a bibliography if you have referred to other sources of information in preparing your submission. Give full details of author, title, publisher and date of publication, and website addresses.
An accurate **word count**.	Record this at the end of the piece. Ensure that the total length of the two pieces is between 1500 and 3000 words.
The **commentary** on each piece.	It is best to place each commentary immediately after the final version of each text, but before the previous drafts.
All **previous drafts** of both pieces – along with any comments/annotations made by teachers and readers.	Arrange these sequentially, from first draft onwards, and label them clearly for ease of reference.
Source materials.	You should include photocopies or printouts of any significant sources of information you have used. This is particularly important for informative texts, where you need to show that you have created a genuinely original piece of writing. Label your sources for ease of reference in your commentaries.
Style models.	Include examples of any style models you have studied when preparing your pieces. Again, label these for ease of reference.

Commentaries

Activity 4

1 In text **A,** note the word play on 'fill the gap', the amusing graphics, the attempts to enthuse readers with words like 'broaden horizons' and 'seize the freedom', and the direct address in the second person. The headline of text **B** links it to the wider 'A-Z of 2003' feature of which it is part, and its apparent 'shock' value – what, no more CDs? – invites readers to read on. Text **C** also goes for a shock effect with its 'prisoner' shot of the typical *Cosmo Girl* reader, which makes clear the meaning of the italicised headline word 'Real'. This, it seems to be saying, could happen to *you*! The opening paragraph is in the present tense and the second person, forcing its readers to undergo imaginatively the experience the article is discussing. The 'trail' for text **D** is provided by the anchor-man's link, and it functions, in effect, as the headline of the piece.

2 The gatefold-leaflet format of text **A** breaks the information into clearly defined sections, each with its own snappy headings. Paragraphing is also very clear, with some icons/symbols and emboldened questions drawing in the eye. Text **B** is a conventional magazine article, with regular paragraphing being the only graphological guide to the structure of the piece. Text **C**, however, uses panels, headings and 'pull quotes' to separate the article into reportage, case study, a set of numbered steps which will follow if someone is caught shoplifting, and a 'help & advice' section.

3 The two voices represent the 'studio' and the 'location' reporters, but in this piece of straight reporting no use is made of SFX or music. The report begins with an overview of the whole match, so there is no 'suspense' involved, but then follows the chronological sequence of first half – second half.

4 It's clear that the writer of text **A** assumes readers know what a 'gap year' means, and the register of the text includes several lexical items which most full-time students will recognise ('placement', 'sponsored events', etc). Some less common terms like the French word *vendange* are implicitly explained. Text **B** assumes in its readers a certain technological familiarity with the world of CDs and their 'skip facility', computing, music and an interest in the record industry generally – which is fair enough, given the medium in which it appears (the *NME*). Less technically, the opening paragraph of text **C** takes it for granted that its readers may be able to identify with the shoplifting scenario it describes and is careful to match the individual case studies to the target audience of the magazine in age and gender. The reporter in text **D** assumes basic interest in the rugby match he describes and a fair degree of familiarity with the terminology of the game, with its 'tries' and 'penalties'.

5 In text **A**, countries and cities are mentioned without explanation – so some basic geography is assumed. The references to students by first names does not imply we know them, but is designed to create an informal, friendly relationship. Text **B** includes unexplained references to technologically or music-related organisations like 'MSN' and 'WinMX', and to several musical artists, but *does* explain the initials 'RIAA' in full the first time it is mentioned. Text **C**'s reference to 'Winona' assumes that its readers will recognise the topical reference to the shoplifting case involving the Hollywood actress Winona Ryder. Text **D** assumes that most listeners may be familiar with the rugby players to whom it refers, though it does provide suitable labels (e.g. 'England and Lions pace man') for the benefit of more casual listeners.

6 No explanations are given by the reporter in text **D** of what 'tries' are or how many points they are worth – the assumption is that listeners are sufficiently informed on these basic aspects of the game.

7 In text **A** several examples of individual students' experiences are included to illustrate some of the general possibilities indicated. Text **B** includes a few facts and figures in straightforward numeric form – the '2.2 billion blank CDs' it mentions is included to convince its readers that there is a problem with music piracy. Text **C** is very much anecdote-led, with the 'true life' stories of two young girls occupying the bulk of the text, and even text **D** uses a human-interest angle to report the rugby game, choosing to focus on one well-known player even though he didn't make a decisive contribution to the game.

8 Standard English is used throughout text **A** but minor sentences like 'Planning a grand tour?', the use of contracted forms like 'they'll' and the slightly light-hearted flavour of some of the examples ('cleaning someone's car with a toothbrush!') don't allow the tone to become too serious. Text **B** is also remarkably formal and serious in tone, even though it includes numerous terms linked to modern music. However, it does slightly subvert 'standard' English practice by beginning sentences with 'Still' or 'So:', and includes some sentences that create the illusion of spontaneity and the spoken word ('Oh, and it's all our own fault'). The register of text **C** is notably different, being closer in places to the colloquial language it imagines its readers use ('scary stuff' . . . 'Mates won't cover for you') and directly quoting the subjects of its case studies extensively.

9 In text **A** some amusing graphics illustrate the main points in each section.

10 The second-person pronoun is used to address the reader throughout text **A** – this establishes an immediate and friendly relationship, and almost feels as if readers are being spoken to rather than written for. This is true to a lesser degree of text **B**, where the feel is still fairly personal, but not as insistently so. Text **C** goes further by forcing its readers to imagine themselves in the present tense carrying out an act of shoplifting. Text **D** remains entirely impersonal.

11 The only uses of first-person singular 'I' in any of the texts occur in passages quoted from specific people. The author of most short informative texts remains anonymous – and unimportant. The writer of text **B** uses the first-person plural, 'we'/'our', to suggest a unity of interest and identity between the writer and readers, but otherwise the texts avoid first-person usage.

12 There is clearly an element of persuasion going on in text **A**, as the Bureau which published the leaflet seems to wish to encourage young people to take a gap year of some kind. Text **B** is only persuasive in so far as it aims to convince its readers of the truth of its argument, but perhaps the pragmatic intention behind text **C** is to deter young people from shoplifting. Text **D** is largely informative but some colourful figurative language ('went off the boil', 'on the comeback trail') is fairly typical of sports reporting and hints at the need to entertain as well as inform listeners.

Activity 9

Text **A** is interesting because it addresses several different audiences – primarily victims but also bullies, parents and carers – all using the second-person pronoun 'you' throughout. It suggests that it has something to say to all of them, and the contents directs each group to its particular section. Celebrity endorsement in the introduction helps victims recognise that their situation is far from unique and can be very successfully overcome. The text uses headings which are phrased as first-person questions ('What can I do if I am being bullied?'), bullet points, and some emboldened and italic text for emphasis. The phrases/sentences in a series of bullets are usually syntactically similar, e.g. all begin with a verb, or contain imperatives. The instructions themselves are imperatives, but these are usually softened by phrases like 'try to . . .' and 'if you can help it'. Reassurance is offered by phrases like 'don't worry' and repeated comments that the recommended actions will make it 'harder' for the bully. The authorship of the text is of no interest or relevance, so the first person is avoided except in the heading already noted, where it is assuming the voice of the reader. Generally, the lexis is straightforward without being patronising – the text presumably has to speak to quite a wide range of students in terms of age and reading ability, so although the vocabulary is fairly simple ('upset', 'angry'), in some ways the language is quite mature ('don't become resigned to . . .').

Jamie Oliver's recipe (text **B**) is an interesting blend of first-person enthusiasm, expressed in short bursts like 'I love this salad', and 'One thing I do', and more straightforward imperatives – 'simply place the figs', 'weave around', etc. He doesn't follow the conventional lay-out for recipes; rather, his continuous prose seems designed to simulate his actual presence in the kitchen, as shown by the real time, future tense of 'At this point you'll think', and the colloquial 'it's pretty damn sexy'. His colourful and interestingly imprecise choice of verbs ('**throw in** some slices', '**rip** over some green or purple basil', '**drizzle** everything with the honey') helps convey something of the energetic personality most readers of the text will recognise from his TV series.

Activity 17

The very first sentence establishes quite a lot about the domestic, Christmas setting and the central character's mood (she 'glowered'). Other details in the paragraph (Tim's grumbling and the 'bare and dismal' nature of the tree) rapidly set the tone of the household as Christmas approaches. Characters are hastily sketched – the boring Uncle with his anecdotes, for instance, is a common enough stereotype. Although the story is told in the third person, it is largely the point of view of Jan we are presented with. She is likely to be the kind of character with whom many *Bella* readers can identify, and many of her thoughts and feelings are directly narrated. Dialogue is used selectively, with fragments of speech bringing to life the domestic episodes described in the story, but the descriptive detail is vital – note the kinds of adjectives used to describe the Christmas decorations ('bare', 'dismal', 'tawdry', 'silly').

Activity 18

It is impossible to reduce children's fiction to a formula, but these extracts do exemplify several features of the most popular titles. The central characters are all recognisable in different ways – Shrek as the unpopular 'loner', and Percy as the cheeky prankster who irritates the older children (represented here by the engines Gordon and James). *Shrek* follows one common narrative pattern by having the main character set out alone, presumably on a series of adventures which include encounters with a witch and a princess, who may represent the possibilities of evil and purity in the world; Percy's story ostensibly takes place in a railway yard but the scenario of practical jokes and pay-back (or 'pay-out' as the 1956 text puts it) may be a feature of many school playgrounds. When Percy gets his come-uppance (as he does later) a lesson about the consequences of 'naughty' or cheeky behaviour is duly learned. *Shrek* makes rather more playful and adventurous use of language; the writer does not shy away from words like 'vent' and 'cowed', 'copse' and 'blithe', though the immediate contexts in which they occur (including a picture on each page, not all reproduced here) provide plenty of clues. Note too the playful language in the rhymes and the rhyming of 'Pheasant, peasant? What a pleasant present!'.

Activity 19

The *Shelter* appeal is insistently personal, with the Director of Housing Services, Christine Parrish, identifying herself and her feelings of anger throughout. This works because of who she is – a significant figure within the organisation. The use of the first-person plural ('Ours is supposed to be a civilised society', 'We can't let this go on', etc.) binds her to her readers and appeals to our sense of collective responsibility for the crisis she describes. Finally she addresses readers in the second person ('If you are wondering . . .', 'your £2 a month') to make her appeal as direct as possible. The piece claims to be have arisen from anger rather than being 'cool and unemotional about it', though there is *some* appeal to our intellects in the form of some statistical information. The logic is straightforward – we aspire to be a 'civilised' society; but many people live in very poor conditions – therefore, something should be done. You can afford to give a little, and a little can go a long way, so you should make a monthly donation of £2.

However, the appeal is primarily to our emotional response, whether it be compassion or a sense of shared guilt. The use of an individual case study is more emotionally effective than simply sticking to facts and figures, and there are plenty of overtly rhetorical techniques (such as the triad 'It's degrading, inhuman and plain **wrong**'). The contrast between the 'civilised' values of our society and the conditions of the homeless is underlined by many lists including a string of emotive adjectives such as 'filthy', 'stinking', etc.

The *Observer* piece is less emotional, rhetorical and personal in style; the author takes a back seat and persuades us by providing evidence to support the conclusion that the Fairbridge organisation does good work and fulfils an important social need. It announces this conclusion early in the piece, and then backs it up with a mixture of general statements, facts, figures and quotes. It makes no direct appeal to readers for cash – the opportunity to donate appears elsewhere in the newspaper – but allows the case to speak for itself.

Glossary

accent The pronunciation characteristic of a particular region or social group *p66*

adjacent pair The basic unit of turn-taking in conversation *p46*

adjectives A word that gives more information about or describes a noun or pronoun *p46*

adverbs A word that gives more information about a verb, an adjective or another verb *p46*

agenda In conversation, the topic(s) covered by the discourse *p59*

alliteration Repetition of similar (usually initial) consonant sounds in successive words *p50*

colloquialism Literally, the language of speech; in practice, very informal use of language *p20*

compound sentence Sentences which consist of several clauses joined by *and, but, or* or *so p72*

conjunctions Words such as *and, but* and *because* which join elements of a sentence together *p46*

connotation The implied or associated meanings of a word or phrase (see also **denotation**) *p*

context-bound/context-free The degree to which the meanings in a spoken or written text refer to elements of the contexts in which they are produced and received *p23*

covert prestige The unofficial prestige that non-standard varieties of accent or dialect may enjoy within a speech community *p132*

data Any sample of spoken or written language gathered for research and analysis *p3*

declarative The most common sentence type, a statement *p42*

deficit model View of language in which varieties which do not correspond to the dominant prestige variety are viewed as inferior or corrupt *p119*

deictic references Words such as *this, that, there,* which refer to people, places or things beyond the text in which they appear *p72*

denotation The literal, primary meaning of a word or phrase (see also **connotation**) *p52*

dialect The distinctive vocabulary and grammar of a geographical area within a language community *p64*

dialectology The study of dialectal variations *11*

digraph A combination of two letters (such as – *sh*) which consistently represents a single **phoneme** *p48*

discourse structure The way in which spoken and language texts are organised and sequenced *p35*

double/multiple negative The use of two or more negative elements or markers in non-standard verb constructions *p74*

dramatic monologue Form of narrative in which a sole narrator 'talks' directly to the reader/audience in a continuous monologue *p165*

dysphemism A deliberately blunt expression of a delicate subject *p53*

ephemera Texts which are designed only to have a short-term use and not to be permanent *p24*

euphemism A polite or understated reference to subject of some delicacy *p53*

eye-dialect Term used to describe the non-standard spelling and punctuation used by some writers to give the impression of a regional variety of speech *p122*

figurative language Language which uses metaphors, simile and other non-literal expressions *p53*

forensic linguistic The application of linguistic study to problems of authorship of texts, sometimes in a criminal context *p64*

generic form Form of a word which refers to a whole class/type *p104*

genre A recognisable type of text/discourse with characteristic elements or ingredients *p69*

grammar The system which enables words to be combined meaningfully into different kinds of texts. Usually includes **mophology** and **syntax** *p40*

graphology Those features which contribute to the visual appearance of a text on the page *p69*

hedges Words/phrases used to indicate a degree of uncertainty or tentativeness *p109*

idiolect The distinctive features of a person's language which mark them as an individual *p43*

imperative The command form of a verb or sentence *p42*

influential power The power to persuade and influence *p88*

instrumental power Power used to apply and exert power and authority *p88*

interrogative The question form of a sentence *p42*

jargon Usually the specialise, technical language associated with a specific field of activity *p64*

language repertoire The range of language styles which an individual speaker uses *p82*

lexis The collective term for the word stock, or vocabulary, of a language or text *p45*

linguistic relativism The view that every language embodies a unique way of thinking about the world, associated with the linguists Sapir and Whorf *p105*

marked/unmarked forms Marked forms of words indicate explicitly the gender, tense or person involved; unmarked forms do not *p104*

maxims Guiding principles associated with H P Grice's analysis of conversational discourse *p91*

metalanguage The language used to discuss language itself *p5*

minimal responses In conversation, short utterances made in response to a speaker (such as *yes, mm, I see*) *p128*

mode Usually, whether a text is spoken or written *p14*

morpheme The smallest units of meaning *p43*

morphology The study of the ways in which the forms of words vary according to grammatical meaning *p43*

noun Class of words which refer to people, places, & objects (**proper** and **concrete**), feelings and ideas (**abstract**) *p44*

onomatopoeia The phonetic imitation in language of actual sounds (e.g. buzz, pop) *p50*

oratory The craft of public speaking *p100*

overt prestige The obvious and official high status and authority of such forms as Standard English and Received Pronunciation *p114*

paralinguistic features Gestures and accompanying facial expressions which contribute to the communication of meanings in speech *p72*

parallelism The successive repetition of similar phrase or sentence structures *p128*

parody A text which imitates and exaggerates distinctive features of another text for humorous effect *p185*

pastiche A text which successfully imitates the distinctive features of another text *p185*

person When referring to verb use, 1st person = I/we, 2nd person = you, etc *p144*

phatic talk In conversation, (small) talk whose primary function is to develop/reinforce social relationships *p90*

phonemes The basic sounds (vowels and consonants) on which a language is based *p48*

phonology The study of the sound system of a language *p48*

present perfect tense Verb tense indicating an action completed in the past that is relevant now such as *I have walked here, I have not told her*, etc. *p76*

pragmatics The study of the meanings which are implied and understood in the way we use language *p54*

prepositions Class of words which define positions and relationships (*to, below, under, into*, etc) *p46*

prescriptivism Approach to language which attempts to impose (or prescribe) 'rules' of 'correct' usage *p119*

progressive tenses Those verb tenses formed with the morpheme *–ing p76*

pronouns Class of words which are used to substitute for and refer to nouns (*she, it, us*, etc) *p46*

prosodic features Those aspects of the use of the voice (intonation, stress, tempo, pitch) which contribute to meanings communicated in speech *p23*

question tag Short question forms which occur at the ends of phrases *p109*

Received Pronunciation (RP) The accent of educated professional speech *p26*

schwa The most common short vowel sound in English (='uh') *p49*

register Either the level or formality or degree of topic-specific language in a text *p69*

rhetoric Term used to describe a range of techniques associated with powerful and persuasive language *p100*

semantic field A group of words with related or similar meanings *p51*

semantics The study of meanings *p51*

sentence boundaries The points in a text where sentences begin or end *p73*

slang Informal language *p20*

Standard English The accepted vocabulary and grammar of educated, 'correct' English *p20*

stress The emphasis placed on a particular word or syllable *p51*

style model An example of a type of text which serves as a model for original writing *p136*

sub-text The implied or intentional meanings in a text *p60*

syntax The aspect of grammar concerned with the construction of sentences and word-order *p41*

taboo Language which is considered offensive (includes 'swear words') *p20*

transcript A written record of spoken language *p9*

verbs Class of words which describe actions, feelings and states *p45*

vulgarism Language which falls short of **taboo** but which is regarded as coarse or impolite *p20*